PARALEGAL LITIGATION
FORMS AND PROCEDURES

PARALEGAL LITIGATION FORMS AND PROCEDURES
THIRD EDITION

MARCY FAWCETT-DELESANDRI
North Harris College

ASPEN LAW & BUSINESS
A Division of Aspen Publishers, Inc.
Gaithersburg   New York

This publication is designed to provide accurate and authoritative information in regard to the subject matter covered. It is sold with the understanding that the publisher is not engaged in rendering legal, accounting, or other professional services. If legal advice or other professional advice is required, the services of a competent professional person should be sought.

—From a *Declaration of Principles* jointly adopted by
a Committee of the American Bar Association and a
Committee of Publishers and Associations.

Copyright © 2001 by Aspen Law & Business
A Division of Aspen Publishers, Inc.
A Wolters Kluwer Company

Printed in the United States of America

Permissions
Aspen Law & Business
1185 Avenue of the Americas
New York, NY 10036

Printed in the United States of America

ISBN 0-7355-1676-6

2 3 4 5 6 7 8 9 0

Library of Congress Cataloging-in-Publication Data

Fawcett-Delesandri, Marcy, 1951-
    Paralegal litigation: forms and procedures / Marcy Fawcett-Delesandri.—3rd ed.
        p. cm.
    "Paralegal practice library."
    Includes index.
    ISBN 0-7355-1676-6
        1. Civil procedure—United States. 2. Civil procedure—United States—Forms. 3. Legal assistants—United States—Handbooks, manuals, etc. I. Title.

KF8841 .F38 2000
347.73'5—dc21

00-048109

About Aspen Law & Business
Paralegal Practice Library

In 1997, Aspen Law & Business welcomed Wiley Law Publications, the legal publishing division of John Wiley & Sons, Inc., into its growing business—already established as a leading provider of practical information to legal practitioners.

At the heart of this acquisition is a powerful synergy created by two closely related yet complementary product lines. Since its founding, Wiley Law Publications has gained a reputation as a leading publisher of high-quality, solutions-based resources for legal and paralegal professionals. The *Paralegal Practice Library* offers a range of practical, hands-on resources, which supply paralegals with the essential tools required to assist the attorney with any case quickly and efficiently.

Both Aspen customers and Wiley Law customers now have access to a substantially greater selection of high-quality products and services. You, our valued customer, can continue to expect the same uncompromising commitment to quality that is the hallmark of Aspen publications.

ASPEN LAW & BUSINESS
A Division of Aspen Publishers, Inc.
A Wolters Kluwer Company
www.aspenpublishers.com

SUBSCRIPTION NOTICE

This Aspen Law & Business product is updated on a periodic basis with supplements to reflect important changes in the subject matter. If you purchased this product directly from Aspen Law & Business, we have already recorded your subscription for the update service.

   If, however, you purchased this product from a bookstore and wish to receive future updates and revised or related volumes billed separately with a 30-day examination review, please contact our Customer Service Department at 1-800-234-1660, or send your name, company name (if applicable), address, and the title of the product to:

ASPEN LAW & BUSINESS
A Division of Aspen Publishers, Inc.
7201 McKinney Circle
Frederick, MD 21704

ABOUT THE AUTHOR

Marcy Fawcett-Delesandri received her B.A. in English from San Diego State University, and graduated with honors from the University of San Diego Lawyer's Assistant's Program. She began her legal career at the defense firm of Thorndal, Backus & Maupin in Las Vegas, Nevada in 1981 where she was intensely involved in the MGM Grand Fire Litigation for three years.

In 1984, Marcy and her family moved to Houston, Texas, and she applied her big case experience to the Continental Air Lines Bankruptcy case as a legal assistant for Dotson, Babcock & Scofield. As legal assistant to the firm's head litigation partner, she was active in assisting with the firm's move toward automation. She has worked extensively in personal injury, insurance defense, product liability, commercial litigation, and oil and gas litigation. Marcy has also been active in the Houston Legal Assistants Association, State Bar of Texas Legal Assistant Division, and the Legal Assistant Management Association.

In July 1988, Marcy left Dotson, Babcock & Scofield to accept a faculty position with the new legal assistant program at North Harris College in Houston, Texas. In addition to her teaching, she has been a frequent seminar speaker across the country. As an independent consultant to law firms and commercial entities, she has performed in-house training seminars and videos for their legal assistants and support staff.

Marcy makes her home in Clear Lake Shores, TX, with her family.

This book is dedicated with enormous respect and admiration to Gene Backus, of Thorndal, Backus and Maupin in Las Vegas, Nevada, who believed in me, patiently guided me, and gave me the opportunity to develop the skills and experience the variety of responsibilities which have allowed me to enjoy such satisfaction and success from my career.

And to the loving memory of my beloved mother who always told me I could do anything I set my mind to—and I believed her.

SUMMARY OF CONTENTS

CONTENTS

CONTENTS

Chapter 3
CALENDARING, DOCKET CONTROL, AND FILE MANAGEMENT 181

CONTENTS

CONTENTS

CONTENTS

CONTENTS

CONTENTS

CONTENTS

CONTENTS

PREFACE

Paralegal Litigation: Forms and Procedure, Third Edition contains everything you need to manage your litigation successfully. Written by veteran paralegal Marcy Fawcett-Delesandri, it includes model interrogatories, demand letters, sample motions, and checklists and practice tips. This book picks up where your form file leaves off—supplying all the forms, pleadings, and instructions needed for most types of litigation. In addition to the sample forms, there is information on meeting with clients and witnesses, preparing exhibits, summarizing files and depositions, investigation, document control, and countless other time-consuming and crucial tasks. Wherever possible, information available on the Internet is included to make your job easier and faster.

Clear Lake Shores, TX   MARCY FAWCETT-DELESANDRI
November 2000

ACKNOWLEDGMENTS

Books are seldom written by the author alone. In this case, the actual writing of the book was secondary to the help and support that I received from the people who care about me. I want to thank both my family and my friends for encouraging me throughout my writing of this book and for their understanding during those times when my writing had to take precedent over my time with them. I want to thank Steve Scholl at Dotson, Babcock & Scofield, for his never-ending support and motivation of my professional development. I want to thank Brenda Turner, my secretary, without whose unselfish help, this book truly would never have been possible.

PARALEGAL LITIGATION
FORMS AND PROCEDURES

CHAPTER 1

CLIENT CONTACT

§ 1.1   Introduction

As a paralegal,[1] you are an invaluable aid to the attorney for maintaining relations with clients. Many attorneys feel that client contact is the most important job the

---

[1] The terms paralegal and legal assistant are completely interchangeable. Many people think they are two different things. The terms vary regionally. While Californians call themselves "paralegals,"

paralegal does. Because the attorney's schedule keeps him in trial, deposition, and settlement negotiations a good part of the time, it is important that someone remain accessible o the client. The paralegal is instrumental in obtaining and keeping the client's confidence, holding his hand when necessary, and making sure he feels his case is important to your office. Often you need only be a good listener to accomplish this task.

The paralegal plays an important role in communicating with clients by telephone and regular correspondence. The client needs to be informed of deadlines throughout the lawsuit, as well as dates for hearings, depositions and trial. The paralegal is the chief conduit of information between the client and the attorney, providing fast, accessible answers to the client's questions and problems. It is the paralegal's duty to relay the attorney's advise or answers expediently to the client. The paralegal also keeps in contact with the client during times of inactivity on the file, to reassure the client that his legal matters are being handled on a timely basis.

Throughout the lawsuit you will probably maintain more contact with the client than will the attorney. You will be the one to take the client's call when he has a small problem or when he needs assistance in matters related to his lawsuit. It is important that you maintain a professional but friendly relationship with him. You will also be the one to contact him when his signature is required on documents and when additional information is needed. You will be forwarding copies of the pleadings to him and answering questions he may have about them.

Paralegals, or legal assistants, are bound by the same ethics as attorneys, and are obligated to protect the confidentiality of the client's matters. They are also bound by the same ethics which govern conflict of interest and the obligation of delivering competent legal services to the client. Paralegals may not quote fees to a client, and therefore, the details of the financial arrangements of the case should be handled by the attorney, including the signing of the fee agreement by the client.

Whether the paralegal conducts the initial client interview with the client is a matter of personal preference to be decided by the attorney or the firm. Sometimes the paralegal is not brought into the case until after the initial client interview has taken place between the attorney and the client. The paralegal is often present during the initial interview so that he or she will be up to speed on the case facts and can proceed immediately with the fact gathering and discovery process.

In the beginning it is best to sit down with the client and explain to him the mechanics of a lawsuit and how it progresses through the various stages until settlement or trial. This is also a good time to address the types of things that he will most likely encounter during this period. Advise him not to give statements or information to anyone without clearing it through your office first, tell him of the possibility of surveillance by insurance company investigators or investigators hired by opposing counsel. Most of these things will have been discussed with him by your attorney, but the follow up on your part is important.

---

the trend in the rest of the country is toward the use of the term "legal assistant." For purposes of consistency, the term paralegal is used throughout this book.

§ 1.2   Client Contact Guidelines

It is extremely important for the paralegal to establish a good working relationship with the client. The following guidelines are essential for establishing necessary client rapport:

1. Be professional, but friendly.
2. Give the client 100 percent of your attention during the contact.
3. Remember ethical considerations.
4. Set a good tone for the client/firm relationship.
5. Explain the paralegal's role to the client.
6. Explain the client's role to him. Tell him what is expected of him.
7. Be considerate of the client's time, energy, and convenience.
8. Follow up on client requests immediately.
9. Prepare fully before any meeting or phone call with the client.
10. Return the client's phone calls promptly.
11. Be aware of the client's apprehensions and concerns.
12. Refrain from being judgmental.
13. Help the client to keep track of ongoing damages.
14. Educate the client regarding the litigation process.
15. Maintain contact on a regular basis, whether or not there has been any activity on the file.
16. Learn to read body language and respond accordingly.
17. Ask permission before tape-recording any interview, whether in person or by phone.
18. Be responsive and accessible to the client.
19. Empathize; do not sympathize.
20. LISTEN, LISTEN, LISTEN.

§ 1.3   Initial Client Interview

This chapter is written with the assumption that the paralegal is conducting the initial client interview. Emphasis is put on the mechanics and psychology of conducting a productive and proper interview, gaining the maximum amount of information from the client, and building a confidence-based rapport with the client during that interview. During the initial interview with the client you and your attorney will begin a fact-gathering process which will be the backbone of your case. Attention to detail during the initial stage will save hours of footwork later. Primarily for this reason, and because you are a trained observer, it is preferable to obtain the information needed from him in a personal interview rather than handing the client

3

a clipboard with a lengthy questionnaire and asking him to take a seat in the foyer and complete it.

There are psychological considerations to conducting a good interview which, if ignored, can be disastrous. Most times, the interview will go smoothly, and the client will be eager and cooperative to assist you in gathering the necessary information; however, there are times when the interview does not go as planned and adjustments must be made. The paralegal should be prepared to deal with such circumstances spontaneously. Dealing with clients is 99 percent common sense. It is usually easy to anticipate possible difficulties by placing yourself in the client's role and imagining how you would like to be treated under the same circumstances.

If you were to walk into the office of someone who was going to be handling very personal and important matters for you, you would not feel confident in that person's abilities to take care of your personal affairs if that person's office looked like a hurricane had just come through. Not only would you feel that your matters would not be dealt with competently, but you would feel that every person walking into that office would be able to see your file contents strewn about. Therefore, it is imperative that you clean your desk and office before conducting interviews there. If it is impossible to do so because of lack of storage space, hold the interview in another office or conference room.

People like to think that their matter is the most important, if not the only matter, which takes your attention. Therefore, it is terribly rude to accept phone calls on any other matters, and especially your own personal matters, while the client is in your office. It is also inexcusable to be condescending or patronizing to the client. No matter how small his matter may be, he must never be told that his case is small or insignificant. If is probably the most important thing in his life, or he would not be in your office discussing it in the first place.

A client also likes to think that you remember him and the intricate details of his case. If a client calls to discuss a matter with you, never begin the conversation until you have the file in front of you. Never leave anything to memory either. Every conversation should be documented with a memo to the file, and placed there immediately, so that the file remains complete at all times. Do not guess if a client asks you about a matter concerning his file. Tell him you will find out and call him back with the answer, and then do it promptly. Clients often feel that we do not deal with their matters with a sense of urgency.

Be prepared for the interview and do not waste the client's time. Have everything you will need organized and at hand, including documents the client will need to sign. I often discuss these documents early in the interview so that they can be prepared and brought into the interview before the client is ready to leave instead of waiting until the end of the interview and then having to make the client wait for the documents to be prepared.

Give the client your undivided attention. Do not fool with your clothing or hair or adjust things on your desk while he is talking. Always listen intently and maintain direct eye contact. Encourage him with smiles and positive body language such as leaning toward him as you speak. Ask if there is anything you can do to assist him right away, and then put it into motion immediately. He will go away with a feeling of well-being that his matters are important to you and that your will deal with him compassionately.

Sometimes, it becomes evident that the client has a problem speaking to you either because of your gender or because you are a paralegal instead of an attorney. Most times, this is because he is misinformed. Try to find out what the problem is and address it. Do not ignore it. Do not become defensive, or take it personally. Your job is to accommodate the client, who is paying for your services; it is not to inform the client that he is mistaken in his views. One possible solution to this problem is to ask the client outright if he would feel more comfortable discussing matters with the attorney. If he replies affirmatively, call the attorney and ask him to step into your office for a few moments. When he arrives, say something such as, "Mr. Attorney, Mr. Client has suggested that perhaps he will feel more comfortable discussing these matters with you, and I have assured him that we will do whatever he felt most comfortable with." The attorney will take your lead now, and begin a dialogue with the client so that a solution can be found. Most times, after a few minutes of conversation, the client will state that he now feels comfortable and will talk to the paralegal about the matter.

Sometimes you will need to go to the attorney after the interview and tell him that you feel the client is not comfortable with you, thereby giving the attorney the opportunity to amend the situation. Sometimes, the situation simply cannot be resolved and the attorney must assume full responsibility for any contact with the client, but that is rare. The attorney should always be given the opportunity to decide what is best for these situations. More often than not, the problem is a lack of understanding on the part of the client as to what a paralegal is, what her credentials are, and what role she assumes in the law office. The attorney can curtail most of these types of problems by introducing the paralegal to the client, explaining what the paralegal's role is, and giving the client the impression that the attorney has the utmost confidence in the paralegal's abilities to perform that role. The attorney should also clearly state to the client that the attorney wishes the client to communicate directly with the paralegal because it will enable the firm to handle the client's matters more quickly and efficiently. If your attorney does not presently practice these methods, perhaps you can sit down with him and discuss with him how important it is to your successful relationship with the client.

§ 1.4 Client Interview Checklist

The checklist that follows is designed for you to use as a guide in the interview of the client, to assure that no major or minor facts will be overlooked. The checklist is meant to make the client think and remember additional facts he may not even realize he has catalogued about the incidents leading up to the filing of the lawsuit. You may want to explain why some of your questions are relevant to the preparation of the case. Many times a client will not think to tell you something he knows about the incident because he does not think it is important or that it could help you in any way.

CLIENT CONTACT

Before beginning, be sure your client is seated comfortably with a soft drink or coffee. Situate yourself in a chair where you are able to easily carry on a conversation and are able to watch his body language and expressions. Try to avoid the traditional seating arrangement of the client seated in front of your desk and you behind it. Your goal is to make him as comfortable as possible.

As you go through the questions with your client, take thorough notes and explore additional facts which arise from standard questions. You do not want any surprises to come up during discovery, and it is essential that you know your case better than anyone else to protect the rights of your client.

The following checklist is to be used as a guideline in preparing for a successful interview. The different categories of information are meant only to prompt the paralegal into developing tailored questions for each specific lawsuit. This is never to be used as a generic questionnaire or given to the client to fill out.

____	**1.**	Review file and prepare interview questions.
____	**2.**	Clear desk and office.
____	**3.**	Hold all calls.
____	**4.**	Arrange for refreshments to be brought into the office for the interview.
____	**5.**	Greet the client personally, shake hands, and maintain eye contact.
____	**6.**	Make sure the client is comfortable.
____	**7.**	Remove barriers to intimidation (for example, stiff, formal seating arrangements, or suit jackets, to make a less formally dressed client feel more comfortable).
____	**8.**	Smile warmly, and often.
____	**9.**	LISTEN, LISTEN, LISTEN.
____	**10.**	Remember how important this case is to the client and the trauma it causes him.
____	**11.**	Never become jaded or hardened to the impact of the litigation on the client.
____	**12.**	Educate the client about the litigation process to take the mystery out of the process for him.
____	**13.**	Explain the paralegal's role to the client and state your credentials, if necessary, but do so with pride and confidence, not as an apology.
____	**14.**	Read client body language and facial expressions and react to correct any developing problems or misunderstandings.
____	**15.**	Try to find the source of resistance, if necessary, and correct it without being overbearing or pushy.
____	**16.**	If you sense that the client would rather speak to an attorney than a paralegal, assist him in making an appointment to see the attorney without reacting negatively.
____	**17.**	Keep the interview as short as possible.
____	**18.**	Never use a standard interview questionnaire except as a guide.

Give the client something to do.

Tell them to keep in touch w/ you

make notes instead of asking a quest. right away

___ 19. Allow the client to tell the story in his own words without interruption.

___ 20. Never assume you know more about the subject matter than the client does.

___ 21. Have the client sign all documents (such as authorizations) needed to begin the case.

___ 22. Explain the client's role in the litigation and the importance of keeping in touch.

___ 23. Remind the client to continue compiling damage information.

___ 24. Remind the client to keep all matters concerning the litigation confidential.

___ 25. Remind the client to follow the attorney's advice.

___ 26. Be aware of your ethical obligations, during the interview, and refrain from saying anything which could be construed as giving legal advice.

___ 27. Do not say or do anything during the interview which could be interpreted by the client as a statement of assurance that he will prevail in the lawsuit or that he will receive a judgment of "x" number of dollars.

___ 28. Remember to adhere to the goals of the interview. Identify the

    ___ A. Facts,

    ___ B. Witnesses,

    ___ C. Damages ($), and

    ___ D. Injuries (physical, mental or property).

§ 1.5 The Client's Role in Litigation

The paralegal needs to establish with the client that there are certain responsibilities that the client must fulfill during the lawsuit in order to accomplish the goals of the litigation. The following guidelines will help the client understand his role and responsibilities. Go over these guidelines personally with the client and answer any questions he may have.

1. Do not talk to anyone about this case, no matter how harmless the conversation may be. We do not want you to inadvertently waive a privilege concerning information which may be confidential and would not have otherwise been subject to discovery.

2. Do not make or sign statements for other attorneys, insurance investigators, or other persons. Refer all these persons to your attorney.

3. Notify your attorney if any persons of the type described in Number 2 attempt to contact you or if anyone is harassing you for information. It is unethical for opposing counsel or any person on his behalf to attempt to contact you without the permission of your attorney.

4. Save all documents which are related to your case and immediately forward them to your attorney. By documents, we mean bills, records, or any other documents which have any relation whatsoever to your case, whether or not they seem directly relevant.

5. Please stay in touch with your attorney at all times. Notify this office if you are going to go on vacation, change residence addresses, change jobs, change telephone numbers, or experience any other changes which would make it difficult for this office to contact you immediately.

6. Remain available to this office to assist in responding to discovery requests such as interrogatory answers, requests for admissions, depositions, and so forth. We will strive to give you as much notice as possible when your presence is required to give testimony at hearings, depositions, or trial.

7. Please maintain an appropriate demeanor throughout this case in deference for the serious matter which a lawsuit is. It may hurt your case to project a disrespectful or cocky attitude toward these proceedings.

8. Please follow all advice given to you by this office or any other professional employed to represent you in this case. If your case involves the necessity to remain under the care of a physician, it is especially important that you keep your appointments with the doctor and follow the doctor's advice and orders to the letter. Please do not stop attending rehabilitation or therapy sessions until formally released by your physician, even if you are experiencing a great improvement in how you feel.

9. Be forthright and timely with your attorney. Please comply with all requests from this office with your most urgent effort, and advise him of the complete truth of all matters relating to your case, however remote the connection may seem. It is imperative that your attorney have your complete cooperation and the benefit of all available information in order to represent you fully and skillfully.

§ 1.6   Client Checklist

Form 1–1 is a checklist for the paralegal to use to formulate questions suitable to a specific case.

FORM 1–1
SAMPLE CLIENT CHECKLIST

A.   Client Identification

Name _____

Address _____

Phone _____

§ 1.6   CLIENT CHECKLIST

Social Security number _____

Military status _____

Date of birth and age _____

Marital status _____

Dependents _____

Occupation _____

Employer name, address, and phone number _____

_____

Membership in union or professional organizations _____

_____

Police record (if any) _____

_____

Have you ever filed bankruptcy? If so, when? _____

_____

B.   Employment History

Type of work _____

Job title _____

Immediate supervisor's name _____

Salary or hourly rate _____

Number of hours worked before and after accident _____

Benefits (Company car, pension plan, vacation, home computer, and so forth) _____

_____

_____

C.   Insurance Coverage for Plaintiff

Name of carrier _____

Carrier's address and phone number _____

Policy number _____

Insurance agent's name, address, and phone number _____

_____

Collision coverage amount _____

Deductible amount _____

Liability coverage amount _____

CLIENT CONTACT

Medical payment amount _____

Uninsured motorist coverage amount _____

Cash policy for accidents _____

Dates of coverage _____

Group policy number (where applicable) _____

D.   Insurance Coverage for Defendant

Name of carrier _____

Policy number _____

Collision coverage amount _____

Liability coverage amount _____

Medical payment coverage amount _____

Uninsured motorist coverage amount _____

E.   Accident Facts (Personal injury or property damage)

Date _____

Day of week _____   Time of day _____

Location _____

Description of accident (Auto, gunshot, construction, and so forth) _____

_____

Name and address of all parties involved, including auto passengers

   1) _____

_____

_____

_____

   2) _____

_____

_____

_____

   3) _____

_____

_____

_____

§ 1.6   CLIENT CHECKLIST

4) _____

_____

_____

_____

5) _____

_____

_____

_____

6) _____

_____

_____

_____

7) _____

_____

_____

_____

Identification of all vehicles involved _____

_____

Name of police agency at scene _____

_____

Any arrests? _____

Any charges? _____

What were you doing? _____

_____

_____

Where were you going? _____

_____

Were you working? _____

If so, for whom? _____

F.   Accident Scene* (personal injury)

Number of lanes _____

Direction of travel _____

CLIENT CONTACT

Hills? _____

Width of lanes _____

Speed limit _____

Stop signs, signals, etc. _____

Road surface _____

Weather _____

Obstructions to vision _____

*Have client prepare sketch

G.   Outline of Accident* (personal injury)

Direction of travel of each vehicle _____

_____

Speed of each vehicle _____

_____

Signal equipment working? _____

Did either vehicle take evasive action? _____

_____

Location of skid marks _____

Location of physical debris _____

_____

_____

Point of impact _____

_____

Final resting place of vehicles _____

_____

Did anyone give statements? _____

If so, to whom and in what capacity? _____

Witnesses _____

_____

*Obtain written narrative statement from client

H.   Property Damage

Photographs? _____

_____

§ 1.6   CLIENT CHECKLIST

Damage to vehicle _____

Damage to buildings, city property, and so forth _____

_____

I.   Bodily Injuries (Plaintiff)

Conscious? _____

Extent of injury _____

_____

Ambulance required? _____

Nature of treatment _____

_____

X-rays? _____

Dates of treatment _____

_____

Drugs and medications _____

_____

Did your injury aggravate any pre-existing medical problems? _____

_____

J.   Bodily Injuries (Other parties)

Conscious? _____

Extent of injury _____

_____

Ambulance required? _____

K.   Previous Medical History

Any pre-existing conditions _____

_____

Prior injuries _____

_____

L.   Damages

How have these injuries changed your lifestyle? _____

CLIENT CONTACT

a) Loss of consortium (Husband, wife, or children) _____

_____

_____

b) Sports _____

_____

c) Sexual activities _____

_____

d) Social activities _____

_____

e) Job duties _____

_____

f) Household chores _____

_____

Have you had to hire domestic help? _____

_____

How do you feel you have been damaged? _____

_____

_____

a) If you feel you have been damaged emotionally by these injuries, please explain in detail how you have been damaged _____

_____

b) If you feel you have been damaged physically by these injuries, please explain in detail how you have been damaged_____

_____

_____

c) If you feel you have been damaged financially by these injuries, please explain in detail how you have been damaged _____

_____

M. Miscellaneous

Have you signed any authorizations to release information to anyone? _____

_____

Have you given any statements to anyone? _____

_____

§ 1.6 CLIENT CHECKLIST

Have you signed any releases? _____

_____

Have you received any insurance benefits? _____

_____

Have you been judged partially or permanently disabled by any administrative
agency? _____

_____

N. Have Client Sign Authorizations

O. Other Damages

How have you been damaged by the actions or omissions of the defendant?

    a) Lost or missed business opportunity _____

_____

_____

_____

    b) Financial damage or hardship _____

_____

_____

_____

    c) Personal reputation damage _____

_____

_____

_____

    d) Professional reputation damage _____

_____

_____

_____

P. Corporate or Business Information

If plaintiff is a corporation or business, the following information is needed:

    a) Name of business entity _____

_____

    b) Principal place of business (address) _____

_____

CLIENT CONTACT

c) Corporation, partnership, sole proprietorship, and so forth? _____

_____

d) Is business registered under the corporation or partnership laws of any state?___

_____

_____

State _____

Corporation or partnership number _____

Name and address of registered agent _____

_____

_____

Date of incorporation or filing of partnership _____

_____

Names and addresses of all directors:

1) _____

_____

_____

2) _____

_____

_____

3) _____

_____

_____

4) _____

_____

_____

5) _____

_____

_____

6) _____

_____

_____

7) _____

_____

_____

8) _____

_____

_____

9) _____

_____

_____

10) _____

_____

_____

Names and addresses of all officers:

President _____

_____

_____

Vice-president _____

_____

_____

Secretary _____

_____

_____

Treasurer _____

_____

_____

   e)   Business liability insurance coverage

Name of carrier _____

Address of carrier _____

_____

Policy number _____

Policy coverage dates _____

Policy liability coverage amounts _____

_____

Director or officer liability coverage amount _____

_____

§ 1.7   Authorizations

At the end of the initial interview, have the client execute the necessary authorization forms. **Forms 1–2** through **1–7** and **Form 1–9** exemplify various authorizations. Once these authorizations have been executed, photocopies may be made to accompany your brief letter to each hospital, doctor, place of employment, or entity your client has listed. The authorizations are necessary to obtain the needed information, and you will probably be asked by opposing counsel to supply the authorizations to the defendant so that he, too, may obtain the information he needs to defend his case.

The official forms for the Internal Revenue Service Information Request (**Form 1–8**) may be obtained from any Internal Revenue office, and should be mailed immediately to avoid any delay in receipt of the information.

It sometimes is difficult to obtain records from a busy hospital or doctor's office, so you should calendar a date two to three weeks into the future for follow-up. You may want to offer your services to the doctor's office to copy the needed records. In many instances, doctors simply are not staffed to handle requests of this nature easily.

§ 1.8   —Medical Records Authorization

FORM 1–2
SAMPLE MEDICAL RECORDS AUTHORIZATION FORM

TO: [name]

This will authorize you to furnish to the law firm of [name of law firm] or its representative, orally or in writing, as requested, all documents pertaining to [name of patient] as a result of injuries sustained by [reason for injuries] on or about the [date].

For purposes of this Medical Authorization, the word "documents" means, without limitation, the following items, whether printed, or recorded or reproduced by any other mechanical process, or written or reproduced by hand: Agreements, communications, correspondence, telegrams, memoranda, summaries or records of personal conversations or interviews, diaries, graphs, reports of consultants, photographs, motion picture films, any marginal comments appearing on any documents, billings, X-rays, and all other writings.

It is agreed that a photocopy of this authorization is to have the same force and effect as the original.

§ 1.8 MEDICAL RECORDS

DATED: [date]

[signature] _____

SUBSCRIBED AND SWORN to before me on this the [date] day of [month], [20__].

[signature of notary public] _____
NOTARY PUBLIC
State of [state] at Large
My Commission Expires: [date]

FORM 1–3
SAMPLE MEDICAL RECORDS AUTHORIZATION FORM
(ANOTHER FORM)

Name of Hospital

_____

_____

ATTN: Medical Records Department

Re: Name _____ [client's name] _____

Address _____ [client's address] _____

_____

E.R. Date: _____

Admission Date: _____

Dear Sir/Madam:

Consistent with the provisions of Public Health Law [section], I hereby request a copy of my hospital record and bill. In accordance with the further provisions of this request, I hereby authorize you to forward the records to my attorneys, [name of firm, address], upon payment by them of the statutory fees for such records.

_____ [name of client] _____

State of [state]   )
County of [county]   ) ss.:

On this ___ day of _____, 20__, before me personally came and appeared [client's name], to me known and known to me to be the individual described in and who executed the foregoing instrument, and who duly acknowledged to me that (s)he executed the same.

_____
Notary Public

§ 1.9 —Employment Records Authorization

FORM 1–4
SAMPLE EMPLOYMENT RECORDS AUTHORIZATION FORM

TO WHOM IT MAY CONCERN: [name]

This Authorization, or a photocopy thereof, will permit the law firm of [name], or its representative or the bearer, to inspect, review, and make copies, including photocopies, of any and all employment records regarding myself, including, but not limited to, application for employment, medical leave, vacation leave, sick leave, termination papers, and any other material contained in said employment records of the undersigned.

[name of client] _____

[attorney for client] _____

§ 1.10 Request for Student's Attendance Record

FORM 1–5
SAMPLE REQUEST FOR STUDENT'S ATTENDANCE RECORD

[school name and address]
ATTN: [name]
    Re: [accident date]

To Whom It May Concern:

Please be advised that we represent [name of student] in connection with claims for injuries sustained in an accident on [date], unrelated to the school.

We request a letter, on your stationery, setting forth the attendance record of the student following the accident.

An authorization for the release of this information is contained herein.

Thank you for your prompt attention to our request.

Very truly yours,

_____

§ 1.11   Request for Lost Earnings Statement

FORM 1–6
SAMPLE REQUEST FOR LOST EARNINGS STATEMENT

[Client's name and address]

Re: Lost Earnings Statement

Dear [client's name]:

We are presently assembling all information which we will require in connection with establishing your losses resulting from the accident. In connection therewith, we have requested the medical records, and we also require a statement from your employer relating to the time lost from employment.

Please deliver the enclosed letter to the proper department of [employer] and request that a statement of lost earnings, due to the injuries you sustained in the accident of [date] 20__, be forwarded to my office.

We will keep you advised as to the progress of the case. If at any time you have any questions, please feel free to contact us.

Very truly yours,

_____

§ 1.12 —Power of Attorney and Declaration of Representative (I.R.S. Form 2848)

FORM 1–7
SAMPLE I.R.S. FORM 2848

Form **2848** (Rev. October 1983) Department of the Treasury Internal Revenue Service	**Power of Attorney and Declaration of Representative** ► See separate Instructions	OMB No. 1545-0150

PART I. — Power of Attorney

Taxpayer(s) name, identifying number, and address including ZIP code (Please type or print)

For IRS Use Only		
File So.		
Level		
Receipt		
Powers		
Blind T.		
Action		
Ret.Ind.		

hereby appoints (name(s), CAF number(s), address(es), including ZIP code(s), and telephone number(s) of individual(s)) ▪

as attorney(s)-in-fact to represent the taxpayer(s) before any office of the Internal Revenue Service for the following tax matter(s) (specify the type(s) of tax and year(s) or period(s) (date of death if estate tax)):

Type of tax (Individual, corporate, etc.)	Federal tax form number (1040, 1120, etc.)	Year(s) or period(s) (Date of death if estate tax)

The attorney(s)-in-fact (or either of them) are authorized, subject to revocation, to receive confidential information and to perform any and all acts that the principal(s) can perform with respect to the above specified tax matters (excluding the power to receive refund checks, and the power to sign the return (see regulations section 1.6012-1(a)(5), Returns made by agents), unless specifically granted below).

Send copies of notices and other written communications addressed to the taxpayer(s) in proceedings involving the above tax matters to:

1 ☐ the appointee first named above, or

2 ☐ (names of not more than two of the above named appointees) ....

Initial here ► .... if you are granting the power to receive, but not to endorse or cash, refund checks for the above tax matters to :

3 ☐ the appointee first named above, or

4 ☐ (name of one of the above designated appointees) ► ....

This power of attorney revokes all earlier powers of attorney and tax information authorizations on file with the Internal Revenue Service for the same tax matters and years or periods covered by this power of attorney, except the following:

....

....

(Specify to whom granted, date, and address including ZIP code, or refer to attached copies of earlier powers and authorizations.)

Signature of or for taxpayer(s)
(If signed by a corporate officer, partner, or fiduciary on behalf of the taxpayer, I certify that I have the authority to execute this power of attorney on behalf of the taxpayer.)

....
(Signature) (Title, if applicable) (Date)
(Also type or print your name below if signing for a taxpayer who is not an individual.)

....
(Signature) (Title, if applicable) (Date)

▪ You may authorize an organization, firm, or partnership to receive confidential information, but your representative must be an individual who must complete Part II.

For Privacy Act and Paperwork Reduction Act Notice, see page 3 of the instructions.   Form **2848** (Rev. 10-83)

§ 1.12 POWER OF ATTORNEY

FORM 1–7
(continued)

If the power of attorney is granted to a person other than an attorney, certified public accountant, enrolled agent, or enrolled actuary, the taxpayer(s) signature must be witnessed or notarized below. (The representative must complete Part II. Only representatives listed there are recognized to practice before the Internal Revenue Service.)

The person(s) signing as or for the taxpayer(s): (Check and complete one.)

☐ is/are known to and signed in the presence of the two disinterested witnesses whose signatures appear here:

_____   _____
(Signature of Witness)   (Date)

_____   _____
(Signature of Witness)   (Date)

☐ appeared this day before a notary public and acknowledged this power of attorney as a voluntary act and deed.

Witness: _____   _____   NOTARIAL SEAL
(Signature of Notary)   (Date)   (if required by State law)

PART II.—Declaration of Representative

I declare that I am not currently under suspension or disbarment from practice before the Internal Revenue Service, that I am aware of Treasury Department Circular No. 230 as amended (31 C.F.R. Part 10), Regulations governing the practice of attorneys, certified public accountants, enrolled agents, enrolled actuaries, and others, and that I am one of the following:

1 a member in good standing of the bar of the highest court of the jurisdiction indicated below;
2 duly qualified to practice as a certified public accountant in the jurisdiction indicated below;
3 enrolled as an agent prusuant to the requirements of Treasury Department Circular No. 230;
4 a bona fide officer of the taxpayer organization;
5 a full-time employee of the taxpayer;
6 a member of the taxpayer's immediate family (spouse, parent, child, brother or sister);
7 a fiduciary for the taxpayer;
8 an enrolled actuary (the authority of an enrolled actuary to practice before the Service is limited by section 10.3(d)(1) of Treasury Department Circular No. 230);
9 Commissioner's special authorization (see instructions for Part II, item 9) _____ ;

and that I am authorized to represent the taxpayer identified in Part I for the tax matters there specified.

Designation (insert appropriate number from above list)	Jurisdiction (State, etc.) or Enrollment Card Number	Signature	Date

☆U.S.GPO:1985-0-483-221 ☆E.I.#430814326

CLIENT CONTACT

§ 1.13 —Tax Information Authorization and Declaration of Representative (I.R.S. Form 2848-D)

FORM 1–8
SAMPLE I.R.S. FORM 2848-D

Form **2848-D** (Rev. October 1983) Department of the Treasury Internal Revenue Service	**Tax Information Authorization and Declaration of Representative** ▶ See separate instructions.	OMB No. 1545-0150

PART I.—Tax Information Authorization

Taxpayer(s) name, identifying number, and address including ZIP code (Please type or print)

For IRS Use Only		
File So.		
Level		
Receipt		
Powers		
Blind T.		
Action		
Ret. Ind.		

hereby authorizes (name(s), CAF number(s), address(es) including ZIP code(s), and telephone number(s))

to receive from or inspect confidential tax information in any office of the Internal Revenue Service for the following tax matter(s).

Type of tax (Individual, corporate, etc.)	Federal tax form number (1040, 1120, etc.)	Year(s) or period(s) (Date of death if estate tax)

Initial here ▶ _ _ _ _ _ _ _ If you do NOT want the above named designee(s)* to act as the representative(s) of the taxpayer(s) before the Internal Revenue Service and to make written or oral presentations of fact or argument on behalf of the taxpayer for the above tax matters.

Send copies of notices and other written communications (excluding refund checks and routine mailings of tax forms) addressed to the taxpayer(s) in proceedings involving the above tax matters to:

1 ☐ the representative first named above, or

2 ☐ (names of not more than two of the above named representatives) _

Unless specified to the contrary below, this tax information authorization automatically revokes all earlier tax information authorizations, but does NOT revoke earlier powers of attorney, on file with the Internal Revenue Service for the tax matters and years or periods covered by this authorization.

_ _ _ _ _ _ _ _ _ _ _ _ _ _ _ (Specify any exceptions to the above, indicating to whom granted, date, and address.) _ _ _ _ _ _ _ _ _ _ _ _ _ _ _

Signature of or for taxpayer(s)

(If signed by a corporate officer, partner, or fiduciary on behalf of the taxpayer, I certify that I have the authority to execute this tax information authorization on behalf of the taxpayer.)

_ _ _ _ _ _ _ _ _ _ _ _ _ _ _ (Signature) _ _ _ _ _ _ _ _ _ _ _ _ _ _ _ (Title, if applicable) _ _ _ _ (Date)

(Also type or print your name below if signing for a taxpayer who is not an individual.)

_ _ _ _ _ _ _ _ _ _ _ _ _ _ _ (Signature) _ _ _ _ _ _ _ _ _ _ _ _ _ _ _ (Title, if applicable) _ _ _ _ (Date)

*If you initial this space, thus authorizing your designee(s) only to receive and inspect confidential information about your tax matters, your designee(s) may be an organization, firm, or partnership. If you do not initial this space, intending that your designee(s) act as your representative(s), your representative must be an individual who must complete Part II.

For Privacy Act and Paperwork Reduction Act Notice, see page 1 of separate instructions.   Form **2848-D** (Rev. 10-83)

§ 1.13   TAX INFORMATION AUTHORIZATION

FORM 1–8
(continued)

Form 2848-D (Rev. 10-83)   **Page 2**

PART II.—Declaration of Representative

I declare that I am not currently under suspension or disbarment from practice before the Internal Revenue Service, that I am aware of Treasury Department Circular No. 230 as amended (31 C.F.R. Part 10), Regulations governing the practice of attorneys, certified public accountants, enrolled agents, enrolled actuaries, unenrolled return preparers, and others, and that I am one of the following:

1 a member in good standing of the bar of the highest court of the jurisdiction indicated below;

2 duly qualified to practice as a certified public accountant in the jurisdiction indicated below;

3 enrolled as an agent pursuant to the requirements of Treasury Department Circular No. 230;

4 a bona fide officer of the taxpayer organization;

5 a full-time employee of the taxpayer;

6 a member of the taxpayer's immediate family (spouse, parent, child, brother or sister);

7 a fiduciary for the taxpayer;

8 an enrolled actuary (The authority of an enrolled actuary to practice before the Service is limited by section 10.3(d)(1) of Treasury Department Circular No. 230);

9 an unenrolled return preparer pursuant to section 10.7(a) (7) of Treasury Department Circular No. 230;

10 Commissioner's special authorization (see instructions for Part II, item 10) _ ;

and that I am authorized to represent the taxpayer identified in Part I for the tax matters there specified.

Designation (Insert appropriate number from above list)	Jurisdiction (State, etc.) or Enrollment Card Number	Signature	Date

§ 1.14 —General Authorization

FORM 1–9
SAMPLE GENERAL AUTHORIZATION FORM

NO. [case number]

[plaintiff name]	) IN THE DISTRICT COURT OF
	)
Plaintiff,	) [county] COUNTY,
	)
vs.	) [judicial district] JUDICIAL DISTRICT
	)
[defendant name]	)
	)
Defendant.	)

AUTHORIZATION

I, [client, parent/legal guardian of], hereby authorize and permit any person, firm, or entity (, including without limitation [names of persons/entities],) to release for inspection and copying to [name/entity], [firm name and address], or their authorized representative, any and all of the matters enumerated below that pertain to [name, date of birth, and Social Security number]. The matters to be released pursuant to this authorization are the following: any and all medical reports or records, x-rays, diagnostic studies, laboratory slides, clinical abstracts, histories, charts, and other information, documents, and opinions relevant to past, present, or future physical condition, treatment, care or hospitalizations. (In addition, the matters to be released include the following: any and all employment records, personal records, applications for employment, W-2 forms and other tax forms, documents related to the beginning of and termination of employment, and all documents, papers, checks, and ledgers showing wages, salaries, other earnings and employee benefits, and amount of time and number of days worked.) The release of the matters listed above is being authorized for purposes of a lawsuit entitled [case name], Case No. [case number], pending in the [district] District Court, in and for [county] County, [state]. A copy of this authorization is agreed by the undersigned to have the same effect and force of an original. Any person, firm, or entity that releases matters pursuant to this authorization is hereby absolved from any liability that might otherwise result from the release of those matters.

[plaintiff's name]

This instrument was acknowledged before me on the [date] day of [month], [20__].

[name of notary public]
Notary Public in and for
The State of [state]

§ 1.15 COVER LETTER CONCERNING AUTHORIZATIONS

FORM 1–10
SAMPLE GENERAL AUTHORIZATION FORM (ANOTHER FORM)

<u>AUTHORIZATION FOR THE RELEASE OF RECORDS</u>

TO: <u>[person or entity in possession of records]</u>

I hereby authorize you, by this form, to furnish <u>[name/entity, firm name and address]</u>, or a bearer, with a copy of the records of my <u>[identify records]</u>, the release of which requires my written authorization. (If records are of an infant, incompetent, or decedent, in my capacity as parent/attorney-in-fact, administrator, or executor.)

<u>A COPY OF THIS FORM SHALL HAVE THE SAME EFFECT AS THE ORIGINAL</u>

Dated: <u>[date]</u>   _____

NAME: [client's name]

ADDRESS: [client's address]

STATE OF <u>[state]</u>, COUNTY OF <u>[county]</u>) ss.;

On <u>[date]</u> , before me personally came and appeared the individual described in and who executed the foregoing instrument, and who duly acknowledged to me that he/she executed the same.

_____

Notary Public

§ 1.15   Cover Letter to Client
Concerning Authorizations

If your client does not sign the necessary authorizations while in your office, the authorizations can be sent to the client with the following cover letter.

FORM 1–11
AUTHORIZATION COVER LETTER

<u>[date]</u>

<u>[client's name]</u>
<u>[client's address]</u>

   Re: Your accident case

CLIENT CONTACT

Dear [client's name]:

Enclosed please find various authorizations which require your signature. Kindly sign same where indicated with an "X" and return them to us immediately in the self-addressed, postage-paid envelope which has been enclosed for your convenience.

If you have any questions, please do not hesitate to contact the undersigned.

Thanking you, I remain,

Very truly yours,
 [firm name]

_____
Paralegal

Encls.

§ 1.16 Client Damage Expense Records

The following form (**Form 1–12**) is useful in helping your personal injury client keep track o the continuing expenses he incurs as a result of his injury. Give it to your client during the initial interview and explain its use to him. It is a good idea to have this checklist printed on the outside of an 11" x 14" manila envelope. Expenses may be documented on the outside of the envelope, and the actual receipts stored inside.

FORM 1–12
SAMPLE DAMAGE EXPENSE RECORD FORM

PHYSICIANS BILLS

	NAME OF PHYSICIAN	DATE OF VISIT	CHARGES	PARKING CHARGES & MILEAGE	LOST TIME FROM WORK
1.	_____	_____	_____	_____	_____
2.	_____	_____	_____	_____	_____
3.	_____	_____	_____	_____	_____
4.	_____	_____	_____	_____	_____
5.	_____	_____	_____	_____	_____
6.	_____	_____	_____	_____	_____
7.	_____	_____	_____	_____	_____
8.	_____	_____	_____	_____	_____

§ 1.16   DAMAGE EXPENSE RECORDS

9. _____ _____ _____ _____ _____
10. _____ _____ _____ _____ _____

PHYSICAL THERAPY BILLS

NAME OF PHYSICAL THERAPIST	DATE OF VISIT	CHARGES	PARKING CHARGES & MILEAGE	LOST TIME FROM WORK
1. _____	_____	_____	_____	_____
2. _____	_____	_____	_____	_____
3. _____	_____	_____	_____	_____
4. _____	_____	_____	_____	_____
5. _____	_____	_____	_____	_____
6. _____	_____	_____	_____	_____
7. _____	_____	_____	_____	_____
8. _____	_____	_____	_____	_____
9. _____	_____	_____	_____	_____
10. _____	_____	_____	_____	_____

MEDICATIONS AND ORTHOPEDIC EQUIPMENT

NAME OF PRESCRIBING PHYSICIAN	NAME OF DRUG OR EQUIPMENT	DATE	AMOUNT
1. _____	_____	_____	_____
2. _____	_____	_____	_____
3. _____	_____	_____	_____
4. _____	_____	_____	_____
5. _____	_____	_____	_____
6. _____	_____	_____	_____
7. _____	_____	_____	_____
8. _____	_____	_____	_____
9. _____	_____	_____	_____
10. _____	_____	_____	_____

CLIENT CONTACT

WAGE LOSS

	DATE	HOURS MISSED	EARNINGS LOST
1.	_____	_____	_____
2.	_____	_____	_____
3.	_____	_____	_____
4.	_____	_____	_____
5.	_____	_____	_____
6.	_____	_____	_____
7.	_____	_____	_____
8.	_____	_____	_____
9.	_____	_____	_____
10.	_____	_____	_____

BENEFITS LOSS

	DATE	BENEFIT LOST	DOLLAR VALUE
1.	_____	_____	_____
2.	_____	_____	_____
3.	_____	_____	_____
4.	_____	_____	_____

RENTAL CAR EXPENSE

	NAME OF RENTAL COMPANY	DATE	CHARGES
1.	_____	_____	_____
2.	_____	_____	_____

§ 1.17 Declining Representation

Sometimes your firm will decide not to represent a prospective client for any of a number of reasons. When this happens, a letter will have to be sent to the individual explaining in lay terms why the firm has decided not to represent him or her. Whatever the reasons for declining the representation, the prospective client should be treated with the same deference and respect as any other client of the firm. It is important not only to preserve that person's rights, but also to protect the firm from the liability of malpractice. The decision to decline representation should be made as early as possible to avoid prejudice to the client's case.

There have probably been court decisions in your state which outline the responsibilities of the law firm in this regard. When a person comes to an attorney and entrusts his legal matters to the attorney, then the attorney and his firm is responsible for advising that person so that his rights are not prejudiced, even if the firm decides not to take the case.

For example, the statutes of limitation should be assessed immediately and calendared. The answer date to a complaint or petition should also be calendared and the prospective client should be notified immediately of the need for responding by the appropriate date. The firm should always allow enough time for the client to gain other representation in time to meet these deadlines, and should make sure the client is not only informed about, but also understands the consequences of inaction by that date.

Sometimes the problem is more complicated than a simple checking of the statute of limitation. If there is possible liability on the part of a governmental agency, for example, this question should be researched immediately. Although the statute of limitations may not have run, there is a possibility of a very short-lived window of time in which a claimant may give notice to such an agency that damages have been incurred and litigation is being contemplated. Sometimes this time frame is as short as six weeks, and may have already run before the prospective client reaches your office. You will find information on your state's statutes of limitation in the civil code for your state. For links to state statutes on the Internet, go to *www.findlaw.com.*

Your firm may want to assist the prospective client by directing him to other legal counsel who may be able to help. Sometimes a firm will turn down representation because the subject matter is outside its area of expertise, but the firm can refer the client to another attorney who handles these types of claims. It is always preferable to do this than to turn down a prospective client and leave him with no information on how to proceed. It is always preferable to speak to the prospective client in person when representation is declined, and to follow up with a letter. (See **Form 1–13**.) The file materials should be returned to the client immediately.

FORM 1–13
SAMPLE LETTER DECLINING REPRESENTATION

[name]
[address]

Dear [name]:

We have had an opportunity to review the file materials which you left with us regarding your possible lawsuit for [cause of action] against [name of party]. We regret that we will not be able to represent you in this action. [Insert appropriate explanation here, for example,

1) creation of conflict of interest

2) outside attorney's area of expertise

3) cost of prosecution of case would exceed expected damages award

4) statute of limitations has run

5) facts insufficient to support a cause of action.]

We have determined that the statute of limitations on your cause of action will expire on [date]. If you desire to pursue this litigation, you must contact an attorney to file this action for you before that date. If the action is not filed before that date, under the law your right to pursue your claim will be automatically waived.

We have returned your file materials by messenger and ask that you sign for their receipt. We wish you luck with your legal matters and urge you to seek other legal counsel as soon as possible.

Respectfully yours,

[name]
Attorney at Law

Enc.
Return Receipt Requested

§ 1.18   Client Contact—Execution of Documents

Arranging for the client to come in to the office to execute documents is usually the responsibility of the paralegal. It will be necessary to obtain you client's signature on medical, tax, employment and other authorizations, his deposition, certain pleadings, and settlement documents. Be sure to have you client's signature notarized when necessary to avoid any later inconvenience to him or yourself. Be prompt when your client arrives and make every contact with him a professional and pleasant one.

It is best to have the client come to the office to execute documents, but at times this may be difficult for the client, particularly one who is elderly or disabled. If you choose to have the documents sent to the client, be sure to include very explicit instructions. A numbered, step-by-step list is probably the most effective way to set out such instructions. Take nothing for granted. If a document must be notarized, make sure the client understands that the document must be executed in front of a notary. It is not uncommon for a client to simply sign the document, thinking that you will notarize it upon receipt. In some cases it may be best to deliver the documents to the client personally.

§ 1.19   —Keeping the Client Up-to-Date

Send copies of all pleadings to your client as they are received or generated. It is best to dictate a brief cover letter to accompany the documents explaining their significance in lay terms. This process may save you an inquiring phone call later. Even when there is no activity on the file you should be in regular contact with the client advising him of the status. Use these contacts as an opportunity to obtain any supplementary information your client may have gathered.

Clients want to know what is happening in their case, why it is happening, and what will happen next. One of the most effective means of providing a client with this information is by letter. Even in firms where such letters are to come from the attorney, the attorney will often expect the paralegal to at least draft the letter. (Of course, letters providing legal advice or opinions must come from the attorney.)

Some guidelines should be followed when you write to a client:

1. **Keep it simple.** Avoid "legalese." Legalese can make any writing difficult to understand, but use of legalese in a letter to a client may make the letter impossible to understand or, worse, result in the client coming to an incorrect conclusion.

2. **Get to the point.** Clients are apt to get nervous when they receive a letter from their attorney. They might simply scan the letter until they get to what they think is the point. Keep the pleasantries brief and say what you have to say.

3. **Consider your audience.** The writing style you use in your letter should vary depending upon the sophistication of the client. A letter to an executive or physician should not be worded in the same way as one directed to a laborer.

§ 1.20   —Aiding the Client

During the course of the lawsuit, the client may require your assistance in matters related to his injuries. For example, in a personal injury traffic accident case, it is not uncommon for the paralegal to act as the liaison between the defendant's insurance company and the plaintiff to arrange for rental car transportation for the plaintiff while his car is being repaired or replaced. It is also common practice to assist the client in setting up doctor's appointments and physical therapy sessions. In cases of worker's compensation claims, the job of filling out the forms and maintaining telephone contact with state worker's compensation offices will fall upon the paralegal. The important thing to remember is that your client has been traumatized and your handling of some of the accident-related details will make things easier for him.

One thing to avoid is assisting your client to the point where he becomes totally dependent on you and helpless without your assistance. It will do neither you nor your client any good if you allow him to call your office several times each day with a myriad of complaints and problems. If this happens, explain to your client that his case is being handled efficiently and professionally and everything possible is being done to bring his case to a speedy and satisfactory conclusion. It is always helpful to arrange for periodic phone contacts between your attorney and these types of clients.

Ninety-nine times out of a hundred, the call from your client is seeking nothing more than reassurance and positive reinforcement. Learn to be sensitive to your client's emotional needs, and assist him to the best of your ability in coping with the other problems associated with his injury. Generally, business clients require less assistance than personal injury clients, but you should be equally attentive to their needs and requests. Just because your client is a businessperson does not mean he is any less apprehensive about the litigation.

§ 1.21 —Instructions to Client: Medical Examination

Part of keeping the client fully informed means instructing the client as to how to handle an opponent's request for the client's medical examination. Sample client instructions follow:

Instructions to Client
Medical Examinations

A medical examination of you has been requested by the defendant's attorney or insurance company. Before your examination, please read the following instructions.

1. BE AS COOPERATIVE AS YOU CAN. Remember that the doctor is not examining you so that he or she can treat your medical condition, but in order to testify for the defendant against you at your trial.
2. TELL THE TRUTH. Be sure to tell the doctor about all the pain, discomfort, and suffering you have experienced because of the incident. Be sure to describe all the things that you are unable to do now because of the incident. Describe in detail the activities you are unable to perform and how the incident has affected your ability to perform them. If you fail to tell the doctor about any of your problems, he or she will not include them in his or her report, and this will affect the value of your case.
3. DO NOT sign any papers, records, or documents.
4. DO NOT give any information about the incident itself, except that it occurred. Do not describe it or give any other information. Advise the doctor or other medical personnel to contact your lawyer if more information is desired.
5. BE CAREFUL IN REPEATING WHAT OTHER DOCTORS HAVE TOLD YOU. If you are asked what other doctors have said about your medical condition, answer in a very general way. For example: "He says that I will have trouble the rest of my life," or "He says that I am getting better, but that it is going to take time."

6. DO NOT allow any laboratory tests, puncturing of skin, or taking of blood or urine unless the doctor obtains your lawyer's written permission. You may submit to X-rays.

7. DO NOT volunteer or give information about past incidents, medical history, past claims, or family history, unless you were specifically instructed to do so by your lawyer or your own doctor.

8. DO NOT permit more than one doctor to examine you.

9. Cooperate with the examining doctor during the examination, but do not be too friendly or give information not requested.

10. Be observant. Take careful note of all words spoken, remarks made, and the places where discussions and examinations took place.

11. Make a note of the time you arrived, the time spent in the waiting room, and the exact time spent by the doctor in taking your history and examining you. Also take note of the time spent on X-rays.

12. REMEMBER THAT THE EXAMINATION BEGINS AS SOON AS YOU ENTER THE OFFICE. The doctor may be watching you from the time you enter the office. The doctor may watch you take off your coat and note whether you have any trouble doing so. The doctor may watch how you walk about the room. It is impossible to fool the doctor, and you should be honest about your problem.

§ 1.22 Practice Tips

Because you will have so much contact with the client, it is almost certain that at one point or another he will ask you for advice. It is essential to remember that, as a paralegal, it is neither legal nor ethical for you to give legal advice to anyone. When this situation arises, tell your client you may not advise him, but will be happy to relate his question to your attorney and either you or he will get back to him promptly with an answer.

Some attorneys are more accessible to their paralegals than others. If you have difficulty finding an opportune time to discuss the developments of a case with your attorney, it is a good idea to schedule an office conference with him at an agreed time every day or week. If this is not feasible, communication by interoffice memo is the next best thing. Keep your attorney apprised of your conversations with your client, and the developments that they bring. Never rely on memory to relate the contents of a client conversation. Get in the habit of taking notes during your phone contact with your client and immediately upon conclusion of the call, dictate a memo to the file. Be sure to follow up on obtaining answers for any questions the client may have had.

CHAPTER 2

INITIATION OF THE SUIT

§ 2.1   Introduction

Whether it is called a complaint or a petition, this document is the initial pleading filed in a case and will always contain certain elements. A complaint must state the names of the parties, show why jurisdiction is proper in the particular court in which you are filing the document, state the causes of action against the defendants, give statements showing how the plaintiffs have been damaged, and include a prayer for relief.

Under the Federal Rules of Procedure, notice pleading is used. Many states have adopted based on the Federal Rules of Civil Procedure with slight variances, and therefore, also subscribe to notice pleading. There are several states, however, that use a more complex codified system. In these states, a more detailed fact pleading system is subscribed to. As notice pleading is the more common, the references herein will be addressed to that system.

This chapter includes the forms for a civil cover sheet (**Form 2–1**) and a summons (**Form 2–2**) used in federal court. The civil cover sheet is an easy document to fill out, and contains its own set of instructions on the back of the document. One of these forms is necessary when filing an original complaint with the clerk of the court. The summons is to be filled out for every defendant you wish to have served. When you present this summons at the time of filing of the complaint, the clerk will issue the summons so that process may be served on the defendant.

§ 2.1 INTRODUCTION

Filing fees vary from court to court. In federal court there is a one-time filing fee to be paid at the time of filing of the complaint. Most state courts, however, will assess different fees for the filing of different pleadings throughout the lawsuit.

FORM 2–1
SAMPLE CIVIL COVER SHEET

JS 44
(Rev. 07/86)

CIVIL COVER SHEET

The JS-44 civil cover sheet and the information contained herein neither replace nor supplement the filing and service of pleadings or other papers as required by law, except as provided by local rules of court. This form, approved by the Judicial Conference of the United States in September 1974, is required for the use of the Clerk of Court for the purpose of initiating the civil docket sheet. (SEE INSTRUCTIONS ON THE REVERSE OF THE FORM.)

I (a) PLAINTIFFS

DEFENDANTS

(b) COUNTY OF RESIDENCE OF FIRST LISTED PLAINTIFF _____
(EXCEPT IN U.S. PLAINTIFF CASES)

COUNTY OF RESIDENCE OF FIRST LISTED DEFENDANT _____
(IN U.S. PLAINTIFF CASES ONLY)
NOTE: IN LAND CONDEMNATION CASES, USE THE LOCATION OF THE TRACT OF LAND INVOLVED

(c) ATTORNEYS (FIRM NAME, ADDRESS, AND TELEPHONE NUMBER)

ATTORNEYS (IF KNOWN)

II. BASIS OF JURISDICTION *(PLACE AN - IN ONE BOX ONLY)*

□ 1 U.S. Government Plaintiff
□ 2 U.S. Government Defendant
□ 3 Federal Question (U.S. Government Not a Party)
□ 4 Diversity (Indicate Citizenship of Parties in Item III)

III. CITIZENSHIP OF PRINCIPAL PARTIES *(PLACE AN × IN ONE BOX FOR PLAINTIFF AND ONE BOX FOR DEFENDANT)*
(For Diversity Cases Only)

	PTF	DEF		PTF	DEF
Citizen of This State	□ 1	□ 1	Incorporated or Principal Place of Business in This State	□ 4	□ 4
Citizen of Another State	□ 2	□ 2	Incorporated and Principal Place of Business in Another State	□ 5	□ 5
Citizen or Subject of a Foreign Country	□ 3	□ 3	Foreign Nation	□ 6	□ 6

IV. CAUSE OF ACTION (CITE THE U.S. CIVIL STATUTE UNDER WHICH YOU ARE FILING AND WRITE A BRIEF STATEMENT OF CAUSE

DO NOT CITE JURISDICTIONAL STATUTES UNLESS DIVERSITY)

V. NATURE OF SUIT *(PLACE AN × IN ONE BOX ONLY)*

CONTRACT	TORTS		FORFEITURE /PENALTY	BANKRUPTCY	OTHER STATUTES
□ 110 Insurance	**PERSONAL INJURY**	**PERSONAL INJURY**	□ 610 Agriculture	□ 422 Appeal 28 USC 158	□ 400 State Reapportionment
□ 120 Marine	□ 310 Airplane	□ 362 Personal Injury — Med Malpractice	□ 620 Food & Drug	□ 423 Withdrawal 28 USC 157	□ 410 Antitrust
□ 130 Miller Act	□ 315 Airplane Product Liability		□ 630 Liquor Laws		□ 430 Banks and Banking
□ 140 Negotiable Instrument		□ 365 Personal Injury — Product Liability	□ 640 R.R. & Truck		□ 450 Commerce/ICC Rates/etc
□ 150 Recovery of Overpayment & Enforcement of Judgment	□ 320 Assault, Libel & Slander	□ 368 Asbestos Personal Injury Product Liability	□ 650 Airline Regs	**PROPERTY RIGHTS**	□ 460 Deportation
□ 151 Medicare Act	□ 330 Federal Employers Liability		□ 660 Occupational Safety/Health	□ 820 Copyrights	□ 470 Racketeer Influenced and Corrupt Organizations
□ 152 Recovery of Defaulted Student Loans (Excl Veterans)	□ 340 Marine	**PERSONAL PROPERTY**	□ 690 Other	□ 830 Patent	□ 810 Selective Service
	□ 345 Marine Product Liability	□ 370 Other Fraud		□ 840 Trademark	□ 850 Securities/Commodities/ Exchange
□ 153 Recovery of Overpayment of Veteran's Benefits	□ 350 Motor Vehicle	□ 371 Truth in Lending	**LABOR**	**SOCIAL SECURITY**	□ 875 Customer Challenge 12 USC 3410
□ 160 Stockholders' Suits	□ 355 Motor Vehicle Product Liability	□ 380 Other Personal Property Damage	□ 710 Fair Labor Standards Act	□ 861 HIA (1395ff)	□ 891 Agricultural Acts
□ 190 Other Contract	□ 360 Other Personal Injury	□ 385 Property Damage Product Liability	□ 720 Labor/Mgmt Relations	□ 862 Black Lung (923)	□ 892 Economic Stabilization Act
□ 195 Contract Product Liability			□ 730 Labor/Mgmt Reporting & Disclosure Act	□ 863 DIWC (405(g))	□ 893 Environmental Matters
				□ 863 DIWW (405(g))	□ 894 Energy Allocation Act
REAL PROPERTY	**CIVIL RIGHTS**	**PRISONER PETITIONS**		□ 864 SSID Title XVI	□ 895 Freedom of Information Act
□ 210 Land Condemnation	□ 441 Voting	□ 510 Motions to Vacate Sentence	□ 740 Railway Labor Act	□ 865 RSI (405(g))	□ 900 Appeal of Fee Determination Under Equal Access to Justice
□ 220 Foreclosure	□ 442 Employment	□ 530 Habeas Corpus	□ 790 Other Labor Litigation	**FEDERAL TAX SUITS**	
□ 230 Rent Lease & Ejectment	□ 443 Housing/ Accommodations	□ 540 Mandamus & Other	□ 791 Empl. Ret. Inc Security Act	□ 870 Taxes (U.S. Plaintiff or Defendant)	□ 950 Constitutionality of State Statutes
□ 240 Torts to Land	□ 444 Welfare	□ 550 Civil Rights		□ 871 IRS — Third Party 26 USC 7609	□ 890 Other Statutory Actions
□ 245 Tort Product Liability	□ 440 Other Civil Rights				
□ 290 All Other Real Property					

VI. ORIGIN *(PLACE AN × IN ONE BOX ONLY)*

□ 1 Original Proceeding
□ 2 Removed from State Court
□ 3 Remanded from Appellate Court
□ 4 Reinstated or Reopened
□ 5 Transferred from another district (specify)
□ 6 Multidistrict Litigation
□ 7 Appeal to District Judge from Magistrate Judgment

VII. REQUESTED IN COMPLAINT: CHECK IF THIS IS A **CLASS ACTION** □ UNDER F.R.C.P. 23
DEMAND $
Check YES only if demanded in complaint:
JURY DEMAND: □ YES □ NO

VIII. RELATED CASE(S) IF ANY (See instructions)
JUDGE _____ DOCKET NUMBER _____

DATE

SIGNATURE OF ATTORNEY OF RECORD

UNITED STATES DISTRICT COURT

INITIATION OF THE SUIT

FORM 2–1
(continued)

INSTRUCTIONS FOR ATTORNEYS COMPLETING CIVIL COVER SHEET FORM JS-44

Authority For Civil Cover Sheet

The JS-44 civil cover sheet and the information contained herein neither replaces nor supplements the filings and service of pleadings or other papers as required by law, except as provided by local rules of court. This form, approved by the Judicial Conference of the United States in September 1974, is required for the use of the Clerk of Court for the purpose of initiating the civil docket sheet. Consequently a civil cover sheet is submitted to the Clerk of Court for each civil complaint filed. The attorney filing a case should complete the form as follows:

I. (a) Plaintiffs - Defendants. Enter names (last, first, middle initial) of plaintiff and defendant. If the plaintiff or defendant is a Government Agency, use only the full name or standard abbreviations. If the plaintiff or defendant is an official within a government agency, identify first the agency and then the official, giving both name and title.

(b) County of Residence. For each civil case filed, except U.S. plaintiff cases, enter the name of the county where the first listed plaintiff resides at the time of filing. In U.S. plaintiff cases, enter the name of the county in which the first listed defendant resides at the time of filing. (NOTE: In land condemnation cases, the county of residence of the "defendant" is the location of the tract of land involved).

(c) Attorneys. Enter firm name, address, telephone number, and attorney or record. If there are several attorneys list them on an attachment, noting in this section "(see attachment)".

II. Jurisdiction. The basis of jurisdiction is set forth under Rule 8 (a), F.R.C.P. which requires that jurisdiction be shown in pleadings. Place an "X" in one of the boxes. If there is more than one basis of jurisdiction, precedence is given in the order shown below.

United States plaintiff. (1) Jurisdiction is based on 28 U.S.C. 1345 and 1348. Suits by agencies and officers of the United States are included here.

United States defendant. (2) When the plaintiff if suing the United States, its officers or agencies, place an X in this box.

Federal question. (3) This refers to suits under 28 U.S.C. 1331 where jurisdiction arises under the Constitution of the United States, an amendment to the Constitution, and act of Congress or a treaty of the United States. In cases where the U.S. is a party, the U.S. plaintiff or defendant code takes precedence and box 1 or 2 should be marked.

Diversity of citizenship. (4) This refers to suits under 28 U.S.C. 1332 where parties are citizens of different states. When Box 4 is checked, the citizenship of the different parties must be checked. (See Section III below.) (Federal question actions take precedence over diversity cases.)

III. Residence (citizenship) of Principal Parties. This section of the JS-44 is to be completed if diversity of citizenship was indicated above. Mark this section for each principal party.

IV. Cause of Action. Report the civil statute directly related to the cause of action and give a brief description of the cause.

V. Nature of Suit. Place an "X" in the appropriate box. If the nature of suit cannot be determined, be sure the cause of description, in Section IV above, is sufficient to enable the deputy clerk or the statistical clerks in the Administrative Office to determine the nature of suit. If the cause fits more than one nature of suit, select the most definitive.

VI. Origin. Place an "X" in one of the seven boxes.

Original Proceedings. (1) Cases which originate in the United States district courts.

Removed from State Court. (2) Proceedings initiated in state courts may be removed to the district courts under Title 28 U.S.C., Section 1441. When the petition for removal is granted, check this box

Remanded from Appellate Court. (3) Check this box for cases remanded to the district court for further action. Use the date of remand as the filing date.

Reinstated or Reopened. (4) Check this box for cases reinstated or reopened in the district court. Use the reopening date as the filing date.

Transferred from Another District. (5) For cases transferred under Title 28 U.S.C. Section 1404(a). Do not use this for within district transfers or multidistrict litigation transfers.

Multidistrict Litigation. (6) Check this box when a multidistrict case is transferred into the district under authority of Title 28 U.S.C. Section 1407. When this box is checked do not check (5) above.

Appeal to District Judge from Magistrate Judgment. (7) Check this box for an appeal from a magistrate's decision.

VII. Requested in Complaint. Class Action. Place an "X" in this box if you are filing a class action under Rule 23, F.R.Cv.P.

Demand. In this space enter the dollar amount (in thousands of dollars) being demanded or indicate other demand such as a preliminary injunction.

Jury Demand. Check the appropriate box to indicate whether or not a jury is being demanded.

VIII. Related Cases. This section of the JS-44 is used to reference relating pending cases if any. If there are related pending cases, insert the docket numbers and the corresponding judge names for such cases.

Date and Attorney Signature. Date and sign the civil cover sheet.

(07/86)

40

§ 2.1 INTRODUCTION

FORM 2–2
SAMPLE FEDERAL COURT SUMMONS

AO 440 (Rev. 5/85) Summons in a Civil Action ●

United States District Court

SOUTHERN _____ DISTRICT OF _____ TEXAS

SUMMONS IN A CIVIL ACTION

V.

CASE NUMBER:

TO: (Name and Address of Defendant)

YOU ARE HEREBY SUMMONED and required to file with the Clerk of this Court and serve upon

PLAINTIFF'S ATTORNEY (name and address)

an answer to the complaint which is herewith served upon you, within _____ days after service of this summons upon you, exclusive of the day of service. If you fail to do so, judgment by default will be taken against you for the relief demanded in the complaint.

_____ Jesse E. Clark, Clerk _____   _____
CLERK   DATE

BY DEPUTY CLERK _____

41

FORM 2–2
(continued)

AO 440 (Rev. 5/85) Summons in a Civil Action

RETURN OF SERVICE	
Service of the Summons and Complaint was made by me[1]	DATE
NAME OF SERVER	TITLE

Check one box below to indicate appropriate method of service

☐ Served personally upon the defendant. Place where served: _____
_____ _____

☐ Left copies thereof at the defendant's dwelling house or usual place of abode with a person of suitable age and discretion then residing therein.
Name of person with whom the summons and complaint were left: _____

☐ Returned unexecuted: _____
_____
_____

☐ Other (specify): _____
_____
_____

STATEMENT OF SERVICE FEES		
TRAVEL	SERVICES	TOTAL

DECLARATION OF SERVER

I declare under penalty of perjury under the laws of the United States of America that the foregoing information contained in the Return of Service and Statement of Service Fees is true and correct.

Executed on _____ _____
Date   Signature of Server

_____
Address of Server

1) As to who may serve a summons see Rule 4 of the Federal Rules of Civil Procedure.

42

§ 2.2   Changes in Method of Service

The method of service under the Feral Rules of Civil Procedure has been completely altered according to Federal Rule of Civil Procedure 4(d)(2). The plaintiff now delivers a notice of initiation of the lawsuit along with a request for the defendant voluntarily to waive service of the summons to the defendant. The notice must allow the defendant a reasonable amount of time (at least 30 days from the date on which the request was sent) to return the waiver. If the defendant is addressed outside any judicial district of the United States, he or she must be given 60 days to return the waiver. The defendant is instructed in the document of his affirmative obligation to avoid the unnecessary costs of service of a summons by completing and returning the enclosed waiver of service. (Both forms are provided in this section. See Notice of Lawsuit and Request for Waiver of Summons (**Form 2–3**) and Waiver of Service of Summons (**Form 2–4**).) If the defendant complies with the request by returning the waiver within 30 days, he is then given 60 days in which to respond to the pleading rather than the traditional 20 days under the old rule. A defendant who is addressed outside any judicial district of the United States will have 90 days to serve an answer if he or she complies.

The notice must be in writing and addressed directly to the defendant, if the defendant is an individual, or else to an officer or managing or general agent authorized by appointment or law to receive service. Significantly, the notice may be dispatched by first-class mail or other reliable means.

A defendant who does not return the waiver must be served in one of the more traditional ways, as set out in Rule 4 of the Federal Rules of Civil Procedure.

The plaintiff must send the forms to the defendant along with a copy of the complaint and a prepaid means of returning the waiver, such as a stamped, self-addressed envelope.

If the defendant does not return the waiver, the court, under the new rules, is required to tax the costs of service of the summons and complaint to the defendant unless there is a showing of good cause by the defendant.

If the defendant does waive service by returning the waiver, the plaintiff must file the waiver with the court, which then serves as proof of service. The date of the filing of the waiver serves as the date of the tolling of the statute of limitations. Notice that the language in the waiver preserves the rights of the defendant, and does not waive his rights to object to venue or personal jurisdiction. Service using a notice of initiation is not complete unless the defendant returns the waiver. Mere proof that the defendant received the notice is not sufficient. So, for example, if the notice is mailed by certified mail and the plaintiff receives the return receipt, this may be proof that the defendant received the notice, but service is still not complete unless the defendant returns the waiver. Thus, it is incorrect to refer to Rule 4(d) as a "service by mail" provision. The key to the rule is the defendant's waiver.

Another new provision of Rule 4 of the Federal Rules of Civil Procedure also extends the court's jurisdiction by allowing the court to seize the assets of the defendant found within that court's jurisdiction (*in rem* or *quasi-in-rem*) if the serving of a summons cannot be effected in any other way.

INITIATION OF THE SUIT

FORM 2–3
SAMPLE NOTICE OF LAWSUIT AND
REQUEST FOR WAIVER OF SUMMONS

IN THE UNITED STATES DISTRICT COURT

[judicial district] JUDICIAL DISTRICT OF [state]

[judicial division] DIVISION

[name of plaintiff]	)	
	)	
Plaintiff	)	Civil Action No. [case number]
	)	
vs.	)	
	)	
[name of defendant]	)	
Defendant	)	

NOTICE OF LAWSUIT AND REQUEST FOR WAIVER OF SUMMONS

TO: [name of defendant] [as [title, or other relationship of individual to corporate defendant] of [name of any corporate defendant, if any)]

A lawsuit has been commenced against you (or the entity on whose behalf you are addressed). A copy of the complaint is attached to this notice. It has been filed in the United States District Court for the [judicial district] District and has been assigned docket number [case number].

This is not a formal summons or notification from the court, but rather my request that you sign and return the enclosed waiver of service in order to save the cost of serving you with a judicial summons and an additional copy of the complaint. The cost of service will be avoided if I receive a signed copy of the waiver within thirty (30) days after the date designated below as the date on which this Notice and Request is sent. I enclose a stamped and addressed envelope [or designate other means of cost-free return] for your use. An extra copy of the waiver is also attached for your records.

If you comply with this request and return the signed waiver, it will be filed with the court and no summons will be served on you. The action will then proceed as if you had been served on the date the waiver is filed, except that you will not be obligated to answer the complaint before 60 days from the date designated below as the date on which this notice is sent (or before 90 days from that date if your address is not in any judicial district of the United States.)

If you do not return the signed waiver within the time indicated, I will take appropriate steps to effect formal service in a manner authorized by the Federal Rules of Civil Procedure and will then, to the extent authorized by those Rules, ask the court read the statement concerning the duty of parties to waive the service of the summons, which is set forth at the bottom of the waiver form.

§ 2.2   CHANGES IN METHOD OF SERVICE

I affirm that this request is being sent to you on behalf of the plaintiff this [date] day of [month], [20___].

_____

[signature of plaintiff's attorney
or unrepresented plaintiff]

FORM 2–4
SAMPLE WAIVER OF SERVICE OF SUMMONS

IN THE UNITED STATES DISTRICT COURT

[judicial district] JUDICIAL DISTRICT OF [state]

[judicial division] DIVISION

[name of plaintiff]	)	
	)	
Plaintiff	)	
	)	
vs.	)	Civil Action No. [case number]
	)	
[name of defendant]	)	
	)	
Defendant		

WAIVER OF SERVICE OF SUMMONS

TO: [name of plaintiff's attorney or unrepresented plaintiff]

I acknowledge receipt of your request that I waive service of a summons in the action of [case name], which is case number [case number] in the United States District Court for the [judicial district] (district) of [state]. I have also received a copy of the complaint in the action, two copies of this instrument, and a means by which I can return the signed waiver to you without cost to me.

I agree to save the cost of service of a summons and an additional copy of the complaint in this lawsuit by not requiring that I (or the entity on whose behalf I an acting) be served with judicial process in the manner provided by Rule 4.

I (or the entity on whose behalf I am acting) will retain all defenses or objection to the lawsuit or to the jurisdiction or venue of the court except for objections based on a defect in the summons or in the service of the summons.

I understand that a judgment may be entered against me (or the party on whose behalf I am acting) if an answer or motion under Rule 12 is not served upon you with 60 days after [date request was sent].

[date]
Date

_____
Signature
[printed/typed name]
{as [description of representation]}

§ 2.3 Lawsuit Initiation Checklist

The following checklist may help you organize the facts and the information in order to initiate the lawsuit.

1. If defendant is a corporation, call the Secretary of State to determine the registered agent for service of process. If the defendant is a natural person, determine the proper address for service of process, including apartment or suite number.

2. Check the Rules of Civil Procedure for drafting, filing, and service of process requirements.

3. Calendar the statute of limitations.

4. Identify the client's goals in the litigation.

5. Asses the cost projections for litigation versus the reasonable expectation for award of damages.

6. Determine what type of legal action is necessary to reach the client's desired goal or objective (that is, temporary restraining order (TRO), claim for relief, declaratory judgment, specific performance, and so forth).

7. Review file for completeness of facts. If incomplete, begin immediate investigation to supply the needed facts.

8. If a contract case, review contract for any mandatory arbitration clauses which would bar traditional litigation and instead prescribe binding arbitration to settle disputes.

9. Draft a demand letter if one is statutorily required or strategically preferable to filing the claim without one.

10. Identify the elements of causes of action which must be proven and inventory the facts that prove them.

11. Research the expected jury verdict for this type of claim in you jurisdiction.

12. Research jurisdictional questions, if any.

13. Obtain copies of pleadings filed in similar actions or forms to use as drafting guidelines.

14. Draft initial pleading.

§ 2.4   Local Rules of Court

Every court district utilizes state and federal rules, but is also impelled to follow the local rules indigenous to that district. The local rules will address such things as the number of copies to be filed with an original pleading, whether sincere effort conferences must be held with opposing counsel before filing a motion to compel discovery, and whether discovery is filed with the court in that district.

Even though you may be familiar with state or federal rules on a certain procedure, it is imperative that you check the local rules to make sure there are no deviations before filing a document. Local rules often limit the number of discovery requests that can be made. Violations of these rules can be the basis for sanctions against you and your client, and, in the more severe instances, may be the cause for pleadings being struck by the court. (See **Appendix C.**)

§ 2.5   Registered Agents for Corporations

One of the primary steps in the preparation of the complaint is to determine the proper parties to the lawsuit. If one of the parties to be sued is a corporation, it will be necessary to determine the proper person to accept service of process for that corporation. If the corporation appears to be doing business in your state, the most obvious place to start your search is with the Secretary of State for your state. If the corporation was incorporated in your state, the Corporations Department of the Secretary of State will tell you the name of the person designated as the registered agent. This person's name and address should be included in the body of the complaint, and he is the person upon whom the summons is served.

Although the rules for partnerships vary from state to state, you will generally be able to determine partnership information by calling the Secretary of State also. As a general rule, a partnership may be served by service of process on one of the partners of the partnership, but it is imperative that you check your local and state rules for the particulars on proper service. Remember that it is very easy for a defendant to have service quashed if it has been improper. This mistake is correctable, but it is one of the areas where both time and money can be saved by proper procedure the first time around.

Although corporations are required to maintain updated information with the Secretary of State, you may find it a time-saving device to verify the information you have received regarding registered agents before sending a process server out to that location. In some instances, the addresses you will be given may list the street address of a 50- or 60-story office building with no suite number. A process server will be unable to effectuate service with such an incomplete address.

Two ways of obtaining registered agent information from the Corporation Department of the Secretary of State are by phone and by letter. **Form 2–5** is a directory which lists the phone numbers for corporation information in the Secretary of State's office. **Form 2–6** is a sample letter which illustrates a request for registered agent information.

FORM 2–5
DIRECTORY: SECRETARY OF STATE
CORPORATION INFORMATION

1.	Alabama	www.sos.state.al.us/business/corporations.cfm	(205) 242-5324
2.	Alaska	www.dced.state.ak.us/bsc/bsc.htm	(907) 465-8530
3.	Arizona	www.sosaz.com/	(800) 222-7000
4.	Arkansas	www.sosweb.state.ar.us	(501) 682-3409
5.	California	www.ss.ca.gov/business/business.htm	(916) 653-2121
6.	Colorado	www.sos.state.co.us/	(303) 894-2251
7.	Connecticut	www.sots.state.ct.us/	(203) 566-8570
8.	Delaware	www.state.de.us/sos/corp.htm	(302) 739-3073
9.	Florida	www.dos.state.fl.us/doc/index.html	(850) 488-9000
10.	Georgia	www.sos.state.ga.us/corporations/	(404) 656-2817
11.	Hawaii	www.state.hi.us/forms/	(808) 586-2727
12.	Idaho	www.accessidaho.org/apps/sos/corp/search.html	(208) 334-2300
13.	Illinois	www.sos.state.il.us	(800) 252-8980
14.	Indiana	www.state.in.us/sos bus_service/corps	(317) 232-6576
15.	Iowa	www.sos.state.ia.us/corpweb	(515) 281-5204
16.	Kansas	www.kssos.org/corpfee.html	(785) 296-4654
17.	Kentucky	www.sos.state.ky.us/	(502) 564-2848
18.	Louisiana	www.sec.state.la.us/crpinq.htm	(225) 925-4704
19.	Maine	www.state.me.us/sos/cec	(207) 287-3676
20.	Maryland	www.dat.state.md.us	(410) 767-1184
21.	Massachusetts	www.state.ma.us/sec/cor/	(617) 727-9640
22.	Michigan	www.sos.state.mi.us	(517) 334-6302
23.	Minnesota	www.sos.state.mn.us	(612) 296-2803
24.	Mississippi	www.sos.state.ms.us/	(800) 256-3494
25.	Missouri	www.mosl.sos.state.mo.us	(573) 751-4936
26.	Montana	www.state.mt.us/sos/business_services	(406) 444-3665
27.	Nebraska	www.nol.org/home/sos/htm/services.htm	(402) 471-4079
28.	Nevada	http://sos.state.nv.us/	(775) 684-5708
29.	New Hampshire	www.state.nh.us/sos	(603) 271-3242
30.	New Jersey	www.state.nj.us/state/	(609) 984-1900
31.	New Mexico	www.nmprc.state.nm.us/ftq.htm	(505) 827-4508
32.	New York	www.state.ny.us	(518) 473-2492
33.	North Carolina	www.secstate.state.nc.us/	(919) 807-2225
34.	North Dakota	www.state.nd.us/sec/default.htm	(701) 224-4284
35.	Ohio	www.state.oh.us/sos/info.html	(614) 466-3910
36.	Oklahoma	www.sos.state.ok.us/	(405) 522-4560
37.	Oregon	www.sos.state.or.us/corporation	(503) 986-2200
38.	Pennsylvania	www.dos.state.pa.us/corps/corp.html	(717) 787-1057
39.	Rhode Island	www.corps.state.ri.us/corporations.htm	(401) 222-1309
40.	South Carolina		(803) 734-2158
41.	South Dakota	www.state.sd.us/sos/corpadm.htm	(605) 773-4845
42.	Tennessee	www.state.tn.us/sos/	(615) 741-2286
43.	Texas	www.sos.state.tx.us	(512) 463-5555
44.	Utah	www.commerce.state.ut.us/	(877) 526-3994
45.	Vermont	www.sec.state.vt.us	(802) 828-2386
46.	Virginia	www.state.va.us/sec/index.html	(804) 371-9967
47.	Washington		(206) 753-7115
48.	West Virginia		(304) 558-6000
49.	Wisconsin	www.wdfi.org/corporations.default.htm	(608) 261-7577
50.	Wyoming	http://soswy.state.wy.us	(307) 777-5334
51.	District of Columbia		(202) 727-7283

52.	Bermuda	(809) 295-5151
53.	Cayman Islands	(809) 949-7900
54.	Bahamas	(809) 322-3316
55.	Alberta	(403) 427-2311
56.	British Columbia	(604) 387-5101
57.	Saskatchewan	(306) 787-2962
58.	Manitoba	(204) 983-3227
59.	Quebec	(418) 643-5260
60.	New Brunswick	(506) 453-2703
61.	Nova Scotia	(902) 424-7771
62.	Ontario	(416) 596-3725

FORM 2–6
SAMPLE LETTER REQUESTING REGISTERED AGENT INFORMATION

Secretary of State
Corporate Information Department
[address]
[city, state, zip code]

Date [date]

Dear [name]:

Please send me the name and address of the registered agent for [name] Corporation, an entity duly incorporated under the laws of this state. If the information is available, I would also appreciate receiving a list of the names and addresses of the officers of the corporation as well as the name and address of the corporation's principal place of business.

Please send the requested information to my attention at the letterhead address listed above at your earliest convenience. I thank you for your assistance in this matter.

Very truly yours,

[name]

§ 2.6 Process Servers

Service of process requirements vary greatly from state to sate. Some states require that original petitions or complaints be served by constables or similar legal entities. In some places, service of process can be handled through the clerk of the court, while other states place the burden for service of process directly upon the plaintiff. Keep in mind also, that service of process for the original petition or complaint may be done entirely differently from the process used to serve depositions, subpoenas, or other pleadings.

Consult your state and local rules to determine service of process requirements. Generally, you will be required to supply a copy of the complaint and the summons form for your particular state. On a lighter note, some of these summons are really quite comical. In Nevada, for instance, the summons begins "Greetings. You have been sued."!

No matter whether process is to be served by a legal entity or private process server, the paralegal should do considerable research to ensure that the address listed for service of process is a good one. If process is to be served on an individual, it is also necessary to have several addresses where that person may be found. Any information regarding that person's employment, family, friends, or known habits, can be very helpful to the process server.

§ 2.7 Timetable for Filing and Service of Documents

Table 2–1 illustrates these requirements in a very useful manner. Note: The column titled "State" has been left blank so that you might fill in the requirements for a specific state.

Table 2–1

Timetable for Filing and Service of Documents

DOCUMENT	FEDERAL	STATE
COMPLAINT	Fed. R. Civ. P. 4(m) Serve Summons within 120 days after filing.	
SUMMONS	Fed. R. Civ. P. 4 *et seq.* Service with complaint within 120 days.	
ANSWER	Fed. R. Civ. P. 12(a) Service within 20 days after service of summons (Same applies to answer to cross-claim or third party complaint) Fed. R. Civ. P. 13 and 14(a).	
	Fed. R. Civ. P. 12(a)(1)(B). If the defendant is served with a Notice of Service of Summons and waives service, the defendant has 60 days to answer.	

Table 2–1
(*continued*)

DOCUMENT	FEDERAL	STATE
DEFAULT	Fed. R. Civ. P. 55(b) No time stated when entered by clerk of court; 3 days notice to party who has already appeared when entered by court.	
DISMISSAL	Fed. R. Civ. P. 41(a)(1) *et seq.* Voluntarily any time before service of answer or motion for summary judgment.	
	Fed. R. Civ. P. 41(c) Voluntary dismissal of counterclaim, cross–claim, or third-party claim before service of responsive pleading or introduction of evidence at time of trial.	
	Fed. R. Civ. P. 4(m) Without prejudice within 120 days if service of summons and complaint not made within 120 days after filing of complaint.	
MOTIONS	Fed. R. Civ. P. 6(d) Service of written motion, supporting affidavits, and notice of hearing not later than 5 days before time specified for hearing.	
AMENDED PLEADINGS	Fed. R. Civ. P. 15(a) Before responsive pleading served or within 20 days if no response is permitted and action not on trial calendar.	

Table 2–1

(continued)

DOCUMENT	FEDERAL	STATE
	Fed. R. Civ. P. 15(a) By leave of court or written stipulation at any time.	
SUPPLEMENTAL PLEADINGS	Fed. R. Civ. P. 15(d) By motion for leave of court and upon reasonable notice to the opposing party.	
REPLY	Fed. R. Civ. P. 7(a) To answer if ordered by court, within 20 days.	
	Fed. R. Civ. P. 12(a)(2) To counter-claim within 20 days after service of answer.	
RESPONSIVE PLEADING	Fed. R. Civ. P. 15(a) To amended pleading within 10 days after service of same or during the time remaining to respond to original pleading, whichever is longer.	
	Fed. R. Civ. P. 15(d) To supplemental pleadings as ordered by the court.	
THIRD-PARTY PRACTICE	Fed. R. Civ. P. 14(a) No leave of court needed if third-party complaint filed no later than 10 days after serving original answer, otherwise by leave of court.	

§ 2.7 TIMETABLE FOR FILING AND SERVICE

Table 2–1
(*continued*)

DOCUMENT	FEDERAL	STATE
INTERROGATORIES	Fed. R. Civ. P. 33(a) and 26(d) Timing and sequence of discovery. Except when authorized under these rules or by local rule, order, or agreement of the parties, a party may not seek discovery from any source before the parties have met and conferred as required by subdivision (f). Unless the court upon motion, for the convenience of parties and witnesses and in the interests of justice, orders otherwise, methods of discovery may be used in any sequence, and the fact that a party is conducting discovery, whether by deposition or otherwise, shall not operate to delay any other party's discovery.	
DEPOSITIONS	Fed. R. Civ. P. 30(b) Notice of taking with reasonable notice to every party. Fed. R. Civ. P. 30(f)(3) and Fed. R. Civ. P. 31(c) Notice of taking to be filed promptly.	

Table 2–1
(continued)

DOCUMENT	FEDERAL	STATE
PRODUCTION OF DOCUMENTS	Fed. R. Civ. P. 34(b) and 26(d) Request may be served on plaintiff any time after commencement of action provided that the parties have met and conferred as required by 26(f). On any other party with or after service of complaint and summons.	
	Fed R. Civ. P. 34(b) Response to request within 30 days or a shorter or longer time as directed by the court or as agreed to in writing by the parties.	
ADMISSIONS	Fed. R. Civ. P. 36(a) May be served on plaintiff after commencement of the action provided that the parties have met and conferred as required by 26(f).	
	Fed. R. Civ. P. 36(a) Answers or objections must be served within 30 days of service of the request.	
MOTION FOR SUMMARY JUDGMENT	Fed. R. Civ. P. 56 *et seq.* Plaintiff may file 20 days after commencement of action or after service of motion for summary judgment by adverse party. Defending party may file at any time.	
MOTION FOR NEW TRIAL	Fed. R. Civ. P. 59(b) Must be served not later than 10 days after entry of judgment.	

Table 2–1
(*continued*)

DOCUMENT	FEDERAL	STATE
APPEAL	Fed. R. App. P. 4(a)(1) Within 30 days of entry of judgment or order.	
MOTION TO AMEND JUDGMENT	Fed. R. Civ. P. 59(e) Must be served within 10 days of entry of judgment.	

In calculating any time period set out in the Federal Rules of Civil Procedure, the day of the act from which the time period begins to run is not included. If the last day of the period falls on a Saturday, Sunday, or legal holiday, the period runs until the next day that is not a Saturday, Sunday, or legal holiday. The period will also run until the next day if the district court clerk's office is inaccessible as a result of weather or other conditions on the last day of the period.

If the period of time in question is less than 11 days, intermediate Saturdays, Sundays, and holidays do not count. Legal holidays include New Year's Day, Martin Luther King's Birthday, Washington's Birthday, Memorial Day, Independence Day, Columbus Day, Veteran's Day, Thanksgiving, and Christmas.

§ 2.8 Verification

This is one area where the rules differ greatly between state and federal procedure. Under Rule 11 of the Federal Rules of Civil Procedure, the signature of an attorney on the pleading is a certification that he has read the pleading, that it is not a frivolous pleading, and that it has not been filed solely for reasons of delay. Federal pleadings do not require additional sworn affidavits of verification as a general rule. Many states, however, do have this requirement. *Verification* is simply a sworn statement signed by the party and notarized by a notary public stating that the facts contained in the pleading are true and correct to the best of the person's knowledge, information, and belief. All pleadings must be either verified or subscribed to by the party or his attorney. Be sure to check your state and local rules to determine which pleadings are required to be verified in your local. **Form 2–7** is a sample complaint verification. **Forms 2–8** and **2–9** are answer verifications.

INITIATION OF THE SUIT

FORM 2–7
SAMPLE COMPLAINT VERIFICATION

State of [state]   )

) SS

County of [county]   )

[name], being duly sworn according to law, deposes and says that he/she is the Plaintiff in the foregoing matter, and that the facts set forth in the Complaint attached hereto are true and correct to the best of his/her knowledge, information and belief.

_____
[plaintiff name]

Sworn and subscribed before me this [day] day of [month], 20[year].

_____
Notary Public

My Commission Expires: [date].

FORM 2–8
INDIVIDUAL VERIFICATION OF ANSWER

STATE OF NEW YORK   )

COUNTY OF NEW YORK   ) ss.:

I, [defendant's name], being sworn, say:

I am the defendant in the within action; I have read the foregoing VERIFIED ANSWER AND COUNTERCLAIM and know the contents thereof; the same is true to my knowledge, except as to the matters therein stated to be alleged on information and belief, and as to those matters I believe it to be true.

_____
[defendant's signature]

Sworn to before me this
___ day of _____, 20___.

_____
NOTARY PUBLIC

FORM 2–9
CORPORATE VERIFICATION OF ANSWER

STATE OF NEW YORK   )
COUNTY OF NEW YORK   ) ss.:

I, [name of corporation's representative],being sworn, says:

I am an [representative's position] of [name of corporation], domestic corporation and party in the within action; I have read the foregoing VERIFIED ANSWER and know the contents thereof; and the same is true to my own knowledge, except as to the matters therein stated to be alleged upon information and belief, and as to those matters I believe it to be true. This verification is made by me because the above party is a corporation and I am an officer thereof. The grounds of my belief as to all matters not stated upon my own knowledge are as follows: from personal knowledge and information contained in my files and records.

_____
[corporate representative's signature]

Sworn to before me this
_____ day of _____, [20__].

_____
        NOTARY PUBLIC

§ 2.9   Demand for Jury Trial

Before completion of the preparation of the complaint, check the rules of the court in which you are filing the document to determine how a demand for jury trial is to be handled. Determine if a fee is necessary and if there is a time limit in which the demand must be made. Some attorneys prefer to demand a jury trial at the time of the filing of the complaint; others may wish to wait until the case has been developed more fully to make this determination. Discuss this point with your attorney and make note of his preference. If he chooses to wait until a later date, and the local rules allow for this, be sure you calendar the date.

The format for demanding a jury trial will vary in different jurisdictions. It is sometimes handled as a clause in the caption of the pleading, and it is sometimes handled as a separate pleading. Some jurisdictions dictate that the phrase "a jury trial is demanded," or similar phrase, is sufficient when it is included in the body of the complaint. (See **Form 2–10**.)

In general, the right to a jury trial may be waived if the party seeking one fails to follow the proper procedure for demanding such a trial. If an issue triable by a jury is commenced in the federal courts, any party may demand a jury trial on that issue by serving the other parties with a demand for a jury trial at any time after commencement of the action, but not later than 10 days after the service of the last pleading directed at that issue. The demand may be included as part of a pleading. The demand for a jury trial must also be filed.

In federal court, the party may indicate in the demand for a jury trial which issues the party wants tried by a jury. If the party does not specify, the party will be deemed to have requested a jury trial for all issues triable by a jury. If a party demands a jury trial for only some of the issues, any other party may make a demand for a jury trial on any other issue within 10 days of service of the other party's jury demand (or within a shorter period of time specified by the court). A demand for a jury trial may not be withdrawn without the consent of the parties.

FORM 2–10
SAMPLE DEMAND FOR JURY TRIAL

IN THE UNITED STATES DISTRICT COURT

[judicial district] JUDICIAL DISTRICT OF [state]

[court division] DIVISION

[name]	)	
	)	
Plaintiff,	)	Civil Action no. [case number]
	)	
vs.	)	
	)	
[name]	)	Demand for Jury Trial
	)	
defendant(s).	)	

COMES NOW, the plaintiff, by and through its attorneys [name of plaintiff's attorney], and demands a jury trial of all of the issues in the above matters.

Dated this [day] day of [month], [20___].

[name of law firm]

By: _____

[attorney's name]
[address]
ATTORNEY FOR PLAINTIFF

§ 2.9 JURY TRIAL DEMAND

FORM 2–11
DEMAND FOR TRIAL BY JURY

NO. _____

[PLAINTIFF(S) NAMES]
   Plaintiffs,)
)
)
)
)
)
)
)
)
v.)
)
[DEFENDANT(S) NAMES])
   Defendants)
	IN THE DISTRICT COURT OF
	
	_____ COUNTY,
	
	_____ JUDICIAL DISTRICT

DEMAND FOR TRIAL BY JURY

TO THE HONORABLE JUDGE OF SAID COURT:

COMES NOW _____, Plaintiff in the above styled and numbered cause, and pursuant to Rule _____ of the _____ Rules of Civil Procedure, makes and files this Demand for Trial by Jury in the above styled and numbered cause.

Contemporaneously with the filing of this jury demand, the Plaintiff has deposited the required jury fee with the County Clerk of _____ County, _____.

Plaintiff, _____, requests that this case be set on the jury docket of the court for disposition in due order and as soon as practicable.

WHEREFORE, PREMISES CONSIDERED, the Plaintiff, _____, prays that this case be placed upon the jury docket for a jury trial, and for such other relief, both general and special, at law and in equity, to which she may show herself justly entitled.

Respectfully submitted,

NAME OF FIRM

_____

Name of Atty
Atty's Bar #
Address
City, State, Zip
Phone #

CERTIFICATE OF SERVICE

I hereby certify that a true and correct copy of the foregoing Demand for Trial by Jury has been served in compliance with Rules _____ and _____ of the _____ Rules of Civil Procedure on the _____ day of _____, [20____].

_____

§ 2.10   Chart of Life Expectancy

When figuring the damages in a wrongful death case, a life expectancy chart is used to calculate the number of years the decedent would have remaining to live had he not died. In using such a chart, look at the age column on the left and follow it down to the decedent's age when he died. Then follow that line across the page and stop under the column which denotes the decedent's sex and race. This gives you the average number of years the decedent would have lived past the age of his death.

In most cases, employment damages should only be figured to expected age 65 unless the decedent was self-employed. Other factors should also be taken into account. For instance, if the decedent did some sort of physical labor, his work life could arguably be considered to end somewhat sooner than age 65. These are the types of things that a defense firm will bring up to try to mitigate damages.

§ 2.11   Emergency Relief

There are times when the wheels of the legal justice system turn too slowly to afford a party the relief he desperately needs. In most civil litigation, the plaintiff files suit to recover monetary damages for wrongs done to him in the past. Emergency or injunctive relief is available in special situations to afford the plaintiff immediate relief from actions or omissions which are causing the plaintiff irreparable harm. Because injunctive relief is considered by the court to be an extreme remedy, it is mandatory that the application set forth specific facts supporting the allegations of imminent or concurring, irreparable damage to person or property which could not be recompensed monetarily. There must not be any adequate remedy at law for the damages suffered.

It is important to remember that injunctive relief is proper only when irreparable harm is being done or when it is anticipated that irreparable harm will be done. *Irreparable harm* is defined as harm which cannot be undone or harm which creates a situation for which no other kind of remedy or compensation is adequate to restore the status quo. The allegation of expected irreparable harm must be incredible specific in order for the judge to grant the order. General or abstract allusions are not enough for a judge to grant an ex parte order for injunctive relief.

§ 2.11 EMERGENCY RELIEF

Applications for injunctive relief are not proper if the harmful act has already occurred or if the element of imminent danger is absent. Such applications are also considered to be improper when another kind of compensation such as monetary damages would be adequate or when there is no genuine emergency. Under no circumstances is injunctive relief to be used as a vehicle for vengeance. The following are good examples of instances when emergency or injunctive relief is proper and likely to be granted by the court:

1.   Application for order to stop a building developer from cutting down historical 100-year-old oak trees to build a parking lot;
2.   Application for order to stop an industrial plant from depleting the water supply underneath a private party's agricultural property; and
3.   Application by estranged wife for order to stop spouse whom she is suing for divorce from bulldozing the family home and community property in attempt to keep the estranged wife from leaving the marriage with any material assets.

By filing an Application for Temporary Restraining Order (**Form 2–12**), the plaintiff may petition the Court to grant an ex parte order (**Form 2–13**) (without notice to the defendant) prohibiting the defendant from doing certain actions or mandating the defendant to do certain actions, whichever will preserve or restore the status quo until a bilateral hearing on the issues may be had. The plaintiff must sign a verified affidavit or a verified petition in order to secure a Temporary Restraining Order, and must tender a surety bond (**Form 2–14**) to court to cover the costs of the plaintiff in the event the Temporary Restraining Order was not proper. **Form 2–15** illustrates a writ for a Temporary Restraining Order. The Temporary Restraining Order remains in force only until the hearing on the Preliminary or Temporary Injunction (**Form 2–16**), usually a period of ten (10) days.

If, after the hearing, an order is granted by the court for further or continuing injunctive relief, that order is referred to as a preliminary or temporary injunction and will remain in effect pending further order of the court. Once the Temporary or Preliminary Injunction hearing has been held, the matter is generally set for trial on the merits. At the time of trial, the judge may decide whether a Permanent Injunction is necessary or whether the judgment itself has provided a solution to the original problem.

FORM 2–12
SAMPLE APPLICATION FOR TEMPORARY RESTRAINING ORDER

NO. [case number]

[name]	)	IN THE DISTRICT COURT OF
	)	
Plaintiff	)	[name] COUNTY, [state]
	)	
vs.	)	[judicial district] JUDICIAL DISTRICT
	)	
[name]	)	
	)	
Defendant	)	

APPLICATION FOR TEMPORARY RESTRAINING ORDER

TO THE HONORABLE JUDGE OF SAID COURT:

COMES NOW, [name], Plaintiff, and files for this Plaintiff's Application for Temporary Restraining Order complaining of [name], Defendant, and for cause of action would respectfully show this Court as follows:

I. PARTIES

Plaintiff is [name], an individual who resides in [city], [county] County, [state]. Defendant, [name], is an individual who resides at [address] in [county] County, [state], and may be served with Citation at that address.

II.

On [date], [20__], [state specific facts on which cause of action is based].

III.

Plaintiff has made numerous attempts to discuss the matter with Defendant and Defendant has, each time, refused to cease and desist said behavior which is the subject of the cause of action in this suit.

IV.

Plaintiff has no adequate remedy at law or otherwise for the harm or damage done by Defendant herein because [state reasons why usual remedies such as monetary damages are not appropriate in this case].

§ 2.11   EMERGENCY RELIEF

V.

As a result of Defendant's continuing actions, Plaintiff will suffer irreparable damage, harm and injury unless the conduct of Defendant is enjoined because [state reasons why irreparable harm or damage is being done] as evidenced by [state supporting facts].

VI.

It is essential that Defendant be restrained from the aforementioned conduct immediately and without notice hereof or hearing hereon, because [state reasons why Temporary Restraining Order should be issued ex parte].

WHEREFORE, PREMISES CONSIDERED, Plaintiff prays for the following:

1) That a Temporary Restraining Order be issued restraining Defendant from the aforementioned behavior;

2) That Plaintiff recover all costs and expenses incurred herein;

3) That Plaintiff have such other and further relief to which he may be entitled, including court costs expended in its behalf.

Respectfully submitted,

_____

Attorney for Plaintiff
[address]
[telephone number]

THE STATE OF [state]   )
)
COUNTY OF [county]   )

BEFORE ME, the undersigned authority, on this date personally appeared [plaintiff], known to me, who being by me first duly sworn upon this oath to tell the truth stated and deposed that he is the Plaintiff in the above entitled and numbered cause, and that in such capacity he has full authority to make this affidavit and is fully competent to make the same, that he has read the foregoing Application for Temporary Restraining Order; that he is familiar with matter and facts therein stated; and that the same are of his personal knowledge true and correct.

_____

[name of plaintiff]

SUBSCRIBED AND SWORN to before me by the said [name], on this [date] day of [month], [20__].

_____

Notary Public, in and for
The State of [state]

63

INITIATION OF THE SUIT

FORM 2–13
SAMPLE ORDER GRANTING TEMPORARY RESTRAINING ORDER

NO. [case number]

[name]	) IN THE DISTRICT COURT OF
	)
Plaintiff	) [county] COUNTY, [state]
	)
vs.	) [judicial district] JUDICIAL DISTRICT
	)
[name]	)
	)
Defendant	)

ORDER GRANTING TEMPORARY RESTRAINING ORDER

On [date], [20__], this court heard the verified application of Plaintiff [name] for a temporary restraining order without notice to the Defendant, [name], and the court, having considered the facts set forth in said verified application, finds that immediate and irreparable harm and injury will result to the Plaintiff before notice could be served and hearing had thereon because [state facts and reasons] and that the Defendant will continue with this injurious behavior unless restrained immediately by a temporary restraining order as authorized by [state authorizing statute or rule of civil procedure], and the court further finds that such behavior should be restrained and enjoined.

It is therefore ordered and adjudged that Defendant, [name], be and [he/she] hereby is temporarily restrained and enjoined from [state specific behavior], and that the clerk of this court issue a temporary retraining order, in full force and effect until and pending the hearing below ordered, restraining and enjoining Defendant, [name] from [state specific behavior].

It is further ordered that Plaintiff, [name] post bond in the amount of [amount of bond] to be paid to the clerk of this court in connection with this temporary restraining order.

It is further ordered that a hearing for Temporary Injunction is hereby set for [time] [A.M./P.M.] in the District Court, [judicial district] Judicial District, [county] County, [state], and that the temporary restraining order herein granted remain operative until and pending said hearing.

Signed on this [date] day of [month], [20__] at [time] [A.M./P.M.]

_____

Judge Presiding

Entered on this [date] day of [month], [20__].

_____

Clerk of Court

§ 2.11 EMERGENCY RELIEF

FORM 2–14
SAMPLE BOND FOR TEMPORARY RESTRAINING ORDER

NO. [case number]

[name]	)	IN THE DISTRICT COURT OF
	)	
Plaintiff	)	[county] COUNTY, [state]
	)	
vs.	)	[judicial district] JUDICIAL DISTRICT
	)	
[name]	)	
	)	
Defendant	)	

BOND FOR TEMPORARY RESTRAINING ORDER

WHEREAS, [name], Plaintiff in the above-captioned cause, has commenced an action herein against Defendant, [name] and has made application to the court for a temporary restraining order against said Defendant, enjoining and restraining [him/her] from the commission of certain behavior, more particularly described and set forth in the Plaintiff's verified Application for Temporary Restraining Order on file herein;

Now, therefore, we, the undersigned, [name], Plaintiff in the above-captioned cause, as principal, and [name], as surety in [county] County, [state] in consideration of the issuance of said temporary restraining order, and other good and valuable consideration, do hereby jointly and severally undertake, in the sum of [amount] and promise to the effect that Plaintiff will be bound by the decision which is to be made in this cause, and will pay all costs and monies adjudged against plaintiff should such temporary restraining order be found to be improper.

Dated this day [date] of [month], [20__].

_____
Plaintiff and Principal

_____
Surety

FORM 2–15
SAMPLE WRIT FOR TEMPORARY RESTRAINING ORDER

The State of [state]

To: [defendant]

[name], Plaintiff, filed a verified application in the District Court of [county] County, [state], on [date], [20__], in a suit numbered [case number] on the docket of said court, wherein [name] is Plaintiff and [name] is Defendant alleging as follows:

INITIATION OF THE SUIT

[state allegations of Application for Temporary Restraining Order here]

The Honorable [name of judge], judge of the [judicial district] District of [county] County, [state], upon presentation of said application to him made an order thereon, a copy of which is attached hereto.

The Plaintiff has executed and filed with the clerk of said court a bond set by the court and approved in the sum of [amount] made payable and conditioned as required law.

Therefore you, [defendant], are temporarily enjoined and restrained as ordered and provided for in the copy of the court's order attached hereto, until and pending the hearing of an Application for Temporary Injunction by Plaintiff before the judge of said court at [time] [A.M./P.M.] on [date], [20__], in the courtroom of the District Court in the [county] County Courthouse, [city], [state], when and where you will appear to show cause why a temporary injunction as prayed should not be granted, effective until final judgment in such suit.

Issued under my hand and seal of said Court, at my office in the City [city], [state], on [date], [20__], at [time] [A.M./P.M.]

_____

[seal and signature of court clerk]

FORM 2–16
SAMPLE TEMPORARY INJUNCTION

NO. [case number]

[name]		IN THE DISTRICT COURT OF
	Plaintiff)	[county] COUNTY, [state]
vs.	)	[judicial district] JUDICIAL DISTRICT
[name]	)	
	Defendant)	

TEMPORARY INJUNCTION

On [date], [20__], a hearing was held on Plaintiff's Application for Temporary Injunction restraining Defendant [name].

I.

The plaintiff in this action is [name]. The defendant in this action is [name].

II.

The court finds these to be the reasons to grant injunctive relief: [state specific reasons for granting injunctive relief].

III.

The security to be tendered to the Court by Plaintiff [name] is a surety bond in the amount of $[amount] to be filed with the Clerk of this Court by [time] [A.M./P.M.] on [date], [20__].

It is therefore ORDERED, ADJUDGED AND DECREED that:

[list specific rulings of the court which define the restraint ordered.]

SIGNED and dated this [date] day of [month], [20__].

_____
Judge Presiding

Entered on this [date] day of [month], [20__].

_____
Clerk of Court

§ 2.12 Affidavits

Affidavits are written statements of facts, signed by the party making the affidavit, the affiant, regarding the facts needed to prove something, and sworn to before an officer authorized by the court to administer an oath. Generally, affidavits are sworn to in front of a notary public, who attests the person's signature and administers the oath to the affiant regarding the truth of the matters contained therein.

Affidavits can be independent documents in a lawsuit or can be attached to other documents, motions, or pleadings as exhibits. Affidavits are commonly used to support pleadings and papers or to serve as an explanation to the court why a particular motion should be granted.

There are several elements that are common to affidavits:

1. County and state in which the affidavit is to filed
2. Style or caption of the case
3. Notarization and sworn oath of the affiant
4. Affidavit is set out in the affiant's name
5. Affidavit contains a statement of the facts sworn to by the affiant
6. Official attestation and seal of the certified officer
7. Date of signature and oath

8. Signature and seal of an authorized officer (generally a notary public)
9. Statement that the affiant is competent to testify to the matters contained therein (personal knowledge)
10. Statement confirming the source of the affiant's personal knowledge
11. Statement confirming why the affiant is competent to make the statements contained therein

An affidavit must be based on the personal knowledge of the affiant. An affiant may swear to things which would be considered to be hearsay under the Rules of Evidence. Affidavits are also written only in the first or third person, (e.g., "that he is qualified to make this statement . . .", or "that he is twenty-one years of age, . . ."). Forms **2–17** and **2–18** are two examples of affidavits.

FORM 2-17
SAMPLE FIRST-PERSON AFFIDAVIT

NO. [case number]

[name]		)	IN THE DISTRICT COURT OF
		)	
	Plaintiff	)	[county] COUNTY, [state]
		)	
vs.		)	[judicial district] JUDICIAL DISTRICT
		)	
[name]		)	
		)	
	Defendant	)	

AFFIDAVIT OF [name of affiant]

STATE OF [state]	)
	)
COUNTY OF [county]	)

BEFORE ME, the undersigned, a Notary Public, on this day personally appeared [name], who is personally known to me, and first being duly sworn according to law, upon his oath deposes and says as follows:

1. That my name is [name of affiant]; I am over the age of eighteen, and I reside at [street address, city], [county] County, [state].

2. That I have never been convicted of a crime, and that I am fully competent to make this affidavit.

3. That I have personal knowledge of the facts stated herein, and that they are all true and correct.

4.   That I have resided at the above address for all of my life, and have always considered and do consider this address to be my home and permanent residence.

_____
[name of affiant]

SUBSCRIBED AND SWORN TO before me on the [day] day of [month], [20__]. To certify which witness my hand and official seal.

_____
Notary Public in and for
the state of [state]
My commission expires:
([date])

FORM 2–18
SAMPLE THIRD-PERSON AFFIDAVIT

NO. [case number]

[name]		)	IN THE DISTRICT COURT OF
		)	
	Plaintiff	)	[county] COUNTY, [state]
		)	
vs.		)	[judicial district] JUDICIAL DISTRICT
		)	
[name]		)	
		)	
	Defendant	)	

AFFIDAVIT

STATE OF [state]	)
	)
COUNTY OF [county]	)

BEFORE ME, the undersigned, a Notary Public, on this day personally appeared [name], who is personally known to me, and first being sworn according to law, upon his oath deposes and says:

1.   That his name is [name of affiant].

2.   That his age is [age].

3.   That he resides at [street address, city], [county] County, [state].

4.   That he has never been convicted of a crime, and that he is fully competent to make this affidavit.

5.   That he has personal knowledge of the facts stated herein and that the facts are all true and correct.

6.   That he is the President of Acme Coyote Destroyers, and has held that office since [date].

7.   That on [date], Acme Coyote Destroyers applied for and received a patent for the Super Coyote Blaster.

8.   That on [date], Acme Coyote Destroyers became aware of a patent infringement on their Acme Coyote Destroyer, manufactured by AAA Varmint Control.

9.   That on [date], [company A] sent a certified mail, return-receipt requested cease and desist letter [company B] warning of the patent infringement.

10.   That [company B] did ignore and continues to ignore [company A]'s repeated requests and warnings to cease and desist from infringing on the patent of [patented article].

11.   That [company A] is experiencing, and continues to experience financial and professional damages from this patent infringement.

_____
[name of affiant]

SUBSCRIBED AND SWORN TO before me on the [date] day of [month], [20__], to certify which witness my hand and official seal.

_____
Notary Public in and for the State of [state]

My commission expires:
[date]

§ 2.13   Demand Letters

In many instances, your attorney may choose to send a demand letter to the defendant or the defendant's insurance company before initiating the lawsuit. A demand letter can be used at different stages of the lawsuit. When used prior to filing the lawsuit, the content is somewhat more abbreviated and compact than demand letters used for settlement purposes later in the lawsuit.

The demand letter should contain the same elements as a petition. A brief statement of the facts followed by a brief description of all damages incurred. The last paragraph of the letter should demand a dollar amount payment for your client's damages and include a deadline for payment of those damages. It is important to calendar the deadline date and follow through with any described action you have stated in your letter. An unanswered demand letter should never be allowed to languish in the file with no action. Credibility is a valuable asset to a law firm.

If you have a very strong case, a detailed statement of the facts may set the stage for a settlement. In many cases, however, you will not want to set forth all your legal theories and supporting case law, playing your hand prematurely and giving opposing counsel ample time to prepare his defenses. Even then, your demand letter should contain enough persuasive facts and law to evoke a settlement offer. (**Forms 2–19** through **2–22** illustrate three different types of demand letters.)

FORM 2–19
SAMPLE AUTO ACCIDENT DEMAND LETTER

CERTIFIED MAIL
RETURN RECEIPT REQUESTED,
REGULAR MAIL and
HAND DELIVERY

[name] _____
[address] _____

Re: [client]

Dear [name]:

We have been retained by [client] to represent [him/her] concerning injuries and damages [he/she] has incurred as a result of an accident which involved you client [name].

On [date], [20__], at approximately [time] [A.M./P.M.], our client was driving [his/her] vehicle in a [description of direction] direction on [name] Avenue in the vicinity of its intersection with [name] Drive. Your client failed to stop [his/her] vehicle at the stop sign located at said intersection and drove [his/her] automobile into the intersection with wanton disregard for the approach of the vehicle driven by our client, thereby causing [his/her] vehicle to collide with that of our client.

As a result, our client was hospitalized with severe internal injuries for a period of two months and has suffered permanent and disabling injuries. Medical costs incurred to date total $[amount].

Our client has not been able to return to work since the time of the accident and has suffered additional monetary damages in the amount of $[amount] for wage and benefit loss.

In addition, our client's vehicle was deemed to be a total loss, and [he/she] has suffered $[amount] in property damages.

INITIATION OF THE SUIT

We are therefore making a demand upon your client to pay our client for the damages incurred, plus attorneys' fees. If no response is made to this letter within 30 days, we will be forced to serve you with a lawsuit.

Very truly yours,

_____
[attorney name]
[firm name and address]

FORM 2–20
SAMPLE PROMISSORY NOTE DEMAND LETTER

CERTIFIED MAIL
RETURN RECEIPT REQUESTED,
REGULAR MAIL and
HAND DELIVERY

[name] _____
[address] _____

Re: [describe promissory note]

Dear [name]:

Please be advised that the above-referenced Promissory Note ("Note") became due and payable on [date], [20__], and is presently due and owing.

We have been requested by [name of lender] ("Lender"), the holder of the Note, to make this demand on you for Payment in full of all amounts currently owing on and under the Note. You may contact [name] at [bank], [address], [phone number] to obtain the exact amount now due and payable on and under the Note. All payments on the Note should be made to Lender at the foregoing address.

If payment is not received from you of all sums now due and payable on the Note on or before [time], [date], [20__], Lender will exercise its right to accelerate the entire amount due and owing along with the accrued, earned and unpaid interest as of the date of acceleration pursuant to the terms and conditions of the Note.

Should you continue to ignore your obligations, Lender will institute and prosecute litigation designed to enforce your obligations under the Note. You are hereby specifically notified that you failure to pay your obligations herein will result in increased liability by the way of attorneys' fees and costs of Court incurred by Lender in the institution and prosecution of litigation designed to enforce such obligations.

Nothing herein shall be deemed a waiver of any other defaults, whether matured or unmatured, and whether enumerated above or not, existing or hereafter arising under the Note or any other agreement, instrument or document executed in connection with or as security for the Note, or a waiver or abandonment of any rights or remedies available to Lender (whether against you or any other person or any property) each of which rights or remedies is hereby specifically reserved (including, without limitation, the right to seek judgment and/or to proceed against personal property).

Very truly yours,

[name of law firm]

By: _____

FORM 2–21
SAMPLE PROMISSORY NOTE DEMAND LETTER

CERTIFIED MAIL
RETURN RECEIPT REQUESTED,
REGULAR MAIL, and
HAND DELIVERY

[name]_____
[address]

Re: [describe promissory note]

Dear _____:

This is to advise you that you are in default under the terms of the promissory note dated _____, for failure to make the payments due thereunder on _____.

The total amount due for those payments is $_____. It is imperative that full payment be received on or before ten (10) days from the date of this letter, or the term for payment of your indebtedness will be accelerated and the entire principal balance and any unpaid interest will become immediately due and payable and proper legal action will be taken to enforce payment thereof.

As you are aware, the terms of the promissory note provide that interest accrues from the date of default at the highest rate allowable by law, and you are liable, upon default, for all costs and reasonable attorney's fees incurred in collection.

Very truly yours,

[Name of law firm]

By: _____

§ 2.14 Plaintiff's Request for Insurance Information

It is important for a plaintiff to know whether the defendant has insurance coverage for any liability the defendant may have incurred. The existence of such coverage may have an important impact on settlement considerations. Your attorney may also want to attempt to reach a settlement with the insurance company before commencing an action. The following letter (**Form 2–22**) can be used to have the defendant put his or her insurance company in touch with your office.

FORM 2–22
SAMPLE PLAINTIFF'S REQUEST FOR INSURANCE INFORMATION

Re: Accident Date:
       Claimant:

Dear [defendant's name]:

Please be advised that we are the attorneys for the above named in connection with the prosecution of all claims arising out of the accident of the above date, involving the motor vehicle driven by you.

Kindly forward this letter to your insurance carrier and advise them to communicate with the undersigned.

Very truly yours,

_____

cc: [your client]

FORM 2–23
SAMPLE DECEPTIVE TRADE PRACTICES DEMAND LETTER (TEXAS)*

CERTIFIED MAIL
RETURN RECEIPT REQUESTED,
REGULAR MAIL and
HAND DELIVERY

[name]_____
[address]_____

Re: Violations of Texas Deceptive Trade Practices Act

Dear [name]:

Pursuant to Section 17.50A, Deceptive Trade Practices—Consumer Protection Act, Tex. Bus. & Com. Code Ann. (Supp. 1980) ("DTPA"), [name] Corporation, hereby gives you notice that [person A], his agents, servants, or employees have breached certain provisions of the DTPA directly affecting [name] Corporation's lease of property situated in [city], [county] County, Texas, commonly known as [property name], and more particularly described as follows: [specify detailed property description]

Section 17.45, DTPA defines "consumer" as follows: "'Consumer' means an individual, partnership, corporation, or governmental entity who seeks or acquires by purchase of lease, any goods or services." (emphasis added). The same section defines "goods" as follows: "'Goods' means tangible chattels or real property purchased or leased for use." (emphasis added). The Act therefore applies to [person A] as the landlord of [property name], being the successor in interest of [person B], the original owner of the above-described premises.

Section 17.50(a) DTPA provides, in pertinent part, the following:

A consumer may maintain an action where any of the following constitute a producing cause of actual damages:

1.   The use or employment by any person of a false, misleading, or deceptive act or practice that is specifically enumerated in a subdivision of Subsection (b) of Section 17.46 of this subchapter;

2.   Any unconscionable action or course of action by any person. . . .

Section 17.46(b) D.T.P.A., provides, in pertinent part, the following:

Except as provided in Subsection (d) of this section, the term "false, misleading, or deceptive acts or practices" includes, but is not limited to, the following acts:

*   *   *   *

(12)   Representing that an agreement confers or involves rights, remedies, or obligations which it does not have or involve, or which are prohibited by law;

(13)   Knowingly making false or misleading statements of fact concerning the need for parts, replacement, or repair service. . .

The specific complaints which are alleged to be in violation of the DTPA are as follows:

(1)   [Person A] has violated express and implied warranties. The lease itself provides the express warranty that "the lessee shall and may peaceably and quietly have, hold and enjoy possession of the Premises for and during the full term of the lease." This warranty has been violated. Further, [person A] has violated these implied and expressed warranties of quiet enjoyment. [person A] has violated these implied and expressed warranties of quiet enjoyment and peaceable possession by pursuing an appeal of the case [person A] v. [name] Corporation, No. [case number], Justice Court, Precinct 1, [county] County, Texas, which was tried on [date], 20[year]. Judgment was rendered unanimously in favor of [name] Corporation by a six-member jury panel. After only a ten minute deliberation, the jury returned, finding that grounds for forfeiture did not exist and that [person A]'s suit was frivolous. To further pursue this cause after such a

decisive verdict amounts to a breach of expressed and implied warranties in violation of DTPA § 17.50(a)(2). Further, by tortuously interfering with contractual relations under the lease, [person A] has broken implied warranties that [person A] would not so interfere. Further, to continue to pursue this case after the clear verdict in the case above cited amounts to malicious prosecution which breaches implied warranties under the DTPA.

(2)   Through letters from [person A], [person A]'s agents, servants or employees, and via Plaintiff's Original Petition in the case above cited, representations have been made that the lease confers rights, and remedies upon [person A] to allow a present right to have the lease forfeited. The continued pursuit during the pendency of this appeal demonstrates that [person A] continues to represent to [name] Corporation that the lease agreement confers a present right and remedy of forfeiture, when, in fact, the lease does not confer nor involve such a present right, and this is a violation of DTPA § 1746(b)(12).

(3)   Further, [person A] has knowingly made false or misleading statements of fact concerning the need for replacement or repair to the glass in the showcase windows of the leased premises, and continues to make such claim by pursuing an appeal of this cause all of which are in violation of DTPA § 1746(b)(13).

(4)   Continuing to attempt to evict Defendant when no grounds for eviction are present is an "unconscionable action or course of action" in violation of DTPA § 17.50(a)(3).

All conduct of [person A], as described herein, was committed "knowingly." All such actions of [person A] have been a producing cause of damages to [name] Corporation.

[Name] Corporation hereby gives notice that from the date of the appeal of the above cited case, it has been damaged in the amount of [amount] actual damages (for settlement purposes), in addition to expenses, including attorneys fees reasonable incurred in asserting these claims against [person A], if a claim under the DTPA were successfully asserted by [name] Corporation against [person A].

Your prompt attention to this matter will be appreciated.

Very truly yours,

[name of law firm]

By: _____
[attorney name]

*Note: Form 2–23 is representative of the Texas Deceptive Trade Practices—Consumer Protection Act.

§ 2.15   The Complaint

The complaint is the initial pleading in a case and should be drafted with several purposes in mind: 1) to name all the parties who are to be defendants, 2) to ask for

§ 2.15 COMPLAINT

relief from alleged causes of action against the defendants, and 3) to give notice of the basic facts giving rise to the plaintiff's claim. The complaint should contain a short and plain statement of the claim showing that the pleader is entitled to relief. If there is more than one claim, each should be set forth separately. In federal court, the complaint must also contain a statement of the grounds upon which the court's jurisdiction depends, unless the court already has jurisdiction and no new grounds are needed to support it. In the federal courts and in many states, very little factual detail is required. However, in federal court some matters, such as fraud, must be pleaded with greater specificity. Keep in mind that statements made in the complaint are binding on the party making them. At the top of the complaint, or petition, as it is sometimes called, is the case caption, or style, containing the names of the plaintiff and defendant, the case number assigned by the court, and the number of the judicial district. An example of a caption, or style, follows in **Form 2–24**:

FORM 2–24
SAMPLE CASE CAPTION

No. [case number]

[name]		)	In The District Court of
		)	
	Plaintiff,	)	[county] County, [state]
		)	
vs.		)	[judicial district] Judicial District
		)	
[name]		)	
		)	
	Defendant.	)	

The lead paragraph of the complaint introduces the plaintiff and advises the court of whom he is complaining. This is the paragraph which traditionally begins "COMES NOW. . . ."

The second paragraph contains statements which set the stage for jurisdiction in the Court. The county and state of residence of the parties is recounted here, or the state of incorporation and principal place of business of any party who is a corporation.

The third paragraph, or series of paragraphs, state the facts that comprise the plaintiff's cause of action.

Following the facts, a series of paragraphs should follow which state the allegations constituting the plaintiff's reasons for believing that the defendant's actions were the proximate cause of the damages suffered by the plaintiff. This is where the plaintiff's allegations of negligence, wilful and wanton disregard, malicious intent, and so forth.

The following paragraphs should contain information explaining how the plaintiff has been damaged by the defendant's actions. Specific dollar amounts of damages are appropriate here.

The final paragraph of the complaint is known as the prayer, and generally begins:

"WHEREFORE, PREMISES CONSIDERED, the plaintiff prays. . . ."

This paragraph should contain the summation of what the plaintiff wishes to be awarded as compensation for damages. These requests should include compensatory damages, exemplary damages, punitive damages, and attorneys' fees, if appropriate.

Lastly, check your state and local rules to determine if the complaint must contain a verification of truth by your client.

It is important to be familiar with different types of complaints. **Forms 2–25** through **2–30** and Forms **2–32** through **2–35** illustrate many different situations.

§ 2.16 —Complaint Drafting Checklist

The following checklist can be very helpful in organizing the information to prepare the complaint properly:

_____ Determine names and addresses of parties.

_____ Determine proper court for filing.

_____ Research jurisdictional and venue issues.

_____ List causes of action and determine if necessary elements exist.

_____ Obtain sample copy of similar complaint.

_____ Check applicable procedural rules for specific court.

_____ Include proper court caption.

_____ Draft jurisdictional allegation.

_____ Draft venue allegation.

_____ If parties include corporations, list registered agents for service.

_____ Draft service of process allegations.

_____ Draft facts of case.

_____ Draft causes of action, including damages sustained.

_____ Draft prayer for relief.

_____ If verification required, draft same.

§ 2.17 —Necessary Elements for Selected Causes of Action

Before filing a complaint, it is imperative to establish whether the elements necessary to prove the cause of action in the complaint exist. This section lists several common causes of action and the elements needed to prove each cause of action.

§ 2.17   NECESSARY ELEMENTS

Breach of Contract:
1. Parties have legal capacity to enter contract
2. Offer
3. Acceptance
4. Consideration

Negligence:
1. Defendant has duty of due care to plaintiff
2. Defendant has breached applicable standard of care
3. Defendant's breach of duty is proximate cause of plaintiff's injuries
4. Plaintiff has suffered some compensable damage

Assault:
1. Fear or apprehension of being harmed
2. Intent—Wilful and knowing misconduct on defendant's part
3. Defendant's action is proximate cause of plaintiff's fear or apprehension

Intentional Infliction of Emotional Distress:
1. Defendant commits extreme or outrageous act
2. Defendant intended to cause severe emotional distress to plaintiff
3. Plaintiff suffered severe emotional distress
4. Defendant's actions were proximate cause of plaintiff's severe emotional distress

False Imprisonment:
1. Defendant deprives plaintiff of right of freedom of movement
2. Defendant intentionally confined plaintiff
3. Defendant's acts were causation of plaintiff's confinement
4. Plaintiff was harmed by confinement or was conscious of confinement

Trespass:
1. Entrance upon plaintiff's property without consent of plaintiff
2. Physical intrusion of property
3. Intent (knowledge) to intrude
4. Defendant's actions are proximate cause of plaintiff's injury or damages

Conversion:
1. Plaintiff is in possession of, or is entitled to possession of, certain property
2. Defendant has intent to exercise control over said property or convert it to his own use

3. Defendant deprives plaintiff of his rightful use of said property
4. Defendant's actions are proximate cause of plaintiff's injury or damages

Nuisance:
1. Use of defendant's land in such a way that it interferes with plaintiff's quiet enjoyment or use of plaintiff's own land
2. Knowledge or intent of interference
3. Defendant's actions are proximate cause of plaintiff's injury or damages

Battery:
1. Defendant touches plaintiff in a harmful or offensive way
2. Intent or knowledge that said touching would be harmful or offensive to plaintiff
3. Defendant's actions are proximate cause of plaintiff's injuries

Slander:
1. Defendant has spoken a defamatory statement about plaintiff
2. Defamatory statement was made in presence of a third party
3. Defamatory statement has caused damages to plaintiff
4. Defendant's statement was proximate cause of damages to plaintiff

Libel:
1. Defendant has written a defamatory statement about plaintiff
2. Defamatory statement was published or made public
3. Defamatory statement has caused damages to plaintiff
4. Defendant's statement was proximate cause of damages to plaintiff

Strict Liability:
1. Product is defective
2. Product is unreasonably dangerous
3. Defendant is seller of product
4. Product causes damages to person or property of plaintiff

Breach of Implied Warranty of Merchantability:
1. Sale of goods to plaintiff by defendant
2. Defendant is a merchant of goods of that kind
3. Goods are not merchantable under the meaning of the Uniform Commercial Code
4. Defendant's breach of warranty of merchantability is proximate cause of plaintiff's damages

5. Damages

Breach of Implied Warranty of Fitness for a Particular Purpose:
1. Sale of goods to plaintiff by defendant
2. Seller has reason to know or is told particular reason for buying the goods
3. Seller knows that the seller's skill, judgment, or expertise will be relied upon by buyer in making the decision to purchase said goods
4. Purchased goods are not fit for the purpose for which they were intended
5. Unfitness of goods is proximate cause of plaintiff's damages
6. Damages

Negligence Per Se:
1. Statute exists regulating certain activities for purposes of safety
2. Defendant has violated statute
3. Defendant's actions were proximate cause of plaintiff's injuries or damages

Fraud:
1. Defendant makes false representation or fails to disclose material fact or circumstance
2. Intent
3. Defendant knows or should know that plaintiff is relying on the false representation
4. Plaintiff has justification to rely upon representations of defendant
5. False representation or failure to disclose material fact or circumstance is proximate cause of injury or damages to plaintiff

§ 2.18   —Auto Accident Complaint

FORM 2–25
SAMPLE AUTO ACCIDENT COMPLAINT

No. [case number]

[name],	)	IN THE DISTRICT COURT OF
	)	
Plaintiff,	)	[county] COUNTY, STATE OF
	)	
vs.	)	[state]
	)	
[name],	)	[judicial district] JUDICIAL DISTRICT
	)	
Defendant.	)	

81

INITIATION OF THE SUIT

COMPLAINT

COMES NOW, plaintiff, [name], and for plaintiff's complaint, alleges as follows:

I.

Plaintiff, for all times mentioned herein, was a resident of the County of [county], State of [state].

II.

Plaintiff is informed and believes and thereon alleges that defendant, [name], was and is a resident of the County of [county], State of [state].

III.

Plaintiff is informed and believes and thereon alleges that at all times and places herein mentioned defendant, [name], was operating a certain [vehicle description], [state] License No. [number], owned by [name of owner].

IV.

At all times herein mentioned plaintiff was and now is the owner of a certain [vehicle description], [state] License No. [number].

V.

At all times herein mentioned [street A] was and now is a public street and highway running in a general easterly and westerly direction in the City of [city], County of [county], State of [state] and [street B] was and now is a public street and highway in said city and county, running in a general northerly and southerly direction and intersecting [street A], and at that intersection, governmental authorities had caused an arterial stop sign to be erected which required all northbound traffic on [street B] to stop for [street A], which is a thoroughfare.

VI.

On or about [date], [20__], at about the hour of [time] [A.M./P.M.], plaintiff was operating plaintiff's automobile in a prudent and careful manner in a general easterly direction upon and along [street A] in the vicinity of its intersection with [street B]; at said time and place defendant was operating said [vehicle description] along [street B] in a general northerly direction; at said time and place defendant failed to stop said vehicle at the stop sign located south of the intersection of [street B] and [street A], or at any time prior to entering the intersection; but rather, drove defendant's automobile into the intersection with wanton disregard of the approach of the vehicle driven by the plaintiff.

§ 2.18 AUTO ACCIDENT COMPLAINT

VII.

At said time and place, defendant with gross negligence and wanton disregard for the safety of others, drove and operated defendant's automobile so as to cause the same to collide with great force and violence with the automobile which the plaintiff was driving.

VIII.

Defendant operated his vehicle in a reckless and negligent manner and in violation of several [state] State Statutes, including, but not limited to: [list violations with statute numbers].

IX.

Plaintiff was injured as a direct result of the collision, the same having been directly and proximately caused by the negligent, wanton conduct of defendant and by defendant's total heedless and reckless disregard of the rights of others.

X.

By reason of said negligence and collision aforesaid, and as a proximate result thereof, plaintiff suffered injuries consisting of, but not limited to, severe injuries, bruises, contusions, strain to all the muscles of his body, lacerations of both knees, and severe lacerations of his forehead of a permanent disfiguring nature; the injuries thus received by plaintiff have greatly impaired plaintiff's health, strength and activity and have thereby caused and continue to cause plaintiff great mental, physical, and nervous pain and suffering and extreme shock to plaintiff's nervous system; and the plaintiff is informed and believes, and thereon alleges, that the injuries will result in some disability to plaintiff, all to his general damage in an amount in excess of [statutory amount for jurisdiction of court].

XI.

In addition to the general damages sustained by plaintiff, plaintiff has suffered substantial expenses, which plaintiff has incurred and will continue to incur, including, but not limited to, expenses for medical treatment including the services of doctors, hospitals and the like, all in an amount in excess of [amount], the exact amount to be proven at time of trial.

XII.

As a further proximate result of the hereinabove alleged carelessness and negligence of said defendant, plaintiff lost the use of his automobile for a period of time, all to his further special damage in an amount equal to the reasonable value of said loss of use.

XIII.

As a further, direct and proximate result of the carelessness and negligence of the defendant, plaintiff was prevented from attending to his usual occupation or any occupation whatsoever and has been damaged in an amount not yet ascertainable, plaintiff is informed and believes and thereon alleges that by reason of said carelessness and negligence of defendant, plaintiff will, in the future, be prevented from attending to his usual occupation for an undetermined period of time, all to his further special damage in an amount to be proven at trial.

WHEREFORE, plaintiff, [name], prays for judgment against the defendant, [name], for

1. General damages in excess of [amount];

2. Special damages in excess of [amount];

3. Reasonable attorneys fees and costs of suit; and

4. Such other and further relief as the Court may deem proper.

[name of law firm]

By: _____
[attorney's name and
firm address]

§ 2.19 —Product Liability Complaint

FORM 2–26
SAMPLE PRODUCT LIABILITY COMPLAINT

No. [case number]

[name]	)	
Plaintiff,	)	In the District Court of
vs.	)	[county] County, State of
[name]	)	[state]
Defendant.	)	[judicial district] Judicial District

COMPLAINT

COMES NOW the plaintiff and for cause of action against the defendant, alleges as follows:

I.

Defendant, [name] Corporation was and is a [type of corporation] corporation doing business in the State of [state] as [name] Corporation in [city, state].

§ 2.19   PRODUCT LIABILITY COMPLAINT

II.

At all times mentioned herein, defendant [name] Corporation was engaged in the business of selling food preparation appliances to the general public.

III.

On or about [date], [20__], plaintiff [name] purchased a food processor manufactured by [name] Corporation through their retail showroom at [street address], [city, state].

IV.

On or about [date], [20__], plaintiff [name] was slicing potatoes in said food processor. Plaintiff stopped the machine and began to disassemble the machine per the enclosed instructions when said machine suddenly engaged without warning, causing deep cuts and serious contusions to plaintiff's hands.

V.

At the time of plaintiff's purchase, the food processor was defective and unsafe for its intended purpose.

VI.

As a direct and proximate result of defendant's careless and negligent manufacture of said product plaintiff was injured in her health, strength, and activity, sustaining shock and injury to her nervous system and person, causing plaintiff mental and physical pain and suffering and resulting in her disability.

VII.

As a direct and proximate result of the said negligence and carelessness on the part of the defendant, plaintiff [name] was disabled and may be disabled in the future and thereby be prevented from attending to the duties of her usual occupation. Plaintiff has therefore lost earnings and income and may lose further earnings and income in the future, all in amounts presently unknown to her. Plaintiff, therefore, asks leave to amend this complaint so as to show the amount of her lost earnings and income when ascertained, or to prove said amount at the time of trial.

WHEREFORE, plaintiff prays judgment against the defendant as follows:

1.   For general damages;

2.   For special damages as alleged or proven at the time of trial;

3.   For lost wages according to proof;

4.   For costs of suit; and

5.   For such other and further relief as the court may deem proper.

INITIATION OF THE SUIT

Dated this [date] day of [month], [20__].

> Respectfully submitted,
>
> [name of law firm]
>
> By _____
> [attorney name]
>
> _____
> [firm address]

§ 2.20 —Medical Malpractice Complaint

FORM 2–27
SAMPLE MEDICAL MALPRACTICE COMPLAINT

No. [case number]

[name],	)	IN THE DISTRICT COURT OF
	)	
Plaintiff,	)	[county] COUNTY, STATE OF
	)	
vs.	)	[state]
	)	
[name],	)	[judicial district] JUDICIAL DISTRICT
	)	
Defendant.	)	

COMPLAINT

COMES NOW, plaintiff, [name], and for his complaint, alleges as follows:

I.

Plaintiff, for all times mentioned herein, was a resident of the County of [county], State of [state].

II.

Plaintiff is informed and believes and thereon alleges that defendant, [name] was and is a medical doctor duly licensed and authorized to practice medicine in the County of [county], State of [state].

III.

At all times mentioned herein, defendant [name] was engaged in the practice of internal medicine.

IV.

On or about [date], [20__], plaintiff [name] began to experience severe abdominal pains and consulted defendant [name], who informed plaintiff that [he/she] was suffering from acute appendicitis and needed emergency surgery. Plaintiff was immediately admitted to [hospital name] Hospital and defendant [name] performed the emergency appendectomy on plaintiff.

V.

On or about [date], [20__], approximately three days following surgery, plaintiff began to run a high fever and experience severe discomfort and pain in the area of the aforementioned surgery. Although given medication, the fever and pain increased until on [date], [20__], lapsed into a coma. Emergency surgery was again performed by defendant [name], and it was discovered that the source of the fever and pain was an infection caused by a surgical sponge left in plaintiff's abdominal cavity by defendant during the initial surgery.

VI.

As a direct and proximate result of defendant's careless and negligent conduct, plaintiff was injured in [his/her] health, strength and activity, sustaining shock and injury to [his/her] person, causing plaintiff extreme mental and physical pain and suffering and resulting in [his/her] disability.

VII.

As a direct and proximate result of the said negligence and carelessness on the part of the defendant, plaintiff [name] was disabled and may be disabled in the future and thereby be prevented from attending to the duties of [his/her] usual occupation. Plaintiff has therefore lost earnings and income and may lose further earnings and income in the future, all in the amounts presently unknown to [him/her]. Plaintiff, therefore, asks leave to amend this complaint so as to show the amount of [his/her] lost earnings and income when ascertained, or to prove said amount at the time of trial.

WHEREFORE, plaintiff prays judgment against the defendant as follows:

1.   For general damages;

2.   For special damages as alleged or proven at the time of trial;

3.   For lost wages according to proof;

4.   For costs of suit; and

5.   For such other and further relief as the court may deem proper.

Dated this [date] day of [month], [20__].

INITIATION OF THE SUIT

Respectfully submitted,

[name of law firm]

By _____
[attorney name]

_____
[firm address]

§ 2.21 —Slip and Fall Complaint

FORM 2–28
SAMPLE SLIP AND FALL COMPLAINT

No. [case number]

[name],	)	IN THE DISTRICT COURT OF
	)	
Plaintiff,	)	[county] COUNTY, STATE OF
	)	
vs.	)	[state]
	)	
[name],	)	[judicial district] JUDICIAL DISTRICT
	)	
Defendant.	)	

COMPLAINT

COMES NOW, the plaintiff and for cause of action against the defendant, alleges as follows:

I.

Defendant [name] was and is a [type of corporation] corporation doing business in the State of [state] as the [name] Hotel in [city, state].

II.

At all times mentioned herein, defendant [name], a corporation, was engaged as an innkeeper or hotel establishment operating for the use of the general public.

III.

On or about [date], [20__], plaintiff [name] was a guest at the [name] Hotel located in [city, state]. While attending a convention at the [name] Hotel in [city, state], and as she was about to enter the coffee shop located in the lobby of the hotel, she slipped on a butter-like substance on the floor, causing her to fall to the floor with great violence.

IV.

Defendant maintained a dangerous and unsafe condition which exposed patrons of their establishment to undue harm.

V.

The defendant operated the hotel in such a negligent manner that as a proximate result plaintiff was injured in her health, strength, and activity, sustaining severe shock and injuries to her nervous system and person, causing plaintiff mental and physical pain and suffering and resulting in her disability.

VI.

As a direct and proximate result of said carelessness and negligence of the defendant, plaintiff was compelled to and did incur expenses for medical care, hospitalization, and other incidentals, and will have to incur additional like expenses in the future, all in the amounts presently unknown to her. Plaintiff, therefore, asks leave either to amend the complaint so as to show the amount of her medical expenses when ascertained or prove said amount at the time of trial.

VII.

As a direct and proximate result of said carelessness and negligence of the defendant, plaintiff has been generally damaged in a sum to be determined at trial.

VIII.

As a direct and proximate result of the said negligence and carelessness on the part of the defendant, plaintiff [name] was disabled and may be disabled in the future and thereby be prevented from attending to the duties of her usual occupation. Plaintiff has therefore lost earnings and income and may lose further earnings and income in the future, all in the amounts presently unknown to her. Plaintiff, therefore, asks leave to amend this complaint so as to show the amount of her lost earnings and income when ascertained, or to prove said amount at the time of trial.

WHEREFORE, plaintiff prays judgment against the defendant as follows:

1.   For general damages;

2.   For special damages as alleged or proven at the time of trial;

3.   For lost wages according to proof;

4.   For costs of suit; and

5.   For such other and further relief as the court may deem proper.

DATED: [date], [20__]

INITIATION OF THE SUIT

Respectfully submitted,

[name of law firm]

By _____
[attorney name]

_____
[firm address]

§ 2.22 —Complaint for Suit Against Municipal Transit Authority

FORM 2–29
SAMPLE COMPLAINT FOR SUIT AGAINST MUNICIPAL TRANSIT AUTHORITY

[court] OF THE STATE OF [name]
COUNTY OF [county]

[name] 　　Plaintiff(s),	)))	Index No. _____ VERIFIED COMPLAINT
	)	
-against-	))	
[name] 　　Defendant(s)	))	

Plaintiff [name], as Administratrix and individually, and plaintiff [name], individually, by the attorneys, [firm name], complaining of the defendant herein, set forth as follows:

AS AND FOR A FIRST CAUSE OF ACTION
ON BEHALF OF [name], AS ADMINISTRATRIX
OF THE GOODS, CHATTELS, AND CREDITS WHICH
WERE OF [name], DECEASED

1. At all times hereinafter mentioned, plaintiffs, [name] and [name], were residents of the County of [county], City of [city],State of [state].

2. At all times hereinafter mentioned, defendant, CITY TRANSIT AUTHORITY, has been and still is a public benefit corporation, duly authorized and existing under and by virtue of the laws of the State of [state].

3. That by a decree of the Surrogate's Court of the County of [county], dated June 7, 1994, the plaintiff, [name], was appointed Administratrix of the goods, chattels, and credits of [name], deceased, copy of affidavit of [administrator of estate], dated May 31,

§ 2.22 SUIT AGAINST MUNICIPAL TRANSIT AUTHORITY

1994, Exhibit "A" and certified copy of Letters of Administration, Exhibit "B" annexed hereto.

4. Heretofore and prior to the commencement of this action and within ninety (90) days after plaintiffs' claims against defendant, CITY TRANSIT AUTHORITY, arose, a notice sworn to by the plaintiffs was served on or about July 25, 1994, upon the defendant, CITY TRANSIT AUTHORITY, in compliance with the law, which notice set forth the name and post office addresses of the plaintiffs and their attorneys, the nature of plaintiff's claim against said defendant, the time, place, and manner in which said claim arose and the items of damage and injuries claimed to have been sustained.

5. At least thirty (30) days have elapsed since service of such notice and adjustment of payment of such claim has been neglected or refused, although plaintiffs have demanded that the same be paid and adjusted.

6. The action has been commenced within one year and ninety (90) days after the happening of the events upon which the defendant's claim is based.

7. At all times hereinafter mentioned, and, more particularly, on May 22, 1994, defendant, CITY TRANSIT AUTHORITY, owned, operated, managed, and controlled a bus at or about Grant Avenue at or near its intersection with Howard Avenue, in the City of [city] and State of [state].

8. At all times herein mentioned, the defendant [name], an employee of the defendant, CITY TRANSIT AUTHORITY, was operating, driving and controlling the aforesaid bus, owned by the defendant, CITY TRANSIT AUTHORITY.

9. At all times herein mentioned, said bus, which was owned by the defendant CITY TRANSIT AUTHORITY, was driven and operated by its employee, the defendant [name], with the knowledge, permission, and consent of the defendant.

10. At all times herein mentioned, Grant Avenue at or near its intersection with Howard Avenue situated in the City of [city] and State of [name] was and still is a much-traveled public highway in common use by the residents of said city and others.

11. On or about May 22, 1989, while the decedent [name] was lawfully riding his bicycle across the intersection of Grant Avenue and Howard Avenue as aforesaid, he was negligently and recklessly struck and knocked down by the bus owned by the defendant CITY TRANSIT AUTHORITY which was then and there being driven and being operated by the defendant [name], and that it caused fatal injuries to the decedent, [name], resulting in his death on May 22, 1994.

12. This accident and the resulting death of [name] was caused solely by the negligence of the defendants and without any contributory negligence on the part of the decedent hereto.

13. That the aforesaid occurrence took place solely as the result of the negligence of the defendant in the ownership, operation, management, and control of the said bus.

INITIATION OF THE SUIT

14. By reason of the aforesaid, [name] has incurred, become liable for, and paid for hospital and funeral expenses in diverse amounts individually and as the representative of the decedent's estate.

15. The amount of damages sought in this First Cause of Action exceeds the jurisdictional limit of all lower courts which would otherwise have jurisdiction.

AS AND FOR A SECOND CAUSE OF ACTION
ON BEHALF OF [name], AS ADMINISTRATRIX
OF THE GOODS, CHATTELS, AND CREDITS WHICH
WERE OF [name], DECEASED

16. Plaintiffs repeat, reiterate, and reallege each and every allegation contained in paragraphs 1 through 15 of this complaint as if fully set forth at length herein.

17. The deceased, [name], prior to his death on May 22, 1994, sustained great, severe, and fatal injuries to his body, head, and limbs; and suffered great pain, shock, and physical and mental anguish as a result of the aforesaid occurrence.

18. The amount of damages sought in this action exceeds the jurisdictional limits of all lower courts which would otherwise have jurisdiction.

AS AND FOR A THIRD CAUSE OF ACTION
ON BEHALF OF [name] AND
[name], INDIVIDUALLY

19. Plaintiffs repeat, reiterate, and reallege each and every allegation contained in paragraphs 1 through 18 of this complaint as if fully set forth at length herein.

20. Plaintiffs [name] and [name] were the parents of the decedent, [name], who was born on August 17, 1981.

21. At all times herein and until the date of his wrongful death, the decedent was a loyal, dutiful, and devoted son.

22. At the time of his death and prior to sustaining the injuries previously mentioned, the decedent, [name], was in good health.

23. By reason of the foregoing, plaintiffs are now and will continue to be deprived of the love, care, and affection of their son, decedent, [name].

24. By reason of the foregoing, the plaintiffs [name] and [name], individually, have been deprived of the comfort, society, and services of the decedent.

25. The amount of damages sought in this action exceeds the jurisdictional limits of all lower courts which would otherwise have jurisdiction.

WHEREFORE, plaintiffs demand judgment against the defendants on all causes of action in an amount commensurate with the injuries and damages sustained herein all together with the costs and disbursements of this action.

Dated: [city, state]

_____, 20__

                    Yours, etc.,

                    [firm name, address, and telephone number]

§ 2.23   —Complaint for Suit on Sworn Account

FORM 2–30
SAMPLE COMPLAINT FOR SUIT ON SWORN ACCOUNT

No. [case number]

[name],		)	IN THE DISTRICT COURT OF
		)	
	Plaintiff,	)	[county] COUNTY, STATE OF
		)	
vs.		)	[state]
		)	
[name],		)	[judicial district] JUDICIAL DISTRICT
		)	
	Defendant.	)	

PLAINTIFF'S ORIGINAL PETITION

TO THE HONORABLE JUDGE OF SAID COURT:

COMES NOW, [name], plaintiff, complaining of [name], defendant, and for cause would show the Court as follows:

I.

Plaintiff is a corporation, with its principal place of business in [city], [county] County, [state]. Defendant is an individual whose residence is located in [county] County, [state]. Service of process may be had by serving defendant with citation at his residence at [address], [city], [state].

II.

On twenty separate occasions from [date], [20__] to [date], [20__], as evidenced by the verified account which is attached hereto as Exhibit A, plaintiff sold and delivered to defendant merchandise consisting of [description of merchandise] as specifically itemized on Exhibit A attached hereto. Such sales were made at the request of defendant, and were sold and delivered in the regular course of business. In consideration of such sales, of which a systematic record has been kept, defendant promised and became bound and liable to pay plaintiff the prices charged for such goods in the total amount of $[amount], being a reasonable charge for such items, as further shown on the attached Exhibit A. Despite numerous demands by plaintiff upon defendant for payment, defendant has refused and failed to pay the account, to plaintiff's damage in the amount of $[amount], plus interest and attorneys' fees.

III.

On [date], [20__], plaintiff presented account to defendant for payment. Plaintiff found it necessary to employ the services of the undersigned attorneys and to incur attorneys' fees of $[amount].

IV.

Plaintiff would further show that he is entitled to interest at the rate of [interest rate] (__%) per annum, commencing on the [number] day from and after the time when the sum is due and payable, as allowed by statute number [statute] of the laws of the state of [state]. Plaintiff is therefore entitled to prejudgment interest from the [number] day after each unpaid item of the account became due and payable, which was [number] days after the delivery date set forth in the attached Exhibit A, until date of judgment.

WHEREFORE, plaintiff prays that defendant be cited to appear and answer and that upon final trial, plaintiff have judgment against defendant for $[amount] plus interest before and after judgment as provided by law, attorneys' fees in the amount of $[amount] and for such other and further relief to which plaintiff is justly entitled.

Respectfully submitted,

[name of law firm]

By: _____
[attorney's name and address]

Note: The following affidavit (**Form 2–31**) should be attached to Exhibit A.

FORM 2–31
SAMPLE AFFIDAVIT FOR SUIT ON SWORN ACCOUNT

The State of [state],
County of [county]

BEFORE ME, the undersigned Notary Public in and for the County of [county], State of [state], on this day personally appeared before me [name], known to me, and after being duly sworn, stated on oath that the foregoing and duly attached account in favor of [name] Corporation and against [defendant] for the sum of $[amount] is within the knowledge of affiant, just and true, that it remains due and unpaid, and that all just and lawful offsets, payments and credits have been allowed.

[signature of affiant]

SWORN AND SUBSCRIBED TO BEFORE ME, on this the [date] day of [month], [20___].

Notary Public in and
for the County of [county],
State of [state]

§ 2.24 —Breach of Contract Complaint

FORM 2–32
SAMPLE BREACH OF CONTRACT COMPLAINT

No. [case number]

[name],	)	IN THE DISTRICT COURT OF
	)	
Plaintiff,	)	[county] COUNTY,
	)	
vs.	)	[state]
	)	
[name],	)	[judicial district] JUDICIAL DISTRICT
	)	
Defendant.	)	

PLAINTIFF'S ORIGINAL PETITION

COMES NOW, [name] plaintiff, complaining of [name] defendant, and for cause of action would show the Court as follows:

I.

Plaintiff is an individual residing in [county] County, [state]. Defendant is a corporation, duly formed and existing under the laws of the State of [state], and may be served with process by serving [name], its registered agent for service, at [address, city], [county] County [state].

II.

On or about [date], [20___], plaintiff and defendant executed the written contract which is attached as Exhibit A and incorporated herein by reference. Under the terms of the contract, for consideration in the amount of $[amount], defendant promised to repair a certain portion of the roof of plaintiff's residence at [address], [county] County,

INITIATION OF THE SUIT

[state]. Defendant agreed to complete such repairs within a ten-day period from the date of the signing of said contract and to at all times protect the inside of the residence from any damages caused by the repairs or weather conditions during that ten day period.

III.

Plaintiff has fully performed his contract by paying defendant $[amount] in cash, receipt for which is hereby attached as Exhibit B.

IV.

On [date], [20__], one day after the parties executed the above-mentioned contract, defendant sent workers to the residence to strip the roof of existing shingles and tar paper. When plaintiff returned home from work at 6:00 P.M. that evening, the workers were gone and plaintiff observed that the portion of the roof to be repaired was exposed to bare plywood, and had neither protective plastic covering nor other weather-protective material. Plaintiff left repeated messages with defendant's answering service that evening, but defendant failed and refused to return plaintiff's calls.

V.

On the following morning, plaintiff again telephoned defendant at his office and finally was successful in talking to defendant. Plaintiff advised defendant that his roof had been left unprotected and exposed to the elements during the previous evening, and that this was expressly forbidden by the contract. Defendant apologized for the oversight by his crews and promised to rectify the situation immediately.

VI.

That evening, upon returning from work at 6:00 P.M., plaintiff observed that no work had been done on his roof that day and that the roof remained unprotected. Plaintiff immediately called defendant's office and told the answering service that the situation was an emergency since severe thunderstorm warnings had just been issued for his area.

VII.

Despite several calls to defendant's office explaining the urgency of the situation, defendant failed to return plaintiff's phone calls, and plaintiff attempted to cover his roof with plastic tarpaulins, which he purchased at a nearby hardware store at an expense of $[amount].

VIII.

At approximately 8:30 P.M., severe thunderstorms accompanied by high winds hit the area of plaintiff's residence. Despite the extensive efforts of plaintiff and his neighbors to hold the plastic tarpaulins on the roof, plaintiff's residence sustained such severe water damage that it was necessary to summon the fire department for assistance. The fire marshal's report is hereby attached as Exhibit C.

§ 2.24   BREACH OF CONTRACT COMPLAINT

IX.

Plaintiff's residence suffered damages to carpeting, wallpaper, plaster, and personal furnishings in an amount exceeding $[amount] as a result of this incident.

X.

Defendant has, as of the date of this petition, failed and refused to perform his remaining work as agreed in the contract which is relative to this cause of action. Defendant also refuses any and all obligation of liability as to the damages suffered by plaintiff as a result of the water damage on [date], [20__].

XI.

Plaintiff alleges that defendant's failure to perform the obligations of his written contract was the proximate cause of damages to the plaintiff's residence.

XII.

Plaintiff alleges that defendant has wrongfully breached the terms of the contract by failing to complete the work he promised to perform.

XIII.

WHEREFORE, plaintiff requests that defendant be cited to appear and answer, and that on final trial, plaintiff have judgment as follows:

1.   For general damages in an amount exceeding the minimum jurisdictional amount of the court.

2.   For any and all damages to plaintiff's residence as a result of the incidents described herein, in an amount to be determined later.

3.   For return of the original $[amount] paid to defendant in consideration for the work described in the contract.

4.   For attorney's fees in the sum of $[amount].

5.   For costs of suit incurred herein.

6.   For interest at the legal rate on the foregoing sums from the date of judgment until paid.

7.   For such other and further relief, at law or in equity, to which plaintiff may be justly entitled.

Respectfully submitted,

[name of law firm]

INITIATION OF THE SUIT

By: _____
[attorney name]
[Address]
[signature of attorney]
Attorney for Plaintiff

§ 2.25 —Wrongful Discharge Complaint

FORM 2–33
SAMPLE WRONGFUL DISCHARGE COMPLAINT

No. [case number]

[name],	)	IN THE DISTRICT COURT OF
	)	
Plaintiff,	)	[county] COUNTY,
	)	
vs.	)	[state]
	)	
[name],	)	[judicial district] JUDICIAL DISTRICT
	)	
Defendant.	)	

PLAINTIFF'S ORIGINAL COMPLAINT

TO THE HONORABLE JUDGE OF SAID COURT

COMES NOW, [name], plaintiff, complaining of [name], defendant, and for cause of action would show the Court as follows:

I.

Plaintiff is an individual residing in [county], County, [state]. Defendant is a corporation, duly organized and qualified to do business under the laws of the state of [state] and may be served with process by service upon its registered agent, [name of registered agent] at [address].

II.

On or about [date], [20__], plaintiff and defendant entered into an oral contract whereby it was agreed by the parties that plaintiff would work for defendant in the capacity of [job description] for a period of [time period] beginning on [date], [20__] and ending on [date], [20__]. The defendant agreed to pay plaintiff compensation in the amount of $[amount] per year, payable in 24 equal installments on the 15th day and last day of every calendar month.

§ 2.25 WRONGFUL DISCHARGE COMPLAINT

III.

As duly agreed upon, plaintiff began performing the duties of plaintiff's employment and oral contract on [date], [20__]. Plaintiff continued to perform the duties of his contract in full accordance with its provisions until [date], [20__], when plaintiff was discharged by defendant without just cause or provocation. Plaintiff remains willing and able to continue to perform according to the provisions of the contract, but has been prevented from doing so by actions of the defendant.

IV.

Up until the date that defendant wrongfully discharged plaintiff, defendant had paid plaintiff the sum of $[amount], as provided under the contract. The last payment to the plaintiff was made on [date], [20__]. There remains a sum of $[amount] due and owing to plaintiff under the provisions of the contract. Plaintiff maintains that since the contract date has now expired, plaintiff is entitled to recover from defendant all sums of wages due from [date], [20__] to the end of the contract, [date], [20__], plus interest computed at the rate of [interest rate]%, representing the statutory allowable interest rate.

V.

Plaintiff presented the above claim to defendant for payment on [date], [20__] by certified mail, return receipt requested. Said letter is attached hereto as Exhibit A. [Number] days (must usually be over 30 days) have elapsed since presentation of this claim, but defendant has refused, and continues to refuse payment of said claim to plaintiff. It has therefore become necessary for plaintiff to obtain the services of legal counsel in this matter. Plaintiff therefore is entitled to recover the additional sum of $[amount], which sum is a reasonable fee for legal services in this action. In the event of appeal, plaintiff would be further entitled to a sum of $[amount] as reasonable attorney's fees.

WHEREFORE, PREMISES CONSIDERED, plaintiff requests that defendant be cited to appear and answer and that, upon final trial plaintiff have judgment as follows:

1. Damages in the sum of $[amount] representing wages owed under the contract plus the legal interest rate from the date each payment became due until date of judgment.

2. Interest after judgment at the statutory rate.

3. Costs of court.

4. Reasonable attorney's fees in the amount of $[amount].

5. Such other and further relief to which plaintiff may be justly entitled.

INITIATION OF THE SUIT

Respectfully submitted,

[name of law firm]

By: _____
[attorney name]

[address]

[signature]_____
Attorney for Plaintiff

§ 2.26 —Promissory Note Complaint

FORM 2–34
PROMISSORY NOTE COMPLAINT

No. [case number]

[name],	)	IN THE DISTRICT COURT OF
	)	
Plaintiff,	)	[county] COUNTY,
	)	
vs.	)	[state]
	)	
[name],	)	[judicial district] JUDICIAL DISTRICT
	)	
Defendant.	)	

PLAINTIFF'S ORIGINAL PETITION

TO THE HONORABLE JUDGE OF SAID COURT:

COMES NOW, [name], plaintiff, complaining on [name], defendant, and for cause of action, would show as follows:

I.

Plaintiff is an individual residing in [county] County, [state]. Defendant is an individual residing in [county] County, [state], and may be served with process be serving him at his residence address, [address, city, state].

II.

On or about [date], [20__], at [city], [state], defendant executed and delivered a promissory note to plaintiff dated [date], [20__], whereby defendant promised to pay to plaintiff the amount of $[amount], with interest at the rate of [interest rate]% per annum, due and payable in monthly installments of $[amount], due on the 1st day of each

100

calendar month for the life of the note at [city], [state]. A true and correct copy of said note is attached hereto as Exhibit A and incorporated by reference herein. Plaintiff is the legal owner and holder of said note.

III.

On or about [date], [20__], defendant ceased to make payments on the note as provided for therein, leaving a sum of $[amount] remaining due and payable to plaintiff. Defendant has failed and refused and continues to fail and refuse to pay plaintiff the remaining sums due and payable under the terms of the note.

IV.

As a result of the defendant's failure to pay the sums due and owing on the note, plaintiff has found it necessary to obtain the services of an attorney to enforce collection of the note. Plaintiff is entitled to recover $[amount], which sum is a reasonable charge for attorney's fees in this action. In the event of an appeal, plaintiff would be entitled to an additional $[amount], as a reasonable attorney's fee.

WHEREFORE, PREMISES CONSIDERED, plaintiff requests that defendant be cited to appear and answer, and that on final trial, plaintiff have judgment as follows:

1.   Judgment against defendant for the sum of $[amount], with interest at the rate of [interest rate in note] from [date], [20__], until judgment.

2.   Attorney's fees in the sum of $[amount], with interest at the rate of [statutory rate] from [date of default], [20__], until paid.

3.   Interest after judgment at the rate of [statutory rate] until paid.

4.   Costs of suit.

5.   Such other and further relief to which plaintiff may be justly entitled.

Respectfully submitted,

[name of law firm]

By: _____
[attorney name]

[address] _____

[signature] _____
Attorney for Plaintiff

§ 2.27 —Deceptive Trade Practices Complaint

FORM 2–35
SAMPLE DECEPTIVE TRADE PRACTICES COMPLAINT

No. [case number]

[name],	)	IN THE DISTRICT COURT OF
	)	
Plaintiff,	)	[county] COUNTY, [state]
	)	
vs.	)	[judicial district] JUDICIAL DISTRICT
	)	
[name],	)	
	)	
Defendant.	)	

PLAINTIFF'S ORIGINAL PETITION

TO THE HONORABLE JUDGE OF SAID COURT:

COMES NOW, [name], Plaintiff, complaining of [name], Defendant, and for cause of action would respectfully show the Court as follows:

I.

Plaintiff [name], (hereinafter referred to as "Plaintiff") resides at [address] and is a resident of [city], [county] County, [state].

Defendant [name], (hereinafter referred to as "Defendant") resides at [address, city], [county] County, [state], and may be served with process at that address

II.

At all times relevant to this Suit, Plaintiff was acting as a consumer as defined in Section [cite sections] of [state] Deceptive Trade Practices—Consumer Protection Act and Defendant was engaged in "Trade and Commerce" as defined in Section [cite section] of the [state] Deceptive Trade Practice Consumer Protection Act, hereinafter referred to as DTPA, in [county] County.

III.

This Suit is filed pursuant to the provisions of Section [cite section] et seq. of the [state] DTPA upon the grounds that the acts and procedures of Defendant as described herein are prohibited by said Statute including but not limited to sections: [cite specific section references].

§ 2.27 DECEPTIVE TRADE PRACTICES

IV.

That on or about [date], Plaintiff answered an advertisement in the newspaper regarding the sale of "a [vehicle description] in excellent condition." Defendant was the legal owner of said vehicle and had placed said advertisement in the newspaper. A copy of said advertisement is attached hereto and incorporated by reference in Exhibit "A."

V.

[State other pertinent facts, if necessary.]

VI.

Based on the representations made by defendant as to the condition of the vehicle offered for sale, Plaintiff made an offer to purchase said vehicle. Said Defendant was aware of or should have been aware of the fact that Plaintiff's offer to purchase said vehicle and price offered thereto were based on the representation that said vehicle was in excellent condition.

VII.

The Defendant, knowingly and intentionally made the following certain oral misrepresentations including but not limited to the following false and untrue statements of material fact: [state the false and deceptive representations here].

VIII.

That all of the statements made by the Defendant referred to in paragraph VII above, should have been known to be false and untrue through the exercise of due care and diligence or that said Defendant was negligent in not ascertaining the truth of falsity of his statements or that said Defendant made said statements recklessly without any knowledge of the truth thereof as though said statements were positive assertions of fact. Said Defendant knew or should have known that the statements referred to in paragraph VII were not true, false, incorrect, or misleading, and that Defendant had a duty to disclose any and all defects known to him regarding said vehicle.

IX.

That said Defendant referred to in paragraph VII herein made the statements referred to in paragraph VII herein with the intent of or knowledge thereof of inducing Plaintiff to purchase a consumer item, namely the vehicle described in paragraph III herein.

X.

That Plaintiff relied upon the truth and/or accuracy of said Defendant's statements and representations referred to in paragraph VII above and as a result of same, Plaintiff purchased the vehicle referred to in paragraph III herein. Plaintiff would not have entered into said transaction but for Defendant's statements and representations regarding the same.

INITIATION OF THE SUIT

XI.

Further, the Defendants impliedly warranted to Plaintiffs pursuant to [state] Business and Commerce Codes Sections [cite sections] and Section [cite section] of the [state] DTPA that the vehicle in question would:

(a) Be fit for the ordinary purposes for which such vehicles are used, and;

(b) Be fit for the particular purpose for which vehicle was required.

At the time the Plaintiff purchased the vehicle the Defendant knew or should have known the purpose for which Plaintiff purchased said vehicle and that Plaintiff was relying on Defendant to furnish a vehicle suitable and fit for that purpose. As a direct and proximate result of Defendant's breach of implied warranties, Plaintiff sustained extensive direct and consequential damages. Defendant has also thereby committed violations of Section [cite section] of the [state] DTPA, by representing that the vehicle was of a particular standard, quality or grade when in fact it was of another.

XII.

Plaintiff has now suffered and continues to suffer injury and damages as a result of the misrepresentations referred to hereinabove. As a result of said misrepresentation Plaintiff has incurred the following losses and expenses: [state the specific expenses and damages here, including attorney's fees and court costs].

Plaintiff reserves the right to plead and prove the damages to which he is entitled at the time of trial.

XIII.

That as a result of Defendant having committed the above described violations of the [state] DTPA and/or willfully and knowingly making false representations referred to herein, Defendant is liable to Plaintiff for three times the amount of Plaintiff's actual damages [check state statue for precise amount] pursuant to Section [cite section] of the [state] DTPA.

XIV.

That Plaintiff has made demand upon Defendant for payment of said sums more than thirty (30) days prior to the filing of this Petition, and Plaintiff would show this Court that the recovery of attorney's fees is authorized, made and provided under and according to the provisions of the [state] DTPA and Rule of the [state] Rules of Civil Procedure. Plaintiff further asks recovery of and from Defendant for such reasonable attorney's fees, inasmuch as Plaintiff has been required to employ the undersigned attorney to file this suit and has agreed to pay him a reasonable fee for his services, all of which Plaintiff alleges to be the amounts prayed for in paragraph XII hereinabove.

XV.

In the alternative, but not waiving any of the above, but specifically insisting upon the same, Plaintiff would show unto the court that Defendant's actions, misrepresentations, and nondisclosures as pleaded above entitle the Plaintiff to rescind the purchase of the vehicle the subject of this lawsuit. Plaintiff would show unto the court that Plaintiff is entitled to rescind his purchase and receive a refund of all the monies expended by Plaintiff for the sale and said vehicle including but not limited to: [state specific expenses and costs here].

XVI.

WHEREFORE, PREMISES CONSIDERED, Plaintiff prays that Defendant be cited to appear and make answer herein, that upon final hearing of this cause, Plaintiff have and recover judgment against the Defendant for:

1) [plead DTPA treble damages];

2) [plead damages in the alternative];

3) [plead attorney's fees and costs];

4) interest at the rate of [check state statute] percent (__%) per annum from date of judgment until paid;

5) and for all other just and lawful relief to which Plaintiff is duly entitled, including costs of court expended in this behalf, and such further relief, in law and in equity, general and specific, to which Plaintiff may be duly and justly entitled.

Respectfully Submitted,

[name of law firm]

By: _____
[attorney for plaintiff]

[Add certificate of service]

FORM 2–36
PLAINTIFF'S ORIGINAL COMPLAINT [DIVERSITY]
(Violation of Family and Medical Leave Act)

UNITED STATES DISTRICT COURT
DISTRICT OF _____

[PLAINTIFF(S) NAMES]	)	
Plaintiffs,	)	
	)	
	)	CASE NO:_____
	)	
	)	
v.	)	
	)	
[DEFENDANT(S) NAMES]	)	
Defendants	)	

INITIATION OF THE SUIT

PLAINTIFF'S ORIGINAL COMPLAINT [Diversity]

Plaintiff, _____, hereby states the following as her causes of action against defendant _____:

1. Plaintiff _____ is an individual resident of _____, _____ County, _____, and formerly a resident of _____, County, _____.

2. Defendant _____ is a corporation duly existing and organized under the laws of the state of _____, with its principal place of business in the state of _____. Defendant may be found and served in _____ County, _____, and venue is proper herein because Plaintiff was employed with Defendant in _____, _____.

3. Jurisdiction is founded under a) 28 U.S.C. § 1331 as Plaintiff asserts her claims under Count I under 26 U.S.C. § 2601 et seq.; b) 28 U.S.C. § 1332 as this action is between citizens of different states and the matter in controversy exceeds the sum of $75,000.00 exclusive of interest and costs; and c) the doctrine of pendent jurisdiction.

COUNT I
VIOLATION OF FAMILY AND MEDICAL LEAVE ACT

4. Plaintiff incorporates by reference the allegations of paragraphs 1 through 3, <u>supra.</u>

5. Defendant is engaged in commerce and employs fifty or more employees for each working day during twenty or more calendar workweeks at the work site where Plaintiff was employed for more than two years, within the meaning of the FMLA and its accompanying regulations.

6. Plaintiff has been employed with Defendant for at least 1,250 hours of service for the twelve-month period preceding Plaintiff's need for leave under the Family and Medical Leave Act (FMLA).

7. Beginning in 1998, Plaintiff suffered from a serious health condition within the meaning of FMLA, and its accompanying regulations, in that Plaintiff was diagnosed with rheumatoid arthritis in her knees in _____, 20___. Further, on _____, 20___, Plaintiff took a leave of absence due to a serious health condition, in that she was under the care of a psychologist and had a diagnosable mental condition requiring her to be off work with Defendant.

8. Defendant was aware of Plaintiff's serious health conditions and her need for leave as a result of one or more of such serious health conditions, on the occasions at issue.

9. Defendant interfered with Plaintiff's medical leave by contacting a prospective employer while Plaintiff was on leave and providing false information concerning Plaintiff and Plaintiff's leave of absence; by having a discriminatory policy related to FMLA leaves of absences in violation of § 825.309(a) of the regulations to the FMLA; and by making

the terms and conditions of Plaintiff's employment intolerable as a result of Plaintiff's requests for FMLA leave, thereby forcing Plaintiff to resign her position.

10. As a direct result of Defendant's violations of the FMLA, Plaintiff has suffered damages, including the loss of past and future wages and benefits, medical expenses, attorneys' fees, expert witness fees, and costs. Further, Plaintiff is entitled to double damages under FMLA.

WHEREFORE, under Count I, Plaintiff requests reinstatement and other equitable relief, past and future wages and benefits, compensatory and double damages as provided by the FMLA, interest at the highest lawful rate, attorneys' fees, expert witness fees and costs, and such further relief as the Court finds just and proper.

COUNT II
SERVICE LETTER VIOLATION

11. Plaintiff incorporates by reference paragraphs 1 through 10 of this Complaint.

12. Plaintiff was employed by Defendant at its location in _____, _____ for at least ninety (90) days.

13. Within a reasonable period of time after Plaintiff's termination of employment with Defendant, Plaintiff sent to Defendant a written request for a service letter with specific reference to the statute and in compliance with _____.

14. Defendant failed to issue a service letter to Plaintiff within forty-five (45) days of receipt of the request, which set forth the nature and character of Plaintiff's services with Defendant, and the true cause for Plaintiff's termination, in violation of _____, thereby entitling Plaintiff to nominal, actual, and punitive damages.

15. Defendant's failure to issue a service letter to Plaintiff was based upon an evil motive or reckless disregard for Plaintiff's rights, entitling Plaintiff to an award of punitive damages.

WHEREFORE, under Count II of her Petition, Plaintiff prays that the Court award against Defendant nominal and actual damages under the statute, punitive damages, interest at the highest lawful rate, for statutory interest, Plaintiff's costs, and such other relief as is just and proper.

COUNT III
TORTIOUS INTERFERENCE WITH BUSINESS EXPECTANCY

16. Plaintiff incorporates by reference the allegations of paragraphs 1 through 15.

17. On or about _____, 20___, Plaintiff took a leave of absence from employment with Defendant, after being advised to do so for medical reasons.

18. On or about _____, 20___, Plaintiff received a job position with _____.

INITIATION OF THE SUIT

19. In early _____, 20___, Defendant's agents and employees, acting in the course and scope of their employment with Defendant, contacted or were contacted by _____ and became aware that Plaintiff was to be or was employed with _____. During the course of such contact, Defendant maliciously, intentionally, and without justification or excuse made defamatory statements concerning Plaintiff, including, without limitation, that Plaintiff had provided false information to _____ concerning her leave of absence, and /or had falsely or fraudulently requested disability benefits.

20. Plaintiff had an expectation of continued employment with _____.

21. The statements made by Defendant were false, were known to be false, or were made with reckless disregard for the truth or falsity of such statements.

22. As a result of such statements by Defendant, _____ terminated Plaintiff's employment and provided Plaintiff the opportunity to resign first, and Plaintiff was thereby forced to resign and was constructively discharged.

23. As a result of such tortious interference by Defendant, Plaintiff has suffered damages, including, without limitation, loss of her job position at _____, damage to her career and professional record, loss of past and future wages, moving expenses, emotional distress, and other nonpecuniary losses.

24. Defendant's tortious interference was based upon an evil motive or conscious disregard for Plaintiff's rights, entitling her to an award of punitive damages.

WHEREFORE, under Count III, Plaintiff prays for judgment against Defendant _____ for actual and punitive damages, for interest at the highest lawful rate, and for such other relief as is just and proper.

COUNT IV
SLANDER

25. Plaintiff incorporates by reference paragraphs 1 through 24 of this Complaint.

26. On or about late _____, 20___ or early _____, 20___, an employee of Defendant, while acting in the course and scope of employment with Defendant, published a defamatory statement concerning Plaintiff. Specifically, Defendant's employee stated that Plaintiff had provided false information to _____ with respect to the application process, that Plaintiff had provided false information to _____ concerning her leave of absence, and/or had fraudulently requested disability benefits at _____.

27. The statement(s) were false at the time made, were known to be false, or were made with reckless disregard for the truth or falsity of such statements.

28. The statements were made maliciously, and in reckless and conscious disregard for Plaintiff's rights, thereby entitling Plaintiff to the recovery of punitive damages.

29. As a result of such defamation, Plaintiff has suffered damages, including mental distress, embarrassment, humiliation, and damage to her reputation, the loss of her job position at _____, past and future wage loss, moving expenses, and damage to her job record.

WHEREFORE, under Count IV, Plaintiff prays for judgment against Defendant for actual and punitive damages, for interest at the highest lawful rate, and for such other relief as the Court deems proper.

Respectfully submitted,
NAME OF FIRM

_____

Name of Atty
Atty's Bar #
Address
City, State, Zip
Phone #

CERTIFICATE OF SERVICE

I hereby certify that a true and correct copy of the above and foregoing document has been forwarded to all counsel of record by facsimile and/or certified mail/R.R.R. on this _____ day of _____, 20___.

_____

FORM 2–37
PLAINTIFF'S ORIGINAL COMPLAINT [DIVERSITY]
(Employment Drug Testing)

UNITED STATES DISTRICT COURT
DISTRICT OF _____

[PLAINTIFF(S) NAMES]	)	
Plaintiffs,	)	
	)	
	)	CASE NO: _____
	)	
	)	
v.	)	
	)	
[DEFENDANT(S) NAMES]	)	
Defendants.	)	

INITIATION OF THE SUIT

PLAINTIFF'S ORIGINAL COMPLAINT [Diversity]

COMES NOW Plaintiff _____, (hereinafter called "Plaintiff"), and for his cause of action against Defendant _____ (hereinafter called "Defendant") respectfully states to the Court as follows:

1. Plaintiff is and was at all times hereinafter mentioned, domiciled in and a citizen of the State of _____.

2. Defendant was and is now a corporation duly organized, existing under the laws of the State of _____, with its principal place of business in the State of _____.

3. Defendant _____ (hereinafter called "Defendant X") is, and was at all times hereinafter mentioned, domiciled in and a citizen of the State of _____, and was employed by Defendant when this cause of action arose.

4. This action is of a civil nature involving, exclusive of interest and costs, a sum in excess of $75,000.00 for each count stated herein. Every issue of law and fact herein is wholly between two citizens of different states.

5. The acts complained of in this complaint occurred in _____ County, _____, a county within the _____ District of _____.

6. This court has jurisdiction of this state law claim by virtue of 29 U.S.C. § 1332.

COUNT I
General Allegations

7. At all times herein mentioned, Defendant was the servant, agent, and employee of Defendant _____, and was acting within the scope of her employment.

8. On _____ _____, 20___, Plaintiff voluntarily submitted to a drug test while attempting to obtain employment with the Defendant. The results of this test were received on _____, 20___, and indicated that the Plaintiff had tested NEGATIVE to all five drugs being tested for, including amphetamine, cocaine, opiate, phencyclidine, and cannabinoids. (See Exhibit "B" attached.)

9. On or about _____, 20___, at the city of _____, County of _____, _____, Defendant, acting within the scope of her employment with Defendant, and in furtherance of her principal's business, maliciously and falsely spoke about and published a facsimile transmission concerning Plaintiff to and in the presence and hearing of _____ of _____ indicating that the Plaintiff was not hired by Defendant because he had, as stated by Defendant, "Failed Pre-Employment Drug Screen." (See Exhibit "A" attached.)

10. That each and every statement made by Defendant X on behalf of and in the scope of her employment with Defendant, both in speech and by facsimile with regard to the Plaintiff and his drug screening were and are false and untrue and were made by Defendant for the purpose of injuring Plaintiff and harming his standing and reputation within the trucking industry.

11. That Defendants falsely spoke and/or published information regarding Plaintiff on his DMV transcript of driver's history, knowing that such information was false and knowing that such information would prevent Plaintiff from obtaining further employment as a truck driver, and that Defendants published such information for the purpose of injuring Plaintiff and harming his standing and reputation within the trucking industry.

12. As a direct and proximate result of the false, malicious, and untrue statements of Defendants as aforesaid, Plaintiff suffered damage by reason of injury to his reputation, credit, and standing in seeking employment in the trucking industry in an amount in excess of $75,000.00.

WHEREFORE, Plaintiff prays the Court to grant him the following relief:

(A)   A judgment against Defendants and in favor of Plaintiff for the damages in excess of $75,000.00 for injuries he sustained as a result of Defendant's actions, including damages for injury to his reputation, credit, standing in seeking employment, and lost wages and benefits;

(B)   A judgment against Defendants and in favor of Plaintiff for punitive damages in an amount as will deter Defendants and others similarly situated from engaging in such conduct;

(C)   For his attorney fees, costs, and expenses of litigation; and

(D)   For such other and further relief as the Court deems just and proper.

COUNT II

COMES NOW Plaintiff, by and through counsel, _____, and for his claim for punitive damages against Defendants, states to the court as follows:

1. Plaintiff hereby realleges and incorporates by reference, as if more fully set forth herein, the allegations in paragraphs 1 through 12 of Count I of this Complaint.

2. By means of the practices alleged more specifically in paragraphs 1 through 12 of Count I of this complaint, Defendants willfully and maliciously falsely spoke and published information about Plaintiff knowing that said information was false.

3. That Defendant's statements were willful and malicious, in that Defendants had in their possession documentation which proved Plaintiff's drug tests were negative, but Defendants proceeded to publish false information regarding the results of the drug tests knowing said information was false and knowing that the false information would injure Plaintiff and harm his standing and reputation within the trucking industry.

4. As a result of Defendants' actions, Plaintiff has sustained damages as more specifically alleged in paragraph 1 through 12 of Count I.

INITIATION OF THE SUIT

WHEREFORE, plaintiff prays the Court to grant him the following relief:

(A) A judgment against Defendants and in favor of Plaintiff for the damages in excess of $75,000.00 for injuries he sustained as a result of Defendants' actions, including damages for injury to his reputation, credit, standing in seeking employment, and lost wages and benefits;

(B) A judgment against Defendants and in favor of Plaintiff for punitive damages in an amount as will deter Defendants and others similarly situated from engaging in such conduct;

(C) For his attorney fees, costs, and expenses of litigation; and

(D) For such other and further relief as the court deems just and proper.

Respectfully submitted,
NAME OF FIRM

_____

Name of Atty
Atty's Bar #
Address
City, State, Zip
Phone #

CERTIFICATE OF SERVICE

I hereby certify that a true and correct copy of the above and foregoing document has been forwarded to all counsel of record by facsimile and/or certified mail/R.R.R. on this _____ day of _____, 20___.

_____

FORM 2–38
PLAINTIFF'S ORIGINAL COMPLAINT FOR CONVERSION

NO. _____

[PLAINTIFF(S) NAMES]	)	
Plaintiffs,	)	
	)	
	)	IN THE DISTRICT COURT OF
	)	
_____	)	_____COUNTY,
	)	
v.	)	
	)	_____ JUDICIAL DISTRICT
[DEFENDANT(S) NAMES]	)	
Defendants.	)	

§ 2.27 DECEPTIVE TRADE PRACTICES

PLAINTIFF'S ORIGINAL COMPLAINT FOR CONVERSION

TO THE HONORABLE JUDGE OF SAID COURT:

COMES NOW _____, Plaintiff, complaining of _____, Defendant, and for cause of action would respectfully show the Court as follows:

I.

Plaintiff, _____ (hereinafter referred to as "Plaintiff"), resides at _____ and is a resident of _____, _____ County, _____.

Defendant, _____ (hereinafter referred to as "Defendant"), is, and at all times herein mentioned was, a resident of the City of _____, County of _____, State of _____, and may be served with process at that address.

II.

At all times herein mentioned, and in particular on or about _____, 20___, Plaintiff was and still is entitled to the possession of the following personal property, namely, one hundred (100) pounds of pecans.

On or about _____, 20___, and at _____, _____ County, _____, the above-mentioned property had a value of $600.

On or about _____, 20___, Defendant took the above-mentioned property from Plaintiff's possession and converted the same to his own use. Defendant was seen to be gathering pecans in his yard which had fallen from Plaintiff's pecan trees. Plaintiff then witnessed Defendant selling said pecans from a stand on his driveway.

On or about _____, 20___, Plaintiff demanded the immediate return of the above-mentioned property, but Defendant failed and refused, and continues to fail and refuse, to return the property to Plaintiff. A copy of Plaintiff's written demand for return of the property is attached hereto as Exhibit "A" and made a part hereof.

As a proximate result of Defendant's conversion, Plaintiff suffered the following damages which are the natural, reasonable, and proximate results of the conversion: damages in the amount of $600.00.

The aforementioned acts of Defendant were willful, wanton, malicious, and oppressive, were undertaken with the intent to defraud, and justify the awarding of exemplary and punitive damages in the amount of $1,000.00.

WHEREFORE, Plaintiff prays judgment against Defendant, as follows:

1.   For the value of the property converted in the sum of $600.00.

INITIATION OF THE SUIT

2. For interest at the legal rate on the foregoing sum pursuant to _____, from and after _____, 20___;

3. For punitive and exemplary damages in the sum of _____;

4. For costs of suit herein incurred; and

5. For such other and further relief as the Court may deem proper.

Respectfully submitted,
NAME OF FIRM

_____
Name of Atty
Atty's Bar #
Address
City, State, Zip
Phone #

CERTIFICATE OF SERVICE

I hereby certify that a true and correct copy of the above and foregoing document has been forwarded to all counsel of record by facsimile and/or certified mail/R.R.R. on this _____ day of _____, 20___.

_____

FORM 2–39
PLAINTIFF'S ORIGINAL COMPLAINT FOR BREACH OF CONTRACT

NO. _____

[PLAINTIFF(S) NAMES] Plaintiffs,	)))	
	)	IN THE DISTRICT COURT OF
	)	
_____	)	_____ COUNTY,
	)	
v.	)	
	)	_____ JUDICIAL DISTRICT
[DEFENDANT(S) NAMES] Defendants.	))	

§ 2.27 DECEPTIVE TRADE PRACTICES

PLAINTIFF'S ORIGINAL COMPLAINT FOR BREACH
OF CONTRACT

TO THE HONORABLE JUDGE OF SAID COURT:

COMES NOW _____, Plaintiff, complaining of _____, Defendant, and for cause of action would respectfully show the Court as follows:

I.

Plaintiff, _____ (hereinafter referred to as "Plaintiff"), resides at _____ and is a resident of _____, _____ County, _____.

Defendant, _____ (hereinafter referred to as "Defendant"), is, and at all times herein mentioned was, a corporation organized and existing under the laws of the State of _____ with principal offices located in the City of _____, County of _____, State of _____, and may be served with process at that address.

II.

On _____, 20___, in _____ County, _____, Defendant entered into a written contract with Plaintiff herein, a copy of which is attached hereto as Exhibit _____ and made a part hereof. By the terms of the contract, Defendant was to build and complete a certain back yard deck to be erected on real property situated at _____, _____, County, _____, which real property is owned by Plaintiff.

Pursuant to the agreement Defendant proceeded with the construction of the building and improvements and caused to be erected on the property a patio deck which to the present time still has not been completed in accordance with the contract.

No notice of completion for the building has been filed.

The construction of the building has not been completed in accordance with the contract between the parties hereto in the following particulars :

1. The railing has not been completed or installed.
2. The deck has boards extending beyond the deck, creating a hazardous condition.
3. The deck has not been sealed or waterproofed.
4. The electrical outlets and light receptacles have not been finished or installed.

Under the terms of the contract, Defendant agreed to complete the building, or to pay for the completion of such unfinished work, but has failed to do so.

INITIATION OF THE SUIT

Plaintiff has made demand on Defendant to complete the work but Defendant has failed, refused, and neglected to do so; Plaintiff has thereby suffered damage in the amount of $4,500.00, the amount Plaintiff must pay for the completion of the unfinished work; all of the foregoing items and the total sum thereof are reasonable.

The patio deck was not and could not be occupied by the Plaintiff herein until _____, 20___; the occupancy was delayed for a period of six (6) months after the date agreed on in the building contract between the parties hereto.

The delay in completion of the building was caused solely by the carelessness, neglect, and failure of the Defendant to complete the building in accordance with the terms of his written contract; by reason of Defendant's failure and neglect, and by reason of his breach of the contract, Plaintiff has suffered damage in loss of use for a period of six (6) months in a total amount to be determined later.

Plaintiff has faithfully and fully performed all of the conditions and covenants required of him to be performed.

WHEREFORE, Plaintiff prays for judgment against Defendant, as follows:

1. For compensatory damages in the sum of $___;
2. For interest on the sum of $_____ from and after _____, 20__ to date of judgment;
3. For reasonable attorney fees according to proof;
4. For costs of suit herein incurred; and
5. For such other and further relief as the Court may deem proper.

Respectfully submitted,
NAME OF FIRM

_____

Name of Atty
Atty's Bar #
Address
City, State, Zip
Phone #

CERTIFICATE OF SERVICE

I hereby certify that a true and correct copy of the above and foregoing document has been forwarded to all counsel of record by facsimile and/or certified mail/R.R.R. on this ____ day of _____, 20___.

_____

§ 2.27   DECEPTIVE TRADE PRACTICES

FORM 2–40
COMPLAINT FOR SPECIFIC PERFORMANCE

NO. _____

[PLAINTIFF(S) NAMES]	)	
Plaintiffs,	)	
	)	
	)	IN THE DISTRICT COURT OF
	)	
	)	_____COUNTY,
_____	)	
	)	
v.	)	
	)	_____JUDICIAL DISTRICT
[DEFENDANT(S) NAMES]	)	
Defendants.	)	

COMPLAINT FOR SPECIFIC PERFORMANCE

TO THE HONORABLE JUDGE OF SAID COURT:

COMES NOW _____, Plaintiff, complaining of _____, Defendant, and for cause of action would respectfully show the Court as follows:

I.

Plaintiff, _____ (hereinafter referred to as "Plaintiff"), resides at _____ and is a resident of _____, _____ County, _____.

Defendant, _____ (hereinafter referred to as "Defendant"), is, and at all times herein mentioned was, a resident of the City of _____, County of _____, State of _____, and may be served with process at that address.

II.

On or about _____, 20___, in the City of _____, County of _____, State of _____, Plaintiff and Defendant entered into a written agreement, a copy of which is attached hereto as Exhibit "A" and made a part hereof. By the terms of said written agreement, Defendant agreed to sell to Plaintiff a restaurant on the beach in _____ County, _____.

The consideration set forth in the agreement was fair and reasonable.

INITIATION OF THE SUIT

Plaintiff has performed all conditions, covenants, and promises required by him on his part to be performed in accordance with the terms and conditions of the contract.

Defendant has failed and refused, and continues to fail and refuse, to perform the conditions of the contract on his part, in that he refuses to complete the sale of the property to Plaintiff.

Plaintiff entered into the contract to buy the property because of the unique way that the surf hits the restaurant windows, adding credibility to his surf theme restaurant. Plaintiff has no adequate legal remedy at law, in that the property in dispute is so unique that monetary damages will be inadequate to compensate.

By the terms of said written agreement, the Plaintiff is entitled to recover reasonable attorney fees incurred in the enforcement of the provisions of the agreement. By reason of the aforementioned breach by the Defendant, the Plaintiff has been forced to secure the services of the legal firm of _____ to prosecute this lawsuit.

WHEREFORE, Plaintiff prays judgment against Defendant as follows:

1. For damages in an amount to be determined later.
2. For an order requiring Defendant to complete the sale of the property to Plaintiff.
3. For such other and further relief as the Court may deem proper.

Respectfully submitted,
NAME OF FIRM

_____
Name of Atty
Atty's Bar #
Address
City, State, Zip
Phone #

CERTIFICATE OF SERVICE

I hereby certify that a true and correct copy of the above and foregoing document has been forwarded to all counsel of record by facsimile and/or certified mail/R.R.R. on this ____ day of _____, 20___.

_____

[Note: Extraordinary remedy complaints generally require verifications in most jurisdictions.]

FORM 2–41
PLAINTIFF'S ORIGINAL COMPLAINT FOR NEGLIGENCE
(DOG BITE)

NO. _____

[PLAINTIFF(S) NAMES]	)	
Plaintiffs,	)	
	)	
	)	IN THE DISTRICT COURT OF
	)	
_____	)	_____ COUNTY,
	)	
v.	)	
	)	_____ JUDICIAL DISTRICT
[DEFENDANT(S) NAMES]	)	
Defendants.	)	

PLAINTIFF'S ORIGINAL COMPLAINT FOR NEGLIGENCE
[DOG BITE]

TO THE HONORABLE JUDGE OF SAID COURT:

COMES NOW _____, Plaintiff, complaining of _____, Defendant, and for cause of action would respectfully show the Court as follows:

I.

Plaintiff, _____ (hereinafter referred to as "Plaintiff"), resides at _____ and is a resident of _____, _____ County, _____.

Defendant, _____ (hereinafter referred to as "Defendant"), is, and at all times herein mentioned was, a resident of the City of _____, County of _____, State of _____, and may be served with process at that address.

II.

At all times herein mentioned, Defendant _____ was, and still is, the owner of a certain Rottweiler dog, which caused the injuries and damage hereinafter complained of. This dog had a vicious nature, disposition, and propensity, which was known or should have been known by Defendant.

On or about _____, 20___, at about ___.M., Plaintiff was walking on the sidewalk in front of Defendant's residence. Defendant's Rottweiler dog was sitting in Defendant's front yard. The dog was not under any form of restraint or control of a competent person. The area is traveled by pedestrians and business people. At this time and place, Plaintiff proceeded to walk past the house and was suddenly and with no

INITIATION OF THE SUIT

warning viciously attacked by the dog. The dog severely bit the Plaintiff about the ankles, legs, buttocks, right arm, and face.

As a proximate result of the actions of Defendant's dog, Plaintiff sustained the following injuries, all to his damage in a sum to be determined after investigation and discovery:

[Specifically list all injuries.]

As a further proximate result of the actions of Defendant's dog, Plaintiff was required to and did employ physicians and surgeons to examine, treat, and care for his multiple injuries and incurred additional medical expenses for hospital bills and other incidental medical expenses in an amount to be determined after investigation and discovery.

Plaintiff is informed and believes, and on such information and belief alleges, that he will incur some additional medical expenses, the exact amount of which is unknown. Plaintiff will ask leave of Court to amend his complaint to insert the correct amount of such medical expenses when the same have been ascertained.

As a further proximate result of the actions of Defendant's dog, Plaintiff has suffered a loss of income and earnings, and his earning ability is, and will remain, impaired and diminished by reason thereof, and he will continue to suffer a further loss of earnings and income for an indefinite period of time, and Plaintiff prays leave to amend this complaint and insert the true amounts when the same shall be ascertained.

Defendant _____ negligently failed to have the dog under restraint or to take any other precautions to prevent the dog from attacking Plaintiff or other persons. Defendant was also negligent in that he failed to post a sign or take other measures to warn of the presence of a vicious dog.

WHEREFORE, Plaintiff prays judgment as follows:

1. For general damages in a sum to be determined after investigation and discovery.
2. For medical and incidental expenses according to proof.
3. For damages for loss of income and earnings and impairment of earning ability according to proof.
4. For costs of suit herein incurred.
5. For such other and further relief as the Court may deem proper.

Respectfully submitted,
NAME OF FIRM

_____
Name of Atty
Atty's Bar #
Address
City, State, Zip
Phone #

§ 2.28 CLASS ACTION COMPLAINT

CERTIFICATE OF SERVICE

I hereby certify that a true and correct copy of the above and foregoing document has been forwarded to all counsel of record by facsimile and/or certified mail/R.R.R. on this _____ day of _____, 20___.

_____

§ 2.28 —Complaint for Class Action

FORM 2–42
SAMPLE CLASS ACTION COMPLAINT

PLAINTIFF'S ORIGINAL PETITION

TO THE HONORABLE JUDGE OF SAID COURT:

Plaintiffs, by counsel, for themselves and all others similarly situated who purchased _____ tractors from Defendant during the period from _____through _____, say:

Parties

1. Plaintiffs are residents of _____ County, _____ [jurisdiction].

2. Defendant is a _____ corporation which does business within _____ County, _____ [jurisdiction], and which has its principal offices located in _____ [jurisdiction].

Class Action Allegations

3.1 Class. This action is brought by Plaintiffs for themselves and all other persons similarly situated whose joinder in this action is impracticable because the class is so numerous. The class consists of persons who purchased at retail from Defendant during the period _____ through _____, _____ farm tractors manufactured and retailed by Defendant, such purchasers numbering approximately _____ persons and entities.

3.2 Common Questions. There are questions of law or fact common to the members of the class that predominate over questions of law or fact affecting only individual members. The questions of law or fact common to all members of the class are whether Defendant intentionally and negligently misrepresented its _____ farm tractor engines to be rated at and to produce _____ horsepower when, in fact, such engines were rated at and produced only _____ horsepower.

3.3 Typical Claims. The claims of the named Plaintiffs are for money damages proximately caused by Defendant's intentional and negligent misrepresentations which is true of the claims of the entire class and, therefore, are typical of the claims of the class.

3.4 Representation. Plaintiffs _____ and _____ are representative of all persons who were materially injured by Defendant's intentional and negligent misrepresentations surrounding Defendant's sale of its _____ farm tractors and Plaintiffs will, as a representative party, fairly and adequately protect the interests of the class.

3.5 Superiority of Class Action. The maintenance of this action as a class action is superior to other available methods of adjudication in promoting the convenient administration of justice.

Count I

4. During the period _____ through _____, Defendant was engaged in the manufacture and retail sale of _____ farm tractors.

5. During the period _____ through _____, Defendant sold to Plaintiffs and approximately 100,000 other purchasers, at retail, Defendant's _____ farm tractors which Defendant represented, both expressly and impliedly, to be rated at _____ horsepower and to be capable of producing _____ horsepower.

6. Defendant's representations that its _____ farm tractors were rated at _____ horsepower and was capable of producing _____ horsepower were in fact intentionally and negligently false in the following respects:

   (a) the tractors were rated at only _____ horsepower and not _____ horsepower; and
   (b) the tractors were capable of producing only _____ horsepower and not _____ horsepower.

7. Plaintiff's and the _____ other purchasers of Defendant's tractors at retail relied upon Defendant's aforesaid misrepresentations.

8. Following the purchases of their tractors from the Defendant, Plaintiffs and the _____ other purchasers discovered the aforesaid misrepresentations by Defendant and discovered that they had each been materially damaged to the extent of $_____, that being the difference in market value between a _____ horsepower farm tractor and a _____ horsepower farm tractor.

9. The amount in controversy exceeds $10,000.

Relief Requested

WHEREFORE, Plaintiffs for themselves and all others similarly situated, request entry of this court's judgment against Defendant as follows:

(a) Awarding compensatory damages at the rate of $_____ for each of the _____ class members for a total of $_____;

(b) Assessing costs and reasonable attorney fees; and

(c) Granting such other and further relief as the court may deem proper.

Respectfully submitted,

[Date]
[Counsel]
[Address of Counsel]

§ 2.29   Lis Pendens

If the subject matter of your lawsuit is a parcel of real property, or if the lawsuit involves a question of rights or interests, liens, or encumbrances against a parcel of real property, you will want to file a Notice of Lis Pendens (**Form 2–43**) with the county clerk in the county where the real property is found. This notice will stay with the property during the course of the suit, and if the property title is transferred during that time, the new owner will own only that portion of the title which would have remained with the original owner at the final decision of the trial. It is designed to protect the plaintiff against losing his interest in the property through transfer by the defendant to a third party.

FORM 2–43
SAMPLE NOTICE OF LIS PENDENS

STATE OF [state]   )
)
COUNTY OF [county]   )

NOTICE IS HEREBY GIVEN that Cause No. [case number] styled [plaintiff] vs. [defendant], was commenced in the [court name] Court of [county] County, [state] on [date], [20__], and is now pending in said court.

The action involves [a lien, a right to interest in, a right to title in, and so forth], real property situated in [county] County, [state] and described as follows: [legal description].

SIGNED THIS [date] day of [month] [20__].

_____

ACKNOWLEDGMENT

STATE OF [name]   )
)
COUNTY OF [county]   )

BEFORE ME, the undersigned Notary Public, on this day personally appeared [name], known to me to be the person whose name is subscribed to the foregoing instrument and acknowledged to me that [he/she] executed that same for purposes and consideration therein expressed.

GIVEN under my hand and seal of office this [date] day of [month], [20__].

_____
NOTARY PUBLIC IN AND FOR
[county] County, [state]
My commission expires: [date]

§ 2.30 Answers

When your client has been served with a lawsuit, it must be noted on what exact day he was served with process, and if he was properly served. Consult your court's general and local rules for the time period within which your client must file an answer. This is one deadline which is disastrous to miss as it will result in an automatic default judgment against your client. Once you have determined the proper answer date, make sure the service of process was proper according to your jurisdiction's rules of procedure. If it was not proper, you may wish to file a Motion to Quash Service (**Form 2–46**), which will satisfy the requirements to answer within the specified time.

Sometimes the service is proper, but the lawsuit is filed in the wrong jurisdiction. In this case, you will want to file an Answer Subject to Motion to Transfer (**Form 2–47**). This, too, satisfies the requirements of an answer.

In most cases, a General Denial (**Form 2–49**) is sufficient. This is a simple form which essentially denies all the allegations of the complaint. Of course, any exceptions to the complaint should also be noted in this answer. Some jurisdictions do not allow a General Denial, but require that every allegation in the complaint be either denied, taken exception to, or an affirmative defense be stated in the answer.

Under Rule 5 of the Federal Rules of Civil Procedure, the answer must be served upon the attorney for the plaintiff. This may be done in person, by handing the answer to the attorney or leaving it at the attorney's office with a clerk or other person in charge. An answer may also be served by mail, in which case service is deemed completed upon mailing. If a party is represented by more than one attorney, service on any one of them will be deemed sufficient.

§ 2.30 ANSWERS

FORM 2–44
ANSWER OF DEFENDANT

NO. _____

[PLAINTIFF(S) NAMES]	)	
Plaintiffs,	)	
	)	
	)	IN THE DISTRICT COURT OF
	)	
	)	_____COUNTY,
	)	
v.	)	
	)	_____JUDICIAL DISTRICT
[DEFENDANT(S) NAMES]	)	
Defendants.	)	

ANSWER OF DEFENDANT

TO THE HONORABLE JUDGE OF SAID COURT:

COMES NOW _____, defendant in the above cause, to file this answer to the original petition of _____, plaintiff herein, and would respectfully show the Court as follows:

I.

The defendant is without knowledge or information sufficient to form a belief as to the truth of those allegations and claims contained in Paragraph ____ of plaintiff's Petition and therefore denies the same.

II.

The defendant admits those allegations and claims contained in Paragraph ___ of plaintiff's Petition.

III.

The defendant specifically denies those allegations and claims contained in Paragraph ____ of plaintiff's Petition and therefore requires strict proof thereof.

IV.

For further answer and defense, the defendant states as follows:

[Choose all affirmative defenses that apply.]

The Petition fails to state a claim against defendant upon which relief can be granted.

125

INITIATION OF THE SUIT

Plaintiff was negligent, and such negligence on the part of plaintiff proximately caused or contributed to the accident and plaintiff's damage, if any, and such negligence on the part of plaintiff comparatively was greater than the negligence of defendant and plaintiff is therefore not entitled to recover.

Plaintiff was negligent, and such negligence on the part of plaintiff proximately caused or contributed to plaintiff's damage, if any, and such negligence on the part of plaintiff comparatively was greater than the negligence of defendant and plaintiff is therefore not entitled to recover. In this regard, plaintiff was negligent in one or more of the following: [list].

Plaintiff's driver, _____ , was negligent. Such driver was at all times complained of herein acting as the agent, servant, and employee of plaintiff, and with whom plaintiff was then and there engaged in a joint mission or enterprise. Such negligence on the part of plaintiff's driver proximately caused or contributed to the accident and plaintiff's damage, if any, and such negligence on the part of plaintiff's driver, together with the negligence of plaintiff, comparatively was greater than the negligence of defendant and plaintiff is therefore not entitled to recover.

Plaintiff's driver was negligent. Such driver was at all times complained of herein acting as the agent, servant, and employee of plaintiff, and with whom plaintiff was then and there engaged in a joint mission or enterprise. Such negligence on the part of plaintiff's driver proximately caused or contributed to the accident and plaintiff's damage, if any, and such negligence on the part of plaintiff's driver, together with the negligence of plaintiff, comparatively was greater than the negligence of defendant and plaintiff is therefore not entitled to recover. In this regard, plaintiff was negligent in one or more of the following: [list].

Defendant was confronted with a sudden emergency not brought about by his own negligence, and in reacting to that emergency, defendant acted as a reasonable and prudent person would have acted under such circumstances.

The accident was an unavoidable accident, casualty, and misfortune that occurred without negligence on the part of defendant.

The action is barred by the statute of limitations.

The accident was proximately caused by the negligence of a third party over whom this defendant had no control, and for those acts this defendant is not responsible.

Plaintiff was at fault and such fault on the part of plaintiff proximately caused or contributed to plaintiff's damage, if any, and such fault on the part of plaintiff was greater than the fault of defendant and plaintiff is therefore not entitled to recover.

Plaintiff was negligent, and such negligence on the part of plaintiff proximately caused or contributed to the accident and plaintiff's damage, if any, and such negligence on the part of plaintiff comparatively was greater than the negligence of the alleged uninsured tortfeasor and plaintiff is therefore not entitled to recover.

§ 2.30 ANSWERS

The alleged uninsured tortfeasor was confronted with a sudden emergency not brought about by his own negligence, and in reacting to that emergency, the alleged uninsured tortfeasor acted as a reasonable and prudent person would have acted under such circumstances.

The accident was an unavoidable accident, casualty, and misfortune that occurred without negligence on the part of the alleged uninsured tortfeasor.

Plaintiff assumed the risk of injury resulting from the negligence of defendant, if any, by voluntarily and unreasonably exposing himself to injury with knowledge and appreciation of the danger and risk involved.

The product allegedly manufactured by this defendant was being used in an abnormal, unintended, and unforeseen manner at the time of the alleged accident, constituting misuse of the product for which this defendant is not liable.

Any injury or damage suffered by plaintiff as a result of the alleged accident described in his Petition was the sole and proximate result of plaintiff's or a third person's alterations, modifications, and changes to the product allegedly manufactured by this defendant and therefore this defendant is not liable to plaintiff.

Any defect in the product allegedly manufactured by this defendant was not in existence when the product left this defendant's possession and control and therefore this defendant is not liable to plaintiff.

The injuries complained of in plaintiff's Petition are the result of preexisting health problems that were neither caused nor aggravated by this defendant and for which this defendant is not liable.

The injuries complained of in plaintiff's Petition are the result of health care problems that developed subsequent to the date of the alleged accident, which were neither caused nor aggravated by this defendant and for which this defendant is not liable.

The named defendant is not a proper party defendant to the cause of action alleged in plaintiff's Petition.

To dismiss the action on the ground that this Court lacks jurisdiction over the subject matter.

To dismiss the action on the ground that this Court lacks jurisdiction over the person of the plaintiff.

To dismiss the action on the ground that improper venue exists.

To dismiss the action or, in lieu thereof, to quash the summons on the ground of insufficiency of process.

INITIATION OF THE SUIT

To dismiss the action or, in lieu thereof, to quash the return of service of summons on the ground of insufficiency of service of process.

To dismiss the action on the ground that plaintiff has failed to state a claim upon which relief can be granted, as a result of [name reason].

To dismiss the action on the ground that plaintiff has failed to join a party under Rule _____ of the _____ Rules of Civil Procedure.

To dismiss the action on the ground that another action is pending between the same parties for the same claim.

To dismiss the action on the ground that defendant, _____, lacks the capacity to be sued.

To dismiss the action on the ground that plaintiff lacks the capacity to bring suit.

WHEREFORE, PREMISES CONSIDERED, defendant prays that plaintiff take nothing by reason of this suit, and that defendant go hence without delay with his costs, and be granted such other and further relief, both general and special, to which defendant may be justly entitled, either at law or equity.

Respectfully submitted,

NAME OF FIRM

_____

Name of Atty
Atty's Bar #
Address
City, State, Zip
Phone #

CERTIFICATE OF SERVICE

I hereby certify that a true and correct copy of the above and foregoing document has been forwarded to all counsel of record by facsimile and/or certified mail/R.R.R. on this _____ day of _____, 20___.

_____

§ 2.30 ANSWERS

FORM 2–45
AMENDED ANSWER AND SPECIAL EXCEPTIONS (DEFENDANT)

NO. _____

[PLAINTIFF(S) NAMES] Plaintiffs,	)))) IN THE DISTRICT COURT OF)) _____ COUNTY,)) _____ JUDICIAL DISTRICT)
v.	
[DEFENDANT(S) NAMES] Defendants.	

DEFENDANT, _____ COUNTY'S FIRST AMENDED ANSWER
AND SPECIAL EXCEPTIONS

TO THE HONORABLE JUDGE OF SAID COURT:

COMES NOW Defendant _____ County, by and through its attorney of record, _____ of _____, and files this answer to the plaintiff's petition.

WHEREFORE, PREMISES CONSIDERED, Defendant prays that its Motion to Transfer Venue be set for hearing and that upon final hearing hereof, this case be transferred to _____ County.

SPECIAL EXCEPTIONS

1. _____ County Beach and Parks Department specially excepts to paragraph __ in plaintiff's petition in that the _____ County Beach and Parks Department is not a legal entity that is subject to suit and is merely a department of the County.

2. _____ County specially excepts to pleadings for negligence in paragraphs ___ and ___ on the grounds that they do not allege all the elements necessary to state a cause of action. The plaintiff incorrectly stated the status of the plaintiff and the corresponding duty of the defendant. The corresponding duty of the defendant is no greater than that owed to a trespasser.

3. _____ County specially excepts to paragraph __ in that it states unliqui-dated damages. Under the _____ Rules of Civil Procedure, Rule ____, the defendant requests that the plaintiff amend his complaint so as to state the maximum amount claimed.

INITIATION OF THE SUIT

ANSWER
GENERAL DENIAL

4. Defendant denies, each and every, all and singular, the allegations in Plaintiff's Original Petition and demands strict proof thereof as required by law.

AFFIRMATIVE DEFENSES
5. Defendant would show that it is a political subdivision of the State of _____ and is immune from suit and liability except to the extent that such has been waived by _____[section]_____ of the _____[Civil Code]_____.

6. In the alternative, defendant alleges that the acts or omissions of _____ were the proximate cause of the accident. The County further alleges that the plaintiff was contributorily negligent, such that his percentage of responsibility was greater than 50 percent, thereby excluding any right to damages under _____[Civil Code]_____.

7. Defendant alleges that the sole proximate cause of the occurrence made the basis of this suit was the act or omission of some third person or persons over which the County had no control, and for which the County is not in law responsible.

8. Defendant alleges that the duty owed to plaintiff is no greater than that owed to a trespasser as set out in Chapter ___ of the _____[Civil Code]_____.

9. Defendant alleges that it is not liable for any injury to one individual caused by the act of the plaintiff under Chapter ___ if the _____[Civil Code]_____.

WHEREFORE, PREMISES CONSIDERED, the defendants pray that this case be dismissed and that they go hence without delay and with their costs.

Respectfully submitted,

NAME OF FIRM

_____

Name of Atty
Atty's Bar #
Address
City, State, Zip
Phone #

CERTIFICATE OF SERVICE

I hereby certify that a true and correct copy of the above and foregoing document has been forwarded to all counsel of record by facsimile and/or certified mail/R.R.R. on this ____ day of _____, 20___.

_____

FORM 2–46
SAMPLE MOTION TO QUA

NO. [case number

[name],	)	IN THE DISTRIC
	)	
Plaintiff,	)	[county] COUNT
	)	
vs.	)	[state]
	)	
[name],	)	[judicial district] JUDICIAL DISTRICT
	)	
Defendant.	)	

MOTION TO QUASH SERVICE

Defendant, [name], specially appearing for the sole and only purpose of contesting the validity of the purported service of a summons and complaint and for no other purpose whatsoever, by and through his attorney of record, [name], moves this Honorable Court for an order quashing the purported service of summons upon the grounds that the alleged service was not made upon the defendant pursuant to [State] Rules of Civil Procedure, Rule [rule number], nor pursuant to any other statute in [State] providing for a different method of service, and that said process is deficient for this reason.

This motion is made and based upon all of the papers and pleadings on file herein.

Respectfully submitted,

[name of law firm]

By: _____
[attorney name]
[firm address]

FORM 2–47
SAMPLE ANSWER SUBJECT TO MOTION TO TRANSFER

NO. [case number]

[name],	)	IN THE DISTRICT COURT OF
	)	
Plaintiff,	)	[county] COUNTY,
	)	
vs.	)	[state]
	)	
[name],	)	[judicial district] JUDICIAL DISTRICT
	)	
Defendant.	)	

MOTION TO TRANSFER UNDER RULE [citation]
AND ORIGINAL ANSWER OF DEFENDANT

TO THE HONORABLE JUDGE OF SAID COURT:

COMES NOW [name], defendant in the above cause, to file concurrently with the answer below this motion to transfer under Rule [citation], and would respectfully show the Court as follows:

I.

The cause of this action arises out of [state specific reasons for cause of action]. Defendant alleges, pursuant to Rule [citation], that the venue of this case should be transferred because (1) the county where the action is pending is not a proper county (2) mandatory venue of the action in another county is prescribed be the following specific statutory provisions: [describe specific statutory provisions].

II.

Defendant specifically denies the following venue allegations made in plaintiff's original petition:

[List all venue allegations you wish to deny.]

_____

_____

_____

§ 2.32 MOTION TO TRANSFER

[insert any legal or factual basis for the allegation that venue is improper.]

_____

_____

_____

III.

Defendant requests by this motion that this cause should be transferred to [county] County, [state]. Venue is [maintainable/mandatory] in that County under Statute [citation]. In support of this request for transfer, defendant alleges the following facts:

[specify facts in support of request.] _____

_____

_____

Respectfully submitted,

[name of law firm]

By: _____
[attorney name]
[firm address]

ORIGINAL ANSWER SUBJECT
TO MOTION TO TRANSFER

Subject to the foregoing motion to transfer and without waiving same, COMES NOW [name], defendant in the above cause, and files this original answer to the original petition of [name], plaintiff herein, and would respectfully show the Court as follows:

I.

Defendant specially excepts to the following allegations in paragraph [number], page [number] of plaintiff's original petition:

[list exceptions to allegations in the complaint] _____

_____

_____

Defendant is entitled to know the specific acts and omissions upon which the plaintiff bases his allegations of negligence on the part of defendant.

INITIATION OF THE SUIT

II.

Defendant also specially excepts on the ground that plaintiff has alleged damages exceeding the minimum jurisdictional amount. Defendant is entitled to know the maximum amount of damages claimed and each element of those damages.

III.

Subject to all stipulations and admissions that may hereafter be made, defendant asserts a general denial as is authorized by Rule [citation] of the [state] Rules of Civil Procedure, and defendant respectfully requests that the plaintiff be required to prove the charges and allegations against defendant by a preponderance of the evidence as is required by the Constitution and the Laws of the State of [state].

IV.

Defendant expressly reserves his right to subsequently amend this Answer to assert any counterclaims or causes of action defendant may have against plaintiff, and to aver any affirmative defenses available to defendant.

V.

For further answer, if necessary, defendant says that the sole proximate cause or a proximate cause of the accident in question was the failure of the plaintiff to exercise that degree of care under the existing circumstances as would have been used by a person of ordinary prudence in the exercise of ordinary care under the same or similar circumstances.

VI.

Defendant further shows that the sole proximate cause or a proximate cause of said accident was the conduct or breach of duty of the driver of the car that defendant was occupying, over whom defendant possessed no right of control and for whose acts defendant is not in law responsible.

VII.

Defendant also says that just before this accident occurred, defendant was faced with an emergency not created by his own negligence, that defendant exercised ordinary care in acting under said emergency, and that said emergency was the sole proximate cause of the accident in question.

VIII.

In the alternative, the accident in question was an "unavoidable accident" as the term "unavoidable accident" is defined by the laws of the State of [state].

§ 2.32 MOTION TO TRANSFER

IX.

In the unlikely event that defendant is found liable to the plaintiff, defendant affirmatively pleads that he is entitled to a credit or an offset for any and all sums plaintiff has received or may hereafter receive by way of any and all settlements arising from plaintiff's claims and causes of action. As allowed by Rule [citation] of the [state] Rules of Civil Procedure, defendant alternatively asserts his right to a proportionate reduction of any damages found against defendant based upon the percentage of negligence attributable to any settling tortfeasor under Statute [citation].

WHEREFORE, PREMISES CONSIDERED, defendant prays that plaintiff take nothing by reason of this suit, and that the defendant go hence without delay with his costs, and be granted such other and further relief, both general and special, to which defendant may be justly entitled either at law or equity.

Respectfully submitted,

[name of law firm]

By: _____
[attorney name]
[firm address]

FORM 2–48
DEFENDANT'S MOTION TO TRANSFER VENUE AND ORIGINAL
ANSWER SUBJECT THERETO

NO. _____

[PLAINTIFF(S) NAMES]	)	
Plaintiffs,	)	
	)	
	)	IN THE DISTRICT COURT OF
	)	
	)	_____ COUNTY,
v.	)	
	)	_____ JUDICIAL DISTRICT
[DEFENDANT(S) NAMES]	)	
Defendants.	)	

DEFENDANT'S MOTION TO TRANSFER VENUE AND
ORIGINAL ANSWER SUBJECT THERETO

TO THE HONORABLE JUDGE OF SAID COURT:

COMES NOW Defendant _____, by and through its attorney of record, _____ of _____, and moves the Court pursuant to Rule _____, _____ Rules of Civil Procedure, to transfer venue of

INITIATION OF THE SUIT

this cause to _____ County, _____, and in support thereof would show unto the Court the following:

1. This action should be transferred to _____ County, _____, which is a proper venue because _____ County where the action is pending is not a proper county of venue.

2. Defendant denies that defendant has its principal office in this state in _____ County, _____. Defendant would show that its principal office in this state is located in _____, _____ County, _____, and therefore venue is proper in _____ County, _____, pursuant to ___[section number]___ of the ___[Civil Code]___. Further, venue is not proper in _____ County, _____, because all or substantial part of the events or omissions giving rise to the claim occurred in a county other than _____ County, _____.

3. Defendant asserts that joinder of all plaintiffs in this one suit is not proper. Defendant further invokes the provisions of ___[section]___ of the ___[Civil Code]___, which requires that each plaintiff must independently of any other plaintiff establish proper venue. In the unlikely event that venue is proper as to any plaintiff in _____ County, defendant maintains that as to any plaintiff which does not establish proper venue in _____ County, this cause of action should be dismissed or transferred to _____ County, _____, which is a county of proper venue.

4. Defendant also seeks transfer of this cause for the convenience of parties and in the interest of justice as provided in ___[section]___ of the ___[Civil Code]___.

WHEREFORE, PREMISES CONSIDERED, defendant prays that its Motion to Transfer Venue be set for hearing and that upon final hearing hereof, this case be transferred to _____ County.

ORIGINAL ANSWER SUBJECT TO MOTION TO TRANSFER VENUE

1. Pursuant to Rule _____ of the _____ Rules of Civil Procedure, defendant denies, each and every, all and singular, the material allegations contained in plaintiff's pleadings filed herein, and demands strict proof thereof, as required by the laws of this state of persons or entities who bring suit as the plaintiff does in the instant case.

2. Defendant respectfully reserves the right at this time to amend this original answer to the plaintiff's allegations after said defendant has had the opportunity to more closely investigate these claims, as is the right and privilege of said defendant under the Rules of Civil Procedure and the laws of the State of _____.

WHEREFORE, PREMISES CONSIDERED, the above-named defendant, having fully answered herein, prays that it go hence without delay for costs, and for such other and further relief, both special and general, at law and in equity, to which the said Defendants may be justly entitled.

DEFENDANTS RESPECTFULLY DEMAND A TRIAL BY JURY.

Respectfully submitted,

NAME OF FIRM

_____

Name of Atty
Atty's Bar #
Address
City, State, Zip
Phone #

VERIFICATION

THE STATE OF _____)
)
COUNTY OF _____)

    BEFORE ME, the undersigned authority, on this day personally appeared _____, who, being by me duly sworn on his oath, stated that he is the attorney of record for the Defendant _____ in the above-entitled and numbered cause and has read the statements contained in the foregoing instrument and to the best of his information and belief, all statements contained therein are true and correct.

_____

    SUBSCRIBED AND SWORN TO BEFORE ME, by the said _____ on this the ____ day of _____, 20___, to certify which witness my hand and official seal of office.

_____

NOTARY PUBLIC,
STATE OF _____

CERTIFICATE OF SERVICE

    I hereby certify that a true and correct copy of the above and foregoing document has been forwarded to all counsel of record by facsimile and/or certified mail/R.R.R. on this ____ day of _____, 20___.

_____

INITIATION OF THE SUIT

ORDER

Having read the above motion and being otherwise advised in the law and the premises,

IT IS HEREBY ORDERED, ADJUDGED, AND DECREED that said motion is in all respects granted.

DATED this _____ day of _____, 20___.

_____

JUDGE PRESIDING

§ 2.33 —General Denial

FORM 2–49
SAMPLE GENERAL DENIAL

NO. [case number]

[name],	) IN THE DISTRICT COURT OF
	)
Plaintiff,	) [county] COUNTY,
	)
vs.	) [state]
	)
[name],	) [judicial district] JUDICIAL DISTRICT
	)
Defendant.	)

DEFENDANT'S ORIGINAL ANSWER

TO THE HONORABLE JUDGE OF SAID COURT:

COMES NOW [name], defendant in the above cause, to file this answer to the original petition of [name], plaintiff herein, and would respectfully show the Court as follows:

I.

Defendant specially excepts to the following allegations in paragraph [number], page [number] of plaintiff's original petition:

[list of exceptions to plaintiff's allegations] _____

_____

_____

§ 2.33   GENERAL DENIAL

Defendant is entitled to know the specific acts and omissions upon which the plaintiff bases his allegations of negligence on the part of defendant.

II.

Defendant also specially excepts on the ground that plaintiff has alleged damages exceeding the minimum jurisdictional amount. Defendant is entitled to know the maximum amount of damages claimed and each element of those damages.

III.

Subject to all stipulations and admissions that may hereafter be made, defendant asserts a general denial as is authorized by Rule [citation] of the [state] Rules of Civil Procedure, and defendant respectfully requests that the plaintiff be required to prove the charges and allegations against defendant by a preponderance of the evidence as is required by the Constitution and the Laws of the State of [state].

IV.

Defendant expressly reserves his right to subsequently amend this Answer to assert any counterclaims or causes of action defendant may have against plaintiff, and to aver any affirmative defenses available to defendant.

WHEREFORE, PREMISES CONSIDERED, defendant prays that plaintiff take nothing by reason of this suit, and that the defendant go hence without day with his costs, and be granted such other and further relief, both general and special, to which defendant may be justly entitled either at law or equity.

Respectfully submitted,

[name of law firm]

By: _____
[attorney name]
[firm address]

INITIATION OF THE SUIT

FORM 2–50
DEFENDANT'S ORIGINAL ANSWER

NO. _____

[PLAINTIFF(S) NAMES] Plaintiffs,	))))))))))	IN THE DISTRICT COURT OF _____ COUNTY,
v.		_____ JUDICIAL DISTRICT
[DEFENDANT(S) NAMES] Defendants.		

DEFENDANT'S ORIGINAL ANSWER

COMES NOW _____, Defendant herein, and makes and files this Original Answer to Plaintiff's pleadings and in support thereof would show the Court the following:

I.

Defendant asserts a general denial to Plaintiff's allegations.

II.

The matters complained of by Plaintiff were proximately caused by the negligence of the Plaintiff.

WHEREFORE, PREMISES CONSIDERED, _____, named Defendant herein, respectfully prays that Plaintiff take nothing against them and that they be discharged, without liability to anyone, and shall recover their costs of Court and for such other and further relief to which Defendant may be entitled.

Respectfully submitted,

NAME OF FIRM

_____

Name of Atty
Atty's Bar #
Address
City, State, Zip
Phone #

CERTIFICATE OF SERVICE

I hereby certify that on _____, 20___, a true and correct copy of the foregoing instrument was forwarded to all counsel of record by certified mail, return receipt requested, and that the above instrument was filed with the Clerk of the Court, together with this proof of service.

_____

§ 2.34   Affirmative Defense Checklist

An *affirmative defense* is a defense that is based on new factual allegations by the defendant which were not contained in the plaintiff's allegations. These defenses are facts which defend or justify the defendant's behavior or actions and defeat the plaintiff's claims.

When raising an affirmative defense, the defendant either expressly or impliedly treats the factual allegations in the complaint as true, but then goes on to assert new matter that eliminates or limits the defendant's liability arising from those allegations.

When your client has been sued and an answer to the complaint is being prepared, any affirmative defenses which set forth additional matters serving to relieve your client of liability should be included in that answer. Affirmative defenses are placed immediately following the denials in the answer. Generally, failure to plead an affirmative defense will result in its waiver. Consult Rule 8(c) of the Federal Rules of Civil Procedure and corresponding state procedural rules for applicable affirmative defenses in your jurisdiction. The following is a checklist of the most commonly used affirmative defenses with their respective definitions:

Accord and Satisfaction: When the parties have entered into an agreement, a dispute arises and a new agreement or accord is reached, the terms of which are known as satisfaction. When both parties in the transaction are in agreement that the new agreement was reached in an effort to resolve the dispute by compromise, the acceptance of the new satisfaction takes the place of the original agreement, and payment of that satisfaction precludes any recovery of the amounts prescribed in the original agreement.

Arbitration and Award: When parties are in disagreement over a transaction and agree to have the dispute settled by a neutral third party, or panel, such process is known as arbitration. The determination and award determined by the arbitrators becomes binding and cannot be pursed further by either party in a court of law.

Assumption of the Risk: If a hazard or danger is known and understood, or is readily apparent to the plaintiff and he voluntarily continues on his course of action, and this action results in his injury, harm, or damage, the plaintiff is barred from his recovery under the assumption of the risk doctrine. An example of a situation in which this doctrine would be employed is a case in which the plaintiff is struck and injured by a train while walking on a railroad trestle. The plaintiff certainly knew that his action was dangerous, and chose to proceed anyway.

Contributory Negligence: In common law theory, a plaintiff is completely barred from recovering in a claim in which the plaintiff's own negligent actions cause or contribute to his own injury, harm or damage. An example of contributory negligence is personified in the case where a pedestrian crossing against the traffic light is hit by a speeding car. Even though the car was speeding, the pedestrian contributed to the cause of the accident by entering the street improperly. Many states have now abolished the common law doctrine of contributory negligence and, instead, have adopted the doctrine of comparative negligence, which, instead of completely barring recovery upon the finding of contributory negligence, assigns the plaintiff and defendant respective percentages of negligence responsibility, adjusting the monetary damage award accordingly.

Bankruptcy Discharge: If a person or corporation has filed bankruptcy and the judge has signed a court order which legally absolves the debtor of his responsibility to repay certain debts, the creditors whose receivables are affected by that court order may not file a legal claim for those monies.

Duress: The enforcement of any promise which is extracted from a person under threat of bodily harm, death, or property damage, even if said promise would otherwise be legally binding, is barred under common law and may be used as an affirmative defense when appropriate.

Estoppel: This affirmative defense is commonly employed in cases where breach of contract has been alleged. In a situation where Party A chooses to continue with a contract after becoming aware of a breach by Party B, Party A's decision to continue with his obligations under the contract constitutes a waiver, and precludes Party A from recovering for breach of contract. Party A is said to be estopped from recovery. Therefore, Party B may use waiver of estoppel as an affirmative defense if sued for breach of contract by Party A.

Failure to State a Claim upon Which Relief Can be Granted: This affirmative defense is also sometimes referred to as a demurrer. Simply stated, if, upon reading of the complaint, the defendant believes that even if all facts alleged therein were proven that the sum total of all said facts would not be sufficient to allow plaintiff's recovery against defendant, then defendant would be correct to plead failure to state a claim upon which relief can be granted as an affirmative defense.

Fraud: The defendant may use fraud as an affirmative defense if his actions were based upon reliance on fraudulent misrepresentations by the plaintiff which were known by the plaintiff to be fraudulent at the time of the representations, and that said representations were made in order to deliberately deceive defendant.

§ 2.34 AFFIRMATIVE DEFENSE

Illegality: Plaintiffs are barred from recovering damages resulting from their own illegal transactions. An affirmative defense of illegality may be used by the defendant when the plaintiff has based his or her claim on such an illegal action or act. Just as a contract which is governed by the statute of frauds is unenforceable when not complying with necessary elements thereof, so are actions for damages based on illegal acts unenforceable.

Laches: In contract law, a plaintiff may be barred from recovery on a claim even if the statute of limitations has not yet run if the plaintiff acted negligently in failing to discover the mistake which is presently at controversy, or if there was unreasonable delay in filing the claim after discovery of the mistake.

License or Privilege: The defendant may use the affirmative defense of license or privilege if he had an express or implied right, authority, or permission to perform the act or action which is the subject matter of the controversy. Such rights or authorities are often granted to policemen or governmental entities, such as the rights of police to utilize reasonable force in making arrests and the right of government to take property by the doctrine of eminent domain for the better good of the public as a whole. Such actions without authorization or license would be illegal.

Payment: Many times agreements are made in which the consideration for such agreements is renegotiated at a later time. If the plaintiff has accepted a renegotiated consideration as payment in full for the debt or agreement, he is barred from recovery of the original agreed upon amount at a later time. This is the reason that such payments are usually marked as "Payment in full" and are signed by the recipient in acknowledgement of that fact.

Release: If a party has accepted a settlement offer from the opposing party and has singed an agreement releasing the other party from all liability in the matter, the party receiving such settlement cannot litigate the matter at a later time in pursuit of more damages, If such party were sued for further damages in a court of law, release would be an appropriate affirmative defense.

Res Judicata: If a judgment on the merits has already been had, the parties are barred under the doctrine of res judicata from retrying the same causes of action based upon the same facts. This doctrine may be likened to its criminal counterpart of double jeopardy in which an accused person cannot stand trial for the same crime twice.

Statute of Limitations: Each state has its own statutes of limitation which invoke specified time limits in which different types of claims must be filed. Claims filed after this time period are said to be barred by the statute of limitations. Some statutes run from the time of occurrence of the wrongdoing, and others run from the time of discovery of the wrongdoing which is the subject matter of the litigation.

§ 2.35 —Boilerplate Language for Affirmative Defenses

It is important to state the affirmative defense correctly in the Answer. This section takes each affirmative defense listed in **§ 2.34** and illustrates the boilerplate wording necessary to state these affirmative defenses correctly. **Form 2–51** is a sample answer exemplifying the use of affirmative defenses.

Accord and Satisfaction:

Defendant admits owing the obligation to plaintiff which is alleged in Paragraph [number] of the plaintiff's complaint in this action; however, defendant alleges that on [date], a[n] [oral/written] agreement was reached between plaintiff and defendant that plaintiff would accept $[amount] from defendant as payment in full of this obligation. [A copy of said written agreement is attached hereto as Exhibit [number] and incorporated herein by reference.]

Further, defendant alleges that on [date], defendant tendered to plaintiff a check in the amount of $[amount], such check notated with the inscription "Payment in full" on the face of said check. Defendant further alleges that plaintiff legally endorsed and cashed said check on [date]. A copy of said check is attached hereto as Exhibit [number] and incorporated herein by reference. Defendant maintains that the cashing of this check and the acceptance of the funds thereto, constitute full accord and satisfaction under the laws of this state and that plaintiff is barred from further recovery in this action under the doctrine of accord and satisfaction.

Arbitration and Award:

Further, as an affirmative defense, defendant would show that a written agreement to arbitrate the matter in controversy was entered into on [date], wherein the parties agreed to abide by the determination of the arbitrators and to consider such determination as legally binding. A copy of said agreement is attached hereto as Exhibit [number] and incorporated herein by reference.

Defendant therefore alleges that the decision of the arbitrators is binding, and that defendant is released therefore from any further liability in this matter. Plaintiff is therefore barred from further recovery in this matter pursuant to the doctrine of arbitration and award.

Assumption of the Risk:

Plaintiff was aware of the risks, dangers and hazards inherent with [state specific activity]. Plaintiff therefore assumed the risk of potential injury resulting therefrom.

Contributory Negligence:

Plaintiff acted negligently and without the amount of due care legally requisite under the circumstances, in that [state specifics which denote allegations of negligence] and in direct violation of [list applicable regulations, statutes or ordinances]. Plaintiff's actions were the [direct/proximate] cause of his [injuries/damages]. Plaintiff is therefore barred from recovery by the doctrine of contributory negligence.

§ 2.35 BOILERPLATE LANGUAGE

Bankruptcy Discharge:

Plaintiff's claim which is the subject matter of the pending action at bar regards a debt which was owing by the defendant to the plaintiff at the time defendant filed for protection under Chapter [number] of the U.S. Bankruptcy Code. Said bankruptcy petition was filed in [state name of court and district] on [date], a copy of which is attached hereto as Exhibit A and incorporated herein by reference.

As a result of that petition for relief, an order was entered on [date] effectively discharging debtor (defendant herein) from the debt owing to plaintiff herein. A copy of the discharge order is attached hereto as Exhibit B and incorporated by reference herein.

Plaintiff is therefore barred from recovery in this action as a result of the Bankruptcy Court order attached hereto as Exhibit B.

Duress:

Defendant alleges that the contract which is the subject matter of this action is invalid and unenforceable by law because defendant did not sign said contract under his own free will. Defendant was forced to enter into said contract under duress inflicted by the plaintiff, said duress being [describe specific acts of duress]. Defendant maintains that absent such duress, he would not have entered into said contract. Therefore, defendant alleges that plaintiff is barred from recovery by virtue of the manner in which the contract was effectuated, namely duress, and that said contract is null and void and unenforceable by law.

Estoppel or Waiver:

Defendant maintains that plaintiff is estopped from bringing this cause of action due to the fact that defendant's actions were done with the full knowledge of plaintiff, said actions being [describe actions], and that absent any objections by plaintiff to said actions, defendant believed, and had a right to believe, that said actions were fully acceptable to plaintiff. By virtue of the fact that plaintiff offered no objections at the time of the occurrence of said actions, plaintiff's absence of objection constituted a waiver of any rights to a future recovery under this claim.

Failure to State a Claim upon Which Relief Can Be Granted:

Plaintiff's complaint fails to state a claim upon which relief can be granted. Said complaint does not contain facts sufficient to support plaintiff's claims.

Fraud:

Defendant alleges that the contract which is the subject of controversy in this matter is null, void, and unenforceable by law. Defendant, in entering into the contract, relied, and had reason to rely on the fraudulent misrepresentations of plaintiff. Defendant further maintains that said fraudulent misrepresentations were made by plaintiff in order to induce defendant into entering into said contract. Plaintiff is therefore barred from recovery in this matter because of the element of fraud in the inducement.

INITIATION OF THE SUIT

Illegality:

Plaintiff's cause of action is based on an act which is illegal, such act being prohibited under the laws of the state of [state]. Pursuant to the doctrine of illegality, plaintiff's cause of action is therefore unenforceable by law.

Laches:

Defendant alleges that plaintiff had knowledge of the incident [or actions] which [is/are] the subject matter of this controversy for a period of [years/months] prior to bringing the instant action. Defendant maintains that plaintiff is guilty of laches in that he unnecessarily and inexplicably caused an inordinate delay in the filing of this action under the circumstances, and as such, said action, if allowed to be brought at this time, will result in undue prejudice to the defendant in that [state such examples of prejudice, such as the unavailability of witnesses, destruction of material evidence, and so forth.].

License:

Defendant was acting within his right under the circumstances to [describe act], which right is afforded to him through an [express/implied] license granted by and through the laws of the State of [state], specifically [state statute].

Payment:

Defendant would show as an affirmative defense to this cause of action that on [date], defendant tendered to plaintiff, and plaintiff accepted, a check in the amount of $[amount] as full payment and good and valuable consideration in exchange for [state services or goods delivered]. Said check was endorsed by plaintiff with the words "payment in full," and cashed on [date]. A copy of said check is attached hereto as Exhibit [number] and incorporated herein by reference. Plaintiff is therefore barred from further recovery in this matter under the doctrine of payment.

Release:

In consideration for the receipt of $[amount] from defendant, plaintiff signed a release on [date], relieving defendant of all liability in this matter. A copy of said release is attached hereto as Exhibit [number] and incorporated herein by reference.

Res Judicata:

Defendant maintains that plaintiff is barred from bringing the cause of action which is the subject matter of the controversy in the instant case in that plaintiff brought the same cause of action against defendant supported by the same facts in a prior litigation in [name court] on [date], in a matter entitled and numbered [name of action and cause number]. A copy of said action is attached hereto as Exhibit [number] and incorporated by reference herein. Said matter was fully adjudicated and judgment was rendered by that court in favor of defendant on [date]. A copy of said judgment is attached hereto as Exhibit [number] and incorporated herein by reference. Said judgment remains in full force and effect and has not been overturned by any court of law. Therefore, plaintiff is barred from bringing this action under the doctrine of res judicata.

Statute of Limitations:

[Name of state] Statute [number of statute] bars recovery for [type of claim] after [insert statutory length of time allowed for filing of claims]. Plaintiff first became aware of [describe the incident which is the subject matter of this litigation occurred] on [date]. This claim has been filed [length of time] after the statutory bar date, and therefore plaintiff is precluded from recovery on this claim.

§ 2.36   —Answer Setting Forth Affirmative Defenses

FORM 2–51
SAMPLE ANSWER SETTING FORTH AFFIRMATIVE DEFENSES

NO. [case number]

[name],	)	IN THE DISTRICT COURT OF
	)	
Plaintiff,	)	[county] COUNTY, [state]
	)	
vs.	)	[judicial district] JUDICIAL DISTRICT
	)	
[name],	)	
	)	
Defendant.	)	

DEFENDANT'S ORIGINAL ANSWER

TO THE HONORABLE JUDGE OF SAID COURT:

COMES NOW, [name], defendant in the above-entitled cause, to file this, his answer to the original [petition/complaint] of [name], plaintiff herein, and would respectfully show unto the Court the following:

I.

Defendant specially excepts to the following allegations in paragraph [number], page [number] of plaintiff's original [complaint/petition]: [state allegations to which the defendant specially excepts]. Defendant is entitled to know the specific acts and omissions upon which plaintiff bases his allegations of negligence on the part of defendant.

INITIATION OF THE SUIT

II.

Defendant also specially excepts on the grounds that plaintiff has alleged damages exceeding the minimum jurisdictional amount. Defendant is entitled to know the maximum amount of damages claimed and each element of those damages.

III.

Defendant asserts a general denial as authorized by Rule [citation] of the [state] Rules of Civil Procedure, and defendant respectfully requests that plaintiff be required to prove the charges and allegations against defendant by a preponderance of the evidence as is required by the laws of the State of [state].

IV.

As an affirmative defense, defendant alleges that plaintiff failed to use that degree of care which a person of ordinary prudence in the exercise of ordinary care would have used under the same or similar circumstances and that said failure on the part of plaintiff was a proximate cause of the accident in which plaintiff alleges his injuries occurred.

V.

Defendant further says that a proximate cause of said accident was the conduct or breach of duty of some party other than defendant, over whom defendant possessed no right of control and for whose acts defendant is not responsible under the laws and statutes of this state.

VI.

Defendant also says that immediately prior to this accident, defendant was faced with an emergency not created by his own negligence, that defendant exercised ordinary care in acting under said emergency, and that said emergency was a proximate cause of the accident in question.

VII.

In the unlikely event that defendant is found liable to plaintiff, defendant affirmatively pleads that he is entitled to an offset or credit for any and all sums plaintiff has received or may hereafter receive by way of any and all settlements arising from plaintiff's claims and causes of action.

WHEREAS, PREMISES CONSIDERED, Defendant prays that Plaintiff take nothing by this action; that Defendant recover all costs; and that Defendant be granted all other and further relief to which he is entitled.

[name of firm]

By: _____
[name of attorney]
Attorney for Defendant
[address]
[telephone number]

[Add certificate of service]

§ 2.37 Special Exceptions

A Special Exception may be the same thing as a special demurrer in the area where you practice. Basically, a special exception challenges the sufficiency of a pleading by making a prompt objection and thus possibly avoiding the expense and duration of an extended lawsuit when either the plaintiff has failed to state a proper cause of action or the defendant has failed to plead a sufficient defense. Special exceptions are generally objections to form rather than substance.

Examples of instances when special exceptions are proper are as follow:

1. A pleading without a proper verification as required by the rules of civil procedure;
2. A pleading which fails to plead damages in a specific amount rather than by a phrase such as "in excess of the minimum jurisdictional amount" as required by code of statute;
3. A pleading has failed to specifically state the acts or omissions upon which it is bases its allegations of negligence if required by code of stature; or
4. A pleading which does not contain any of the several designated elements necessary as outlined in that jurisdiction's rules of civil procedure.

In some jurisdictions, a defendant's special exceptions are filed separately from the answer rather than as a paragraph included in the original answer. **Form 2–52** is a simple form for filing the special exceptions of the defendant. You can delete any paragraph that does not apply to your case. **Form 2–53** is an example of an order which sustains special exceptions.

FORM 2–52
SAMPLE DEFENDANT'S SPECIAL EXCEPTIONS

NO. [case number]

[name],	)	IN THE DISTRICT COURT OF
	)	
Plaintiff,	)	[county] COUNTY,
	)	
vs.	)	[state]
	)	
[name],	)	[judicial district] JUDICIAL DISTRICT
	)	
Defendant.	)	

DEFENDANT'S SPECIAL EXCEPTIONS

COMES NOW, [name], defendant in the above cause, to file these special exceptions to the original petition of [name], plaintiff herein, and would respectfully show the Court as follows:

I.

Defendant specially excepts to the following allegations in paragraph [number], page [number] of plaintiff's original petition:

[specify exceptions to plaintiff's allegations]. _____

_____

_____

Defendant is entitled to know the specific acts and omissions upon which the plaintiff bases his allegations of negligence on the part of defendant.

II.

Defendant also specially excepts on the ground that plaintiff has alleged damages exceeding the minimum jurisdictional amount. Defendant is entitled to know the maximum amount of damages claimed and each element of those damages.

III.

Defendant specially excepts to the following allegations in paragraph [number], page [number] of plaintiff's original petition:

[specify exceptions to plaintiff's allegations]. _____

_____

_____

IV.

Defendant specially excepts to the following allegations in paragraph [number], page [number] of plaintiff's original petition:

[specify exceptions to plaintiff's allegations]. _____

_____

_____

WHEREFORE, PREMISES CONSIDERED, [name], defendant herein, prays that the Court sustain these special exceptions in all respects and award all other and further relief to which defendant is entitled.

[name of law firm]

By: _____
[attorney name]
[attorney address]
Counsel for Defendant

FORM 2–53
SAMPLE ORDER SUSTAINING SPECIAL EXCEPTIONS

No. [case number]

[name]	)	IN THE DISTRICT COURT OF
	)	
Plaintiff	)	[county] COUNTY, [state]
	)	
vs.	)	[judicial district] JUDICIAL DISTRICT
	)	
[name]	)	
	)	
Defendant	)	

ORDER SUSTAINING SPECIAL EXCEPTIONS

BE IT REMEMBERED that on the [date] day of [month], [20__], came on for consideration the special exceptions of [name], defendant herein, to the original [complaint/petition] of [name], plaintiff herein, and that the Court has decided to grant and sustain said special exceptions [in part/in all respects].

It is therefore, ORDERED, ADJUDGED, and DECREED that defendant's special exceptions be and the same are hereby sustained and granted, in the following respects: [reiterate special exceptions, stating for each one how it is to be rectified, such as " by amending that portion of the pleading . . ."].

It is further ORDERED, ADJUDGED, and DECREED that plaintiff amend his original [complaint/petition] in the manner set forth above within [number] days from the entry of this Order.

SIGNED this [date] day of [month], [20___].

_____
Judge Presiding

§ 2.38   Default Judgments

If, within the prescribed number of days allotted for a response, the defendant does not answer your petition or complaint, you should immediately prepare a Motion for Default Judgment. The motion is usually accompanied by an affidavit stating that the defendant has not paid the money due, has not answered the petition, is not in the military, and therefore not entitled to that defense for nonresponse, and accordingly, the default judgment is proper.

Under the Federal Rule of Civil Procedure, Rule 55 states that a default judgment may be obtained by filing a Request for Entry of Default (**Form 2–54**) along with an affidavit (**Form 2–55**). A military service affidavit (**Form 2–56**) is also required.

Under Federal Rule of Civil Procedure 55(b)(2), a judgment of default may not be entered against an infant or incompetent person unless the infant or incompetent is represented by a guardian or committee.

FORM 2–54
SAMPLE REQUEST FOR ENTRY OF DEFAULT

IN THE UNITED STATES DISTRICT COURT
[judicial district] DISTRICT OF [state]
[judicial division] DIVISION

[name]

                    Plaintiff   )   Civil Action No. [case number]

vs.

[name]

                    Defendant   )

§ 2.38 DEFAULT JUDGMENTS

REQUEST TO CLERK FOR ENTRY OF DEFAULT

The Plaintiff hereby requests the clerk for the [specify court] Court to enter the Defendant's default in the above-entitled action. The Defendant has failed to appear or otherwise answer the complaint, and is therefore in default as set out in the accompanying affidavit.

Respectfully submitted,

_____
[attorney for plaintiff]
[address]
[city, state, zip code]
[telephone number]

FORM 2–55
SAMPLE AFFIDAVIT FOR DEFAULT JUDGMENT

IN THE UNITED STATES DISTRICT COURT
[judicial district] DISTRICT OF [state]
[judicial division] DIVISION

[name]	)	
	)	
Plaintiff	)	Civil Action No. [case number]
	)	
vs.	)	
	)	
[name]	)	
	)	
Defendant	)	

AFFIDAVIT FOR DEFAULT JUDGMENT

[Name of attorney], being duly sworn, deposes and says:

1. That he is attorney for Plaintiff in the above-entitled action and that he has personal knowledge of the facts set forth in this affidavit.

2. That on the [date day of [month] [20__], the Plaintiff herein filed his complaint against the Defendant in this cause of action.

3. That the Defendant was served with a copy of the complaint and summons by the United States Marshal on the [date] day of [month], [20__].

4. That more than twenty days have passed since the service of the complaint and summons in this action.

5.   That the Defendant is not an incompetent, infant, or in the military service.

6.   That the Defendant has failed to answer Plaintiff's complaint.

7.   That the amount due Plaintiff by Defendant is justly owed and remains unpaid.

8.   That this affidavit is executed by the affiant herein in accordance with Rule 55(a) of the Federal Rules of Civil Procedure, for the purpose of obtaining an entry of default against the Defendant herein, as entitled for the defendant's failure to answer the Plaintiff's complaint herein.

Respectfully submitted,

_____
[attorney for plaintiff]
[address]
[city, state, zip code]
[telephone number]

[notarization]

FORM 2–56
SAMPLE AFFIDAVIT OF MILITARY SERVICE OF DEFENDANT

IN THE UNTIED STATES DISTRICT COURT
[judicial district] DISTRICT OF [state]
[judicial division] DIVISION

[name]		)
		)
	Plaintiff	) Civil Action No. [case number]
		)
vs.		)
		)
[name]		)
		)
	Defendant	)

AFFIDAVIT OF MILITARY SERVICE OF DEFENDANT

[name of attorney], being duly sworn, deposes and says:

1.   I am legal resident of the United States being over the age of eighteen years.

2.   My resident address is [address, city, state, zip code].

3.   I am attorney for the Plaintiff in the above-entitled cause of action and have full knowledge of the facts relating thereto.

4.   That Defendant is engaged in the business of [description of business] in the city of [city], and is not in the military service of the United States.

Respectfully submitted,

_____

[attorney for plaintiff]
[address]
[city, state, zip code]
[telephone number]

§ 2.39   Removal to Federal Court

The defendant in a lawsuit is afforded the same privilege of choice of forum that the plaintiff enjoys when filing his lawsuit. 28 U.S.C. §§ 1441 *et seq.* states that any civil action filed in a state court which could have been heard originally in a federal court, that is, where there is concurrent original jurisdiction, may be removed by the defendant to the federal court in the same jurisdiction in which the state court action is presently pending. However, an exception to this doctrine is the prohibition of removal of a civil action not arising from federal law to federal court if the defendant is a resident of the state where the original action was filed. 28 U.s.c. § 1441 states:

(a)   Except as other wise expressly provided by Act of Congress, any civil action brought in a State Court of which the district courts of the United States have original jurisdiction, may be removed by the defendant or the defendants, to the district court of the United States for the district and division embracing the place where such action is pending. For the purposes of removal under this chapter, the citizenship of defendants sued under fictitious names shall be disregarded.

(b)   Any civil action of which the district courts have original jurisdiction founded on a claim or right arising under the Constitution, treaties or laws of the United States shall be removable without regard to the citizenship or residence of the parties. Any other such action shall be removable only if none of the parties in interest properly joined and served as defendants is a citizen of the State in which such action is brought.

(c)   Whenever a separate and independent claim of or cause of action within the jurisdiction conferred by section 1331 of this title is joined with one or more otherwise nonremovable claims or causes of action, the entire case may be removed and the district court may determine all issues therein, or, in its discretion, may remand all matters in which State law predominates.

The decision to remove a case to federal court is usually made by the client after recommendation of the attorney. The attorney's recommendation for the change in the choice of forum is generally influenced by details such as the speed of court calendars and the length of time in which a case may come to trial, the geographic convenience to the attorney and/or his client, the historical record of jury verdicts in a particular court system, the differences in discovery procedures or facility of practice within that court system, the differences in the rules of evidence, between the two court systems, and the professional and personal reputations of certain judges in the respective court systems.

An amendment to Title 28 of U.S.C. which went into effect on November 19, 1988 changed the name of the Petition for Removal to Notice of Removal. The judge no longer signs an order granting the removal: payment of the filing fee and filing of the Notice of Removal is all that is required at the federal level. The Notice of Removal (**Form 2–57**) must be filed within 30 days of receipt of the original state court summons (or citation) and complaint (or petition).

As of November 19, 1988, the necessity of posting a surety bond was abolished. The bond was previously used to guarantee plaintiff's costs for the removal procedure should it have been determined that the action may not have been removed under the stature. Be sure and check your local rules regarding this change, as some federal local rules now requiring the attachment of all state papers (including discovery papers) as exhibits to the Notice of Removal.

Another recent rule change which affects federal removal practice is the changeling of the "amount in controversy" requirement for diversity jurisdiction. That amount is now $75,000.

Federal Rules of Civil Procedure 81 (c) states that once the action is removed to federal court, it is not necessary to replead the cause of action or the demand for jury trial if previously pled, unless the federal court directs the party to do so.

The following checklist is useful in organizing a complaint removal:

1. Answer the original state complaint or petition within the statutory time limit (usually 20 days) to avoid default.

2. Make sure that the action qualifies for removal under 28 U.S.C. § 1441. Pay special attention to the $75,000 jurisdictional minimum and the provisions of subsection (b).

3. File the Notice of Removal within 30 days of accepting service of the original state court summons (or citation) and complaint (or petition).

4. Check with the Federal District Court Clerk to determine the filing fee.

5. File the following in federal court:
   a. Notice of Removal with exhibits. Exhibits consist of copy of original state court complaint (or petition) and summons (or citation), the latter showing proof of service. (Some jurisdictions may also require discovery documents.)
   b. Copy of Notice to Clerk of State District Court (**Form 2–58**).

6. Pay filing fee to the federal court.

7. File the following in state court where the original action was filed.
   a. Copy of Notice of Removal with exhibits. Exhibits consist of copy of original state court complaint (or petition) and summons (or citation), the latter showing proof of service.

    b. Notice to Clerk of State District Court.

8. Serve the plaintiff's attorney with the following:

    a. Copy of Notice of Removal with exhibits (Exhibits consist of copy of original state court complaint (or petition) and summons (or citation), the latter showing proof of service.

    b. Copy of Notice of Clerk of State District Court.

FORM 2–57
SAMPLE NOTICE OF REMOVAL

IN THE UNITED STATES DISTRICT COURT
[judicial district] DISTRICT OF [state]
[judicial division] DIVISION

[name]	)	
	)	
Plaintiff	)	Civil Action No. [case number]
	)	
vs.	)	
	)	
[name]	)	
	)	
Defendant	)	

NOTICE OF REMOVAL

TO THE HONORABLE JUDGE OF SAID COURT:

COMES NOW [name], defendant in the above cause, and files this notice of removal of said cause from a State Court to this Court, and for such notice would show the Court as follows:

I.

This is a pending civil action brought by plaintiff against defendant petitioner in the District Court of [county] County, [state], [judicial district] Judicial District, of which the United States Courts have original jurisdiction.

II.

This suit involves a controversy between citizens of different states in that at all times pertinent hereto plaintiff has been and is a citizen and resident of the State of [state] and the defendant has been and is a citizen and resident of the State of [state].

INITIATION OF THE SUIT

III.

The amount of the matter in controversy in this suit exceeds $75,000 exclusive of interest and costs. (in diversity cases.)

IV.

This notice is filed within thirty (30) days after the date of service of process upon the defendant herein as required by statute [check local federal rules] and defendant has not filed any pleadings in this cause in the State Court prior to filing of this notice of removal.

V.

Copies of all pleadings and papers served upon defendant in this action are filed with this notice.

VI.

Immediately upon the filing of this notice of removal, written notice of such filing is being given by defendant to the plaintiff as required by law, and a copy of this petition is simultaneously being filed with the Clerk of the State Court in which this cause was originally filed.

WHEREFORE plaintiff is hereby notified that said action is removed from the State Court to this Court.

_____

[attorney for defendant]

[certificate of service.]

FORM 2–58
SAMPLE NOTICE TO CLERK OF STATE DISTRICT COURT

NO. [case number]

[name],	)	IN THE DISTRICT COURT OF
	)	
Plaintiff,	)	[county] COUNTY, [state]
	)	
vs.	)	[judicial district] JUDICIAL DISTRICT
	)	
[name],	)	
	)	
Defendant.	)	

NOTICE TO CLERK OF STATE DISTRICT COURT

Please take notice that the undersigned, attorney for [name] in the above entitled and numbered cause, hereby certifies that a signed and acknowledged copy of the Notice of Removal filed by said defendant in the United States District Court for the [judicial district] District of [state] Civil No. [case number] on the docket of said court, was filed with the Clerk of the District Court of [county] County, [state], by mailing a true copy to said Clerk, in the United States Mail, on this the [date] day of [month], [20___].

_____
[attorney for defendant]

[Add certificate of service.]

§ 2.40 Demurrers

Rule 12(b) of the Federal Rules of Civil Procedure contains at lease six possible defenses which may be made in the form of a Motion for Dismissal prior to filing an Answer to the Complaint.

1. Lack of subject matter jurisdiction,
2. Lack of personal jurisdiction,
3. Improper venue,
4. Improper service of process,
5. Failure to state a claim on which relief may be granted, and
6. Failure to join an indispensable party.

Many of the same grounds for dismissal are available in the state courts.

The function of a motion to dismiss in federal court is to test the sufficiency of the complaint. Such a motion does not resolve contests surrounding the facts, the merits of a claim, or the applicability of defenses. In federal court and, generally, in state courts, when considering a motion to dismiss for failure to state a claim, the court will not look outside the complaint. The standard approach taken by the courts to a motion to dismiss is to make all reasonable inferences in favor of the nonmoving party and not to dismiss any count unless it appears beyond a doubt that recovery would be impossible under any set of facts that could be proven.

However, when a motion has been made in federal court to dismiss for lack of subject matter jurisdiction, the court will look beyond the jurisdictional allegations in the complaint and view whatever evidence has been submitted on the issue to determine whether subject matter jurisdiction exists.

When similar motions are filed in state courts, they are often known as demurrers. However, demurrers are not used in all state courts. Basically, a *demurrer* is a technical challenge to the wording of the complaint, and may result in a dismissal of the complaint or an amendment of the pleadings to correct the insufficiency. In many cases, the attorney must sign an affidavit which states that the demurrer has not been filed simply as a stall tactic.

The form for a demurrer (**Form 2–59**) is very simple and uncomplicated. A basic motion is used with paragraph insertions such as the following: The following examples illustrate three different defenses:

1. The complaint does not contain sufficient facts to establish a claim upon which relief can be granted.

2. The Court does not have personal jurisdiction over the defendant in the instant matter as defendant has never been present in the state of [state name] and the criteria for minimum contacts has not been met.

3. Venue in this Court is improper as the statute calls for venue to be primarily proper in the county of the occurrence of the incidence which is the subject matter of this action.

Form 2–59 is a sample demurrer. It is representative of a demurrer for California.

FORM 2–59
SAMPLE DEMURRER (CALIFORNIA)

ATTORNEYS FOR DEFENDANTS

SUPERIOR COURT OF THE STATE OF [state]

FOR THE COURT OF [court division]

[name]		
	Plaintiffs,	) NO. [case number]
		)
		) DEMURRER TO COMPLAINT
		) AND MEMORANDUM OF
vs.		) POINTS AND AUTHORITIES
		)
		) DATE: [date]
[name]		) TIME: [time]
	Defendants.	) DEPT: [judicial]

To plaintiffs and to their attorney of record,

PLEASE TAKE NOTICE that on [date], [20___], at [time], or as soon thereafter as counsel may be heard in Department [judicial department] of the above-entitled court, located at [address], [city], [state], defendants [names] will and do hereby demur to the complaint of [specify complaint].

Said demurrer will be based on this notice, the attached memorandum of points and authorities, the pleadings, records and files herein, and any and all matters raised at the time of the hearing of the motion.

DATED: [date]

§ 2.40   DEMURRERS

DEMURRER TO COMPLAINT

Defendants [names] hereby demur to the complaint of [specify complaint] on the ground that the second cause of action fails to allege facts sufficient to constitute an award of punitive damages.

DATED: [date]

MEMORANDUM OF POINTS AND AUTHORITIES

I.

PLAINTIFFS HAVE FAILED TO STATE A CAUSE OF ACTION FOR PUNITIVE DAMAGES

Plaintiffs [names] files their complaint for damages for personal injuries on [date].

The action stems from an automobile accident where plaintiff was a passenger on or about [date].

With respect to defendants [names], plaintiffs allege in their second cause of action, *inter alia*, that defendants [specify cause of action (example: "allowed 12 pupils, including the driver, as well as baseball equipment, into the 1974 Chevrolet pick-up truck driven by _____. There were three students in the front passenger compartment, and nine students seated in the rear truck bed. From the time the students met at _____ in preparation for their being transported to _____ for the Junior Varsity baseball game, all of the students driven be _____ in the vehicle driven by _____ were under the supervision and control of _____." Plaintiffs further alleged that _____ was operating, controlling and maintaining the 1974 Chevrolet pick-up truck with the permission and consent of _____.) Finally, plaintiffs add, *inter alia,* in Paragraph VIII of the Second Cause of Action, "In so doing the things herein alleged, Defendant, and each of them, acted recklessly and wantonly by reason thereof, and Plaintiff request punitive and exemplary damages in a sum to be determined according to proof at trial."

The cases that interpret Civil Code Section 3294 have consistently held that *animus malus* or evil motive is an essential element of malice and an important component to sustain a cause of action for punitive damages. *J.D. Searle & Co. v. Superior Court*, 49 Cal. App. 3d 22 (1975); *Davis v. Herst*, 160 Cal. 143 (1911); *Gombos v. Ashe*, 158 Cal. App. 2d 517 (1958).

Moreover, the malice alleged must be malice in fact as opposed to malice in law.

> Certainly the mere characterization of the conduct challenged as willful, reckless, wrongful and unlawful is not of itself sufficient to charge the malice in fact required to sustain a cause of action for punitive damages. *Gombos*, at 529.

A conscious disregard for the safety of others may constitute malice pursuant to Civil Code Section 3294. However, "in order to justify an award of punitive damages on this basis, the plaintiff must establish that the defendant was aware of the probable dangerous consequences of his conduct, and that he willfully and deliberately failed to avoid those certain consequences." *Taylor v. Superior Court*; 24 Cal. 3d 890, 896 (1978).

It is clear from the face of the pleading that plaintiffs have enunciated allegations containing only conclusional allegations concerning defendants [names]. Nowhere does the pleading state any malicious intent. The bottom line in this regard is that "mere negligence, even gross negligence, is not sufficient to justify such an award." *Gombos*, 158 Cal. App. 2d 517 (1958), at 527; *J.D. Searle & Co.* 158 Cal. App. 2d 517 (1958), *Ebaugh v. Rankin*, 22 Cal. App. 3d 891 (1972).

California law "does not favor punitive damages and they should be granted with the greatest of caution." *Beck v. State Farm Mut. Auto. Ins. Co.*, 54 Cal. App. 3d 347, 355 (1976).

It is therefore duly submitted that this demurrer be granted without leave to amend.

DATED: [date]

§ 2.41   Cross-Complaints and Counterclaims

Sometimes a defendant may feel that the plaintiff has neglected to name a party whom he feels may be culpable in the action or that another defendant should be sued by him to indemnify himself in this action. In these instances, the defendant will choose to file a cross-claim. A *cross-claim* is filed against one party by another party for a cause of action which arises out of the same transaction, or incident, which is the subject matter of the original action.

Unlike counterclaims, which are claims against the plaintiff by the defendant, the cross-claim does not have to be brought in the original answer to prevent waiving its privilege. The cross-action may be brought at any time permitted under the local rules for amendment of pleadings. Although the Federal Rules of Civil Procedure do not specify a time limit in which cross claims must be filed, the unwritten rule is that the filing and service of such a claim should not be done so late as to unfairly delay the trial of the plaintiff's original claim.

If the defendant being sued in the cross-claim has already appeared and answered in the original action, the defendant filing the cross-claim need only serve counsel of the cross-defendant in the manner specified in the rules for service of documents other than original complaints. If, however, the cross- defendant has not yet answered or appeared in the original action, and therefore counsel for the cross-de-fendant is unknown or the cross-defendant has not yet been served with the original complaint and summons, the cross-claim should be served in the manner in which an original complaint and summons is served in that jurisdiction.

As amended in 1993, Rule 11 of the Federal Rules of Civil Procedure states in part:

§ 2.41 CROSS-COMPLAINTS AND COUNTERCLAIMS

(b)   Representations to Court. By presenting to the court (whether by signing, filing, submitting, or later advocating) a pleading, written motion, or other paper, an attorney or unrepresented party is certifying to the best of the person's knowledge, information and belief, formed after an inquiry reasonable under the circumstances,—

(1)   It is not being presented for an improper purpose, such as to harass or to cause unnecessary delay or needless increase in the cost of litigation;

(2)   the claims, defenses, and other legal contentions therein are warranted by existing law or by a nonfrivolous argument for the extension, modification, or reversal of existing law or the establishment of new law;

(3)   the allegations and other factual contentions have evidentiary support or, if specifically so identified, are likely to have evidentiary support after a reasonable opportunity for further investigation or discovery; and

(4)   the denials of factual contentions are warranted on the evidence or, if specifically so identified, are reasonably based on a lack of information or belief.

A *counterclaim* is essentially a complaint, or petition, containing a claim or claims for relief asserted by the original defendant (counter-defendant) against the original plaintiff (counter-plaintiff). There are two types of counterclaims: (1) permissive and (2) compulsory.

The Rules of Civil Procedure state that compulsory counterclaims must be asserted in the defendant's original answer. *Compulsory counterclaims* are those which arise out of the same occurrence or transaction which is the basis of the plaintiff's original cause of action. If the defendant neglects to assert a compulsory counterclaim in his original answer, he loses his right to bring that action in that, or any other, lawsuit. Some jurisdictions do not have rules of civil procedure regarding compulsory counterclaims. In those instances, counterclaims are strictly permissive.

If a defendant has a claim or claims against the plaintiff which are not related to the same transaction or occurrence that is the basis of the plaintiff's original cause of action, he may either assert his claim in his original answer in the form of a permissive counterclaim, or, if he chooses, in a separate lawsuit.

Other than the specific rules regarding compulsory and permissive counterclaims mentioned above, counterclaims are subject to the same rules regarding any other claim for relief asserted in an original complaint or petition. That is to say that jurisdictional requirements shall be observed, and no claim shall be allowed to be asserted in existing claim for relief over which the trial court cannot have jurisdiction. In such a case, the court will require that the offending claim be bifurcated, or severed , into a separate and independent lawsuit, to be filed in a court of appropriate jurisdiction.

Counterclaims are drafted by the same rules of civil procedure as are complaints and petitions, and are subject to the same dispositive motions and defenses as the original complaint or petition. Counterclaims must be answered in the form of a reply within 20 days of service of the counterclaim, as are answers to original complaints and petitions. When combined with the defendant's original answer, counterclaims are asserted in the answer after any appropriate affirmative defenses.

INITIATION OF THE SUIT

The correct name of the document in that instance is DEFENDANT'S ORIGINAL ANSWER AND COUNTERCLAIM.

Two sample cross-claims are exemplified in this section. **Form 2–60** is a sample Answer and Cross-Complaint. **Form 2–61** is a sample Original Cross-Action.

FORM 2–60
SAMPLE CROSS-COMPLAINT

No. [case number]

[name]		)	IN THE DISTRICT COURT OF
		)	
	Plaintiff	)	[county] COUNTY, [state]
		)	
vs.		)	[judicial district] JUDICIAL DISTRICT
		)	
[name]		)	
		)	
	Defendant	)	

DEFENDANT'S ORIGINAL ANSWER AND CROSS-CLAIM
AGAINST CO-DEFENDANT

TO THE HONORABLE JUDGE OF SAID COURT:

COMES NOW [name], one of the Defendants in the above styled and numbered cause, and files this its original answer to the Plaintiff's original petition, and would respectfully show unto the Court the following:

I. GENERAL DENIAL

Subject to such stipulations and admissions as may hereinafter be made, Defendant, [name], asserts a general denial as authorized by Rule [citation] of the [state] Rules of Civil Procedure, and said Defendant respectfully requests that the Plaintiff be required to prove the charges and allegations against this Defendant by a preponderance of the evidence as required by the Constitution and laws of the State of [state].

II. CROSS-ACTION

Separately from the foregoing answer and affirmative defense, Defendant, [name], complaint of Co-Defendant, [name], and for cause of action shows the following by way of cross-claim:

[state causes of action here just as in an original complaint or petition, referencing that the cross-claim arises out of the same transaction or occurrence that is the subject of the current litigation].

Defendant would further show that Co-Defendant, is or may be liable to Defendant for all or part of the claims asserted by Plaintiff in the above entitled and numbered cause of action.

[state allegations and basis thereof here as well as damages].

Defendant, [name], additionally seeks to recover all sums which defendant is required to pay as a result of the above entitled cause of action, including attorney's fees and Court costs.

WHEREFORE, PREMISES CONSIDERED, Defendant, [name], requests judgment of the Court that Plaintiff take nothing by this suit and that Defendant, [name], recover all of its costs together with such other and further relief to which it may be justly entitled. Furthermore, if the Court finds judgment for the Plaintiff and against Defendant, [name], this Defendant requests judgment of the Court that Co-Defendant, [name], be adjudicated liable to Defendant, [name], for the amount of such judgment together with all costs including attorney's fees and Court costs and for such other and further relief to which he may be justly entitled.

Respectfully submitted,
[name of firm]

By: _____
Attorney for Defendant
and Cross-Plaintiff

[add certificate of service.]

FORM 2–61
SAMPLE ORIGINAL CROSS-ACTION

No. [case number]

[name]	)	IN THE DISTRICT COURT OF
	)	
Plaintiff	)	[county] COUNTY, [state]
	)	
vs.	)	[judicial district] JUDICIAL DISTRICT
	)	
[name]	)	
	)	
Defendant	)	

ORIGINAL CROSS-ACTION

TO THE HONORABLE JUDGE OF SAID COURT:

COMES NOW [name], hereinafter called cross-plaintiff, complaining of and against [name], hereinafter called cross-defendant, and for his cause of action would respectfully show unto the Court the following:

INITIATION OF THE SUIT

I.

Cross-plaintiff and cross-defendant have previously appeared in this case, and therefore, personal service of this cross-action is not necessary. In the alternative, service upon the cross-defendant shall be made by certified mail. return receipt requested, in compliance with Rule [citation] of the [state] Rules of Civil Procedure.

II.

Plaintiff, [name], brought this original cause of action for [state original causes of action], alleging that cross-plaintiff and cross-defendant breached ceratin and various legal duties owed to plaintiff and that the breach of said duties was the legal cause of plaintiff's damages. Cross plaintiff has denied, and continues to deny any liability to plaintiff.

III.

In the unlikely event that cross-plaintiff is found liable, cross-plaintiff says that cross-plaintiff is entitled to complete indemnity from cross-defendant. Cross-plaintiff asserts that the sole proximate cause of any damages to the plaintiff was the conduct or breach of legal duty of cross-defendant.

WHEREFORE, PREMISES CONSIDERED, cross-plaintiff [name] prays that, upon final hearing of this cause, cross-plaintiff have judgment against cross-defendant for complete indemnity; and that cross-plaintiff have all other and further relief to which he is entitled.

> [name of firm]
>
> By: _____
> [attorney's name]
> Attorney for Cross-Plaintiff
> [address]
> [telephone number]

[Add certificate of service]

§ 2.42 Amended Pleadings

The first and cardinal rule of amended pleadings is to proofread, proofread, proofread! There is a great danger in omitting anything that was pled in the original complaint, thereby waiving your client's right to that particular cause of action. Conversely, the same danger in omitting items is inherent in the amendment of Answers.

Each state has its own rules regarding the times that amended pleadings are allowed. Some states allow pleadings to be amended right up to the time of trial, while others have strict time constraints during which amended pleadings may be filed.

Some jurisdictions allow amended pleadings to be filed without requesting leave of court. For those jurisdictions which require such a motion to the court before amendment is permitted, an example follows.

The reasons for amending a pleading are many and varied. Many times during discovery additional facts are uncovered which change the complexion of the case. This may result in the need for bringing other parties into the action, or the addition or deletion of causes of action. It is the duty of the attorney to bring such matters to the attention of the court as well as opposing parties in the case. (See **Forms 2–62** through **2–67**.)

The purpose of a motion to amend the pleadings is to allow the party to cure certain deficiencies or errors in the pleadings, ensuring that a claim will be considered on the merits and not barred by a technicality.

A motion to amend to add counterclaims should be granted where the motion is made in good faith, is timely, and will not prejudice the opposing party.

A pleading amended after the statute of limitations has run may "relate back" to the filing of the original complaint if the claim or defense in the amended pleading arose out of the conduct, transaction, or occurrence set forth in the original complaint. Under these circumstances, in federal court an amended pleading changing the party who is the target of the claim will relate back if, before the statute of limitations ran, the new party: (1) had such notice of the commencement of the action that his or her rights will not be prejudiced, and (2) knew or should have known that, but for a mistake concerning the identity of the proper party, the action would have been brought against the new party.

§ 2.43   —Motion to Disqualify Counsel

FORM 2–62
SAMPLE MOTION TO DISQUALIFY COUNSEL

NO. [case number]

[name]	)	IN THE DISTRICT COURT OF
	)	
Plaintiff	)	[county] COUNTY, [state]
	)	
vs.	)	[judicial district] JUDICIAL DISTRICT
	)	
[name]	)	
	)	
Defendant	)	

MOTION TO DISQUALIFY COUNSEL

TO THE HONORABLE JUDGE OF THIS COURT:

INITIATION OF THE SUIT

[Movant], [plaintiff/defendant] respectfully moves this Motion to Disqualify Opposing Counsel and in support of his motion would show the Court as follows;

I.

[Opposing counsel] formerly served as counsel to movant. Specifically, [opposing counsel] served as counsel to movant during the time frame of [date] to [date]. The matter in which [opposing counsel] represented movant is [the same or substantially related to the present matter in that . . .] (or in the alternative) [commonly related to the issues in the instant matter]. The nature of the former representation is more fully described in the affidavit of [affiant] attached hereto as Exhibit [number] and incorporated by reference herein.

II.

In the course of the representation of movant, [opposing counsel] obtained confidential information which [opposing counsel] could use to the disadvantage of movant in the current matter. Movant has not given consent, express or implied, to the disclosure or use of any information obtained in the course of the former representation, and objects to [opposing counsel] or any member of [his/her] firm serving in this matter.

WHEREFORE, PREMISES CONSIDERED, [plaintiff/defendant] prays that his matter be set for hearing and that on final hearing the court rule that [opposing counsel] and all other members of his firm are disqualified from serving as counsel in this matter, that no work product generated prior to this motion be made available to which movant may be justly entitled.

Respectfully submitted,

_____

[attorneys name]

[add certificate of service]

FORM 2–63
ORDER GRANTING MOTION FOR SUBSTITUTION OF COUNSEL

NO. _____

[PLAINTIFF(S) NAMES]	)	
Plaintiffs,	)	
	)	
	)	IN THE DISTRICT COURT OF
	)	
	)	_____ COUNTY,
	)	
v.	)	
	)	_____ JUDICIAL DISTRICT
[DEFENDANT(S) NAMES]	)	
Defendants.	)	

§ 2.43 MOTION TO DISQUALIFY COUNSEL

ORDER GRANTING MOTION FOR SUBSTITUTION OF COUNSEL

On the date signed below came on to be heard the Motion for Substitution of Counsel filed herein by the attorneys of record for Defendant, _____, in the above-numbered and entitled cause, and it appearing to the Court that such Motion should be granted; it is, therefore,

ORDERED, ADJUDGED, AND DECREED that _____ of the law firm of _____ be allowed to withdraw as the attorneys of record for Defendant, and that _____, _____, and _____ and the law firm of _____ be substituted in as attorneys of record for all purposes and in all phases of litigation in the above-entitled and numbered cause.

Signed this the _____ day of _____, 20___.

JUDGE PRESIDING

FORM 2-64
MOTION FOR SUBSTITUTION OF COUNSEL

NO. _____

[PLAINTIFF(S) NAMES]	)	
Plaintiffs,	)	
	)	
	)	IN THE DISTRICT COURT OF
	)	
	)	_____ COUNTY,
_____	)	
v.	)	
	)	_____ JUDICIAL DISTRICT
[DEFENDANT(S) NAMES]	)	
Defendants.	)	

MOTION FOR SUBSTITUTION OF COUNSEL

TO THE HONORABLE JUDGE OF SAID COURT:

Comes now _____, Defendant in the above entitled and numbered cause, and respectfully moves the Court to substitute _____, _____, and _____ of the law firm of _____, as his attorney of record and to withdraw _____ of the law firm of _____.

169

INITIATION OF THE SUIT

Our attorneys would show the Court that no undue delay or prejudice will result by the said substitution of attorneys.

Respectfully submitted,

NAME OF FIRM

_____

Name of Atty
Atty's Bar #
Address
City, State, Zip
Phone #

CERTIFICATE OF SERVICE

I hereby certify that a true and correct copy of the foregoing MOTION FOR SUBSTITUTION OF COUNSEL was forwarded to all counsel of record by CERTIFIED MAIL/RETURN RECEIPT REQUESTED in compliance with Rules _____ and _____ of the _____ Rules of Civil Procedure on the _____ day of _____, 20___.

_____

FORM 2–65
MOTION AND ORDER TO WITHDRAW AS COUNSEL

NO. _____

[PLAINTIFF(S) NAMES]	)	
Plaintiffs,	)	
	)	
	)	IN THE DISTRICT COURT OF
	)	
	)	_____ COUNTY,
	)	
_____	)	
	)	
v.	)	
	)	_____ JUDICIAL DISTRICT
[DEFENDANT(S) NAMES]	)	
Defendants.	)	

MOTION AND ORDER TO WITHDRAW AS COUNSEL

TO THE HONORABLE JUDGE OF SAID COURT:

COMES NOW _____, attorney of record for defendant, _____, and moves the court for an order granting her leave to withdraw

170

as attorney for said defendant, _____. This motion is made pursuant to Rule _____ of the _____ Rules of Civil Procedure and on the grounds and for the reasons that _____ has dismissed and terminated the undersigned as his attorney and has requested that the undersigned withdraw as his attorney of record.

DATED this _____ day of _____, 20___.

Respectfully submitted,

NAME OF FIRM

_____
Name of Atty
Atty's Bar #
Address
City, State, Zip
Phone #

CERTIFICATE OF SERVICE

I hereby certify that a true and correct copy of the above and foregoing document has been forwarded to all counsel of record by facsimile and/or certified mail/R.R.R. on this _____ day of _____, 20___.

_____

ORDER

Having read the above motion and being otherwise advised in the law and the premises,

IT IS HEREBY ORDERED, ADJUDGED, AND DECREED that said motion is in all respects granted.

IT IS FURTHER ORDERED that defendant, _____, appoint another to appear, or appear in person by filing a written notice with the Court stating how he will represent himself, within twenty (20) days from the date of this order.

DATED this _____ day of _____, 20___.

_____
Judge Presiding

§ 2.44 —Motion for Leave to File

FORM 2–66
SAMPLE MOTION FOR LEAVE TO FILE

NO. [case number]

[name],	)	IN THE DISTRICT COURT OF
	)	
Plaintiff,	)	[county] COUNTY,
	)	
vs.	)	[state]
	)	
[name]	)	[judicial district] JUDICIAL DISTRICT
	)	
Defendant	)	

MOTION FOR LEAVE TO FILE

TO THE HONORABLE JUDGE OF SAID COURT:

COME(S) NOW [name], (one of the) (cross-)defendant(s) in the above cause, to file this motion for leave to file [specify pleading/amendment], and respectfully show(s) to the Court the following:

I.

[State what pleadings you are requesting leave to file, for example, late answer to requests for admission, amended answer, or supplemental answers to interrogatories.] A copy of said [pleading/amendment] is attached hereto and is incorporated herein for all purposes.

II.

[State reasons that justify leave to file.]

WHEREFORE PREMISES CONSIDERED, [name], (cross-)defendant(s) herein, pray(s) that this motion for leave to file be granted and that the Court award all other and further relief to which (cross-defendant(s) (is are) entitled.

[name of law firm]

By: _____
[attorney name]
[state bar no.]
[firm address]
[counsel for (cross-)defendant(s)]

§ 2.45   MOTION FOR THIRD-PARTY PETITION

STATE OF [state]   )
)
COUNTY OF [county]   )

BEFORE ME, the undersigned authority, on this day personally appeared [name], known by me to be the person whose name is subscribed below, who, having first been duly sworn, stated under oath that [he/she] is attorney of record for [name], (cross-)defendant(s) in the above cause, and is, therefore, entitled to make this affidavit; and that the statements and allegations in said motion are true and correct (according to [his/her] personal knowledge).

_____
[attorney name]

SUBSCRIBED AND SWORN TO before me on the [date] day of [month] [20__].

[name of notary public]
Notary Public in and for
The State of [state]

[Add certificate of service.]

§ 2.45   —Motion for Leave to File Third-Party Petition

FORM 2–67
SAMPLE MOTION FOR LEAVE TO FILE THIRD-PARTY PETITION

NO. [case number]

[name]	)	IN THE DISTRICT COURT OF
	)	
Plaintiff,	)	[county] COUNTY,
	)	
vs.	)	[state]
	)	
[name]	)	[judicial district] JUDICIAL DISTRICT
	)	
Defendant.	)	

MOTION FOR LEAVE TO FILE THIRD-PARTY PETITION

TO THE HONORABLE JUDGE OF SAID COURT:

COME(S) NOW [name], (one of the) (cross-)defendant(s) in the above cause, to file this Motion for Leave to File Cross-action against [name], hereinafter called third-party defendant(s), and respectfully show(s) to the Court the following:

INITIATION OF THE SUIT

I.

In this case the (cross-)plaintiff(s) allege(s) that [state nature of case].

II.

Attached as an exhibit hereto is a true copy of the proposed cross-action against third-party defendant(s). Third-party defendant(s) [is/are] alleged to be liable on the following grounds: [state liability grounds].

III.

The proposed cross-action against third-party defendant(s) will not unduly delay the trial or progress of this case and is not submitted for that purpose. Instead, said cross-action is proposed for the purpose of bringing all parties before this Court in one action rather than having these matters adjudicated in separate suits, which will have the effect of saving judicial time and resources.

WHEREFORE, PREMISES CONSIDERED, [name], (cross-)defendant(s), herein, respectfully pray(s) that the Court grant this motion in all respects and award all other and further relief to which (cross-)defendant(s) (is are) entitled.

[name]

By: [attorney name]
[state bar no.]
[firm address]
Counsel for (Cross-)Defendant(s)

FIAT

On this the [date] day of [month], [20__], at request of the (cross-)defendant(s), the Court set the above motion to be heard at [time] [A.M./P.M.] on the [date] day of [month], 20__.

[name]
JUDGE PRESIDING

[Add certificate of service]

§ 2.46 Motion for Severance

Motions for severance (**Form 2–68**) are not generally looked upon with favor by the court unless the motion is absolutely necessary to protect the rights of a party, avoid prejudice against a party, or to ease the disposition of the lawsuit. The party requesting the severance must be able to show that the original cause included an action which was improperly joined under the Rules of Civil Procedure, that if the cause is not severed, it will result in undue hardship or expense to the movant, or that the nonseverance of the action would unnecessarily confuse the jury.

Severance does not relate to issues, but rather to causes of action, and an order for severance **(Form 2–69)** demands that the original action be divided into two or more separately docket numbered actions, each with its own independent judgment. Severance differs from separate trials in that separate trials can be had on separate issues of a cause of action without those issues being severed, the result of which is one final judgment.

FORM 2–68
SAMPLE MOTION FOR SEVERANCE

NO. [case number]

[name]		)	IN THE DISTRICT COURT OF
		)	
	Plaintiff	)	[county] COUNTY [state]
		)	
vs.		)	[judicial district] JUDICIAL DISTRICT
		)	
[name]		)	
		)	
	Defendant	)	

MOTION FOR SEVERANCE

TO THE HONORABLE JUDGE OF SAID COURT:

COMES NOW, [name], [plaintiff/defendant] in the above-entitled action, and respect-fully requests the Court to sever the following claim [specify cause of action], making it the subject o fa separate action, and in support thereof, would show the Court as follows:

I.

The above-named and numbered cause primarily relates to [describe cause of action] and the claim of [name] relates to [describe cause of action] and comprises a complete cause of action in and of itself and can stand alone as a separate lawsuit.

II.

(The claim of [name] against [name] relating to [describe cause of action] is improperly joined in this action in that [describe any circumstance which directly supports the argument for severance, such as the fact that the claims involve different parties and do not arise out of the same transaction or occurrence, or the fact that each claim is uniquely diverse in question of law of fact].)

(It would be prejudicial and cause undue hardship, expense, and delay to movant to require movant to participate in a trial of all claims joined in this action in that _____

INITIATION OF THE SUIT

[describe circumstances, such as the fact that the movant is ready to go to trial on the claims relating to movant and the other parties are not prepared to proceed at this time]. Accordingly, the trial on the merits of the movant's claim will be delayed for a period of [number] days unless severance is ordered. Said delay would be prejudicial to movant because [describe ramifications].)

WHEREFORE, PREMISES CONSIDERED, [name] [plaintiff/defendant] requests that this Court order that the cause between [name] and [name] relating to [describe cause of action] be severed, made the subject of a separate suit, and assigned its own docket number on the docket of this Court, and make such other orders as the Court deems fair and just.

Respectfully submitted,

[attorney name]
[address]
[telephone number]
[Add certificate of service]

FORM 2–69
SAMPLE ORDER FOR SEVERANCE OF ACTIONS

NO. [case number]

[name]		)	IN THE DISTRICT COURT OF
		)	
	Plaintiff	)	[county] COUNTY [state]
		)	
vs.		)	[judicial district] JUDICIAL DISTRICT
		)	
[name]		)	
		)	
	Defendant	)	

ORDER FOR SEVERANCE OF ACTIONS

On the [date] day of [month], 20__, came on to be considered plaintiff's motion for severance in the above-entitled and numbered cause. The Court, being satisfied that due notice of the filing of such motion and of the hearing thereon was given, and after considering the pleadings and arguments of counsel, is of the opinion that such motion should be granted.

IT IS, THEREFORE, ORDERED , DECREED AND ADJUDGED that the cause of action asserted by [name], [plaintiff/defendant] against [name], [plaintiff/defendant] and relating to [described cause of action] be, and the same hereby is severed from this action and made the subject of a separate action, and that it proceed as such to final judgment or other disposition in this Court under the style of [name] vs. [name] and bear docket number [docket number].

§ 2.44A MOTION TO APPEAR PRO HAC VICE

IT IS FURTHER ORDERED, ADJUDGED AND DECREED that separate judgments be entered in the severed causes, each judgment to be final and to dispose completely of all of the issues between all parties in the respective suits.

SIGNED this [date] day of [month] [20__].

_____

Judge Presiding

§ 2.47 Pleading Verification Checklist

1. Answer
2. Cross-Complaint
3. Preliminary Injunction
4. Answers to Interrogatories
5. All petitions, including, but not limited to;
   a. Petition for Writ of Mandate
   b. Petition for Claim to Escheated Property
   c. Petition for Writ of Review
   d. Petition for Writ of Prohibition
6. Actions filed to establish title
7. Action regarding adverse possession

§ 2.48 Motion to Appear Pro Hac Vice

FORM 2-50
MOTION TO APPEAR PRO HAC VICE

UNITED STATES DISTRICT COURT
DISTRICT OF _____

[PLAINTIFF(S) NAMES]	)	
Plaintiffs,	)	
	)	
	)	CASE NO: _____
	)	
	)	
	)	
v.	)	
	)	
[DEFENDANT(S) NAMES]	)	
Defendants.	)	

INITIATION OF THE SUIT

MOTION TO APPEAR PRO HAC VICE

COMES NOW, the attorney for the _____ [Plaintiff/Defendant] _____, _____ [Names of Attorneys] _____ and respectfully requests that the Court allow counsel to appear pro hac vice in this proceeding only to represent the interests of the _____.

Dated this _____ day of _____, 20____.

Respectfully submitted,

NAME OF FIRM

_____

Name of Atty
Atty's Bar #
Address
City, State, Zip
Phone #

FORM 2–71
MOTION FOR ADMISSION PRO HAC VICE

NO. _____

[PLAINTIFF(S) NAMES]	)	
Plaintiffs,	)	
	)	
	)	IN THE DISTRICT COURT OF
	)	
	)	_____ COUNTY,
	)	
_____	)	
	)	
v.	)	
	)	_____ JUDICIAL DISTRICT
[DEFENDANT(S) NAMES]	)	
Defendants.	)	

MOTION FOR ADMISSION PRO HAC VICE

_____, of the firm _____, moves the court pursuant to _____, to admit him to practice before this court solely for the purpose of appearing as counsel in the above-styled case, and shows the court:

1. The following is a list of all courts in which I am authorized to practice law:

[list courts]

2. _____, an active member of the _____ Bar Association and a resident of the State of _____, whose address is stated below, and who has previously entered his appearance in this action, is associated with me as counsel for party in this action.

OR

2. I am a regularly admitted practicing attorney in the courts of record of the state of _____, which by _____ does not require as a condition to the appearance of an _____ attorney representing his client in the courts of _____, the association with him of an attorney resident of and duly admitted to practice in the courts of that state.

> Respectfully submitted,
> NAME OF FIRM
>
> _____
>
> Name of Atty
> Atty's Bar #
> Address
> City, State, Zip
> Phone #

CERTIFICATE OF SERVICE

I hereby certify that a true and correct copy of the above and foregoing document has been forwarded to all counsel of record by facsimile and/or certified mail/R.R.R. on this ____ day of _____, 20___.

_____

§ 2.49   Practice Tips

This stage of a lawsuit is the most crucial as far as making sure that deadline dates are not overlooked. Every step possible should be taken to ensure that all documents are complete, in compliance with local civil rules of procedure, and that service of process is effected in the manner prescribed by law.

Learn the mechanics of initial pleadings early in your career and make them second nature. Become a self-made expert on jurisdiction and service of process. Your attorney will rely heavily on you for your knowledge in these fields.

Become familiar with the personnel in the courthouse who handle these matters for you and learn the workings and idiosyncracies of the system. Most importantly, stay abreast of changes in civil procedure and courthouse procedure. It is your job to refine the mechanics and see that the procedure runs like clockwork, just as it is up to your attorney to stay abreast of changes in statutes and judicial opinions.

CHAPTER 3

CALENDARING, DOCKET CONTROL, AND FILE MANAGEMENT

§ 3.1 Calendaring

Every law office must have a virtually foolproof way of dealing with the calendaring of meetings, depositions, trial and hearing dates, and due dates for documents. There are countless ways of dealing with the calendaring of dates. Some law offices will assign the opening of mail and calendaring of dates to one person in the firm who will keep the master calendar. In other firms, each attorney's individual secretary or paralegal will do the calendaring for him. Whichever the procedure in your firm, chances are that sometime in your career as a paralegal, you will be asked either to set up a procedure for calendaring or to be responsible for keeping one. **Sections 3.2** through **3.8** are devoted to informing you of different calendaring applications and how they work.

§ 3.2 Manual and Computerized Systems

For small law offices which do not have computer capabilities, manual calendaring systems can be just as effective if foolproof systems for entering dates are instituted and enforced. The safest way of doing this is to appoint one person to handle the procedure and to educate the rest of the firm on the importance of cooperation in seeing that nothing slips through the system and that all entries are correct.

All documents coming into the office must be checked for response dates or dates requiring the attorney's attendance. Someone familiar with the state and federal rules of procedure should be designated to enter these dates onto a master calendar. The dates should then be brought to the attention of the attorney's secretary for entering on his personal calendar. The calendar can then be distributed in advance to all attorneys and posted in the coffee room where all personnel will view the calendar at least once a day. Any changes should be posted immediately and distributed to all personnel.

Computerized calendaring systems take many different forms. A manual calendar could easily be kept and updated on a standard word processing format and printed out, distributed, and posted. Ready-made software programs are available for most computer systems for standard legal calendars. Check to see what software is compatible with your computer system and compare the software packages available. Many are or can be preprogrammed to automatically calculate response dates according to the proper rule of civil procedure and to automatically calendar appropriate reminders prior to the deadline. Printouts can be obtained and disseminated on a daily, weekly, or monthly basis for each individual attorney or for the entire firm.

§ 3.3   Document Feed for Master Calendar

No calendar system, be it manual or computerized, will work if there is a breach in the manner that information reaches the person responsible for its maintenance. The best way to ensure the system's continued accuracy is to institute a policy whereby all incoming documents, whether delivered by mail, messenger, or express service, must first go through the person responsible for the master calendar. This procedure will delay the distribution of the document by only a few minutes and is invaluable in making sure that everything is properly calendared.

There will be exceptions to the flow of documents in every office, and it is vital that the documents are dealt with in such a fashion that they are routinely incorporated into the calendar system. For example, many times attorneys will bring documents into the office that they have acquired in court or in meetings with other attorneys. These documents should be immediately routed through the calendar system. Both the attorneys and secretaries should cooperate in seeing that all such stray documents find their way to the master calendar as soon as their presence in the office is discovered.

One other way in which deadline dates enter the office is over the telephone. Many times dates or schedules are changed in telephone conversations. Each attorney and paralegal should be supplied with a pad of Docket Memos (see **Form 3–1**) which can be filled out with the newly acquired information and routed through the master calendar. (Note: Docket is a term which is used interchangeably with calendar in legal circles. A docket can also refer to a judge's calendar. A docket sheet is a record of all pleadings filed in a case.)

FORM 3–1
SAMPLE DOCKET MEMO

Case Name _____

Client/Matter # _____

Attorney _____

Date _____

Deposition of _____

is set for _____

The following extension was granted/received: _____

_____

_____

Other changes, additions and deletions: _____

_____

_____

§ 3.4   Statute of Limitations

Often when a new case comes into the firm, a period of time may elapse before a suit is actually filed. You should research the deadline date for the barring of the filing of the action under the appropriate statute of limitations and enter the date in a prominent place in the file. The date should also be entered in the master calendar system with reminders at appropriate intervals preceding the onset of the deadline. The bar dates for statutes of limitation can often be serveral years into the future and can be easily overlooked, with deadly results. It is grounds for legal malpractice to neglect to file a client's suit before the bar date of the statute of limitations.

§ 3.5   Pleading Response Dates

If you regularly deal with litigation from several jurisdictions, you may want to develop a chart such as the one in **Table 3–1** for easy reference regarding deadline and response dates in each jurisdiction. Be sure to consult local rules for any modification to the chart, and update the chart when changes are made in the Rules of Civil Procedure for that jurisdiction.

§ 3.6   Deadline Reminder Dates

Most attorneys have personal preferences regarding how long before a deadline date they would like to receive a reminder. Discussions should be held and routine schedules of reminder dates instituted into the calendar system. For example, an attorney may wish to receive reminders one month, two weeks, one week, two days, and the day prior to the occurrence of the deadline. Another attorney may only wish to be reminded two days prior to the occurrence. The personal preferences should be noted and observed so that the attorney does not receive so much information that he becomes frustrated and begins to ignore all the printouts of the system.

§ 3.7   Sample Calendars

Forms 3–2 and **3–3** are two samples of calendar printouts which are distributed in a law firm. **Form 3–2** illustrates a weekly deadline notice for an attorney; **Form 3–3** illustrates a daily deadline notice for a paralegal.

Table 3–1
Response Dates

DOCUMENT	TEXAS STATE	LOUISIANA STATE	FEDERAL
Answer	First Monday after 20 days from date of service of petition	15 days from date of service of petition 30 days if served pursuant to Long-Arm (L.A. Rev. Stat. Ann. § 13:3205)	20 days from date of service of complaint
Jury Demand	Any time prior to trial	Within 10 days of service of last pleading direct to issue triable by jury	Within 10 days of answer
Amended Pleadings	Any time until 7 days prior to trial	Plaintiff, anytime before answer. Defendant, within 10 days of service of answer. Otherwise by leave of court.	By leave of court
Interrogatories	30 days	Answer within 15 days or within 30 days of service of petition	30 days
Request for Admissions	30 days	Answer within 15 days	30 days
Request for Production	30 days	Response within 15 days or within 30 days of service of petition	30 days
Hearing Dates	By agreement or court order (5 days prior to date)		By agreement or court order (5 days prior to date)
Appeal	30 days from judgment or from court's refusal for new trial	In general, if an appeal does not suspend the effect or the execution of an appealable order or judgment, 90 days from expiration of delay for applying for new trial or from court's refusal of new trial. If an appeal suspends the effect or the execution of an appealable order or judgment, 15 days from expiration of delay for applying for new trial or from court's refusal of new trial. There are specific periods to appeal from certain types of judgments, e.g., 30 days to appeal from a judgment of divorce.	30 days from entry of judgment order
Depositions	Reasonable notice	15 days after service of process on reasonable notice	Reasonable notice
Motions	10 days		10 days
Motion for New Trial	30 days from entry of judgment	7 clear days from signing of judgment	10 days from entry of judgment

CALENDARING/DOCKET CONTROL/FILE MANAGEMENT

FORM 3–2
SAMPLE WEKLY DEADLINE NOTICE (ATTORNEY)

Weekly Notice of Deadlines for Atty. Robert Wood

Critical Date	Event	Plaintiff	Defendant	File #
11/10/__	Deposition (10:00)	Margaret Hill	Doug Rose	Hill-42
11/10/__	Meeting w/ Client (3:00)	Carl Thompson	Steve Sykes	Thom-24
11/11/__	Answer Due to Us	Monica Brown	Henry Morgan	Brow-13
11/11/__	Response to Request for Production of Documents Due	Lester Wright	Haverly Bros.	Wri-17
11/12/__	Trial	Cory Anderson	Guy Smith	And-4
11/13/__	Trial	Cory Anderson	Guy Smith	And-4
11/14/__	Accident Reconstruction (11:00)	Lester Wright	Haverly Bros.	Wri-17

FORM 3–3
SAMPLE DAILY DEADLINE NOTICE (PARALEGAL)

Daily Notice of Deadlines for Paralegal Natalie Wagner

Critical Date	Event	Plaintiff	Defendant	File #
11/10/__	Deposition (10:00)	Margaret Hill	Doug Rose	Hill-42
11/10/__	Meeting w/ Client (3:00)	Carl Thompson	Steve Sykes	Thom-24
11/10/__	Follow-up Medical Records	Monica Brown	Henry Morgan	Brow-13
11/10/__	Draft of Petition Due	Scott Simpson	Gary Reyes	Simp-05
11/10/__	Venue Research Due	Carla Dysart	Michael Orr	Dys-01
11/10/__	Paralegal Assn. Dinner (7:00)			

§ 3.8   Docket Control

Docket control not only encompasses the calendaring of response dates, dead-lines, and physical appearances, but also the maintenance and organization of pleadings in the file. As part of the master calendar system, all incoming pleadings should be stamped with the date received and logged onto that file's docket sheet or pleading log. It is essential to have a fail-safe record of received documents to which to refer when questions arise as to whether a document ever reached your office.

Docket control is a multilevel area of responsibility and will only work properly when checks and balances and follow-up systems are implemented. **Sections 3.9** through **3.14** are directed toward the design of those systems and their integration into your overall office procedure.

§ 3.9   Checks and Balances

Keeping a pleading log of incoming documents (see **Form 3–4**) is a good foundation on which to build a system of checks and balances. Sometimes a document does not find its way into the pleading board right away and may become temporarily misplaced; when this happens, the pleading log will serve as proof that the document was received and duly noted. Likewise, the pleading log can serve as proof that a document was never received by your office. This log can augment an argument in court when it is alleged that your office was served with a particular document.

The distribution of the master calendar is an automatic check and balance. The more law office personnel who see the master calendar daily, the better the system will work to prevent oversights and errors. Any corrections to the master calendar should be immediately noted on docket memos and routed through the master calendar system.

One person in the firm should be appointed to follow up on the date that deadlines occur to ensure that they are met on that day. This responsibility could also be delegated to the individual paralegal responsible for that file.

§ 3.10   Sample Pleading Log

FORM 3–4
SAMPLE PLEADING LOG

IN THE UNITED STATES [court designation] COURT
[judicial district] DISTRICT
[judicial division] DIVISION

[name]	)	
	)	
Plaintiff,	)	
	)	
vs.	)	No. [case number]
	)	
[name]	)	
	)	
Defendant.	)	

PLEADING LOG

NAME OF DOCUMENT	DATE FILED	DATE REC'D

1. _____   _____   _____

2. _____   _____   _____

3. _____   _____   _____

4. _____   _____   _____

5. _____   _____   _____

6. _____   _____   _____

7. _____   _____   _____

8. _____   _____   _____

    _____

9. _____   _____   _____

    _____

10. _____   _____   _____

    _____

§ 3.11   Tickler Systems

The distribution of weekly and monthly master calendars is an automatic tickler, or reminder, system in and of itself. There are, however, other ways of accomplishing or augmenting this procedure. Some attorneys prefer the use of a card file, or come-up, system. When a document comes into the office, it is logged in and any response date entered into the master calendar system. The name of the document and the response date are then written on several index cards and filed in an index file behind the respective months and days on which you wish to receive a reminder that some action is due. There is no limit to the number of reminder dates under which these cards can be filed. Every day the cards filed under that day's date are pulled and distributed to the responsible attorney or paralegal. The tickler note card, along with the file, can then be placed on the attorney's desk for action.

Another tickler system has copies of the actual document requiring action placed in a full-sized file containing dividers numbered by months and years. In this system, also, the file is checked daily for action requirements.

§ 3.12   Follow-Up Systems

No matter what method is devised for calendar and docket control, its effectiveness is compromised without follow-up systems. Firstly, pleading boards should routinely be compared to the pleading logs to make sure that the pleading boards are complete and up-to-date. Periodic checks of this nature will help eliminate emergency situations arising later when it is suddenly realized that a pleading cannot be located.

Secondly, documents should not be allowed to be filed in the pleading boards without the date received stamp of the master calendar system. This will help ensure that all response and deadline dates have been entered into the system and will appear on the master calendar in due course.

Thirdly, all personnel should be educated to cooperate in making sure that deadlines are met. If a master calendar is posted, for example, the person having performed the necessary action should make that notation on the calendar with the date the action was performed, and his respective initials. This will eliminate the need for time to be spent by someone tracking down the file or the person responsible for the file to make sure that the action was performed within its time limit.

§ 3.13   Docket Checklist

Form 3–5 is a handy one to keep in the front of the file for in-house docket control. You may want to keep duplicates of these forms in one centralized place, such as a notebook or on computer.

FORM 3–5
SAMPLE DOCKET CHECKLIST

No. [case number]

[name]	)	IN THE DISTRICT COURT OF
	)	
Plaintiff,	)	
	)	
vs.	)	[county] COUNTY, [state]
	)	
[name]	)	[judicial district] JUDICIALDISTRICT
	)	
Defendant.	)	

Client Name _____

Client Address _____

Client Phone _____   File No. _____

Attorney Assigned _____   Paralegal Assigned _____

Opposing Counsel _____

   Address _____

   _____

   Phone _____

Date Petition Filed _____

§ 3.13 DOCKET CHECKLIST

Date Served _____

Date Answer Due _____

Date Answered _____

Investigation Materials Received from Client _____

_____

Plaintiff's Interrogatories _____

    Date Served _____

    Date Answer Due _____

    Date Answered _____

Plaintiff's Request for Production _____

    Date Served _____

    Date Answer Due _____

    Date Answered _____

Plaintiff's Request for Admissions _____

    Date Served _____

    Date Answer Due _____

    Date Answered _____

Defendant's Interrogatories _____

    Date Served _____

    Date Answer Due _____

    Date Answered _____

Defendant's Request for Production _____

    Date Served _____

    Date Answer Due _____

    Date Answered _____

Defendant's Request for Admissions _____

CALENDARING/DOCKET CONTROL/FILE MANAGEMENT

Date Served _____

Date Answer Due _____

Date Answered _____

Medical Records Ordered

	Doctor or Hospital	Date Ordered	Date Received
1.	_____	_____	_____
2.	_____	_____	_____
3.	_____	_____	_____
4.	_____	_____	_____
5.	_____	_____	_____
6.	_____	_____	_____
7.	_____	_____	_____
8.	_____	_____	_____
9.	_____	_____	_____
10.	_____	_____	_____

Employment Records Ordered

	Employer	Date Ordered	Date Received
1.	_____	_____	_____
2.	_____	_____	_____

Depositions:

	Witness	Date Scheduled	Date Taken
1.	_____	_____	_____
2.	_____	_____	_____
3.	_____	_____	_____
4.	_____	_____	_____
5.	_____	_____	_____

6. _____   _____   _____

7. _____   _____   _____

8. _____   _____   _____

Discovery Deadline _____

Date Filed _____

Trial Date _____

Trial Book Complete _____

Trial Exhibits Complete _____

Deadline to Amend Pleadings _____

Deadline to File Medical Records _____

Deadline to Designate Expert Witnesses _____

§ 3.14 Docket Chart

Form 3–6 is a chart that I designed to keep track of documents and dates in a situation in which the client was self-insured, and we had the same types of cases coming in day after day. Because many cases were active at the same time, the chart was useful in determining the status of individual cases at a glance. I placed an enlarged version of this chart on the wall in my office and put a clear plastic overlay on the top which allowed me to write on it with erasable markers.

§ 3.15 File Management

File Management is an important function of the paralegal. Attorneys seem to have instant recall for an obscure line in a 400 page document, but invariably, they cannot remember where the document is. It is essential that files be maintained in a logical manner which lends itself to legal thinking. You must have the ability to determine whether correspondence should be separated from its attachment in the file, or if it makes more sense to leave everything together as a unit. Files should be set out with descriptive headings which make it easy to analyze the contents at a glance.

Files should be maintained on a daily basis, so as to avoid plowing through a mountain of documents to locate what your attorney needs at that moment. Daily upkeep also reduces the chances of statutory dates slipping by unnoticed which could result in sanctions against your client or dismissal of his claim. Organization is the single most effective way of running a case efficiently and without error or

FORM 3-6
SAMPLE DOCKET CHART

MATTER	RESP ATTY	CAUSE NO.	ANSWR	DATE DUE OF RESPONSE TO PLAINTIFFS:			DATE DUE OF RESPONSE TO DEFENDANTS			DESGNT WTNSS	FILE MED RCRDS	AMEND PLDNGS	DEADLINES: PRE-TRIAL ORDER DUE	TRIAL DATE
				INTRG	REQ/ PROD	REQ/ ADMS	INTRG	REQ/ PROD	REQ/ ADMS					

omission. It is also helpful if every file is set up in the same manner, so that the attorney will be able to lay his hands on needed documents when you are not in the office. A few moments of efficiency can save you hours of overtime. (The File Management Checklist in **Form 3–7** can help manage each file.)

§ 3.16   File Management Checklist

FORM 3–7
SAMPLE FILE MANAGEMENT CHECKLIST

NO. [case number]

[name]	)	IN THE DISTRICT COURT OF
	)	
Plaintiff	)	[county] COUNTY, [state]
	)	
vs.	)	[judicial district] JUDICIAL DISTRICT
	)	
[name]	)	
	)	
Defendant	)	

1. Plaintiff Counsel _____

    Address _____

    Phone Number _____

2. Defendant Counsel _____

    Address _____

    Phone Number _____

3. Judge _____

    Court Clerk _____

    Phone Number _____

4. Type of Case _____

5. Case Facts Summary _____

    _____

    _____

CALENDARING/DOCKET CONTROL/FILE MANAGEMENT

6. Filing Date of Suit _____

7. Answer Due Date _____

8. Trial Date _____

9. Names of Parties

   Plaintiff _____

   Defendant _____

10. Venue Questions

    Plaintiff's Residence _____

    Accident Location _____

    Accident Date _____

11. Motion to Transfer Venue _____

    Affidavits _____

    Brief Filed _____

    Hearing Date _____

    Order Signed _____

12. Pleading _____

    Dollar Amount of Damages Sought _____

    Answer File Date _____

    Counterclaims _____

    Cross-Claims _____

    Third-Party Actions _____

13. Motions

    Name of Motion _____

    Name of Movant _____

    Date Filed _____

    Date Response Due _____

    Hearing Date _____

§ 3.16 FILE MANAGEMENT CHECKLIST

Order Signed _____

Name of Motion _____

Name of Movant _____

Date Filed _____

Date Response Due _____

Hearing Date _____

Order Signed _____

Name of Motion _____

Name of Movant _____

Date Filed _____

Date Response Due _____

Hearing Date _____

Order Signed _____

Name of Motion _____

Name of Movant _____

Date Filed _____

Date Response Due _____

Hearing Date _____

Order Signed _____

14. Interrogatories

Plaintiff or Defendant _____

Date Served _____

Information Required _____

Answered _____

Supplemented _____

15. Admissions

Plaintiff or Defendant _____

CALENDARING/DOCKET CONTROL/FILE MANAGEMENT

Date Served _____

Information Required _____

_____

_____

Answered _____

Supplemented _____

16. Request for Production of Documents

Plaintiff or Defendant _____

Date Served _____

Information Required _____

_____

_____

Answered _____

Supplemented _____

17. Names of Witnesses to be Deposed

_____

_____

18. Plaintiff's Exhibits

_____

_____

_____

_____

_____

19. Defendant's Exhibits

_____

_____

§ 3.16   FILE MANAGEMENT CHECKLIST

_____

_____

_____

20. Liability Opinion _____

21. Comparative Negligence Projected Percentage to Plaintiff _____

22. Comparative Negligence Projected Percentage to Defendant _____

23. Damages

   Plaintiff's Date of Birth _____

   Family History _____

   Education _____

   Age at Date of Accident _____

   Nature of Plaintiff's Injuries _____

   Nature and Extent of Treatment _____

   Prognosis _____

   Life Expectancy _____

   Work-Life Expectancy _____

   Earnings History _____

   Projected Future Economic Losses _____

   Incapacitating Disability? _____

   Medical History _____

   Projected Future Medical Costs _____

   Pain and Suffering Damages Claimed _____

   Future Pain and Suffering _____

   Plaintiff's Demand _____

24. Projected Jury Verdict Award _____

25. Settlement officers _____

   Date _____

Amount _____

Result _____

26. Motions in Limine _____

27. Desired Juror Profile _____

_____

_____

28. Special Jury Instructions

_____

_____

_____

_____

_____

_____

_____

§ 3.17 Procedure for Creation of Litigation Files; Checklist of Contents

To maximize opportunities for recovery in personal injury litigation, the paralegal should organize a file system so as to efficiently store and retrieve documents, pleadings, witness statements, and other evidence as they accumulate during the course of investigation and litigation. The file system should also enable the litigator to:

- Monitor the progress of the investigation
- Enhance his/her ability to analyze the case at any time during the course of litigation
- Enable the litigator to prepare confidently for trial
- Permit the litigator to gain ready access to any document or piece of evidence during trial
- Provide a means whereby secretaries and other legal assistants can gain access to relevant documents without risking the loss of important evidence or the duplication of effort

§ 3.17   CREATING LITIGATION FILES

Note: An organized file system in litigation is also essential as a means of calendaring the statutes of limitations, crucial court and discovery dates, and for scheduling witness interviews and other stages of the investigation.

Methods

The specific system the paralegal uses will depend upon the size of the case. The size and structure of the office or firm, including the number of people who need access to the files at any point in time, may also determine the type of file system.

A generally accepted method, adaptable to a wide variety of types and sizes of personal injury cases, is a system of accordion or expandable file folders. Each file folder contains a particular type of material (e.g., pleadings, depositions, etc.). The files may be color-coded and/or numbered for easy reference. Any file system should also contain an accessible index of all of the contents and their location. The file should also contain a calendar of important dates. This is in addition to any master calendaring system the office or firm may use to keep track of all of the cases in the office. The scheduling calendar should also generate reminders within an appropriate time before the date or deadline so that the attorney, assistant, or investigator can prepare for it.

Litigation now encompasses a broad variety of "advocacy" opportunities, including (in addition to trials) arbitrations, mediation, "mini" trials, trials before advisory juries, complex multi-day settlement conferences, etc. File maintenance, therefore, should be appropriate to the nature of the case, its complexity, and the probable manner in which it will be resolved. In some cases, for example, an intricate system with computerized file maintenance and document retrieval will be required.

Checklist of Contents

The contents of the file will depend on the nature of the particular case. The extent to which the paralegal cross-indexes the files also will depend on the case and the habits or desires of the responsible attorney. It is essential, however, to cross-index key evidence as it comes in as a prerequisite to efficient trial preparation. The following checklist is highly useful:

Pleadings.   These include the complaint and answer and any amended pleadings. This file may also include any pretrial orders of the court narrowing the issues for trial.

Motions.   Keep pretrial motions, briefs in support and opposition, and resulting court orders, in a separate file. These include motions to dismiss or for summary judgment, and, in a criminal case, demurrers to an indictment and motions to discover evidence.

Legal research.   The paralegal should retain the results of the research in the form of notes, internal memoranda, and annotated copies of important cases. The file may be further subdivided according to subject matter.

Attorney notes.   The paralegal should collect all notes about trial theories, credibility of witnesses, strength or weakness of certain evidence, voir dire strategies, possible grounds for objection to evidence, alternative means of proof, and early drafts of the opening statement and closing argument. A separate file with these notes avoids the possibility that during discovery attorney work-product may accidentally reach the hands of the adverse party.

Witnesses.   The witness files should contain interview notes, witness statements, and any deposition transcripts and summaries of depositions. For each witness, the list should contain the name; home and business addresses and phone numbers; whether or not the witness has been interviewed, a statement taken, a deposition taken or testimony given at a hearing; and whether or not a subpoena may be necessary to bring the witness to trial.

Correspondence.   The paralegal should organize correspondence chronologically or by subject matter, or both.

Documents.   Identify each of the issues to which the document is relevant, identify the source of the document, and outline the foundation testimony that will be necessary for its introduction, including the names of witnesses who can provide the foundation.

Physical evidence.   The paralegal may not be able to hold physical evidence in a file folder, but should find some means of keeping the evidence together in a secure place. (Security is particularly important if the physical condition of the evidence will be an issue at trial—for example, whether it has been tampered with or altered.) Keep the physical evidence or any reports or test results, such as police laboratory tests or reports written by consulting experts relating to the physical evidence, in a separate file.

Interrogatories and answers to requests for admissions.   Include the originals and the answers given or received. Cross-index these to other related evidence.

Discovery disputes.   Automobile accident litigation will often generate disputes over discovery. The file will include both counsel's and the adverse party's requests for discovery, as well as any motions to compel discovery or for protective orders brought by either side.

Things to do.   This is simply a file of reminders to schedule interviews, pursue lines of investigation, conduct research, draft letters, and the like. This may be combined with the calendar system so that reminders are generated at the appropriate time if there is a deadline, or periodically until a task is accomplished.

Calendar.   It is often useful to have a separate calendar of deadlines and relevant dates pertaining to the particular case. A glance at the calendar can help plan investigation and pretrial strategies. It also helps you to set aside time to analyze the case and begin to prepare for trial. This calendar is in addition to the office or firm master calendar containing relevant dates for all cases.

§ 3.18   Sample File Index

The following index in **Form 3–8** represents not only an index but also a logical order in which to organize the files.

FORM 3–8
SAMPLE FILE INDEX

File No. 1	Main File
	1.0 Index
	1.1 Correspondence
	1.2 Memoranda
	1.3 Attorneys' Notes
	1.4 Legal Research
	1.5 Drafts
	1.6 Newspaper Articles
	1.7 List of Players
File No. 2	Pleadings
File No. 3	Special Damages
File No. 4	Client Documents
File No. 5	Depositions and Hearing Transcripts
File No. 6	Document Productions
File No. 7	Medical Records
File No. 8	Witness Files
File No. 9	Exhibits

§ 3.19 Correspondence

Correspondence should be filed with the earliest date on the bottom of the file and the most recent correspondence on the top. According to your attorney's preference, it may or may not be necessary to prepare and maintain an index to the correspondence. This index should be kept on the left hand side of the file opposite the correspondence. Make sure that copies of all correspondence emanating from your office are included in this file so that a continuous and complete record is kept. (Many attorneys keep a reading file, which contains copies of all correspondence they send out on all files. Even though this is a duplication, the letters should always be filed additionally in each respective file.)

Begin and end correspondence files in a logical fashion. They may be separated by month, quarter, or year as they begin to become bulky. Avoid beginning a new file in the middle of the month. When a file is complete, the date of the correspondence contained within should be included on the label (for example, Correspondence—January 1, 20__ to June 30, 20__).

§ 3.20 Pleadings

Pleadings should be organized in a chronological fashion, with the earliest date on the bottom. The date of filing of the document, not the certificate of service date or the date of receipt of the document should be used for these purposes. This will give you an exact duplicate of the court's file, and will make it easier to determine at a later time if documents appear to be missing. The documents should be numbered and indexed with a copy of the index placed in the front of the file. You may find it helpful to write the number of the document in pencil in the lower right hand corner so that it may be easily replaced if it must be removed from the pleading board for any reason. Begin a new pleading board and label it accordingly when the prior pleading board begins to become too large to handle easily. Make sure that the index in the front of the pleading board contains the document number, name of the document, and the date on which it was filed.

§ 3.21 Legal Research

Your attorney may research several points of law in any given lawsuit. The case law on each point of law should be kept together in its own subfile and referenced in the index kept in the front of the legal research file. If research has been done on a subject which your firm encounters often, you may want to duplicate the research for a general staff research file. This will alleviate the attorney having to try to remember which case it was in which this point of law arose before. Consult your attorney to see if he prefers the legal memoranda to be filed in the legal research file with the case law or separately in the memoranda file.

§ 3.22 Memoranda

The memoranda file should be kept chronologically in the same fashion as the correspondence file. It may, or may not, need its own index. The contents of this file will consist of interoffice memoranda, and legal memoranda written to address separate issues as they arise in the lawsuit.

§ 3.23 Witness Files

A file should be constructed for every witness to the case and should consist of any documents which directly apply to that witness or his potential testimony, and any statements, affidavits, or sworn testimony by that witness in the case. Any information, including unrelated newspaper clippings, pertaining to that person may be helpful in preparation for trial.

In the case of expert witnesses, you may want to include testimony from previous cases in which he may have testified, especially if the expert witness is adverse to your cause and the testimony would be helpful in impeaching or discrediting him. You will also want to include biographical information and any literary credits the expert witness may have.

The contents of these files will be used later in the preparaton of trial notebooks and in preparing the case for trial. It is easier and more efficient to keep up these witness files as the case progresses than to wait until the rush for trial preparation begins.

§ 3.24 Special Damages

This file should consist of all receipts, bills, ledgers, and any and all listings of damages to your client, including medical property damages, wage loss and any other accounting of damages which apply. It is also a good idea to keep a current accounting of all legal fees and costs in this file. The attorney should be able to go to this file at a moment's notice and determine the current damages total. It is an especially helpful file for him to refer to when he is engaged in a telephone conversation with opposing counsel over settlement negotiations. Work closely with the client to keep the damages total up-to-date.

§ 3.25 Documents

The client's personal documents should be kept separate from the other documents collected during the course of the discovery process. Often the attorney is entrusted with the custody of irreplaceable original documents belonging to the client and the utmost care should be taken to preserve the authenticity of those documents.

Documents acquired through investigation and document productions should be indexed and kept together in a logical filing fashion to make document retrieval easy and efficient. These files are so important that an entire chapter (**Chapter 6**) later in the book has been devoted to their treatment.

§ 3.26   Practice Tips

Systems are a paralegal's best friend. It is impossible to store all the information a paralegal is responsible for in one person's memory bank. That's not to say that there are not paralegals out there who seem to have computerized databases for memories, but there are just too many important facts to entrust to the human mind. Paralegals who insist on doing this are also missing one other very important point: The whole object of being a paralegal is to assist the attorney in creating order out of chaos. It serves no useful purpose to create a system only one person can de-code.

Forms and Systems are created to enhance organizational capabilities and standardize access to information. Your ultimate goal should be to ensure that any person who needs to obtain information from one of your systems will be able to locate that information easily and quickly without your assistance. Some paralegals feel that easy accessibility somehow threatens their indispensability, when in reality, the ability to create and update these systems is an indispensable talent in and of itself. Keep common goals in mind and avoid the tendency to want to be the keeper of the keys. Your team effort is infinitely more valuable to a law firm that your independent knowledge of any one file.

CHAPTER 4

DISCOVERY

DISCOVERY

§ 4.1 Introduction

There are four types of discovery used in most lawsuits:

1. Interrogatories;
2. Requests for Production of Documents;
3. Requests for Admissions;
4. Depositions.

Each type of discovery has its own purpose which will be described in more detail in this chapter. All discovery, however, is designed to lead to relevant facts on which the attorney builds his case. The courts are generally very liberal in the application of the rules governing what is discoverable. Generally, anything reasonably calculated to lead to the discovery of admissible evidence is permitted.

Certain things are not discoverable even under a liberal application of the rules. Communications between attorney and client are privileged and, therefore, not discoverable. Documents prepared in anticipation of trial are not discoverable by the opposing party unless that party can demonstrate to the court that he cannot obtain the equivalent of the materials by other means without undue hardship and that he has a substantial need of the materials in the preparation of his case. In federal court, these limitations on discovery have not been eliminated by the new open-disclosure requirements of the Federal Rules of Civil Procedure.

Discovery should be a well-organized effort to obtain the information needed to substantiate your case in settlement or in court. Discovery should not be allowed to become disjointed or to lose direction; it is a valuable tool if you use it correctly. There is no doubt that cases are won and lost in the discovery process. In order to maintain a focus on the direction of discovery, the preparation of Interrogatories, Requests for Production of Documents, and Requests for Admissions should be carefully tailored to the circumstances of the individual case. Standard forms should be edited to remove any material which is not relevant, and relevant materials placed in their stead. Especially in jurisdictions where requests are limited, it is important not to waste them on irrelevant points.

Once responses have been received from the opposing party, they should be reviewed with a fine-toothed comb to ferret out facts, concepts, and theories which constitute further discovery and development. Develop and follow up on each one until it either proves to be irrelevant or incorrect, or it becomes a vital building block which strengthens your case. This is the time to use your additional discovery requests.

Depositions are the vital turning point in most cases. If your litigation team has done its job and prepared properly—developing every possible fact and theory and methodically discarding the irrelevant ones until the issues narrow naturally into a fluent direction—you will be in the driver's seat for settlement talks or trial.

§ 4.2 Discovery Checklist—Product Liability

____ 1. Prepare standard product liability interrogatories.

____ 2. Prepare special liability interrogatories.

____ 3. Prepare special damage interrogatories.

____ 4. Prepare standard contention interrogatories.

____ 5. Prepare standard consents and authorizations for medical records.

____ 6. Order medical records.

____ 7. Prepare standard consents and authorizations for IRS, income, and employment records, and order the records.

____ 8. Prepare standard requests for production of documents.

____ 9. Prepare standard requests for admissions.

____ 10. Calendar response dates.

____ 11. Research through NEXIS or library periodical index, all newspaper and periodical articles relating to the product or similar incidents. (Your opposition has already done this!)

____ 12. Research all warranties and representations, made or implied, regarding product.

____ 13. Arrange for independent lab testing of product.

____ 14. Find expert witness.

____ 15. Research applicable safety standards.

____ 16. Evaluate and summarize discovery responses.

____ 17. Summarize medical records.

____ 18. Prepare status report for client.

____ 19. Prepare deposition questions for any needed depositions.

____ 20. Determine witnesses.

____ 21. Interview witnesses.

____ 22. Summarize depositions.

____ 23. Prepare client or witness for deposition.

____ 24. Follow up on materials promised during deposition.

____ 25. Arrange for independent medical exam.

____ 26. Summarize employment and income records.

____ 27. Evaluate and summarize damages.

§ 4.3 —Commercial Litigation

____ 1. Prepare standard damage interrogatories.

____ 2. Prepare standard contention interrogatories.

____ 3. Prepare standard requests for production of documents.

____ 4. Prepare standard requests for admissions.
____ 5. Calendar response dates.
____ 6. Organize and index client documents.
____ 7. Evaluate and summarize client documents.
____ 8. Organize and index documents received in response to discovery requests.
____ 9. Evaluate and summarize discovery responses.
____ 10. Prepare status report for client.
____ 11. Prepare deposition questions for any needed depositions.
____ 12. Find expert witnesses.
____ 13. Determine witnesses.
____ 14. Interview witnesses.
____ 15. Summarize depositoins.
____ 16. Prepare client or witness for deposition.
____ 17. Follow up on materials promised during deposition.
____ 18. Evaluate and summarize damages.

§ 4.4 —Personal Injury

____ 1. Prepare standard personal injury interrogatories.
____ 2. Prepare special liability interrogatories.
____ 3. Prepare special damage interrogatories.
____ 4. Prepare standard contention interrogatories.
____ 5. Prepare standard consents and authorizations for medical records.
____ 6. Order medical records.
____ 7. Prepare standard consents and authorizations for I.R.S., income and employment records, and order the records.
____ 8. Prepare standard requests for production of documents.
____ 9. Prepare standard requests for admissions.
____ 10. Calendar response dates.
____ 11. Evaluate and summarize discovery responses.
____ 12. Summarize medical records.
____ 13. Prepare status report for client.
____ 14. Prepare deposition questions for any needed depositions.
____ 15. Determine witnesses.
____ 16. Interview witnesses.
____ 17. Summarize depositions.
____ 18. Prepare client or witness for deposition.
____ 19. Follow up on materials promised during deposition.

____ 20. Arrange for independent medical exam.

____ 21. Summarize employment and income records.

____ 22. Evaluate and summarize damages.

§ 4.5 Duty of Disclosure

The 1993–4 Federal Rules of Civil Procedure completely changed the way we conduct discovery, and therefore, the role and responsibilities of paralegals in civil litigation. Prior to the changes, the discovery phase was an adversarial process which required skillful implementation of a strategic investigation plan. Parties and their counsel were required to seek out relevant information, facts, witnesses, evidence, and documents possessed by the opposing side and use each wave of information obtained to develop the discovery strategy for the purpose of narrowing the issues and supporting their respective cases. The new mandatory disclosure required under Rule 26(a) of the Federal Rules of Civil Procedure is significant because much of the information formerly disclosed in the adversarial discovery process must now be freely given by both sides without the benefit of a formal request.

Failure to comply with mandatory disclosure is dealt with in Federal Rule of Civil Procedure 37(c)(1):

> A party that without substantial justificaiton fails to disclose information required by Rule 26(a) or 26(e)(1) shall not, unless such failure is harmless, be permitted to use as evidence at trial, at a hearing, or on a motion any witness or information not so disclosed. In addition to or in lieu of this sanction, the court, on motion and after affording an opportunity to be heard, may impose other appropriate sanctions.

As a result of the adoption of Rule 37(c)(1), Rule 11 sancitons no longer apply to compliance violations of Rule 26.

The individual states are beginning to follow the trend for mandatory disclosure. For example, Texas now has a multilevel discovery plan that must be addressed in the initial pleading. There are three levels of discovery, and the appropriate one must be chosen and inserted into the pleading. The levels pertain to the dollar amount and complexities of the cases and control the numbers of discovery requests able to be propounded and the discovery deadline dates of the case. This is a major departure from the traditional rules of civil procedure and discovery procedures.

The following table (**Table 4–1**) is a summary of the changes to Rule 26 of the Federal Rules of Civil Procedure. **Table 4–2** is a summary of the changes to the discovery timetable in Rule 26(a).

Many of the provisions of amended Rule 26 are not binding on the federal district courts. Under the amendments to Rule 26, the district courts may modify or refuse to adopt some of the provisions of the amended rule. In particular, a number of district courts have refused to put into place the mandatory disclosure provisions in amended Rule 26(a).

§ 4.5   DUTY OF DISCLOSURE

Table 4–1

Summary of Rule 26 Changes

26(a)(1): (Note: Any mandatory disclosure obligation deadline may be modified by stipulation, court order or local rule. Be sure to check your local District Court Rules.)	Requires a party to voluntarily disclose the following kinds of information "without awaiting a discovery request:"
	1) Identity, address, and phone number of each individual "likely to have discoverable information relevant to disputed facts alleged with particularity in the pleadings, identifying the subjects of the information."
	2) "A copy of or a . . . description . . . of, all documents, data compilations, and tangible things . . . relevant to disputed facts alleged with particularity in the pleadings."
	3) A computation of the damages and supporting documentation
	4) Indemnifying agreements or insurance agreements
26(a)(2) (Disclosures must be made at least 90 days prior to trial.)	Requires mandatory disclosure of any identifying information for any person who may be used as an expert witness at time of trial.
26(a)(2)(B) (Disclosures must be made at least 90 days prior to trial.)	Mandatory disclosure of expert witness reports including "a complete statement of all opinions to be expressed and the basis and reasons therefore . . . ." Expert qualifications and compensation are also to be disclosed.
26(a)(3) (Disclosure must be made at least 30 days prior to trial.)	Mandatory disclosure of evidence which may be used at trial "other than solely for impeachment purposes."
	Mandatory disclosure of trial witnesses, and designation of deposition testimony, documents, and other exhibits. Objections must be made within 14 days of disclosure.

Table 4–1
(continued)

26(b)(5)	Parties claiming privilege for any otherwise discoverable information are now required to provide an accounting of "the nature of the documents, communications or things not produced or disclosed in a manner that, without revealing information inself privileged or protected, will enable other parties to assess the applicability of the privilege or protection."

Table 4–2

Discovery Timetable under Rule 26(a)

Scheduling Conference under Rule 16(b)	Within 90 days of appearance of defendant and 120 days after service of complaint.
Rule 26(f) Meeting	At least 14 days before the scheduling conference.
Mandatory Disclosures	Within 10 days of meeting of parties under Rule 26(f).
Mandatory Disclosure (Identity of expert witnesses and substance of testimony)	90 days prior to trial
Mandatory Disclosure (Information to be used other than solely for impeachment)	Within 30 days prior to trial.

§ 4.6 Limits on Discovery

As a paralegal preparing discovery motions, be aware that to promote the legislative purposes in enacting discovery legislation, courts are required to construe the statute liberally in favor of discovery. Discovery is a matter of right, but that right is neither absolute nor unlimited. Explicit statutory language or compelling countervailing considerations may act as a bar to discovery.

Unless limited by court order in accord with the act, a party may obtain discovery regarding any nonprivileged matter relevant to the subject matter of a pending action or to the determination of any motion made in the action, providing the matter is admissible in evidence or is reasonably calculated to lead to discovery of admissible evidence. Thus, information sought through discovery must be relevant to the subject matter involved in the action, and must not be privileged.

Though relevance can only be dispositively defined on a case-by-case basis according to the facts of a given case, trial courts are required to resolve doubts as to relevance in favor of granting discovery. A matter is relevant for purposes of discovery if it relates to the subject matter involved in the action, as opposed to the issues framed in the pleadings (the more stringent standard of relevance applicable at trial).

Note: Admissibility of evidence at trial is not generally a prerequisite to its discoverability.

Privileges

Note that privileges protect personal relationships, such as the attorney-client relationship, when confidential communication between persons in such relationships is deemed more important than full disclosure of evidence. A privilege may exempt one possessing it from answering questions about the privileged matter, or may allow that person to prevent another from disclosing privileged information. Thus, relevant information, if privileged, is not discoverable under discovery legislation.

The privileges contained in the legislation of most states is exclusive. Courts are not free to create new privileges unless authorized by some statutory or constitutional provision.

The major evidentiary privileges include:

(1)   Privilege against self-incrimination
(2)   Lawyer-client privilege
(3)   Spousal privilege
(4)   Physician-patient privilege
(5)   Psychotherapist-patient privilege
(6)   Clergy-penitent privilege, and
(7)   Official information privilege

Most courts also recognize "quasi-privileges," such as a newsperson's immunity from contempt sanctions for refusing to divulge a source of information.

There is a statutory presumption that communications made in confidence during lawyer-client, physician-patient, psychotherapist-patient, clergy-penitent, or husband-wife relationships are confidential, and may be privileged. A party opposing a claim of privilege for a communication pursuant to such relationships has the burden of establishing that the communication was not confidential. However, even when confidentiality is presumed, the party claiming privilege continues to bear the burden of proving that the communication was within the terms of the evidentiary privilege.

Most evidentiary privileges are subject to waiver by their holders. Thus, waiver is a defense to a claim of privilege. If the privilege-holder voluntarily discloses a significant part of a privileged communication, or consents to disclosure by another, waiver may occur. Consent to disclosure is manifested by statements or conduct by the privilege-holder indicating consent, including failure to claim the privilege in any proceeding in which the holder has legal standing and opportunity to claim the privilege.

A claim of privilege may be made by objecting and refusing to respond to the discovery request. The objection should be made at the earliest opportunity and should specifically set forth the nature of the privilege claimed in order to avoid a waiver under the jurisdiction's discovery statute.

Work Product Protection

To ensure an attorney's ability to prepare for trial with the privacy necessary to encourage thorough investigation of the case, and to prevent attorneys from taking unfair advantage of their adversary's preparation, discovery legislation provides that attorney work-product is protected from disclosure during discovery. Any writing that reflects an attorney's impressions, conclusions, opinions, legal research, or theories is absolutely protected; it is not discoverable under any circumstances.

Other forms of work product receive qualified protection. They are not discoverable unless a court determines that denial of discovery will result in injustice, or will unfairly prejudice the party seeking discovery in preparing a claim or defense. Conditionally protected work product is material of a derivative or interpretive nature, including charts, diagrams, audit reports, and reports of experts hired by an attorney to analyze evidence.

Practice Tip: In presenting a work-product claim, counsel must do more than state a conclusion that material is work-product. The burden is on counsel to establish preliminary facts showing entitlement to protection.

Work-product protection is waived if not claimed by the holder. A client may assert the work-product rule in the attorney's absence, but the attorney actually holds the protection, and only the attorney may waive it. However, only a disclosure of information wholly inconsistent with work-product protection results in waiver.

Constitutionally Based Limits

Most courts have also recognized limited protection from discovery for confidential communications that come within federal or state constitutional principles. Examples include the right to privacy and freedom of the press. Because judicial discovery orders inevitably involve state-compelled disclosure of presumptively protected information, such constitutional protection is available even in purely private litigation.

§ 4.7 Discovery Sanctions

It is very important for the paralegal to be aware that to the extent authorized by a section governing a particular discovery method or other provisions of the discovery legislation, and after notice to affected parties, persons, or attorneys and an opportunity for hearing, trial courts may typically impose sanctions against anyone engaging in conduct that is a misuse of the discovery process.

Checklist of Misuses of Discovery

Misuses of discovery under most discovery legislation include, but are not limited to, the following:

(1) Persisting, over objection and without substantial justification, in attempts to obtain information or materials that are outside the scope of permissible discovery.

(2) Using a discovery method in a way that does not comply with specified procedures.

(3) Employing a discovery method in a way or to an extent that causes unwarranted annoyance, embarrassment, oppression, or undue burden and expense.

(4) Failing to respond or submit to an authorized discovery method.

(5) Making, without substantial justification, an objection to discovery that is unmeritorious.

(6) Making an evasive response to discovery.

(7) Disobeying a court order to provide discovery.

(8) Making or opposing, unsuccessfully and without substantial justification, a motion to compel or limit discovery.

(9) Failing to confer in person, by telephone, or by letter with an opposing party or attorney in a reasonable, good faith effort to informally resolve any discovery dispute, if the section governing a particular discovery motion requires the filing of a declaration stating facts showing that such an attempt has been made.

Most discovery legislation provides trial courts with five sanctions for abusive discovery behavior: monetary, issue, evidence, terminating, and contempt sanctions. The most common sanction is monetary, the sanction of first resort in dealing with misuses of discovery. The other sanctions are usually more drastic, and thus are not typically available unless a party violates both an obligation imposed by the Act, and a court order to comply with the Act.

Courts may impose monetary sanctions ordering one engaging in misuse, an attorney advising such conduct, or both, to pay reasonable expenses, including attorney fees, incurred by anyone as a result of the conduct. Monetary sanctions are also available against anyone who unsuccessfully asserts that another has engaged in misuse of the discovery process. A court must impose monetary sanctions, if authorized by a provision of the Act, unless it finds that the one subject to sanction acted with substantial justification or that other circumstances make imposition of the sanction unjust.

Least severe of the more drastic sanctions is the evidence sanction. Evidence sanctions prohibit a party from introducing designated matters into evidence. More severe are issue sanctions, in which a court may order designated facts to be taken as established at trial against a party engaging in misuse, or may prohibit that party from supporting or opposing designated claims or defenses.

The most severe sanction is termination. A court may impose terminating sanctions striking out a party's pleadings, staying further proceedings by the party until it obeys a discovery order, dismissing part or all of the party's action, or rendering a default judgment against the party. Generally, terminating sanctions are proper only in cases in which a party has engaged in an egregious, chronic pattern of delay or evasiveness that includes violation of court orders regarding discovery.

One who wishes to obtain sanctions for discovery misuse must make a noticed motion specifying the type of sanction sought, and the person, party, or attorney against whom sanctions are sought. A party may properly include such a notice in the body of a discovery motion. The notice of motion must be supported by a memorandum of points and authorities and, if monetary sanctions are requested, must be accompanied by a declaration setting forth facts supporting the amount sought.

§ 4.8 Interrogatories

Interrogatories are written questions propounded by one party to another to derive answers about the facts of the case. These questions must be answered truthfully and are sworn to and admissible as evidence in trial. Very often, answers to interrogatories will unveil other issues or facts which are incorporated into the discovery process. Interrogatories are usually sent to the opposing party early in the proceedings. The first set of interrogatories is usually very standardized and broad in scope. After answers to these questions are received and reviewed, a second more specific set of interrogatories may be called for. The answers to these questions are usually a basis for further discovery and questions to be asked during depositions.

It is important to word these written inquiries in such a way that they will not be objected to by the other side. Questions which fall under the category of overly broad, burdensome, or irrelevant should be avoided. For example, it is usually considered burdensome and irrelevant to ask for a person's complete salary chronology for the past 20 years when the incident giving rise to the lawsuit occurred only two years prior. Because the number of interrogatories allowed is limited in some jurisdictions, word your questions carefully and address only those issues which are important to the building of your case.

Federal Rule of Civil Procedure 33 for the first time limits the number of interrogatories one party may serve upon another. Prior to this rule change, the limits were reflected only in some local federal district court rules. Rule 33 reflects the optimistic view of the court that the new mandatory disclosure provisions of Rule 26 will lessen the need for interrogatories, and therefore, only 25 interrogatories, including "all discrete subparts" are now permitted. More interrogatories may still be propounded with leave of court. Rule 33 also states that, consistent with Rule 26(f), interrogatories may not be served before the parties have met to plan discovery.

Interrogatories must be responded to within 30 days of service unless stipulations for extensions of time are arranged under Rule 29 of the Federal Rules of Civil Procedure.

Effective interrogatory development is an art. It should be done in a logical manner only after all the known facts and documents have been reviewed. Otherwise, interrogatories are nothing more than fishing expeditions and are usually worthless. Each question should be asked with the issues of the case in mind, and tailored to fit the specifics of the case. (See **Forms 4–2** through **4–9** for examples of interrogatories tailored to fit case specifics.) Avoid using stock or form interrogatories verbatim. They rarely fit your needs exactly, and it is foolish to waste limited questions on irrelevant material. It is also important to remember the following goals for interrogatories:

1. Determine merits of opponent's case.
2. Determine extent of damages or injuries (if defense).
3. Identify witnesses.
4. Identify potentially relevant documents.
5. Identify parties who should be joined.
6. Determine credibility of witnesses.
7. Determine credibility of testimony and evidence.
8. Identify physical evidence.
9. Gather information to assist in future investigation.
10. Gather information to support dispositive motions, such as motions for summary judgment.
11. Determine strategy of opponent's case.
12. Gather information to support position in settlement negotiations.

Develop your own form files of interrogatories. You may even find it helpful to develop files for different ways of asking specific questions. Make sure that you define your terms in the preliminary statement.

Proofread your questions not only for grammatical or technical errors, but for conciseness and clarity of intent. It is sometimes a good idea to have the questions read by someone else to make sure that your intent is clear.

The following checklist is helpful in making sure that the necessary components are included in your interrogatories:

1. Proper caption.
2. Appropriate citations to the Rules of Civil Procedure.
3. Preliminary statement or definition of terms.

4. Interrogatories drafted in compliance with Rules of Civil Procedure.
5. Attorney signature.
6. Jurat.
7. Certificate of service.

§ 4.9 Interrogatory Drafting Guidelines

Table 4–3 is a table that you can fill out to help establish your own guidelines and techniques.

1. Read the documents.
2. Prepare a time line of events.
3. Familiarize yourself with any types of forms or reports used.
4. Make notes regarding meetings, documents mentioned, and phone calls.
5. Create a cast of characters or list of players.
6. Create an organizational chart for commercial cases.
7. Identify the issues
8. Know your local court rules.
9. Consult your judge's notebook for objection ruling information.
10. Consult form interrogatories.
11. Define your terms.
12. Tailor the questions to fit the case.
13. Anticipate objections.
14. Reread your questions for clarity.
15. Proofread your questions for technical and grammatical errors and to see if your intent is clear and the question concise.

Table 4–3

Interrogatory Drafting Guidelines

Criteria—What elements are found in a good set of interrogatories?	How do you achieve those elements?	Tips, Techniques
Questions are tailored to fit the case.	Make sure that all pronouns, adjectives, and adverbs are appropriate for this particular case. Edit any form interrogatories used to reflect the specific needs and vocabulary for this case.	

Table 4–3
(continued)

Criteria—What elements are found in a good set of interrogatories?	How do you achieve those elements?	Tips, Techniques
Quesitons are clearly stated and concise.	Avoid long-winded, complex sentence structure. Avoid legalese. Draft questions so that the intent is clear to any reader and nothing has to be implied or surmised to answer the question.	
Format of interrogatories follows appropriate Rules of Civil Procedure.	Consult appropriate Rules of Civil Procedure and the local rules which affect the filing and serving of interrogatories. Limit the number of questions propounded to numbers allowed by that court's rules of civil procedure. Determine how questions with subparts are numbered and counted in that jurisdiction.	If available, consult a judge's notebook for how the judge rules on various objections which may be made to the interrogatories.
Questions are drafted in such a way that they will not exceed the scope of discovery.	Anticipate objections to avoid asking questions which will be disallowed. See the Rules of Civil Procedure regarding objections to discovery. Define terms such as "you", "agent", "document", etc. prior to stating the first interrogatory to broaden or narrow the scope of the questions asked.	
Questions are directed toward eliciting facts which support or attack the issues of the case.	Read all the documents in the file and all supporting factual analyses of the scenario.	

Table 4–3
(continued)

Criteria—What elements are found in a good set of interrogatories?	How do you achieve those elements?	Tips, Techniques
	Prepare a time line of events for your own use to help you better understand the chronology of the events which gave rise to the litigation.	
Questions are designed to elicit facts, existence of witnesses, and existence of documents.	Make notes regarding meetings, documents mentioned, and phone calls made while reviewing file materials.	
	Create a cast of characters or a list of players to help you understand the relationships of people in the case.	
	If this is a commercial case, create an organizational chart to help you understand the relationships of people and their positions in the case.	

§ 4.10 Interrogatory Checklist

The following checklist is a laundry list of topics to be addressed by the Interrogatories:

____ Basis in fact supporting each allegation made by opposing party in each pleading.

____ Identify fact witnesses.

____ Identify expert witnesses.

____ Existence and custody of statements.

____ Existence and custody of written correspondence, memoranda, relevant documents, and so forth.

____ Dates and substance of meetings or telephone calls.

____ Personal or professional background information regarding opposing party.

§ 4.11   NOTICE OF SERVICE

____   Damage calculations and amounts.

____   Existence of photographs.

____   Existence of relevant insurance coverage.

____   Existence of tests or reports.

____   Claims or representations relied upon.

§ 4.11   Notice of Service of Interrogatories

Form 4–1 is a sample Notice of Service of Interrogatories. It should accompany the Interrogatories.

FORM 4–1
SAMPLE NOTICE OF SERVICE OF INTERROGATORIES

NO. [case number]

[name]	)	IN THE DISTRICT COURT OF
	)	
Plaintiff	)	[county] COUNTY, [state]
	)	
vs.	)	[judicial district] JUDICIAL DISTRICT
	)	
[name]	)	
	)	
Defendant	)	

TO: ([name]) by and through his attorney of record [name and address of opposing counsel];

Pursuant to Rule [number] of the [state] Rules of Civil Procedure, the [plaintiff/defendant] serves these Interrogatories upon you, the answers to which shall be made under oath, separately and fully, in writing on or before thirty (30) days after the service of such record.

Respectfully submitted,

_____

[Attorney's name]

CERTIFICATE OF SERVICE

I certify that this instrument was served in compliance with Rules [number] and [number] of the [state] Rules of Civil Procedure, by certified mail or hand delivery, return receipt requested, on the [date] day of [month], [20__], and was promptly filed with the Clerk of the Court, together with this proof of service.

_____

[Attorney's name]

§ 4.12 Sample Interrogatories—Auto Accident

FORM 4–2
SAMPLE AUTO ACCIDENT INTERROGATORIES

1. Were you the operator of a vehicle involved in an accident with plaintiff on the [date] day of [month], [20__], at about [time] o'clock [A.M./P.M.] at [location] in the County of [county], state of [state]? If not, state the operator's name and address, but if so, please state:
   (a) Is your name correctly stated in the complaint on file in this cause?
   (b) All names by which you have ever been known with the dates during which other names were used;
   (c) Your date and place of birth, Social Security Number, your height, weight, eye and hair colors, and address at the time of said accident;
   (d) The names, addresses, and telephone numbers of your present and former spouses, if any;
   (e) The names, addresses and telephone numbers of all your natural and adopted children residing with you at the time of said accident, if any.

2. With respect to places you resided for the five years prior to your present residence, please state:
   (a) The complete address with inclusive dates of residence;
   (b) Whether a house, apartment, and so forth;
   (c) The names of the owners or managers.

3. With respect to each employment you have engaged in for the five years prior to and including your present employment, please state:
   (a) The name, address, and telephone number of each employer or place of business, with inclusive dates;
   (b) The nature of the work you performed;
   (c) The hours worked per week at such work;
   (d) The names and addresses, and telephone numbers of your immediate superiors or other owners.

4. Did you have a driver's license to operate a motor vehicle on the date of the accident, and if so, please state:
   (a) The type, the date of issuance, and expiration date;
   (b) The state of issuance and number of license;
   (c) All offenses, violations, or restrictions recorded on or against such license.

5. With respect to your driving background, please state:
    (a) How many years driving experience you have had;
    (b) How many years you have been a licensed driver;
    (c) Whether you have ever had a driver's license which contained restrictions of any sort, and if so, the date, state, and type of restriction.

6. Have you ever had a driver's license suspended, canceled, revoked, or been denied the issuance of a driver's license for mental or physical reasons? If so, for each such occurrence, please state:
    (a) The date and state;
    (b) The reason therefor.

7. Do you have normal vision and hearing without the use of corrective apparatus? If not, please state:
    (a) Whether you were wearing corrective apparatus at the time of the accident;
    (b) The present location of said apparatus;
    (c) The date prescribed, and the name and address of the prescriber;
    (d) The date and complete address of the place where said apparatus was purchased.

8. Have you had your vision or hearing examined within the last five years? If so, as to each examination please state:
    (a) The date and reason therefor;
    (b) The name, address, and telephone number of the examiner;
    (c) The results or action taken.

9. At any time prior to the time of this accident had you ever been advised by any physician or other qualified person that you required glasses, corrective lenses, or hearing aids? If so, please state:
    (a) The date, name, and address of the physician or person;
    (b) The reason therefor;
    (c) The action taken by you.

10. Have you ever had any form of mental illness, fits or convulsions, fainting spells, epilepsy, venereal disease, nervous breakdown, tuberculosis, alcoholism or drug addiction? If so, for each such occurrence or reoccurrence within one year prior to this accident, please state:
    (a) A description of the condition;
    (b) The date of onset;
    (c) Your address at the time of onset;
    (d) The names and addresses of all qualified persons treating you for the condition, with inclusive dates of treatment;
    (e) The names and address of all hospitals, institutions, and so forth where you were treated for such condition, whether in-patient or out-patient, and inclusive dates of treatment;
    (f) The date of termination or present status of the condition.

DISCOVERY

11. If you were the operator of a motor vehicle involved in this accident, please state:
   (a) Name, address, and telephone number of each owner of the vehicle, and identify which of same, if any, gave you permission to use the vehicle.

12. If any such owner was your employer on the date of the accident state:
   (a) If you were acting on behalf of said employer at the time of the accident;
   (b) Your hours of employment on said date;
   (c) The purpose of your using said vehicle at the time of said accident.

13. If any owner of the vehicle was related to you at the time of the accident, please state what relationship you were to the owner, and further state:
   (a) Did you reside within the same premises at the time of the accident?
   (b) Was the vehicle you were operating available to you generally from the owner around and including the time of the accident?
   (c) Whether or not you were using the vehicle for any family purposes of the owner, at the time of the accident.

14. If you claim you did not have permission of an owner of the vehicle to operate the vehicle at the time of the accident, state the facts as to how you obtained the vehicle.

15. Have you ever been rejected or exempted from military service? If so, for each such occurrence, please state:
   (a) The date;
   (b) The reason;
   (c) The branch of service and the office or base address.

16. At the time of the accident did you have all of, and full use of all your limbs and extremities? If not, please state:
   (a) The details of any impairment;
   (b) The extremities or limbs affected;
   (c) The dates and cause of impairment.

17. Did you take any drug, narcotic, sedative, tranquilizer, or other form of medication within a 24 hour period preceding the accident? If so, for each such, please state:
   (a) The identity of the medication, and reason for taking;
   (b) The number of times, schedules, and amounts of dosages taken;
   (c) The date and complete address of the place where purchased;
   (d) The name, address, phone number, and occupation of the person by whom prescribed and the prescription number.

18. Were you in an establishment or residence where liquor was dispensed within twenty-four hours prior to the accident? If so, for each such occasion, please state:
   (a) The name and address of the establishment or residence;
   (b) The times of day of your presence therein:
   (c) The name and address of each person accompanying you;
   (d) The name, type, and quantity of each alcoholic beverage consumed;
   (e) The exact time of consumption of each drink;

(f)   The name and address of each person in whose company you consumed each drink.

19.   After the accident, were you requested to undergo any type of sobriety test? If so, for each such test you actually had, please state:
(a)   The type;
(b)   The length of time after the accident;
(c)   The name and address of the person or place where given;
(d)   The results thereof;
(e)   The name and address of the person having present custody of the record thereof;
(f)   If you refused any such tests, the name, address, and telephone number of each person whom you refused.

20.   Describe hourly if possible your general activities for twenty-four hours preceding the accident and specify all your hours of employment.

21.   With reference to the trip you were taking at the time of the accident, please state:
(a)   Where you started from and where you were going;
(b)   The time you started and the time you were scheduled to arrive at your destination;
(c)   The address of each place where you stopped off during the trip;
(d)   The purpose;
(e)   The exact route by street and compass direction;
(f)   The name, address, phone number, and present whereabouts of each passenger during the trip.

22.   At the time of the accident, please state, to your best recollection, the following:
(a)   The exact date, day of the week, and time;
(b)   The direction you were traveling immediately prior to impact;
(c)   The speeds at which you were traveling prior to the point of impact, at the distances of approximately one mile, one-half mile, one-quarter mile, 250 feet and 50 feet;
(d)   The visibility and light conditions;
(e)   The weather, including approximate wind conditions and temperature;
(f)   The general character of the neighborhood.

23.   With respect to the scene of the accident, please state:
(a)   The composition of the road surface and its coloring, and the amount of incline and curve, if any, in the direction you were traveling;
(b)   The nature of irregularities in the physical characteristics of the road, if any;
(c)   The number of driving and parking lanes and describe the type and color of lane markers or dividers, if any;
(d)   All posted speeds from one mile away in the direction you were traveling and the distance of the last one you saw prior to the point of impact.

24.   Were there shoulders or curbs on the sides of the road in the immediate vicinity of the scene of the accident, and if so, please state:

DISCOVERY

(a) Composition of the same;

(b) The dimensions of the same;

(c) Their distance from the midline of the road.

25. State whether or not it was raining and/or if the street was wet at the time of the accident, and if so, please state:

    (a) For how long the condition had existed prior to the time of the accident;

    (b) Whether you contend that the condition was the cause or one of the causes of the accident.

26. If it was raining at the time of the accident, state whether or not your windshield wipers were in operation.

27. Was your attention diverted from traffic at any time within the last approximate 500 feet prior to the point of impact? If so, please state:

    (a) The approximate distance from point of impact;

    (b) The distance you traveled while diverted (in feet or seconds);

    (c) The speeds of your vehicle while diverted;

    (d) By what your attention was diverted;

    (e) Your distance from Plaintiff(s) when you first noticed it after your concentration returned (in feet or seconds).

28. Were there any traffic controls at or near the accident scene? If so, as to each, please state:

    (a) The type of control;

    (b) Whether the control was visible at the time of the collision, and functioning properly;

    (c) The location thereof in relation to the point of impact (in feet and compass direction).

29. State where each party and vehicle involved in the accident was at the instant you first noticed each, in the following manner:

    (a) In feet or seconds of each;

    (b) The compass direction of each;

    (c) The traffic lane each was in.

30. State where each party and vehicle involved in the accident was located at the instant you first realized that there would be an accident, and further state as to each:

    (a) In feet or seconds;

    (b) The compass direction;

    (c) In what traffic lane.

31. If any plaintiff was also driving a vehicle, did you observe it reduce speed or stop prior to the accident? If so, at the time you observed this please state your respective locations in the following manner:

    (a) In feet or seconds from each other;

    (b) In compass direction you were each traveling;

    (c)   The traffic lanes you were each in at such time.

32.   Did Plaintiff(s) remain in your line of vision at all times after first observed until the impact? If not, state why not.

33.   If there was any vehicle (or vehicles) in between yours and the other vehicle and parties involved, within one quarter mile prior to the point of impact, please state the number of vehicles and speed of each, and the compass direction and lane in which each such vehicle was traveling.

34.   Do you claim that any unexpected mechanical failure or malfunction of the vehicle you were then driving and/or any vehicle involved in the accident caused or contributed to the cause of the accident? If so, as to each such occurrence, state:
    (a)   The nature and extent of the same;
    (b)   The amount of time (in seconds) prior to the impact, when you first noticed the same;
    (c)   If you further allege such defect caused or contributed to the cause of the accident, describe how.

35.   With reference to the automobile you were driving at the time of the accident, please state:
    (a)   The year, make, model and color;
    (b)   The weight, length, height and width;
    (c)   The road clearance, and distance of driver's seat from ground level;
    (d)   The horse power and number of cylinders;
    (e)   The type of transmission and brakes system.

36.   At the time of the accident, state whether your vehicle was equipped with lights and, if so, please state:
    (a)   The number of lights and the color of each, specifying their location on the vehicle you were operating;
    (b)   Whether or not any of the lights were on and, if so, which ones.

37.   At the time of the accident, please state whether or not you felt tired, sleepy, or ill, and, if so, describe such condition in detail to your best recollection.

38.   If you were an owner or co-owner of the automobile you were driving at the time of the accident, please state:
    (a)   The date, place, name, and address of the place where purchased;
    (b)   Whether new or used when purchased, and the mileage on it at such time;
    (c)   The date, name, and address of each place where repaired within one year immediately preceding the accident, and describe each repair.

39.   Do you allege that the accident was caused or contributed to by any defect or irregularity on the part of someone or something other than the parties or the vehicles involved, or was unavoidable? If so, please describe in detail all facts upon which you base such allegation.

40.   Did you apply your brakes prior to impact? If so, please state:
    (a)   The distance (in feet or seconds) from the point of impact when applied;

(b) The distance (in feet or seconds) traveled by your vehicle from the point of braking to the place where your vehicle came to rest after the accident;

(c) The distance in feet of skid marks laid down by your automobile prior to the point of impact;

(d) The distance in feet of the marks laid down by your vehicle past the point of impact.

41. Did you swerve, blow your horn, or do anything else whatever in an attempt to avoid the accident? If so, to each act, please state:

(a) The distance (in feet or seconds) prior to the point of impact when you did the same;

(b) Describe what you did, and the resulting effect.

42. Did any plaintiff(s) swerve, blow their horn, or do anything else whatever in an attempt to avoid the accident? If so, to each such act, please state:

(a) The distance (in feet or seconds) prior to the point of impact when such plaintiff(s) did the same;

(b) Describe what such plaintiff(s) did, and the resulting effect.

43. Did you observe the extent of damage to the parties or vehicles involved prior to their being moved from the accident site after the accident? If so, please describe in detail all of such damage.

44. Did you observe the position of the parties or vehicles involved before they left the scene of the accident? If so, please stae:

(a) The compass direction the front end of each was pointing;

(b) The distance in feet each was resting past the point of impact.

45. Did police investigate the accident? If so, please state:

(a) How many minutes after the time of impact the first officer arrived;

(b) The number of officers and name of the department investigating;

(c) Whether you were interrogated by any officer as to how the accident occurred;

(d) Whether any officer required you to make a written statement regarding what happened;

(e) Specify each citation you received as a result of the accident, how you pled to each, and the disposition thereof including the name and address of the court involved.

46. Did you converse with any of the parties or vehicle drivers at the scene? If so, as to each, please state:

(a) Which, if any, admitted responsibility;

(b) Describe what was said by each;

(c) The name, address, and phone number of every witness to each such conversation.

47. State the name, address, and phone number of each person or firm not previously mentioned, known to you, your attorneys, or other representatives acting on your behalf, having or claiming to have knowledge of:

§ 4.12 AUTO ACCIDENT

    (a)   The manner of occurrence of the accident;

    (b)   The conduct, activity, physical condition, or statement of any party to this action during the twenty-four hour period immediately preceding the accident;

    (c)   The conduct, activity, physical condition or statement of any party to this action diuring the twenty-four hour period immediately subsequent to the accident;

    (d)   The statement of any eyewitness relating to the manner of occurrences of the accident (identifying each such eyewitness, time and place of such statement, and each person then present);

    (e)   The damage to property directly or indirectly involved in the accident;

    (f)   The taking or existence of pictures, moving or still, relating to any of the above matters;

    (g)   The condition of the vehicles involved in the accident.

48. State the name, address, and phone number of each person known to you, your attorneys, or other representatives acting on your behalf, who claim to have:

    (a)   Witnessed the accident;

    (b)   Been present at the scene of the accident;

    (c)   Witnessed events immediately preceding the accident or the investigation following.

49. List the name, address, phone number, and job title or capacity of each person known to you, your attorneys, or other representatives acting on your behalf, who investigated the accident.

50. Subsequent to investigation at the scene, have you made a report to any governmental department concerning the accident? If so, as to each, please state:

    (a)   The date made, to whom, and the purpose therefore;

    (b)   The name, address, telephone number, and job title or capacity of each person assisting you.

51. As a result of the accident, were any charts, maps, photographs, plats, drawings, or other graphic representations made by you, on your behalf, or known by you or your attorneys to exist? If so, as to each such, please state:

    (a)   The name, address, and telephone number of the person making the same, and the date made;

    (b)   What objects, scenes, or views were depicted;

    (c)   The name, address, and telephone number of the person having present custody of the same;

    (d)   Please attach a copy to your answers to these interrogatories, if you will do so without a Motion to Produce.

52. Prior or subsequent to the accident, have you ever participated in a collision involving a motor vehicle? If so, as to each such, please state:

    (a)   The date and place of occurrence;

    (b)   The names and addresses of the drivers and passengers involved;

    (c)   The number of vehicles involved and the type of each;

(d) The facts as to what happened;

(e) The nature and extent of any injuries sustained by you;

(f) The name and address of the insurance company, insurance adjusters, attorneys, and/or other representatives acting in your behalf.

53. Have you ever been a party to a civil action involving a motor vehicle accident (not including this lawsuit)? If so, for each such, please state:

(a) The name, and address of the court in which filed, and the date of filing and number of court case;

(b) The name, address, and telephone number of your attorney therein.

54. At any time since the date of this accident, have you filed a form known as "SR-1" with the motor vehicle department, and if so, please state:

(a) The name and address of the company or agent to whom submitted, and date thereof;

(b) The type of report, that is oral, written, and so forth;

(c) The name, address, and telephone number of the person having present custody of same.

55. Did you give any other kind of notice to any insurance company other than your liability insurance carrier or its agents as a result of this accident? If so, for each such notice, state:

(a) The date and type thereof, that is, oral, written, and so forth;

(b) The name, address, telephone number, and occupation of each person who assisted you;

(c) The name and address of the company or agent to whom given;

(d) The name, address, telephone number, and occupation of each other person present when the notice was so given;

(e) The substance of the notice.

56. State how this accident occurred (in factual form with as much detail as possible).

57. Do you deny that this accident was entirely your fault? If so, please state all facts upon which you base such denial.

58. Do you contend the plaintiff herein caused or contributed to the cause of this accident? If so, please state all facts upon which you base such contention.

59. If you admit that you alone caused this accident and do not contend plaintiff caused or contributed to the cause of this accident, do you deny that plaintiff's injuries resulted entirely from this accident? If so, please state all facts upon which you base such denial.

60. Whether or not you intend to use such person as a witness and/or for other evidentiary purposes herein, please state whether or not you have consulted with any expert in regard to the present accident, including, but not limited to any insurance adjuster, attorney, and/or other type of expert, and, if so, please state for each:

(a) Their name, present address, telephone number, place of employment, and job title, if any;

(b) Each date of such consultation;

(c) Each date they performed any service on your behalf as a result of such consultation;

(d) Describe in detail the purpose for each such consultation;

(e) Describe in detail what they did on your behalf as a result of each such consultation and the cost of each such consultation.

61. If the answer to the foregoing question is "yes", please state whether or not any such expert performed any test on your behalf and, if so, for each such test, please state:

(a) What was tested;

(b) The date of each test;

(c) Whether a report was made as a result of each such test and, if so, to whom;

(d) If a written report was made for each such test, please state who has present custody, care and/or control of each such report;

(e) The cost of each such test.

62. Whether or not you intend to use the same as evidence herin, please state whether or not any test not covered by the previous two questions was made on your behalf with respect to the present accident and, if so, please state:

(a) The name, present address, telephone number, employer, and job title of each person making each such test;

(b) What was tested;

(c) The date of each test;

(d) Whether a report was made as a result of each such test and, if so, to whom;

(e) If a written report was made for each such test, please state who has present custody, care, and/or control of each such report;

(f) The cost of each such test.

63. Please state whether or not at the time of the accident herein you were covered with liability insurance whether primary, secondary, or excess, and, if so, please state:

(a) The name of each insurer by whom you were covered and each policy number;

(b) The effective dates of coverage;

(c) Limits of each such liability coverage;

(d) Describe each vehicle covered by each such insurer and identify the particular insurer so covering;

(e) State the named insured in each such policy.

64. Whether or not you intend to use the same as evidence herin, as a result of this accident, state whether or not you, your attorneys, insurance adjusters, and/or other representatives have obtained any statements of any type, whether written, recorded and/or otherwise, from any person, (including any plaintiff(s), relative to some facet of this lawsuit, and if so, for each such statement please state the following:

(a) The name, present address, and telephone number of each person making each such statement;

(b)   The date and place where each such statement was made;

(c)   The type of each such statement, that is, written, recorded, and/or other type;

(d)   The name, present address, and telephone number of the person within whose custody each such statement is.

65.   As to each person referred to in your answers to Interrogatories No. 48 and No. 49, please state:

(a)   Were you personally acquainted prior to said accident?

(b)   Whether you are related by blood or marriage.

66.   Identify by name, firm name, affiliation name, business address, business telephone number, and home address, each person defendant expects to call as a witness at the time of trial of this action.

67.   Identify by name, firm name, affiliation name, business address, business telephone number, and home address, each person defendant expects to call as an expert witness at the time of trial of this action.

68.   If the vehicle was owned or driven by yourself, state whether or not an estimate of repair has been made for said vehicle and if said vehicle has been repaired and further state:

(a)   The actual cost of repair;

(b)   The name, address, firm name, and job title of the person who made said estimate, if any, and/or the place where said vehicle was repaired and the date.

69.   State whether or not you, your representative, agent, and/or attorney, have taken any moving pictures of any plaintiff herein, and if so, state for each taken:

(a)   Name the individual subject of such;

(b)   The date of each such moving picture taken;

(c)   The length of time (in seconds, minutes, or hours) said moving picture consumes when projected from start to end;

(d)   The name, address, and telephone number of each person taking such pictures;

(e)   Identify the scene and site by address or other description sufficient to locate same, where each such moving picture was taken;

(f)   State the name, address, and telephone number of the person having the care, custody, and control of each such moving picture;

(g)   State the name, address, and telephone number of the place where said moving pictures were developed and the date.

70.   Please state the name, address, and job title or capacity of each person assisting you with your answers to these interrogatories.

71.   Please identify by question number and subletter each question herein, the answer to which was provided to you by your representative, agent, and/or attorney (that is, each answer you have given not known personally by you when you signed your answers herein), and further:

(a) Identify specifically the person who so provided you with each answer.

72. Have you ever been convicted of a felony?

§ 4.13 —Slip and Fall

FORM 4–3
SAMPLE SLIP AND FALL INTERROGATORIES

1. State your full name and all names by which you have been known or have used, including nicknames.

2. State your date of birth and birth place.

3. What is your present home address and home telephone number; what is your business address and business telephone number?

4. State the name of any and all witnesses or purported witnesses believed or understood by defendant to have witnessed the accident or incident of [describe incident], [20___] or to have knowledge of events leading up to said accident or incident, or the subsequent investigation and related events of that date. As to each such witness, state the following:
    (a) Name, address, and telephone number;
    (b) Point or position, and distance from which the events in question were observed.

5. Does the defendant have the possession or control of, or know of the existence of, any statements, memoranda or writings concerning any of the events described in No. 4 above, made by the witness referred to above or the defendant, whether or not signed by said witness or the defendant? This interrogatory refers to any statement made by such defendant or witness, including those prepared by someone other than the defendant or witness. If so, as to each such statement state the following:
    (a) The date made;
    (b) Name, address, and telephone number of the person making same;
    (c) Any further information which you have which might aid in locating the person;
    (d) The name, address, and telephone number of the person taking such statement, memorandum, or writing;
    (e) The name, address, and telephone number of the person at whose request such statement, memorandum, or writing was taken;
    (f) The present location of such item and of any copies thereof, and;
    (g) The specific subject matter of each such statement.

6. Does the defendant have the possession or control of, or know of the existence of, any written statement, whether said statement was signed by the plaintiff or was prepared by someone other than the plaintiff or not signed? If so, state:
    (a) The date of each statement;

    (b)   Name, address, and telephone number of the person taking such statement;

    (c)   The name, address, and telephone number of the person at whose request such statement was made;

    (d)   The present location of such statement and any copies thereof, and;

    (e)   The specific subject matter of each statement.

7. Did the plaintiff at any time make any oral statement concerning the events in issue? If so, please state:

    (a)   When and where the statement was made;

    (b)   The specific subject matter of such statement;

    (c)   The name, address, and telephone number of the person or persons present when it was made.

8. Does the defendant have the possession or control of, or know of the existence of, any maps, motion pictures, photographs, plats, drawings, diagrams, measurements, or other written description of the accident, the scene of the accident, the vehicles (if any), or the areas or persons involved? This interrogatory refers to any maps, diagrams, pictures, and so forth, made either before, after, or at the time of the events in question.

9. If the answer to the foregoing interrogatory is in the affirmative, list for each such item:

    (a)   Its nature;

    (b)   Its specific subject matter;

    (c)   The date it was made or taken;

    (d)   The name, address, and telephone number of the person making or taking it;

    (e)   The name, address, and telephone number of the person at whose request such item was made or taken;

    (f)   The present location of said item and any copies thereof.

10. State the names, addresses, and telephone numbers of any and all witnesses or purported witnesses believed or understood by the defendant to have any information concerning the injury or injuries sustained, or claimed to have been sustained by plaintiff.

11. State the names, addresses, and telephone numbers of any and all persons believed or understood by defendant to have any information concerning:

    (a)   Any preexisting disabilities, injuries, ailments, or illnesses of the plaintiff;

    (b)   Disabilities, ailments, illnesses, or injuries of the plaintiff suffered after the date of the accident set forth in plaintiff's complaint.

12. Does the defendant have the possession or control of, or know of the existence of, any written statement, reports, pictures, or writings concerning the medical or physical condition of the plaintiff, whether before or after the date set forth in plaintiff's complaint? If so, state as to each such statement, report, picture or writing:

    (a)   The date of it;

    (b)   The name, address, and telephone number of the person making same;

(c) The name, address, and telephone number of the person taking same;

(d) The present location of such statement, picture, report, or writing and copies thereof;

(e) The specific subject matter of each such item.

13. Specifically, does the defendant have the possession or control of, or know of the existence of, any still or motion picture taken of the plaintiff, either before or after the date of the accident? If so, state as to each such still or motion picture:

(a) The date on which it was taken;

(b) The name, address, and telephone number of the person who requested the taking of such picture;

(c) The name, address, and telephone number of the person who took the picture;

(d) The present location of such picture or pictures and copies thereof.

14. Has the defendant made any reports or statements concerning any of the events in issue? If so, state:

(a) When each such report or statement was made;

(b) To whom it was made;

(c) Who was present when it was made;

(d) Further state the present location of each such statement or report and copies thereof.

15. What is the extent of your formal education?

16. If you are currently employed, what is your present occupation?

17. With respect to each form of employment you have had in the past five years, state:

(a) The name and address of employer;

(b) The dates of employment;

(c) The nature of the employment.

18. Has the defendant ever been convicted of a felony? If the answer is in the affirmative, please state:

(a) The charge upon which convicted;

(b) Whether the defendant pled guilty to the charge or was convicted after trial;

(c) The name and address of the court where the proceedings took place;

(d) The caption and case number of such proceeding.

19. Were any tests, inspections, or measurements taken or made with respect to the accident scene or any object involved? If so, state:

(a) The subject of each test, inspection, or measurement;

(b) The name, address, and telephone number of the person who conducted each test, inspection, or measurement;

(c) The date on which each test, inspection, or measurement was performed;

(d) The name, address, and telephone number of the person now with custody of any written report concerning each test, inspection, or measurement;

    (e)   The name, address, and telephone number of the person who requested such item.

20.   Was an investigation conducted concerning:
    (a)   The accident in question?
    (b)   Plaintiff's alleged injuries?
    (c)   Plaintiff's background?
    (d)   Plaintiff's previous or subsequent medical history and condition?
    (e)   Plaintiff's expenses and damages?
    (f)   Plaintiff's alleged loss of earnings and/or wages?
    If so, state:
        (i)   The name, address, and telephone number of the person who conducted each investigation;
        (ii)   The name, address, and telephone number of the person who requested each investigation be made;
        (iii)   The date on which each investigation was conducted;
        (iv)   The places where each investigation was performed;
        (v)   The name, address, and telephone number of the person now with custody of each written report made concerning each investigation;
        (vi)   The specific subject matter of each such investigation.

21.   Is the defendant's name correctly stated in the complaint on file in this action? If not, state the correct designation of defendant.

22.   Are there any other persons, firms, or corporations connected with and/or responsible for the events and acts described in plaintiff's complaint? If so, state the full name, address, and telephone number of each such person, firm, or corporation.

23.   Give the name, address, and telephone number of any expert or consultant with whom you have communicated in connection with the occurrence which is the subject matter of this action, and state:
    (a)   The last known business and home address of each such person;
    (b)   The name of any business entity with which each such person is associated;
    (c)   The specific area of knowledge of each such person (for example, chemical engineer, structural engineer, medical doctor, and so forth);
    (d)   The date when each person was first contacted;
    (e)   The date of each report rendered by each such person, indicating whether such report was written or oral, and if oral, who the speaker was;
    (f)   Precisely what documentary or written material was provided to each such person, giving the date and the author of each such document or written material;
    (g)   What physical objects were provided to each such person.

24.   Were there other persons, corporation or firms interested in the operation, control, or management of the premises described in plaintiff's complaint at the time stated in plaintiff's complaint? If so, state the full name, address, and telephone number of each such person, corporation, or firm and what such interest was.

25. Does the defendant contend that the plaintiff was in any way negligent; if so, what negligence, if any, contributed to the plaintiff's injury?

26. Does the defendant contend that a third party was in any manner responsible for the events set forth in plaintiff's complaint, and for plaintiff's resulting injuries?

27. Does the defendant contend that the plaintiff in some manner assumed the risk of injury to himself?

28. If the answer to any of the three preceding interrogatories is in the affirmative, set forth each fact upon which defendant bases said contention, state the name of each witness who will testify to each of said facts, and identify the documentary, physical, or expert evidence defendant contends supports such defense.

29. Identify by name, firm name, affiliation name, business address, business telephone number, and home address, each person the defendant expects to call as an expert witness at the time of the trial of this action.

30. With respect to each person the defendant expects to call as an expert witness at the trial of this action, state:
    (a) The subject matter to which each expert is expected to testify;
    (b) The substance of the facts and opinions to which each expert is expected to testify;
    (c) A summary of the grounds for each opinion held by each such expert.

31. Identify by name, firm name, affiliation name, business address, and business telephone number, each expert employed by you in anticipation of this litigation, or in preparation for the trial of this action, who you do not expect to call as a witness at the time of trial.

32. State the names of all insurance companies whose insurance policies afford defendant and the premises, bodily injury or public liability insurance coverage, whether primary or excess, concerning the accident or incident described in plaintiff's complaint, and further state:
    (a) The policy number of each such policy;
    (b) The monetary limits of liability for bodily injury or public liability coverage of each such insurance policy;
    (c) The exact designation of all named insureds on each such policy.

33. Was there in effect at the time of the accident or incident described in plaintiff's complaint any insurance policy where a question, issue, or controversy exists as to whether such policy affords to the defendant any bodily injury or public liability coverage, whether primary or excess, in connection with the accident or incident?

34. If the answer to the preceding interrogatory is in the affirmative, please state:
    (a) The name of each such insurance company;
    (b) The policy number of each policy in question;
    (c) The exact designation of each named insured in each such policy;
    (d) The monetary limits of liability for bodily injury or public liability coverage under each such policy.

35. At the time of the events described in plaintiff's complaint, was there in force and effect one or more insurance policies by or through which any coverage or benefits (either medical, hospital, surgical, nursing, funeral, burial, or otherwise) were made payable to any plaintiff herein, regardless of negligence or fault?

36. If the answer to the preceding interrogatory is in the affirmative, please state as of the time of said accident or incident:
     (a) The total number of such policies;
     (b) The name of the company issuing each such policy;
     (c) The policy number of each policy;
     (d) The exact designation for all named insureds of each policy;
     (e) The limits of coverage or benefits for each policy;
     (f) The nature of the coverage or benefits for each policy, (that is, medical, hospital, surgical, nursing, funeral, burial, or otherwise.)

37. Have other persons, whether patrons, employees, or otherwise, tripped, slipped, or fallen in the area described in plaintiff's complaint prior to the time stated in plaintiff's complaint? If so, state the full name and address, both home and business, of each such person, and summarize what occurred in each of said instances. If a suit was filed, state the name of the action, case number, and place where suit was filed. Further, if defendant has possession or control of any reports or memoranda, or complaints or letters concerning said incidents, state where such documents are located.

38. State who built the area described in plaintiff's complaint, and further state:
     (a) When it was built;
     (b) What repairs, modifications, alterations, or changes were made in the subject area;
     (c) By whom they were made;
     (d) What such alterations, repairs, or modifications consisted of.

39. Did defendant ever receive any complaint or notice, oral or written, that the area described in plaintiff's complaint, or the lighting of the same, was dangerous, hazardous, unsafe, defective, or inadequate?

40. If defendant's answer to the preceding interrogatory is in the affirmative, state:
     (a) The name and address of each person making such complaint;
     (b) The date of each such complaint;
     (c) Which were oral and which were written;
     (d) If oral, the person to whom said complaint was made, and the substance thereof;
     (e) If written, the present custodian of each such writing;
     (f) What action was taken to remedy each such complaint;
     (g) By whom this was done;
     (h) When it was done.

41. After plaintiff's injury as alleged in the complaint, were any changes made to the area described in plaintiff's complaint? If the answer is in the affirmative; state:

§ 4.14 PRODUCT LIABILITY

(a) The date of each such change;

(b) The name and address of each person who made such change;

(c) The name, address, and telephone number of each person who ordered each such change.

42. Are there in existence books, records, memoranda, or writings which show maintenance, repair, servicing, replacement, or upkeep of the area described in plaintiff's complaint?

43. If the answer to the preceding interrogatory is in the affirmative, describe these books, records, memoranda, or writings in detail, and state the full name, address, and telephone number of the present custodian of same.

44. State the name, address, and present occupation of each person or persons whose duty it was to inspect the area described in plaintiff's complaint for the purpose of safety and maintenance for the period of three years prior to the alleged injury to the plaintiff.

45. In the area where plaintiff fell as set forth in the complaint, were there any warning signs or other warning devices to advise persons in the area of dangerous conditions?

§ 4.14 —Product Liability

FORM 4–4
SAMPLE PRODUCT LIABILITY INTERROGATORIES

1. State your full legal name and all names by which you have been known.

2. What is your present address, telephone number, and Social Security Number?

3. If you are a corporation, and will do so without a Request to Produce, please provide us with copies of your Articles of Incorporation and By-laws.

4. State the first date the product in question was manufactured by you.

5. Do you allege that the plaintiff was negligent or careless in his use of your product?

6. Do you have any previous knowledge of any similar incidents with this product?

7. State the name, address, and curriculum vitae of any expert you have retained to review this incident.

Don't do this!

8. If you will do so without a Request to Produce, please provide us with all reports, calculations, and test results developed by your expert witness. Note that in many jurisdictions, this type of interrogatory will not compel the opposing side to produce any kind of documents. Most jurisdictions require a Request to Produce Documents to accomplish this.

9. Has anyone from your company investigated the incident? If you will do so without a Request to Produce, please provide us with all such reports.

241

10. Have you obtained any statements, either written or recorded, from any witnesses to this incident? If so, please produce them.

11. Do you allege that the product is safe?

12. Are you now or have you been in the past involved in any lawsuits relating to this product?

13. Do you admit that there are flaws in the design of the product creating hazardous conditions in its usage?

14. Have any design changes been made to the product since it was first manufactured? If so, why?

15. Describe the recommended use intended for this product.

16. State any warnings which appear on the product or on any accompanying literature regarding the product's use.

17. Do you allege that the average public does not require any special talents or skills to use the product properly?

18. Have you ever recalled this product for any reason?

§ 4.15 —Medical Malpractice

FORM 4–5
SAMPLE MEDICAL MALPRACTICE INTERROGATORIES

1. State your full legal name, residence address, and telephone number, business address, and business telephone number.

2. When and where did you graduate from medical school?

3. Briefly give a history of your experience as a physician beginning with your internship through the present.

4. If you belong to any professional organizations, please list.

5. If you are board certified in any specialty, please describe.

6. If you are incorporated, please provide us with a copy of your Articles of Incorporation and By-Laws.

7. What is the first date that you saw the plaintiff in a professional capacity?

8. What was your diagnosis and treatment of the patient at that time?

9. How many times subsequent to the first visit did you see the plaintiff in your office, and on what dates? Describe each treatment.

10. Did you have in your possession a history of the plaintiff's medical records?

11. State the names of all hospitals where you are privileged to practice.

§ 4.16 EXPERT WITNESS

12. Has your privilege ever been revoked by any hospital? If so, please explain.

13. Were you under the influence of alcohol or drugs on the date of the incident? If so, please explain.

14. Have you ever been reprimanded by any medical association or had your license revoked for any reason? If so, please explain.

15. State the names and addresses of all witnesses you intend to call at time of trial.

16. Do you allege that you provided the plaintiff with the customary standard of care as prevails under these circumstances?

17. Do you disclaim any negligence in this matter?

18. State the name and address of any expert witness you intend to call at time of trial.

§ 4.16 —Expert Witness

FORM 4–6
SAMPLE EXPERT WITNESS INTERROGATORIES

1. Have you employed any person(s), including, but not limited to, automobile accident reconstruction experts, economists, physicians, and so forth?

2. If so, for each such expert state:
   (a) His name, or other means of identification, address, and telephone number;
   (b) His profession or occupation, and the field in which he allegedly is an expert;
   (c) The name of description of the substance, product or object that was tested, analyzed or examined; and
   (d) Whether you intend to call him as a witness during the trial of this action.

3. Has he had a formal education in his field?

4. If so, state:
   (a) The name and address of each school where he received this special education or training;
   (b) The dates when he attended each school; and
   (c) The name and description of each degree he received, including the date when each was received, and the name of the school from which he received the degree.

5. Did he have other special training in his field?

6. If so, state:
   (a) The type of training he received;
   (b) The name and address of the school or place where he received this training; and
   (c) The dates when he received this training.

7. Is he a member of any professional or trade association in his field?

8. If so, state:
    (a) The name of each professional or trade association;
    (b) The date he became a member; and
    (c) A description of each office he has held in each association.

9. Has he written any books, papers, or articles on subjects in his field?

10. If so, for each book, paper, and article, state:
    (a) The title and subject matter;
    (b) The name and address of the publisher; and
    (c) The date of publication.

11. Is he licensed by any governmental authority to practice in his field?

12. If so, state:
    (a) The designation of the authority by whom he was licensed;
    (b) The date when he was licensed;
    (c) The general requirements that he had to meet to obtain this license; and
    (d) How he fulfilled these requirements.

13. Was his license to practice in his field ever revoked or suspended?

14. If so, for each revocation or suspension, state:
    (a) The inclusive dates;
    (b) The designation of the authority who revoked or suspended the license;
    (c) The charges preferred; and
    (d) The punishment imposed.

15. Has he practiced or worked in his field during the past ten (10) years?

16. If so, state:
    (a) Whether he was self-employed, employed by someone else, or associated as a partner;
    (b) Each address where he practiced or was employed:
    (c) The date he was with each employer; and
    (d) The type of duty he performed with each employer.

17. If he has not practiced or worked in his field during the past ten (10) years, what was his employment during this time?

18. What experience, other than that stated above, has he had in his field?

19. Has he had any previous experience in his field which involved problems similar to those encountered in this action?

20. If so, describe each similar problem with which he has had experience.

21. At what address is he presently employed?

22. Between what dates has he been so employed?

23. What are his present duties?

24. As pertains to this case, what did he test, analyze, or examine? Please identify the documents or materials tested, analyzed, or examined with sufficient specificity to allow these plaintiffs/defendants the ability to file a Request for Production pursuant to Rule [citation] of the Federal Rules of Civil Procedure.

25. During what dates did he make this test, analysis, or examination?

26. At what address was this test, analysis, or examination, made?

27. What facts or information were you seeking in having this test, analysis, or examination conducted?

28. Explain in detail the steps used in this test, analysis, or examination.

29. Did anyone assist him?

30. If so, state:
     (a) The name and address of each person who gave assistance;
     (b) The type or amount of assistance given; and
     (c) The inclusive dates that each person gave assistance.

31. Were any results or conclusions reached as a result of his test, analysis, or examination?

32. If so, what were the results or conclusions?

33. What is the name or other means of identification, and address of the person who has present custody of each item that was tested, analyzed or examined?

34. On what date did each such person obtain custody of each item?

35. How did each person obtain custody of each item?

36. Did this expert submit a report, either in writing or orally, of his objective findings?

37. If so, state:
     (a) The date this report was submitted;
     (b) The name or other identification of the person to whom this report was submitted;
     (c) The means by which the report was submitted; and
     (d) If the report was oral, either telephonic or otherwise, were any means used, whatsoever, to make a record of the same?
     If so, state:
          (i)   The means by which the record of such oral report was made;
          (ii) The name and address of the person who has the present custody of the record of such oral report;
          (iii) Whether or not you will attach a copy of the record of the oral report without a Request to Produce to your Answers to these interrogatories.

38. Did he submit a report setting forth his opinions or conclusions reached from the test, analysis, or examination that he conducted?

39. If so, state:
    (a) The date this report was submitted;
    (b) The name or other means of identification of the person to whom this report was submitted;
    (c) The means by which this report was submitted; and
    (d) If the report was oral, either telephonic or otherwise, were any means used whatsoever to make a record of the same?
    If so, state:
        (i) The means by which the record of such oral report was made;
        (ii) The name and address of the person who has present custody of the record of such oral report; and
        (iii) Whether or not you will attach a copy of the record of the oral report without a Request to Produce to your Answers to these Interrogatories.

40. Did he submit any other reports based on the test, analysis, or examination that he conducted?

41. If so, state:
    (a) A description of each report that was made;
    (b) The date that each report was made;
    (c) The name, or other means of identification, of the person to whom each report was submitted; and
    (d) The name and address of the person who has present custody of each report.

42. If you will do so without a Request to Produce, attach to your Answers to these Interrogatories a copy of any reports made by this expert on the basis of his tests, analysis, or examination.

43. Does your expert still have custody of each of the items tested, analyzed, or examined?

44. If so, without a Request to Produce, will you return the items to the individual who forwarded them to your expert?

45. If your expert does not have custody of said items, please state the following:
    (a) Who presently has the custody of said items;
    (b) By what means of transportation the custody was transferred;
    (c) The date said transportation took place;
    (d) The name and address of the transporting agent or company;
    (e) The date said items were received from your expert; and
    (f) By whom said items were received and the address of same.

46. Is the expert to be compensated for his work and efforts in connection with this action?

47. If so, how much is he to be paid?

48. Is he to receive any additional compensation if you are successful in this action?

49. If so, what are the terms of this additional compensation?

§ 4.17 CORPORATION

50. Has he already been paid?

51. If not, when will he be paid?

52. Please set forth the names, addresses, and telephone numbers of all persons whom the Defendants expect to call as expert witnesses or otherwise, together with an outline of the material to which they will testify.

§ 4.17 —Corporation

FORM 4–7
SAMPLE INTERROGATORIES TO A CORPORATION

1. Is the business name of plaintiff, [business name of plaintiff] correctly stated in the proceedings herein? If not, what corrections should be made?

2. Is the plaintiff, [corporation], hereinafter referred to as [name], incorporated under the laws of the state of [state], or of any other state?

3. If the preceding answer is in the affirmative, please state:
    (a) The state of incorporation;
    (b) The address of its principal place of business;
    (c) The date on which the articles of incorporation were filed with the Secretary of State;
    (d) The date on which the articles were filed with the County Clerk of [county] County, [state].

4. What, according to the Articles of Incorporation of [corporation], is:
    (a) The specific or primary business to be engaged in by the the corporation;
    (b) The general purpose for which the corporation was organized;
    (c) The duration, if any, of its corporate existence;
    (d) The total number of originally issued shares of stock;
    (e) The name and address of the person to whom each share was originally issued;
    (f) The date of issuance of each original share.

5. Has any person who was a holder of the shares of stock originally issued by [corporation] transferred his shares to any other person, corporation, or entity?

6. If so, state:
    (a) The name of the person transferring his shares;
    (b) The number of shares transferred;
    (c) The person to whom such shares were transferred;
    (d) The consideration received for the transfer of such shares;
    (d) Whether such transfer occurred in your share certificate book;
    (f) The date of each transfer.

DISCOVERY

7. What is the name and last known address of each of the present stockholders for [corporation].

8. Does [corporation], maintain a share certificate or a share register book?

9. If so, state:
    (a) The name and address of the person having custody of such book;
    (b) The present location of such book.

10. Did [corporation], after incorporation, adopt by-laws?

11. If so, state:
    (a) The time and place of their adoption;
    (b) The name and address of the person who drafted them;
    (c) The name of each person present at the meeting at which time they were adopted.

12. Do such by-laws provide for:
    (a) Time, place, and manner of calling, conducting, and giving notice of directors' meetings;
    (b) Time, place, and manner of calling, conducting, and giving notice of shareholders' meetings;
    (c) A method of publication of notices of meetings of the shareholders or directors when publication is required;
    (d) A method for the execution, revocation, and other use of proxies;
    (e) Appointment of an executive committee or other committee of the board of directors;
    (f) Appointment, duties, compensation, and tenure of office other than directors;
    (g) A method to determine the shareholders of record;
    (h) The making of annual reports and financial statements to shareholders.

13. What provisions are there in the by-laws, if any, relative to the number, qualifications, duties, and compensation of directors?

14. What provisions, other than those already described, are there in the by-laws relative to directors?

15. What is the name and address of each person who has acted as a director of [corporation] from the date of incorporation to the date of these Interrogatories?

16. What was the period of time during which each such director served?

17. Has any salary, fee, or other compensation been paid to any director of [corporation]?

18. If the answer to the preceding Interrogatoruy is in the affirmative, please state:
    (a) The name and address of each director paid;
    (b) The period for which each payment was made in each case;
    (c) The amount of the payment, if money, in each case;

(d) The nature of the payment, if property, in each case;

(e) The date of the payment in each case.

19. If any payment to a director was in a form other than money, in addition to the nature of such payments, state:

(a) The fair value of the property paid;

(b) Whether the board of directors voted approval of any payments mentioned; and

(c) If the board voted approval, which payments were approved.

20. Has the plaintiff, [corporation], had officers from the date of incorporation to the date of these Interrogatories?

21. If the answer to the preceding Interrogatory is affirmative, please state:

(a) The name and address of each;

(b) The period during which each served;

(c) The title of the office of each;

(d) The nature of services performed by each.

22. Has any officer of [corporation] received any salary, fee, or other compensation from the corporation? If so, state:

(a) The name and address of the officer;

(b) The period for which the payment was made in each case;

(c) The amount, if paid in money;

(d) The nature of the payment, if paid in property.

23. If payment to any officer has been made in a form other than money, state in addition to the nature of the property:

(a) The fair value of the property paid;

(b) Whether the fair value was stated by resolution of the board of directors;

(c) Whether the board of directors voted approval of payment;

(d) The name of each member of the board voting such approval.

24. Please state full name and address of the person answering these Interrogatories on behalf of [corporation].

25. Is the person answering these Interrogatories an officer of [corporation] or does he hold another position? If so, state:

(a) The office or title held by said person;

(b) For what period of time said office has been held by said person;

(c) The current address and phone number of said person;

(d) Whether said person is acting within the scope of his authority in answering these Interrogatories.

DISCOVERY

§ 4.18 —Wrongful Discharge

FORM 4–8
SAMPLE WRONGFUL DISCHARGE INTERROGATORIES

1. (a) State your full name and all other names by which you have been known, including the inclusive dates you were so known;
   (b) Set out each address at which you have resided in the last ten years, stating the inclusive dates of residence at each such address;
   (c) Beginning with high school, set out each school you have attended, and with respect to each, the date(s) of attendance, your grade average, your rank in class, any diploma, degree, and honors you received, and your major course of study.

2. State your date and place of birth.

3. Describe fully and specifically all other training and work experience which you have had, including, but not limited to:
   (a) The identity of all your employers other than defendant;
   (b) The identity of all of your supervisors at each such employment;
   (c) A full and complete description of your duties, job title(s), hours of work, and rate(s) of pay;
   (d) The dates of and reasons for all changes in said rates of compensation;
   (e) The dates of each such employment;
   (f) The reason(s) for its termination.

4. If you have previously been a party to any lawsuit (other than this lawsuit), charge, or claim to an administrative agency (other than this charge), please state:
   (a) The nature of such suit, charge or claim (for example, if civil—personal injury, or if criminal—theft) or charge (for example, EEOC—sex or race, OSHA—safety or health) or claim (for example, workers' or unemployment compensation);
   (b) The date of each such suit, charge, or claim;
   (c) The court or agency (state, federal, or local) in which it was brought;
   (d) The name of the other parties to each such suit, charge, or claim and the proper designation (for example, civil action, charge or claim number) of the suit or charge;
   (e) Whether you were plaintiff, defendant, charging, or charged party;
   (f) The disposition of each such lawsuit, charge, or claim.

5. Identify all documents relating to the lawsuit(s), charge(s) or claim(s) identified in Interrogatory No. 4, if any.

6. State with respect to your employment by [name of employer]:
   (a) The inclusive dates of employment;
   (b) Your job title(s) for each position held while in defendants employ, and the inclusive dates of employment for each job;
   (c) A complete and detailed description of the duties of each such job;

250

(d)   Rates of pay for each job;

(e)   Name(s) of your supervisors for each job.

7.   State whether you will utilize or in any way rely upon the opinion of an expert witness in this action and, if so:

(a)   Identify each person you will or may utilize as an expert witness by (1) name, (2) present or last known address and telephone number (business and residential), and (3) occupation, job title, business affiliation, and/or nature of business;

(b)   Summarize the opinions of the expert;

(c)   State each fact underlying each such opinion.

8.   State the full name of each person you will use or may use as a witness in this action, and if not otherwise identified above, state that person's:

(a)   Present or last known address and telephone number (business and residential);

(b)   Occupation, job title, and business affiliation;

(c)   Knowledge of facts relevant to this lawsuit.

9.   (a)   Identify all employers whom you have contacted regarding employment in the last ten years, specifying the date(s) of each contact, the job(s) sought or inquired about, the result(s) of each such contact, and the rate(s) of pay of any jobs offered, and the identity of the persons you contacted at each such employer;

(b)   Identify each employment agency which you have contacted in the last ten years, specifying the date(s) of contact or use, the names of the person(s) you contacted, and the purpose(s) of each such contact;

(c)   Describe fully all efforts other than those set out in response to paragraphs (a) and (b) which you have made to seek employment other than with defendant in the last ten years.

10.   With respect to the allegaiton of paragraph [number] of the [reference number] Cause of Action of plaintiff's complaint, "That on or about [date], Plaintiff and Defendants [names], and each of them, entered into a contract of employment, the terms of which were oral:"

(a)   State every fact that supports plaintiff's contention that plaintiff and the defendant entered into an oral contract of employment;

(b)   Identify every employee of defendant whom you contend participated in the formation of the alleged oral contract;

(c)   Identify each person with knowledge or information concerning facts requested by this interrogatory, specifying the fact(s) of which each such person had knowledge;

(d)   Identify all documents relating to or reflecting facts requested by this interrogatory.

11.   With respect to the allegation of paragraph [number] of the [reference number] Cause of Action of plaintiff's complaint, that, "Under the terms and provisions of said contract, said Defendants agreed to employ Plaintiff as [job description], to begin the position on [date], for so long as his services were satisfactory, to afford

251

him continuing opportunity for promotion and advancement, to provide him and his family with investment, and insurance equal to or better than those reasonably available through employment with any of said Defendants competitors and not to terminate his employment without good cause:"

(a) State every fact that supports said contention;

(b) Identify every employee of defendant whom you contend agreed to the provisions of the oral contract as you allege, and specify with respect to each:

   (i) The exact terms allegedly agreed to;

   (ii) The date upon which such alleged agreements were reached;

(c) Identify each person with knowledge or information concerning facts requested by this interrogatory, specifying the fact(s) of which each such person has knowledge;

(d) Identify all documents relating to or reflecting facts requested by this interrogatory.

12. With respect to the allegation of paragraph [number] of the [reference number] Cause of Action of plaintiff's complaint, "That at all times herein mentioned, Plaintiff faithfully and fully performed all the promises, covenants, and conditions of such contract of employment on his part to be performed, and rendered service to Defendants far in excess of the level required for their good faith satisfaction":

(a) State every fact that supports said contention;

(b) Describe fully each way in which you contend that plaintiff faithfully and fully performed all the promises, covenants, and conditions of such contract of employment;

(c) Identify each person with knowledge or information concerning facts requested by this interrogatory, specifying the fact(s) of which each such person has knowledge;

(d) Identify all documents relating to or reflecting facts requested by this interrogatory.

13. With respect to the allegation of paragraph [number] of the [reference number] Cause of Action of plaintiff's complaint, "That on or about [date], Defendants, and each of them, wrongfully and tortiously discharged Plaintiff from his hereinabove alleged employment without good cause, and, indeed, for no cause at all, upon the pretext that the Plaintiff made clerical errors and that the staff was complaining of his ability as a supervisor:"

(a) Describe fully the circumstances of your termination by defendant, and with respect to those circumstances:

   (i) Set forth fully the facts upon which you base your allegation that you were discharged without good cause;

   (ii) Identify the name(s) and job title(s) of the employee(s) of defendant whom you contend acted in its behalf in wrongfully discharging you;

   (iii) Identify all employees of defendant whose job performance was similar to or poorer than your own and were not discharged;

   (iv) As to each such employee of defendant, state the fact(s) which support(s) your contention that such person's job performance was similar to or poorer than your own.

(b) State the reason(s), if any, given to you by any employee(s) or defendant for your termination, the date(s) such reason(s) was(were) given, and the identity of those employee(s);

(c) Identify each person with knowledge or information concerning facts requested by this interrogatory, specifying the fact(s) of which each such person has knowledge;

(d) Identify all documents relating to or reflecting facts requested by this interrogatory.

14. With respect to the allegation of paragraph [number] of the [reference number] Cause of Action of plaintiff's complaint that, "Said termination was unwarranted and unlawful in that the Defendants terminated the Plaintiff to place Defendants' then friend in Plaintiff's position for Defendants' personal reasons:"

(a) State every fact that supports said contention;

(b) Identify the employee(s) of defendant who you contend was(were) a "friend" of plaintiff's replacement;

(c) State every fact that supports your contention that such employee(s) of defendant was(were) a friend of plaintiff's replacement;

(d) Identify each person with knowledge or information concerning facts requested by this interrogatory, specifying the fact(s) of which such person has knowledge;

(e) Identify all documents relating to or reflecting facts requested by this interrogatory.

15. With respect to the allegation of paragraph [number] of the [reference number] Cause of Action of plaintiff's complaint, "That as a direct and proximate result of Defendants' hereinabove alleged conduct in the premises, Plaintiff has suffered and shall continue to suffer, serious and substantial injury, defamation and disparagement to his reputation in the property management industry, all to his general damage in any amount, yet to be determined, but which Plaintiff is informed and believes, and thereon alleges, to be in excess of $10,000.00:"

(a) Describe fully each fact which supports your contention that, "Plaintiff has suffered and will continue to suffer, serious and substantial injury, defamation, and disparagement to his reputation in the property management industry;"

(b) Identify each person with knowledge or information concerning facts requested by this interrogatory, specifying the fact(s) of which each such person has knowledge;

(c) Identify all documents relating to or reflecting facts requested by this interrogatory.

16. With respect to the allegation of paragraph [number] of the [reference number] Cause of Action of plaintiff's complaint, "That as a further and direct proximate result of the Defendants' herinabove alleged conduct in the premises, Plaintiff was injured in his health, strength, and activity, which injuries caused, and will continue to cause, Plaintiff great mental nervousness, physical and emotional pain and suffering, all to his future general damages in an amount in excess of $10,000.00:"

(a) Specify each type of physical or emotional problem which you have suffered;

(b) State what symptoms you have experienced with respect to each such problem;

(c)   State when each symptom for each condition appeared, and how it evolved;

(d)   Describe what treatment you have received and identify the health care provider involved for each symptom;

(e)   Describe each fact which supports your contention that, "Plaintiff was injured in his health, strength and activity;"

(f)   Identify each person with knowledge or information concerning facts requested by this interrogatory, specifying the fact(s) of which each such person has knowledge;

(g)   Identify all documents relating to or reflecting facts requested by this interrogatory.

17.   With respect to the allegation of paragraph [number] of the [reference number] Cause of Action of plaintiff's complaint, "That as a further direct and proximate result of Defendants' hereinabove alleged conduct in the premises, Plaintiff has lost, and will continue to lose, substantial fringe benefits, including but not limited to , insurance, investment and loss of credit rating, all to his further special damage in an amount to be proven at trial:"

(a)   State the specific way(s) in which plaintiff allegedly will lose the above-specified benefits;

(b)   Identify each person with knowledge or information concerning facts requested by this interrogatory, specifying the fact(s) of which each such person has knowledge;

(c)   Identify all documents relating to or reflecting facts requested by this interrogatory.

18.   With respect to the allegation of paragraph [number] of the [reference number] Cause of Action of plaintiff's complaint, "That in conducting themselves in the premises herein, Defendants, and each of them, acted with fraud, oppression and malice, entitle Plaintiff to an award of exemplary damages in excess of $10,000.00:"

(a)   State the specific way(s) in which you contend defendant acted, "with fraud, oppression, and malice;"

(b)   State each fact upon which you base your contention that defendant acted with fraud and malice;

(c)   Identify each person with knowledge or information concerning facts requested by this interrogatory, specifying the fact(s) of which each such person has knowledge;

(d)   Identify all documents relating to or reflecting facts requested by this interrogatory.

19.   With respect to the allegations of paragraph [number] of the [reference number] Cause of Action of plaintiff's complaint, "That in conducting themselves in the premises, Defendants and each of them, acted outrageously and with the intention of causing Plaintiff, or in reckless disregard of the likelihood that Plaintiff would suffer, severe emotional distress:"

(a)   State the specific way(s) in which you contend that defendants, "acted outrageously and with the intention of causing Plaintiff, or in reckless disregard of the likelihood that Plaintiff would suffer, severe emotional distress;"

(b) State each fact which supports your contention that defendants acted in the above-specified manner;

(c) Identify each person with knowledge or information concerning facts requested by this interrogatory, specifying the fact(s) of which each such person has knowledge;

(d) Identify all documents relating to or reflecting facts requested by this interrogatory.

20. With respect to the allegations of paragraph [number] of the [reference number] Cause of Action of plaintiff's complaint, "That in conducting themselves in the premises, Defendants, and each of them, acted in bad faith and in breach of their duty of good faith and implied-at-law covenant of good faith and fair dealing, contained in Plaintiff's hereinabove alleged contract of employment:"

(a) State the specific way(s) in which you contend that defendants acted in the manner specified in the above allegation;

(b) State each fact which supports your contention that defendants acted in the manner specified in the above allegation;

(c) Identify each person with knowledge or information concerning facts requested by this interrogatory, specifying the fact(s) of which each such person has knowledge;

(d) Identify all documents relating to or reflecting facts requested by this interrogatory.

21. With respect to the allegations of paragraph [number] of the [reference number] Cause of Action of plaintiff's complaint, "That on and after [date], the date on which Defendants tortiously discharged Plaintiff from his employment, as hereinabove more fully appears, Defendants, and each of them, represented to Plaintiff and to third persons that they had terminated his employment because they had good faith reasons to be dissatisfied with his services:"

(a) Identify every employee whom you contend made the representations described in the above allegation;

(b) Specify the date and circumstances in which such representations were allegedly made, including the identity of the person to whom the allegations were made;

(c) Identify each person with knowledge or information concerning facts requested by this interrogatory, specifying the fact(s) of which each such person has knowledge;

(d) Identify all documents relating to or reflecting facts requested by this interrogatory.

22. With respect to the allegations of paragraph [number] of the [reference number] Cause of Action of plaintiff's complaint, "That said represntations were false at the time Defendants made them in that Defendants did not terminate Plaintiff because they had good faith reasons to be dissatisfied with Plaintiff's services and discharged him in bad faith as hereinabove more fully appears:"

(a) State every fact which supports your contention that defendants had no reason to be dissatisfied with plaintiff's services and discharged him in bad faith;

(b) Identify each person with knowledge or information concerning facts requested by this interrogatory, specifying the fact(s) of which each such person has knowledge;

(c) Identify all documents relating to or reflecting facts requested by this interrogatory.

23. With respect to the allegations of paragraph [number] of the [reference number] Caues of Action of plaintiff's complaint, "That Defendants and each of them, made the aforesaid misrepresentations with knowledge that they were false. At the time Defendants made them, they knew, or had every reason to know, that their publications would induce others not to deal with Plaintiff:"

(a) Sate every fact which supports your contention that defendants made the alleged specified misrepresentations with knowledge that they were false;

(b) State every fact which supports your contention that the defendants knew, or had every reason to know, that their publications would induce others not to deal with plaintiff;

(c) Identify each person with knowledge or information concerning facts requested by this interrogatory, specifying the fact(s) of which each such person has knowledge;

(d) Identify all documents relating to or reflecting facts requested by this interrogatory.

24. Do you contend that defendant has acted wrongfully in any manner not covered in your response to the interrogatories set out above? If so:

(a) Describe fully each instance in which you contend that defendant so acted wrongfully, stating with respect to each such instance:

(i) The precise nature of such alleged wrongful treatment;

(ii) The specific time and place at which the alleged wrongful treatment occurred;

(iii) The name(s) and job title(s) of each employee of defendant whom you contend participated in such wrongful treatment, with a description of the action taken by each such employee;

(iv) Any other facts by which you contend that you received such alleged wrongful treatment.

(b) Identify each person with knowledge or information concerning facts requested by this interrogatory, specifying the fact(s) of which each such person has knowledge;

(c) Identify all documents relating to or reflecting facts requested by this interrogatory.

25. Describe fully your efforts to obtain employment since leaving Defendant's employ, including the following:

(a) The date(s) and nature of each such effort;

(b) The employer(s) involved in each such effort;

(c) The name(s) of persons contacted at each such employer;

(d) The job(s) sought and their starting rates of pay;

(e) The results of each such effort.

§ 4.19 SWORN ACCOUNT

26. If you received any payment or other compensation after termination by defendant, other than payments listed in the preceding interrogatory or payments received from defendant, state:
    (a) The amount of each such payment;
    (b) The source of each such payment;
    (c) The date of each such payment;
    (d) The reason for each such payment.

27. Describe and identify any document concerning any payment or other compensation described in response to the two preceding interrogatories.

§ 4.19 —Sworn Account

FORM 4–9
SAMPLE INTERROGATORIES ON SWORN ACCOUNT

1. Please state the following:
    (a) The full and complete name, business and residential street address, and the business and residential telephone numbers of the person responding to these Interrogatories; and,
    (b) That person's position with, or business relation to the defendant (for example, sole proprietor, employee, partner, officer, and so forth) at the time of responding to these Interrogatories and during the period from [date] to [date].

2. Please state the proper name of the defendant and the type of business entity it is.

3. Please state whether the goods, wares, merchandise, and material shown and described on the attached invoices, copies of which are attached to plaintiff's original petition in the above-entitled and numbered cause as part of Exhibit A, were ordered from the plaintiff by the defendant herein, his agent or duly authorized representative.

4. If the answer to the preceding interrogatory is NO, please state all the facts known to you, directly or indirectly, which you contend to be a basis for that denial.

5. Please state whether the goods, wares, merchandise, and material listed and described in the attached invoices referred to in Interrogatory No. 3 were delivered as ordered.

6. If the answer to the proceeding interrogatory is NO, please state if the defendant or any person employed by defendant or any person associated with defendant in the operation of defendant's business received any of the goods, wares, and merchandise described in Exhit A to plaintiff's original Petition; and if so, please set forth precisely which goods and merchandise defendant did and did not receive or were and were not received by any person employed by defendant or any person associated with defendant in the operation of his business; and with respect to materials received, the dates of receipt.

DISCOVERY

7. Please state whether the charges as shown and stated on the invoices referred to in Interrogatory No. 3 were the agreed charges for such goods, wares, merchandise, and material listed on such invoices at the time that the same were purchased from the plaintiff by the defendant.

8. If the answer to the preceding interrogatory is NO, please state the agreed charges for such goods, wares, merchandise, and material listed on said invoices at the time same were purchased from plaintiff by defendant. Point out specifically which charges are erroneous and give the charge agreed upon, or if no charge was agreed upon, explain why each said charge is in error.

9. Please state whether the charges on the invoices referred to in Interrogatory No. 3 were the usual, customary, or reasonable charges for such goods, wares, merchandise, and material at the time of the sale and delivery thereof.

10. If the answer to the preceding interrogatory is NO, please state what the usual, customary, or reasonable charges for each of such goods, wares, merchandise, and material were at the time of the sale and delivery thereof.

11. Please state whether you have at any time prior to the filing of this suit communicated to the Plaintiff any objections to the prices charged in the attached invoices.

12. If the answer to the preceding interrogatory is YES, state specifically the particular prices objected to, the dates the objections were made, the contents of the objections, to whom they were made; and if documented, please attach such documentation.

13. Please state whether defendant herein has sold, used, or otherwise disposed of the goods, wares, merchandise and the material shown and described on the invoices referred to in Interrogatory No. 3.

14. If the answewer to any part of the preceding interrogatory is NO, state which items as shown on the invoices have not been sold, used or otherwise disposed of and in that regard state the present location thereof. [Specify the invoice or invoices on which said goods, wares, merchandise, and material are shown.]

15. Please state whether payment has been made against the account annexed as Exhibit A to plaintiff's original Petition. If so, state the date and amount of each payment.

16. State whether all credits due to defendant have been given to defendant by plaintiff as shown on the account annexed as Exhibit A to plaintiff's original Petition.

17. Please state whether any offsets are due to defendant by plaintiff regarding any business dealing between plaintiff and defendant.

18. Please claim with respect to each offset, payment, or credit which defendant claims, the following information:
    (a) Whether defendant claims an offset, payment, or credit;
    (b) Date of same;
    (c) What the same is for;

(d) Attach and identify any written material you have which you believe supports same;

(e) If you or any officer, director, or employee of defendant have had any conversations with plaintiff regarding same, then state the dates of such conversations, the parties present, the contents of same, and what was said by each party in each such conversation.

19. Please state whether this claim and account has heretofore been presented to defendant for payment.

20. Have you or any officer, director, or employee ever denied to plaintiff, or any of plaintiff's representatives or attorneys, that defendant is indebted upon the account made the basis of plaintiff's original Petition? If so, set forth:

(a) The date upon which each and every such denial was made;

(b) Whether the same was oral or in writing;

(c) The name of the person or persons to whom each such denial was made or given;

(d) If in writing, please annex a copy of such writing to your answers to these Interrogatories or set out in full the content of said writing;

(e) If made orally, state the content of each denial and the reasons for making same.

21. Have you or any officer, director, or employee ever made any claims to plaintiff, or to any of plaintiff's representatives or attorneys, for payments, credits, and/or offsets upon the account made the basis of plaintiff's original Petition? If so, please set forth:

(a) The date upon which each such payment, credit, and/or offset was claimed;

(b) The name, address, and telephone number of the person making such claim;

(c) Name of the representative or attorney of plaintiff to whom the same is made;

(d) Whether the same was oral or in writing;

(e) If in writing, please annex a copy thereof to your answers to these Interrogatories or set out in full the content of said writing.

22. Does defendant acknowledge itself to be indebted to plaintiff for any sum of money upon the account made the basis of plaintiff's original Petition? If so, please set forth the amount of money for which defendant acknowledges itself indebted to plaintiff.

23. If your answer to Interrogatory No. 22 is in the negative, or if your answer to Interrogatory No. 22 is a sum and amount less than that amount shown on Exhibit A attached to plaintiff's original Petition, please set forth each and every reason, ground, and defense upon which you rely to support your contention that defendant is not indebted to plaintiff for the sum and amount shown in Exhibit A.

§ 4.20 Preliminary Statement

In order to tailor a set of interrogatories to a specific case, it is advisable to define any specialized terms which may be of a technical nature and not easily understood by someone not familiar with the subject matter. The preliminary statement is the vehicle by which these definitions may be introduced. The preliminary statement is also a handy tool for defining ordinary terms used in the interrogatories to ensure that the recipient will answer the questions fully and to your satisfaction. The statement can be used to broaden or narrow the scope of the discovery by virtue of the definitions you include and it should immediately precede the first interrogatory. Not all jurisdictions allow preliminary statements so be sure to check your state and local rules. (See **Form 4–10**.)

FORM 4–10
SAMPLE PRELIMINARY STATEMENT

Please answer each of the following interrogatories in writing, under oath, pursuant to the [state/federal] Rules of Civil Procedure. With respect to each of the interrogatories propounded to you, answer the quetions in accordance with the PRELIMINARY STATEMENT.

PRELIMINARY STATEMENT

The following Preliminary Statement and definitions apply to each of the interrogatories set forth hereunder, and they are deemed to be incorporated therein.

1. The terms "you" and "your", as they are used herein, refer to Defendants and include any and all agents, servants, and employees of Defendants including but not limited to Defendants' attorneys, and to any other person or persons acting pursuant to Defendants' direction.

2. The singular number and the masculine gender, as used herein, shall be deemed to include the plural, the feminine, or the neuter, as may be appropriate.

3. The term "person", as used herein, shall be deemed to include, in the plural as well as singular, any natural person, firm, association, partnership, joint venture, corporation, or other legal entity, unless the context otherwise indicates.

4. If you are asked to identify a person, please state for each such person:
    a. That person's full name;
    b. If the person is other than a natural person (for example, corporation, partnership, and so forth), the type of entity it is;
    c. That person's last known home address, and telephone number;
    d. That person's last known business address, and telephone number;
    e. If the person is a natural person, state his relationship (including business, blood, or other relationship), if any, to you;
    f. The particular facts of which each such person has knowledge;
    g. If the person is a natural person, state the name and address of his employer or employers, setting forth a description of his job duties and the dates during which such person was so employed.

§ 4.20 PRELIMINARY STATEMENT

5.   The term "document", as used herein, shall mean originals and all copies, unless identical, of written, recorded and graphic matter, however produced or reproduced, formal or informal, whether for internal or external use, including, but not limited to, correspondence, letters, memoranda, drafts, corporate minutes, diary or appointment book entries, guest calendar entries, telephone logs, telegrams, telexes, notes (including stenographic notes), minutes, reports, contracts, agreements, directives, instructions, court papers, graphic representations, lists of persons or things, books, pamphlets, manuscripts, canceled checks, mechanical and electric sound recordings, charts, tapes, indexes, data sheets, data processing cards and tapes, statistical tables, memoranda made of any telephone communications, and diagrams.

6.   If you are asked to identify a document, as defined in Paragraph 5 above, for each such document, please state:
    a.   A description of the document with sufficient specificity to enable Plaintiff to identify such writing in a Request to Produce, or in a Subpoena Duces Tecum;
    b.   The date the document was prepared;
    c.   The identity of each person signing or executing the document;
    d.   The identity of each person who prepared the document;
    e.   The date on which such person signed or executed such document;
    f.   A statement of contents of the document;
    g.   The name and last known address and telephone number of the person who presently has custody of the document, or if that is not known, the name and address and telephone number of the person who you know or believe last had custody of the document, and the relationship (including business, blood, or other relationship), if any, of that person to you;
    h.   If you will do so without a Request to Produce, please attach a copy of the document to your Answers to these interrogatories;
    i.   The name and last known address and telephone number of each person who received the document or a copy thereof;
    j.   The identity of each person who aided or assisted in the preparation of said document, other than the person (secretary or typist, etc.) who actually caused the document to be prepared.
The term "oral conversation", as used herein, includes, but is not limited to, any oral conversation conducted in person or over the telephone.

7.   These interrogatories call for all information (including information contained in writings) known or available to you, including all information in the possession of your attorneys, accountants, employees, and/or their firms; corporations; and other persons acting on your behalf or under your direction or control.

8.   If you cannot answer any interrogatory fully after exercising due diligence to make inquiry and secure the information requested, please so state and answer each inter-rogatory to the extent you deem possible, specifying the portion of the interrogatory you claim you are unable to fully and completely answer, and specifying the facts upon which you rely to support your contention that you are unable to answer the interrogatory fully and completely, and state what knowledge, information or belief you have concerning the unanswered portion of any such interrogatory.

§ 4.21 Jurats

A *jurat* is simply a sworn, notarized statement by the signing party which states that he or she has read the answers to interrogatories and that they are true and correct. It is attached as the final page of the interrogatories, and should be provided for the opposing party along with the interrogatories as a matter of course. (See **Forms 4–11, 4–12,** and **4–13.**) This will eliminate the possibility of receiving unsworn answers in response to your questions. Conversely, it is necessary for the answering party to sign and swear to the answers after they are prepared by his counsel. It is important that your client read the answers carefully before signing, and make sure that the answers are absolutely correct, as these answers can be used as evidence in court.

FORM 4–11
SAMPLE FEMALE JURAT

THE STATE OF [state]   )
)
COUNTY OF [county]   )

BEFORE ME, the undersigned authority, on this day personally appeared [name], known to me to be the person whose name is subscribed to the foregoing answers to interrogatories and after having been duly sworn stated on her oath that she is the [plaintiff/defendant] in the above captioned case, that she has read the foregoing answers to interrogatories and that they are true and correct.

_____

[Plaintiff/defendant name]

SWORN TO AND SUBSCRIBED before me by the said [plaintiff/defendant] on this the [date] day of [month], [20__].

_____

Notary Public in and for
The State of [state]

FORM 4–12
SAMPLE MALE JURAT

THE STATE OF [state]   )
)
COUNTY OF [county]   )

BEFORE ME, the undersigned authority, on this day personally appeared [name], known to me to be the person whose name is subscribed to the foregoing answers to interrogatories and after having been duly sworn stated on his oath that he is the

§ 4.22   LETTER TO THE CLERK OF COURT

[plaintiff/defendant] in the above captioned case, that he has read the foregoing answers to interrogatories and that they are true and correct.

_____

[Plaintiff/Defendant name]

SWORN TO AND SUBSCRIBED before me by the said [plaintiff/defendant] on this the [date] day of [month], [20__].

_____

Notary Public in and for
The State of [state]

FORM 4–13
SAMPLE CORPORATE JURAT

THE STATE OF [state]   )
)
COUNTY OF [county]   )

BEFORE ME, the undersigned authority, on this day personally appeared [name], or [location], known to me to be the person whose name is subscribed to the foregoing instrument and acknowledged to me that [he/she] is a duly authorized representative of [corporation], and after having been duly sworn stated on [his/her] oath that the foregoing answers to interrogatories are true and correct and that [he/she] is authorized to make this affidavit on behalf of [corporation].

[name of corporation]
(By) [name of corporate representative]

SWORN TO AND SUBSCRIBED before me by the said [corporate representative], on this the [date] day of [month], [20__].

[name of notary public]
NOTARY PUBLIC IN AND FOR
The State of [state]

§ 4.22   Transmittal Letter to Clerk of Court

If you are sending your documents to the court to be filed by messenger, you may not feel it is necessary to include a transmittal letter. You will want to include, however, one extra copy when it is called for by the local court requirements so that the clerk of the court may file stamp your copy for you. This is the copy that should be kept in your pleading file. If you have occasion to mail documents to the court for filing, the following form (**Form 4–14**) is included to use as a cover letter.

FORM 4–14
SAMPLE TRANSMITTAL LETTER TO CLERK OF COURT

[Date]

RE: Cause No. [case number], In the [judicial district]
           Judicial District Court in and for [county] County,
           [state], [plaintiff] vs. [defendant]

[Clerk of court]
[address]

Dear Sir:

We enclose [reference to enclosed documents] in the above styled and numbered cause which we request that you file among the papers in this cause. Please acknowledge receipt and filing of this instrument by placing your file mark on the enclosed copy of this letter and returning it to us. A self-addressed, stamped envelope is enclosed for your convenience in returning the copy to us.

A copy of this pleading has been furnished to the attorneys for the [plaintiff(s)/defendant(s)].

                    Very truly yours,

                    [attorney name]
                    For the Firm of [name of law firm]
                    State Bar No. [number]

§ 4.23   Transmittal Letter to Client

When you receive interrogatories from opposing counsel, you will immediately want to make a copy and forward them to your client for his review. If at all possible, this should be done on the same day that you receive the interrogatories. The earlier that you send the interrogatories to your client, the more time you will have to work with him and develop well thought-out, complete answers which will serve you and your client throughout the remainder of the case.

After the client has had the interrogatories in his possession for approximately one week, you should either contact him by phone or arrange for him to come into the office to discuss the answers. When you have sent the letter to the client, be sure to calendar appropriate follow-up time to insure that the interrogatories will be completed, signed, notarized, and filed within the specified period of time allotted by the rules. (**Form 4–15.**)

§ 4.24   FOLLOW-UP LETTER—ANSWERS

FORM 4–15
SAMPLE TRANSMITTAL LETTER TO CLIENT

Dear [client]:

On [date], [20__], we received these Interrogatories from opposing counsel. By law, we must file answers to these questions by [date]. Since that period of time can go by very quickly, we would like you to review these questions immediately and begin to jot down notes about the answers.

[name], a paralegal in our firm, will be calling you in approximately one week to discuss the answers with you. If necessary, she will set up a meeting with you to go over the questions thoroughly. Once the answers have been prepared, it will be necessary for you to review them and sign them on sworn affidavit in front of a notary public. We will contact you as soon as they are ready.

In the meantime, if you have any questions about the Interrogatories, please call and speak with me or my paralegal.

Very truly yours,

_____

[attorney name]

§ 4.24   Follow-Up Letter to Client— Interrogatory Answers

Form 4–16 is a sample follow-up letter to your client.

FORM 4–16
SAMPLE FOLLOW-UP LETTER TO CLIENT— INTERROGATORY ANSWERS

Re: Answers to Plaintiff's First Set of Interrogatories

Dear [client]:

On [date], we forwarded to you a copy of Plaintiff's First Set of Interrogatories, along with a request that you begin to assimilate information for the preparation of the answers to those questions.

We have not yet received any material from you, and we are now concerned that we may not be able to file and serve the Answers to Interrogatories within the statutorily mandated time frame of the [state/federal] Rules of Civil Procedure. Failure to respond to these interrogatories in a timely fashion can result in the court ordering sanctions against you in the form of monetary fines or the striking of any or all of your claims or defenses in this action.

It is imperative that you contact me immediately to arrange a time to finalize the answers to these interrogatories. Please recognize the urgency of this matter; it is vital to your legal representation. Thank you for your cooperation.

Respectfully yours,

[name of paralegal]
Paralegal to [name of attorney]

§ 4.25 Letter to Client—Overdue Discovery

Form 4–17 is a sample letter that you would send to the client about overdue discovery.

FORM 4–17
SAMPLE LETTER TO CLIENT—OVERDUE DISCOVERY

Dear [client],

We are concerned that we have not yet received your response to the following documents which were forwarded to you on [date], [20__]:

[List the names and dates of the documents here.]

It is crucial that you understand the importance of the statutory deadlines for responding to these types of documents. The [state/federal] Rules of Civl Procedure state that a party must respond to this type of pleading in [number] days from receipt of service of this document or the Court may either on its own volition or upon motion by the opposing party, invoke sanctions upon the party who is delinquent in its response. The sanctions which the Court may choose to invoke in cases of this nature are very severe, and range from monetary fines to imprisonment for civil contempt to striking portions or the entirety of your pleadings before this court, which could virtually eliminate your right to [describe legal right] in this action.

We are sure that you understand that once we have received your response to this document, we must have adquate time to review your responses to protect your rights of privilege and to finalize the document so that it may be filed before the statutory deadline. To that end, we again stress how important it is that we receive the necessary information from you within the next [specified time period]. If there is a problem which will prevent you from being able to produce the material within that period of time, or if there is anything we may do to assist you in this endeavor, please call us immediately so that we may take whatever steps are available to us to try to obtain an extension for you.

We look forward to hearing from you shortly.

Very truly yours,

_____

[attorney's name]

§ 4.26   Protective Orders

Many times there will be information related to a lawsuit that, if made public, would be damaging to one of the parties in a way not related to the lawsuit at all. An example of this type of information would be commercial, or trade, secrets, the divulgence of which would hurt a party's competitive edge in the business world. Another example would be customer or account lists. An individual in a lawsuit may wish to protect a fact such as an adoption of a child to prevent undue hurt to a party. There are basically two ways to protect this kind of information in the discovery process, through a joint confidentiality agreement or a protective order.

In deciding whether to issue a protective order, the court balances the privacy interests in the information asserted by one party with the probative value of that information to the other party. When the probative value of the information is significant, and the privacy interests in the material can be protected by redaction, there is a presumption in favor of discovery.

It has become common practice in the federal courts for the court to enter a protective order on stipulation of the parties. A proposed amendment to Federal Rule of Civil Procedure 26(c) would codify this practice.

The power of the court to enter a protective order includes the power to revoke and modify such orders.

A joint confidentiality agreement can be signed between the parties which spells out both parties' intent to utilize agreed-upon procedures to ensure that the confidentiality of the information is secure.

A second way of preserving the confidentiality of documents is by Protective Order signed by the presiding judge in the case. In this type of order, the judge may rule that he is to view the documents *in camera* and make a decision on how much of the information should be shared, or he may issue a blanket ruling which defines the procedures to be followed in the admission of such information and outline the limitations and restrictions on the use of such information once it is disclosed.

The Protective Order which follows (**Form 4–18**), is written for use in Federal District Court, and is actually in use today in one of the nation's largest litigations.

FORM 4–18
SAMPLE PROTECTIVE ORDER

It appearing to the Court that documents, materials and information subject to discovery in these cases may contain trade secrets, proprietary and/or other confidential

DISCOVERY

information, the further disclosure of which might be injurious to either the Plaintiffs, Defendants or Intervenors, and it further appearing that counsel for the parties have agreed to the entry of this Protective Order to preserve the confidentiality of such documents and information, it is, therefore, ORDERED, pursuant to Rule 26 of the Feederal Rules of Civil Procedure, as follows:

1.   All information supplied or documents exchanged by the parties hereto for inspection and/or copying by any other party shall constitute Confidential Information, and such Confidential Information shall be used solely for the prosecution or defense of these cases and shall not be disclosed to anyone except in accordance with the terms of this Order.

2.   Confidential Information may be disclosed only to the following persons ("Qualified Persons"):
     (a)   Counsel for a party, and persons regularly employed in the offices of such counsel;
     (b)   Outside experts or professional advisers retained by a party to assist in the prosecution or defense of these cases, and persons regularly employed in the offices of such experts or advisers; and
     (c)   Those officers or employees of a party assisting counsel in the prosecution or defense of these cases; provided, however, that prior to such disclosure to them, counsel shall furnish a copy of this Protective Order to the persons described in subparagraphs (b) and (c) above and obtain the written agreement of each person to be bound by the terms of this Protective Order. The requirement of obtaining such written agreement may be satisfied by obtaining the signature of any such person at the foot of a copy of this Order.

3.   Nothing contained herein shall prevent the parties from utilizing any other parties' Confidential Information at the trial of these cases or in any pre-trial proceeding; provided, however, if such Confidential Information is used in answers to interrogatories, admissions, depositions or other discovery, at the request of the party providing such Confidential Information, all portions of the interrogatory answers, admissions, transcripts of depositions, and exhibits thereto or other discovery which refer or relate to such Confidential Information shall be treated as Confidential Information and thus be subject to the provisions of this Protective Order.

4.   Confidential Information shall not be disclosed or made available, in whole or in part, whether in writing, orally, or by other means, to persons other than the Court, Qualified Persons, or the party who designated or provided the Confidential Information, except as required by law, or by any judicial, governmental, or administrative body under any law, regulation, or order; provided, however, that the party being required to disclose Confidential Information shall give five (5) days' prior written notice of such disclosure by certified mail to the party or parties which provided such Confidential Information addressed to the attorneys of record of such party or parties, unless the judicial, governmental, or administrative body's law, regulation or order requires disclosure sooner, than that disclosing party shall give such notice by telephone as soon as practicable.

§ 4.26 PROTECTIVE ORDERS

5.   Nothing herein shall prevent disclosure beyond the terms of this Order if each and every party designating the information as Confidential Information consents to such disclosure, or if the Court, after notice to all affected parties, orders such disclosure.

6.   The restrictions on the use and disclosure of information designated as Confidential Information contained herein shall not apply to such information which the party receiving such information can show:
   (a)   At the time of disclosure to the receiving party was available to the public.
   (b)   Subsequent to the disclosure to the receiving party, the information becomes available to the public through no fault of the receiving party (including the officers or employees of a corporate party) or was disclosed to the receiving party without any obligation of confidentiality by someone not a party to this action who was in lawful possession of such information. However, no information which is specific as to details shall be deemed to be excepted from the restrictions on use and disclosure merely because it is embraced by more general information which is readily available to the public or which is in or comes into the possession of the receiving party, except to the extend such more general information precisely discloses the specific information disclosed to the receiving party. The receiving party shall have the burden of proving that such Confidential Information comes within the scope of one or more of the exceptions contained in this Paragraph 6.

7.   The inadvertent or unintentional production of documents containing, or other disclosure of, confidential or secret information without being designated as Confidential Information at the time of the production or disclosure shall not be deemed a waiver in whole or in part of a party's claim of confidentiality or secrecy, either as to the specific information disclosed or as to any of the information relating thereto or on the same or relating subject matter.

8.   The designation of documents or information as Confidential Information pursuant to this Order is intended solely to facilitate the proceedings in these cases, and such designation shall not be construed as an admission or agreement by other parties that such information constitutes or contains confidential or secret information.

9.   At the conclusion of these cases, all Confidential Information subject to this Protective Order, except for such information that becomes part of the public record in proceedings of this Court, shall, at the written request of the party providing such Confidential Information, be returned to such party by all persons to whom such documents have been furnished.

10.   The provisions of this Protective Order are without prejudice to the right of (a) the party receiving Confidential Information to apply to the Court for an order that any given document or item or information received need not be treated as Confidential Information and is not, therefore, subject to the restrictions contained herein, or (b) the party producing such documents or furnishing information to apply to the Court for an order imposing further restrictions on specified documents or information.

11.   This Order is without prejudice to the right of any party to oppose production or admissibility of documents or information for any reason.

12.   Nothing contained in this Protective Order shall preclude any party from using its own Confidential Information in any matter it sees fit, or from revealing such Confidential Information to whomever it chooses, without the prior consent of any other party or this Court.

13.   The inadvertent or unintentional production of documents or other information containing, or other disclosure of, privileged information or information constituting work product shall not be deemed a waiver in whole or in part of a parties' claim of privilege or work product protection, either as to the specific information disclosed or as to any other information relating thereto or on the same or relating subject matter.

SIGNED this [date] day of [month], (20__].

_____
UNITED STATES DISTRICT JUDGE

§ 4.27   Additional Interrogatories under Limiting Rules

Many state rules, and many more local rules now call for limiting the number of interrogatories that one party may propound to another. Some rules limit the actual number of questions as well as the number of sets you may serve on your opponent. In most cases, this is a good rule that keeps abuse of this discovery tool to a minimum, and forces a party to propound well-thought-out questions designed to obtain relevant information.

The Federal Rules of Civil Procedure limit the number of interrogatories which may be propounded. Prior to this rule change, interrogatories in federal civil practice were limited only by local rules in certain jurisdictions. Rule 33(a) reads as follows:

(a) Availability.   Without leave of court or written stipulation, any party may serve upon any other party written interrogatories, not exceeding 25 in number including all discrete subparts, to be answered by the party served or, if the party served is a public or private corporation or a partnership or association or governmental agency, by any other officer or agent, who shall furnish such information as is available to the party. Leave to serve additional interrogatories shall be granted to the extent consistent with the principles of Rule 26(b)(2). Without leave of court or written stipulation, interrogatories may not be served before the time specified in Rule 26(d).

The principles of Rule 26(b)(2) refer to the limitations imposed by the court with regard to reasonableness and scope of questions which may be propounded according to general discovery principles.

There are times, however, when new information comes to light or a case is especially complex and when a party may feel the need to serve additional interrogatories. Toward that end, most rules provide for a motion asking the judge to permit the party to file additional interrogatories. Be sure to check your state and

270

local rules for your jurisdiction's proper procedure in this instance. (See **Form 4–19.**)

A number of federal district courts have rejected Rule 33's limitation on the number of interrogatories or have adopted their own limitation.

FORM 4–19
SAMPLE MOTION FOR LEAVE TO FILE
ADDITIONAL INTERROGATORIES

NO. [case number]

[name]	)	IN THE DISTRICT COURT OF
	)	
Plaintiff,	)	[county] COUNTY, [state]
	)	
vs.	)	[judicial district] JUDICIAL DISTRICT
	)	
[name]	)	
	)	
Defendant.	)	

MOTION FOR LEAVE TO FILE ADDITIONAL INTERROGATORIES

TO THE HONORABLE JUDGE OF SAID COURT:

COME(S) NOW [name], (one of the) (cross-) defendant(s) in the above cause, to file this motion for leave to file additional interrogatories, and respectfully show(s) to the Court the following:

Alternative ONE

I.

(Cross-)defendant(s) (has/have) previously filed in this case [number] set of interrogatories, which consist of a total of [number] separate interrogatories. (Cross-) defendant(s) now ask(s) for leave of Court to file an additional set of interrogatories. A copy of the proposed set of interrogatories is attached as an exhibit hereto.

Alternative TWO

I.

(Cross-)defendant(s) ask(s) leave of Court to file attached set of interrogatories, which consists of [number] separate interrogatories.

II.

The filing of the proposed additional set of interrogatories or (The filing of interrogatories in a number exceeding [number] is in no way an attempt to harass or to burden the part(y ies) to whom the interrogatories are directed. Instead, the filing of these interrogatories is justified on the following grounds:

[describe grounds for justifying additional interrogatories].

_____

_____

_____

WHEREFORE, PREMISES CONSIDERED, [name], _____, (cross-)defendant(s) herein, pray(s) that the Court grant this motion in all respects and award all other and further relief to which (cross-)defendant(s) (is are) entitled.

[name of law firm]

By: _____
[attorney name]
State Bar No. [number]
[firm address]
Counsel for (Cross-)Defendant(s)

FIAT

On this the [date] day of [month], [20], at the request of the (cross-)defendant(s), the Court set the above motion to be heard at [time] [A.M./P.M.] on the [date] day of [month], [20].

_____
JUDGE PRESIDING

CERTIFICATE OF SERVICE

I certify that this instrument was served in compliance with Rules _____ and _____ of the Rules of Civil Procedure, by certified mail or hand delivery, return receipt requested, on the [date] day of [month], [20__], and was promptly filed with the Clerk of the Court, together with this proof of service.

_____
[Attorney's name]

§ 4.28   Answering Interrogatories

Paraglegals are often asked to prepare the first draft of answers to a set of interrogatories. As with any other aspect of a lawsuit, there are basic rules and guidelines to follow in completing this task. First, provide the client with a copy of the interrogatories so that he can begin to assimilate any information which will aid you in this process.

Second, discuss the questions with the client to obtain a clear understanding on both parts as to the meaning of the questions and the information required to answer them completely. You may wish to ask your client to provide you with his own draft of the answers as a starting point. When you sit down to prepare your first draft, keep in mind that your objective is to answer the questions fairly, accurately and completely, without volunteering any information which is not absolutely essential to properly respond to the questions.

Many jurisdictions have rules which state that the entire question must be repeated preceeding the answer. Even if this is not required in your locale, it is a good habit to get into. This will eliminate the possibility of placing an answer as a response to the wrong question. Is also makes later proofreading jobs easier. Care should also be taken during the preparation of answers to sort out those questions which should be objected to as being irrelevant, burdensome, or seeking privileged information or other information which that party could obtain themselves.

Answers to interrogatories should not be taken lightly. Failure to respond within the time alloted by the appropriate rule of civil procedure could cause the judge to grant sanctions against your client. Care should also be taken to ensure that the final revision of the answers contain well-thought-out, truthful, and concise responses to the questions. The final document must be reviewed and approved by the attorney and signed and sworn to in front of a notary public by the client.

§ 4.29   —Requesting Time Extensions

Many law firms automatically request an extension of time from the propounding party to respond with answers to the interrogatories. The following letter (**Form 4–20**) requesting an extension of time contains two sample paragraphs in brackets giving typical reasons for requesting an extension.

FORM 4–20
SAMPLE LETTER REQUESTING TIME EXTENSION FROM
OPPOSING COUNSEL

[name]
[address]

    Re: [Case Name and Case Number]

Dear [opposing counsel]:

    We are in receipt of Plaintiff's First Set of Interrogatories, which were served on [date]. We have contacted our client regarding the answering of these interrogatories, and have begun to assimilate the information you have requested.

DISCOVERY

(Unfortunately, our client has suffered a death in his family and has informed us that he must leave immediately to take care of emergency family business in another state. It will be necessary for him to remain out of state until [date]. Therefore, we are asking your cooperation in granting our client a three week extension until [date] in order to answer the Plaintiff's First Set of Interrogatories.)

(We are having some difficulty in locating some of the information you have requested and would like to request a two-week extension of time in order to answer the interrogatories properly and completely. If you are so gracious as to allow us the two-week extension, our client's Answers to Interrogatories will be due to you on [date].)

We thank you very much for your cooperation in this matter.

Respectfully yours,

_____

[Name]

Frequently, an attorney or legal assistant will request an extension of time to respond to interrogatories simply by telephoning the counsel for the propounding party. If so, the propounding party will usually grant or deny an extension orally at that time. In this situation, always follow up the telephone call with a confirming letter such as the following sample in **Form 4–21.**

FORM 4–21
SAMPLE LETTER CONFIRMING TIME EXTENSION FROM
OPPOSING COUNSEL

[name]
[address]

Re: [case name and case number]

Dear [opposing counsel]:

This letter is to confirm our telephone conversation today wherein you graciously agreed to grant our client [name] a two-week extension in which to file the Answers to Plaintiff's First Set of Interrogatories, which were originally served on [date]. The Answers will now be due on [date].

We thank you very much for your cooperation in allowing us this additional period of time in which to respond.

Respectfully yours,

_____

[name]

§ 4.29   REQUESTING TIME EXTENSIONS

If you *must* have additional time to respond to interrogatories but the opposing counsel refuses to grant you an extension, you will have to file a motion similar to the one in **Form 4–22** requesting an enlargement of time. **Form 4–23** is a sample order granting enlargement of time.

FORM 4–22
SAMPLE MOTION FOR ENLARGEMENT OF TIME

NO. [case number]

[name]	)	IN THE DISTRICT COURT OF
	)	
Plaintiff	)	[county] COUNTY, [state]
	)	
vs.	)	[judicial district] JUDICIAL DISTRICT
	)	
[name]	)	
	)	
Defendant	)	

MOTION FOR ENLARGEMENT OF TIME

TO THE HONORABLE JUDGE OF SAID COURT:

COMES NOW, [name], [plaintiff/defendant] in the above-entitled and numbered cause, and moves this Court for an Order enlarging the time in which [he/she/it] may (serve answers and objections to [referenced set] Interrogatories to [number of days], [OR] respond to [name of document]) and in support of this motion would show the Court as follows:

As provided for by Rule [citation] of the [state/federal] Rules of Civil Procedure, good cause exists for an Order by this Court to grant this motion as follows: [State facts specifically, such as the client being out of the country and unavailable, or the material needed to necessitate response was unavailable temporarily, or there was an excusable problem at the law firm, such as illness of the attorney.] Therefore, this Court is respectfully requested to grant [plaintiff's/defendant's] motion to enlarge the time in which to [specify act for which motion to enlarge is requested].

WHEREFORE, PREMISES CONSIDERED, [name], [Plaintiff/Defendant] respectfully requests that the Court, upon hearing of this motion, order that [name] [plaintiff/defendant] be permitted [number] days from the service of [name of document] in which to serve [name of document].

Respectfully submitted,

_____

[attorney name]

CERTIFICATE OF SERVICE

I certify that this instrument was served in compliance with Rules ____ and ____ of the _____ Rules of Civil Procedure, by certified mail or hand-delivery, return receipt requested, on the [date] day of [month], [20__], and was promptly filed with the Clerk of the Court, together with this proof of service.

_____
[attorney name]

FORM 4–23
SAMPLE ORDER GRANTING ENLARGEMENT OF TIME

NO. [case number]

[name]		) IN THE DISTRICT COURT OF
	Plaintiff	)
		) [county] COUNTY, [state]
		)
vs.		) [judicial district] JUDICIAL DISTRICT
		)
[name]		)
		)
	Defendant	)

ORDER GRANTING ENLARGEMENT OF TIME

BE IT REMEMBERED that on this the [date] day of [month], [20__], came on for consideration the motion of [name] [plaintiff/defendant] in the above-entitled cause, to grant [plaitiff/defendant] an enlargement of time to [number] days from the service of [name of document] in which to serve and file a response to [name of document]; and that the Court decided to grant such motion in all respects.

It is, therefore, ORDERED, ADJUDGED, and DECREED that [plaintiff/defendant] be hereby granted an enlargement of time to [number] days from the service of [name of document] in which to serve and file a response to [name of document].

SIGNED this [date] day of [month], [20__].

_____
Judge Presiding

§ 4.30 Checklist for Answering Interrogatories

Form 4–24 is a sample checklist for answering interrogatories.

§ 4.30   CHECKLIST FOR ANSWERING

FORM 4–24
SAMPLE CHECKLIST FOR ANSWERING INTERROGATORIES

Date
Accomplished   **Task**

___   1.   **Calendar response date.**
           Immediately notate the required response date according to the appropriate
           rules of civil procedure in the firm's docketing or calendar system. Use tickler
           notices to remind you of the various dates by which you expect a preliminary
           response from your client, the date on which the client must sign, and so
           forth.

___   2.   **Review questions and make preliminary notations regarding:**
           a.   **Any questions which may be legally objected to; and**
           b.   **Where in your documents the answers may be found.**
           Review the objections stated in the checklist found at § 4.30 to determine
           if any of the interrogatories may be objected to.

___   3.   **Confer with attorney to determine if the objections you have notated are**
           appropriate.
           Now make a copy of the interrogatories which either completely leaves out
           any interrogatory to which you plan to object, or shows the objections
           already in place as an answer to that interrogatory for forwarding to the
           client. This should be done before the client sees the interrogatories so as to
           avoid the client becoming distressed or unduly upset by what he perceives
           to be unfair or invasive questions.

___   4.   **Mail copy of interrogatories to client for review along with an explanatory**
           letter which gives all dates by which you need to have responses from
           the client.
           It is also a good idea to telephone the client and let him know that you have
           forwarded the interrogatories to him, and to explain what role he must play
           in the answering of the interrogatories. If your client is a commerical
           enterprise and his files are voluminous, it may be more expedient for you
           to go to his offices and conduct a search of the files for relevant documents.
           You may also choose to work closely with either the client or a knowledge-
           able member of his staff to search for the relevant documents.

___   5.   **Set up office conference or telephone conference with client to go over**
           interrogatory answers before they are put into first draft form.
           In preparation for this office or telephone conference, you should have
           gathered as much information as possible from the files and materials you
           already have to supplement the answers the client is preparing.

___   6.   **Prepare first draft of answers, incorporating information gathered from**
           office or telephone conference with client.
           Remember that answers should be stated in such a way as to emphasize
           devastating effects for a plaintiff or to minimize those effects for a defendant.

___ 7. **Go over first draft of answers with client and make any revisions necessary to promote clarity or to correct misunderstandings.**

___ 8. **Submit first draft of answers to attorney for comment and approval.**

___ 9. **Make any needed revisions pursuant to your conference with the attorney.**
Check the appropriate Rules of Civil Procedure once again to be sure that the answers are prepared properly in substance and form. Have your attorney once again review the answers, and revise again, if necessary.

___ 10. **Go over final answers with client.**
Make sure that the client fully understands the answers that have been given, and that the answers are accurate. This step is imperative, because the client will be asked again and again during the course of the litigation and at trial to refer to answers he made in the interrogatories.

___ 11. **Have the client sign answers before a notary public.**

___ 12. **File the answers (if filing is done in that jurisdiction) and serve the Answers to Interrogatories on opposing counsel and any other parties necessary under the appropriate notice rules.**

___ 13. **Place a file-stamped copy of the Answers to Interrogatories in the file.**

§ 4.31   Answers to Interrogatories

Form 4–25 is a sample form used to answer interrogatories. **Form 4–26** illustrates sample answers to interrogatories.

FORM 4–25
SAMPLE FORM FOR ANSWERS TO INTERROGATORIES

NO. [case number]

[name]   )   IN THE DISTRICT COURT OF
)
            Plaintiff   )   [county] COUNTY, [state]
)
vs.   )   [judicial district] JUDICIAL DISTRICT
)
[name]   )
)
            Defendant   )

§ 4.31 ANSWERS TO INTERROGATORIES

ANSWERS TO INTERROGATORIES

TO: [name]_____
          [address]_____

          _____

Pursuant to Rule [citation], of the [state/federal] Rules of Civil Procedure, [name], (cross-)defendant(s) in the above cause, hereby serve(s) upon [name], (cross-)plaintiff(s) in the above cause, the answers to interrogatories propounded by (cross-)plaintiff(s) in this cause.

[name of law firm]

By: [attorney name]
State Bar No. [number]
[firm address]
Counsel for Defendant(s)

CERTIFICATE OF SERVICE

I certify that this instrument was served in compliance with Rules ____ and ____ of the _____ Rules of Civil Procedure, by certified mail or hand-delivery, return receipt requested, on the [date] day of [month], [20__], and was promptly filed with the Clerk of the Court, together with this proof of service.

_____
[attorney name]

FORM 4–26
SAMPLE INTERROGATORY ANSWERS

1. State your full legal name, residence address, and telephone number and business address and phone number.
   ANSWER: Douglas R.B., M.D.
                  [address]
                  [city, state]
                  [telephone number] (home)
                  [telephone number] (office)

2. When and where did you graduate from medical school?
   ANSWER: [name] University, 1970

3. Briefly give a history of your experience as a physician beginning with your internship through the present.
   ANSWER: Internship: University of [state] Medical Center 1970–1972
                  Residency: [name] University—1973–1975
                  Special Residency in Pediatric Surgery: University of [state]

DISCOVERY

Medical Center 1976—1979
Private Practice: 1979-present

4. Do you belong to any professional organizations?
   ANSWER: I am a member of the American Medical Association, [state] Medical Association, Association of American Surgeons, and Association of Pediatric Surgeons.

5. Are you board certified in any specialty?
   ANSWER: I am a board certified pediatric surgeon.

6. If you are incorporated, please provide us with a copy of your Articles of Incorporation and By-Laws.
   ANSWER: My practice is not incorporated.

7. What is the first date that you saw the plaintiff in a professional capacity?
   ANSWER: I first saw Jamie C. as a patient on [date].

8. What was you diagnosis and treatment of the patient at that time?
   ANSWER: Jamie C. had been referred to me by his pediatrician, Dr. W., for repair of an inguinal hernia. I examined the patient, concurred with Dr. W.'s findings, and scheduled surgery for the following week, [date].

9. How many times subsequent to the first visit did you see the plaintiff in your office, and on what dates? Describe each treatment.
   ANSWER: I saw the patient for routine follow-up and removal of stitches one week following the surgery, on [date]. I saw the patient again two weeks later on [date] for routine follow-up, at which time I released him from my care.

10. Did you have in your possession a history of the plaintiff's medical records?
    ANSWER: I have in my office all medical records on Jamie C. which had been sent to me by Dr. W. and all medical records regarding Jamie C.'s surgery.

11. State the names of all hospitals where you are privileged to practice.
    ANSWER: I have practicing privileges at [hospital A], [hospital B], and [hospital C].

12. Has your privilege ever been revoked by any hospital?
    ANSWER: My practicing privileges have never been revoked at any hospital.

13. Were you under the influence of alcohol or drugs on the date of the incident?
    ANSWER: I was not under the influence of drugs or alcohol at any time on [date].

14. Have you ever been reprimanded by any medical association or had your license revoked for any reason?

ANSWER: I have never been reprimanded by any medical association nor had my license revoked for any reason.

15.   State the names and addresses of all witnesses you intend to call at time of trial.
ANSWER: [doctor A], M.D.
[hospital A]

[nurse B], R.N.
[hospital A]

[doctor C], M.D.
[hospital A]

16.   Do you allege that you provided the plaintiff with the customary standard of care as prevails under these circumstances?
ANSWER: My surgery on Jamie C. was done with the utmost care. The surgery was entirely routine, and there were no complications.

17.   Do you disclaim any negligence in this matter?
ANSWER: I disclaim any negligence whatsoever relating to my surgery on Jamie C.

18.   State the name and address of any expert witness you intend to call at time of trial.
ANSWER: [doctor D], M.D.
University of [state] Health Service Medical Center

§ 4.32   Objections to Interrogatories

You should be familiar with the following standard objections when preparing your answers to Interrogatories.

1.   **Objection**.   This question is not calculated to lead to the discovery of information relevant to the subject matter of this action.

2.   **Objection**.   This question calls for information protected from disclosure by the attorney-client privilege.

3.   **Objection**.   This question is vague, ambiguous, and unintelligible, and any response to same would be based on speculation as to the true meaning of the question.

4.   **Objection**.   This question calls for information which is equally available to all parties and would be burdensome for the plaintiff to respond to.

5.   **Objection**.   This question calls for information which is not reasonably limited in scope by time, and therefore is overly broad.

6.   **Objection**.   This question calls for information which is protected by the attorney work product privilege.

7. **Objection.** The information sought would require a burdensome effort to produce, and is harassing.

8. **Objection.** Plaintiff/Defendant objects to Interrogatory #_____ on the grounds that such interrogatory is too broad in scope, covers too long a period, and is unlimited as to place. In short, such interrogatory does not seek to discover facts or information relevant to the subject matter involved in the pending action. Further, such interrogatory is designed and intended to cause plaintiff/defendant undue annoyance, oppression, and expense.

9. **Objection.** This question calls for information prepared by counsel in preparation for trial and is protected by the attorney work product privilege.

10. **Objection.** This question has been asked and answered previously. See Interrogatory and Answer No. _____ in plaintiff's/defendant's (First, Second, and so forth) Set of Interrogatories.

11. **Objection.** This question calls for information which has previously been protected by a court-ordered protective order dated _____.

12. **Objection.** This question seeks a scientific opinion from a party who is a layperson.

13. **Objection.** This question assumes a fact not in evidence.

14. **Objection.** This question calls for a conclusion which is properly made by the trier of fact at time of trial.

§ 4.33 Motion to Compel and for Sanctions

Sometimes there is difficulty getting the opposing party to file their answers timely to a discovery request. When this happens, your attorney will probably instruct you to place a telephone call or compose a letter to opposing counsel requesting their answers. (See **Form 4–27.**) In some jurisdictions, there is a rule which requires that the two attorneys hold a conference before any motion for contempt is filed. This meeting usually resolves the differences and results in the answers being supplied.

If, however, these alternatives do not work, you may file a motion with the court to compel answers and the court may elect to award sanctions such as attorney's fees or the striking of pleadings. Federal Rule of Civil Procedure 26(a) provides for mandatory disclosure of discovery information. A full discussion of this new rule is found in **§ 4.5.** With this new rule, provisions have been made for sanctions and noncompliance. Essentially, according to Rule 37(c)(1) of the Federal Rules of Civil Procedure, if the witness or information is not disclosed, the offending party will not be permitted to use the evidence at trial. (See **Form 4–28.**)

§ 4.33 MOTION TO COMPEL

FORM 4–27
SAMPLE LETTER PRECEDING MOTION TO COMPEL

[name]
[address]

[date]

Re: [case name and case number]

Dear [opposing counsel],

On [date], we served your office with Plaintiff's First Set of Interrogatories, the answers to which were due on [date] according to Rule [citation] of the [state/federal] Rules of Civil Procedure.

(We have previously contacted you regarding the insufficiency of your answer to Interrogatory [number], and are waiting to receive a full and complete answer to that interrogatory according to the [state/federal] Rules of Civil Procedure.)

We must ask that we receive the full and complete Answers to Plaintiff's First Set of Interrogatories by [date] to avoid the necessity of a Motion to Compel and for Sanctions. Please contact us immediately if you anticipate any problems complying with this request. Thank you very much for your cooperation in this matter.

Respectfully yours,

[attorney name]

FORM 4–28
SAMPLE MOTION TO COMPEL AND FOR SANCTIONS

NO. [case number]

[name]		)	IN THE DISTRICT COURT OF
		)	
	Plaintiff	)	[county] COUNTY, [state]
		)	
vs.		)	[judicial district] JUDICIAL DISTRICT
		)	
[name]		)	
		)	
	Defendant	)	

MOTION TO COMPEL AND FOR SANCTIONS

COMES NOW, [name], plaintiff, by and through his attorney of record, [name of attorney], and moves this Court to compel the defendant [name], to answer Plaintiff's

First Set of Interrogatories and for an Order levying sanctions against the defendant [name], as provided for by Rule [citation] of the [state] Rules of Civil Procedure. In support of his motion, plaintiff would show the Court as follows:

I.

On [date], plaintiff [name] filed with this Court and served on defendant [name], Plaintiff's First Set of Interrogatories. Pursuant to Rule [citation] of the [state] Rules of Civil Procedure, the defendant was bound to provide plaintiff with Defendant's Answers to Interrogatories by [date].

On [date], counsel for defendant was contacted by telephone by plaintiff's counsel at which time defendant's counsel promised to provide answers on [date].

As of this date, defendant [name] has failed to provide plaintiff with said answers, and more than [number] months have elapsed since said answers were originally due.

WHEREFORE, PREMISES CONSIDERED, plaintiff moves this Honorable Court to compel defendant to provide such answers and for an Order for Sanctions, along with attorney's fees and for such other and further relief as the Court may deem proper.

Respectfully submitted,

[Firm Name]

By: _____
[attorney name]
[firm address]

§ 4.34 Depositions

After the initial investigation is complete and discovery, such as interrogatories, requests for production, and requests for admissions, have taken place, the time is right to schedule depositions. Depositions taken prior to these other forms of discovery are seldom more than fishing expeditions and rarely result in usable information. Most depositions are taken by agreement and result in the sworn testimony of a witness being documented by a court reporter and preserved in written transcript form. In most cases, the plaintiff's deposition is the first taken, followed by the defendant and peripheral witnesses.

Preparing for a deposition is a twofold process. The attorney must be knowledge-able about the facts of the case and prepare his client for the workings of a deposition. Often, both jobs will fall to the capable direction of the paralegal. Depositions are a powerful discovery tool and should not be taken lightly.

Depositions are a key aspect of trial preparation, providing an opportunity for both sides to obtain information that can have a major impact on the trial itself. Depositions also offer an opportunity to commit your opponent's witnesses to a particular version of the events in question. Used in a skillful manner, a deposition may result in damaging admissions by the opposing party or his witnesses or demonstrate that the witnesses are biased. Depositions can also be used to authenticate exhibits or documents, although requests to admit may be a more efficient means of obtaining authentication (see **§ 4.57**).

A party may name a corporation, association, or government agency as a deponent. When this is done in the federal courts, Federal Rule of Civil Procedure 30(b)(6) provides that the organization shall designate one or more officers, directors, managing agents, or other persons who consent to testify on the organization's behalf. The deponent may also indicate the matters about which each deponent will testify. A subpoena sent to a nonparty organization must inform the organization of its duty to appoint such a person.

A deposition may be taken either orally or by written question. Depositions by written questions are utilized most often to secure copies of documents such as medical records, in a form admissible for trial. The questions are generally designed to prove up the authenticity of the documents. (An example of such usage is found in **Chapter 5.**)

Oral depositions are commonly taken in cases. The deponent (witness) is asked questions by an attorney while a court reporter takes down the sworn testimony verbatim. Evidence may be presented to the deponent for verification of authenticity during the deposition in the form of exhibits, which will ultimately be attached to the written copy of the transcript of the proceedings.

Depositions are a discovery tool which may be used in questioning both parties and nonparties in an action. Because parties have already submitted to the jurisdiction of the court, they may be commanded to appear for a deposition by serving them with a Notice of Deposition, giving them a reasonable amount of notice. Nonparties to a suit may be deposed by serving them with a deposition subpoena which commands them to appear. Reasonable notice must also be given in this instance. Both the Notice of Deposition and the deposition subpoena state the date, time, and place where the deponent must appear to have his deposition taken.

Rules 30 and 31 of the Federal Rules of Civil Procedure now require leave of court before taking either more than 10 oral or written depositions or before taking a deposition of a witness who has already been deposed of the case. Another change brought about by Rule 30 is that depositions are no longer required to be taken in front of a court reporter. Depositions may now be "recorded by sound, sound-and-visual, or stenographic means, and the party taking the deposition shall bear the cost of the recording." Under the rule, "any party may arrange for a transcription of a deposition taken by non-stenographic means."

Under Rule 30 of the Federal Rules of Civil Procedure, the party taking the deposition must state in the notice the method that will be used to record the testimony. By giving prior notice to the deponent and the other parties, any party can designate a method of recording the testimony in addition to that in the notice; the party requesting an additional method for recording testimony must pay the expense of this additional method.

Videotaped depositions can be particularly useful. It is more effective to show the jury a videotape of a deponent making an admission than it is to have a transcript read to the jury. Of course, taking a videotaped deposition can be more difficult for the same reason: the tape will reveal all that was going on. In addition, while deposition transcripts can be reviewed and changed, no changes can be made to a videotaped transcript.

Rule 30(b)(7) of the Federal Rules of Civil Procedure provides that a deposition may be taken by telephone or other remote means.

Unless the parties agree otherwise, a deposition is conducted before an officer authorized to administer oaths or by a person appointed by the court. The deposition begins with this officer placing on the record his name and business address and the date, time, and place of the deposition; the administration of the oath to the person who will be deposed; and the identities of all persons present. When the deposition has been completed, the officer will state on the record that the deposition is complete. The officer will also state for the record any stipulations entered into by counsel concerning the custody of the transcript or recording and any exhibits.

Federal Rule 29 allows for modifications of these and other discovery rules by stipulations between the parties unless the proposed extension of times would interfere with court mandated times set for completion of discovery.

§ 4.35 Deposition Checklist

The following checklist helps illustrate your duties and your responsibilities when it comes to depositions.

____ 1. Arrange an agreeable date for deposition with opposing counsel and/or counsel of person to be deposed.

____ 2. If necessary, prepare deposition subpoena or subpoena duces tecum, check appropriate rule for fees and service, and have subpoena served, making sure that the return of service is filed timely.

____ 3. Send Notice of Deposition to opposing counsel and any other parties requiring notice.

____ 4. File Notice of Deposition with the court in jurisdictions where discovery documents are filed with the court.

____ 5. Arrange for court reporter to be present at deposition.

____ 6. Send copy of Notice of Deposition to court reporter.

____ 7. Provide court reporter with word list and definitions of terms common to the lawsuit as well as lists with spellings and titles of the principal players and witnesses in the lawsuit. Make sure to provide this list well in advance of the deposition. It will make the court reporter's job much easier, and provide for more standardized spellings of difficult terms and names.

___   8.   Notify court reporter if expedited transcript delivery is necessary.

___   9.   Notify court reporter of proper person to contact within the law firm should questions arise. This is particularly important in large cases with several attorneys and/or paralegals working on the case. It will make it easier for the court reporter, and will avoid the problems of the, "We know it was delivered to the firm, but we do not know who it was sent to" syndrome which sometimes afflicts large firms.

___ 10. Make any necessary conference room arrangements for the deposition.

___ 11. Make travel arrangements for your expert, if necessary, and provide him with any materials he needs to prepare for his attendance at the deposition.

___ 12. Prepare questions for deposition.

___ 13. Meet with attorney and discuss relevant issues for depositions.

___ 14. Gather documents for deposition exhibits and label according to attorney instruction.

___ 15. Follow up on delivery of deposition transcript.

___ 16. Summarize deposition transcript.

___ 17. Arrange for payment of court reporter's bill.

___ 18. If the deposition witness was your client, arrange for review and signature of the deposition transcript.

___ 19. Follow up on correction and signature pages.

___ 20. File deposition with the court in jurisdictions where discovery documents are filed with the court. (In some cases, your court reporter may automatically take care of Numbers 18, 19, and 20. Check to see if this is the case.)

___ 21. Annotate deposition with corrections and make sure all exhibits are attached.

§ 4.36   Motion to Quash

FORM 4–29
MOTION TO QUASH

NO. _____

[PLAINTIFF(S) NAMES] Plaintiffs,	)	
	)	
	)	IN THE DISTRICT COURT OF
	)	
	)	_____ COUNTY,
	)	
_____	)	
	)	
v.	)	
	)	_____ JUDICIAL DISTRICT
[DEFENDANT(S) NAMES]	)	
Defendants.	)	

DEFENDANT'S MOTION TO QUASH DEPOSITION OF
_____ WITH SUBPOENA DUCES TECUM
AND MOTION FOR PROTECTION

TO THE HONORABLE JUDGE OF SAID COURT:

_____ asks that the Court grant this motion to quash Plaintiff's Notice of Intention to take the deposition with subpoena duces tecum of _____, the manager at the time of Plaintiff's alleged incident, as permitted by Rule ____ of the _____ Rules of Civil Procedure.

I.

Plaintiff's claim for negligence is generated from the allegation that a plastic hanger was lying on the floor of the _____ Store on Christmas Eve. Plaintiff alleges that this hanger was an unreasonably dangerous condition. Consequently, Plaintiff brings suit under a premise liability cause of action. Plaintiff then amended her Original Petition to add the cause of action of dangerous condition associated with the shopping carts being provided by Defendant to customers.

II.

On _____, 20__, Defendant received via facsimile Plaintiff's Notice of Intention to take the Deposition of _____ with subpoena duces tecum, scheduled for _____, _____, 20__. _____ was the store manager at the time of Plaintiff's alleged injury; however, he was not on duty at the time of the accident. _____ is no longer employed at the _____ Store in _____, _____. He has been transferred and now works and resides in Puerto Rico.

III.

Pursuant to _____ law, the time and place designated for depositions shall be reasonable: the place of taking a deposition shall be in the county of the witness's residence, or where he is employed or regularly transacts business in person, or at such other convenient place as may be directed by the court in which the cause is pending. Rule _____, _____ Rules of Civil Procedure. _____ currently resides in Puerto Rico. _____ respectfully moves this Court to deny the deposition of _____, who lives and works in Puerto Rico, due to the fact that the time and place are not convenient nor reasonable, nor is the place designated the county of the witness's residence or where he is employed or regularly transacts business. *Wal-Mart v. Street*, 754 S.W.2d 153, 155 (Tex. 1988), *aff'd* 761 S.W.2d 588 (Tex. Ct. App. 1988).

WHEREFORE, PREMISES CONSIDERED, based upon the foregoing reasons, Defendant asks the Court for the relief herein sought, and for such other and further relief to which Defendant may be entitled.

Respectfully submitted,

NAME OF FIRM

_____

Name of Atty
Atty's Bar #
Address
City, State, Zip
Phone #

CERTIFICATE OF CONFERENCE

I hereby certify that a representative of my office has spoken with representatives from the offices of all counsel of record and that no agreement could be reached on this matter, thereby necessitating the filing of this motion.

_____

CERTIFICATE OF SERVICE

I hereby certify that a true and correct copy of the above and foregoing document has been forwarded to all counsel of record by facsimile and/or certified mail/R.R.R. on this _____ day of _____, 20___.

_____

DISCOVERY

FORM 4–30
ORDER TO QUASH

NO. _____

[PLAINTIFF(S) NAMES]) Plaintiffs,)	

[PLAINTIFF(S) NAMES]   )
  Plaintiffs,   )
) IN THE DISTRICT COURT OF
)
) _____ COUNTY,
_____   )
)
  v.   )
) _____ JUDICIAL DISTRICT
[DEFENDANT(S) NAMES]   )
  Defendants.   )

ORDER

CAME ON FOR HEARING, Defendant's Motion to Quash the Deposition of _____ with Subpoena Duces Tecum and Motion for Protection and the Court, after hearing the arguments of counsel, is of the opinion that the Motion is meritorious. It is, therefore,

ORDERED that the deposition of _____ along with the subpoena duces tecum is quashed.

SIGNED this _____ day of _____, 20 ___.

_____
PRESIDING JUDGE

FORM 4–31
SUBPOENA FOR DEPOSITION

DEPOSITION SUBPOENA WITNESS FEE $10.00 ATTACHED YES__/NO__

THE STATE OF _____

To any Sheriff or Constable for the State of _____ or other Person Authorized to Serve Subpoenas as provided in Rule _____, _____ Rules of Civil Procedure. WITNESS SUBPOENA PURSUANT TO RULE _____, _____ Rules of Civil Procedure.

CASE NO. _____ IN THE DISTRICT COURT OF _____ COUNTY, _____

_____ VS.
(Plaintiff/s name)

§ 4.36 MOTION TO QUASH

_____
(Defendant/s name)

YOU ARE HEREBY COMMANDED TO SUMMON:

_____ADDRESS_____ AT _____ OF:
_____ to appear before: _____

ADDRESS: _____
_____ in and for _____County, _____, on the
_____ day of _____, 20__, at _____ o'clock, __.M., and there to
answer under oath to certain oral/written questions to be propounded to you at the
instance of the Plaintiff/s or the Defendant/s (underline one), in a certain suit now
pending in the Court of _____ County, _____, and that the witness bring with
them and produce at said time and place the list of instruments attached hereto, to wit:
(IF ADDITIONAL SPACE IS NEEDED PLEASE ATTACH A LIST OF DOCUMENTS TO BE
PRODUCED) ITEMS: _____
_____

and that the witness continue in attendance from day to day until discharged.

DO NOT FAIL to return this writ to Court, with return thereon, showing the manner of
execution.

Witness my official signature this the _____day of _____, AD 20___.

_____

This subpoena not prepared by the Office of District Clerk
BY: _____

Issuance of Subpoena requested by:_____, Attorney or
Pro/Se Party for the Petitioner or Respondent (circle one)

OFFICER'S OR AUTHORIZED & DISINTERESTED PERSON'S RETURN

Came to hand on the _____ day of _____, 20___ at _____ o'clock ____.M.,
and executed by delivering a copy of this subpoena to the within named witness, in
person at _____ in _____ County,
_____, on the _____ day of _____, 20___, at _____ o'clock
____.M.

NOT EXECUTED as to the witness for the following reasons: _____
_____

SERVICE FEES _____

NAME OF OFFICER OR AUTHORIZED & DISINTERESTED PERSON:
_____

I hereby accept service of this subpoena and will appear on said date and time directed in this subpoena.

Witness Signature:

_____

§ 4.37   Witness/Client Deposition Preparation Checklist

The following is a checklist of points to go over with your witness or client prior to his deposition. Use verbal illustrations to help him understand each point, and make sure he has no questions when you are through.

____ 1. Wear neat, clean, conservative clothes.

____ 2. Refresh your memory by going through all your records and become familiar with all relevant dates and times.

____ 3. Answer all questions audibly and distinctly.

____ 4. Do not guess if you do not know the answer to a question. State that you do not know.

____ 5. If you do not understand the question, ask the attorney to repeat or clarify it.

____ 6. Always tell the truth. There are criminal penalties for perjury.

____ 7. Do not volunteer information. Answer only the question asked.

____ 8. Do not try to figure out why an attorney is asking you a certain question. He is probably fishing, and you may guess wrong.

____ 9. Do not argue with the attorney who is asking you questions.

____ 10. Do not lose your temper. You may be doing exactly what the attorney wants you to do.

____ 11. If you are asked if you have spoken to this attorney prior to this deposition, tell the truth.

____ 12. Do not be sarcastic or hostile toward the attorney.

____ 13. Be courteous to everyone involved in the deposition. Say "yes, sir" and "no, sir."

____ 14. Do not estimate anything unless you clearly state first that you are estimating.

____ 15. If you do not remember the answer to a question, state that you do not recall.

____ 16. Do not anticipate a question. Let the attorney finish the question completely before you answer it.

____ 17. If you know that the attorney has asked you a question incorrectly, do not try to correct him. Merely answer the question he has asked.

____ 18. Do not agree with the attorney just to be nice or agreeable.

19. Watch your attorney for cues, but do not appear as if you are looking to him for direction in answering the questions.

20. If you are interrupted while answering a question, ask permission to finish your answer.

21. Take all the time you need to answer a question.

22. Do not joke. A lawsuit is a serious matter.

23. Rely only on your personal knowledge to answer a question.

§ 4.38   Deposition Question Preparation

Before proceeding with the taking of depositions, all interrogatory answers and initial investigation should be reviewed. When you have determined the witness you wish to depose, make a list of all the incidents the witness has knowledge of that could help you develop or defend your case. You should also put together a list of witnesses who may damage your case. For each issue, devise a question or several questions to ask the witness. Review the statements and testimony of other witnesses. Check to see if other issues have developed that need clarification and testimony. If the witness might have further knowledge of these new issues, develop questions geared to expand on these points.

To the extent possible, your attorney should develop a theory of the case before you prepare the questions for the deposition. Such a theory will provide a focus for your questions. Of course, your attorney may decide to alter his or her theory of the case based on the results of the depositions.

There are various ways to arrange your deposition questions. In some instances, it may be best to proceed chronologically, asking about events in the order in which they took place. In other instances, it may be more effective to arrange your questions by topic, exploring the more important topics first.

Whether to use open-ended questions will depend upon the purpose of the deposition. If the primary purpose of the deposition is to obtain information, open-ended questions can be useful. If the purpose is to make a record that will be read later at the trial, open-ended questions should be avoided.

§ 4.39   Preparing Your Witness for Deposition

Just as you would prepare your witness for trial, you must prepare your witness if he or she is going to testify at a deposition. Proper preparation of a witness who is going to testify at a deposition can be even more important than preparing a witness for trial; many a case is won or lost based on the results of depositions. Be sure to provide your witness with any documents that may be used at the deposition and review these documents with your witness. Discuss with the witness his or her demeanor and style of presentation.

If the witness is to be asked questions of a technical nature, his credentials need to be set out. For example, if your witness is testifying that the mechanical failure which the defendant claims caused the accident is impossible under the circumstances, his employment history of 30 years as a mechanic is very important testimony. The same is true of educational background. A witness' education may often either solidify or weaken the validity of his testimony.

If the person being deposed was an eyewitness to the subject incident, questions should be asked about his ability to see, hear or interpret what he is supposed to have witnessed. For example, if another driver says he saw the entire accident sequence, and under oath, that witness testifies that his attention was momentarily distracted when he dropped his lighted cigarette in his lap, there is a credibility problem with his testimony.

The final list of deposition questions should be presented to your attorney at least a week in advance of the deposition. If possible, go over the list with him and explain your reasons for believing that certain questions have relevance. It is possible that you may have picked up on something of which your attorney is not aware.

§ 4.40 Deposition Summaries

Deposition summaries are one of the most interesting parts of the paralegal's job, and you should take great pride in doing them well. In order to produce the best possible summaries, you must understand what the attorney will use the summaries for. However, it is not necessary to have the attorney spend an inordinate amount of time with you before you summarize the dposition to explain the issues of the lawsuit. You are, after all, simply SUMMARIZING or condensing the material contained in the deposition transcript; you are not drawing conclusions or analyzing the information. You are simply deleting any extraneous material from the transcript to serve as an easy reference to the substantive testimony found therein. (See **Form 4–33.**)

Keeping the mission of the assignment in mind, begin to summarize the transcript using whatever format your attorney has demonstrated a preference for. The following hints may be helpful:

While condensing the testimony, be sure not to use words which will change the original meaning of the witness' account. If you are not sure if the meaning will be changed, do not hesitate to consult a dictionary or thesaurus. When you believe the witness has made a mistake or used the wrong word, use the word "sic" enclosed by brackets to show the reader that you have copied the material just as it appeared but that you believe it is wrong. (See **Form 4–31** for a sample transcript).

Do not summarize the questions. What the attorney asked is not important here. The answers, or the witness' testimony is important. If, however, the witness' answer is a straightforward "Yes" or "No," be sure to summarize the question into the answer so that what the witness is answering "Yes" or "No" to will be evident to the reader. All other answers should include parts of the questions only if necessary to infer the meaning. Avoid phrases such as, "When asked if he had been aware of the ongoing negotiations, the witness answered 'No'." Such a statement could more simply be summarized, "He had not been aware of the ongoing negotiations." Notice how much shorter and concise the second statement is.

It is not necessary to use the name of the deponent or phrases such as the deponent or the witness over and over again in the summary. Pronouns such as he or she are perfectly acceptable and will keep the length of the summary to a minimum. You must be careful, however, in using pronouns when referring to persons other than the witness who are discussed in the testimony. Reread your summary to make sure that every time a pronoun is used that the identity of the person being referred to is extremely clear to the reader. If not, substitute the last name of the subject for the pronoun wherever needed to interject clarity.

Even though the side conversations between the attorneys may be some of the most interesting parts of the deposition, they are not important to the summary, and may be entirely eliminated unless some sort of understanding or stipulation has come about as a result of it. In that case, refer to the stipulation or agreement. Do not leave out or change phrases such as "I think," "I believe," "In my opinion," and so on. It is important that the testimony be truthfully reflected as opinion when it is not fact.

Notice in the example (**Form 4–34**) provided in this section that there are sometimes multiple entries for the same page of testimony. Every time the subject matter changes on a page, the page number is to be entered again. Lines should also be skipped between entries to set them apart. Therefore, the summary should be double-spaced, with extra lines between the entries. Every entry, therefore, has the appearance of being a separate paragraph with lines between each. Sometimes, the subject matter will continue on to the next page. When this happens, hyphenate the page numbers as in the sample summary.

Keep the format of the summary consistent throughout. If you have chosen a style of complete sentences, maintain it throughout. Do not go back and forth between complete and incomplete sentences. (Refer to **§ 4.47** for further tips on summarizing depositions.) **Table 4–4** is helpful in setting up the elements for a good deposition summary.

Table 4-4

Elements of a Good Deposition Summary

Criteria—What elements are found in a good deposition summary?	How do you achieve those elements?	Tips, Techniques
Length of summary does not exceed 10 percent of the length of the deposition transcript.	Use a telegram style if your full sentence structure makes your summary too lengthy. Example: "States he does not remember having conversation with Smith that night." Omit articles and pronouns where possible. Example: "Reviewed contract for merger meeting." Do not summarize conversations between attorneys.	Highly technical deposition summaries may be somewhat lengthier. If using pronouns, make sure the identity of the speaker and the subject is clear. An example of a sentence which would need to be clarified is as follows: "He said that he saw him late yesterday when she was with him." A clarified sentence would read: "Deponent said he saw Brown late yesterday when Charlotte was with Brown."
Summary is a condensation of the testimony, not an interpretation.	Whenever possible, use the words of the deponent. If you need to shorten the passage, do not use words that change the original meaning of the testimony.	If a deponent states that he "thinks" something or "in his opinion", be sure to include those words so that what follows will not be construed as fact rather than opinion.
The testimony is summarized so that no facts are left out.	Assume all facts are important to the case and include them in the summary. Be sure to indicated when a deponent does not know something, because the fact that he does not possess that knowledge may be important in itself.	

Table 4–4
(continued)

Criteria—What elements are found in a good deposition summary?	How do you achieve those elements?	Tips, Techniques
The content of the summary is limited to the facts of the testimony.	Summarize the answers, not the questions. Include parts of the question in the summary of the answer of the deponent if necessary for clarity. For example: Question: "Did you see the man that night?" Answer: "No." Summary: "He did not see the man that night." Do not summarize conversations between attorneys.	
The summary is clear and grammatically correct.	Keep the syntax and verb tense consistent throughout the summary. If using pronouns, make sure the identity of the speaker and the subject is clear. Use correct grammar. Include parts of the question in the summary if needed for clarity.	
Format of the summary is correct.	Type the summary in two columns: page number and narrative. When the subject matter changes on the same page of the deposition transcript, drop down a line on the summary, retype the page number, and summarize the next thought.	

Table 4–4
(*continued*)

Criteria—What elements are found in a good deposition summary?	How do you achieve those elements?	Tips, Techniques
Deposition summary heading is clear and complete.	Use the case style or caption with the name of the deponent and date of the deposition as a heading for the summary. If deposition is multivolume, be sure the volume number is stated in the heading.	
Exhibits are properly identified.	List the exhibit number and a description of the exhibit on the summary page whenever exhibits are introduced.	
Include a separate index page showing the number of the exhibit, the deposition page number where the exhibit is introduced, and a brief description of the exhibit.		

§ 4.41 —Page Summary

The page summary is the most widely-used method of summarizing depositions. The format is simple and straightforward, but detailed enough to be a helpful index to the deposition. The volume of a good page summary should be 10-15 percent of the volume of the deposition itself. That is, if the deposition is 100 pages in length, the summary should be no more than 10-15 pages in length. The summary should be in complete sentences, condensing the important statements of the witness, leaving out any extraneous phrases. For example, if the deposition read as follows:

Question: How far away was the plaintiff's car when you first saw it?

Answer: Well, I'm not sure. It appeared to be . . . I noticed the care about the same time that . . . No, that's not right. It probably was about 100 yards away, I guess. Isn't 100 yards about as long as a football field?

The summary would read:

§ 4.42   SAMPLE TRANSCRIPT EXCERPT

Summary: She is not sure how far away the plaintiff's car was when she first saw it.
She thinks it was about 100 yards away.

and whould be in the following format:

Deposition Summary of (Deponent's name)

Page   **Narrative**

4   She is not sure how far away the plaintiff's car was when she first saw it.
She thinks it was about 100 yards away.

It is better to separate complete thoughts by a space instead of running the entire summary of a page in one continuous paragraph. Skip a line and enter the page number again for the narrative summary relating to the next thought process or idea.

§ 4.42   Sample Deposition Transcript Excerpt

FORM 4–32
SAMPLE DEPOSITION TRANSCRIPT EXCERPT

1	A	The other work with Homecraft had nothing to do	page 18
2		with this project, no.	
3	Q	Have you had any other contact with Peabody	
4		Engineers?	
5	A	No.	
6	Q	Did Montgomery Engineering ever serve as district	
7		engineer for Emerald Forest?	
8	A	We do now, and we did.	
9	Q	When did you start?	
10	A	We started in—our contract is signed by the district	
11		in either July or August of '76.	
12	Q	Have you served in that capacity on a continuous	
13		basis?	
14	A	Yes.	
15	Q	I know this is rather an open-ended question, but	
16		could you describe for me briefly what a district	
17		engineer would do?	
18	A	On any project?	
19	Q	Yes, sir. Just generally.	
20	A	Okay. He generally represents all of the engineering	
21		needs of the district which could be design in	
22		nature; it could be construction. Typically it is design	
23		and construction. But a lot of district engineers'	
24		activities could be best described as consulting,	
25		having to do with	

1		numerous different things of a technical nature	page 19
2		that a district requires be done. We attend all	
3		of the district board meetings. We are available	
4		to recommend and comment on various requests	
5		made of the board, such as connections to their	
6		water, sewerage and drainage systems. I think	
7		you know that the district is only empowered by	
8		law to be concerned with water, sanitary and	
9		drainage activities, and therefore that's all—	
10		that's the scope of my service for them also.	
11	Q	Do you have an annual contract with the district?	
12	A	No. I have an ongoing base contract that	
13		requires that specific services be authorized as	
14		they come up. And so they are normally authorized	
15		in the minutes of the board meeting.	
16	Q	Are you compensated on a project basis?	
17	A	We are—our contract calls for compensation to	
18		us on an hourly basis, and we have a fee	
19		schedule that is revised once a year, by the way,	
20		which may answer your question.	
21	Q	When did you start attending the meetings of the	
22		Emerald Forest Utility District?	
23	A	I believe June of '76 was the first meeting we	
24		went to.	
25	Q	Would you have been the person in Montgomery	
1		Engineering to attend those meetings?	page 20
2	A	Yes.	
3	Q	As far as you know, have you attended the	
4		majority of the meetings?	
5	A	Yes.	
6	Q	Is there anybody else at Montgomery who would	
7		have taken a share of the attending of those	
8		meetings in your place?	
9	A	Yes. Gilbert Flores attended a number of the	
10		meetings. A gentleman by the name of Jerry	
11		Paquette, P-a-q-u-e-t-t-e, attended some of the	
12		meetings.	
13	Q	Where is Mr. Paquette today?	
14	A	Paquette is also in business for himself.	
15	Q	Is that here in Houston?	
16	A	It's here in Houston.	
17		MR. BUSSELL: You are running an	
18		apprenticeship.	
19		THE WITNESS: Right. Kind of a	
20		small Turner, Collie & Braden.	
21	A	His involvement was far less than Flores' and	
22		mine.	
23	Q	(By Mr. Sheehy) Mr. Montgomery, do you have an	
24		opinion as to whether there were any problems	

300

25		with a line which was initially constructed which
1		is the basis of this lawsuit?
2	A	Yes.
3	Q	Before we go into the specific problems with the
4		line, would you tell me what you base your
5		opinion on?
6	A	My opinion is based on an observation of the
7		facts of the physical observation of the line
8		itself through the videotapes, review of the
9		files; correspondence; discussions with other
10		professionals, contractors. And I believe that's
11		the scope of the people and the sources that I
12		would have talked to or reviewed.
13		I was not retained specifically to
14		review and critique this particular project. But
15		there was no way in the course of becoming
16		involved with the district and designing a
17		replacement line and becoming the new engineer
18		for the district, that I could not help but
19		develop an opinion about what happened.
20	Q	Did you make any other observations of the line?
21	A	Other than through the videotape? No.
22	Q	Did you ever see the line when it was uncovered?
23	A	No.
24	Q	When you indicated that you reviewed files, would
25		those be the files which you have with you today?

page 21

§ 4.43 Sample Deposition Transcript Summary

FORM 4–33
SAMPLE DEPOSITION TRANSCRIPT SUMMARY

Page	Narrative
18	The other work with Homecraft had nothing to do with this project.
18	He has had no other contact with Peabody Engineers.
18	Montgomery Engineering has served as district engineer for Emerald Forest on a continual basis since signing the contract in July or August of 1976.
18–19	A district engineer represents all of the construction and design needs of the district and consults on things of technical nature. He attends all district board meetings and makes recommendations and comments on requests to the board concerning connections to the water, sanitary and drainage systems.
19	His ongoing base contract specifies that specific services must be authorized in the minutes of the board meetings as they come up.

19	His contract calls for compensation on an hourly basis, based on a fee schedule which is revised yearly.
19	He attented his first meeting of the Emerald Forest Utility District in June of 1976.
19-20	He is the Montgomery Engineering person who would attend those meetings, and he has attended the majority of them.
20	Gilbert Flores and Jerry Paquette attended some of the meetings. Paquette is in business for himself in Houston. Paquette's involvement was far less than Flores' or the witness'.
20-21	He believes there were problems with the line which is the basis of this lawsuit.
21	He bases his opinion on physical observation of the line through videotapes, file review, correspondence and discussions with other professionals and contractors.
21	He was not retained specifically to review and critique this particular project.
21	He never saw the line when it was uncovered.

§ 4.44   Deposition Summaries—by Line

Line summaries are the same as page summaries except that the line numbers are set out with the page numbers to the left of the narrative. The page and line numbers read as follows: 43:1-6 or 22: 15, which represents page 43, lines 1–6; and page 22, line 15. In every other way, the line summary should be approximately 10-15 percent of the volume of the actual deposition. The line summary is extremely useful for locating exact passages of testimony in a deposition transcript and is an excellent index to the transcript itself.

§ 4.45   —by Key Word or Key Issue

In cases where there are several witnesses with varying accounts of the same incident or fact, key word or key issue summaries are invaluable. They can be done in one of two ways. Each deposition can be summarized individually, or all depositions can be summarized under the common key word or key issue. For example, in a personal injury case resulting from a traffic accident, there may be several different accounts of what color the traffic lights were. In a case such as this, it is very helpful to see what every witness had to say about that issue. The following format (**Form 4–34**) would be used:

FORM 4–34
SAMPLE DEPOSITION SUMMARY—KEY ISSUE

Key Issue: Color of Traffic Signal

Deposition	Page	Narrative
[deponent A]	42	He is positive the light was red.
[deponent B]	23	She is not sure, but thinks the light was still yellow.
[deponent C]	81	Someone told him after the accident that the light had been red.
[deponent D]	12	He has no idea what color the traffic signal was.

This type of summary can be done manually, of course, but there are wonderful computer applications available now which allow you to obtain the deposition on a floppy disk and use it with preprogrammed software to do key word or key phrase searches. If you office is automated, you probably already know what a fantastic development this is.

§ 4.46—Outline of Evidence Based on the Testimony

This type of summary is very similar to the key word or key issue summary. For each issue or key word, list the deposition page and line numbers which can be used to support or refute that topic. Under that same category, also list all exhibits from depositions and documents from document productions that support or refute the topic. Do not forget to include in the listing tangible items such as photographs and physical evidence. (See **Form 4–35.**)

FORM 4–35
SAMPLE OUTLINE OF EVIDENC BASED ON THE TESTIMONY

I.   Issue: Defendant's visibility approaching intersection

SUPPORTING EVIDENCE

A.   Deposition of Robert Carlton, page 101, lines 10–21

Deposition of Susan R. Anthony, page 50, line 4
                                pages 82–96, inclusive

Deposition of David Connors, page 15, lines 1–15
                             page 63, lines 7–8
                             page 85, lines 21–22

    B.   Exhibit 10, Deposition of Susan A.

    C.   Document 0034, Plaintiff's Document Production
         Documents 0025-0036, Plaintiff's Document Production
         Document 002, Defendant's Document Production

    D.   Scene Photographs A, D, L

II.   Issue: Speed of Defendant's Car

SUPPORTING EVIDENCE

    A.   Deposition of David C., page 52, lines 7–12

    B.   Police Report, page 2, paragraph 3

§ 4.47   Deposition Summarizing Tips

The following tips can be useful when you are preparing a deposition summary:

1. Remember you are doing a condensation, not an interpretation.
2. Do not use words which change the original meaning.
3. Use a telegram style if your full sentence structure makes your summary too lengthy. Omit articles and pronouns where possible.
4. Summarize answers, not questions.
5. If using pronouns, make sure the identity of the speaker is clear.
6. Do not summarize conversations between attorneys.
7. When the subject matter changes on the same page, drop down a line, retype the page number, and summarize the next thought.
8. Use the case style or caption with the name of the deponent and date of the deposition as a heading for the summary. If the deposition is multivolume, be sure the volume number is stated in the heading.
9. Keep the length of the summary to 10 percent of the length of the deposition if at all possible. Highly technical deposition summaries may be somewhat lengthier.
10. Learn to scan ahead while summarizing to increase your speed.
11. If a deponent is asked a question to which he answers "no", summarize his response in such a way that the question is evident. The fact that a deponent does not know about something is probably as important as if he did have that knowledge.
12. If a deponent states that he "thinks" something or "in his opinion . . .", be sure to include those words so that what follows will not be construed as fact rather than opinion.

13. Whenever exhibits are introduced, list the exhibit number and a description of the exhibit.

14. Keep the syntax and verb tense consistent throughout the summary so as to avoid confusion for the reader.

15. Proofread, proofread, proofread!

§ 4.48 Letter Advising Client of Deposition

Form 4–36 is a sample letter notifying the client of a deposition.

FORM 4–36
SAMPLE LETTER ADVISING CLIENT OF DEPOSITION

[date]

[plaintiff] _____
[address] _____
_____

Re: Cause No. [case number]; in the [judicial district] Judicial
     District Court in and for [county] County, [state]
     [plaintiff] vs. [defendant].

Dear [plaintiff]:

The defendant in this case, [name], has noticed your deposition for [day] [month], [date], [20__]. As I have previously explained to you, a deposition is an informal setting in which the defendant's attorney will ask you questions regarding the accident. A court reporter will be in attendance to take down your sworn testimony in written form, and sometime afterwards, we will receive a copy of the transcript which you will be asked to review and sign.

I would like to discuss the deposition in greater detail with you, and request that you contact my paralegal, [name], to set up a convenient time for you approximately one week in advance of the scheduled deposition.

Please let us know immediately if the scheduled date of the deposition presents a conflict for you.

Very truly yours,

_____
[attorney name]

§ 4.49 Witness Review of Deposition Transcript

Under Rule 30(e) of the Federal Rules of Civil Procedure, the deponent may review the transcript or recording of the deposition. To do so, the deponent or a party must have requested such a review before completion of the deposition. If this request has been made, the deponent has 30 days after being notified by the officer who presided at the deposition that the transcript or recording is available for review. The deponent may sign a statement reciting any changes in form or substance. Of course, this procedure is of practical use primarily when a deposition has been recorded stenographically. There are obvious limitations on a deponent's ability to claim that portions of a recording, particularly a videotaped recording, are inaccurate.

§ 4.50 Letter Transmitting Deposition Transcript to Witness

Form 4–37 is a sample deposition transcript transmittal letter.

FORM 4–37
SAMPLE DEPOSITION TRANSCRIPT TRANSMITTAL LETTER

[date]

Re: [plaintiff] v. [defendant]

Dear [witness]:

I have enclosed a copy of your deposition in the above-captioned case. Please review it and make any necessary corrections on the amendment sheet which is enclosed separately. Please sign both the amendment sheet and the enclosed signature page and have your signature notarized.

You are welcome to keep this copy of your deposition. Please return the amendment page and notarized signature page to me within TEN (10) days so that I may file them with the court. If they are not filed with the court within this time period, the court reporter will file your deposition with the court without benefit of any amendments you may wish to make.

Please call me at the above-referenced number if I may answer any questions for you.

Very truly yours,

_____

Paralegal

§ 4.51   Notice to Plaintiff to Sign and Return Deposition

If your attorney deposes the plaintiff, **Form 4–38** can be sent with the transcript of the deposition for the plaintiff's signature.

FORM 4–38
NOTICE TO PLAINTIFF TO SIGN AND RETURN DEPOSITION

[court] SUPREME COURT OF THE STATE OF [state]
COUNTY OF [county]

[name]	)	Index No.
	)	
Plaintiff,	)	NOTICE TO SIGN
	)	AND RETURN
-against-	)	DEPOSITION
	)	
[name]	)	
	)	
Defendant	)	

SIR:

   PLEASE TAKE NOTICE that enclosed herewith is an original and a copy of the deposition of the plaintiff, taken on [date], which must be signed, subscribed, and return to the undersigned within thirty (30) days of service of this notice.

   PLEASE TAKE FURTHER NOTICE that if there is a failure to so return the deposition, then in that event it will be used as fully as though signed in this action, pursuant to [Rule of Civil Procedure].

Dated:_____ [city, state]_____
_____
[date]

                                 [name of law firm]
                                 Attorneys for [name]
                                 [address and telephone number
                                 of firm]

TO: _____ [name]_____

307

§ 4.52   Deposition Transcript Errata Sheet

Form 4–39 can be used to list the errors in a deposition transcript.

FORM 4–39
DEPOSITION TRANSCRIPT ERRATA SHEET

ERRATA SHEET FOR TRANSCRIPT OF_____
                                                     (Witness's Name)

RE:_____

DATE TAKEN:____/____/____

PAGE	LINE NUMBER	CORRECTION	REASON FOR
_____	_____	_____	_____
_____	_____	_____	_____
_____	_____	_____	_____
_____	_____	_____	_____
_____	_____	_____	_____
_____	_____	_____	_____
_____	_____	_____	_____
_____	_____	_____	_____
_____	_____	_____	_____
_____	_____	_____	_____
_____	_____	_____	_____
_____	_____	_____	_____
_____	_____	_____	_____
_____	_____	_____	_____
_____	_____	_____	_____
_____	_____	_____	_____
_____	_____	_____	_____
_____	_____	_____	_____
_____	_____	_____	_____

_____
(Witness's Signature)

Subscribed and sworn to before me
this ___ day of _____, 20__

_____
Notary Public

§ 4.53 Deposition Roster

As the deposition stage progresses and you begin to receive transcripts of the actual deposition testimony, a system should be instituted for organization of those transcripts and their summaries. The Deposition Roster (**Form 4–40**) allows you to maintain an index of the transcripts and keep track of whether the original copy has been signed, corrected, and filed, and whether a summary has been prepared. The case heading at the top allows you to determine at a glance which court the case is in, and thus, in which court the originals should be filed.

In some jurisdictions the court reporter will file the original transcripts herself. When that happens you will receive a letter from her notifying you of that fact. Whether you do it yourself or the court reporter does it for you, it is always a good idea to double-check to make sure all transcripts are filed before you proceed to trial.

FORM 4–40
SAMPLE DEPOSITION ROSTER

NO. [case number]

[name]		)	IN THE DISTRICT COURT OF
	Plaintiff,	)	
		)	
vs.		)	[county] COUNTY, [state]
		)	
[name]		)	[judicial district] JUDICIAL DISTRICT
	Defendant.	)	

DEPOSITION ROSTER

Deponent's Name	Deposition Date	Transcript Received	Original Signed	Changes Entered	Summa-rized	Original Filed

DISCOVERY

§ 4.54 Notice of Deposition

As you know, you may take the deposition of any party in the case simply by noticing that deposition. Under Rule 30 of the Federal Rules of Civil Procedure, a party desiring to take the deposition of any person must give reasonable notice in writing to every other party to the action. The notice must contain the name and address of each person to be examined. If the name of the person is not known, the notice must contain a general description sufficient to identify the person or the particular class or group to which the person belongs. The notice must also include the time and place of the deposition. If a subpoena duces tecum is to be served on the deponent, the designation of the materials to be produced as set forth in the subpoena must be attached to or included in the notice. Many depositions are taken by agreement, and do not even go through the formalities of filing a notice. It is always good practice, however, to follow up with a Notice of Deposition (**Form 4–41**) to confirm the date, time, and place to avoid any problems arising at a later date. It is also a good idea to forward a copy of the Notice of Deposition to the court reporter as a courtesy.

FORM 4–41
SAMPLE NOTICE OF DEPOSITION

NO. [case number]

[name]	)	IN THE DISTRICT COURT OF
	)	
Plaintiff,	)	
	)	
vs.	)	[county] COUNTY, [state]
	)	
[name]	)	[judicial district] JUDICIAL DISTRICT
	)	
Defendant.	)	

NOTICE OF DEPOSITION

TO: [name] _____
      [address] _____
      _____

You will take notice that the oral deposition of [name] will be taken at the offices of [firm name], [street address], [city,state] on [day], [date,month], [20__] at [time] [A.M./P.M.].

Respectfully submitted,

[name of law firm]

310

By _____
[attorney name]
[street address]
[city, state]
[telephone number]

Counsel for [plaintiff/defendant]

§ 4.55   Commission to Take Deposition Outside State

Occasionally, it may be necessary to take the deposition of a witness who is not a party to the case and may live outside the court's jurisdiction. It will be necessary to obtain a commission to take the deposition from the clerk of the court in which the case is filed. This commission will then be used to obtain a subpoena from the court jurisdiction in which the witness resides, and will give authority to the court reporter in that jurisdiction to take the sworn testimony of the witness at the deposition. There are many variations of this rule and it is imperative that you consult your jurisdiction's Rules of Civil Procedure for the proper way to approach such a matter. (See **Form 4–42.**)

FORM 4–42
SAMPLE COMMISSION TO TAKE OUT-OF-STATE DEPOSITION

COMMISSION TO TAKE DEPOSITION
OUTSIDE STATE OF [state]

TO: ANY NOTARY PUBLIC OF THE STATE OF [state]:

You are hereby commissioned and fully authorized to take the deposition of [name] in accordance with the Rules of Civil Procedure for the State of [state], at the office(s) of [name] on the [date] day of [month], [20__], commencing at the hour of [time] [A.M./P.M.], and on succeeding days until concluded, or at such other time and place as may be mutually agreed upon by counsel for the respective parties hereto.

You shall put said witness on oath and [his/her] testimony shall be recorded stenographically by someone acting under your direction, and thereafter, transcribed. Objections to evidence presented shall be noted and the evidence shall be taken subject to said objections. When the testimony is fully transcribed, it shall be signed by the respective witness, after a full opportunity to make corrections or changes.

You shall certify on the deposition that the witness was duly sworn by you and that the deposition is a deposition and thereafter place the same in an envelope endorsed with the title of the action and marked "Deposition of [name]" and send it registered mail to the undersigned.

By: _____
CLERK OF COURT

§ 4.56 Subpoena Duces Tecum

A Subpoena Duces Tecum is used when you desire your witness to bring certain documents or things with him to the deposition. The form provided (**Form 4–43**) includes a definition of the term documents, which leaves little to the imagination, making it possible to obtain any and all documents you need to question the witness about. This definition can be expanded to include other specific documents pertinent to your case. Remember that the difference between a Notice of Deposition and a Subpoena Duces Tecum is that any party's deposition may be noticed, but a witness who is not a party to the case must be subpoenaed. Your court clerk will have standard subpoena forms to be used when only the presence of the witness is required at the deposition. A Subpoena Duces Tecum, just like a subpoena, must be issued by the clerk of the court before being served.

FORM 4–43
SAMPLE SUBPOENA DUCES TECUM

SUBPOENA DUCES TECUM

THE STATE OF NEVADA SENDS GREETINGS TO:

[Name of the person being subpoenaed]

WE COMMAND YOU, that all and singular, business and excuses being set aside, you appear at the law offices of [name of law firm], [address], on the [date] day of [month], [20__], at the hour of [time] [A.M./P.M.], then and there to testify on the part of [plaintiff/defendant]. And for a failure to attend you will be deemed guilty of contempt of Court, and liable to pay all lossess and damages sustained thereby to the parties aggrieved and forfeit ONE HUNDRED DOLLARS ($100.00) in addition thereto.

PLEASE BRING WITH YOU any and all records pertaining to [describe requested documents, records, or things].

As used in this Subpoena, the term "records" means, without limitation, the following items, whether printed, or recorded or reproduced by any other mechanical process, or written or reproduced by hand: agreements, communications, memoranda, correspondence (including communications, memoranda, and/or correspondence from [name] attorney), telegrams, summaries or records of personal conversations or interviews, diaries, graphs, reports, notebooks, note charts, drawing sketches, summaries or records of meetings or conferences, opinions or reports of consultants, photographs, motion picture films, and marginal comments appearing on any documents, billings, x-rays, and all other writings.

IN WITNESS THEREOF, I have hereunto set my hand and affixed the seal of said Court this [date] day of [month], [20__].

[name], Clerk

By: _____
       Deputy

Note: This form is used in the State of Nevada. Many states have preprinted forms for this use and the wording will vary slightly.

§ 4.57   Requests for Admissions

Early in the case, you may find several facts which, if clarified, would make further discovery simpler, more direct, and defined. In these instances, a Request for Admissions is a useful tool. In such a Request, the opposing party is asked to either admit or deny certain facts or the truthfulness of certain statements. The admitted facts take on the same significance as if they had been stipulated. Check your local rules concerning admissions. In most states, if the requested admissions are not answered within 30 days, they are deemed admitted. Therefore, they are a very dangerous document to overlook when they are directed to your client. Conversely, an oversight by the opposing party can be used in your client's favor. (See **Form 4-44.**)

The use of admissions is much less restrictive than interrogatories in most jurisdictions. Although the number of interrogatories may be restricted, the number of admission requests are not. The responses to requests for admissions can be used to establish facts conclusively or to remove entire defenses, thereby paving the way either for the narrowing of issues at trial or for summary judgments. The best use of admissions is to restate the answers to previous interrogatories into statements of fact, submitting those statements of fact for admission or denial by the party. Once a fact is admitted under these circumstances, the rules of civil procedure deem that matter conclusively established as fact.

Requests for admissions are often used to prove up documents. The request "Admit that this is a true and correct copy of the . . . ." is commonly used to authenticate documents and put them into admissible form for use at trial. These requests are not to be used in the place of interrogatories. They are to be used mainly to eliminate contention of facts and thereby eliminate the necessity of proof at time of trial and to narrow the issues for trial. You can also use requests for admissions very successfully to force the admissions of facts about which there is no question, leading to the ability to file a motion for summary judgment, either in whole or in part. Unlike many other discovery devices, there are usually no limits on the number of Requests to Admit that can be served. Such Requests can be made at numerous points during the litigation process, right up to the beginning of the trial itself.

Federal Rule of Civil Procedure 36 governs Requests for Admissions. Time limits for responding may be modified by stipulation or court order pursuant to Rule 29 of the Federal Rules of Civil Procedure.

Under Rule 36, the party responding to the Request to Admit may not give lack of information or knowledge as a reason for failing to admit or deny unless the party states that the party has made reasonable inquiry and that the information known or readily obtainable by the party is insufficient to enable the party to admit or deny. Requests to Admit are subject to protective orders.

§ 4.58 —Drafting Guidelines

Both the following checklist and **Table 4–5** are useful tools in drafting Requests for Admissions.

____   1. Use Requests for Admissions for verification of facts regarding the truth of any matters.

____   2. Each request should be specific and singular in theme.

____   3. Requests should be worded in such a way that the elicited answer can be none other than ADMITTED or DENIED.

____   4. Avoid using extraneous modifying words or phrases which tend to editorialize or show bias and remove objectivity, such as "which caused the fire," or "had devastating effects."

____   5. Phrase each Request for Admission in such a way that it cannot be objected to. Check the Rules of Civil Procedure regarding scope of discovery for proper legal objections.

____   6. Use Requests for Admission to elicit admissions regarding the genuineness of documents. (In many state courts, the documents must be attached to the Request for Admissions. Under Rule 36 of the Federal Rules of Civil Procedure, copies of the documents must be served with the request unless they have been or are otherwise furnished or made available for inspection or copying.)

____   7. Keep all Requests for Admissions simple and direct. Do not use elaborate legalese, compound, or conditional sentences.

____   8. Use Requests for Admissions to narrow and define issues prior to trial.

Table 4–5

Admissions Drafting Guidelines

Criteria—What elements are found in a good set of admissions?	How do you achieve those elements?	Tips, techniques
Requests for Admissions are designed to verify the facts of the truth of any matter.	State each fact which is important to the issues of the case in a simple sentence. Example: "Admit or deny that the traffic light was red when you entered the intersection."	Avoid phrases which place blame or interject morality issues into the facts. Example: "Admit or deny that the fire would not have happened if you had properly supervised your son."
		Use Requests for Admissions to verify the facts which support every element of a claim which need to be proven at trial. For example, if the claim is negligence, ask questions, which if admitted, will give every element of proof needed to prove negligence, that is, duty, breach of duty, proximate cause, and damages. Requests for Admissions are useful in supporting Motions for Summary Judgments.
Requests for Admissions are designed to elicit admissions regarding the genuiness of documents in order to prove them up for trial.	Example: Admit or deny that the document attached hereto and designated as Exhibit A is a true and correct copy of the contract which is the subject matter of this litigation.	
	Attach copies of referenced documents to admissions as exhibits.	
Criteria—What elements are found in a good set of admissions?	How do you achieve those elements?	Tips, techniques

Table 4–5
(*continued*)

Requests for Admissions are designed to narrow and define the issues prior to trial.	Break down the facts which comprise the issues. Use Requests for Admissions to verify all the facts possible, thus narrowing the list of facts needed to be determined by a jury. Review all discovery to date, such as deposition testimony, answers to interrogatories and responses to requests for production of documents to gather facts appropriate for addressing in Requests for Admissions.	
Requests for Admissions are stated simply and directly.	Requests should be worded in such a way that the elicited answer can be none other than ADMITTED or DENIED. Each request should be specific and singular in theme. Anticipate objections to avoid making requests which will be disallowed by the Rules of Civil Procedure.	Do not use elaborate legalese, compound, or conditional sentences.
Format of Requests for Admissions follows appropriate Rules of Civil Procedure.	Consult appropriate Rules of Civil Procedure and the local rules which affect the filing and serving of Requests for Admissions.	
Requests for Admissions are drafted in such a way that they will not exceed the scope of discovery.	Anticipate objections to avoid requesting admissions which will be disallowed. See the Rules of Civil Procedure regarding objections to discovery.	

§ 4.59   Sample Request for Admissions

FORM 4–44
SAMPLE REQUEST FOR ADMISSIONS

NO. [case number]

[name]	)	IN THE DISTRICT COURT OF
	)	
Plaintiff,	)	[county] COUNTY, [state]
	)	
vs.	)	[judicial district] JUDICIAL DISTRICT
	)	
[name]	)	
	)	
Defendant.	)	

REQUEST FOR ADMISSIONS

Pursuant to Rule [citation] of the [state] Rules of Civil Procedure, [name], plaintiff in the above cause, requests that [name], defendant in the above cause, admit the truth of the following matters in order to simplify the issues for consideration by the Court. Defendant should answer this request in the manner directed by Rule [citation] and should supplement his answers or inquiries by Rule [citation].

Under Rule [citation], the matters that defendant is requested to admit should be deemed admitted unless defendant delivers or causes to be delivered to plaintiff or his attorney of record, a sworn statement with thirty (30) days after the delivery of this request, either denying specifically the matters of which an admission is requested or explaining in detail why he cannot truthfully either admit or deny these matters. All admissions made pursuant to this request are made for the purpose of this pending action and will not constitute an admission by defendant for any other purpose and may not be used against him in any other proceeding.

Defendant is requested to admit to the following matters:

1.   That Defendant signed a contract dated September 1, 1999, to buy plaintiff's home.

2.   That the agreed upon purchase price for said property was $95,000.

3.   That defendant gave plaintiff an earnest money check for $3,000 dated September 1, 1999.

4.   That defendant agreed to apply in writing for financing within seven days of the signing of the contract.

5.   That plaintiff agreed to remove his home from the market.

6.   That defendant did not apply in writing for financing to any financial institution within the seven day period.

7.   That defendant called plaintiff on September 9, 1999 to say he could not secure financing.

8.   That defendant asked for the return of his earnest money from plaintiff on September 9, 1999.

9.   That defendant made an earnest money deposit of $3,000 on another property on September 6, 1999.

10.   That defendant secured a financing commitment on said other property on September 8, 1999.

> [name of law firm]
>
> By: _____
>   [attorney name]
>   [firm address]
>   Counsel for Plaintiff

§ 4.60 —Sample Request for Admissions— Uninsured Motorist Litigation

FORM 4–45
SAMPLE REQUEST FOR ADMISSIONS— UNINSURED MOTORIST LITIGATION

Attorneys for Claimant(s)
Re: Case No.:
To: Respondent and to Your Attorney(s) of Record:
          Respondent is requested by Claimant(s):

To answer under oath, in accordance with ____, the following Requests for Admissions, within ____ days, plus five for mailing, and to provide all of the information presently available to you in answering these Requests for Admissions.

Dated: _____

1. Admit that claimant was covered by uninsured motorist benefits, under a valid policy issued by respondent in force at the time of the subject collision.

2. Admit that no policy or coverage defenses are raised.

§ 4.60   UNINSURED MOTORIST ADMISSIONS

3. Admit that the adverse vehicle involved in the subject collision was an uninsured motor vehicle as defined in Insurance Code ____.

4. Admit that the driver of the adverse vehicle involved in the subject collision was negligent.

5. Admit that the negligence of the adverse driver involved in the subject collision was the sole cause of the subject collision.

6. Admit that the Claimant was not contributorily negligent in the subject collision.

7. Admit that the Claimant did not assume the risk of the subject collision.

8. Admit that the Claimant suffered property damage to Claimant's vehicle as a result of the subject collision.

9. Admit that the Claimant suffered injuries to Claimant's person, body, mind as a result of the subject collision.

10. Admit that the Claimant continues to suffer injuries to Claimant's body, mind and person as a result of the subject collision.

11. Admit that the Claimant suffered from loss of wages as a result of the subject collision.

12. Admit that no other person or cause was the proximate cause of the subject collision but the adverse vehicle.

13. Admit that the Claimant incurred medical expenses for treatment, diagnosis, and examination as a result of the subject collision.

14. Admit that the medical expenses incurred by the Claimant are reasonable and necessary.

15. Admit that the Claimant continues to incur medical expenses for care, treatment, and/or diagnosis as a result of the subject collision.

16. Admit Claimant continues to suffer from mental and/or nervous pain and suffering as a result of the injuries sustained in the subject collision.

FAILURE TO TIMELY RESPOND TO THE REQUESTS FOR ADMISSIONS HEREIN ABOVE SET FORTH WILL SUBJECT THE RESPONDING PARTY TO THE SANCTIONS AND PENALTIES AS PROVIDED IN _____, WHICH MAY INCLUDE THE ADMISSION OF EACH MATTER REQUESTED.

DISCOVERY

FORM 4–46
REQUEST FOR ADMISSIONS

NO. _____

[PLAINTIFF(S) NAMES] Plaintiffs,	)))	IN THE DISTRICT COURT OF
	)))	_____ COUNTY,
_____	))	
v.	))	_____ JUDICIAL DISTRICT
[DEFENDANT(S) NAMES] Defendants.	))	

REQUEST FOR ADMISSIONS

Pursuant to Rule _____ of the _____ Rules of Civil Procedure, _____, defendant in the above-named cause, admits the truth of the following matters in order to simplify the issues for consideration by the Court. Defendant should answer this request in the manner directed by Rule _____ and should supplement his answers or inquiries by Rule _____ of the _____ Rules of Civil Procedure.

Under Rule _____, the matters that defendant is requested to admit should be deemed admitted unless defendant delivers or causes to be delivered to plaintiff, or plaintiff's attorney of record, a sworn statement within thirty (30) days after the delivery of this request, either denying specifically the matters of which an admission is requested or explaining in detail why he cannot truthfully either admit or deny these matters. All admissions made pursuant to this request are made for the purpose of this pending action and will not constitute an admission by defendant for any other purpose and may not be used against him in any other proceeding.

Defendant is requested to admit to the following matters:

REQUEST FOR ADMISSION NO. 1: ADMIT that you have read and are familiar with all pages of this document.

REQUEST FOR ADMISSION NO. 2: ADMIT that on _____, 20__, at approximately ___.m. you were the driver of a ____[make and model]____ that was _____[direction, street, town]_____.

REQUEST FOR ADMISSION NO. 3: ADMIT that at the date, time, and location as stated in Request for Admission Number 2, you and your vehicle were involved in an automobile accident with a ____[make and model]____ driven by _____.

§ 4.60   UNINSURED MOTORIST ADMISSIONS

REQUEST FOR ADMISSION NO. 4: ADMIT that at the date, time, and location as stated in Request for Admission Number 2, the accident as specified in Request for Admission Number 3 was caused by your negligence.

REQUEST FOR ADMISSION NO. 5: ADMIT that at the date, time, and location as stated in Request for Admission Number 2, the accident as specified in Request for Admission Number 3 could have been prevented but for your inaction.

REQUEST FOR ADMISSION NO. 6: ADMIT that at the date, time, and location as stated in Request for Admission Number 2, the accident as specified in Request for Admission Number 3 was caused solely by your failure to proceed for a green light.

REQUEST FOR ADMISSION NO. 7: ADMIT that at the date, time, and location as stated in Request for Admission Number 2, the accident as specified in Request for Admission Number 3 was caused solely by your own acts or omissions without any negligence on the part of the defendant.

REQUEST FOR ADMISSION NO. 8: ADMIT that the injuries of which you complain were not proximately caused by or related to the accident as stated in your petition.

REQUEST FOR ADMISSION NO. 9: ADMIT that Plaintiff did not devote full time and attention prior to the subject accident and that as a result of said inattention Plaintiff negligently caused said accident to occur, and all damages concomitant thereto.

Respectfully submitted,
NAME OF FIRM

_____

Name of Atty
Atty's Bar #
Address
City, State, Zip
Phone #

CERTIFICATE OF SERVICE

I hereby certify that a true and correct copy of the above and foregoing document has been forwarded to all counsel of record by facsimile and/or certified mail/R.R.R. on this _____ day of _____, 20___.

_____

DISCOVERY

FORM 4–47
REQUESTS FOR ADMISSIONS
(Automobile Collision)

NO. _____

[PLAINTIFF(S) NAMES]
    Plaintiffs,
	)
	)
	) IN THE DISTRICT COURT OF
	)
	) _____ COUNTY,
	)
	v.)
	) _____ JUDICIAL DISTRICT
	[DEFENDANT(S) NAMES])
	    Defendants.)

REQUESTS FOR ADMISSIONS

Pursuant to Rule _____ of the _____ Rules of Civil Procedure, _____, defendant in the above-named cause admits the truth of the following matters in order to simplify the issues for consideration by the Court. Defendant should answer this request in the manner directed by Rule _____ and should supplement his answers or inquiries pursuant to Rule _____ of the _____ Rules of Civil Procedure.

Under Rule _____, the matters that defendant is requested to admit should be deemed admitted unless defendant delivers or causes to be delivered to plaintiff, or plaintiff's attorney of record, a sworn statement within thirty (30) days after the delivery of this request, either denying specifically the matters of which an admission is requested or explaining in detail why he cannot truthfully either admit or deny these matters. All admissions made pursuant to this request are made for the purpose of this pending action and will not constitute an admission by defendant for any other purpose and may not be used against him in any other proceeding.

Defendant is requested to admit to the following matters:

REQUEST NO. 1: Admit or deny that you were involved in an automobile collision with Plaintiff, [name of Plaintiff], on or about [date of accident] at or near the intersection of [location of accident].

REQUEST NO. 2: Admit or deny that you were cited for failing to yield the right-of-way from a stop sign as a result of the above-mentioned collision.

REQUEST NO. 3: Admit or deny that your failing to yield the right-of-way from a stop sign directly caused the above-mentioned collision.

REQUEST NO. 4: Admit or deny that you were in violation of __[statute]__ at the time of the above-mentioned collision.

<u>REQUEST NO. 5:</u> Admit or deny that as a result of the above-mentioned collision, Plaintiff sustained serious personal injuries.

<u>REQUEST NO. 6:</u> Admit or deny that as a result of the above-mentioned collision, Plaintiff was prevented from transacting [his/her] business.

<u>REQUEST NO. 7:</u> Admit or deny that as a result of the above-mentioned collision, Plaintiff has suffered and will suffer pain of mind and body.

<u>REQUEST NO. 8:</u> Admit or deny that as a result of the above-mentioned collision, Plaintiff has incurred and will incur medical expenses.

<u>REQUEST NO. 9:</u> Admit or deny that as a result of the above-mentioned collision, Plaintiff has been disabled.

<u>REQUEST NO. 10:</u> Admit or deny that as a result of the above-mentioned collision, Plaintiff has been disfigured.

Respectfully submitted,
NAME OF FIRM

_____

Name of Atty
Atty's Bar #
Address
City, State, Zip
Phone #

CERTIFICATE OF SERVICE

I hereby certify that a true and correct copy of the above and foregoing document has been forwarded to all counsel of record by facsimile and/or certified mail/R.R.R. on this ____ day of _____, 20___.

_____

§ 4.61   Requests for Production of Documents

Should you believe that there may be documents in the possession of the opposing party which could be useful to the investigation and development of your case, you can request those documents by filing a Request for Production of Documents. (See **Form 4–48**.) There may be specific documents of which you are aware and will want to identify by name in your request. More often that not, however, you will be aware only of the possibility of the existence of such documents and will want to be able to ask for them in general terms. For this reason, the request contains a definition of the word document which is designed to cover all possible forms of documents which may be available. An example of a request might be as follows:

Any and all documents relating to your alleged inability to return to your previous job duties as a result of the injuries received by you in this accident.

(Followed, of course, by the liberal definition of the word "document.")

Rule 34 of the Federal Rules of Civil Procedure governs Requests for Production of Documents. Under this rule, the number of requests a party may make is not limited. The need for formal Requests for Production of Documents may be somewhat lessened by the mandatory disclosure provisions of Rule 26.

The producing party is given 30 days to respond to the requests. The requests must be specific enough as not to be deemed overly broad or objectionable.

FORM 4–48
SAMPLE REQUEST FOR PRODUCTION OF DOCUMENTS

NO. [case number]

[name]	)	IN THE DISTRICT COURT OF
	)	
Plaintiff,	)	[county] COUNTY, [state]
	)	
vs.	)	[judicial district] JUDICIAL DISTRICT
	)	
[name]	)	
	)	
Defendant.	)	

REQUEST FOR PRODUCTION

TO: [name] by and through their/his attorney of record, [name]

Pursuant to Rule [citation] of the [state/federal] Rules of Civil Procedure, [name], defendant/plaintiff] in the above cause, request(s) that [name], defendant(s)/plaintiff(s) in the above cause, produce the documents* listed below:

As directed by Rule [citation], Plaintiff(s) shall file a written response to this request within thirty (30) days after the date of service.

If any documents responsive to any request herein are withheld by reason of any assertion of privilege, Plaintiff(s) shall submit a schedule at the time of production stating, for each document withheld, the following information:

1.   The type of document (for example, letter, memorandum, account statement, prospectus, and so forth);

2.   The date the document was prepared, and the date of any meeting or conversation reflected or referred to therein;

3.   The name of each author, co-author or preparer of the document and the name of each recipient or addressee, including each recipient of a copy thereof;

4.   If the document reflects or refers to a meeting or conversation, the name of each person who was present at or was a party to the meeting or conversation;

5.   The subject matter of the information contained in the document;

6.   The nature of the privilege asserted; and

7.   A brief explanation of why the document is believed to be privileged.

By _____
[attorney name]

COUNSEL FOR
[DEFENDANT(S)/PLAINTIFF(S)]

CERTIFICATE OF SERVICE

I certify that this instrument was served in compliance with Rules ____ and ____ of the _____ Rules of Civil Procedure, by certified mail or hand delivery, return receipt requested, on the [date] day of [month], [20__], and was promptly filed with the Clerk of the Court, together with this proof of service.

_____
[attorney's name]

*"Document" means each of the following that is in the possession, custody, or control of each party named above or that can be obtained by the party through the exercise of a superior right to compel production from a third person: the original and each nonidentical copy (whether different from the original by virtue of notes made or otherwise) and, if the original is not in existence or subject to your control, each nonidentical copy, regardless of origin or location, of any handwritten, typewritten, printed, recorded, transcribed, punched, taped, photocopied, photostatic, telecopied, filmed, microfilmed, or otherwise reproduced, and further including without limitation any papers, book, accounts, drawings, graphs, charts, photographs, phono-records, plans, blueprints, telexes, telegrams, electronic or videotaped or mechanical recordings, magnetic impulses, and any other data compilation from which information can be obtained or translated into reasonably usable form.

DISCOVERY

FORM 4–49
SAMPLE REQUEST FOR PRODUCTION OF DOCUMENTS
(ANOTHER FORM)

[court] COURT OF THE STATE OF [state]
COUNTY OF [county]

[name]		)	Index No.
		)	
	Plaintiff,	)	PLAINTIFF'S FIRST
		)	
		)	REQUEST
		)	
-against-		)	FOR PRODUCTION OF
		)	
		)	DOCUMENTS AND THINGS
[name]		)	
	Defendant	)	

Pursuant to [Rule of Civil Procedure], plaintiff [name] hereby requests that defendant produce for inspection and copying at the offices of [law firm name and address], commencing at or before 10:00 a.m. Eastern Standard Time on July 10, 20__, each document within the possession, custody, or control of defendant described below.

DEFINITIONS AND INSTRUCTIONS
Definitions

A. The term "person" or "persons" includes natural persons, firms, partnerships, associations, joint ventures and corporations, governmental units or agencies, and public corporations of the State of [state].

B. The term "document" shall mean any writing (whether handwritten, typed, printed, or otherwise made), drawing, graph, chart, photograph, phono-record, or electronic or mechanical matter (including microfilm of any kind or nature, tape or recordings), or other data compilations from which information can be obtained (translated, if necessary, by defendants through detection devices into reasonably usable form), and shall include, without limiting the generality of the foregoing, all correspondence, telegrams, teletypes, telexes, agreements, contracts, amendments, messages, memo pads, studies, reports, price lists, quotations, memoranda, minutes, journal entries, notes, books, records, accounts, ledgers, invoices, bank statements, books of account, work sheets, advices, analyses, comparisons, booklets, lists, studies, interoffice communications, transcripts, pamphlets, log books, letters, diaries, data in the memory of a computer, or any other machine-readable matter, bills of lading, newspaper clippings, and any and all other writings or papers of any kind, including drafts and other preliminary material, from whatever source underlying, supporting, or used in the preparation of any documents, copies or reproductions of any of the foregoing, and information stored in computers or other data storage or processing equipment in the possession, custody, or control of the defendant.

C. "Things" means any tangible objects or materials that concern, relate, or refer to defendants or defenses.

D. The term "relating to," in addition to its customary and usual meanings, means discussing, mentioning, pertaining to, assessing, recording, concerning, describing, touching upon, and/or summarizing.

<u>Instructions</u>

A. In responding to each document request, you are to review and search all relevant files of appropriate entities and persons.

B. In responding to each document request, you are to make certain that this document demand is provided to appropriate and responsible persons at defendant so that appropriate persons review the document demand and produce the requested documents.

C. At the time and place of production, you shall serve your responses to this request, setting forth the manner of response to each of the numbered requests contained herein. You are requested to segregate the documents produced to indicate the particular request in response to which they are being produced.

D. Unless otherwise specified, this request calls for the production of documents written, prepared, dated, sent, or received during, relating, or referring to the period from the beginning of the plaintiff's employment to the present.

E. If any documents called for by this demand are withheld under a claim of privilege, please furnish a description for each document for which privilege is claimed, together with the following information as to each such document: name(s) and address(es) of each person who prepared, received, viewed, and has or has had custody of the document and a statement of the basis upon which such privilege is claimed.

F. If any document herein requested was formerly in the possession, custody, or control of the defendant and has been lost or destroyed, the defendants are requested to submit in lieu of each such document a written statement which:

    (a) describes the nature of the document;

    (b) identifies the person who prepared or authorized the document and, if applicable, the person to whom the document was sent;

    (d) specifies, if possible, the date on which the document was lost or destroyed, and, if destroyed, the conditions of and the reasons for each destruction and the persons requesting and performing the destruction.

G. "And" and "or" shall be interpreted to mean and/or.

H. Plural words shall be interpreted to include the singular, and vice versa.

I. This request shall be deemed continuing so as to require further and supplemental production if the defendants obtain additional documents between the time of this initial

DISCOVERY

production and the time of trial herein. This paragraph shall not be construed to alter any obligation to comply with all other instructions in this document demand.

J. Please note that in lieu of personal appearance, you may submit to the undersigned true and complete copies of the items demanded at any time on or before the above-mentioned date.

Documents to Be Produced

1. All documents including, but not limited to, the Security Agreement and Note previously executed by the defendant RALPH LIEBER which are presently held by Fleetwood Financial Corp. to protect their security interest in the subject business.

2. All documents including, but not limited to, the proposed Assignment and Assumption of the Security Agreement and Note that the plaintiff allegedly refused to sign on or about June 29, 20__.

Dated: [city and state]
_____ 20__

Yours, etc.,

[Law firm's name, address, and telephone number]

TO: [name, address, and
telephone number of
opposing counsel]

FORM 4–50
REQUEST FOR INSPECTION OF LAND OR PREMISES

UNITED STATES DISTRICT COURT
DISTRICT OF _____

[PLAINTIFF(S) NAMES] Plaintiffs,	)	
	)	
	)	
	)	CASE NO:_____
	)	
v.	)	
	)	
[DEFENDANT(S) NAMES] Defendants.	)	

REQUEST FOR INSPECTION OF LAND OR PREMISES

To _____[Defendant/Plaintiff]____, ____[name]____, by and through his attorney of record _____[name and address of attorney]_____.

§ 4.62 DOCUMENT REQUEST CHECKLIST

_____[Requesting party]_____, _____[name]_____, requests that _____[responding party]_____ permit _____[requesting party or agent]_____ to enter and inspect land in _____[responding party's]_____ possession, control, or custody located at _____[address]_____, _____[city]_____, _____ County, [State] on _[date at least 30 days after service of demand]_, at _[time]_. Pursuant to Rule 26 of the Federal Rules of Civil Procedure, _[responding party]_ is required to serve a written response to this inspection request within _[30 or as the case may be]_ days from the date of service of this request.

1. [If other related activities are requested, add the following: In addition to entrance on, and inspection of _____(responding party's)_____ property, _(requesting party)_ intends to _(specify other related activities)_.]

2. [Specify manner in which activities other than inspection will be performed; for example: The property involved will be subjected to inspection, measurement, surveying, photographing, testing, and sampling as follows:

a. Photographing of the _____ and related objects or premises located on the property.

b. Sampling of the _____.

c. Testing of _____.

d. Surveying of _____.]

3. [If testing, sampling, or other related activities will permanently alter or destroy the property involved, that fact must be stated; for example: The property involved will be permanently _(altered or destroyed)_ in that _(describe manner and extent of alteration or destruction)_.]

Dated this _____ day of_____ 20___.

> Respectfully submitted,
>
> NAME OF FIRM
>
> _____
> Name of Atty
> Atty's Bar #
> Address
> City, State, Zip
> Phone #

§ 4.62 Document Request Checklist

Each individual case will have its own idiosyncracies, and therefore, no standard checklist will be complete enough to allow you to derive your Request for Production of Documents from it alone. The following checklist is meant to be used as a guideline to jog your thought processes when you are developing your requests. Be sure to ask for every possible document that could be relative to your case or could lead to the discovery of relative information.

____ 1. Any documents which would show identity of witnesses.
____ 2. Any statements, recorded or written, relative to the case.
____ 3. Documentation relied upon to support allegations.
____ 4. Documents proving damages and bill amounts.
____ 5. Permission to test tangible evidence.
____ 6. Permission to enter premises for inspection purposes.
____ 7. Photographs.
____ 8. Television or radio transcripts or recordings.
____ 9. Copies of birth certificates, marriage licenses, driver's licenses, and so forth.
____ 10. Copies of income tax returns.
____ 11. Copies of relevant insurance policies.
____ 12. Documents relating to prior knowledge of hazardous conditions.
____ 13. Copies of reports or tests obtained from expert witnesses.
____ 14. Copies of any covenants not to sue, or any other agreements signed.
____ 15. Medical record authorization.
____ 16. I.R.S. record authorization.
____ 17. Employment record authorization.
____ 18. Claims and warranties of a certain product.
____ 19. Advertising brochures for a certain product.

§ 4.63 Responding to Requests for Production of Documents

There is no doubt that the first time a paralegal is faced with the task of gathering documents responsive to a request for production of documents, the thought of the responsibility attached and the scope of the job is awesome. However, just like everything else we do, there are procedures and guidelines that make the job easier and give us a greater level of self-confidence in its undertaking.

First of all, calendar the date by which you must serve the response on the opposing party, and then set out to survey the job in terms of trimming its overwhelming nature. The most obvious starting place is to read through the requests to see which ones may be objected to under the applicable Rules of Civil Procedure. The next step is to enlist the aid of other persons who will help make your job easier. First, consult with your attorney to validate your decisions about objections. Next, go through the requests with the thought in mind that the client may have certain types of documents in his possession. You have already succeeded in enlisting the help of at least two in this job and things are moving right along. Don't you feel better already?

Before you approach the client about those documents which you need to obtain from him in order to respond to the requests, remove all of those requests to which you know you will be objecting. There is no need to confuse the issue. You will also want to give your client a date by which it is necessary for him to provide you with copies of those documents which he has in his possession so that you will have enough time to prepare the final draft of the response comfortably and have it reviewed by the attorney before the deadline date.

Now that all of those systems are in place and working for you, it is time to review the documents that are in the file and determine which ones must be produced. Instead of taking all the requests into account at once, which is an overwhelming job, start with one request at a time and begin to gather those documents which are responsive. In this original process, even those documents which are responsive but privileged should be included. Label them, however, with a loudly-colored stick-on note which will protrude beyond the edge of the paper. This will ensure that those documents are logged onto a privileged document log and accounted for, but not actually produced in the document production. As you go through the documents in this fashion and move from one request to another, you will probably notice that some of the documents will also be responsive to other requests as well. Make notes of this as you go. Remember that you are not required to produce multiple copies of the same documents, but only to refer the party to those documents which you have previously produced and are responsive to his request.

It is imperative that you know what you have produced when you finish. Therefore, each page of each produced document (as well as those pulled from the stack for privilege) must be numbered with a Bates stamp or computerized number label in the lower right-hand corner of the document. You will also want to create either a manual or computerized index of those documents for later reference. Some attorneys provide copies of these indices with the documents when they are produced, but generally, the feeling is that the indices are produced as work product for your own use and benefit and nothing will prevent the receiving party from devising his own indices if he so chooses.

The documents must be delivered to the party in a responsive manner: that is, all documents responsive to a certain request must be labeled accordingly. It is not acceptable to dump all the documents into a box or boxes and expect the other party to determine which documents are responsive to which requests. This is true whether the document production is small and can be hand-delivered, or extremely voluminous and done by on-site inspection and copying.

Before the documents are released from your offices, make sure that you have a complete copy of what has been produced. You will be referring to these documents innumerable times before the litigation is over. It will be vitally important for you to be able to review the document production at different stages of the litigation in order to determine which documents are available to your opponent as he develops his case.

If the document production is small, a manual index may very well suffice, but it is recommended to use a more sophisticated index such as one sorted by word processor or by computerized litigation support if the volume of the production is in excess of 1,000 documents. There are several different types of indices discussed in **Chapter 6**.

§ 4.64 Checklist for Responding to Request for Production of Documents

_____ 1. Calendar response date.

_____ 2. Forward copy of Request for Production of Documents to attorney.

_____ 3. Go through requests and determine which should be objected to. (Refer to § **4.33** regarding objections.)

_____ 4. Consult with attorney regarding objections.

_____ 5. Go through the Request to determine which responsive documents may be in the possession of your client.

_____ 6. Send copy of Request with letter to client explaining what kind of help you need from him in locating responsive documents, giving him a deadline date to have those documents to you. Be sure to allow yourself enough time for copying and indexing the documents as well as preparing the final draft of the Response. (See § **4.24**.)

_____ 7. In the alternative, arrange a time to go to the client's office and look through the documents yourself to determine responsiveness.

_____ 8. Start compiling documents responsive to one request at a time. Review for privileged information. Make a log of privileged documents and pull these from the documents to be produced. Have the attorney review these documents for privilege confirmation.
Objectives:

_____ a. Identify responsive documents

_____ b. Number documents not already numbered

_____ c. Identify privileged documents

_____ 9. When you have finished compiling all the documents which are responsive to a particular request, copy all the documents, label as being responsive to which specific request, and replace original documents in file.

_____ 10. Check back with the client to be sure there are no other responsive documents to be produced.

_____ 11. Meet with the client and go over the responsive documents. Ask if he is aware of any other responsive documents.

___ 12. Number all documents with a Bates stamp or computerized number labels. Number series would be assigned for each producing party at the beginning of the case or production.

___ 13. Make one additional copy of all the documents to keep for your file, along with a copy of the Response to Request for Production of Documents.

___ 14. Create a manual or computerized index of all the documents which are being produced. (Refer to the form for indexing in Chapter 6. You may also want to add categories showing the date produced and the name of the producing party.)

___ 15. Finalize the Response to Request for Production of Documents.

___ 16. Consult with the attorney regarding final draft, and have the document signed and verified by the attorney or client. (Check the applicable Rule of Civil Procedure.)

___ 17. File the Response to Request for Production of Documents with the court clerk if such documents are filed in your jurisdiction. (Check the applicable Rules of Civil Procedure.)

___ 18. Serve the Response to Request for Production of Documents (**Form 4–51**) on opposing counsel with all documents attached.

§ 4.65 Response to Request for Production of Documents

FORM 4–51
SAMPLE RESPONSE TO REQUEST FOR PRODUCTION OF DOCUMENTS

NO. [case number]

[name]	)	IN THE DISTRICT COURT OF
	)	
Plaintiff	)	[county] COUNTY, [state]
	)	
vs.	)	[judicial district] JUDICIAL DISTRICT
	)	
[name]	)	
	)	
Defendant	)	

RESPONSE TO REQUEST FOR PRODUCTION OF DOCUMENTS

To: [name of requesting party] by and through his attorney of record [name and address of opposing counsel]:

COMES NOW [name of client], [plaintiff/defendant] in the above-captioned and numbered cause, and files this, his Responses to Requests for Production of Documents heretofore served on him:

[Retype the original Requests, and under each one, reference the attached documents which are responsive to that particular request. If the request is objected to, type that objection directly under the request.]

[name of firm]

By: _____
　　　　[attorney name]
　　　　Attorney for [plaintiff/defendant]
　　　　[address]
　　　　[telephone number]

[Add verification if necessary in your jurisdiction.]

[Add certificate of service.]

§ 4.66 Supplementary Discovery

Consult the local rules of court in your district to determine if it is necessary to supplement your Answers to Interrogatories and Responses to Request for Production automatically. The rules differ from district to district, both in federal and state courts, but for the most part you can expect this requirement to be standard.

　　Even where this rule is not standard, opposing counsel will often send a supplementary request (**Form 4–52**) for updated information. When this happens, consult the file to see if additional information has already been gathered on the subject, then contact your client to complete your supplementary response. Be sure to send him a copy of whatever documents are served or filed. (**Form 4–53** is a sample Supplemental Response to Interrogatories.)

　　Rule 26(e) of the Federal Rules of Civil Procedure regarding supplementation of discovery states:

(e) Supplementation of Disclosure and Responses. A party who has made a disclosure under subdivision (a) or responded to a request for discovery with a disclosure or response is under a duty to supplement or correct the disclosure or response to include information thereafter acquired if ordered by the court or in the following circumstances:

(1) A party is under a duty to supplement at appropriate intervals its disclosures under subdivision (a) if the party learns that in some material respect the information disclosed is incomplete or incorrect and if the additional or corrective information has not otherwise been made known to the other parties during the discovery process or in writing. With respect to the testimony of an expert from whom a report is required under subdivision (a)(2)(B) the duty extends both to information contained in the

334

report and to information provided through a deposition of the expert, and any additions or other changes to this information shall be disclosed by the time the party's disclosures under Rule 26(a)(3) are due.

(2) A party is under a duty seasonably to amend a prior response to an interrogatory, request for production, or request for admission if the party learns that the response is in some material respect incomplete or incorrect and if the additional or corrective information has not otherwise been made known to the other parties during the discovery process or in writing.

FORM 4–52
SAMPLE REQUEST FOR SUPPLEMENTATION OF DISCOVERY

NO. [case number]

[name]	)	IN THE DISTRICT COURT OF
	)	
Plaintiff,	)	[county] COUNTY, [state]
	)	
vs.	)	[judicial district] JUDICIAL DISTRICT
	)	
[name]	)	
	)	
Defendant.	)	

REQUEST FOR SUPPLEMENTATION OF DISCOVERY

TO: [name]_____

         [address]_____

COME(S) NOW [name], (cross-)defendant(s) in the above case, to request under Rule [citation] of the [state/federal] Rules of Civil Procedure that [name], (cross-)plaintiff(s) in the above case, supplement (his/her/its/their) answers and responses to the discovery mentioned below with any additional information acquired after (his/her/its/their) previous answers or responses to the following:

[specify pleadings for which supplemental discovery is being requested.]_____

_____

_____

_____

_____

(Cross-)defendant(s) request(s) that (cross-)plaintiff(s) file [his/her/its/their] supplemental answers thirty (30) days after the service of this request for supplementation.

[name of law firm]

By: _____
    [attorney name]
    State Bar No. [number]
    [firm address]
    Counsel for (Cross-)Defendants(s)

CERTIFICATE OF SERVICE

I certify that this instrument was served in compliance with Rules _____ and _____ of the _____ Rules of Civil Procedure, by certified mail or hand delivery, return receipt requested, on the [date] day of [month], [20__], and was promptly filed with the Clerk of the Court, together with the proof of service.

_____
[attorney's name]

FORM 4–53
SAMPLE SUPPLEMENTAL RESPONSE TO INTERROGATORIES

NO. [case number]

[name]	)	IN THE DISTRICT COURT OF
	)	
Plaintiff,	)	[county] COUNTY, [state]
	)	
vs.	)	[judicial district] JUDICIAL DISTRICT
	)	
[name]	)	
	)	
Defendant.	)	

PLAINTIFF'S FIRST SUPPLEMENTAL RESPONSE TO DEFENDANT'S
FIRST WRITTEN INTERROGATORIES

TO THE HONORABLE JUDGE OF SAID COURT:

COMES NOW [name], plaintiff in the above-numbered and entitled action and files [this/its] First Supplemental Response to Defendant's First Written Interrogatories, pursuant to Rule [citation] of the [state/federal] Rules of Civil Procedure, and for same would show unto the Court the following:

Interrogatory No. [number]:

[Recite entire original interrogatory to be supplemented, with its original number.]

ANSWER: [State all additional information to be divulged.]

STATE OF [state]   )
)

COUNTY OF [county]   )

BEFORE ME, the undersigned authority on this day personally appeared [name], known to me to be the person whose name is subscribed to the foregoing First Supplemental Response to Defendant's First Written Interrogatories and after having been duly sworn on his oath stated that he is the attorney of record for [name] in the above-captioned case and that he has read the foregoing answers to interrogatories and that they are true and correct.

[name] _____

SUBSCRIBED AND SWORN to before me this [date] day of [month], [20__].

[name] _____
NOTARY PUBLIC IN AND FOR
THE STATE OF [state]

Respectfully submitted,

[name of law firm]

By: _____
[attorney name]
[address]

Attorneys for Plaintiff

§ 4.67   Independent Medical Examinations   *Rule 35*

Personal injury cases often involve the necessity of submitting the plaintiff to an independent physical or mental examination. Under Rule 35(a) of the Federal Rules of Civil Procedure, the adverse party may request that the other party undergo an examination if good cause exists or if the nature of the condition is in controversy.

Normally these medical examinations can be arranged informally with agreement between the parties, but if that is not possible, the requesting party may file a Motion for Compulsory Physical (or Mental) Examination (**Form 4–54**). The requesting party chooses the examining physician and bears the costs of the exam. The physician supplies the requesting party with a written report detailing his findings in the examination. It is often the paralegal's responsibility to keep files on physicians who are used by the law firm in giving independent exams, as well as setting up the actual appointment and handling payment and party contact. (**Form 4–55** is a sample Order Granting Motion for Physical Examination.)

FORM 4–54
SAMPLE MOTION FOR PHYSICAL EXAMINATION

[case number]

[name]	)	IN THE DISTRICT COURT OF
	)	
vs.	)	[county] COUNTY, [state]
	)	
[name]	)	[judicial district] JUDICIAL DISTRICT

MOTION FOR PHYSICAL EXAMINATION

TO THE HONORABLE JUDGE OF SAID COURT:

COMES NOW [name], the defendant in the above cause, to file this motion under Rule [citation] of the [state/federal] Rules of Civil Procedure to require [name], plaintiff in the above cause, to submit to a physical examination to be made by [name of physician], at [address], in [city], [state], and respectfully show the Court as follows:

I.

This is a case in which the Plaintiff alleges that he suffered permanent and disabling injuries as a result of an automobile accident between his car and that of the defendant on [date], [20___], in [city], [state]. The plaintiff alleges that said accident was directly and proximately caused by the negligence of defendant.

II.

Defendant denies the allegations made by the plaintiff concerning his injuries and disabilities. Accordingly, the physical condition of plaintiff is in controversy.

III.

Defendant's investigation has revealed that the plaintiff has retained the same employment position and pay since the time of the accident, and that defendant has continued all prior physical and recreational activities since the time of the accident, including a skiing trip to [ski area] seven days ago.

IV.

Defendant has requested plaintiff to submit to a voluntary examination, and has been heretofore denied that request.

V.

Defendant requests that the plaintiff be ordered by the Court to submit to an independent medical examination at the offices of [name of physician], at [address], in [city], [state], on [date], at [time].

WHEREFORE, PREMISES CONSIDERED, [name], defendant herein, prays that the Court grant this motion in all respects and award all other and further relief to which defendant is justly entitled.

Respectfully submitted,

_____

Attorney for [defendant/plaintiff]

FORM 4–55
SAMPLE ORDER GRANTING MOTION FOR PHYSICAL EXAMINATION

[case number]

[name]	)	IN THE DISTRICT COURT OF
	)	
vs.	)	[county] COUNTY, [state]
	)	
[name]	)	[judicial district] JUDICIAL DISTRICT

ORDER GRANTING MOTION FOR PHYSICAL EXAMINATION

BE IT REMEMBERED that on this the [date] day of [month], [20__], came on for consideration the motion of [name], defendant in the above cause, to require [name], plaintiff in the above cause, to submit to a physical examination to be made by Dr. [name of physician], [city], [state]; and that the Court decided to grant such motion in all respects.

It is therefore ORDERED, ADJUDGED, and DECREED that plaintiff, [name], appear before Dr. [name], [address], [city], [state] on the [date] day of [month], [20__], at [time] [A.M./P.M.], then and there to submit to a physical examination to be made by that physician.

It is further ORDERED, ADJUDGED, and DECREED that the cost of the examination be borne by defendant.

SIGNED this [date] day of [month], [20__].

_____

Presiding Judge

§ 4.68   Practice Tips

Use the discovery process wisely. Pay close attention to the Rules of Civil Procedure for answering or receiving answers to discovery. There is never an excuse for a deadline going by without either answering a request or contacting the opposing counsel for an extension. By the same token, if you are having problems receiving answers from the opposing party, especially if the trial date is drawing near, do not hesitate to use your procedural rights to file a motion to compel and/or for sanctions. If you develop a reputation for answering on time and staying on top of due dates when answers are due to you, you will eventually begin to see an improvement in your response time.

Begin the discovery process early in the case and be as thorough as you possibly can. You owe it to your client to take advantage of every opportunity to obtain documentation to support his claim.

CHAPTER 5

INVESTIGATION

INVESTIGATION

§ 5.1 Introduction

If you are like most paralegals, this is probably the aspect of the profession that you enjoy the most. It is exciting, challenging, and provides a variety of ever-changing tasks. Some of the investigatory duties are routine, of course, but the excitement of possibly uncovering a gem of information really keeps the adrenaline flowing. Thoroughness is the best quality a good investigator can have. Follow-up is likewise essential. Leave no stone unturned, and go forth and uncover!

Never overlook your client as a source of information. Your client is likely to have a wealth of information, as well as documents, that can be used in order to advance his case. In the case of a corporation, do not assume that the information provided to you by the client is all of the information that exists. With the client's permission, it may be necessary to conduct your own investigation, interviewing your client's employees and examining your client's files. Such an investigation may be necessary, for your client's own protection, to avoid damaging surprises.

§ 5.2 Accident and Fire Marshall Reports

If your client has been involved in a traffic accident, the most obvious way to start your investigation is to order a copy of the accident report from the police department if one was taken (**Form 5–1**). You will be able to obtain several pieces of information from this one document. The report will list every driver's name and address, as well as the names and addresses of each witness, if any exist. There will be a diagram of the accident and a report of the weather and road conditions. The time of day and date of the accident will be noted, and if a ticket was issued to either party by the officer, that, too will be noted. Whether there were injuries, whether anyone was transported to the hospital, and the name of the ambulance and hospital will also be found on the form. Last, but not least, the police officer will state his version of how the accident happened along with statements taken at the scene from witnesses and parties.

Any time fire is involved in an injury, whether it be industrial, an automobile accident, or a building fire, obtain a copy of the fire marshall's report. Firefighters are excellent trained observers and are fanatics about details. These reports always contain a wealth of information and theories on causation. You will find that when you compare the fire marshall's report with the police report you will receive many more insights from the former report. Follow up on any theories or facts you are able to discover in these reports.

§ 5.3   Accident Reconstruction in Automobile Litigation

To prepare for effective discovery in automobile accident litigation, it is essential for the paralegal to go to the scene as soon as possible after the accident and begin the process of accident reconstruction. Many conditions can change quickly.

For example, skid marks will disappear with the first rain. Other vehicles driving over the scene will erase the length of the skid marks and, eventually, all of the marks within a short period of time. Other conditions may also change, such as the re-asphalting of the streets or traffic lanes being re-striped. Lighting conditions, road surfaces, warning or traffic signs or signals, new or different curbings, traffic patterns and flows may also change. It is best to document and preserve as much of the scene, vehicle damage and other property damage, as close to the time of the incident as possible. Documentation should include photographs, measurements, expert inspections, names of investigators and witnesses, photos of the property, damage of all the vehicles, non-vehicle property damage at the scene, and photos of the scene taken for all directions of travel.

The paralegal should take photographs of the roadway, shoulder area, and any off-road areas that any of the vehicles may have traveled over before and after the accident. Skid marks will change depending upon the difference in surfaces as the vehicles move from one surface to another. This will be critical to the expert's reconstructing of the accident, including forming opinions of speeds and rotations of the vehicles, points of impacts, and points of rests.

Skid-mark evidence.   The automobile accident case often presents an excellent opportunity to make use of skid-mark evidence. In many cases, the alleged negligence on the part of the driver will consist either of excessive speed or failure to keep a proper lookout. In such situations, the total length of the skid marks can be valuable evidence of the speed at which the automobile was traveling. The place at

FORM 5–1
SAMPLE REQUEST FOR COPY OF PEACE OFFICER'S ACCIDENT REPORT

REQUEST FOR COPY OF PEACE OFFICER'S ACCIDENT REPORT
(Please Submit in Duplicate)

Statistical Services
Texas Department of Public Safety
P. O. Box 15999
Austin, Texas 78761-5999

Date of Request _____

Claim or Policy No. _____

Enclosed is a (check) (money order) payable to the Texas Department of Public Safety in the amount of $ _____ for (check service desired):

☐ Copy of Peace Officer's Accident Report - $4.00 each

☐ Certified Copy of Peace Officer's Accident Report - $6.00 each

for the accident listed below:

Please provide as accurate and complete information as possible.

ACCIDENT DATE _____
                MONTH   DAY   YEAR

ACCIDENT LOCATION _____   _____   _____
                      COUNTY   CITY   STREET OR HIGHWAY

WAS ANYONE
KILLED IN THE ACCIDENT? _____ If So, Name of one Deceased _____

INVESTIGATING AGENCY AND/OR OFFICER'S NAME (IF KNOWN) _____

| DRIVER'S FULL NAME | DRIVER INFORMATION (If Available) | | ADDRESS |
	DATE OF BIRTH	TEXAS DRIVER LICENSE NO.	
1.			
2.			
3.			

Texas Statutes allow the investigating officer 10 days in which to submit his report.
Requests should not be submitted until at least 10 days after the accident date to allow time for receipt of the report.

The Law also provides that if an officer's report is not on file when a request for a copy of such report is received, a certification to that effect will be provided in lieu of the copy and the fee shall be retained for the certification.

Mail To _____

Mail Address _____

City _____ State _____ Zip _____

Requested By _____ Phone # _____

FOR DPS USE ONLY:

Date Received _____ Receipt No. _____ Clerk _____

☐ Report Sent   Date _____ Clerk _____

☐ Report Not On File   Date Searched _____ Clerk _____

ST-91 Rev. 7/85

Note: This accident report request is only for Texas. Other states may have their own version of this request.

which the skid marks began can show where the driver first applied the brakes, thus helping to indicate the point at which he first actually saw the pedestrian, as compared with the point at which he had the first opportunity to see the pedestrian.

To estimate speed from skid marks laid down during the accident, test skids are ordinarily made. Because the condition of the brakes (and other factors) can vary from vehicle to vehicle, even among vehicles of the same make and year, it is best to perform tests with the vehicle involved in the accident, if possible. By the same token, since the type of road surface and other road conditions can constitute variables, tests are best performed at the scene of the accident. The weather and the time of day should be duplicated as nearly as possible. Tests should be performed as soon as possible after the accident, before the brakes of the accident vehicle become more worn, or are adjusted or otherwise serviced. Photographs of the actual skid marks produced by the accident should be taken promptly, and certainly before any skid-mark testing is performed at the same location. Of course, the driver's reaction time, and the time then required to put his or her foot on the brake pedal, are also part of the equation. Similarly, the size and weight of the vehicle and the type of brakes with which it is equipped can make a difference both in the place at which the skid marks began and their total distance.

Skid marks should be photographed in their entirety, including impending skids. In photographing the skid marks, pictures should be taken with a measuring tape alongside the skid marks to document the accuracy of the dimensions of the skid marks, in terms of length and width, including "yaw marks" (centrifugal force marks).

§ 5.4 Checklist of Information to Be Gathered

In order to assist in reconstruction of the accident, the paralegal should obtain the following photos and other information:

1. Photos of all vehicles.
2. Photos of all non-vehicle property damage (curbs, benches, signs, telephone poles).
3. Photos of the scene of the accident.
4. Photos of the scene indicating skid marks, gouge marks, road marks.
5. Measurements and identification of the marks in relationship to the accident scene, such as number of feet from the east or west curb line, number of feet from the north or south curb line.
6. Photos of the tires of the vehicles, indicating tread, depths, and conditions of the tires.
7. The weather conditions at the time of accident.
8. The visibility at the time of the accident.
9. Obstructions of drivers or witnesses at the scene.

10. Condition of the vehicles, including brakes, steering, windshield, lights.

11. Dimensions and specifications of vehicles, such as weight, length, width, horsepower of engine, type of transmission, type of braking system, steering, turning radius.

12. Vehicle inspections by experts, and by others.

13. Information as to whether the vehicle has been dismantled or otherwise made unavailable without inspection.

14. Vehicle parts taken from vehicle and maintained for evidence.

15. Comparison of police report information.

Practice Note: After the initial investigation and gathering of information, it is good practice to prepare a written memo to the file listing liability considerations and issues. In preparation of the memo, the paralegal should state all of the liability issues, favorable and unfavorable to the client's position. With the help of experts, the lawyer should be able to identify the key issues to be resolved in the case. The paralegal should mention the evidence supporting each of these issues or the missing evidence or inquiries needed to support these issues. In addition, issues favorable to the opponent should be stated and the evidence in support of those issues noted. Also, the opposition's theories of liability and the evidence supporting those positions should be anticipated.

The questions or opinions necessary to resolve liability should be stated and whether or not an expert is needed to give their opinion to meet the burden of proof. For example, if the client was allegedly driving in excess of the speed limit just before impact, an expert opinion is needed on the speed of the vehicles prior to braking and at the moment of impact.

§ 5.5   Newspaper Articles

Even if an incident or accident took place several months or a year prior to your first contact with your client, research the newspapers during the time period to get copies of any articles that may have been written regarding the incident or similar incidents. Also, research the videotape libraries of the television stations' news broadcasts for possible evidence. Begin to create a history with these articles and make it a point to interview any prospective witnesses or persons experiencing similar incidents, such as problems at the same intersection or similar mechanical problems with the same type of car.

§ 5.6   U.S. Patent Office

Product liability cases are investigated in slightly different ways. A good place to begin is by ordering a copy of the product's patent from the U.S. Patent Office. These patents usually contain detailed diagrams and explanations of the product and how it works. These can be studied in-house for possible inherent defects or supplied to your expert witness to do the same.

A request for copies of a patent should be directed to:

U.S. Patent and Trademark Office
P.O. Box 9
Washington, D.C. 20231
(703) 308-4357 or 1-800-786-9199
www.uspto.gov/web/menu/pats.html

The U.S. Patent Office does not provide a specific form for requesting copies of a patent, but the letter (**Form 5–2**) which follows this section may be used for that purpose. Patent searches may also be performed online at the above site.

FORM 5–2
SAMPLE LETTER REQUESTING PATENT INFORMATION

U.S. Patent and Trademark Office
P.O. Box 9
Washington, D.C. 20231

[date]

To Whom it May Concern:

My law firm is presently involved in litigation in which the product [product name] is involved. Therefore, I am interested in receiving a copy of U.S. Patent No. [patent number]. I have enclosed a check for _____ as required to cover the costs of receiving this document. Please forward the patent to my attention at the above address at your earliest convenience. If there are any problems in obtaining the patent I have requested, I would appreciate your notification by telephone. My direct office number is [telephone number].

I thank you for your assistance.

Very truly yours,

[name of paralegal]

§ 5.7 Product Standards

Another good place to start looking for leads in a product liability case is to obtain a copy of the product standards governing that particular product and see if the product involved actually meets the required standards. If it does not, and the deficiencies have been the cause of injury to your client, you may well want to involve the attorney general's office and avail yourself of their investigative services. Of course, this type of discovery also opens the door for punitive damages when you file your suit. You may also want to obtain product information and research data on similar products which appear to be safer for use in comparison.

The Consumer Product Safety Commission's website is a virtual Pandora's box of information. The site lists recall notices, warnings, and reports on specific products and Freedom of Information Act information. As an example, there are reports on the site regarding all-terrain vehicle safety, crib safety, and national statistics on deaths and injuries related to certain products. This would be an excellent starting point for nonlegal research in a product liability case. There are graphs, statistics, and analyses of data on everything from shopping cart injuries to pool alarm reliability.

Form 5–3 is a sample letter requesting product standards. For the address of the nearest regional center or field office of the Consumer Product Safety Commission, www.cpsc.gov, see **§ 5-8.**

FORM 5–3
SAMPLE LETTER REQUESTING COPY OF PRODUCT STANDARDS

[name and address of appropriate agency]

[date]

To Whom it May Concern:

I would like to request a copy of your product standards for the following product: [name] (include the following identifying information to the agency:

1) Name of product
2) Name of manufacturer
3) Specified performance for the product
4) Material product is made of
5) Any other helpful identification information.)

I am also interested in learning if the standards for this product developed by your agency are statutorily binding on the manufacturer.

I understand that you will contact me to let me know the fee for the copying charges related to this request. I may be reached by phone at [telephone number] or by mail at the above letterhead address.

Thank you very much for your assistance in this matter.

Very truly yours,
[name of paralegal]

Note: In the alternative, use the sample Freedom of Information Act request letter found in § **5.15.**

§ 5.8 Consumer Product Safety Commission Directory—Regional Centers and Field Offices

Central Regional Center/CPSC
230 South Dearborn Street,
   Room 2945
Chicago, Illinois 60604
(312) 353-8260

Eastern Regional Center/CPSC
201 Varick St., Rm. 903
New York, New York 10014
(212) 620-4120

Western Regional Center/CPSC
1301 Clay St., Ste. 610 N.
Oakland, Ca. 94612
(510) 637-4050

Albuquerque Field Office/CPSC
Albuquerque Technical Vocational
   Institute
604 Bueno Vista, S.E.
Albuquerque, New Mexico 87106
(505) 766-2108

Atlanta Field Office/CPSC
730 Peachtree Street, N.E., Suite 871
Atlanta, Georgia 30365
(404) 347-2231

Baltimore Field Office/CPSC
City Hall Annex
303 East Fayette Street, Lower Level
Baltimore, Maryland 21202
(301) 962-0622

Boston Field Office/CPSC
Federal Office Building
10 Causeway Street, Room 224
Boston, Massachusetts 02222
(617) 565-7730

Buffalo Field Office/CPSC
111 W. Huron Street
P.O. Box 3001
Buffalo, New York 14202
(716) 846-4116

Charleston Field Office/CPSC
L. Mendel River Federal Office
   Building
Room 124
334 Meeting Street
Charleston, South Carolina 29403
(803) 724-4470

Charlotte Field Office/CPSC
222 S. Church Street, Suite 408
Charlotte, North Carolina 28202
(704) 371-1615

Cincinnati Field Office/CPSC
Federal Office Building, Room 3527
550 Main Street
Cincinnati, Ohio 45202
(513) 864-2872

Cleveland Field Office/CPSC
1 Playhouse Square
1375 Euclid Ave., Room 606
Cleveland, Ohio 44115
(216) 522-3886

Dallas Field Office/CPSC
1100 Commerce Street, Room 1C10
Dallas, Texas 75242
(214) 767-0841

Denver Field Office/CPSC
961 Stout Street, Room 1185
Denver, Colorado 80294
(303) 844-2904

Detroit Field Office/CPSC
McNamara Federal Building
477 Michigan Ave., Room M-24
Detroit, Michigan 48226
(313) 226-4040

Fort Lauderdale Field Office/CPSC
299 East Broward Blvd., Room 202-F
Ft. Lauderdale, Florida 33301
(305) 527-7161

Honolulu Field Office/CPSC
P.O. Box 50052
Honolulu, Hawaii 96850
(808) 541-1779

Houston Field Office/CPSC
405 Main Street, Room 605
Houston, Texas 77002
(713) 226-2814

Indianapolis Field Office/CPSC
Federal Building
Corporate Square West-Bldg. 20
Suite 1000
5610 Crawfordsville Road
Indianapolis, Indiana 46224
(317) 248-4100

Kansas City Field Office/CPSC
1009 Cherry Street
Kansas City, Missouri 64106
(816) 374-2034

Little Rock Field Office/CPSC
Arkansas Department of Health
4815 W. Markham
Little Rock, Arkansas 72201
(501) 378-6631

Los Angeles Field Office/CPSC
4221 Wilshire Blvd., Suite 220
Los Angeles, California 90010
(213) 251-7464

Milwaukee Field Office/CPSC
Federal Building, Room 602
517 East Wisconsin 53202
(414) 291-1468

New Orleans Field Office/CPSC
800 Commerce Road, East
New Orleans, Louisiana 70123
(504) 589-3742

Orlando Field Office/CPSC
c/o F.D.A.
7200 Lake Ellenor Drive, Room 246
Orlando, Florida 32809
(407) 648-6261

Philadelphia Field Office/CPSC
2nd & Chestnut Street
Custom House Building, Room 603
Philadelphia, Pennsylvania 19106
(215) 597-9105

Phoenix Field Office/CPSC
CPSC, c/o DHHS, IHS, Env. Health
3738 North 16th Street, Suite A
Phoenix, Arizona 85016-5981
(602) 241-2397

Pittsburgh Field Office/CPSC
Federal Building, Room 2318
1000 Liberty Avenue
Pittsburgh, Pennsylvania 15222
(412) 644-6582

Portland Field Office/CPSC
U.S. Courthouse, Room 207
620 S.W. Main Street
Portland, Oregon 97205
(503) 221-3056

Seattle Field Office/CPSC
6046 Federal Office Building
909 First Avenue
Seattle, Washington 98174
(206) 442-5276

St. Louis Field Office/CPSC
808 North Collins
St. Louis, Missouri 63102
(314) 425-6281

Trenton Field Office/CPSC
City Hall, First Floor Annex
319 E. State Street
Trenton, New Jersey 08608
(609) 989-2062

Tulsa Field Office/CPSC
333 West 4th St., Room 3097
Tulsa, Oklahoma 74103
(918) 581-7606

Twin Cities Field Office/CPSC
Federal Courts Bldg., Room 128
316 N. Robert Street
St. Paul, Minnesota 55101
(612) 290-3781

Washington Field Office/CPSC
11820 Coakley Circle
Rockville, Maryland 20852
(301) 443-1152

§ 5.9   Streets and Highways

The streets and highways departments of the different states, counties, and cities keep records on road conditions and construction projects on all the streets and highways in their jurisdiction. If you are in doubt as to whether any conditions or construction may have had a causal effect on the accident in question, research their records and request printouts on that section of the road for that particular date. As a side comment, it is also a good idea to check with the weather bureau and get a copy of that day's weather at that particular time and also obtain the times of sunrise and sunset on the day in question so that light conditions can be figured. The street and highway departments will also be able to supply you with a history of accidents at that location. This information alone is often very revealing and useful.

§ 5.10   Government Agencies and Departments of Licenses and Inspections

Government agencies are wonderful sources of scores and scores of paper and forms, as we all know too well when we have to fill all those forms out! A good paralegal, however, puts the red tape to work and uses the system to his or her advantage. In cases of injury on a property, check the building permits, inspection records, and required licenses to make sure that the building was in compliance with all requirements. Deficiencies in any regard are a great place to begin investigation.

Both state and federal agencies, as well as their local counterparts are a very common source for the information gathering exercise. Learn to use the Freedom of Information Act (FOIA) in obtaining those records which will help you investigate or prove up your case. The laws vary from state to state and agency to agency regarding what records are available to you in your investigation. It is a good idea to start a form file early in your career in which you collect forms and instructions for obtaining different kinds of information from different entities. You will use it over and over again. Whether you anticipate having use for the form or not, it is a good idea to keep it on hand for future reference.

§ 5.11 Freedom of Information Act and Privacy Act of 1974

In 1966 Congress passed the Freedom of Information Act (FOIA) (see **Appendix A**). Prior to that time, any person wanting access to government records had to prove that he should be allowed access to those records. With the passage of this act, the informational records covered under the act may be obtained without showing a need for those records. The law set guidelines regarding which records are available for public inspection, what procedures to follow, and what remedies are available if a person is denied access to those records. The important thing to remember is that records are obtainable, not generalized information. If the law states that the public has a right to access a certain type of information, it is available by requesting the proper document. The government is not obliged to create new documents to secure that information for you. The statute requires a full disclosure by the governmental agency.

For a terrific government pamphlet on the FOIA, go to *www.access.gpo.gov* and order *A Citizen's Guide on How to Use the Freedom of Information Act and the Privacy Act Requesting Government Documents*.

The Privacy Act of 1974 allows individuals to seek records containing information about themselves. The statute protects the individual in that the agencies are bound to keep that information accurate and complete, void of irrelevant information. You can challenge the accuracy of your own records under the Privacy Act, and there are civil remedies for those whose rights have been violated.

The Privacy Act also requires that each federal agency publish a description of each type of record of personal information that it maintains.

There are, however, certain categories of information which are recognized by both laws which restrict the access to information in order to protect trade secrets, national security, criminal investigations, and other types of confidential information.

Under the FOIA, federal agencies are required to publish the following:

1. Descriptions of agency organization and office addresses

2. Statements of the general course and method of agency operation
3. Rules of procedure and description of forms
4. Substantive rules of general applicability and general policy statements
5. Final opinions made in the adjudication of cases
6. Administrative staff manuals that affect the public.

All of the above information is available without the formality of a FOIA request.

§ 5.12   State Open Records Acts

The state counterpart of the FOIA is each individual state's open records act. It provides access to the state's agencies' public records by emulating the FOIA at the state level. Each state's laws vary in the information protected or disclosed under the appropriate Open Records Act. Each law will have its own regulations regarding forms for requests, types of information available, and costs. In Houston, for example, there is a well-known investigative reporter who specializes in governmental abuse and uses the Texas Open Records Act liberally and frequently to research his stories. He accesses the same kinds of information that a paralegal uses in the investigation of a lawsuit. A full-text version of the Texas Open Records Act may be found at *http://www.applink.net/opengovt/coppell/file/law_tx/oract.htm*. Similarly, other states' open records acts may be found either with an independent search on a search engine like *www.altavista.com* or at *www.findlaw.com*. (See **Appendix A**.)

§ 5.13   FOIA—Statutory Exemptions

There are statutory exceptions to the FOIA of which you should be aware. The following list sets out both the exemption and a description of the exemption:

1. Classified documents—Information labeled as confidential, secret, or top secret under the procedures of the executive order on security classification may be withheld.
2. Internal personnel rules and practices—Trivial administrative rules or practices of an agency or administrative manuals, the disclosure of which would risk circumvention of law or agency regulations.
3. Information exempt under other laws—Information which has already been established as confidential, such as tax returns or identifiable census data is not available under the FOIA.
4. Confidential business information—Trade secrets and commercial or financial information obtained from an individual are not available under the FOIA.

5. Internal government communications—This exemption protects against the premature disclosure of agency policies before their final adoption and enables the government officials to enter into frank discussions of policy matters with confidentiality intact. This exemption, however, is only in effect until the policy is adopted.

6. Personal privacy—This exemption protects the confidentiality of an individual's personnel and medical files which would constitute an invasion of privacy.

7. Law enforcement—Any information which, if released, would impede law enforcement proceedings is not available under the FOIA. It protects the confidentiality of sources and the techniques and procedures utilized in law enforcement investigations. No information which could conceivably endanger the life or physical safety of any individual is available under the FOIA.

8. Financial institutions—Information related to the examination, operation or condition of a financial institution which has been prepared by or for such agencies as the Federal Deposit Insurance Corporation (FDIC) is not available under the FOIA.

9. Geological information—This exemption covers geological and geophysical information, data, and maps about wells, but this exemption is rarely used.

§ 5.14   —Request Checklist

The following checklist details how you should go about obtaining information.

____ 1. Identify the specific agency which maintains the records you are seeking. If you are not sure of the proper agency, consult the United States Government Manual which is available in public libraries and United States Government bookstores.

____ 2. Make your request in writing. (See **Form 5–4.**)

____ 3. Include necessary elements of a request. The necessary elements follow:

    ____ a) State that the request is being made under the FOIA;

    ____ b) Identify specifically the requested records;

    ____ c) Include the name and address of the requestor;

    ____ d) Include your telephone number if you desire;

    ____ e) Indicate if there is a limit on the fees you are willing to pay without being contacted first;

    ____ f) Include any requests for fee reductions or waivers.

____ 4. Address the letter to the agency's FOIA Officer or the head of the agency. The outside envelope must be marked on the lower left-hand corner with the words "Freedom of Information Act Request." Check

355

the agency's regulations in the *Code of Federal Regulations* to find the name and address of the current FOIA officer. You can search the U.S. Code online at *http://uscode.house./govusc.htm.*

§ 5.15 —Request Letter

FORM 5–4
SAMPLE FOIA REQUEST LETTER

[agency head/or FOIA officer]
[name of agency]
[city, state, zip code]
Re: Freedom of Information Act Request

Dear [name]: _____

Pursuant to the provisions of the Freedom of Information Act, 5 U.S.C. § 552, I am requesting a copy of the following records: [identify the records with as much specificity as possible].

If any fees are to be incurred and assessed to me in the process of searching for information and filing this request, please contact me first (or please supply the records without contacting me first as long as the fees do not exceed $[amount]).

(I request a waiver of fees pertaining to this request as the information is to be used for a purpose primary benefitting the public [explain in detail] and will not be used for my commercial interest.)

Thank you for your consideration of my request.

        Sincerely,

        [name]
        [address]
        [city, state, zip code]

§ 5.16 Privacy Act Request for Access Letter

Form 5–5 is a sample letter requesting access to records under the Privacy Act of 1974.

FORM 5–5
SAMPLE PRIVACY ACT ACCESS REQUEST LETTER

[privacy act officer or system of records manager]
[name of agency]
[address]
[city, state, zip code]
Re: Privacy Act Request for Access

Dear [name]: _____

This is a request under the Privacy Act of 1974.

I request a copy of any records (or specifically named records) about me maintained by your agency.

(To assist you in locating my records, please note that I have had the following written contacts with your agency:)

(This request is made also under the Freedom of Information Act. If there are additional records which may be provided under this Act, please include them with my request.)

(Please supply the records to me without contacting me first if the fees do not exceed $_____.)

Enclosed please find [identifying document] which will verify my identity.

Thank you for your consideration of this request.

> Sincerely,
> [name]
> [address]
> [city, state, zip code]

§ 5.17   FOIA Request Forms

Forms 5–6 through **5–10** represent several different types of FOIA request forms. **Forms 5–9** and **5–10** are Texas forms.

§ 5.18 —Last Known Address

FORM 5–6
SAMPLE LAST KNOWN ADDRESS FORM

POSTMASTER:

As provided under the Freedom of Information Act, please advise the last known change of address for:

Name: _____

Address: _____

City, State, ZIP: _____

- -

Signature of Requestor: _____

Firm or Agency: _____

Address: _____

City, State, ZIP: _____

- -

Information provided: _____

Furnished by: _____
                        [employee name & postal unit]

Date: _____

____ Check one: ( )   Required $1.00 fee collected; receipt (Form 3544)
                              attached.
                     ( )   Authorized law enforcement agency; no fee required.

POSTAL CLERK: Retain this form in File 352.4, Administrative Support Manual.

SCF/FTW/409 (9/83)

§ 5.19 —Military Records

FORM 5–7
SAMPLE REQUEST PERTAINING TO MILITARY RECORDS

REQUEST PERTAINING TO MILITARY RECORDS	Please read Instructions on the reverse. If more space is needed, use plain paper.

PRIVACY ACT OF 1974 COMPLIANCE INFORMATION. The following information is provided in accordance with 5 U.S.C. 552a(e)(3) and applies to this form. Authority for collection of the information is 44 U.S.C. 2907, 3101, and 3103, and E.O. 9397 of November 22, 1943. Disclosure of the information is voluntary. The principal purpose of the information is to assist the facility servicing the records in locating and verifying the correctness of the requested records or information to answer your inquiry. Routine uses of the information as established and published in accordance with 5 U.S.C.a(e)(4)(D)

Include the transfer of relevant information to appropriate Federal, State, local, or foreign agencies for use in civil, criminal, or regulatory investigations or prosecution. In addition, this form will be filed with the appropriate military records and may be transferred along with the record to another agency in accordance with the routine uses established by the agency which maintains the record. If the requested information is not provided, it may not be possible to service your inquiry.

SECTION I—INFORMATION NEEDED TO LOCATE RECORDS (Furnish as much as possible)

1. NAME USED DURING SERVICE (Last, first, and middle)	2. SOCIAL SECURITY NO.	3. DATE OF BIRTH	4. PLACE OF BIRTH

5. ACTIVE SERVICE, PAST AND PRESENT (For an effective records search, it is important that ALL service be shown below)

BRANCH OF SERVICE (Also, show last organization, if known)	DATES OF ACTIVE SERVICE		Check one		SERVICE NUMBER DURING THIS PERIOD
	DATE ENTERED	DATE RELEASED	OFFICER	ENLISTED	

6. RESERVE SERVICE, PAST OR PRESENT   If "none," check here ▶ ☐

a. BRANCH OF SERVICE	b. DATES OF MEMBERSHIP		c. Check one		d. SERVICE NUMBER DURING THIS PERIOD
	FROM	TO	OFFICER ☐	ENLISTED ☐	

7. NATIONAL GUARD MEMBERSHIP   (Check one): ☐ a. ARMY   ☐ b. AIR FORCE   ☐ c. NONE

d. STATE	e. ORGANIZATION	f. DATES OF MEMBERSHIP		g. Check one		h. SERVICE NUMBER DURING THIS PERIOD
		FROM	TO	OFFICER ☐	ENLISTED ☐	

8. IS SERVICE PERSON DECEASED ☐ YES ☐ NO If "yes," enter date of death.	9. IS (WAS) INDIVIDUAL A MILITARY RETIREE OR FLEET RESERVIST ☐ YES ☐ NO

SECTION II—REQUEST

1. EXPLAIN WHAT INFORMATION OR DOCUMENTS YOU NEED; OR, CHECK ITEM 2; OR, COMPLETE ITEM 3	2. IF YOU ONLY NEED A STATEMENT OF SERVICE check ☐ here

3. LOST SEPARATION DOCUMENT REPLACEMENT REQUEST (Complete a or b, and c.)

	a. REPORT OF SEPARATION ☐ (DD Form 214 or equivalent)	YEAR ISSUED	This contains information normally needed to determine eligibility for benefits. It may be furnished only to the veteran, the surviving next of kin, or to a representative with veteran's signed release (item 5 of this form).
	b. DISCHARGE ☐ CERTIFICATE	YEAR ISSUED	This shows only the date and character at discharge. It is of little value in determining eligibility for benefits. It may be issued only to veterans discharged honorably or under honorable conditions; or, if deceased, to the surviving spouse.

c. EXPLAIN HOW SEPARATION DOCUMENT WAS LOST

4. EXPLAIN PURPOSE FOR WHICH INFORMATION OR DOCUMENTS ARE NEEDED	6. REQUESTER
	a. IDENTIFICATION (check appropriate box)
	☐ Same person identified in Section I ☐ Surviving spouse
	☐ Next of kin (relationship) _____
	☐ Other (specify) _____

b. SIGNATURE (see instruction 3 on reverse side)	DATE OF REQUEST

5. RELEASE AUTHORIZATION, IF REQUIRED (Read instruction 3 on reverse side)

I hereby authorize release of the requested information/documents to the person indicated at right (item 7).

VETERAN SIGN HERE ▶ _____

(If signed by other than veteran show relationship to veteran.)

7. Please type or print clearly —   COMPLETE RETURN ADDRESS

Name, number and street, city, State and ZIP code _____

TELEPHONE NO. (include area code) ▶

180-106
NSN 7540-00-142-9360
STANDARD FORM 180 (Rev. 7-86)
Prescribed by NARA (36 CFR 1228.162(a))

INVESTIGATION

FORM 5–7

(continued)

INSTRUCTIONS

1. Information needed to locate records. Certain identifying information is necessary to determine the location of an individual's record of military service. Please give careful consideration to and answer each item on this form. If you do not have and cannot obtain the information for an item, show "NA," meaning the information is "not available." Include as much of the requested information as you can. This will help us to give you the best possible service.

2. Charges for service. A nominal fee is charged for certain types of service. In most instances service fees cannot be determined in advance. If your request involves a service fee you will be notified as soon as that determination is made.

3. Restrictions on release of Information. Information from records of military personnel is released subject to restrictions imposed by the military departments consistent with the provisions of the Freedom of Information Act of 1967 (as amended in 1974) and the Privacy Act of 1974. A service person has access to almost any information contained in his own record. The next of kin, if the veteran is deceased, and Federal officers for official purposes, are authorized to receive information from a military service or medical record only as specified in the above cited Acts. Other requesters must have the release authorization, in item 5 of the form, signed by the veteran or, if deceased, by the next of kin. Employers

and others needing proof of military service are expected to accept the information shown on documents issued by the Armed Forces at the time a service person is separated.

4. Location of military personnel records. The various categories of military personnel records are described in the chart below. For each category there is a code number which indicates the address at the bottom of the page to which this request should be sent. For each military service there is a note explaining approximately how long the records are held by the military service before they are transferred to the National Personnel Records Center, St. Louis. Please read these notes carefully and make sure you send your inquiry to the right address. Please note especially that the record is not sent to the National Personnel Records Center as long as the person retains any sort of reserve obligation, whether drilling or non-drilling.

(If the person has two or more periods of service within the same branch, send your request to the office having the record for the last period of service.)

5. Definitions for abbreviations used below:
NPRC—National Personnel Records Center   PERS—Personnel Records
TDRL—Temporary Disability Retirement List   MED—Medical Records

SERVICE	NOTE: (See paragraph 4 above.)	CATEGORY OF RECORDS — WHERE TO WRITE ADDRESS CODE ▼		
AIR FORCE (USAF)	Except for TDRL and general officers retired with pay, Air Force records are transferred to NPRC from Code 1, 90 days after separation and from Code 2, 150 days after separation.	Active members (includes National Guard on active duty in the Air Force), TDRL, and general officers retired with pay.		1
		Reserve, retired reservist in nonpay status, current National Guard officers not on active duty in Air Force, and National Guard released from active duty in Air Force.		2
		Current National Guard enlisted not on active duty in Air Force.		13
		Discharged, deceased, and retired with pay.		14
COAST GUARD (USCG)	Coast Guard officer and enlisted records are transferred to NPRC 7 months after separation.	Active, reserve, and TDRL members.		3
		Discharged, deceased, and retired members (see next item).		14
		Officers separated before 1/1/29 and enlisted personnel separated before 1/1/15.		6
MARINE CORPS (USMC)	Marine Corps records are transferred to NPRC between 6 and 9 months after separation.	Active, TDRL, and Selected Marine Corps Reserve members.		4
		Individual Ready Reserve and Fleet Marine Corps Reserve members.		5
		Discharged, deceased, and retired members (see next item).		14
		Members separated before 1/1/1905.		6
ARMY (USA)	Army records are transferred to NPRC as follows: Active Army and Individual Ready Reserve Control Groups: About 60 days after separation. U.S. Army Reserve Troop Unit personnel: About 120 to 180 days after separation.	Reserve, living retired members, retired general officers, and active duty records of current National Guard members who performed service in the U.S. Army before 7/1/72.*		7
		Active officers (including National Guard on active duty in the U.S. Army).		8
		Active enlisted (including National Guard on active duty in the U.S. Army) and enlisted TDRL.		9
		Current National Guard officers not on active duty in the U.S. Army.		12
		Current National Guard enlisted not on active duty in the U.S. Army.		13
		Discharged and deceased members (see next item).		14
		Officers separated before 7/1/17 and enlisted separated before 11/1/12.		6
		Officers and warrant officers TDRL.		8
NAVY (USN)	Navy records are transferred to NPRC 6 months after retirement or complete separation.	Active members (including reservists on duty)—PERS and MED		10
		Discharged, deceased, retired (with and without pay) less than six months, TDRL, drilling and nondrilling reservists	PERS ONLY	10
			MED ONLY	11
		Discharged, deceased, retired (with and without pay) more than six months (see next item)—PERS & MED		14
		Officers separated before 1/1/03 and enlisted separated before 1/1/1886—PERS and MED		6

*Code 12 applies to active duty records of current National Guard officers who performed service in the U.S. Army after 6/30/72.
Code 13 applies to active duty records of current National Guard enlisted members who performed service in the U.S. Army after 6/30/72.*

ADDRESS LIST OF CUSTODIANS (BY CODE NUMBERS SHOWN ABOVE)—Where to write / send this form for each category of records

1	Air Force Manpower and Personnel Center Military Personnel Records Division Randolph AFB, TX 78150–6001	**5**	Marine Corps Reserve Support Center 10950 El Monte Overland Park, KS 66211–1408	**8**	USA MILPERCEN ATTN: DAPC-MSR 200 Stovall Street Alexandria, VA 22332–0400	**12**	Army National Guard Personnel Center Columbia Pike Office Building 5600 Columbia Pike Falls Church, VA 22041
2	Air Reserve Personnel Center Denver, CO 80280–5000	**6**	Military Archives Division National Archives and Records Administration Washington, DC 20408	**9**	Commander U.S. Army Enlisted Records and Evaluation Center Ft. Benjamin Harrison, IN 46249–5301	**13**	The Adjutant General (of the appropriate State, DC, or Puerto Rico)
3	Commandant U.S. Coast Guard Washington, DC 20593–0001	**7**	Commander U.S. Army Reserve Personnel Center ATTN: DARP-PAS 9700 Page Boulevard St. Louis, MO 63132–5200	**10**	Commander Naval Military Personnel Command ATTN: NMPC-036 Washington, DC 20370–5036	**14**	National Personnel Records Center (Military Personnel Records) 9700 Page Boulevard St. Louis, MO 63132
4	Commandant of the Marine Corps (Code MMRB-10) Headquarters, U.S. Marine Corps Washington, DC 20380–0001			**11**	Naval Reserve Personnel Center New Orleans, LA 70146–5000		

☆ U.S. Government Printing Office: 1987—181-247/40207

STANDARD FORM 180 BACK (Rev. 7-86)

§ 5.20   —Statement of Earnings (Social Security Administration)

FORM 5–8
SAMPLE REQUEST FOR STATEMENT OF EARNINGS
(SOCIAL SECURITY ADMINISTRATION)

FOLD HERE

REQUEST FOR STATEMENT OF EARNINGS
(PLEASE PRINT IN INK OR USE TYPEWRITER)

FOR SSA USE ONLY
AX
SP

I REQUEST A SUMMARY STATEMENT OF EARNINGS FROM MY SOCIAL SECURITY RECORD

NH | Full name you use in work or business
First | Middle Initial | Last

SN | Social security number shown on your card | Your date of birth
DB | Month | Day | Year | A

MA | Other Social Security number(s) you have used | Your Sex
SX | ☐ Male | ☐ Female

AK | Other name(s) you have used (Include your maiden name)

FOLD HERE

PRIVACY STATEMENT

The Social Security Administration (SSA) is authorized to collect information asked on this form under section 205 of the Social Security Act. It is needed so SSA can quickly identify your record and prepare the earnings statement you requested. While you are not required to furnish the information, failure to do so may prevent your request from being processed. The information will be used primarily for issuing your earnings statement.

I am the individual to whom the record pertains. I understand that if I knowingly and willingly request or receive a record about an individual under false pretenses I would be guilty of a Federal crime and could be fined up to $5000.

Sign your name here: (Do not print) | Date

I AUTHORIZE YOU TO SEND THE STATEMENT TO THE NAME AND ADDRESS BELOW: *(To be completed in all cases)*

PN | Name of the addressee

AD | Street number and name

City and state | ZP | Zip Code

Form **SSA-7004 PC**   OP 3   (9-82) Previous Editions are Obsolete

INVESTIGATION

FORM 5–8
(continued)

SOCIAL SECURITY ADMINISTRATION
ALBUQUERQUE DATA OPERATIONS CENTER
P.O. BOX 4429
ALBUQUERQUE, NM 87196

YOUR SOCIAL SECURITY EARNINGS RECORD

For a *free* statement of earnings credited to your social security record. complete other side of this card. Use card for only *one* person.

All covered wages and self-employment income are reported under your *name* and social security *number*. So show your name and number *exactly* as on your card. If you ever used another name or number, show this too.

Be sure to put a stamp on this card or it won't be delivered.

If you have a separate question about social security, or want to discuss your statement when you get it, the people at any social security office will be glad to help you.

§ 5.21   —Driver's License Records (Texas)

FORM 5–9
SAMPLE REQUEST FOR INFORMATION FROM TEXAS
DRIVER LICENSE RECORDS

REQUEST FOR INFORMATION FROM TEXAS DRIVER LICENSE RECORDS   LIDR-1 (Rev. 9/91)
(Mail To: LIDR, Texas Department of Public Safety, Box 15999, Austin, Texas 78761-5999)
MAKE CHECK PAYABLE TO: TEXAS DEPARTMENT OF PUBLIC SAFETY
TO BE COMPLETED BY PERSON REQUESTING INFORMATION

CHECK TYPE SERVICE DESIRED:

☐ 1. Date of birth-License status-Latest address.   Fee $ 4.00
☐ 2. Date of birth-License status-List of accidents and violations in record within immediate past 3 year period.   Fee $ 6.00
☐ 2A. Same as #2 (above)-Certified. **THIS RECORD NOT ACCEPTABLE FOR DDC COURSE.**   Fee $10.00
☐ 3. Date of birth-License status-List of all accidents and violations in record.
       THIS RECORD FURNISHED TO LICENSEE ONLY.   Fee $ 7.00
☐ 3A. Same as #3 (above)-Certified. **THIS RECORD FURNISHED TO LICENSEE ONLY. ACCEPTABLE FOR DDC COURSE.**   Fee $10.00

INFORMATION REQUESTED ON: DATE OF BIRTH

TEXAS DRIVER LICENSE NO.	SOCIAL SECURITY NO.	Month	Day	Year

LAST NAME	FIRST	MIDDLE/MAIDEN

NAME OF PERSON OR FIRM REQUESTING RECORD

MAILING ADDRESS	STREET/BOX NUMBER

CITY	STATE	ZIP CODE

INVESTIGATION

§ 5.22 —Motor Vehicle Information (Texas)

FORM 5–10
SAMPLE REQUEST FOR MOTOR VEHICLE INFORMATION (TEXAS)

REQUEST FOR MOTOR VEHICLE INFORMATION

```
Texas Vehicle License Plate No.
```

AND/OR

```
Vehicle Identification Number
```

I request that the State Department of Highways and Public Transportation Division of Motor Vehicles furnish to me information checked below for the vehicle listed.

CHECK INFORMATION REQUESTED:

       []   Title and registration verification (record search) $2.00

       []   Certified title and registration verification $5.00

       []   Title history $5.00

       []   Certified title history $8.00

            I HEREBY CERTIFY THAT THIS INFORMATION IS REQUESTED FOR A
                     LAWFUL AND LEGITIMATE PURPOSE.

Name:_____

Address:_____

City:_____

This request must be submitted with cash, cashier's check, or money order in the amount indicated.

SIGNATURE: _____   DATE: _____

State Department of Highways and Public Transportation
Division of Motor Vehicles
Austin, Texas 78779-0001

§ 5.23 Vital Statistics Information Directory

This directory lists the name and address of each state bureau and the fee for obtaining a birth or death certificate.

State   Fee

ALABAMA
Birth or Death Certificate $12.00
Center for Health Statistics
State Department of Public Health
P.O. Box 5625
Montgomery, Alabama 36103-5625
(334) 206-5418
www.alapubhealth.org/vital/vitalred.htm

ALASKA
Birth or Death Certificate $10.00
Department of Health and Social Services
Bureau of Vital Statistics
P.O. Box 110675
Juneau, Alaska 99811-0675
(907) 465-3038
www.hss.state.ak.us/dph/bvs/bvs_home.htm

ARIZONA
Birth or Death Certificate $9.00
Vital Records Section
Arizona Department of Health Services
P.O. Box 3887
Phoenix, Arizona 85030
(602) 255-3260
www.his.state.az.us/plan/ohpes.htm

ARKANSAS
Birth Certificate $5.00
Death Certificate $4.00
Division of Vital Records
Arkansas Department of Health
4815 West Markham St.
Little Rock, Arkansas 72205
(501) 661-2336
www.state.ar.us

CALIFORNIA
Birth Certificate $12.00
Death Certificate $ 8.00
Vital Statistics Section
Department of Health Services
304 S Street
Sacramento, California 95814
(916) 445-2684
www.dhs.cahwnet.gov/

COLORADO
Birth or Death Certificate $15.00
Vital Records Section
Colorado Department of Health
4300 Cherry Creek Drive South
Denver, Colorado 80222-1530
(303) 756-4464
www.cdphe.state.co.us/hs/certs.asp

CONNECTICUT
Birth or Death Certificate $5.00
Department of Health Services
Vital Records Section
Division of Health Statistics
State Department of Health
150 Washington St.
Hartford, Connecticut 06106
(860) 509-7897
www.state.ct.us/dph/OPPE/hpvr.htm

DELAWARE
Birth or Death Certificate $5.00
Office of Vital Statistics
Division of Public Health
Jesse Cooper Bldg. Room 144
Federal & William Penn Streets
Dover, Delaware 19901
(302) 739-4721

FLORIDA
Birth Certificate $9.00
Death Certificate $5.00
Department of Health and Rehabilitative Services
Office of Vital Statistics
P.O. Box 210

1217 Pearl Street
Jacksonville, Florida 32202
(904) 359-6900
www.doh.state.fl.us/

GEORGIA
Birth or Death Certificate $10.00
Georgia Department of Human Resources
Vital Records Unit
Room 217-H
47 Trinity Avenue, SW
Atlanta, Georgia 30334
(404) 656-4900
www.ph.dhr.state.ga.us/vital/vitalrec.htm

HAWAII
Birth or Death Certificate $10.00
Office of Health Status Monitoring
State Department of Health
P.O. Box 3378
Honolulu, Hawaii 96801
(808) 586-4533
www.state.hi.us/health/records/vr_howto.html

IDAHO
Birth or Death Certificate $8.00
Bureau of Vital Statistics, Standards, and Local Health Services
450 West State Street
State Department of Health and Welfare
Statehouse Mail
Boise, Idaho 83720-9990
(208) 334-5988
www.state.id.us/dhw/hwgd_www/home.html

ILLINOIS
Birth or Death Certificate $15.00
Division of Vital Records
State Department of Health
605 West Jefferson Street
Springfield, Illinois 62702-5097
(217) 782-6553
www.idph.state.il.us/vital/vitalhome.htm

INDIANA
Birth Certificate $6.00

INVESTIGATION

Death Certificate $4.00
Division of Vital Records
2 North Meridian Street
Indianapolis, Indiana 46204
(317) 233-2700
www.state.in.us/isdh/bdcertifs/birth_and_death_certificates.htm

IOWA
Birth or Death Certificate $10.00
Iowa Department of Public Health
Vital Records Section
Lucas Office Building
231 East 12th Street
Des Moines, Iowa 50319-0075
(515) 281-5871
www.idph.state.ia.us/pa/vr.htm

KANSAS
Birth Certificate $10.00
Death Certificate $ 7.00
Office of Vital Statistics
Kansas State Department of Health and Environment
900 S.W. Jackson St.
Topeka, Kansas 66612-2221
(785) 296-1400
www.kdhe.state.ks.us./vital/

KENTUCKY
Birth Certificate $9.00
Death Certificate $6.00
Office of Vital Statistics
Department for Health Services
275 East Main Street
Frankfort, Kentucky 40621
(502)564-4212
http://cfc-chs.chr.state.ky.us/vital.htm

LOUISIANA
Birth Certificate $15.00
Death Certificate $ 5.00
Vital Records Registry
Office of Public Health
325 Loyola Avenue
New Orleans, Louisiana 70112

(504) 568-8353
www.dhh.state.la.us/OPH/vital/index.htm

MAINE
Birth or Death Certificate $10.00
Office of Vital Statistics
Maine Department of Human Services
Station 11
State House
Augusta, Maine 04333-0011
(207) 287-3181
www.janus.state.me.us/dhs/faq.htm

MARYLAND
Birth or Death Certificate $6.00
Division of Vital Records
Department of Health and Mental Hygiene
6550 Reistertown Road
Baltimore, Maryland 21215-0020
(410) 764-3038
www.dhmh.state.md.us/html/vitalrec.htm

MASSACHUSETTS
Birth or Death Certificate $11.00
Registry of Vital Records and Statistics
470 Atlantic Avenue, 2nd Floor
Boston, Massachusetts 02210-2224
(617) 753-8600
www.state.ma.us/dph/vitrecs.htm

MICHIGAN
Birth or Death Certificate $13.00
Office of the State Registrar and Center for Health Statistics
Michigan Department of Public Health
P.O. Box 30195
Lansing, Michigan 48909
(517) 335-8656
www.mdch.state.mi.us/PHA/OSR/VITALREC.HTM

MINNESOTA
Birth Certificate $14.00
Death Certificate $ 8.00
Minnesota Department of Health
Section of Vital Statistics
717 Delaware St., SE
P.O. Box 9441

Minneapolis, Minnesota 55440
(612) 676-5120
www.health.state.mn.us/topic.html

MISSISSIPPI
Birth Certificate $12.00
Death Certificate $10.00
Vital Records
State Board of Health
2423 North State Street
Jackson, Mississippi 39216
(601) 576-7981
www.msdh.state.ms.us/phs/index.htm

MISSOURI
Birth or Death Certificate $10.00
Missouri Department of Health
Bureau of Vital Records
1730 East Elm
P.O. Box 570
Jefferson City, Missouri 65102-0570
(573) 751-6387
www.health.state.mo.us/

MONTANA
Birth or Death Certificate $5.00
Bureau of Records and Statistics
State Department of Health and Environmental Sciences
Helena, Montana 59620
(406) 444-2614
www.dphhs.mt.gov/

NEBRASKA
Birth Certificate $10.00
Death Certificate $ 7.00
Bureau of Vital Statistics
State Department of Health
301 Centennial Mall, South
P.O. Box 95007
Lincoln, Nebraska 68509-5007
(402) 471-2871
www.hhs.state.ne.us/ced/cedindex.htm

§ 5.23   VITAL STATISTICS INFORMATION DIRECTORY

NEVADA
Birth Certificate $11.00
Death Certificate $ 8.00
Division of Health—Vital Statistics
Capitol Complex
505 East King Street #102
Carson City, Nevada 89710
(702) 885-4480

NEW HAMPSHIRE
Birth or Death Certificate $10.00
Bureau of Vital Records
Health and Welfare Bldg.
6 Hazen Drive
Concord, New Hampshire 03301
(603) 271-4654

NEW JERSEY
Birth or Death Certificate $4.00
State Department of Health
Bureau of Vital Statistics
South Warren and Market Streets
CN 370
Trenton, New Jersey 08625
(609) 292-4087
www.state.nj.us/health/vital/vital.htm

NEW MEXICO
Birth Certificate $10.00
Death Certificate $ 5.00
Vital Statistics Bureau
New Mexico Health Services Division
1105 St. Francis Drive
Santa Fe, New Mexico 87503
(505) 827-2338
www.health.state.nm.us/website.nsf/frames?ReadForm

NEW YORK
Birth or Death Certificate (New York City only) $15.00
Division of Vital Records
Department of Health of New York City
125 Worth Street
New York, New York 10013
(212) 788-4520

INVESTIGATION

Birth or Death Certificate $15.00
Vital Records Section
State Department of Health
Empire State Plaza
Tower Bldg.
Albany, New York 12237-0023
(518) 474-3075
www.health.state.ny.us

NORTH CAROLINA
Birth or Death Certificate $10.00
Department of Environment, Health and Natural Resources
Division of Epidemiology
Vital Records Section
1903 MSC
Raleigh, North Carolina 27699-1903
(919) 733-3526
www.schs.state.nc.us/SCHS/certificates/

NORTH DAKOTA
Birth Certificate $7.00
Death Certificate $5.00
Division of Vital Records
State Capitol
600 East Boulevard Avenue
Bismarck, North Dakota 58505
(701) 328-4508
www.health.state.nd.us/ndhd/admin/vital/

OHIO
Birth or Death Certificate $7.00
Bureau of Vital Statistics
Ohio Department of Health G-20
65 South Front Street
Columbus, Ohio 43266-0333
(614) 466-2531
www.odh.state.oh.us/records/records-f.htm

OKLAHOMA
Birth or Death Certificate $5.00
Vital Records Section
State Department of Health
1000 Northeast 10th Street
P.O. Box 53551
Oklahoma City, Oklahoma 73152

(405) 271-4040
www.health.state.ok.us/program/vital/index.html

OREGON
Birth or Death Certificate $15.00
Oregon Health Division
Vital Statistics Section
P.O. Box 14050
Portland, Oregon 97293
(503) 731-4095
www.ohd.hr.state.or.us/cdpe/chs/certif/certfaqs.htm

PENNSYLVANIA
Birth Certificate $4.00
Death Certificate $3.00
Division of Vital Records
State Department of Health
Central Bldg.
101 South Mercer St.
P.O. Box 1528
New Castle, Pennsylvania 16103
(412) 656-3100
www.health.state.pa.us/HPA/apply_bd.htm

RHODE ISLAND
Birth or Death Certificate $15.00
Division of Vital Records
Rhode Island Department of Health
Room 101, Cannon Bldg.
3 Capitol Hill
Providence, Rhode Island 02908-5097
(401) 277-2811

SOUTH CAROLINA
Birth or Death Certificate $17.00
Office of Vital Records and Public Health Statistics
South Carolina Department of Health and Environmental Control
2600 Bull St.
Columbia, South Carolina 29201
(803) 898-3630
www.state.sc.us/dhec/vitalrec/

SOUTH DAKOTA
Birth or Death Certificate $5.00
State Department of Health

Center for Health Policy and Statistics
Vital Records
525 E. Capitol
Pierre, South Dakota 57501
(605) 773-3355
www.state.sd.us/doh/VitalRec/Vital.htm

TENNESSEE
Birth Certificate $10.00
Death Certificate $ 5.00
Tennessee Vital Records
Department of Health
Central Services Building
Nashville, Tennessee 37247-0350
(615) 741-1763
www.state.tn.us/health/vr/index.html

TEXAS
Birth Certificate $11.00
Death Certificate $ 9.00
Bureau of Vital Statistics
Texas Department of Health
1100 West 49th St.
Austin, Texas 78756-3191
(512) 458-7111
www.tdh.state.tx.us/bvs/default.htm

UTAH
Birth Certificate $5.00
Death Certificate $9.00
Bureau of Vital Records
Utah Department of Health
288 North 1460 West
P.O. Box 16700
Salt Lake City, Utah 84116-0700
(801) 538-6105
www.health.state.ut.us/bvr/

VERMONT
Birth or Death Certificate $7.00
Vermont Department of Health
Vital Records Section
Box 70
60 Main St.

Burlington, Vermont 05402
(802) 863-7275

VIRGINIA
Birth or Death Certificate $8.00
Division of Vital Records
State Health Department
P.O. Box 1000
Richmond, Virginia 23208-1000
(804) 225-5000
www.vdh.state.va.us/misc/f_08.htm

WASHINGTON
Birth or Death Certificate $13.00
Center for Health Statistics
P.O. Box 9709
Olympia, Washington 98507-9709
(206) 753-5936
www.doh.wa.gov/EHSPHL/CHS/cert.htm

WEST VIRGINIA
Birth or Death Certificate $5.00
Vital Registration Office
Division of Health
State Office Building No. 3, Room 516
Charleston, West Virginia 25305
(304) 558-2931
www.wvdhhr.org/bph/oehp/hsc/vr/birtcert.htm

WISCONSIN
Birth Certificate $12.00
Death Certificate $ 7.00
Vital Records
1 West Wilson Street, Room 158
P.O. Box 309
Madison, Wisconsin 53702
(608) 266-1374
www.dhfs.state.wi.us/vitalrecords/index.htm

WYOMING
Birth Certificate $12.00
Death Certificate $ 6.00
Vital Records Services
Hathaway Building
Cheyenne, Wyoming 82002

(307) 777-7591
www.wdhfs.state.wy.us/vital_records/DEFAULT.HTM

DISTRICT OF COLUMBIA
Birth or Death Certificate $18.00
Vital Records Branch
825 N. Capitol Street, NE
Washington, D.C. 20002
(202) 442-9009

§ 5.24   Surveys

A dramatic increase has arisen in the use of survey evidence in recent years. The use of sampling techniques of surveys provides a practical alternative to using huge amounts of data taken from the entire population. The Manual for Complex Litigation, Third, published by the Federal Judicial Center, notes that a distinction should be drawn between sampling for the purpose of generating data about a population to be offered for its truth and sampling designed to measure a population's opinions, attitudes, and actions. In the case of information gathered for its truth, the user must be sure that:

1.   The population was properly chosen and defined.
2.   The chosen sample was representative of that population.
3.   The data was reported accurately.
4.   Accepted statistical principles were used to analyze the data.

If the purpose of the survey is to measure the attitudes and opinions of a population, you should consider whether the survey was conducted:

1.   Using questions that were clear and not leading
2.   By qualified persons
3.   Using proper interview procedures
4.   In order to insure objectivity.

Manual for Complex Litigation, Third (Federal Judicial Center, 1995) 21.493.

§ 5.25   Working with Public Documents

Whether you work in commercial litigation, probate, or a nonrelated specialty of law, you need to be familiar with the most common public corporation documents and information sources. The following information is meant to be an introduction to those documents and where to obtain them:

§ 5.25 PUBLIC CORPORATION DOCUMENTS

Public Corporation Documents

Form 10K. An annual report required by the Security and Exchange Commission (SEC) *www.sec.gov/* to be filed within 90 days of the close of the publicly-held company's fiscal year. This regulatory agency document contains a detailed accounting of the company's business dealings, history, holdings, financial statements, names and addresses of management officials, and an auditor's report or letter. The auditor's letter will be a good indicator of the true financial condition of the company. This document is a better source of information for straight financial information than the company-produced annual report, which often is a glossy marketing magazine published to impress the company's stockholders. The 10K Form may also contain exhibits evidencing actual financial documents and contracts which affect the financial condition of the company. The 10K form may be ordered from the SEC or through service bureaus. Much of this information is now on online and searchable through the EDGAR database.

8K. The 8K is yet another report which is required to be filed by publicly held companies; however, this document is filed only to report unusual events such as mergers, acquisitions, legal judgments and such.

10Q. The 10Q report must be filed quarterly with the SEC. It describes the quarterly financial condition of the publicly-held company as well as any important or unusual events which have occurred that quarter and which may affect the financial condition of the company. As with the 10K, this report is accompanied by exhibits evidencing the relevant dealings. This document is different from the company-produced quarterly report in the same way as the 10K is different from the annual report. The 10Q is available from the SEC and from service bureaus specializing in SEC documents.

Quarterly Report. Like the Annual Report, the Quarterly Report is a glossy publication produced by the company for its shareholders. The Quarterly Report accompanies the dividend checks mailed to the shareholders. As with the Annual Report, this document is a marketing tool reporting on the financial status of the company in an editorial fashion. The report, however, may be important for its written representations. The Quarterly Report is often more difficult to obtain than the company's Annual Report, and may need to be obtained from a shareholder.

Annual Report. As stated above, the Annual Report is a marketing tool which contains much of the same information as the SEC 10K Form, but in a more editorialized form. Although the 10K Form is a more accurate source of financial information, statements and representations made by company officials in the Annual Report may be used as evidence in a court of law. Annual Reports are easily obtained from the company's corporate offices.

§ 5.26   Tax Rolls

Tax rolls, or records, come in handy when you want to determine if a party has any assets and therefore if it would be worthwhile to file suit against him at all. This information will supply you with the name of the property owner who receives the tax bills, and a description of the property with its appraised value. This method is also used often in skip-tracing or tracking down parties to serve them with process. All of this information, of course, is public information.

These records are generally kept by either the county tax assessor or county recorder. The custodian of these records may also be called the county clerk in some locales. The records are generally kept on microfiche and are usually searchable by property owner's name, street address, or legal description of a property. Even the owner of a vacant parcel of land can be identified in this manner. One would simply locate the property on a map in the county recorder's office and then use the legal description found there to perform a search of the records for the owner.

§ 5.27   Court Records

Court records can be a useful source of information for your case. In court records you may find information about previous litigation involving the parties in your case. A review of the records from these other cases may provide you with important facts and information—perhaps even witnesses—useful to your case.

§ 5.28   Data Banks and the Internet

An increasing amount of information is available from the ever-growing collection of on-line services. Much legal and factual information that may be useful to your case is also increasingly available through the Internet.

§ 5.29   Advertising Claims

When a product of any kind is responsible for injury to your client, immediately begin research by collecting all magazine, newspaper, direct mail, or any other type of media advertising claims about the product. Obtain an original packing container and accompanying instructions, warnings, and warranties. All claims made by the manufacturer are vitally important to your suit. Do research to see if there have been lawsuits for similar incidents against the manufacturer and if they have changed the design, prescribed usage, or warnings since your client purchased the product. You will probably want to hire an expert to test the product to see if it lives up to the advertising claims and works properly.

§ 5.30   Photographs

Photographs are an absolute must. If your firm does not own a good quality 35mm camera and a knowledgeable operator, by all means, hire a professional. You might do well to take photography classes yourself and become proficient at photographing evidence of all kinds. Pictures should be taken from all angles of intersections where an accident has occurred, and it is also a good idea to videotape the approach of your client's car from the inside of the windshield so that the jury will be able to view the road as your client saw it.

It is also a wonderful evidentiary tool to take pictures of damages sustained, defective parts of a product, or even a videotape of a product in the process of malfunctioning. Juries are very moved by visual scenes, and sometimes opposing counsel will offer early settlement negotiations when confronted with such incriminating evidence. An emotionally difficult, but necessary thing to do also, is to obtain before and after pictures of your client's injuries and disfigurement, if that applies, in a personal injury case. This alone could be your most valuable evidence.

Photographs are especially effective in commercial litigation. If the subject of your lawsuit is something with which the average juror (or even judge) is probably not familiar, a basic explanation of how it works, accompanied by visual aids, is priceless. For example, even in Texas, where oil rigs are sometimes mistaken for the state bird, attorneys will begin the most complex commercial litigation with photographs or videotapes designed to walk the judge and jury through a basic understanding of how the oil is drilled, extracted, and transported away from the well. If a juror has a basic understanding and mental picture of how it works before he begins to hear the facts of the case, he can focus more on the issues that are important in the lawsuit without losing his way in a frustrated attempt to understand what it all means.

§ 5.31   Document Authenticity

There may be times in your investigation of cases when a question is raised as to the genuineness of a document. While most paralegals cannot profess to be handwriting or forensic experts, there are still many things a paralegal can do to help such an investigation along. Because a paralegal's work is document-intensive, things will often appear to jump right off the page to them if something appears different, or out-of-the-ordinary. Discuss your hunches and findings with your attorney and use the information contained in this section to get started. If you have determined, after your investigation, that discrepancies exist in a document, you may want to hire a professional forensic document examiner to complete the investigation. Your local legal directory is a good source for locating such and expert. **Form 5–11** is helpful when the genuineness of a document is questionable.

§ 5.32 Document Authenticity Checklist

FORM 5–11
SAMPLE DOCUMENT AUTHENTICITY CHECKLIST

____ 1. Chain of possession of the document.

_____

_____

_____

____ 2. Evidence of tampering, editing, erasure, or other changes.

_____

_____

_____

____ 3. Obvious editing-out of any information.

_____

_____

_____

____ 4. Original document available or photocopy only?

_____

_____

_____

____ 5. Difference in type or writing in different portions of the document.

_____

_____

_____

____ 6. Is grammar usage and verb tense consistent throughout the document?

_____

_____

_____

____ 7. Is there something obviously different about the signature on the document as opposed to the same signature on other available documents?

_____

_____

_____

___   8.   Did the document mysteriously reappear after a noticeable absence?

_____

_____

_____

___   9.   Does anything on the document appear to have been added after the fact?

_____

_____

_____

___   10.   Are any witnesses available to testify as to the authenticity of the document?

_____

_____

_____

§ 5.33   Checklist of Documents Containing Handwriting Samples

The documents in the following list are a good source of handwriting samples:

1. Credit card transactions
2. Bank records
3. Insurance records
4. Correspondence
5. Voting records
6. Library cards
7. School records
8. Licenses or applications for licenses
9. Passports
10. Corporate records
11. Lease agreements
12. Income tax forms
13. Vehicle titles
14. Military records
15. Court records
16. Social Security records
17. Club or union records
18. Utility deposits

19. Wills
20. Real estate records

§ 5.34 Development of Witnesses

The development and interviewing of witnesses is a fine art at which you will learn to excel with experience. As with anything else, practicing good fundamentals is an important part of the success you achieve. Preparedness is the primary fundamental in the development of witnesses. Know your goals and objectives before seeking information from a witness, and remain true to those goals and objectives. Have the ability, however, to pursue the unexpected twists and turns of an interview without losing sight of your original objective. Keep in mind the following general objectives about information you want to discern from the interview:

1. Facts
2. Insights or opinions of the witness
3. Credibility of the witness
4. Credibility of the testimony
5. Existence of physical evidence
6. Existence of documents
7. Timing sequence or chronology of events.

Go thru documents thoroughly

make a "players list" potent. witnesses

§ 5.35 Witness Statements

A lawsuit can take years to come to trial. In that long span of time, the memories of events fade, and details surrounding the events become a hazy recollection. Important facts and impressions may be lost forever. To preserve the accuracy of a witness's account of an event, time is of the essence. As soon as you become aware that someone may be a possible witness in your case, locate him and take a statement. Always go out of your way to accommodate a witness and make him comfortable. Do not insist that he be inconvenienced by a trip into your office. Go to see him where he is comfortable. If that means meeting him in a restaurant or at his home, do so. Ask open-ended questions and encourage the witness to talk freely, even if he strays from the subject. When this happens, listen attentively, respond accordingly, and gently bring him back to the subject.

Take notes throughout the interview, using the phrases and words of the witness. At the end of the interview, write a statement for the witness to sign, using his own words. Have the witness read it, initial any changes he wants to make, and have him sign the statement. The last paragraph of the statement should be a standard testament stating that the "foregoing is a true and correct account."

The main advantages of taking a witness's statement rather than a deposition, are that you do not have to have the opposing party in attendance, it is cost-efficient, and you do not have to let the opposing party know you have the witness statement. The statement is attorney work product. Under most rules of civil procedure, you do not have to produce it unless the other party can prove they need it, cannot get the substantial equivalent on their own, and that not having the statement would create an undue hardship.

On the other hand, if you are trying to obtain a copy of a witness statement, talk to the witness and remind him that he is entitled to have a copy of his own statement. You may have better luck obtaining the statement from him than from opposing counsel.

§ 5.36   Determination of Witnesses

Every scrap of paper you have collected in connection with your discovery process and your investigative process should be gone over with a fine-toothed comb to come up with names of possible witnesses. Interview every witness you discover. Even if a witness does not have actual firsthand knowledge of the incident, chances are he will make at least one statement or mention one fact or theory of which you were not previously aware. Take these facts and theories and follow up on them, no matter how ludicrous they may seem. Law is a surprising profession, and you never know when you have a diamond in the rough right in your hands.

The most obvious place to begin to look for witnesses is in the documents. As you go through the documents, keep lists of witnesses according to the subject matter of their knowledge about the facts of the case. In commercial cases, you may want to develop charts resembling family trees or organizational charts of corporations to keep the chain of command or structure straight in your mind.

After you have developed all the witnesses possible from the documents and statements that you have regarding the case, begin to think about where you would look for information if you had no leads at all. Who would have been in a position to have known anything about one particular fact? In the case of eyewitnesses to an incident, who would have been in a position to have seen anything happening in that locale on any given day? In a commercial case, who in the chain of command would be most likely to be privy to the day to day operations surrounding the subject matter of the controversy? Once you have developed a list of probable or possible witnesses by this method, incorporate your questions into the interview with the witnesses that you know to have facts about the case.

During the course of an interview with a witness, names or identities of other possible witnesses will automatically come up. The whole purpose of interviewing a witness is to find out what he knows about a particular incident, and the most valuable information you may come across is the name of a witness of whom you were previously unaware. Many times a witness may not know who else definitely has information on the subject matter, but they will have ideas about who should

INVESTIGATION

have information. Many times this type of information can shed a whole new light on your case.

Informal discovery can be very useful in locating witnesses and finding out what they have to say. However, while informal discovery is not prohibited, it is generally not required or mandated. Therefore, although a party might attempt to conduct such discovery, the object of that discovery need not go along with it.

§ 5.37 Guidelines to Witness Development

Use the following guidelines as a reference for discovering possible witness:

1. Go through all documents with a fine-toothed comb.
2. Decide who would have logically been in a position of knowledge of any question of fact.
3. Decide who logically would have been in a position to be an eyewitness to an incident.
4. Decide who in the chain of command of a business organization would be most likely to be privy to the normal day to day operations surrounding the subject matter of the controversy.
5. During other witness interviews, confirm your theories about the existence of other probable witnesses.
6. Follow up on all probable witness leads, no matter how remote the possibilities seem.
7. Do not make a witness feel that by naming another probable witness they will get that person into trouble.
8. Always assume that the witness knows more about the facts of the case than you do. This will keep your mind open to new leads.

§ 5.38 —Witness Statement

The following guidelines are helpful in taking a witness statement:

1. Make plans to take the statement as soon as you identify the witness.
2. Contact the witness and set up a time for interview.
3. Choose the interview location where the witness will be comfortable.
4. Make a good impression and begin to establish a rapport.
5. Do not inconvenience the witness if at all possible.
6. Be friendly, but professional.
7. Use psychology in making the witness at ease.
8. Prepare—so that you can keep the interview as short as possible.

9. Empathize, don't sympathize.

10. Ask open-ended questions.

11. Let the witness tell the story in his own words.

12. Gently lead the witness back to the subject if he strays.

13. Develop unexpected leads which arise in the course of the interview.

14. BE A GOOD LISTENER!

15. Remember your ethics. Do not disclose attorney/client privileged information, no matter how curious the witness is.

16. Do not offer legal advice to the witness. If he asks for legal advice, tell him that you are not an attorney, and therefore are unable to advise him.

17. Tape the interview whenever possible, always asking the witness's permission first.

18. Prepare the statement for the witness's signature. Use vocabulary and grammar similar to the witness's own. Do not fill the statement with legalese.

19. The witness is entitled to a copy of his own statement, but remember that if he has it, it may very well fall into the hands of opposing counsel. Handle this decision as delicately as possible.

§ 5.39 —Witness Location

The following guidelines will help you in locating a witness:

1. Talk to the witness's former coworkers.

2. Talk to former neighbors.

3. Find out what church he attended.

4. Find out where he had his clothes dry cleaned, who his doctors were, and so forth.

5. Research his former telephone number through a cross-directory such as Cole's.

6. If you think he has moved to another city, check out the professional association memberships in his profession.

7. Try writing a friendly letter asking him to call you. Be sure to mark the envelope "Please Forward."

8. Use the Freedom of Information Act Last Known Address Form (**Form 5–6**).

9. Search Motor Vehicle and Driver's License Records (**Forms 5–9** and **5–10**).

10. Check the tax assessor's records.

11. Search motor vehicle and driver's license records.

12. Check the real property transaction records.

13. Check the divorce records at the County Clerk's office.

14. Check the marriage license records.

15. Locate and talk with relatives of the witness. Try checking the telephone book for people with the same last name.

16. Check utility company records, if they are available to you.

17. Check voter registration records.

18. Brainstorm with a colleague about your next area of search.

19. The Internet:
    - http://www.findlaw.com/directories/reverse.html
      Reverse directory for addresses and phone numbers for locating people
    - http://www.switchboard.com/
    - http://people.yahoo.com/
    - www.whowhere.com
    - http://www.usps.gov/ncsc/lookups/lookup_zip+4.html
      Looks up zip codes
    - www.anywho.com
    - http://www.lookupusa.com/homesite/index.html

§ 5.40 Witness Questionnaire

Once again, rather than mailing a form questionnaire to a prospective witness or calling him in to your office to fill out such a form, take the time to interview him personally over the phone or in-person in a place comfortable or convenient to him. The following questionnaire (**Form 5–12**) is a rough outline to follow during an interview concerning a traffic accident.

FORM 5–12
SAMPLE WITNESS QUESTIONNAIRE (TRAFFIC ACCIDENT)

1. When did the accident occur?

   _____

2. Where did the accident occur?

   _____

3. What is your complete name and address?

   _____

   _____

4. What is your telephone number? _____

   _____

§ 5.40 WITNESS QUESTIONNAIRE

5. What is your occupation and who is your employer? _____

    _____

6. What were you doing when the accident occurred? _____

    _____

    _____

7. Did you actually see the accident happen? _____

    _____

8. What did you observe? _____

    _____

    _____

    _____

9. How fast do you think the two cars were going? _____

    _____

    _____

10. Did either vehicle run a red traffic light or a stop sign? _____

    _____

    _____

11. Did either vehicle fail to yield the right-of-way? _____

    _____

    _____

12. Was either vehicle travelling on the wrong side of the street? _____

    _____

    _____

13. Did either vehicle make an unsafe lane change? _____

    _____

    _____

INVESTIGATION

14. Did either vehicle use directional signals? _____

_____

_____

15. Did either vehicle have its headlights on? _____

_____

_____

16. Was there any construction in the area? _____

_____

_____

17. Was either driver trying to avoid some sort of obstacle?

_____

18. Do you think either driver was under the influence of drugs or liquor at the time of the accident? _____

_____

_____

_____

19. Did you overhear any statements made by either driver after the accident?

_____

_____

_____

_____

20. Who do you think was to blame for the accident? _____

_____

_____

21. Prior to the accident, did you observe the vehicle you felt to be at fault doing anything illegal or reckless?

_____

_____

_____

_____

22. Are you related to or do you personally know either of the drivers? _____

_____

_____

23. Is there anything else you can think of that you feel would be helpful for us to know? _____

_____

_____

_____

§ 5.41   Driver's License Records

In most states, the easiest way to locate someone's current address is to file a request through the Department of Public Safety or the Department of Motor Vehicles requesting information on the driver's license of that person. Some states, however, will not allow those records to be released without the authorization of the individual because the records are considered private and are protected by the Open Records Act or a similarly-named act in another state. This is because the driver's license records contain information which opens the gateway to discovering an infinite amount of information about the individual, and some states have decided that this privacy must be protected. Check with the individual agencies in each state to see if this information is protected before you request it. This information has become even harder to get subsequent to passage of 18 U.S.C. § 2721, which is commonly called the Driver's Privacy Protection Act of 1997. There is a nifty little site at http://www.carbuyingtips.com/dmv.htm that lists the motor vehicle sites for all 50 states. Check the site for information on the state in which you are requesting records.

§ 5.42   Expert Witnesses   *only ones who are pd. for testim.*

Many cases need the added perspective given by an expert in the field to sway the jury and prove up your case. Picking an expert witness whose credibility is beyond reproach and who possesses the courtroom savvy to deliver testimony effectively is a job which should not be taken lightly. There are thousands of experts available in any given field. Under the newest amendments to Rule 26 of the Federal Rules

Only ones who are allowed to give opinion

of Civil Procedure, the other party must prepare a written report prepared by the testifying expert, and this report must be prepared without waiting for a discovery request. The report must contain such information as the expert witness's opinions, reasoning, and data or other information considered by the expert witness in forming those opinions. Expert witnesses can be located through recommendation, advertisements in periodicals of interest to the legal field, legal directories, direct mail advertisements, LEXIS, or professional societies in their respective fields. Still others can be located through trade journals in which they author articles. It is possible you will run across some of these in your normal investigation.

It is important to pick an expert who not only is outstanding in his field, but also one whose personality will be accepted favorably by a jury. He must possess the ability to relate his findings and opinions in such a way that the average juror can understand what he is talking about. It will do you no good, and perhaps even hurt you, if your expert speaks in such technical terms that everything he says goes above the jury's heads.

Experts are particularly important in commercial litigation. Not only do experts testify about how something works, or how something could have happened, but they also are very effective in testifying as to whether procedures followed in a certain instance are accepted standards in a specific industry. If your client is being sued for negligence, for example, and your client maintains that he was not negligent but followed widely-accepted normal procedures or practices in that industry, you will want to locate a qualified expert witness who can testify that what your client maintains is true.

An expert witness can be someone other than a professional consultant or expert witness. If, for example, you need someone to testify as to normal and accepted banking procedures and practices, go out into your community and find the most highly respected banker you can with years of experience behind him. Your attorney will know how to lay the foundation for qualifying him as an expert witness.

The expert witness receives special treatment in many aspects of the case compared to other witnesses. An expert witness is the only type of witness who is allowed to testify regarding his opinions at trial. Under Rule 701 of the Federal Rules of Evidence, general witnesses are not allowed to express opinions. Under Rule 26(b)(4) of the Federal Rules of Civil Procedure, interrogatories may be addressed to the opposing party to discover not only the expert's identity, and the subject matter about which he is expected to testify at trial. The interrogatories may ask the basis of fact for each opinion the expert will testify about at time of trial, but the expert's report is not discoverable. It is more difficult to discover the opinions of an opposing party's expert if the expert is not expected to testify at trial. This situation almost always requires a motion to be granted by the court if the court agrees with the argument that the information or opinions held by that expert are indispensable to your case and there is no other way for you to obtain that information on your own. If you file one of these motions, you can automatically expect opposition form opposing counsel.

§ 5.43 EXPERT CONSULTANT OR WITNESS

Under Rule 35 of the Federal Rules of Civil Procedure, if your client has been required to undergo a physical or mental examination, you may obtain a copy of the examiner's written report.

Witnesses generally may give opinion testimony only when based on their own perceptions (*see* Federal Rule of Evidence 602). An expert witness may testify based on information not acquired firsthand, including facts or data presented to the expert and hearsay evidence which would be otherwise inadmissible if the expert's scientific, technical, or other specialized knowledge will assist the jury to understand the evidence to determine a fact in issue (*see* Federal Rule of Evidence 702). Among permissible bases are the expert's own perceptions, hypothetical facts, the perceptions and opinions of others (including other experts), and data and documents that the expert has studied.

The opinion must be based on data or information of a type that reasonably may be relied on by experts in forming an opinion on the subject to which the testimony relates. A common example is a physician's basing his or her diagnosis and treatment on a nurse's report or X-rays. One expert may rely on the opinion of another if it is of a type reasonably relied on by experts in the field.

The expert's reliance on potentially inadmissible data constitutes an important exception to the hearsay rule. For example, it permits a treating physician to testify to subjective symptoms as described by the patient— otherwise, probably inadmissible through the doctor's testimony—because, while the physician's statements about symptoms are not admissible for the truth of what they assert, they are permitted to establish the facts upon which the physician's expert opinion is based.

Practice Note: When inadmissible matter is relied on by an expert, opposing counsel should request that the court instruct the jury that such matter is not offered for its truth and is, instead, offered only to explain the basis of the opinion (*Paddack v. Dave Christensen, Inc.,* 745 F.2d 1254, 16 Fed. R. Evid. 1280] (9th Cir. 1984)).

While the expert may testify to opinions without prior disclosure of the bases for them, he or she may be required to disclose the underlying bases on direct or cross-examination. (*See* Fed. R. Evid. 705).

§ 5.43 Expert as Consultant or Witness

An expert may be retained to serve as a consultant, as a witness, or as both. The critical difference for trial planning purposes is that in civil cases the identity of the expert consultant and his or her reports are not discoverable except in exceptional circumstances where there is a showing of need (*see* Fed. R. Civ. P. 26) while the identity of the expert witness, and any material upon which his or her opinion is based, are generally subject to discovery (*see* Fed. R. Civ. P. 35). In criminal cases, however, the prosecutor must make known to the defendant the identity of all experts.

Role as consultant.   Discovery law generally encourages thorough investigation of both the favorable and unfavorable aspects of the case by protecting the privacy of investigations and preventing other attorneys from obtaining the fruits of investigations by their opponents. For example, confidential communications, including technical data given to a consultant in the course of investigation and trial preparation, may be protected by the attorney-client and work product privileges. While the attorney-client privilege is not generally applicable to communications with a consultant (since the consultant is not a client), the privilege may apply if the communications were reasonably necessary to further the purpose for which the attorney was employed. In such instances, the courts treat the consultant as the attorney's agent and, therefore, for purposes of pretrial discovery, entitled to the shield of the privilege.

Matters prepared in anticipation of litigation, such as a consultant's reports to counsel or any material that includes a consultant's findings, opinions, or reports may be protected by the work-product privilege. This may also include purely advisory work, such as when an expert helps the attorney prepare pleadings, decide how to present proof, and develop appropriate direct and cross-examinations of other witnesses. The work-product privilege is strongest with respect to an attorney's impressions, conclusions, opinions, or legal research or theories, known as "derivative" matters, because it is presumed that an attorney's ideas and direction are reflected in the consultant's work. Other matters ("non-derivative") enjoy only a qualified protection, and are subject to disclosure on a showing of good cause. (*See,* e.g., F.R.C.P. 26(b); Hickman v. Taylor (1947), 329 U.S. 495, 91 L.Ed. 451, 67 S. Ct. 385, 34 Ohio Ops. 395).

Practice Note: In this area, it is particularly important to study applicable case law in your jurisdiction. The appellate opinions governing disclosure of expert-consultant work are "fact-specific," thus making it difficult (and dangerous) to over-generalize concerning this issue.

Role as witness.   Under most state law, the identity of an expert who will testify as a witness, and the results of any tests or reports upon which he or she relies in reaching an opinion, are discoverable. F.R.C.P. 26(b)(4) provides that a party may be required to identify expert witnesses and state the subject matter of the anticipated testimony (facts and opinions) and the grounds of each opinion.

If you decide that your expert consultant should also serve as a witness, and you disclose your decision to opposing counsel as required by law, the client is presumed to have waived the attorney-client privilege as to the expert, and the opposing attorney may have a reasonable time in which to conduct discovery. Reports prepared by the expert are generally discoverable if they contain opinions and information concerning the subject matter about which the expert will testify.

§ 5.44   —Strategy Considerations

The safest approach to assuring at least the initial confidentiality of your investigation is to initially retain an expert as a consultant. When you are certain that your theories of the case coincide with the expert's, engage that expert as a witness.

However, this approach will not necessarily protect the confidentiality of all work performed by the expert witness in his or her earlier consultant capacity. Work-product rules are designed to protect a party's expense and industry in seeking out expert testimony, not to sanction suppression of evidence; work-product rules cannot be relied on to protect the work of the consultant-turned-witness.

Therefore, although it is not clear in the abstract whether a court would deny the work-product privilege for work done before the change in status, the better practice is to assume that all work done by an expert witness in preparation for trial will be discoverable, and to hire a separate consultant if you would prefer to retain the work-product privilege. Should you engage both an expert witness and a consultant, do not permit them to exchange views or materials; if the expert relies on any of the consultant's materials, they may no longer be privileged from discovery.

Practice Note: The work-product rule protects only the work of an expert acting as an agent of the attorney, not the work of an expert retained by the client. If the client has already retained an expert for consultation, draft a separate attorney-expert agreement to ensure protection of work done at your request, since the protection is generally unavailable for work done prior to such an agreement.

§ 5.45   Scope of Expert's Testimony

Expert testimony at trial is generally limited to the specific topics identified as the general substance of expected testimony disclosed in pretrial discovery required by procedural statutes. Ordinarily, however, the expert will be deposed prior to trial; once an expert has been deposed, that expert's opinion, even if not disclosed earlier, may be used at trial. Failure to disclose experts and their anticipated areas of testimony can result in exclusion of the expert's testimony or in judicial sanctions, such as continuance of the trial and attorney's fees.

An expert's opinion is generally permitted only with respect to matters as to which the expert is qualified. If an expert, qualified to testify in one area, attempts to offer an opinion in a different area, the testimony concerning the issue as to which the expert is not qualified may not be admitted (with the concomitant result that the witness may lose credibility in the eyes of the jurors). However, there are many cases where this limitation is inapplicable or questionable:

- Can a radiologist testify to the malpractice of a chiropractor?
- Can a commercial banker testify to the reasonable business practice of a mortgage banker in a case involving breach of a lending commitment for a $5 million hotel loan?

- Can a hospital nurse testify to the standard of care of an office nurse who allegedly failed to inform the doctor of a suspicious drug reaction?
- Can a C.P.A. testify to the present value of a lifetime of lost wages when his assumptions are at odds with a Ph.D. economist who testified for the other side? What if one expert was a Ph.D. in statistics with an M.B.A. and 20 years' experience and the other was a bookkeeper with only an A.A. degree?
- Can an ex-state trooper testify as an accident reconstruction expert against a Ph.D. in biomechanics and computer design analysis (CAD-CAM)?
- Can a general dentist with 16 hours of post-graduate seminars give an opinion on the malpractice of an orthodontist who has caused temporomandibular joint derangement by the placement of braces?

The answer to each hypothetical situation described above will depend on the trial judge's interpretation of expert testimony law. Generally, however, any deficiencies in an expert's qualifications should go to the weight of his or her testimony, and not to its admissibility. Since experts are given such broad testimonial power, learning how to use and control them is essential.

§ 5.46 Sources for Locating Expert Witnesses

Use the following source list to help locate expert witnesses:

1. NEXIS (expert witness database)
2. *Forensic Services Directory*
3. *Guide to Periodic Literature* (authors of articles are often experts in their fields)
4. *Lawyer's Desk Reference*
5. *AMERICAN BAR JOURNAL*
6. *Best's Guide to Insurance Attorneys*
7. State legal directories
8. Colleges/universities
9. Newspaper articles
10. Radio and TV interview files and tapes
11. Professional journals
12. Professional associations
13. Your law firm's files on experts
14. Courthouse—(check other pleadings)
15. Other attorneys or paralegals
16. State bar journals
17. Government agencies

18. State bar associations
19. American bar associations
20. *Who's Who* ~~don't use~~
21. Private companies
22. Legal newspapers
23. Hospitals
24. Medical examiner's office
25. The client
26. *Encyclopedia of Associations*
27. *Jury Verdict Research, Inc.* (LRP Publications) An online alternative is found at www.bluesheet.com
28. *Dialog*—(on-line computerized database)
29. *Index Medicus*
30. Expert Pages www.expertpates.com/index.htm
31. http://www.expert4law.org/
32. ExpertLaw.com
33. http://www.onlineexperts.net/
34. Technical Assistance Bureau http://www.tabexperts.com/
35. http://www.expertnetwork.com/
36. http://www.findlaw.com/13experts/directories.html
37. Site containing many more links to experts http://www.pimall.com/nais/n.exp.html
38. http://www.expertwitness.com/

Experts may be found in a variety of places. Word-of-mouth is probably the most reliable source; the expert recommended by a colleague on the basis of a satisfactory prior experience is often more likely to prove successful than one located in a published directory. A recommendation from a colleague, however, is not always possible.

The following additional suggestions may aid your search:

(1) *Recommendation by colleague.* As noted above, this is generally the most reliable source for locating an expert.

(2) *Percipient witness.* Percipient witnesses are subject to the normal non-expert witness discovery processes. Nevertheless, they may be the source of valuable opinion testimony. A treating physician, for example, may be an excellent expert. You will not need to explain the whole case to such a witness, and his or her opinion or conclusion might carry more weight than would an independent expert's because it is based on direct perception of the facts rather than on the testimony of others or on other physician's records and charts.

(3) *Expert files.* If your firm or office routinely handles cases where expert testimony is required, there may be a central file of experts that members of the firm have used before. If not, individual attorneys in the firm or office may have some suggestions. In addition, do not hesitate to call attorneys outside your firm or office whom you know have previously engaged the type of expert you need.

(4) *Professionals* (other than attorneys). Other professionals who use the same type of experts may be consulted for recommendations. Banks and realtors, for example, often use appraisers.

(5) *The client.* If your client is in a specialty business or profession, he or she may qualify as an expert or may know who else in the field is qualified to be an expert. Such a client also should be able to evaluate the qualifications of potential experts.

(6) *Recent cases dealing with the same issues.* Publications which report jury verdicts, for example, usually identify experts and often provide the substance of their testimony at trial. Reports of appellate decisions often involve facts or issues similar to those in your case. Appellate counsel may be consulted to learn who tried the cases, and trial counsel may become a valuable source of experts.

(7) *Reference books of experts.* For example: Directory of Medical Specialists (Marquis' Who's Who, Chicago, Ill.); Lawyers Desk Reference (Bancroft-Whitney, San Francisco, CA); New Directory of Experts and Attorney Services (California Trial Lawyers Association); Locating Scientific and Technical Experts, 2 Am. Jury Trials 293; Expert Witness Index (Defense Research Institute, Milwaukee, WI); Forensic Services Directory (National Forensic Center, Fairlawn, N.J.).

(8) *Legal periodicals.* These publications often carry advertisements by experts, or by services that locate experts. Consult, for example, legal newspapers, and trial magazines published by ATLA and the state bar.

(9) *Specialty publications.* Professional publications in other fields, such as medical journals or reference materials, may yield authors or other persons who are considered experts within a particular area.

(10) *Private organizations.* There are several organizations that specialize in finding expert witnesses for attorneys. They include: TASA (Technical Advisory Service for Attorneys), which now has a computer data base with nearly 10,000 experts in over 3,500 categories; Consulting Institute of America; and the Association of Trial Lawyers of America, which sponsors the Exchange Network.

(11) *Consulting firms.* These include: Failure Analysis Associates, National Economic Research Associates, Inc., and JurEcon.

(12) *Universities.* Witnesses from university faculties are often considered by jurors to be particularly credible.

(13) *Professional organizations.* By reviewing the membership rosters of particular professional organizations, you may be able to locate specialists (such as Board-certified neurosurgeons, psychiatrists, toxicologists, or metallurgists).

(14) *Trade Associations.*

(15) *Records of court-appointed experts.*

(16) *Yellow pages.*

Curriculum vertae? (CV)

§ 5.47   Expert Witness Qualification Checklist

Use the following checklist to establish your expert witness guidelines:

1. Education (degrees and names of institutions)
2. Publications written (articles and books)
3. Level of experience
4. Name recognition in his field (local or national)
5. Previous litigation testimony experience
6. Membership in professional associations
7. Honorary degrees and awards
8. Communications skills, appearance, and jury appeal
9. Potential conflicts of interest
10. Cost.

§ 5.48   Desirable Qualities in an Expert

To a certain extent, the qualities to look for in an expert will depend on whether you envision the expert as consultant, witness, or both. Your preferences will also be guided by your personal style, the nature of the case, and the jurisdiction in which the case will be tried. For example, jurors in a small rural community may resent even a highly credentialed expert who seems to be a "city slicker."

In other words, generalizations concerning appropriate qualities to look for in experts are difficult to draw in absolute terms. With this caveat in mind, consider the following matters when choosing an expert:

(1) *Personality.* Seek someone who will communicate clearly, effectively, and honestly with you, to opposing counsel as a deponent, and later with the jury. Avoid the arrogant or sarcastic expert. If you respond negatively to your expert's personality, the jury probably will, too.

(2) *Experience.* You may split the responsibilities and work with a less well-known but enthusiastic expert (who will charge a lower fee) as a consultant, and then find an older, well-respected specialist to testify when it becomes clear that testimony is required. Generally, avoid specialists who spend most of their time in the courtroom and little time in practice, and those who testify exclusively for one side or the other. They may be perceived as "hired guns"; and their testimony, while smooth and practiced, may lack depth. It is often more effective to prepare a knowledgeable but forensically inexperienced person to become a competent witness.

(3) *Ability to use diagrams or other aids to explain or illustrate ideas.* The expert may serve as a teacher, explaining complex concepts in lay terms but without

patronizing the jury. Often, someone with teaching experience is at home in this role.

(4) *Expert qualifications.* As good as your expert may be, his or her opinion will not be admissible in court unless he or she is qualified by education or experience as an expert. And, although admissible, the opinion may not carry much weight unless his or her qualifications are outstanding. Thus, while a family practice M.D. will often be qualified to deliver an opinion on neurological damage, such an opinion will not have much weight when compared with that of the board-certified neuro-surgeon testifying for the opposing party.

Practice Note: Although not common, there have been instances in which consultants and experts have exaggerated or even falsified their credentials. If you have any doubt as to your expert's qualifications, investigate them with care.

(5) *Ability to think creatively.* Your expert should be able to help develop new theories to accommodate new information, as well as to identify flaws in an existing theory.

(6) *Adequate time to prepare the case.* The most qualified expert is of no use to you if he or she is overcommitted. Inquire as to the extent of other matters currently on your expert's calendar, and explain both how much time you will need and the generally known dates and deadlines for the case.

(7) *Involvement in case preparation.* Some experts are available only to testify at deposition and in court as to their opinions. They have neither the time nor the desire to be involved in developing the case. The extent of the expert's involvement should be made clear at the outset so that you will have time to retain another expert, if necessary, to perform pretrial consulting work. Determine also whether the expert needs to perform tests or studies and whether appropriate resources are available for the work anticipated.

(8) *Fees.* Determine the fees charged by the expert for consultations, travel time, depositions, and trial testimony. Some experts charge more for the stressful work of deposition or courtroom testimony.

(9) *Credibility and persuasive effect.* If the expert will testify, consider his or her ability to communicate. Evaluate the credibility of your witness from the point of view of the jury.

§ 5.49   Keeping Biographical Files

As a routine matter, it is a good idea to keep files on expert witnesses used by other attorneys as well as those you use regularly and other experts you become familiar with. Each file should contain copies of articles authored by the expert, newspaper articles, or magazine articles written about the man, excerpts of his testimony in previous cases, copies of his curriculum vitae (summary of his personal history and professional qualifications), and summaries of how his testimony affected the outcome of previous cases in which he testified.

There are certain obvious things to research when looking for an expert: 1) Find out if he is plaintiff or defendant-oriented, 2) check articles he has written to make sure he has not changed his opinions about important issues, 3) check his testimony in other court cases to make sure he has not contradicted himself and may be easily impeached, 4) check his website if he has one.

The information in your biographical files can be supplemented by biographical sketches found in various literary sources such as the prolific series of *Who's Who* books. These particular books should never be exclusively relied upon, however, because the information found in these publications is voluntarily submitted by the prospective expert himself, and may be exaggerated.

§ 5.50   Determining Credibility

If you are planning to use a person as an expert witness, you will need to become knowledgeable about everything about him. Know his politics, if they are obvious, know what type of attorneys and cases he has testified for previously, and be aware of his professional reputation. Read articles he has written, and analyze his testimony in previous cases to make sure his position is consistent and not at variance with your theories and style of presentation. One last thing to be concerned with is his personality. Is the jury going to like him and respect him, or is he going to come across as a haughty, sarcastic person who answers questions in a condescending manner? Juries will not like that, and the opposing counsel will try to rip him apart on the stand. If you have the slightest feeling that he would be received in this manner, recommend a change in expert witnesses. It could cost you your case.

§ 5.51   The Doctor as an Expert Witness

In some cases, the testimony of a doctor is essential. For example, in a medical malpractice case, expert testimony by a doctor is generally required in order to establish the standard of care expected of a doctor and the breach of that standard.

When selecting a doctor as an expert witness, the selection should not be based completely on the doctor's credentials. Care must also be exercised to ensure that the doctor's communications skills will make him a convincing witness. It is also usually better to select a doctor who has actually treated your client, rather than one who has only reviewed the medical records.

The doctor as an expert witness is a different kind of duck, as the saying goes, and requires special handling. Let's say, for example, that in reviewing your client's medical records, you come upon the name of a doctor who treated your patient and has stated in his records that, in his opinion, your client is incapable of resuming his former job duties as a result of the injuries suffered in the accident. Obviously, this doctor's expert testimony is invaluable to your client's claim for damages relating to loss of future earning capacity and disruption of lifestyle. In this case, the doctor should be approached cautiously, with great respect and deference to his schedule.

Many doctors are very, very reluctant to commit their time more than a few days in advance and for more than an hour at a time.

Do not, however, allow your respect and deference to get in the way of preparing the doctor to testify. Go over the doctor's testimony with him, looking for any discrepancies or "holes" in his testimony. Review the medical records and make sure that the doctor has had an opportunity to review them. Also make sure the doctor knows what he will be asked and provide any help needed to ensure that the doctor's answers will be clear to a jury of lay persons. Finally, make sure that he is prepared for the questions that will be asked during cross-examination.

You may want to give the doctor the option of taking his deposition to preserve his testimony so that he will not have to be inconvenienced at time of trial. Anything you can do to accommodate the doctor's schedule is advisable, and will certainly be appreciated by the doctor and his staff. Always be straightforward with doctors regarding the reasons you wish to speak to them. Most doctors are reluctant to second-guess another doctor's diagnosis or treatment or testify against a fellow doctor. Some may even refuse to speak to you at all unless they are subpoenaed. For the most part, however, your contacts with doctors will be rewarding and pleasurable if you employ consideration in your dealings with them.

§ 5.52   Working with Expert Witnesses

Your relationship with the expert witness on your case is a vital one. It is entirely possible that you will be spending more time with him, both in person and on the telephone, than your attorney will. You will be the liaison and, often, the only contact that the expert has with your office until the trial. It will be your responsibility to work with the expert and to see that he has the information and materials he needs to do the best job of analysis and consultation for your client.

Your assistance to the expert witness will probably be extremely varied in scope. It could range from picking him up at the airport and accompanying him to the site of physical evidence in the case to entertaining him or providing him with tickets to entertainment events while he is in town. In the office, of course, you will be working with him to develop a case and provide him with materials from the file which help him to create a substantive backbone for your case. It may be necessary for you to make travel arrangements for the expert for attendance at depositions or trial.

During the time you spend with the expert on the preparation of the case, you will be assessing his oral communication effectiveness. You will also be observing his mannerisms, and whether he has any which are liable to irritate or antagonize the jury. His jury appeal is every bit as important as his expertise in his field. Because you will probably spend more time with him than the attorney in the early part of the case, you may pick up on some of his mannerisms or weaknesses long before the attorney notices them. Any potential problems should immediately be reported to the attorney so that he may have time to assess them for himself and determine if these types of things may be improved by proper preparation and, perhaps, videotaping sessions.

There is much that you, as a paralegal, can do to help eliminate these types of hurdles to effective testimony. By working your witness preparation techniques into your relationship with the expert, you can accomplish many of the things that would be awkward if you were to bring them up at a single session with your expert. Instead of making him feel that something about him has to be changed to improve the delivery of his testimony, it should be approached in generalities, telling him that it has been noted that juries usually prefer a certain kind of delivery or that a certain style of dress is generally more effective with a jury. If you coach your expert in a manner so that he feels he is working with you as part of a team for the good of the client, and the team is using all methods known to them to ensure the effectiveness of their testimony and production of evidence in the courtroom, your job of preparation will come much easier, and there will be no misunderstandings or hurt feelings. For example, if you have an expert whose dressing habits remind you of the absentminded professor, sooner or later, you will have to approach him about the importance of his being crisply and conservatively dressed for his testimony at trial. Instead of dictating to him how he is going to have to change his style of dress, approach the subject by telling him how you and your attorney dress for trial and tell him why. He may not know that such things have an effect on the jury.

Besides preparing the expert in terms of jury appeal, you will be helping to prepare him throughout the case by supplying him with materials which he needs from the file. Years ago, it was fairly well accepted that anything your expert did in preparation for the trial was covered by the attorney work product privilege, and there was not a problem in showing him anything he needed to prepare his case. In recent years, however, there has been a tendency by judges to construe the procedural rules in a slightly different manner. Now, it is not uncommon for a judge to rule that any material shown to an expert in preparation for his testimony, whether that material was covered by privilege or not, is discoverable by the other side. You can see right away what kind of problems this presents. It is imperative that you clear everything through your attorney before your give copies of it to the expert. Your attorney will want to make the decision regarding whether he wants to take the chance of having the privilege waived by supplying that information to the expert. There may be other ways of giving the same information to the expert without having to waive the privilege on certain documents. This is an extremely important concept for paralegals to understand and monitor.

Expert witnesses are invaluable in helping to assess the need and types of visual aids to be used for trial exhibits. Your expert will have countless ideas about what type of exhibits would best illustrate important elements of his testimony, and even about how to develop those exhibits. If you listen carefully throughout your working relationship with the expert, you should be able to pick out and develop several helpful ideas for these exhibits as you go along. He will have a good idea about which ideas may seem foreign or too highly technical for a jury to grasp, and how they might be best illustrated to alleviate that problem. Many experts have computer software packages which they use regularly to develop charts and graphs for such purposes, and some are even able to produce three-dimensional or scale models. Experts are also helpful in assessing the exhibits you may have already been considering for use and advising you on ways to improve their effectiveness.

§ 5.53   Experts' Fees

Various acceptable expert fee arrangements are possible, depending on the size and complexity of the case, the resources of your client, and the demands of the expert. The particular arrangement you reach will be a result of the tension between (1) your need to know what your approximate expenses will be and your unwillingness to commit yourself to an hourly rate of pay for an unknown quantity of hours, and (2) the expert's income needs and his or her unwillingness to agree to a flat fee or project rate before the extent of work involved is known.

Generally, you can arrive at a preliminary flat fee for case evaluation based on a mutual estimate of the finite time required. This may be an hourly or a daily fee. A different arrangement, at a smaller hourly or daily rate, may cover tests, reports, assistance with discovery, and other items intended to help you to prepare for litigation. Because the expert is guaranteed employment for a certain period of time for case evaluation, he or she may be willing to accept a lower fee per unit of time for trial preparation. Expert witnesses often charge the most for the time they are being deposed or testifying at trial.

When you have reached an appropriate agreement, draft a retainer letter setting out the terms. Exercise caution in choosing language, as the contents of the letter may be discoverable. Emphasize that you are retaining the expert to evaluate the case or, at most, to explore whether a particular set of facts might lead to a particular result, rather than to espouse a particular opinion.

§ 5.54   Checklist for Preparing Expert Witnesses for Testimony

When preparing your expert witness for testimony, use the following checklist as a guideline:

1. Do not use highly technical language that the jury will not understand.
2. Dress conservatively, but professionally. A conservative, dark-colored suit is appropriate. A sports coat or casual slacks or jeans are not appropriate court attire. Ties should also be conservative.
3. Confine your answers to the questions you are asked. Do not try to volunteer information outside the scope of the questions. Your attorney will give you the opportunity to clarify any misconceptions which may have occurred in questioning by opposing counsel.

4. Do not become belligerent or argumentative when questioned by opposing counsel. That is exactly the response he hopes to evoke.

5. Do not speculate or guess to answer questions you are not sure how to answer. Admit that you do not know the answer to the question. The jury will see you as merely being human.

6. When you speak, watch your tone of voice and body language. Never cross your arms or speak in a condescending or sarcastic tone of voice.

7. Do not let opposing counsel badger you into changing your testimony. Stick to your original testimony and do not let opposing counsel intimidate you.

8. Answer every question truthfully.

9. If asked whether you received payment for your testimony, tell the truth, and give amounts if asked. Remember that the other side's expert is subject to the same types of questions. Your attorney will see to it that the jury understands this to be common and accepted practice.

10. Please tell us now if you have ever written anything or testified to anything that could be construed as being converse to what you are going to testify here. Opposing counsel may use information of this type to try to impeach you. We would like to prepare for this possibility ahead of time.

11. We may choose to videotape your testimony here in our offices prior to trial or deposition so we can play your testimony back for you and work with you on the points we have discussed. It is not our intention to change your testimony, but to refine your delivery so that the value of the testimony is enhanced to its greatest impact. You will find this process very helpful and confidence-inspiring.

12. If you feel that any visual aids, graphics, or models would help to convey the meaning of highly technical ideas to the jury, please discuss this with us and let us know how we may assist in obtaining these aids for you.

Under amended Federal Rule of Civil Procedure 26, a party must disclose expert witness information without waiting for a discovery request. In written reports prepared by the testifying experts, the parties must disclose, among other things, the expert witnesses' opinions, reasoning, and data or other information considered by the expert witnesses in forming their opinions. This includes information that the expert considered but did not rely on. (See § **8.14**.)

§ 5.55   Discoverability of Expert Witness Material

Just as it is important for a journalist to be able to protect his sources and keep them confidential in order to be able to ensure the quality of his writing, so must the attorney be free to seek out experts and consultants in confidentiality to help him assess and develop his case to the best of his ability for his client. The court

INVESTIGATION

recognizes the need for this confidentiality, and thus protects most aspects of that relationship by privilege.

Not all experts will be hired with trial testimony in mind. Some of them are hired purely as consultants to analyze the technical elements of a case and to assist the attorney in determining the impact of those elements. The work and opinions of experts who are hired only as consultants without the intention of utilizing their testimony at trial, are not discoverable to the other party except in extreme circumstances. Those circumstances include a provision in the rules of procedure whereby a party may be able to discover such material if he can prove to the court that his case will be prejudiced without benefit of such information, and that there is not other practical or nonprohibitive manner in which to secure that type of information. As an example, the court may rule the material discoverable in cases where something was analyzed by the expert and, in the process of that analyzation, the material evidence was totally destroyed or used up and is not longer available for analysis by another party's expert, or in cases where procuring such evidence would be prohibitively expensive. (See **Forms 5–13** and **5–14.**)

Generally speaking, the expert witness's report to the attorney is not discoverable. The other party may ask for and receive information regarding the subject matter about which the expert is going to testify at trial, what opinions he has formulated on the subject, and what material and facts he has used to come to that conclusion. The most common way of procuring this information is through interrogatories propounded on the other party through his attorney (see FRCP 26(b)(4)(A)).

FORM 5–13
SAMPLE MOTION TO COMPEL PREPARATION AND PRODUCTION OF WRITTEN REPORT OF EXPERT NOT PRESENTLY DESIGNATED AS A WITNESS

NO. [case number]

[name]	)	IN THE DISTRICT COURT OF
	)	
Plaintiff	)	[county] COUNTY, [state]
	)	
vs.	)	[judicial district] JUDICIAL DISTRICT
	)	
[name]	)	
	)	
Defendant	)	

MOTION TO COMPEL PREPARATION AND PRODUCTION OF
WRITTEN REPORT OF EXPERT CONSULTANT

COMES NOW, [name] [plaintiff/defendant] in the above-entitled action, and pursuant to Rule [citation] of the [state/federal] Rules of Civil Procedure, files this, his motion to compel the preparation and production of written report of the expert consultant retained by [name], [plaintiff/defendant] herein, and in support of his motion would respectfully show unto the Court as follows:

I.

[Plaintiff/Defendant] is informed and believes and thereon alleges that [plaintiff/defendant] has hired and retained [name] as an expert consultant to examine, study, and report on [specify nature of experts] examination].

_____

_____

_____

II.

[Plaintiff/Defendant] further says that he cannot adequately evaluate this case or prepare for trial without the information requested above and that there are exceptional circumstances such as are allowed by Rule [citation] of the Rules of Civil Procedure [use applicable rule which parallels Rule 26(b)(4)(B) of the Federal Rules of Civil Procedure] which make it impracticable for [plaintiff/defendant] to obtain facts or opinions on the same subject by other means. The exceptional circumstances which substantiate the need for the production of said materials are: [outline extraordinary circumstances].

WHEREFORE, PREMISES CONSIDERED, [plaintiff/defendant] prays that the Court grant this motion in all respects and award all other and further relief to which [plaintiff/defendant] is entitled.

[name of firm]

By: _____
    [name of attorney]
    Counsel for
    [plaintiff/defendant]
    [address]
    [telephone number]

[Add certificate of service.]

INVESTIGATION

FORM 5–14
SAMPLE ORDER MANDATING PREPARATION AND PRODUCTION OF WRITTEN REPORT OF EXPERT NOT PRESENTLY DESIGNATED AS A WITNESS

NO. [case number]

[name]	)	IN THE DISTRICT COURT OF
	)	
Plaintiff	)	[county] COUNTY, [state]
	)	
vs.	)	[judicial district] JUDICIAL DISTRICT
	)	
[name]	)	
	)	
Defendant	)	

ORDER MANDATING PREPARATION AND PRODUCTION OF WRITTEN REPORT OF EXPERT CONSULTANT

On [date], [20__], came on to be heard [plaintiff's/defendant's] motion to compel preparation and production of written report of expert consultant, [name], an expert hired by [plaintiff/defendant] and not presently designated as a witness for trial.

The Court, having read and heard oral argument on the motion, is of the opinion that the exceptional circumstances outlined by [plaintiff/defendant] in his motion, conform to the true spirit of Rule [citation] of the [state/federal] Rules of Civil Procedure, and should permit the discovery of the materials sought herein.

It is therefore ORDERED, ADJUDGED, and DECREED that [plaintiff's/defendant's] motion be granted in all respects.

SIGNED and dated this [date] day of [month], [20__].

[name]
Judge Presiding

ENTERED this [date] day of [month], [20__].

_____
Clerk of Court

§ 5.56 —Exchange of Expert Witness Lists

Most states have statutes which provide guidelines for demanding and exchanging expert witness lists. Generally, the demand and exchange will occur shortly after the case is set for trial. In addition to the expert's name, business address, and qualifications, the disclosure may include a listing of the expert's fees and a brief narrative statement summarizing the gist of the expert's testimony. It is important to consult local rules for guidance.

Failure to comply with appropriate expert disclosure statutes may preclude your calling experts to testify at trial. In addition, if you comply in part, but fail to disclose a particular expert when you submit your list of experts, an opposing party may object to the nondisclosed expert's testimony. However, the court may permit late disclosure of expert witnesses under certain circumstances, for example, where a good faith effort has been made to comply with the statutes. The court will generally consider whether the opposing parties have relied on the list that was served, and how disadvantaged the objecting party will be if the court permits late disclosure.

Federal Rules provide guidelines for discovery of facts known and opinions held by experts retained in anticipation of litigation or for trial (Fed. R. Civ. P. 26(b)(4)). A party may, through interrogatories, discover the identity of each expert the other side expects to call at trial, as well as the subject matter of the expected testimony, including the substance of the facts and opinions to which the expert is expected to testify, and a summary of the grounds for each opinion (F.R.C.P. 26(b)(4)(A)(i)). And in *Scott & Fetzer Co. v. Dile* (1981, CA9 Ariz.) 643 F.2d 670, 211 U.S.P.Q. 401, 8 Fed. R. E. 421, 31 F.R. Serv. 2d 424, the Ninth Circuit Court of Appeals held that the District Court abused its discretion in allowing plaintiff to use undisclosed witnesses and exhibits to support a previously undisclosed theory of the case in view of plaintiff's failure to supplement responses to interrogatories in violation of Fed. R. Civ. P. 26(c).

Practice Note: The identity of an expert called for impeachment or rebuttal does not have to be disclosed, on the theory that you do not know that you are going to use a rebuttal witness until after the case-in-chief has been completed. This rule should be used with caution, however, particularly where there exists a possibility that the trial judge will find your "impeachment" or "rebuttal" witness to be an expert who should have been disclosed prior to trial.

§ 5.57   Expert Interrogatories

The 1995 amendments to Rule 26 of the Federal Rules of Civil Procedure make it easier to learn about the other party's experts. Without waiting for a discovery request, the other party must provide a written report prepared by the testifying expert. The report must contain such information as the expert witness's opinions, reasoning, and data or other information considered by the expert witness in forming those opinions. As a result, there is less of a need than in the past to use interrogatories to obtain information about the experts who will testify for the other party in federal court. However, in many state courts resort to the more traditional use of interrogatories to obtain information about experts may still be necessary. It may also be necessary in those federal courts that have modified or rejected some or all of the mandatory disclosure requirements of Rule 26.

The use of interrogatories to obtain information about experts who are not expected to testify but who have been retained by the other party in anticipation of litigation or in preparation for the trial is limited. Federal Rule of Civil Procedure 26(b)(4)(B) states that a party may use interrogatories in order to:

> [D]iscover facts known or opinions held by an expert who has been retained or specially employed by another party in anticipation of litigation or preparation for trial and who is not expected to be called as a witness at trial only as provided in Rule 35(b) [dealing with physical and mental examinations] or upon a showing of exceptional circumstances under which it is impracticable for the party seeking discovery to obtain facts or opinions on the same subject by other means.

If a party makes use of interrogatories to obtain information about a non-testifying expert, the court must require the party seeking discovery to pay the other party a fair portion of the fees incurred by the latter party to obtain opinions from the expert.

§ 5.58 Expert Witness Depositions

Under Rule 26 of the Federal Rules of Civil Procedure, a party may depose any person who has been identified as an expert whose opinions may be presented at trial. If the expert is required to file a report under the mandatory disclosure provisions of Rule 26, the deposition shall not take place until after the report is provided. Unless manifest injustice would occur, the party seeking discovery must pay the expert a reasonable fee for the time spent in responding to discovery.

Upon a showing of exceptional circumstances, a party may also depose an expert who is retained by the other party in connection with the case but who is not expected to testify.

§ 5.59 Advantages and Disadvantages of Deposing the Opposing Expert

It is helpful to consider the following factors in deciding whether to depose an opponent's expert. Most trial lawyers considering these factors conclude that discovery from the opposing expert is a useful and even necessary pretrial activity:

(1) *Trial preparation.* Deposition of the opposing expert serves the primary functions of discovery: it prevents surprises at trial and helps you to prepare your case. For example, it commits the expert to theories and conclusions announced at the deposition and thus makes it difficult for him or her to change them at trial.

(2) *Settlement.* It may give you a practical view of the strengths and weaknesses of both sides of the case, so that you can negotiate a realistic settlement.

(3) *Case evaluation.* Deposing the opposing expert may allow you to discover the weaknesses in your case, and alert you to tests your expert should perform or additional preparation that should be made. You will be able to evaluate the witness's qualifications, credibility, and strength, and compare them with the qualities of your own expert. If your opponent's expert is extremely convincing, and if you believe that your own expert will not be as persuasive with the jury, you may be able to find another expert, subject to pretrial time constraints and the cut-off of discovery, whose sole function will be to testify.

(4) *Learning about your opponent's case.* While not a recommended practice, the fact is that counsel sometimes do not prepare experts as carefully for deposition as they do for trial, because of the time and cost involved. Hence, you may be able to learn the other side's theories, elicit favorable admissions, and pin the expert down to a firm statement of opinion that may be used at trial for impeachment if the expert's testimony changes.

(5) *Danger of prompting your opponent to prepare.* If the expert is not deposed, your opponent may not begin case preparation early enough to discover flaws in the opponent's theory or proof. Preparation of an expert for deposition may enable opposing counsel to uncover and remedy any such flaws well before trial.

(6) *Danger of revealing too much.* Your cross-examination of the opposing expert will provide a preview of cross-examination at trial, revealing your style as an interrogator, your ideas about the weaknesses in your opponent's case, and the methods you intend to use to discredit the witness. Many attorneys, however, are uncomfortable going to trial without having deposed the opposing experts. One compromise approach is to conduct the expert's deposition as a pure discovery deposition, using primarily open-ended questions and reserving cross-examination questions for trial.

§ 5.60   Motion to Prohibit Examination of Expert Used Solely for Consultation

Sometimes it is necessary to file a motion to prohibit the examination of your expert witness especially when the expert witness was used solely for consultation. Use **Form 5–15** under these circumstances. **Form 5–16** is a sample order confirming your motion.

INVESTIGATION

FORM 5–15
SAMPLE MOTION TO PROHIBIT EXAMINATION OF EXPERT USED SOLELY FOR CONSULTATION

NO. [case number]

[name]	)	IN THE DISTRICT COURT OF
	)	
Plaintiff	)	[county] COUNTY, [state]
	)	
vs.	)	[judicial district] JUDICIAL DISTRICT
	)	
[name]	)	
	)	
Defendant	)	

MOTION TO PROHIBIT EXAMINATION OF EXPERT USED SOLELY FOR CONSULTATION

COMES NOW, [name], [plaintiff/defendant] in the above-entitled action, and files this his motion for protection under Rule [citation] of the [state/federal] Rules of Civil Procedure, and would show unto the Court as follows:

I.

[Plaintiff/Defendant] [name] has served on [plaintiff/defendant] a notice to take the oral deposition of [name], an expert in the field of [description of field of expertise], and who has been retained by [name] in conjunction with said notice of oral deposition, has served on [expert] a subpoena duces tecum ordering and requiring him to produce at the deposition certain records and reports concerning an investigation of [specify nature of requested records]

_____

_____

which is pertinent to the subject matter of this suit.

II.

The above-entitled action involves highly intricate and technical matters, and [plaintiff/defendant] has hired [expert] as a consultation expert only to aid and assist counsel in the preparation of the matters of this suit for trial, and is not designated as an expert witness, nor is he anticipated to be designated as an expert witness prior to trial in this matter. The records and reports prepared by [expert] are protected by attorney work product privilege as detailed in Rule [citation] of the [state/federal] Rules of Civil Procedure, and as such are not subject to discovery.

410

§ 5.60 MOTION TO PROHIBIT EXAMINATION

WHEREFORE, PREMISES CONSIDERED, [Plaintiff/Defendant] prays that this motion be granted and the subpoena duces tecum be quashed and that [expert] be ordered not to produce any of the records or reports, and that [plaintiff/defendant] be awarded all costs and attorneys' fees in connection with this motion.

[name of firm]

By: _____
           [name of attorney]
           Counsel for
           [plaintiff/defendant]
           [address]
           [telephone number]

[Add certificate of service.]

FORM 5–16
SAMPLE ORDER BARRING THE DEPOSITION AND PRODUCTION OF RECORDS OF EXPERT CONSULTATION

NO. [case number]

[name]		)	IN THE DISTRICT COURT OF
		)	
	Plaintiff	)	[county] COUNTY, [state]
		)	
vs.		)	[judicial district] JUDICIAL DISTRICT
		)	
[name]		)	
		)	
	Defendant	)	

ORDER BARRING THE DEPOSITION AND PRODUCTION OF
RECORDS OF EXPERT CONSULTANT

On [date], [20__], came on to be heard the motion of [plaintiff/defendant] for an order directing that the deposition of [expert] and the accompanying subpoena duces tecum noticed for [date] be quashed and that said expert not be compelled to appear for such examination.

The court is of the opinion that movant has shown good cause for the sustaining of this motion, and it is therefore

ORDERED, ADJUDGED, and DECREED that the deposition and subpoena duces tecum previously served upon [expert] is hereby quashed.

SIGNED and dated on this [date] day of [month], [20__].

[name]
Judge Presiding

ENTERED on this [date] day of [month], [20__].

_____

Clerk of Court

§ 5.61   Case Evaluation Forms

Between the time that discovery ends and the trial begins, you will want to be able to present your attorney with a capsulized accounting of the facts and figures of the case. Use the case evaluation forms exemplified in **Forms 5–17** and **5–18** for this purpose.

FORM 5–17
SAMPLE CASE EVALUATION FORM—PERSONAL INJURY

Date of Evaluation [date]

NO. [case number]

[name]	)	IN THE [type] COURT OF
	)	
Plaintiff,	)	[county] COUNTY, [sate]
	)	
vs.	)	[judicial district] JUDICIAL DISTRICT
	)	
Defendant.	)	

Date of Accident: [date] _____

Special Damages

Medical Expenses

1. [List names of all doctors, hospitals, and dates of treatment.]   [List all dollar expenses.]

2. [List names of all doctors, hospitals, and dates of treatment.]   [List all dollar expenses.]

3. [List names of all doctors, hospitals, and dates of treatment.]   [List all dollar expenses.]

4. [List names of all doctors, hospitals, and dates of treatment.]   [List all dollar expenses.]

Total Medical Expenses to Date   [amount]

§ 5.61   CASE EVALUATION FORMS

Expected Future Medical Expenses

1.	[List expected future treatment.]	[dollar amount]
2.	[List expected future treatment.]	[dollar amount]
3.	[List expected future treatment.]	[dollar amount]

Lost Wages Damages

[List number of days and dates multiplied by daily compensation.]	[dollar amount]

Other Related Expenses

EXAMPLES:

1.	Property damage [describe	[dollar amount]
2.	Other	[dollar amount]

Future Related Expenses

EXAMPLES:

1.	Loss of career advancement opportunity due to disability	[dollar amount]
2.	Loss of business partnership opportunity	[dollar amount]

Total Medical, Lost Wages-Related Expenses and Future Damages	[dollar amount]

Injuries

1.	[List all injuries incurred.]
2.	[List all injuries incurred.]
3.	[List all injuries incurred.]
4.	[List all injuries incurred.]
5.	[List all injuries incurred.]
6.	[List all injuries incurred.]

Medical Treatment

[Insert a chronological summary of patient's medical treatment and progress.]

How Injuries Have Changed Life of Injured Person

[Insert a detailed description of the client's life-style before and after the accident, and how the injuries have affected and changed that lifestyle.]

Damages Asked for Disability, Disfigurement, Pain, Suffering, and Change of Lifestyle	[dollar amount]
Researched Expected Jury Verdict in this Jurisdiction	[dollar amount]

INVESTIGATION

Acceptable Settlement Figure   [dollar amount]

List of Exhibits

1.

2.

3.

4.

5.

6.

List of Bills

1.

2.

3.

4.

5.

6.

Summary and Recommendations

[Two or three paragraph summation]

FORM 5–18
SAMPLE CASE EVALUATION FORM—COMMERCIAL LITIGATION

Date of Evaluation [date]

NO. [case number]

[name]	)	IN THE [type] COURT OF
	)	
Plaintiff,	)	[county] COUNTY, [state]
	)	
vs.	)	[judicial district] JUDICIAL DISTRICT
	)	
[name]	)	
	)	
Defendant.	)	

Summary of Claim: [summarize claim.] _____

_____

_____

_____

Damages

1. [List specific damages claimed in petition and discovery responses.]   [dollar amount]

2. [List specific damages claimed in petition and discovery responses.]   [dollar amount]

3. [List specific damages claimed in petition and discovery responses.]   [dollar amount]

4. [List specific damages claimed in petition and discovery responses.]   [dollar amount]

Total Damages to Date   [dollar amount]

Expected Future Damages

1. [List all future damages claimed in petition and discovery responses.]   [dollar amount]

2. [List all future damages claimed in petition and discovery responses.]   [dollar amount]

3. [List all future damages claimed in petition and discovery responses.]   [dollar amount]

4. [List all future damages claimed in petition and discovery responses.]   [dollar amount]

Lost Wages Damages (if applicable)

[List number of days and dates multiplied by daily compensation.]   [dollar amount]

Other Related Damages

Examples:

1. Property damage (describe)   [dollar amount]

2. Loss of business opportunity (lost contracts, and so forth)   [dollar amount]

3. Business interruption   [dollar amount]

4. Lost interest   [dollar amount]

Figure Related Damages

1. [List all future foreseeable damages using prior-listed damages as guide.]   [dollar amount]

2. Other   [dollar amount]

Total Future Damages   [dollar amount]

Total Past and Future Damages   [dollar amount]

Expected Jury Verdict in this Jurisdiction   [dollar amount]

Acceptable Settlement Figure   [dollar amount]

List of Exhibits

1.

2.

3.

4.

5.

Summary and Recommendations

[Two or three paragraph summation]

§ 5.62 Status Report (Interoffice Memo)

At different time periods during the case, you should prepare a status report to be placed in the file. This document should chronologically report the events and progress of the case from start to finish in small, concise, journalistic-style paragraphs. The style is similar to that used in deposition summaries. In a personal injury suit, the report should flow in a story-like manner, encompassing statements made by the client as to his or her physical condition, any contact he or she has had with any attorneys or investigators, and any comments the client has on how the accident is affecting his or her life.

A similar status report in a commercial lawsuit should outline developments in the lawsuit itself and its investigation. The majority of commercial cases do not continue to accumulate damages other than monetary items like interest or contract payments once a lawsuit is filed. This is attributed to the fact that the plaintiff's attorney will file an immediate injunction against the other party to stop irreparable damages until a jury can decide a case on its merits.

§ 5.63 Investigation Checklist

This checklist can serve as a guideline to follow during the investigation stage of a case. Not all points will be relevant in all cases, but they will give you ideas for starting points.

	1.	Police reports
____	2.	Photographs of scene
____	3.	Actual physical evidence
____	4.	Police officer's notes
____	5.	Autopsy report
____	6.	Traffic ticket disposition
____	7.	Motor vehicle ownership report

____   8.   Driving record

____   9.   Newspaper articles and photographs

____ 10.   Videotapes from television news stations

____ 11.   Highway department history of accidents at that location

____ 12.   Maps and diagrams of area

____ 13.   Determine witnesses

____ 14.   Interview witnesses

____ 15.   Medical records

____ 16.   Medical bills

____ 17.   Property damage bills

____ 18.   Police records of parties and possible witnesses

____ 19.   Insurance company statements

____ 20.   Rental car agency statements

____ 21.   Statements to employers

____ 22.   Employment records

____ 23.   Lost wages record

____ 24.   Social Security records

____ 25.   Income tax records

____ 26.   Weather conditions on day of accident

____ 27.   Safety manuals

____ 28.   Warning literature

____ 29.   Vehicle maintenance and repair records

____ 30.   Consumer Product Safety Commission

____ 31.   Retrace steps of defendant and interview persons he came into contact with before accident (coworkers, bartenders, and so forth)

____ 32.   Credit bureau

____ 33.   Registrar of Voters

____ 34.   Docket search for involvement in other lawsuits

____ 35.   County recorder records

____ 36.   Fire marshall reports

____ 37.   Product standards

____ 38.   Advertising claims

§ 5.64 Skip Tracing

While the term skip tracing is normally associated with the tracking down of debtors who have reneged on payment of money owed to creditors, the techniques used in this method of investigation are often very helpful in locating witnesses who have disappeared for one reason or another. A word of caution should be inserted here:

The paralegal must adhere to a strict code of ethics, some of which may conflict with certain well-known skip tracing techniques or methods of gathering information. The paralegal should always be certain that any type of investigation is done within the bounds of good legal ethics.

For example, it is perfectly ethical to use a Social Security number as a starting place to determine your missing witness's probable home state, where he may have returned or has family ties. (See § **5.66**.) It is not, however, ethical to misrepresent who you are or why you are looking for that particular person. There are many ethical crossroads which the paralegal will approach during an investigation, and each decision must be handled on an individual basis. For the paralegal assimilating information for trial, where the information came from, or how it was acquired, can be just as vital as the information itself. If you have any doubt whatsoever that an investigation technique might be in conflict with American Bar Association (ABA) ethics, discuss it with your attorney before proceeding.

§ 5.65 Skip Tracing Checklist

The checklist which follows outlines some of the skip tracing information sources which paralegals may safely utilize in their jobs. Be aware that some of these sources may not be available in your state because of confidentiality laws. (Refer to § **5.39** for other ideas.)

____ **1.** Landlords
____ **2.** Neighbors
____ **3.** Moving companies
____ **4.** Professional or occupational licenses
____ **5.** Tax records
____ **6.** Divorce records
____ **7.** Previous employers
____ **8.** Social Security number (state of issuance is normally home state)
____ **9.** Voter registration records
____ **10.** Credit reporting agencies
____ **11.** Utility companies
____ **12.** Process servers
____ **13.** Cable TV companies

§ 5.66 Directory—Social Security Number Identification by State

If you have the Social Security number of the witness you are trying to locate, then this directory can be very helpful to you because the witness will often return to his home state. The first three numbers of a Social Security number may identify the state where the number was issued. Social Security numbers now are derived from the zip code in the mailing address on the application for a card. The numbers in this directory refer to the first three digits of a Social Security number.

001-003	New Hampshire	486-500	Missouri
004-007	Maine	501-502	North Dakota
008-009	Vermont	503-504	South Dakota
010-034	Massachusetts	505-508	Nebraska
035-039	Rhode Island	509-515	Kansas
040-049	Connecticut	516-517	Montana
050-134	New York	518-519	Idaho
135-158	New Jersey	520	Wyoming
159-211	Pennsylvania	521-524	Colorado
212-220	Maryland	525,585	New Mexico
221-222	Delaware	526-527	Arizona
223-231	Virginia	528-529	Utah
232-236	West Virginia	530	Nevada
237-246	North Carolina	531-539	Washington
247-251	South Carolina	540-544	Oregon
252-260	Georgia	545-573	California
261-267	Florida	574	Alaska
268-302	Ohio	575-576	Hawaii
303-317	Indiana	577-579	District of Columbia
318-361	Illinois	581-585	Puerto Rico, Guam,
362-386	Michigan		American Samoa,
387-399	Wisconsin		Philippine Islands
400-407	Kentucky	586	Guam, American Samoa,
408-415	Tennessee		Mariana Island
416-424	Alabama	588	Mississippi
425-428	Mississippi	589-595	Florida
429-432	Arkansas	596-599	Puerto Rico
433-439	Louisiana	600-601	Arizona
440-448	Oklahoma	602-626	California
449-467	Texas	627-645	Texas
468-477	Minnesota	646-647	Utah
478-485	Iowa	648-649	New Mexico

§ 5.67   Medical Records Services

There are two methods of obtaining medical records. The first is to send a request to each doctor and hospital with a copy of the signed authorization. The second, and more time-efficient, method, is to supply a medical records service with a copy of the authorization and the names of the hospitals and doctors and let them do the rest. The marvelous thing about using records services is that it eliminates the inevitable follow-up calls and, in most cases, you will receive the records sooner. The records service will not only prepare all subpoenas, depositions upon written questions, and all other pertinent documents, but also they will make sure the records are complete and they will follow up on them until they are delivered. That alone is worth whatever price the records cost. The services often have an ongoing rapport with the doctors' offices and will go out and copy the records so that the doctor's staff is not inconvenienced. Unfortunately, there are some jurisdictions which do not provide for the acquisition of records in this fashion. Be sure to check your jurisdiction's rules of civil procedure.

§ 5.68   Medical Reports

Occasionally it is helpful to request a medical report from a physician. If, after reviewing the medical records of a patient, you believe that one or more of the physician's opinions would be helpful to your case, send a written request to the doctor asking for a report. Doctors generally charge anywhere from $150 to $300 and more for doing these reports, but they are a dynamic settlement tool. They contain in a capsule what the doctor would testify to at the time of trial. Many times the opposing counsel will realize that the weight of the testimony would be an overwhelming obstacle at trial and serious settlement negotiations will ensue.

§ 5.69   Summarizing Medical Records

Today many of the megafirms in large cities are using registered nurses to summarize medical records in their personal injury cases. This trend emphasizes the importance of this portion of the discovery process. In actuality, summarizing medical records is not as intimidating as it might seem. There are several ways of going about it but, the important thing to keep in mind is that your attorney is not a physician. Many of the terms you see in the medical records are as foreign to him as they are to you. A summary filled with technical terms is as useless to him as trying to sift through the records themselves. Use a good comprehensive medical dictionary, and express technicalities in layman's terms.

The most useful format for a medical records summary is chronological to show a natural progression of the patient's recovery or relapse. It is helpful to begin the chronology with any significant medical history the patient may have, followed by the medical treatment received as a result of the injury or accident, including follow up treatment such as office appointments and physical therapy. This summary can take several forms. The most common form is a typed narrative with the date of the event or office visit on the left with a brief description of the patient's symptoms, complaints, diagnoses, and treatment on the right. A second, less common but, very effective and helpful visual form is to use an actual blank calendar and place the narrative information in the square of the corresponding date. A third method is to use a timeline, which is a straight line across the middle of a sheet of paper or at the bottom of the paper, with intersecting perpendicular lines, at the top of which are typed the dates and narrative events.

To complete a medical records summary (see **Table 5–1**) such as the chronological narrative summary you should begin by reading each and every page of the medical records, creating a three-column summary (date, provider, and description), and entering information into the three columns from each and every page. Do not try to put the summary into chronological order until you have summarized the information on every page.

The medical records summary is different from a deposition summary in that a deposition summary requires you only to condense the material and not draw conclusions or make judgments about what parts of the material are important. Medical records summaries, on the other hand, ONLY contain information regarding remarkable, or abnormal information. Therefore, things like normal temperature readings and the like are left out of the summary unless there is some significance to the fact that the findings are normal.

While you are doing the summary, it is important to remember who the document is being prepared for (the attorney), and that the document must be helpful to him and serve as a substitute for reading the entirety of the medical records until such time that he deems it necessary to do so. Therefore, be sure to define complex medical terms in parentheses behind the word, for example, mandibular (jaw).

While the volume of material being summarized is generally large, the actual summary itself is not. A summary of a typical three-day hospital stay for a patient generally does not exceed one to one and one-half typewritten, double-spaced pages, for example. This is accomplished by eliminating many of the chronological entries which are duplicative. Once you have put the information into chronological order, the duplicate entries will become evident, and may be culled out. This entire process can be done in one step by typing the material into sort columns on a word-processing package, and then sorting by chronological order.

INVESTIGATION

Table 5–1

How to Summarize Medical Records

Criteria—What elements are found in a good summary of medical records?	How do you achieve those elements?	Tips, techniques
Complex medical terms are defined in parentheses following the use of the medical term in the summary.	Look the medical term up in a good medical dictionary.	Remember that you are preparing the summary for a lawyer to read and that he may not have extensive medical background. He will need the complex terms defined for him in order to understand and be able to utilize the summary.
Records are summarized in chronological order.	Use date of occurrence or event rather than any later date on which the document itself had been prepared.	
Medical records are summarized in three columns: date, provider, and description.	Summarize everything in the record first and then cut and paste into chronological order or sort in chronological order on word processor.	Use date of the occurrence in date column, name of doctor or categorical entity making notes, that is, nurses' notes in provider column, and description of treatment or complaint in description column.

Include a summary of how the injury occurred, past medical history, and beginning diagnoses. |
| Remarkable, rather than unremarkable, data found in medical records are noted in the medical summary. | Refer to laboratory reports for interpretation of laboratory test results. | Medical record summaries analyze factors which tell a story of unusual events which help to assess facts or liabilities based on what is not normal about the health or physical well-being of the patient or claimant. |

Table 5–1
(continued)

Criteria—What elements are found in a good summary of medical records?	How do you achieve those elements?	Tips, techniques
Medical records summary is based on complete medical record.	Look for gaps or unexplained occurrences in chronology of records. When writing in medical records is illegible, try to refer to other parts of the record to interpret, or make arrangements to view the original.	Pay special attention to nurses' notes and compare them to doctors' notes and orders to see if orders were carried out properly.
Late entries or alterations in the record are notated.	Look for inconsistencies or things which do not appear to make sense.	
Original medical records are not written on or defaced during the summarization process.		
Summary contains a note of discharge instructions to the patient.		

§ 5.70   Medical Terms

Table 5–2 is a useful source for medical terms that will help you with the medical record summaries.

Table 5–2

Medical Terms

abdomin	abdomen	bar	weight	cec	bline
acid	sour	bi	two	cele	brain
aden	gland	blephar	eyelid	cent	puncture
alg	pain	brady	slow	cephal	head
ante	before	bucc	cheek	cerebr	cerebrum
anti	against	capit	head	cervic	neck
arthr	joint	carcin	cancer	chrondr	cartilage
aur	ear	cardi	heart	crani	skull

423

Table 5–2
(continued)

cut	skin	mast	breast	plas	shap
cyst	bladder	medi	middle	platy	broad
dent	tooth	mega	large	pleur	rib
diplo	two	melan	black	pne	breathing
dors	back	mening	membrane	pneumo	lung
dur	hard	ment	mind	pod	foot
dys	bad	micr	small	poly	too many
ect	outside	mon	only	pre	before
ede	swell	morph	form	pro	before
end	inside	my	muscle	proct	anus
erythr	red	myel	marrow	pseud	false
eu	good	narc	numbness	psych	mind
faci	face	nas	nasal	pub	adult
febr	fever	ne	new	pulmo	lung
flect	bend	necr	corpse	pur	pus
fract	break	neur	nerve	py	pus
galact	milk	nutri	nourish	pyel	pelvis
gangli	swelling	ocul	eye	pyl	orifice
gastr	stomach	odont	tooth	pyr	fire
glott	tongue	opthalm	eye	rachi	spine
glyc	sweet	or	mouth	radi	ray
grav	heavy	orchi	testicle	re	again
hem	blood	orth	straight	ren	kidneys
hemi	half	oss	bone	retro	backwards
hom	same	ost	bone	rhag	burst
hydr	water	ot	ear	rhin	nose
hyper	above	ov	egg	sanguin	blood
hypn	sleep	oxy	sharp	sarc	flesh
hypo	under	pachy	thicken	scler	hard
ile	intestines	para	beyond	scop	look at
infra	beheath	ped	child	sect	cut
inter	among	pend	hang	semi	half
intra	inside		down	sep	decay
is	equal	peps	digest	sial	saliva
ischi	hip	per	through	sin	hollow
junct	join	peri	around	somat	body
labi	lip	pha	speak	spers	scatter
laryng	windpipe	phag	eat	spher	ball
later	side	pharmac	drug	spin	spine
leuk	white	pharyng	throat	spirat	breathe
lig	tie	phleb	pain	splen	spleen
ly	dissolve	phob	fear	sten	narrow
lymph	water	phon	sound	ster	solid
macr	large	phos	light	strep	twist
mal	abnormal	phot	light	strict	draw tight
mamm	breast	phylac	guard	sub	under
man	hand	pil	hair	super	above

Table 5–2
(*continued*)

syn	together	thorac	chest	ur	urine
tact	touch	thromb	lump	vagin	sheath
tel	end	tom	cut	vas	vessel
tele	at a	tox	poison	vesic	bladder
	distance	trache	windpipe	vit	life
temper	temple	trich	hair	zo	life
tens	stretch	troph	nurture	zym	ferment
therap	treatment	tuber	node		
therm	heat	un	one		

§ 5.71 Checklist—Analyzing Medical Records

Refer to the elements in the following checklist to help you analyze medical records.

____ 1. Check all records for possible deletions and alterations.

____ 2. Pay particular attention to nurse's notes in hospital records, especially those mentioning that no physicians' orders have been received. Nurse's notes should also be scrutinized for details on patient's tolerances for pain, medication, and physician's orders of any type. Patients tolerating procedures very well in hospitals often give depositions later stating what extreme pain they were in during their hospital stay.

____ 3. Review records with impeachment in mind. They can be used to contradict other sworn testimony.

____ 4. Look for other possible claims in the medical records. Regardless of the subject matter of the original claim, other incidents may have taken place which give rise to other claims for relief. This is likewise true for mitigation of damages.

____ 5. In the case of hospital records, look for negligence based in under-staffing situations.

____ 6. Carefully review all elements of the medical record, matching actual test results to lab reports.

____ 7. Hospital records should contain the following information:

    ____ a. Admission history

    ____ b. Admission physical

    ____ c. Physician's notes

    ____ d. Physician's orders

    ____ e. Nurse's notes

    ____ f. Laboratory and x-ray reports

INVESTIGATION

____ g. Operative reports

____ h. Anesthesiologist's report

____ i. Recovery room report

____ j. Postoperative reports by physician and anesthesiologist

____ k. Medication records

____ l. Emergency room records

____ m. Physical therapy reports

____ n. Radiology reports

____ o. Vital signs charts and flow sheets

____ p. Consultation reports

____ q. Ambulance and transfer records

____ r. Discharge summary with physician's orders

____ s. Final diagnosis

____ 8. Compare physician's notes with nurse's notes from the same time period. Often the nurse's notes will be contradictory to a perfunctory satisfactory note made by the physician. This is especially important in medical malpractice claims.

____ 9. Check discharge summaries for instructions given to the patient. They may figure in malpractice claims when improper or incomplete treatment was rendered.

____ 10. Hospital bills should be reviewed carefully, matching equipment and supplies billed to the patient with other hospital records which may have not mentioned the use or administration of those supplies.

____ 11. Every person making notations in the record would be considered as a possible witness, whose qualifications are subject to review. Was that person qualified to do that particular job, or was he filling in during period of short or under-staffing?

§ 5.72 Medical Records Summary Guidelines

Use the following guidelines to help you prepare your medical summaries properly:

1. Define complex medical terms in parentheses following medical term in summary.
2. Summarize records in chronological order, using date of occurrence or event rather than any later date on which the document itself has been prepared.
3. Summarize medical records in three columns: date, provider, and description.
4. Notate remarkable, rather than unremarkable data in medical records.

5. Refer to laboratory reports for interpretation of laboratory test results.

6. Look for gaps or unexplained occurrences in chronology of records.

7. Determine completeness of medical records.

8. Pay special attention to nurses' notes and compare them to doctors' notes and orders to see if orders were carried out properly.

9. When writing in medical records is illegible, try to refer to other parts of the record to interpret, or make arrangements to view the original. If copies are illegible, contact the source for better copies or arrange to view the original.

10. Notate late entries or alterations in the record.

11. Summarize everything in the record first and then cut and paste into chronological order or sort in chronological order on word processing.

12. Use a good medical dictionary to verify spellings and define complex medical terms.

13. Do not write on or deface original medical records.

14. Include a summary of how the injury occurred, past medical history, and beginning diagnoses.

15. Make a note of discharge instructions to the patient.

§ 5.73 Obtaining Medical Records

Most law firms in major cities now use medical records services to obtain medical records for them, but many paralegals in many parts of the country must still accomplish this task independently. The documents which follow in §§ 5.74 and 5.78 are designed to facilitate that process.

In order to make medical records admissible evidence for use in a court of law, the records must be proven up in accordance with the rules of evidence for that appropriate state or federal court. Records obtained from a medical provider's custodian of records must be accompanied by an affidavit (**Form 5–23**) swearing to the authenticity of the records. The questions propounded in the Deposition Upon Written Questions are designed to elicit responses to prove up the medical records within the boundaries of the exceptions to the hearsay rule which allow the admissibility of business records when they have been kept in the normal course of business. Medical records acquired without subpoenas, affidavits, and depositions upon written questions are said to be in nonadmissible form. (See **Forms 5–19** through **5–23.**)

§ 5.74 Subpoena for Medical Records

FORM 5–19
SAMPLE SUBPOENA FOR MEDICAL RECORDS

SUBPOENA

The state of [state]

COUNTY OF [county]

To the sheriff, constable, or any other person authorized to serve and execute subpoenas as provided in Rule [citation], [state/federal] Rules of Civil Procedure.

Greetings:

You are hereby commanded to subpoena and summon the following witness: Custodian of Records for : [name of entity]

to be and appear before a Notary Public with [name of firm or medical records service with address] or their designated agent on the forthwith day of instanter at the office of the summoned witness

> to bring and produce for inspection and photocopying any RECORDS, INCLUDING, BUT NOT LIMITED TO, hospital records, employment records, insurance records, office notes, bills, reports and correspondence in the possession, custody or control of the said witness, and every such record to which the witness may have access, pertaining to:

[name of patient]

Then and there to give evidence at the instance of the Defendant in that certain Cause No. [case number] pending on the docket of the [type] Court of the [judicial district] Judicial District of [state], [county] County, [state], styled

[caption of case]

and there remain from day to day and time to time until discharged by me according to law.

Witness my hand, this the [date] day of [month], [20__].

[name of notary public]
Notary Public, Officer of the State of
[state] as provided in Rule [citation].
My Commission expires [date].

_____ Officer's Return [date]

§ 5.75 NOTICE TO COURT—DEPOSITION

CAME TO HAND [date], [20__], and executed by delivering same to the within named witness [name], and tendering all lawful fees on [date], [20__].

Notary Public, Officer of the state of [state] as provided in Rule [citation]. My Commission expires [date].

§ 5.75 Notice to Court—Deposition upon Written Questions

FORM 5–20
SAMPLE NOTICE TO COURT—DEPOSITION UPON WRITTEN QUESTIONS

Clerk of the [judicial district] District Court
[county] County Courthouse

NO. [case number]

[name]	)	IN THE DISTRICT COURT OF
	)	
Plaintiff	)	[county] COUNTY, [state]
	)	
vs.	)	[judicial district] JUDICIAL DISTRICT
	)	
[name]	)	
	)	
Defendant	)	

Re: Deposition by Written Questions to the Custodian of Records for:

[name of medical provider]

The witness was duly sworn and the transcript attached is a true record of the testimony given by the witness. The deposition was signed by the witness and returned on [date]. Changes made by the witness, if any in the transcript are attached or incorporated hereto. The original deposition transcript, together with copies of all exhibits, were provided to the attorney or party who asked the first question appearing in the transcript for safekeeping and use at trial in a manner specified by [state/federal] Rules of Civil Procedure [citation]. The charges for preparation of the completed deposition transcript and any copies of the exhibits are to be paid for by the attorney for the Defendant and total $[amount].

I certify that a true and correct copy of the foregoing instrument was mailed to the respective parties or attorneys of record, postage prepaid, or was hand delivered.

Date: [date]   By: [name]

Sworn to and subscribed before me on this the [date] day of [month], (20__).

_____

Notary Public in and for the State of
[state]

My Commission expires
[date]

§ 5.76 Deposition by Written Questions— Custodian of Records

FORM 5–21
SAMPLE DEPOSITION BY WRITTEN QUESTIONS— CUSTODIAN OF RECORDS

NO. [case number]

[name]	)	IN THE DISTRICT COURT OF
	)	
Plaintiff	)	[county] COUNTY, [state]
	)	
vs.	)	[judicial district] JUDICIAL DISTRICT
	)	
[name]	)	
	)	
Defendant	)	

DEPOSITION BY WRITTEN QUESTIONS PROPOUNDED TO
THE WITNESS, CUSTODIAN OF RECORDS FOR:

[name of medical provider]

1.   Please state your name, business address and occupation.

2.   Did you receive a subpoena to appear and bring with you for inspection and photocopying any and all records pertaining to [name of patient]?

3.   Are you able to identify these records as the original or true and correct photostatic copies of the originals?

4.   Were these records made and kept in the regular course of your business?

5.   In the regular course of your business, did the person who signed or otherwise prepared these records either have personal knowledge of the entries of these records

or obtain the information to make such records from sources who have such personal knowledge?

6. Are these records under your care, supervision, direction, custody or subject to your control?

7. Are these records made at or near the time of the act, event or condition recorded on these records or reasonably soon thereafter?

8. Were these records kept as described above?

9. Will you hand all of such records as outlined in the subpoena duces tecum to the Officer taking your deposition for inspection and photocopying?

_____
WITNESS, CUSTODIAN OF RECORDS

I, [name], A Notary Public in and for the State of [state] do hereby certify that the foregoing answers of the witness were made by the said witness and sworn to and subscribed before me. The records attached hereto are exact duplicates of the original records.

GIVEN UNDER MY HAND AND SEAL OF OFFICE on this the [date] day of [month], [20__].

_____
Notary Public in and for the State of [state]

My commission expires [date].

§ 5.77 Deposition by Written Questions—Custodian of Records re Medical Charges

FORM 5–22
SAMPLE DEPOSITION BY WRITTEN QUESTIONS—CUSTODIAN OF RECORDS RE MEDICAL CHARGES

NO. [case number]

[name]	)	IN THE DISTRICT COURT OF
	)	
Plaintiff	)	[county] COUNTY, [state]
	)	
vs.	)	[judicial district] JUDICIAL DISTRICT
	)	
[name]	)	
	)	
Defendant	)	

INVESTIGATION

DEPOSITION BY WRITTEN QUESTIONS PROPOUNDED TO THE WITNESS, CUSTODIAN OF RECORDS FOR:

[name of medical provider]

1.   Please state your name, business address, and occupation.

2.   Did you receive a subpoena to appear and bring with you for inspection and photocopying any and all records pertaining to [name of patient].

3.   Are you able to identify these records as the original or true and correct photostatic copies of the originals?

4.   Were these records made and kept in the regular course of your business?

5.   In the regular course of your business, did the person who signed or otherwise prepared these records either have personal knowledge of the entries on these records or obtain the information to make such records from sources who have such personal knowledge?

6.   Are these records under your care, supervision, direction, custody or subject to your control?

7.   Are these records made at or near the time of the act, event or condition recorded on these records or reasonably soon thereafter?

8.   Were these records kept as described above?

9.   Will you hand all of such records as outlined in the subpoena duces tecum to the Officer taking your deposition for inspection and photocopying?

10.   Please state the full amount of the charges in the treatment of the patient, [amount].

11.   Please state whether or not such charges are reasonable for like or similar services rendered in the vicinity in which they were incurred.

12.   Please state whether or not the charges are reasonable and the services performed were necessary for the proper care and treatment of the patient.

_____
WITNESS, CUSTODIAN OF
RECORDS

I, [name], A Notary Public in and for the State of [state] do hereby certify that the foregoing answers of the witness were made by the said witness and sworn to and subscribed before me. The records attached hereto are exact duplicates of the original records.

GIVEN UNDER MY HAND AND SEAL OF OFFICE on this the [date] day of [month], [20__].

Notary Public in and for the State of [state]

My Commission expires [date].

§ 5.78   Affidavit—Custodian of Records

FORM 5–23
SAMPLE AFFIDAVIT—CUSTODIAN OF RECORDS

NO. [case number]

[name]		) IN THE DISTRICT COURT OF
		)
	Plaintiff	) [county] COUNTY, [state]
		)
vs.		) [judicial district] JUDICIAL DISTRICT
		)
[name]		)
		)
	Defendant	)

AFFIDAVIT

RECORDS PERTAINING TO: [name of patient]

Before me, the undersigned authority, personally appeared [custodian of records], who by me being duly sworn, deposed as follows:

I, the undersigned, am over eighteen (18) years of age, of sound mind, capable of making this affidavit, and personally acquainted with the facts herein stated;

I am the CUSTODIAN OF RECORDS FOR: [name of medical provider].

Attached hereto are [number] pages of records. These said records are kept in the regular course of business, at the office of the above, for an employee, or representative, or a doctor, with personal knowledge of the act, event or condition, opinion, or diagnosis recorded to make the memorandum or record or to transmit information hereof to be included in such memorandum or record; and the memorandum or record was made at or near the time of the act, event or condition recorded or reasonably soon thereafter.

The records attached hereto are the originals or exact copies of the originals and nothing has been removed from the original file before making these copies. The attached records include all hospital records, employment records, insurance records, office notes, bills, reports and correspondence contained in the file on the named patient.

_____

Affiant

SUBSCRIBED AND SWORN TO BEFORE ME this the [date] day of [month], [20__].

Notary Public in and for the state of [state]

My commission expires [date].

§ 5.79 Sample Medical Records Summaries

This section contains three different examples of medical records summaries: A chronological narrative summary (**Form 5–24**), a calendar summary (**Figures 5–1** and **5–2**) and a time line summary (**Figure 5–3**).

FORM 5–24
SAMPLE CHRONOLOGICAL NARRATIVE SUMMARY

DATE	PROVIDER	DESCRIPTION
06/26/__	CCMH ER	Patient admitted to Central City Memorial Hospital after auto accident. Treated by ER physician Dr. Conrad and consultation by Dr. Herman.
		COMPLAINTS: Does not recall circumstances of accident. Tenderness right mandibular (jaw) region, lower back, and midcervical region. Multiple lacerations of the face, which were sutured, and abrasions of the arm and lower back.
		FINDINGS: X-rays show compression fracture of L1, 2 and 3. Lumbosacral corset ordered to be worn for six weeks. Fracture of nasal bones. Cervical spine normal except for minor discogenic degenerative changes at C6-7. Analgesics administered. To be followed in office.
06/29/__	Conrad	Patient discharged from CCMH.
08/01/__	Herman	Last office visit to Dr. Herman.

08/26/__	CCMH	Patient admitted to Central city Memorial Hospital for septal rhinoplasty (straightening of the nasal bridge) and excision of the scars of the eyelid and dermabrasion of forehead scars. Dr. Anderson did surgery.
08/30/__	CCMH	Patient discharged to be followed in Dr. Anderson's office.
10/__	Anderson	Patient doing fine. Sutures removed. Follow-up in six weeks.
11/25/__	Anderson	Patient has overgrowth of the cartilage over the nasal bridge. Also complaining of pain over the left T.M. joint (as opposed to right jaw pain on the day of the accident); may need further surgery to correct hump over nasal bridge and may need to see DMD or DDS for T.M. joint.
05/19/__	Baker	Patient presents complaining of lower back pain since accident. Referred to Dr. Koslow and back to Baker for diathermy treatments (electromagnetic heat to muscles).
05/27/__	Koslow	Found patient has diminished motion in the lumbar spine to approximately 40 degrees of a normal range of motion. "Remaining pain, discomfort and restriction of motion the patient now has represents his permanent disability of his low back." Patient is unlikely to improve.
06/10/__	Baker	Diathermy treatment.
06/11/__	Baker	Office Visit—no details.

June 20___

SUNDAY	MONDAY	TUESDAY	WEDNESDAY	THURSDAY	FRIDAY	SATURDAY
		1	2	3	4	5
6	7	8	9	10	11	12
13	14	15	16	17	18	19
20	21	22	23	24	25	26 Auto accident. Patient admitted to CCMN. Nasal fractures, right jaw tenderness, compression fracture L1, 2, and 3.
27	28	29 Patient discharged from CCMH	30			

Figure 5-1. Sample Calendar Summary of Medical Records (June).

436

August 20___

SUNDAY	MONDAY	TUESDAY	WEDNESDAY	THURSDAY	FRIDAY	SATURDAY
	1 Last office visit to Dr. Herman	2	3	4	5	6
7	8	9	10	11	12	13
14	15	16	17	18	19	20
21	22	23	24	25 Patient admitted to CCMH for septal rhinoplasty and plastic surgery on facial scars	26	27
28	29	30 Patient discharged from CCMH. To be followed in Anderson's office	31			

Figure 5-2.   Sample Calendar Summary of Medical Records (August).

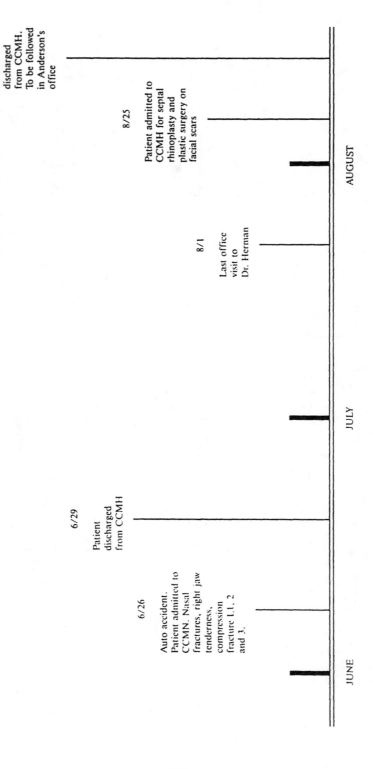

Figure 5-3. Sample Time Line of Medical Records.

§ 5.80 Expected Jury Verdict

Whether you are working on the plaintiff or defense side, preparation of your case is not complete without researching the expected jury verdict. There are several ways of doing this, and it may be best to utilize all of them to gain the most complete information available from which to make an educated determination of what can be expected in your particular case. Your county law library probably subscribes to a loose-leaf service which lists recent jury verdicts with a small abstract of the case facts and the corresponding awards. This service will further break down jury award statistics by specific injury or damage and by area of the country.

Another way to research jury verdicts is by studying the court's records in your jurisdiction for decisions on similar facts or instances. LEXIS is also a wonderful tool for finding information in this regard. NEXIS, also, will lead you to newspaper and periodical articles on the subject. The next step to complete the process would be research of newspaper libraries in the appropriate jurisdiction.

Your state or local bar journals and legal newspapers are mediums you should monitor for this information. You may find it helpful to begin a scrapbook of clippings that appear in these pieces of literature and in your local newspapers for future reference.

Special attention should also be paid to trends in certain jurisdictions where juries tend to be extremely oriented in either, the plaintiff or defendant direction, or in which the awards are abnormally high or low.

All of the above factors should be considered when trying to arrive at a projected jury verdict in your case. Demographics play a very important part in decisions of juries. You may want to consider the employment of the consultant who specializes in jury selection psychology if you feel it is warranted in your case. These consultants are being used with increasing frequency by law firms across the nation, and with incredible success.

§ 5.81 Preservation of Evidence— In General

In order to draft forms effectively, the paralegal must assist counsel in insuring that all possible litigation evidence is preserved for a possible trial. This is essential in order to be able to draft settlement requests, pleadings, motions to produce, interrogatories, and all discovery devices.

§ 5.82 —Property Damage Photographs

Photographs of the property damage in the case are most important to preserve as evidence. In automobile litigation, for example, the photographs should include all areas of damage to the car, whether or not related to the incident. Areas that are related should be photographed in such a way that the full extent of impact can be visualized. For example, many rear-end collisions when photographed directly from behind seem to be very minor. However, the same vehicle when photographed from the side, at an angle, may show greater deformation and damage to the vehicle. Likewise, damage underneath the vehicle or to the interior should be photographed.

At least one of the photographs should show the vehicle license plate and any manufacturer, emblems, or names.

If there is an issue regarding hit-and-run or identification of another vehicle, then close-up photographs are necessary to document the paint transfer and scrapes.

Depending on the budget established for the case and the seriousness of injury, interior photographs may be the most important evidence to corroborate the client's injuries and support the reconstruction expert's opinion. This is particularly crucial if the expert was unable to inspect the vehicle.

Interior marks, such as a bending or deformation of the door panels, dashboards, headliners, frame around the doors or the windows, rear-view mirrors, instrument panel, steering wheel, under the dashboard, on the pedal of the accelerators, gearshift, and seat may be used by an engineer or biomechanical expert to determine the kinematics (the study of motion and forces) of the occupant and related injuries.

Today, many automobile cases will involve seat belt issues. Photographs of the type of seat belts that were available both to the driver and passengers should be documented. If the seat was loosened or came off its track, photographs of both the seat and the attachment mechanism, such as the nut and bolt, are critical to preserve evidence.

Also, mechanical damage may be an issue in the case. For example, in one case the police officer checked the brakes and they were not functioning after the accident. Photographs were taken showing the severing of the brake line, that the master cylinders were without fluid, and that fluid had splattered over the entire engine compartment.

Note: In an uninsured motorist hit-and-run case where identification of the other driver and vehicle are not obtained, there must be contact to establish the client's claim.

Illustration: In one case, a claimant alleged slight contact on her driver's door. A very slight indentation was captured in a photograph. However, the indentation could have been caused by another car door hitting the side of the car in a parking lot. Due to the severity of the injuries, the car was maintained in a storage yard for a few years. Both sides agreed to use an accident reconstruction expert. Upon inspection, there was a paint transfer found underneath the driver's side rear-view mirror that was the same color as the hit-and-run vehicle. Also, there was a slight transfer of the same color paint from the vehicle that was hit on the front of the hit-and-run vehicle that had been totally collapsed and folded in. Only upon a very careful inspection was the paint located and photographed.

§ 5.83   —Photographs and Videos of the Scene

Photographs of the scene are important to fully understand the accident. These photographs are also valuable in reviewing the accident scene with the client, who may or may not remember all of the important events and surrounding landmarks or objects, number of lanes, speed limit signs, or lighting conditions. These photographs should be reviewed with the client before the client gives statements, depositions, or testimony at trial, since it will enhance the client's confidence and credibility.

Photographs taken immediately will preserve the condition of the scene of the accident. Subsequent changes to the scene of the accident may occur, such as re-asphalting, thereby changing the coefficient of friction. Repainting or relining of the lanes of traffic, turn lanes, and/or changing the speed limit signs, signals, markings, and stop signs may also change the scene.

For example, in one case, at arbitration, the defendant claimed that the client had a stop sign in his direction of travel. This was contradicted by photographs that were taken immediately after the incident indicating no stop sign at that location. After the incident, a stop sign was installed and posted in the client's direction of travel. The defendant was impeached by the photographs.

Videotapes of the scene can be quite effective. Videotapes may depict a re-enactment of the incident, traffic flow, lighting conditions, and defective or deceptive conditions. Videotapes are much like watching television and capture the full attention of the viewer. Once viewed, it is hard to dispute the perception and impact of the video. Additionally, videotapes with sound can place the trier of fact at the scene of the accident, just as though perceiving the actual event.

§ 5.84   —Chain of Custody

Great care must be taken in preserving evidence in the chain of custody so that evidence is not lost, changed, or disputed as unreliable. Review all evidence considerations regarding the chain of custody and foundation needed to introduce the evidence at trial. For example, if a part was removed from a vehicle, the person dismantling and removing the part will be a percipient witness in proving foundation and authentication of that part.

Caution: Given the opportunity, your opponent will question the chain of custody, whether or not there have been changes or modifications to the evidence. It is good practice to have the expert who is going to testify to that evidence, or other reliable person, maintain and store the evidence. Also, that person should take photographs, videotapes, or use other identifying procedures to enable him or her to testify as to the quality of the preservation of the evidence and the chain of custody. For example, in a vehicular case where criminal investigation has been pursued, the local authorities will maintain the evidence in a storage locker. This can prove quite helpful at time of trial in the civil case. The police officer in uniform will testify to having maintained the evidence from the time of the incident without any changes.

§ 5.85 —Notice to Maintain and Preserve Evidence

Critical evidence may be lost, destroyed, or dismantled if arrangements are not made to maintain and preserve it. With cooperative individuals, a confirming letter should be sent indicating the importance and responsibility of the custodian to preserve evidence in proper condition. With uncooperative individuals or entities, notice of potential liability regarding spoilation of evidence, including punitive damages, should be sent, such as when an automobile is being stored by a dismantler or an insurance company facility. They may be tempted to remove parts or destroy the vehicle, unless immediate action is taken to place those individuals on notice that they are destroying evidence in a potential or pending lawsuit.

Both telephone and written notice should be communicated to the persons in charge of their obligation to maintain and preserve evidence. They must be told that if the evidence is lost, altered, or spoiled, they will be held accountable. Spoilation of evidence can give rise to a cause of action in tort and for punitive damages.

Once placed on notice, any sensible facility or insurance carrier should abide by such notification and avoid the risk of exposure regarding a cause of action for spoilation of evidence. However, without proper communication and written documentation, evidence may be altered, changed, and destroyed.

§ 5.86 Practice Tips

The investigation state is a wonderful, exhilarating time of a lawsuit. All of us probably have a little frustrated detective blood in us, and it is easy to get carried away with the excitement. Always keep your primary goal in mind and try not to stray too far from the issue at hand.

Develop a personal rapport with personnel at the agencies you contact most frequently. You will find that it will be easier and faster to get your information from someone who knows you and understands how you work. Be honest with the people you deal with. Do not try to be cagey; it will only cause them to distrust you and hinder your efforts to obtain the needed information. You will make better contacts and get more cooperation by being honest.

The most important aid to you in this process is the personal files you develop containing forms and information on how to request information. Even if you become aware of something along those lines and do not ever anticipate having a need for that information in the future, save it and put it into a file where you may retrieve it easily later. You just never know what type of case you will be working on next and what you will need to use.

Become familiar with the Freedom of Information Act and the types of information available to you pursuant to that act. You may also want to purchase a copy of

§ 5.86   PRACTICE TIPS

The United States Government Manual, which is available from government bookstores and is searchable online at www.access.gpo.gov/nara/browse-gm.html. This wonderful source contains information about every governmental agency that exists today. Another excellent tool is The National Directory put out by Southwestern Bell. It lists telephone numbers and addresses for thousands of agencies and other helpful information on a state-by-state basis.

Most importantly, look for links in the investigative materials you gather. Think of them as pieces of a jigsaw puzzle and try to figure out how they fit together. If that thought process produces a theory, investigate it. Be thorough, confirm your sources, put facts together logically, and most of all, have fun doing it!

CHAPTER 6

DOCUMENT CONTROL

§ 6.1 Introduction

If you have ever experienced the frustration that comes from trying to locate a document that has been misplaced in a file, you realize the importance of document control. Document control not only gives your files organization for easy document retrieval but also provides a method of determining which documents, if any, are missing. How often have you looked for something that was never there in the first place?

There are any number of acceptable methods for organizing and controlling documents. The important thing is to choose one of them and be consistent with it. Do not let documents mount up before integrating them into the filing system. That is a surefire way to lose something. Every day, as documents become available, see that they are indexed or abstracted immediately and made part of a file. The one hazard to stay away from is setting up a system that does not follow a logical, legal thinking process. The system is only as good as its ease of retrieval. Because several different people will probably have to access these documents, the logic used should be universal.

§ 6.2 Document Organization—Chronological Order

Any time you accumulate documents, chronological progression is an acceptable organization method. The documents with the most current dates should be in the front, or on top, of the file with dates descending behind them. It may also be helpful to designate separations of calendar years in some fashion, such as ending one file and starting another. Chronological groupings tell a story, and are often more helpful than other types of files for that reason. Even if a different filing system is decided on, chronological files may be desired as an auxiliary file. This can be done by duplicating the hard copies in the file or by creating a chronological index. (See **Form 6–1.**)

FORM 6–1
SAMPLE CHRONOLOGICAL INDEX

Date of Document	Document Number	Primary Addressee	Author	Description

§ 6.3 —by Player

Much the same as witness files, these file are set up to contain all documents pertaining to, authored by, addressed to, or copied to a player in the lawsuit. Groupings of this nature will give you an idea of what that person knew about a particular issue at a particular time. These files may contain background information as well as documents obtained by document production. Here again, the files may be subfiles to a main file that are organized in a different fashion. The files can be duplicated or simulated by the creation of an index. (See **Form 6–2.**)

FORM 6–2
SAMPLE FILE INDEX BY PLAYER

Name of Player	Document Number	Date of Document	Is Player Author, Addressee, CC'd, or Mentioned in Document?	Description

§ 6.4 —by Issue

More complicated cases may call for organizing the documents by issue. In some instances, this organization becomes even more complex as the issues overlap or are difficult to determine. This is a process, however, that you are inevitably going to encounter in preparation both for trial and the search for evidence. Sometimes it makes more sense to group documents by issue than to integrate them into a larger file. If the integrity or continuity of the documents will be interrupted by the separation of the file, or if the documents become unintelligible when separated, it is probably a good idea to keep them together. (See **Form 6–3.**)

FORM 6–3
SAMPLE FILE INDEX BY ISSUE

Issue	Document Number	Document Date	Primary Addressee	Author	CC's	Description

§ 6.5 —by Logical Groupings

The integrity of certain files is often more important than breaking them down by player or issue. For example, if you receive a file on your client's work-related injury from the state disability office, you will want to keep that file together, grouping it under an identifying name. The same is true of a highway department file on the history of accidents at a certain location. You will be able to identify those files easily which should remain intact. Remember that the most important thing in document control is to set up a logical, consistent system to aid in your quick and easy retrieval of documents. (See **Form 6–4.**)

FORM 6–4
SAMPLE FILE INDEX BY ORIGINAL FILE NAME

Origin of File (Party or Agency)	Name of Original File	Document Number	Date of Document	Author	Addressee	Description

§ 6.6 Indexing Documents—Necessary Elements

Before preparing an index to any documents, you must first determine what your needs will be for retrieving that information at a later date. At the very least, the following information should be derived from each document and listed in the index:

1. Document number
2. Date
3. Author
4. Addressee
5. CCs (who was sent a copy of the document)
6. Description.

If you are lucky enough to have access to a computer or word processor, setting these columns up across the top of the page with the document numbers running down the left side will allow you to be able to sort the documents by column. This will give you the ability to reprint an entire index, limiting the scope to only those issues, names, or dates you are searching for at that time. If you do not have computer capability, an index done in this fashion will at least make a manual search easier. Be sure to keep a master index away from the file so that you will have a copy in case the index becomes separated from the file.

§ 6.7 —Narrative Description

The narrative description should go directly to the main point of the document in a clear and concise manner. The description by necessity should be brief and follow the same rules as a good journalistic piece of writing: who, what, when, where, and why. The index is used as a device for quickly locating possible relevant documents, so the description should contain enough verbiage to make possible an intelligent decision as to the relativity of the document. If you get too wordy in your description, however, it loses its effectiveness.

§ 6.8 —Cross-Indexing

As you are indexing the documents, be alert for documents either that may be relevant to more than one issue or that you may want to look for in more than one category as the case progresses. It is more expedient to cross-index a document at the beginning than it is to try to rely on your memory to locate that document later. How many times have you remembered that you saw a document somewhere in those stacks and stacks of paper that you think addressed the particular issue you are now researching, but you cannot remember where you filed it? Save yourself the countless hours of frustration by cross-indexing properly at the outset.

§ 6.9   Programming for Document Retrieval

In automated systems for document retrieval, the programming of the information is vitally important to the quality of the retrieval of the information. There are two major systems of automated document retrieval. One system is using your firm's in-house personal computers and litigation support software. The software is available from a variety of legal litigation support software firms. In this system, the programming is done in-house by paralegals and attorneys.

The second system is a shared document retrieval system, which is commonly used in complex litigation with multiple defendants. In this system, the documents are usually abstracted and the data input by the computer firm setting up the system. In some instances, a selected team of attorneys from the lawsuit will meet to review and abstract the documents. The documents are then loaded into the system by the computer firm. In these instances, all parties to the case need to have compatible computers with phone modems to connect into the system.

You can also opt to hire a litigation support firm to program your in-house system. The foremost question in your mind should be whether the issues can be decided by an outside firm or whether that is best left to your in-house staff.

§ 6.10   —Deciding the Issues

Deciding the issues is the most difficult part of the whole document retrieval process. It is very difficult to determine early in the case which issues may rise to unexpected importance at a later time. There will be, of course, those major issues which are glaringly obvious from the outset, but there are also "sleeper" issues which will crop up at a later date. The best way to handle this problem is to live by the old adage that two heads are better than one. Having a brainstorming session with the attorneys and paralegals on the case will invariably produce a more complete list of possible issues than could be produced by one person alone.

§ 6.11   —Document Profile Form

The form that follows is typical of the forms used for abstracting documents in preparation for programming the retrieval system. If the form is properly filled out, all the needed information will be available to aid the input process. Each document should be given an identifying number and have a document profile form filled out for it. (See **Form 6–5.**)

FORM 6–5
SAMPLE DOCUMENT PROFILE FORM

DOCUMENT NO. _____

AUTHORS _____

DATE OF DOCUMENT (year, month, day) _____

EXHIBIT NO. (if applicable) _____

TITLE OR SUBJECT OF DOCUMENT _____

_____

PROGRAMMER'S NAME _____

REVIEWER'S NAME _____

ISSUES RELATIVE: (PREDETERMINED)

1) ☐ (for example, damages/liability) _____   4) ☐ _____

2) ☐ _____   5) ☐ _____

3) ☐ _____   6) ☐ _____

PERSONS MENTIONED IN DOCUMENT:
1) _____   4) _____

2) _____   5) _____

3) _____   6) _____

KEYWORDS:
1) _____   4) _____

2) _____   5) _____

3) _____   6) _____

REVIEWER'S REMARKS: _____

_____

_____

§ 6.12 —Programming Checklist

Short of scanning the full text of each document into your retrieval system, the most reliable way of ensuring consistency and completeness in your programming is to use the following checklist as a guideline when abstracting a document. The checklist is meant to provide a consistent minimum of information.

____   1.   Document identifying number
____   2.   Author(s) of document
____   3.   Date of document origination
____   4.   Exhibit numbers where applicable
____   5.   Addressees of document
____   6.   Names of person cc'd on document
____   7.   Title or subject of document
____   8.   ALL issues addressed by document
____   9.   Names of persons mentioned in document
____ 10.   Keywords mentioned in document
____ 11.   Name of person who reviewed and abstracted document
____ 12.   Name of programmer
____ 13.   Reviewer's remarks about document

§ 6.13   Document Production

Document Production does not have to be a dirty word, or phrase, as the case may be. In fact once you become comfortable with the procedures of a document production, you will begin to enjoy them immensely. This is the stage of the game where you can actually roll up your sleeves and discover pieces of information that can lead you to wonderful clues and aids to preparing your case. It is an opportunity to show how valuable a paralegal can be and it can provide you with a sense of accomplishment. The following sections (**§§ 6.14–6.24**) will take the mystery out of the document production process.

If at all possible, know what to expect before you arrive at the production site. You will want to be well equipped and prepared. Do not be caught off-guard by thinking that this production is one which you will slip in between summarizing that deposition which is due this morning and the motion which needs to be drafted by tomorrow morning only to walk in and be faced with a room full of boxes and an impossible task to perform in the allotted time period. Also, beware of other people's interpretations of how large the production is. Ask for specifics. Your attorney's idea of a roomful of documents may be three boxes, but you will know right away that three boxes are approximately 6000 pages, if those boxes are full, because the average box holds around 2000 pages. You may want to keep that formula to yourself and maintain some of the mystique in your ability to estimate production size off your cuff! Don't you just love it when they say, "How do YOU DO that?" with such admiration in their voices!

Before you go on-site to the production, have a plan for reviewing and copying the documents. Are you going to give a cursory review to the documents, estimate their numbers, and then request copies of all documents, or are you going to do an extensive review of all documents and request only those documents which you think are responsive to the requests? You should also know before you leave your office how the copying of the documents is to be handled. Are you going to have the documents sent out to be copied? Is the producing party going to be making the copies at their office after you have designated those documents you want copied? Are you going to be allowed to make the copies of the documents yourself? If the producing party is making the copies, are you going to be able to take the copies with you at the close of the production, or will you have to wait several days or weeks before receiving the copies? The answers to these questions will have a great impact on how you do your initial review of the documents. If the copies are not going to be available to you for some time, you will most certainly want to take more extensive notes at your review. You may also want to spend a great deal of time taking notes on which document are being produced and which you have ordered copies of to compare with the documents you actually receive days or weeks later. If at all possible, know whether the bulk of the documents are single-paged letters, or hundred-page contracts. It will make a big difference in how long the production will take to finish and what information you hope to find.

Remember that you are looking for documents that respond to specific request made by your firm in its request for production of documents. You will have to make judgments as to whether the documents designated by the producing party actually are responsive to the requests or whether they are incomplete. The same forms which you use to index or abstract documents will be helpful to you at the production site for recording information from the documents. (See §§ **6.19** and **6.23** for further information.)

§ 6.14   Document Numbering

After the documents have been organized in the fashion that you feel will be most helpful, the documents should be numbered consecutively for identification.

The most common device for this process is called a Bates numbering stamp. Not only can the numbers be adjusted to begin where you desire, there is also a switch on the back of the hand-held stamp which allows you to change the number of times the machine will stamp the same number consecutively. This feature is extremely useful when you have two or more duplicate sets that must be stamped, as when you must produce a set of documents and wish to retain one for your records. The numbers will provide a positive means of identification which is extremely useful in evidentiary proceedings.

§ 6.15   Preassigning Document Production Numbers

When dealing with litigation in which you expect large numbers of documents to be produced, it is usually helpful to work with all parties in the lawsuit to distribute number assignments for each party's document production. This will avoid the possibility of each party numbering its documents with the same numbers which can cause many problems later on in the litigation. These preassigned numbers can be used not only in document productions but also for any documents which are to be introduced as exhibits at depositions.

In order to facilitate a preassigned numbering system such as this, it is necessary to be able to determine with some accuracy how many documents each party is likely to produce. For example, if you believe a total of 1000 documents will be produced by each of five parties, the following numbering system would apply:

Party A	1-1000
Party B	1001-2000
Party C	2001-3000
Party D	3001-4000
Party E	4001-5000

§ 6.16   Color-Coding Document Production Files

Each lawsuit contains files which grow in size as the case progresses, and efficient management of those files is imperative. The paralegal is the one most often charged with the responsibility of the file organization and maintenance, and most often is the one to develop the systems which are used for that purpose. It is to your benefit to develop a number of ways to keep the integrity of the file and to facilitate the use of the file contents during the progression of the lawsuit.

Standardization is one of the most helpful tools used in file management. (See **Chapter 3.**) Easy recognition and identification of file contents is another extremely helpful tool to employ. The paralegal organizes the file not only for his or her own personal use during the lawsuit, but also for the use of anyone else in the lawfirm who has occasion to work on the file. It stands to reason that if the same type of standardization is used on all files, anyone in the office will have no trouble locating a necessary document in the file or realizing its source of significance. Color is one of the simplest and most visually effective ways of accomplishing this. For example, if all files containing original client documents are red, then everyone in the office becomes familiar with such files and realizes their significance. The chances of the misplacement or misuse of those files becomes greatly diminished. Choose a color which will serve for the primary opposing party in all cases, and use this color to code all files containing documents produced by that party. Other colors may be employed to code the files of each additional party producing documents in the case. Check your office supply catalog for available colors of file folders or file labels. You may place a color-coded chart using colored dots to designate the color for each party in the file or post the chart nearby for easy reference.

§ 6.17 Client Documents

No matter what kind of case you are working on, the client will generally come to the office with documents in hand. Sometimes the documents will be given to you in a neat organized manner, and sometimes they will be turned over in what can best be described as mass mayhem in a box. Your first order of business is to put the documents into some sort of logical order, if they are not already organized, and to prepare them for indexing and labeling.

Remember that the documents brought to your office by the client are his personal property. Often they are one-of-a-kind originals that will be used during the course of the litigation and then returned to the client at the close of trial. Therefore, it is imperative that you treat the documents as originals. Do not spindle, mutilate, hole-punch, number, tear, or deface them in any way. The safest way to handle the documents is to make working copies and put the originals away under lock and key for safekeeping until they must be produced at time of trial. If you must keep the originals in the working file, seal them in manila envelopes or at the very least, put them into color-coded file folders with the word **ORIGINALS** stamped in very large red letters on the outside of the file folders. You are trying to prevent the unwitting disfigurement or unexplained misplacement of any of the client's original files by firm members during the course of the litigation. Therefore, the best policy is to keep only working copies in the file so that no one will mistake the originals for working copies.

If the documents do not arrive in some logical and congruent fashion, devise some sort of order for them before numbering and indexing them. If the documents of a business case are in the order in which they came out of the business files, it is best to leave them in that order, as WHERE the documents were found is just as important as the fact that they exist. You may be asked later to produce the documents and to declare their source.

If there is no order to the documents whatsoever and it is left up to you to devise one, it is best to use the most logical groupings and sequencing possible. Contract documents, for example, should be kept together, as should correspondence or the entire contents of a supervisor's personal files. This type of logical grouping will make it easier to index and identify documents throughout the case. After the documents have been organized, color-coded, and put into file folders, it is time to number the working copies to facilitate the indexing.

§ 6.18 Indexing Client Documents

Once you have determined how to organize the client's documents, continue to handle them as if they were a document production from another party. Index the documents using the methods discussed in §§ **6.6** through **6.8**. Not only do you want to preserve an accurate record of the documents which your client has given or loaned to you, but you also will want to put the information into a format which will facilitate determination of responsive documents for purposes of production.

You will also want to begin to identify those documents which you determine to be privileged so that they can either be pulled from the file and placed in a separate location to avoid inadvertent production or identified in some fashion which accomplishes the same end. Remember that you will have to produce a log of privileged documents along with the documents you are producing in order to show which documents may be responsive, but are being withheld for privilege.

The same index which you have initially prepared for your client documents should be done in such a way that it will be helpful to you throughout the case in identifying facts for evidentiary purposes.

§ 6.19   Document Index Forms

The following form (**Form 6–6**) is a good guideline to use when indexing or abstracting documents. After the documents are organized and numbered with a Bates stamp, you should create an index listing the document number, the date of the creation of the document, the person or entity to whom the document was addressed or for whom it was prepared, the name of the person who authored or prepared the document, and a brief description of the substantive content of the document. This last entry is very important because you will be using it later to decide if the document relates to whatever research you are conducting at the time.

FORM 6–6
SAMPLE DOCUMENT INDEX FORM

Document #	Date	Primary Addressee	Author	Description

§ 6.20   Monitoring Document Productions

Essentially there are two ways of producing documents. One is to make copies of the requested documents and to send them to the opposing party. The other way is to arrange for the opposing party to review the documents at a prearranged location. Under the Rules of Civil Procedure, this option is allowed to the producing party when large numbers of documents are going to be produced. The process is sometimes called inspection and copying. In these instances, you are often asked to sit in and monitor the review to be sure the integrity of the documents is preserved. This is done frequently in large cases of complex litigation, when document productions may go on for a month or longer. It is also the paralegal's role in this case not only to assist the opposing party by making copies of those documents he wishes to take with him but also to act as a liaison for your firm and to clarify any questions which might arise.

When asked to monitor a document production, you may be told that you are not to carry any other work into the production area with you, such as a deposition you need to summarize, and so forth. This is generally the rule for two reasons: (1) because you are to pay very close attention to what is going on during the document production and (2) because of the preservation of the confidentiality of another client's file or attorney work product. What, then, are your responsibilities during this production? The Document Production Checklist (**Form 6–7**) should be useful in helping you to understand your responsibilities and to make document productions progress smoothly and efficiently.

§ 6.21   Document Production Checklist— Paralegal Responsibilities

____ 1. Arrange to use the conference room or office. Be sure comfortable seating and sufficient working space are available. Be sure the room is equipped with a telephone.

____ 2. Arrange for office personnel to make copies for the opposing counsel if you are not permitted to leave the room during the production.

____ 3. Arrange for a tray of coffee, water, soft drinks, and ice to be available throughout the production so you will not have to leave the room to obtain refreshments.

____ 4. Arrange for another paralegal to relieve you from time to time so that you will be able to return to your office to check your messages, make phone calls, or use the restroom.

_____ 5. Arrange the boxes of documents around the perimeter of the room or on top of the table. Remove the box tops, and be sure that no markings on the boxes or files reflect notes or opinions of your firm which should be protected under the attorney work-product privilege. For example, if a box is designated HOT DOCUMENTS or TRIAL EVIDENCE, replace the box with a clean one for the production.

_____ 6. If you wish opposing counsel to mark the documents for copying in a certain way, such as with paper clips, provide an ample supply for his use. Supply a small number of pens or pencils if needed.

_____ 7. Do not answer substantive questions about the production or the case if asked by opposing counsel. Refer all such questions to your supervising attorney. Watch out for questions such as "Are these all the documents that pertain to the contract negotiations?" Attorneys try to get paralegals to give them information. If a paralegal said, "These are *all* the documents," it would be unauthorized practice of law, besides beyond the scope of his or her job.

_____ 8. Do not engage in more than a cursory amount of casual conversation with opposing counsel. Show by your demeanor that you are a professional and are there to perform a specific job function. You should always be courteous, but not overly friendly.

_____ 9. As opposing counsel is through with each box of documents, return the documents to their box and original order before the volume of documents displaced from their boxes makes it impossible to do so.

_____ 10. Clarify to opposing counsel the hours which he will be allowed to remain at the document production site. If he is to leave for a lunch break at the same time you do, make that point clear to him at the beginning of the session. You should have already discussed starting and stopping times with your supervising attorney. Determine in advance whether opposing counsel will be allowed to stay past normal office hours to work on the document production. As you must stay as long as the production is in progress, determine what the production hours are, especially if you have outside obligations. Never leave the hours up to the opposing counsel, because this leaves you at his mercy.

_____ 11. Last, update your Document Production Log (see **Form 6–7**) so you will have an accurate record of all documents produced and copied by opposing counsel.

DOCUMENT CONTROL

§ 6.22   Document Production Log

FORM 6–7
SAMPLE DOCUMENT PRODUCTION LOG

Name of Reviewing Party	Date of Review	Document Nos. of Documents Requested by Reviewer	Initial Document Production Monitor	Comments

§ 6.23 Off-Site Document Production

When the number of documents produced in a case is extremely large, the chances are good that you will be reviewing the documents off-site. Many paralegals are becoming specialists in out-of-town document productions and are sent out-of-town every time their firm is involved in such a case. It takes an extremely organized person to be able to go into an office or warehouse miles away from her own office and come home with an organized, relative, and meaningful group of documents. The tendency, of course, when there are multitudes of documents, is to walk into a room, gasp with shock, and immediately order copies of everything. After all, if opposing counsel produced them all, they all must be relevant, right? Wrong! Chances are that the opposing counsel did not want to go through all those documents either. The privileged documents have most likely been removed, but unless you have the file space and your client does not mind spending thousands of dollars for copies of irrelevant documents, you must sit down and go through every single piece of paper.

The fact that the production is far away from home means that supplies must be taken with you and arrangements made for copies in an unfamiliar town. The final challenge is shipping the boxes of documents home. Use the checklist in **§ 6.24** for making sure that you have remembered everything before you leave on an off-site document production. As your own experience grows with these types of productions, add to the list or modify it with the hints that you have found helpful.

Finally, be sure to speak with different vendors and give them a chance to quote on the copying job. Many vendors now are going out-of-town to do document productions, and this part alone can save you time, money, and headaches. Remember that the culling out and analyzation of the documents takes much more time than the copying in most cases, so give yourself and your team a head start before you bring on the copy machines or you will be paying for idle time.

§ 6.24 Off-Site Document Production Checklist

I. To Do Before Departure:

____ 1. Find out estimated number of documents being produced.
____ 2. Have several vendors give you a firm bid for copying the documents
____ 3. Find competent temporary help agencies in the production town.
____ 4. Find a good office supply store near the production site and arrange for credit.
____ 5. Find suitable lodging close to the production site.
____ 6. Find out if you will have sufficient room for your needs at the production site or if you will have to rent additional space for on-site copying.
____ 7. Make sure you will be allowed to take the documents off-site for copying before you arrange to do so.

	8.	Find out what hours you will be allowed to work at the site.
	9.	Arrange for computer hookups.
	10.	Make arrangements for shipping office supplies to the site.
	11.	Make arrangements for shipping the boxes to your office.
	12.	Find a local establishment to rent copy machines from.

II.   Things To Take With You:

	1.	A copy of the pleadings.
	2.	A good secretary, if possible.
	3.	Pens, pencils.
	4.	Staples, staplers, staple removers, paper clips, rubber bands.
	5.	Huge supply of stick-on notes.
	6.	File folders, labels.
	7.	Archive boxes.
	8.	Notebooks to put your finished indices in.
	9.	Computer and supplies.
	10.	Huge supply of legal pads.
	11.	Marking pens.
	12.	Rulers.
	13.	A sense of humor.

§ 6.25   Practice Tips

Document control is not a difficult task. You can easily build a reputation for yourself as a dynamic paralegal by mastering this aspect of your profession. The magic words that make up this mastery are consistency, logic, organization, and persistence. The persistence comes into play when you have to train your attorneys to replace in the proper position documents they have removed, and to force yourself to keep up with the documents on a daily basis so that they will not snowball and become a distasteful chore.

When organizing your document system, be sure to consider how your fellow paralegals and attorneys will look for each document. The best systems are those in which a person not familiar with the file can readily locate what he needs without your assistance. It is by no means a feather in your cap to produce a system which only you know how to use. To be successful, think where each document should be filed for easy retrieval.

CHAPTER 7

INSURANCE DEFENSE

§ 7.1   Introduction

Insurance defense work lends itself well to the use of tailored forms that streamline the personal injury defense case. An important part of your job as an insurance defense paralegal is to keep both the insurer and its insured informed. You will find the checklists and memoranda in this section helpful in retrieving up-to-date information at a glance. Also included in this section are forms for status letters to clients.

§ 7.2   Acknowledgment Letter to Client

Upon receipt of the complaint and summons from your client's insurance company, the following letter (**Form 7–1**) should be prepared and sent to the insured. It is important that you have the confidence and cooperation of the insured for the defense of his case. In many instances, you will find that the insured does not really understand either how his defense is to be brought about or the roles that he, the attorney, and the insurance company will play in the action. It is also important that you educated the insured concerning his communications with other persons or parties regarding the action.

   If you have received no reply to this letter within two weeks, follow up by making personal contact with the insured. You should not assume that the letter has been received and understood. Being sued is probably the most traumatic event that has occurred in the insured's life, and it may be difficult for him to grasp at first.

FORM 7–1
SAMPLE ACKNOWLEDGMENT LETTER TO CLIENT

[defendant's name]
[defendant's address]

Re: [name of case]_____

Dear [defendant]:

This law firm has been retained by your insurance carrier, [name], to represent you relative to the above-referenced matter. During the course of this litigation we will need to consult with you, and naturally desire your full cooperation, in the defense of this legal action in accordance with the provisions of your insurance contract.

It is essential that we know of your current address and telephone number at all times. Should you move, even temporarily, please advise us as we may need your assistance and cooperation in answering some legal inquiry.

Because this lawsuit concerns our mutual interests, please do not discuss this matter or give any written or oral statements to anyone other than a properly identified representative of this office or [name of insurance company]. If you have any questions, please do not hesitate to call us.

In order that we may properly and effectively defend this lawsuit in your behalf, it is imperative that we be furnished copies of all correspondence and other documents you may have accumulated in connection with this incident. Please forward the requested documentation to me as soon as possible. I would appreciate it if you would address this question at your earliest possible convenience.

Respectfully yours,

[name of attorney]_____

§ 7.3 Preliminary Evaluation Letter to Client

When you receive a new file from your client's insurance company, look for discrepancies in service of process, venue, and jurisdiction to determine the proper appearance to be made on behalf of the client. Prepare a letter to your client acknowledging receipt of the file and outlining your proposed plan of action. This letter contains only cursory information and will be followed up by more detailed reports to the client at later points of development in the case. (See **Form 7–2.**)

§ 7.4   INITIAL FILE SUMMARY MEMORANDUM

FORM 7–2
SAMPLE PRELIMINARY EVALUATION LETTER TO CLIENT

Dear [client]:

We are in receipt of the [name of matter] file which you forwarded to us on [date]. We would like to thank you for referring this file to us.

(Because of the improper service of this complaint on [date], our first action will be to file a motion to quash service.) All (other) components of the complaint seem to be in order, and (as soon as proper service is effected,) we will proceed immediately with an answer. As usual, we will forward our standard predeposition interrogatories to the plaintiff when we file our answer.

Our investigation will begin by obtaining a copy of the accident report and a visual inspection of the scene. We also plan to order a history of accidents at that intersection from the Highway Department.

As soon as we have received the plaintiff's answers to interrogatories and have evaluated the above information, we will forward to you our initial suit evaluation.

Thank you again for the referral. We appreciate your continued confidence.

Respectfully yours,

[name of attorney]

§ 7.4   Initial File Summary Memorandum

This form (**Form 7–3**) should be filled out with information gleaned from the complaint and from the investigation file you receive from the insurance company. Place the memorandum in a portion of the file that will be readily accessible to your attorney. One of the major benefits of this memorandum is that, if it is kept up-to-date, the attorney will be able to pick up the file and, with one glance, determine the important elements, numbers, and issues of the case. Because the memorandum is a perfect tool for telephone settlement negotiations, up-dated information must be added to the memorandum as it becomes available.

INSURANCE DEFENSE

FORM 7–3
SAMPLE INITIAL FILE SUMMARY MEMORANDUM

[name]
                  Plaintiff,   ) IN THE [judicial district] JUDICIAL
) DISTRICT OF THE STATE
) OF [state] IN
) AND FOR THE COUNTY OF

vs.   )
) [county]
) Case No. [number]
[name]   )
                  Defendant.   )

Internal File No. _____

Name of Client _____

Client Address, Phone _____

_____

Attorney in Charge _____

Paralegal Assigned _____

Opposing Counsel (Address and Phone No.) _____

Date of Loss _____

Date Complaint Filed _____

Date Answer Filed _____

Statute of Limitations Bar Date Followed? _____

If no, list bar date _____

Venue Proper?   YES _____   NO _____

Service Proper?   YES _____   NO _____

Jurisdiction Proper?   YES _____   NO _____

Judge Assigned _____

Jury Trial?   YES _____   NO _____

Insurance coverages and established procedures: _____

_____

_____

Brief description of claim or accident: _____

_____

_____

_____

Brief description of injuries, medical specials, and lost wages: _____

_____

_____

_____

Special legal issues: _____

_____

_____

Probable defenses: _____

_____

_____

_____

Investigation and discovery recommendations: _____

_____

_____

_____

DEMANDS (PLAINTIFF)		DEMANDS (DEFENDANT)	
DATE _____	AMOUNT _____	DATE _____	AMOUNT _____
DATE _____	AMOUNT _____	DATE _____	AMOUNT _____
DATE _____	AMOUNT _____	DATE _____	AMOUNT _____

§ 7.5 Initial Defense Checklist

Use this checklist (**Form 7–4**) as an easy reference for the initial steps to be taken upon receipt of the summons and complaint. Once all the steps in this checklist have been completed and the dates entered under the column entitled "Date Accomplished," you are ready to move into the investigation and discovery aspects of the case. Refer to **Chapters 4** and **5** for information on these steps.

FORM 7–4
SAMPLE INITIAL DEFENSE CHECKLIST

[name]		)
	Plaintiff,	) IN THE [judicial district] JUDICIAL
		) DISTRICT OF THE STATE
		) OF [state] IN
		) AND FOR THE COUNTY OF
vs.		)
		) [county]
		) Case No. [number]
[name]		)
	Defendant.	)

Date Accomplished:

___ 1. Date of Summons is _____.

___ 2. Answer is due _____.

___ 3. Send acknowledgment letter to client (insured).

___ 4. Send preliminary evaluation letter to client (insurance company).

___ 5. Prepare Initial File Summary Memorandum.

___ 6. Prepare defendant's answer.

___ 7. Ascertain if method of service was proper. If not, prepare Motion to Quash Service.

___ 8. Ascertain if venue is proper. If not, prepare Answer Subject to Motion to Transfer Venue.

___ 9. File and service defendant's answer.

___ 10. Request insurer to send excess letter to insured.

___ 11. Make jury demand.

___ 12. Begin with investigation. Make initial contact with important witnesses and expert witnesses.

___ 13. Amend original answer, if necessary, after initial investigation. Initiate third-party action if deemed appropriate and necessary.

___ 14. Forward copies of pleadings to insurer and insured.

§ 7.6   Contention Interrogatories

The following interrogatories in **Form 7–5** are specially designed defense interrogatories, to be tailored to each particular complaint and its specific allegations.

§ 7.5 INITIAL DEFENSE CHECKLIST

FORM 7–5
SAMPLE CONTENTION INTERROGATORIES

1. Please state each and every fact which supports or tends to support or prove, in whole or in part, your allegations that you are informed and believe, and thereon allege in paragraph [number] of your Complaint, that [state necessary facts].

_____

_____

(Examples:

    (a)   the defendant was responsible in some manner for the events and happenings referred to, thereby proximately causing the injuries and damages to you;

    (b)   as a direct and proximate result of the alleged negligence, carelessness, and recklessness of the defendant, you did thereby incur injuries and damages;

    (c)   the defendant's willful and wanton disregard was the proximate cause of your injuries and damages;

    (d)   the illegal acts of the defendant were the proximate cause of your injuries and damages.)

2. Please identify each and every person having knowledge of the facts set forth in your answer to Interrogatory No. 1, above.

3. Please identify each and every document which is evidence of, refers to, or mentions any of the facts specified in your answer to Interrogatory No. 1, above.

4. Please identify each and every oral conversation which supports or tends to support or prove, in whole or in part, the fact or facts set forth in your answer to Interrogatory No. 1, above.

(Note: Continue this series of four interrogatories until all allegations of the complaint have been addressed. Then proceed with standard defense personal injury interrogatories, as follows.)

No. _____   Were you involved in an accident or incident occurring on or about the [date] day of [month], [20__]?

No. _____   State your full name and all names by which you have been known.

No. _____   What is your present address, telephone number, and Social Security number?

No. _____   List each of your residence addresses during the past five years and the inclusive dates of your residence at each such address.

No. _____   State your date of birth and birthplace.

No. _____   Have you ever been married? If so, state:

    (a)   how many times;

    (b)   the name and present address of each spouse;

    (c)   the date and place of each marriage;

    (d)   the date and place of termination of each marriage; and

(e)   the name, address, and age of each child born of each marriage.

No. ____   Have you ever been a member of the armed forces? If so, state:

(a)   when and where you were discharged, and

(b)   the type of discharge you received.

No. ____   Have you resided with any person since the date of the accident referred to in Interrogatory No. 1? If so, state:

(a)   the name and present address of the person;

(b)   the relationship to you, if any, of the person; and

(c)   the address of the place where you resided together.

No. ____   State the name and address of each person known to you or your attorney who has investigated the accident which is the subject of this litigation.

No. ____   State the name and address of each witness to the accident mentioned known to you, your attorney, agent, investigator, or detective employed by you or your attorney or anyone acting on your behalf.

No. ____   State the name and address of each person, including doctors, known to you, your attorney, agent or any investigators, or detective employed by you or your attorney or anyone acting on your behalf, having knowledge of facts relevant to the subject matter of this action.

No. ____   Give the name of any expert or consultant with whom you have communicated in connection with the occurrence which is the subject matter of this action, and state:

(a)   the last known business and home address of each such person;

(b)   the name of any business entity with which each such person is associated;

(c)   the specific area of knowledge of each such person (for example, chemical engineer, structural engineer, medical doctor, and so forth);

(d)   the date when each such person was first contacted;

(e)   the date of each report rendered by each such person, indicating whether the report was written or oral and, if oral, who the speaker was;

(f)   precisely what documentary or written material was provided to each such person, giving the date and author of each such document or written material; and

(g)   what physical objects were provided to each such person.

No. ____   Do you, your attorney, or any of your other representatives have in your possession or under your control, any notes, reports of conversations, phonetic recordings of conversations, stenographic verbatim reports of conversations, transcriptions of phonetic recordings, or any other memoranda whatsoever related or communicated by defendant which pertains in any manner to this accident or to the issues arising therefrom? If so, state:

(a)   the nature thereof;

(b)   the time and date obtained;

(c)   the place obtained;

(d)   the name and address of the person soliciting;

(e)   the names and addresses of those present at the solicitation; and

(f)   the name and address of the person having present custody thereof.

§ 7.5 INITIAL DEFENSE CHECKLIST

No. ____ Have you overheard any conversation between defendant and any other person concerning the accident? If so, state:
(a) your best recollection of the conversation;
(b) when it occurred;
(c) where it occurred; and
(d) the names and addresses of all persons present.

No. ____ What were you doing immediately prior to the accident?

No. ____ What was the defendant doing immediately prior to the accident?

No. ____ How did the accident happen?

No. ____ You have alleged in your complaint that defendant was negligent. State all facts upon which you base that allegation. (Note: this interrogatory may be repetitive because of Interrogatories No. 1-4.)

No. ____ State the name and address of each person known to you or your attorneys who has knowledge of those facts stated in your answer to the preceding Interrogatory.

No. ____ If you claim to have suffered personal injuries in the accident, list all such injuries or ailments and symptoms experienced by you.

No. ____ State the name and address of each hospital, if any, in which you have been hospitalized since the accident, and further state:
(a) the dates of hospitalization;
(b) whether each such hospitalization was either wholly or partially the result of injuries or symptoms resulting from said accident;
(c) the total amount and the amount of each item incurred for any such hospitalization and incidental expense necessitated wholly or partially by reason of injuries or symptoms resulting from said accident; and
(d) the name and address of each doctor or physician who has advised you that you will in the future require further hospitalization for any injury or symptom wholly or partially resulting from said accident, and the purpose of such hospitalization.

No. ____ State the full name and business address of each doctor or physician who has examined, treated or consulted with you since the accident, and further state:
(a) the date of each such examination, treatment, or consultation;
(b) whether each such examination, treatment, or consultation was wholly or partially required by reason of said accident;
(c) the present total amount of the bill, and the amount of each item in such bill, of each such doctor or physician having examined, treated, or consulted with you since said accident, wholly or partially by reason thereof;
(d) whether such course of treatment with such doctor or physician has terminated, and the date of such termination; and
(e) whether you were examined or treated by any of these doctors or physicians prior to this accident, and the purpose of each such examination or treatment.

INSURANCE DEFENSE

No. ____ Have you, your agent or representative received any written reports concerning your physical condition from any doctor or physician? If so, state:
  (a) by whom the report was made and the date of each report; and
  (b) if you will do so without a Request for Production, attach a copy of each report to your answers to these Interrogatories.

No. ____ State whether your doctor, hospital or medical bills have been paid, and further state the name of any person or organization making such payment.

No. ____ State whether you have made application or claim for benefits under any medical pay coverage of a policy of insurance under any public or private group medical benefits plan or any state, federal or local workmen's compensation plan, as a result of injuries arising out of the accident referred to in Interrogatory No. 1, and further state:
  (a) the name of the insurance company, governmental body, or organization to which such application or claim was made;
  (b) the date of such claim or application;
  (c) the claim, application or policy number; and
  (d) the date of payment.

No. ____ Give the date and place of each accident, other than this accident, wherein you sustained any injuries whatsoever which required or resulted in any medical care, consultation, examination, or treatment, and further state:
  (a) the nature of the injuries and symptoms;
  (b) the name and address of each doctor and each hospital from which you received such care, consultation, examination, or treatment; and
  (c) whether any such injuries left residual symptoms which had not disappeared at the time of this accident, and the nature of any such symptoms.

No. ____ Have you had an accident or illness since the accident described in your complaint? If so, state:
  (a) when the accident occurred or the illness arose;
  (b) where the accident occurred or illness arose;
  (c) the circumstances surrounding the accident or illness;
  (d) the nature and extent of the injuries arising from the accident or illness;
  (e) any complaints that you now have as a result of the accident or illness; and
  (f) the name and address of each doctor who treated you as a result of the accident or illness.

No. ____ State whether you have ever made, prior to the present action, a claim against any person or organization for damages for personal injuries or damage to your property, and further state:
  (a) the name and address of such person or organization;
  (b) the date and place of the accident or occurrence out of which such claim arose; and
  (c) the name of the judicial or administrative tribunal, if any, in which such claim was prosecuted, and the case or proceeding number.

No. ____ State your business or occupation during the past five years, and further state:

    (a)   the name and address of each of your employers during such period or whether self-employed;

    (b)   the name and address of your immediate boss, foreman, supervisor, or other person to whom you were responsible at the time of the accident;

    (c)   the name and address of your immediate boss, foreman, supervisor, or other person to whom you are presently responsible;

    (d)   your rate of pay or compensation at the time of the accident and for the year immediately prior thereto; and

    (e)   your rate of pay or compensation from the time of said accident to the present date.

No. ____ State whether you have lost any salary, compensation, or income since the accident, and further state:

    (a)   the amount of such loss which has resulted solely by reason of injuries sustained in said accident;

    (b)   the total amount of time lost from your employment, business, or occupation since the accident and solely by reason of injuries suffered in said accident;

    (c)   the date you returned to work; and

    (d)   the amount of time lost from your employment, business, or occupation resulting from reasons other than because of injuries suffered in said accident, and the reasons for such loss of time.

No. ____ With respect to each of the past five years, state:

    (a)   your yearly gross income;

    (b)   your yearly net income; and

    (c)   the name and address of the person, firm, or corporation having custody of any papers pertaining to your income.

No. ____ List in detail all expenses which you have incurred solely by reason of the accident.

No. ____ State whether you consumed any intoxicating beverages within 24 hours preceding the accident, and further state:

    (a)   the time and place of each drink;

    (b)   the kind and amount of intoxicating beverages consumed; and

    (c)   the name and address or each person present at the consumption of each drink.

No. ____ Have you ever been convicted of a felony? If so, state:

    (a)   the nature of the felony;

    (b)   the date of each conviction; and

    (c)   the place of each conviction.

No. ____ State whether plaintiff has received any money, promise to pay money, loan, advance of money, or payment of any kind, from any person, firm, or corporation in payment, settlement, or compromise of any claim resulting from or growing out of the claims alleged in the complaint, and further state:

    (a)   the name and address of the party with whom the above-mentioned transaction was made;

    (b)   whether said transaction is in writing and, if so, the date and the name and address of the custodian of the same;

(c)   the consideration for said transaction; and

(d)   the amount of money involved in the transaction.

No. _____   State whether plaintiff, his agents, representatives, attorneys, or anyone acting in his behalf, has executed a Covenant Not to Sue, Covenant Not to Execute, Release, or any other contract or agreement releasing any party or third person from any past, present, or future liability which does or may result from any claim associated with, or growing out of, any claim mentioned in the complaint or any acts or omissions associated with any party or third person as mentioned in the complaint. If so, state:

(a)   the name and address of the person having custody of said document;

(b)   the consideration for execution of said document; and

(c)   the name and address of all parties to each covenant, release, contract, or agreement.

§ 7.7   Status Letter to Client

Use the following form (**Form 7–6**) to inform your contact at the insurance company that answers to the interrogatories have been received from the plaintiff. The same form may be used throughout the case to keep the client up-to-date regarding information compiled from depositions, investigation, and other discovery tools. At the very minimum, the client should receive this type of status letter from you after your receipt of interrogatory answers from the plaintiff, after every round of depositions, and after any settlement negotiations. Prior to trial, the attorney may want to include much of this information in his final status letter, with recommendations to the client.

FORM 7–6
SAMPLE STATUS LETTER TO CLIENT

Dear [insurance adjuster]:

The following is a summary of plaintiff's answers to our initial interrogatories.

FACTS

Plaintiff's full name is [name]   .

He was born [date of birth]   , in [city, state]   ,

and currently resides at [current address]   .

His Social Security number is [Social Security number]   .

In reference to plaintiff's version of the accident, plaintiff states as follows:

[statement regarding the accident].

_____

_____

_____

_____

With reference to the facts on which plaintiff bases his allegations of negligence, plaintiff states:

[statement regarding allegations of negligence]._____

_____

_____

_____

The plaintiff lists [names of witnesses] _____

_____

_____

as witnesses to the accident.

INJURIES AND MEDICAL HISTORY

Plaintiff states that he suffered injury to [description of injuries]._____

_____

_____

Following the accident, he was hospitalized at [name of hospital]_____

_____

_____

from [date]_____ to [date]_____. His treating physicians were:

[list names and addresses]_____

_____

_____

Plaintiff states that he has had no previous accidents and no accident or illness since the accident here involved.

(Plaintiff states that he has had [number] previous accidents and [number] illnesses and accidents since the accident here involved.)

EMPLOYMENT RECORD

The plaintiff claims to have been employed as a [description of employment] for the past [number] years, employed by [name of employer]. He claims he was earning $[amount] per hour (or per week, month, and so forth) and has lost approximately $[amount] in wages. Lost time since the accident totals [number] days.

SPECIAL DAMAGES CLAIMED

In answer to our interrogatory as to what expenses plaintiff has incurred, he lists the following:

[list of expenses]

_____

_____

RECOMMENDATIONS

[Have attorney complete this section.]

We will keep you advised as matters further develop herein.

Respectfully yours,

[name of attorney]

§ 7.8   Legal Research Files

Most law firms have specific recurring legal issues that are indigenous to their type of practice. Rather than researching these issues over and over again, legal research files are set up to address them. For example, there may be an area in your locale which is the subject of controversy regarding jurisdiction by two governmental agencies. If this type of issue arises frequently in your practice, set up a file with the background material to support your firm's memorandum of law on the subject. Another hotly-debated issue in your area may be the proper venue for a case to be heard. In some metropolitan areas, this can be a problem and can become a routine element in filing your answer.

Case law on liability and allowance for pain and suffering differs from locale to locale. Make a thorough check of the prevailing court opinions influencing your area on these subjects. Also ask the attorneys in your firm what other issues they address frequently and set up corresponding files.

§ 7.9 Practice Tips

Remember that in defense work your client has been accused of wrongdoing or that his actions have been the proximate cause of harm or damages to the plaintiff. Therefore, you must work twice as hard to prove the allegations untrue. The way to accomplish this is to leave no stone unturned.

A good insurance defense paralegal must learn to read in between the lines of everything and explore all possibilities that those insights present. This is not to say that you should read things into something that are not there, but rather to investigate statements or facts thoroughly which could lead to the discovery of other pertinent and revealing facts which may help your client.

For example, if, while you are examining the medical records of a plaintiff complaining of lower back pain, you discover that an escalation in the plaintiff's pain seems to coincide with a weight gain of 35 pounds a year after the accident, you should bring this fact to the attorney's attention. It could be used to show that the plaintiff has done something to exacerbate his injuries, which could very well reduce your client's exposure to liability. Investigate the credibility of witnesses and follow up on all your hunches, no matter how far-fetched they may seem at the time. These are qualities that distinguish a terrific paralegal from an adequate one.

CHAPTER 8

TRIAL READINESS AND SETTLEMENT

§ 8.1   Introduction

Anticipate, anticipate, anticipate! These are the watchwords throughout a lawsuit. Trials are by nature a very hectic time, and the added chaos and confusion of last minute preparation is an unwanted guest. Prepare for trial from the very beginning of the lawsuit. It takes no extra time to make duplicate copies of substantive pleadings and deposition summaries for the trial book as you go along. Even evidence can be tagged early and readied for trial. Certainly there is nothing to prevent placing a set of stock jury instructions in the file for the attorney to revise as he goes along, rather than at 10:00 P.M. the night before trial begins. All the sections in this chapter will help you to organize yourself and your attorney to become the best-prepared trial team in the courthouse. There is much to be said for organization and preparedness. After all, it leaves much more spare time to analyze your opponent!

§ 8.2   Letter Advising Client or Witness of Trial Date

Once the trial date has been established, you should notify either the client or the witness of that date. Use the following letter (**Form 8–1**) for notification.

FORM 8–1
SAMPLE LETTER ADVISING CLIENT OR WITNESS OF TRIAL DATE

Re: [case caption]

Dear [name]_____:

   This is to advise you that the trial of the above-entitled matter has been scheduled, on a stacked basis, starting on the [date] day of [month], [20___]. In cases of this nature, the Court, as a matter of judicial economy, stacks several cases back to back so there will not be any periods of time wasted between trials. As a result, it is very difficult to know the exact date and hour the trial will commence. We do wish to advise you at this time that you should be available during that entire week.

TRIAL READINESS AND SETTLEMENT

We ask that you keep us advised of your whereabouts at all times because we will need to be in contact with you to give you a more accurate trial date and to discuss this case with you in detail.

If for any reason you find you will not be available during this time please call our office immediately because your testimony is necessary at trial.

Very truly yours,

_____

[paralegal/attorney]

§ 8.3   Trial Certification Request

The procedure followed for placing a trial on the court's docket differs greatly from jurisdiction to jurisdiction. Sometimes it is done by order of the court after a pretrial conference, but many times it is done by request of one of the parties in the action. This is known as a Trial Certification Request. It is a document which simply states that the party is ready to proceed to trial and would like to reserve a date for that trial on the court's calendar. Because it is a request submitted by one of the parties, the requesting party must obtain the approval of the other party in order to get the case certified for trial. This ensures that the court's time is not wasted by setting a trial date for which the parties will not be ready. (See **Forms 8–2 and 8–3.**)

Both **Forms 8–2 and Forms 8–3** are Trial Certification Requests for Texas.

FORM 8–2
SAMPLE TRIAL CERTIFICATION REQUEST

NO. _____

IN RE:		JURY
_____ VS	|	NON-JURY
	|	_____ JUDICIAL DISTRICT OF TEXAS
_____	|	DATE_____

Ray Hardy, District Clerk
Houston, Texas 77002

Please set the above entitled and number cause for trial on the merits on the General Docket for Monday, _____, 20__

In accordance with Rule 3, Rules of the District Courts of Harris County, Texas, I, the undersigned, hereby certify the following:

§ 8.3   TRIAL CERTIFICATION REQUEST

X_____
Signature of Party Making Request and Certification

(a)   That the pleadings are in order;

(b)   That counsel upon whom the request for setting is served has not withdrawn from the case;

(c)   That all written and filed agreements to take depositions and to produce a party for physical examination have been accomplished;

(d)   That all necessary ad Litem appointments have been made;

(e)   That all matters preliminary to trial have been accomplished;

(f)   That all parties and counsel of record have been supplied with copies of the request for setting; and

(g)   That the case is ready for trial;

(h)   That I have in good faith negotiated to settle the case and have communicated my best offer in writing to the other party or parties.

FIRM _____   FIRM _____
BY _____   BY _____
ADDRESS _____   ADDRESS _____
PHONE _____   PHONE _____
          Attorneys for Plaintiff   Attorneys for Defendant

OTHER PARTIES AND COUNSEL

FIRM _____   FIRM _____
BY _____   BY _____
ADDRESS _____   ADDRESS _____
PHONE _____   PHONE _____

NOTICE   LOCAL COURT RULES SHOULD BE READ FOR PROCEDURE REQUIREMENTS COPY OF RULES WILL BE SUPPLIED BY DISTRICT CLERK UPON REQUEST

J-33-R

FORM 8–3
SAMPLE TRIAL CERTIFICATION REQUEST—CIVIL TRIAL DIVISION

TRIAL CERTIFICATION REQUEST: DISTRICT COURTS—CIVIL TRIAL DIVISION
Ray Hardy, District Clerk, Harris County, Texas

_____ Judicial District
_____ Case number

_____

VERSUS

_____

TRIAL READINESS AND SETTLEMENT

PREFERENCE:

_____ Jury
_____ Non-Jury

_____ Workers' Compensation
_____ Injunction
_____ Other (Article 2166a or Local Rule 4), please specify:
_____

Under Local Rule 3 the undersigned represents that this case is ready for trial and requests certification to the trial docket.

PARTY: _____
CAPACITY: (Pl, Df, Intv'r, etc.) _____
SIGNITURE: (Attorney) _____
STATE BAR NUMBER: _____
FIRM: _____
ADDRESS: _____
TELEPHONE: _____
DATE: _____

ATTORNEY REQUESTING CERTIFICATION MUST SECURE SIGNATURES OF ALL COUNSEL REPRESENTING PARTIES TO THIS SUIT.

PARTY: _____
CAPACITY: (Pl, Df, Intv'r, etc.) _____
SIGNITURE: (Attorney) _____
STATE BAR NUMBER: _____
FIRM: _____
ADDRESS: _____
TELEPHONE: _____
DATE: _____
Matters precluding setting: _____
_____ Agree _____ Contest

Copies of this request must be furnished to all parties per Local Rule 12 and Rule 72, Texas Rule of Civil Procedure.

PARTY: _____
CAPACITY: (Pl, Df, Intv'r, ect.) _____
SIGNITURE: (Attorney) _____
STATE BAR NUMBER: _____
FIRM: _____
ADDRESS: _____
TELEPHONE: _____
DATE: _____
Matters precluding setting: _____
_____ Agree _____ Contest

§ 8.4   WITNESS SUBPOENAS

PARTY: _____

CAPACITY: (Pl, Df, Intv'r, etc.)   _____

SIGNITURE: (Attorney)   _____

STATE BAR NUMBER: _____

FIRM: _____

ADDRESS: _____

TELEPHONE: _____

DATE: _____

Matters precluding setting: _____

_____ Agree _____ Contest

CONFERENCE SCHEDULE (For Court Use Only)

Conference Date Scheduled: _____   _____ Teleconference   _____ In Person

DISPOSITION (For Court Use Only)

Setting Request: _____ Granted   _____ Denied

Request Granted; Conditions:

_____

_____

Request Denied; Reasons:

_____

_____

Re-hearing on DENIED Motion Set: _____

_____   _____
Judge Presiding   Date

J 125

§ 8.4   Witness Subpoenas

As soon as the trial date has been certified, begin preparations for notifying friendly witnesses. Prepare subpoenas for all other witnesses, including those who may be friendly but prefer to testify with the formality of a subpoena, and make arrangements for service under Rule 45 of the Federal Rules of Civil Procedure, or the applicable state rule of civil procedure. Check the jurisdictional rule to see what mileage fees and witness fees need to be attached to the subpoena before releasing it for service. Subpoenas should be served upon the witnesses with enough time to allow the return of service to be filed with the court before the witness is due to testify at trial. (**See Form 8–4.**)

Rule 45 of the Federal Rules of Civil Procedure underwent significant changes in 1994. Several aspects of the procedures regarding use and issuance of subpoenas have been revised. Among these changes are:

Issuance: Subpoenas no longer must be issued under seal of court. Formerly, subpoenas could only be issued by the clerk of the court. Now, under the new rule changes, any attorney, as an officer of the court, may also issue a subpoena. Clerks may still issue subpoenas and must sign the subpoena, but do not have to apply the seal of the court.

Attorneys may now issue subpoenas in any court in which they are authorized to practice or in any other district in which a production of documents or deposition is taking place. In the latter case, the subpoena should be issued in the name of the court where such deposition or document production is to occur. The attorney need not be a member of the bar in that district or admitted to practice pro hac vice in order to issue a subpoena in an action pending in a court in which that attorney is authorized to practice. This new rule change makes it easier for an attorney to take a foreign deposition without the often confusing process of acquiring the deposition subpoena from a foreign district.

Nonparty Subpoenas: Nonparties are no longer required to attend a deposition when subpoenaed to produce documents. Fees also do not have to be paid to nonparty witnesses when their attendance is not required. Nonparties may also be subpoenaed to allow inspection of property or other things. They do not have to appear for the inspection and no fees are required to accompany the subpoena.

Notice of Subpoena: Prior notice of any commanded production of documents and things or inspection of premises before trial must be served on each party as prescribed by Rule 5(b) of the Federal Rules of Civil Procedure. The notice serves the same function and may follow the same format as a Notice of Deposition.

100-Mile Rule: A deposition, trial, or production subpoena may be served at any place within the district of the court by which it is issued, or at any place outside the district that is within 100 miles of the place of the deposition, hearing, trial, production, or inspection, according to Federal Rule of Civil Procedure 45(b)(2).

Quashing a Subpoena: Subpoenas may be quashed or modified by the court for the following reasons:

1. A timely motion by a deponent or producer who is a nonparty and is requested to come more than 100 miles;
2. A trial subpoena requires a witness to travel more than 100 miles at substantial expense;
3. The subpoena requires the disclosure of a trade secret or other confidential or protected material;
4. The subpoena does not allow a reasonable time for compliance;

5. The subpoena subjects a person to undue burden or unreasonable expense;
6. The subpoena requires the disclosure of the opinions of an unretained expert.

The court may either quash subpoenas meeting the above criteria, or wherever appropriate, opt to order the persons issuing the subpoena to reasonably compensate the party.

Proof of Service: Proofs of service of subpoenas need only be filed in cases of controversy or dispute.

Objections: The length of time in which a person may object to a production subpoena has been lengthened from 10 days to 14 days. The nonparty must also be protected by the court from any significant expense associated with copying or production.

Justification for Withholding of Documents: Rule 45(d)(2) of the Federal Rules of Civil Procedure specifies that when information subject to a subpoena is withheld on a claim that it is privileged or subject to protection as trial preparation materials, the claim shall be made expressly and shall be supported by a description of the nature of the documents, communications, or things not produced that is sufficient to enable the demanding party to contest the claim.

Organization of Documents: A person responding to a subpoena to produce documents shall produce them as they are kept in the usual course of business or shall organize and label them to correspond with the categories in the demand, according to Rule 45(d)(1) of the Federal Rules of Civil Procedure.

Contempt: Failure to obey a subpoena still carries the punishment for contempt, except in cases where a person is required to travel in excess of 100 miles. In those cases, filing of a motion to quash is unnecessary.

FORM 8–4
SAMBLE WITNESS SUBPOENA (TEXAS)

THE STATE OF TEXAS

TO ANY SHERIFF OF CONSTABLE OF THE STATE OF TEXAS OR OTHER PERSON AUTHORIZED TO SERVE SUBPOENAS UNDER RULE 178 T.R.C.P.

WITNESS SUBPOENA IN CASE NO. _____

TRIAL READINESS AND SETTLEMENT

_____
Plaintiff

vs.   IN THE _____ JUDICIAL DISTRICT
                                           COURT OF HARRIS COUNTRY, TEXAS

_____
Defendant

    YOU ARE HEREBY COMMANDED TO SUMMON:

_____

Address _____
in_____ County, Texas, and who is represented to reside within one hundred
miles of the Court House of Harris County, Texas, in which the above suit is pending or
who may be found within such distance at the time of the trial, to appear before the
_____ Judicial District Court in and for Harris Country, in Houston, Texas, on the ___day
of ___, 20___, at _____. M., to testify as a witness in behalf of the Plaintiff/Defendant
in the above styled Civil Action, to attend from day to day until lawfully discharged;
    And that he bring with him a produce in Court the following:

_____
_____
_____

    Issued at the instance of Plaintiff/Defendant by _____

    DO NOT FAIL to return this writ to said Court, with return thereon, showing the
manner of execution.
    Witness my official signature this the ___ day of _____, A.D., 20___.

                    RAY HARDY,
                    District Clerk, Harris County, Texas
                    301 Fannin St., Houston, TX 77002
                    By _____ Deputy

          OFFICER'S RETURN

    Came to hand the _____ day of _____, 20___, at _____ o'clock __. M., and
executed by delivering a copy of the Subpoena to the within-named _____
in person at _____ in _____ County,
Texas, on the ____ day of _____, 20__, at _____ o'clock __. M., and tendered
to the witness a fee of $ _____ in cash.
    Not executed as to the witness _____ for the
following reasons: _____
_____

                    _____ Sheriff
                                  Constable
                    _____ County, Texas

ACCEPTANCE OF SERVICE OF
SUBPOENA BY WITNESS PER
RULE 178 T.R.C.P.

By _____ Deputy

OR

By _____
Person who is not a party and is not
less than 18 years of age.
Per Rule 178 T.R.C.P.

I hereby accept service of the attached
subpoena and will appear in said court
on said date and time directed in this
subpoena.

_____
WITNESS

FEE: _____

_____
DATE

F-5 R-1-84

Note: This sample subpoena is a Texas subpoena.

§ 8.5   Your Role at Trial

When dressing for trial, remember that the jury will form an opinion of you just as they do of the attorneys who address them. The jury's impression of the trial team can affect your client's verdict heavily. Therefore, it is a good idea to wear a simple, well-fitting, conservative suit and to make sure your hair and makeup are business-like and not dramatic.

Where you sit at trial is a matter of your attorney's personal preference. Some attorneys wish to have their paralegal or an associate sit next to them at the trial table, and some prefer to have only their client sit with them there. Know your attorney's preference before you enter the courtroom so as to avoid confusion on the day of the trial. Wherever you sit, be sure to pay close attention to the proceedings so you can anticipate the needs of your attorney. Avoid making comments during testimony and try to maintain a poker face. Remember that you are being observed not only by the jury, but by the opposing trial team as well.

Smile at jury members if you run into them in the courthouse halls or in restaurants, but UNDER NO CIRCUMSTANCES speak to jury members during a trial. Doing so, even if the circumstances are entirely innocent, could lead to a mistrial or a reprimand of your attorney by the judge. You do not want to compromise the effectiveness of your trial team or prejudice the court against them.

Jury selection is a large part of the paralegal's role at trial. Sometimes we all have feelings about something which are not necessarily backed by facts but nevertheless, are important impressions. These feelings play a part in jury selection. Be sure to voice your concerns or impressions to your attorney or other members of the trial team so that that input can be made useful in the jury selection process.

If you pay strict attention during the trial and learn to take excellent notes, you will become a valuable member of the trial team. Even if he does not ask for one, your attorney will appreciate a typed summary of the trial day's events. You may want to send a copy of your morning's notes back to your secretary to type and have ready for the afternoon, and have a secretary standing by to type your afternoon notes so that your attorney can look them over by 6:00 P.M. that evening.

It is your responsibility to keep track of the flow of the trial transcripts so that you can keep your attorney apprised of their turnaround schedule. He will want to see them daily, if they are available. You may be asked to dictate daily summaries of the trial transcripts.

Another area which becomes your responsibility during trial is that of witness readiness. Work with your witnesses to make sure they have everything they need to arrive at the courthouse in time, prepared to testify. If that entails a side talent as a travel agent, then so be it!

Your final and most important role at trial is to make sure that everything your attorney needs for his presentation is ready and available to him in the courtroom. Make preparations well ahead of time for any needed audiovisual equipment, check the courtroom for electrical outlet accessibility, and make sure all your exhibits are in final form. Make arrangements for oversized exhibits and any necessary documents to be taken to the courtroom every day. Always be the first member of the trial team in the courtroom each day, making sure that everything is in its place and in final form.

Paying strict attention to your attorney will enable you to anticipate his introduction of exhibits into evidence. Have the proper exhibit marked and ready to hand to him so that he does not miss a beat and lose his train of thought. Every time an exhibit is introduced by either side in the courtroom, it should be marked on your exhibit log. If your attorney has introduced an exhibit, but failed to offer it formally into evidence, find a subtle way of bringing that point to his attention so that he may do so.

§ 8.6   Checklist—The Paralegal's Role at Trial

The following items outline the paralegal's role at trial.

_____ **1.** Assist in jury selection.

_____ **2.** Take copious notes.

_____ **3.** Locate documents, testimony, or evidence to help attorney impeach a witness.

_____ **4.** Witness coordination.

_____ **5.** Do impromptu legal research.

_____ **6.** Keep in touch with office to keep attorney abreast of important developments in the status of other cases or the needs of other clients.

_____ **7.** Handle trial exhibits and demonstrative evidence.

____   **8.**   Anticipate attorney's needs.

____   **9.**   Use an exhibit list or exhibit log to keep track of all exhibits as they are introduced and admitted.

____   **10.**   Operate and take charge of all audiovisual equipment.

____   **11.**   Keep track of trial transcripts.

____   **12.**   Make copies of new documents as necessary.

____   **13.**   Stay with documents and exhibits during lunch breaks in courtroom.

____   **14.**   Arrange for any necessary changes in demonstrative evidence which are brought about by unexpected testimony.

____   **15.**   Pay close attention to all courtroom testimony and action.

____   **16.**   Arrange for any needed overtime help at the office to stay after hours to help prepare for the next day's testimony in court.

§ 8.7   Jury Selection

Some jurisdictions make available to the public a list of the names of people who are available for jury selection during that particular period of time. If this is the case in your jurisdiction, utilize the list to develop background information for your attorney. Prospective juror's job titles and any relationship to facts being presented in the case will be very helpful to your attorney during voir dire.

During voir dire, the entire trial team will size up the answers given by a prospective juror to determine if he or she would be likely to give a favorable verdict to your client. Many times, comments are made out of the hearing of the attorney conducting the voir dire, or you may pick up on body language or facial expressions which will be helpful in gaining insight into a juror's tine feelings. Sometimes you may even be able to alert your attorney to friendships between potential jurors which can indicate how a juror may lean. Anything of this nature should be reported to your attorney so that he can consider it along with his own impressions before making a choice in the jury selection.

The Jury Seating Chart (**Form 8–5**) is a helpful tool both during the voir dire and once the jury panel is seated. It provides spaces to fill in the name of the juror, his address, and his occupation. Use a Jury Selection Form (**Form 8–6**) for taking more extensive notes during voir dire. If possible, fill in as much information ahead of time as you have available on the prospective juror so that your attorney can ask more pertinent questions of that juror in making his jury selection decision. These notes will be used by the trial team in conferences outside the courtroom during which time challenges and decisions to strike a juror are discussed.

The Rules of Civil Procedure on the process of jury selection vary wildly from state to state and from state to federal. Most state rules allow for the questioning of prospective jurors by the attorneys and have some kinds of limits on the number of questions which can be asked as well as the subject matter of the questions. Federal Rule of Procedure 47 gives the court complete discretionary rights whether to conduct the examination itself or to allow, "the parties or their attorneys to supplement the examination by such further inquiry as it deems proper or shall itself submit to the prospective jurors such additional questions of the parties or their attorneys as it deems proper." Although the federal rules allow the attorney to conduct his own examination, most federal judges exercise their discretion to conduct the examination themselves. Consequently, jury selection in federal cases is much different from most state cases in which the attorneys do their own questioning and are allowed much latitude by the court.

However, in recent years the number of federal judges permitting participation by the attorneys has grown considerably. Under a proposed amendment to Federal Rule of Civil Procedure 47, the court would be required to conduct the jury selection, but the court would also have to permit "the parties to orally examine the prospective jurors to supplement the court's examination within reasonable limits of time, manner, and subject matter." The court would be allowed to terminate examination by an attorney who violates these limits.

In both state and federal court, attorneys and their parties are allowed to challenge, or excuse, a prospective juror for a number of reasons. The first kind of challenge is called a peremptory challenge. It is designed to allow the attorney to excuse a prospective juror for any reason without having to justify a basis in law to the court. This challenge is used when an attorney has a feeling that a prospective juror may not be a good prospect for a juror in this particular case, but the attorney may not be able to put that feeling into justifiable record. Recent court rulings have chipped away at the traditional right of an attorney to challenge any juror for any reason by peremptory challenge. Attorneys may not, under the new court rulings, challenge a juror on the basis of gender, race, religion, or any other commonly protected civil liberty protected by discrimination laws. The number of peremptory challenges allowed to each party is limited by federal or state statute and is usually few in number. The appropriate rules of civil procedure should be checked for each individual case, as there are usually rules which define whether each party is given a certain number of challenges or whether the number of challenges is given to each side. Most rules allow for special circumstances in which there are multiple parties and, in some cases, allow the court discretion in equalizing the number of challenges awarded to all parties.

An attorney may also challenge a prospective juror for cause. For cause means that there is some statutory or common law basis preventing the prospective juror from being able to serve in that capacity. Reasons for excusing a prospective juror for cause include obvious bias, being a relation or friend to one of the parties or attorneys, or convictions of some offenses. These challenges are unlimited in number, but must be approved by the court.

The number of jurors seated for the trial is also governed by the appropriate rules of civil procedure. Rule 48 of the Federal Rules of Civil Procedure states:

> The court shall seat a jury of not fewer than six and not more than twelve members and all jurors shall participate in the verdict unless excused from service by the court pursuant to rule 47(c). Unless the parties otherwise stipulate, (1) the verdict shall be

unanimous and (2) no verdict shall be taken from a jury reduced in size to fewer than six members.

Under a proposed amendment, Rule 48 would read as follows:

The court shall seat a jury of twelve members. All jurors shall participate in the verdict unless excused from service under Rule 47(c). Unless the parties stipulate otherwise, (1) the verdict shall be unanimous, and (2) no verdict may be taken from a jury of fewer than six members.

The psychology of jury selection has become a profession in and of itself lately. Consultants are often hired to advise a trial team as to a profile of a prospective juror who would be best suited to render a favorable verdict for the client. Most attorneys, however, still do their own profiling and structuring of questions designed to elicit the desired information from the prospective jurors. There are two ways of looking at the objective of the questioning process: (1) is the purpose to select a juror who is most likely to vote for a favorable verdict for your client, or (2) is it to eliminate those prospective jurors who are most likely to vote for an unfavorable verdict for your client? Very likely, it is the latter, because the opposing trial team will do everything in its power to make sure that you do not realize your first objective.

Keeping your objective in mind, questions should be designed to expose preexisting biases of prospective jurors, which is often difficult, because there is a tendency for people to give politically correct answers to questions instead of divulging their true feelings or attitudes. Because prospective jurors feel pressured to give the correct answer rather than the true answer, attorneys often must ask questions which are designed to give related or parallel responses. For instance, instead of asking a person whether he considers himself to be a liberal thinker, ask instead which newspapers or books he enjoys reading, or to which organizations he belongs. Before any questions can be designed, you must know what result you are trying to achieve. Generalizations can usually be made about different kinds of attitudes which are encountered in the jury selection process, but it is vital to understand how those attitudes will culminate in a verdict. For example, it is fairly easy to design questions which would expose a close-minded, morally self-righteous, prejudgmental attitude in a juror, or to recognize a prospective juror who is condescending to those persons whom he sees as inferior to himself, but it is quite another thing to put that information into perspective and determine how those attitudes will affect the outcome of the verdict. Some of the conclusions drawn based on this information can be surprising. This is where the experience of the trial attorney guides the trial team in the proper direction. That is not to say that intuition is not valuable, but rather that the process is one in which both intuition and experience should be weighed appropriately.

The use of open-ended questions can be helpful. Such questions give the prospective jurors more of a chance to talk and allow them to express themselves in their own words.

The use of supplemental questionnaires for the jury should also be considered. Such questionaires can be useful in obtaining specific information on juror attitudes on the issues in the case. The use of such questionnaires should be cleared with the other party and the court.

§ 8.8 Checklist—Jury Selection Observation

Watch the prospective jury pool for the following:

1. Body language;
2. Facial expressions;
3. Signs of agreement, nonagreement, disgust, boredom, or condescension;
4. How prospective jurors fill the slack time and entertain themselves that is, read (and if so, what are they reading?), converse with other people, and so forth;
5. Signs of group dynamics forming, such as persons who naturally take on leadership roles, and so forth;
6. Lack of attention or constant looking at watches, and so forth;
7. Avoiding direct answers to questions;
8. Expensive clothing, jewelry, or accessories;
9. Muttering of sidebar comments either under their breath or to other prospective jurors;
10. Friendships, either old or newly-forming;
11. Seeming inability to understand the proceedings.

§ 8.9 Jury Seating Chart

FORM 8–5
SAMPLE JURY SEATING CHART

JURY SHEET

_____ vs _____

No._____

Date._____

Name	Name	Name	Name	Name	Name
Address	Address	Address	Address	Address	Address
Occupation	Occupation	Occupation	Occupation	Occupation	Occupation

Name	Name	Name	Name	Name	Name
Address	Address	Address	Address	Address	Address
Occupation	Occupation	Occupation	Occupation	Occupation	Occupation

Name	Name	Name	Name	Name	Name
Address	Address	Address	Address	Address	Address
Occupation	Occupation	Occupation	Occupation	Occupation	Occupation

§ 8.10 Jury Selection Form

FORM 8–6
SAMPLE JURY SELECTION FORM

JURY SELECTION

Name:_____ Res._____ Sec. of town._____

Time in County_____ Previous Res._____

Married_____._____ Spouse Occupation_____ Spouse Prev. Occup._____

Occupation_____ Name of Employer_____ How long_____

Prev. occupation_____ Name of Employer_____ How long_____

Prior Jury serv._____ When_____ Type of case_____

Prejudice against one who sues for damages due to neg. which results in P. I._____

Ever been sued for damages_____

Ever sued for damages_____ When_____ Type of case_____ Recover_____

JURY SELECTION

Name:_____ Res._____ Sec. of town._____

Time in County_____ Previous Res._____

'Married_____ Spouse Occupation_____ Spouse Prev. Occup._____

Occupation_____ Name of Employer_____ How long_____

Prev. occupation_____ Name of Employer_____ How long_____

Prior Jury serv._____ When_____ Type of case_____

Prejudice against one who sues for damages due to neg. which results in P. I._____

Ever been sued for damages_____

Ever sued for damages_____ When_____ Type of case_____ Recover_____

JURY SELECTION

Name:_____ Res._____ Sec. of town._____

Time in County_____ Previous Res._____

Married_____ Spouse Occupation_____ Spouse Prev. Occup._____

Occupation_____ Name of Employer_____ How long_____

Prev. occupation_____ Name of Employer_____ How long_____

ior Jury serv._____ When_____ Type of case_____

Prejudice against one who sues for damages due to neg. which results in P. I._____

Ever been sued for damages_____

Ever sued for damages_____ When_____ Type of case_____ Recover_____

§ 8.11   Locating a Jury Consultant

Locating a consultant or consulting firm to assist with a particular case may require some time and effort. The best place to begin the search for a consultant or consulting firm is to check with colleagues. Although the number of competent july consultants and consulting firms has increased, there are still only a small number of firms with long-standing, nationwide reputations for integrity and excellence. Word-of-mouth remains the best means of identifying potential consultants. The most successful consultants in the country, like any other profession, have outstanding reputations and obtain most of their clients from referrals, If a consultant cannot be located through colleagues, there are a number of resource publications that provide listings of jury and trial consultants, as discussed below.

It is not uncommon for a consultant to provide services to either a plaintiffs attorney or a defense attorney. In fact, experience with cases from both perspectives generally serves to sharpen the skills and insights of a consultant. However, some consultants, who have provided assistance on one side of a particular type of case, decline to provide assistance for the other side, at any time. For example, some firms who have provided assistance to plaintiffs on sexual or racial harassment claims, will decline to take on defense cases on that issue even when the parties, jurisdiction, facts, and counsel are completely different. Others will provide assistance to either side of an issue, providing there is no current conflict with the case.

Practice Tip: Martindale-Hubbell provides a listing of jury and trial consultants, both in its hardbound directories and through its on-line service. Consultants are listed by city. It may be important to look under the larger cities in a state to find listings.

The search may be expanded to include display advertising in regional publications, or publications that focus on counsel's area of practice. For example, the plaintiff's bar often produces a local publication. If counsel is representing a plaintiff and is interested in locating a consultant who specializes in undertaking plantiff cases, it is often possible to identify two or three prospects who have advertised in the publication. Display advertising can be somewhat expensive. The fact that a firm has a large ad doesn't indicate much, but repetition does. Counsel should look through several issues of the publication to be sure the firm has been around for some period of time and is not a start-up with little experience. Most long standing firms run continuous advertising. Counsel should look for a statement in the ad about the number of years the firm has been in business. Those with experience will state it. Those without it, will avoid mentioning it.

For defense counsel, finding firms in defense publications is not as easy because many publications produced by the defense bar do not permit display advertising. In these instances, referring to major statewide publications will often produce a number of potential consulting firms in the trial jurisdiction.

Note: In many communities, a directory or resource manual of experts and consultants is published by the local Bar Association. Increasingly, these publications are including headings for jury consultants and trial consultants.

There is a national directory of jury and trial consultants currently published and available in most law libraries. It is not an exhaustive directory of consultants, but rather a listing of the members of the American Society of Trial Consultants. The directory provides the names and addresses of firms throughout the country.

Finding someone "local" is not of paramount concern. It is not always possible to locate a consulting firm within close proximity. It is relatively unimportant that the consulting firm be headquartered in the trial jurisdiction. Most all of the research undertaken by a consulting firm is undertaken with jury-eligible community residents drawn from the trial jurisdiction, relying on the specific facts of the case. There is limited value to claims of "familiarity with the trial jurisdiction." Truly meaningful data is not based upon historical data from previous trials in the jurisdiction, but rather from direct information and analysis of the facts of the case at hand.

Note: In most instances, it would be unusual to find a local trial consultant, except in large metropolitan areas. Most national consulting firms strive to contain travel costs such that the distance factor is kept minimal. It is slightly more expensive to call upon a firm that is headquartered some distance away, but counsel will be obtaining the same data as if the firm resided in the community.

§ 8.12   Use of Focus Groups

A focus group consists of eight to twelve jury-eligible community residents recruited for a small group discussion on the issues of the case. The focus group is a relatively new tool. It is a less-formalized exercise than a mock trial, discussed above, but still yields a rich amount of data.

A focus group allows the attorney to test sensitive issues and obtain reactions to case themes in far greater depth than can obtained in a mock trial. The pace of the focus group allows each component of the case to be explored in detail before moving to the next level. Possible argument strategies are identified and unproductive themes can be eliminated quite early.

As with the mock trial, counsel can obtain feedback on the impact of potential exhibits and documents from the focus group participants. Prototypes of exhibits can be circulated to focus group members and their reactions sought. Counsel can also see what aspects of a document or exhibit confuse jurors, and obtain instructions from the focus group on how to make the exhibit clearer.

The impact of photographs can also be pretested in the focus group. Frequently, day-in-the-life videos are pretested in focus groups or mock trials. Many plaintiff's attorneys have abandoned interest in presenting a day-in-the-life video after obtaining feedback from jurors in a focus group. Similarly, defense counsel have often learned that their planned strategy for "attacking" a plaintiff would be too harsh, and that it would elicit a ricochet effect from jurors. A focus group allows the defense attorney to gauge how strongly he or she can attack the plaintiff, without overstepping the bounds.

Note: In cases where only one research tool is required, the focus group is the one most frequently utilized. The focus group is used in these cases because they can be put together with a minimum of preparation time for the trial team and the consultant. They provide a general overview of a case and are flexible enough to allow the testing of a small number of exhibits or videotaped excerpts from key witnesses or experts.

Like mock trials, a focus group involves recruiting jury-eligible community residents to participate in the study, and many of the same considerations apply. Thus, the jury consultant recruits focus group participants without informing them which side is undertaking the exercise, and the same precautions regarding confidentiality of the exercise should be taken.

As with the mock trial, counsel and the consultant should discuss the procedures for ensuring that participants in the focus group are not currently on jury duty or anticipate being called for jury duty during the time the case may come to trial.

The participants are provided with a summary of the trial issues in a step-by-step fashion. Their points of view, opinions, and reactions are solicited by the focus-group monitor, generally, the trial consultant, at each level of discussion. The goal is to allow the attorneys to understand jurors' thinking and to learn to view the case as jurors' perceive it.

Counsel should attend the focus group and be an active participant in the discussions following the guidance of the jury consultant in terms of how to elicit meaningful responses from jurors. The jury consultant will raise issues with the group and ask open-ended questions to elicit comments from jurors.

At each stage of the focus group, jurors are given information from both the plaintiff and defense perspectives. Jurors thus hear a balanced presentation.

After eliciting reactions to the strengths and weaknesses of each side's case, the focus-group monitor will redirect the discussion exclusively toward one side and probe for specific suggestions on how the attorney can strengthen his or her case.

Because there is no need to undertake the preparations of a formalized presentation to the group, a focus group requires less preparation time far the attorney than a mock trial. While it is important to develop a clear outline that builds the case in a series of progressive stages, the time devoted to developing the agenda with the trial consultant should be relatively minimal. Generally, focus groups are also of much shorter duration than mock trials. The entire procedure can be conducted in an evening, or at most, in a single day.

At the end of the procedure, jurors are debriefed. There are a number of debriefing strategies which leave participants feeling not only like they participated in a very educational evening, but pleased with their ability to assist in providing feedback that will help resolve what is clearly a significant conflict.

TRIAL READINESS AND SETTLEMENT

§ 8.13   Trial Exhibits

Keeping track of the exhibits introduced at trial is a very important function. You may even be asked by the judge to confirm whether a particular exhibit has been formally offered into evidence, or what the number of a particular exhibit was. It is vital that you have an organized and professional method of keeping track of the exhibits. The Exhibit Log used here is an excellent one for such purposes and should serve you well. (See **Form 8–7**.)

FORM 8–7
SAMPLE EXHIBIT L06

UNITED STATES DISTRICT COURT
[Judicial district] DISTRICT OF [state]
[judicial division] DIVISION

CASE NO. [case number]

_____ : JUDGE _____
      :
_____ : Courtroom Deputy _____
      :
  vs.   : Court Reporter
      :
_____ : COURT TRIAL/JURY TRIAL/HEARING
      :
_____ : Held at _____

DATE _____

EXHIBIT LIST OF _____   Attorney _____

Page 1of ___ Pages

EX.	DESCRIPTION	Marked	Offered	Objected	Admit	Date	Disposition after trial

500

§ 8.13   TRIAL EXHIBITS

_____ DISTRICT

EXHIBIT LIST OF _____   CASE NO. _____

Page _____ of _____ Pages

EX. NO.	DESCRIPTION	Marked	Offered	Object	Admit	Date	Disposition after trial

§ 8.14   Designation of Expert Witnesses

Most courts have procedural rules which require the designation of expert witnesses prior to the beginning of trial. A failure to designate the experts under these rules disqualifies the testimony of the expert at trial. The following is a simple form used for the purpose of designating such experts, and is filed prior to the trial and usually before or just after the pretrial conference. (See **Form 8–8.**)

Federal Rule of Civil Procedure 26(a) requires voluntary disclosure of discovery. Two portions of this new rule pertain to the designation of expert witnesses in federal litigation. Rule 26(a)(2)(A) states "In addition to the disclosures required by paragraph (1), a party shall disclose to other parties the identity of any person who may be used at trial to present evidence under Rules 702, 703, or 705 or the Federal Rules of Evidence." While the identity of experts has always been disclosed in the past, the rules now require that the parties disclose a detailed report by any expert witness who is retained or specially employed as an expert witness. The report must include the qualifications of the expert, his compensation for his services, and his opinions and basis thereof concerning the subject matter of the litigation for which he has been hired to give testimony. The report must also include, according to Rule 26(a)(2)(B), any data or other information considered by the witness in formulation of his opinion, any exhibits expected to be used as support for the opinions, a list of all publications the expert has written in the past 10 years, and a list of all other cases in which he has testified either at trial or by deposition within the past four years.

Federal Rule of Civil Procedure 26(a)(2)(C) requires that absent any other directions from the court or stipulations by the parties (such as provision made for this date in the planning meeting required under Rule 26(f)), the disclosures concerning the expert witness shall be made no later than 90 days before the trial date, or "if the evidence is intended solely to contradict or rebut evidence on the same subject matter identified by another party under paragraph 2(B), within 30 days after the disclosure made by the other party."

In the many jurisdictions that do not have the expert disclosure provisions of the Federal Rules of Civil Procedure, more traditional discovery devices may have to be used. (See **Forms 8–8** and **8–8A.**)

FORM 8–8
SAMPLE DESIGNATION OF EXPERT WITNESSES FORM

NO. [case number]

[name]	)	IN THE DISTRICT COURT OF
	)	
v.	)	[county] COUNTY, [state]
	)	
[name]	)	[judicial district] JUDICIAL DISTRICT

§ 8.14 DESIGNATION OF EXPERT WITNESSES

DEFENDANTS'S DESIGNATION OF EXPERT WITNESSES

TO THE HONORABLE JUDGE OF SAID COURT:

COMES NOW, [name], Defendant herein, and pursuant to the Court's Order designates its expert witnesses.

I.

EXPERT WITNESSES

[Defendant] may call as expert witnesses in the trial of this case the following individuals:

[list expert witnesses]

_____

II.

DESIGNATION OF ADDITIONAL EXPERTS

In the event it is determined that additional expert witnesses may be necessary, [defendant] will amend this designation to include such witnesses.

Respectfully submitted,
[name of law firm]

By: _____
    [attorney name]
    State Bar No. [number]
    [firm address]

[Add certificate of service]

FORM 8–9
DEMAND FOR EXPERT INFORMATION

[court] COURT OF THE STATE OF [state]
COUNTY OF [county]

[name]	)	
	)	
Plaintiff(s),	)	Index No.
	)	DEMAND FOR
-against-	)	EXPERT INFORMATION
	)	
[name]	)	
	)	
Defendant(s).	)	

TRIAL READINESS AND SETTLEMENT

SIR:

PLEASE TAKE NOTICE that pursuant to Section 3101(d) of the Civil Practice Law & Rules, the defendant, [name], hereby demands that you furnish the undersigned attorney for the defendant, [name], within ten (10) days of the service of this Demand, the following:

1. Identify each person whom you expect to call as an expert witness at trial;
2. Disclose in reasonable detail the subject matter on which each expert is expected to testify;
3. Disclose the substance of the facts on which each expert is expected to testify;
4. Disclose the substance of the opinions on which each expert is expected to testify;
5. Disclose the qualifications of each expert witness;
6. Set forth a summary of the grounds for each expert's opinion.

PLEASE TAKE FURTHER NOTICE that this demand shall be deemed to continue during the pendency of this action, including the trial thereof, and if you fail to comply with this demand, a motion will be made seeking an Order precluding you from introducing the testimony of any undisclosed expert at the trial of this action upon the grounds of your noncompliance.

PLEASE TAKE FURTHER NOTICE, that in the event of plaintiff's failure to comply with the foregoing demand within twenty (20) days, the defendant will move to preclude the offering of any evidence as to the matters herein demanded, together with the costs of such application.

Dated: [city, state]
       [date]

                                          Yours etc.,

                                          [firm name]

                                        Attorneys for Defendant [name]
                                        [firm address and
                                        telephone number]

TO: [name, address, and
     telephone number of
     plaintiff's firm]

§ 8.14   DESIGNATION OF EXPERT WITNESSES

FORM 8–10
DESIGNATION OF EXPERT WITNESSES

NO. _____

[PLAINTIFF(S) NAMES]	)	
Plaintiffs,	)	
	)	
	)	IN THE DISTRICT COURT OF
	)	
_____	)	_____ COUNTY,
	)	
v.	)	
	)	_____ JUDICIAL DISTRICT
[DEFENDANT(S) NAMES]	)	
Defendants.	)	

DESIGNATION OF EXPERT WITNESSES

TO THE HONORABLE JUDGE OF SAID COURT:

Comes Now _____, Defendant in the above-entitled and numbered cause, and pursuant to Court order and/or in supplementation of any discovery previously served, hereby designates the following experts who may be consulted and give testimony in this cause:

1. Defendant does not intend to call any expert witnesses retained by or for Defendants, at this time.

2. Defendant does, however, reserve the right to call as adverse expert witnesses any medical or mental health providers, or their custodian of records, who have been previously identified and designated by Plaintiff or other party Defendants in pleadings served in this cause.

It is anticipated that these experts will testify regarding the treatment and prognosis of their patient, and/or regarding the contents of their records provided in discovery.

Respectfully submitted,

NAME OF FIRM

_____

Name of Atty
Atty's Bar #
Address
City, State, Zip
Phone #

CERTIFICATE OF SERVICE

I hereby certify that a true and correct copy of the foregoing Defendant's Designation of Expert Witnesses has been served in compliance with Rules _____ and _____ of the _____ Rules of Civil Procedure on the _____ day of _____, 20___.

_____

§ 8.15   Pretrial Conferences and the Pretrial Order

Prior to 1983 the pretrial conference which took place in federal district court litigation was a meeting between counsel for the parties and the judge in his chambers just prior to the trial. It was a meeting in which the judge routinely asked the attorneys present if they were ready to proceed to trial and whether there was any hope of settlement prior to trial.

Rather than being a mere formality, the role of the pretrial conference has expanded to the point that the first meeting takes place within 90 days after the appearance of a defendant and within 120 days after the complaint has been served upon the defendant. During these conferences, the judge and the counsel for the parties actually plan the management of the case and actively pursue settlement possibilities.

The purpose of the pretrial conference is to encourage settlement, expedite the disposition of the case by good case management, and ease the crowded nature of the court's docket.

Items considered at the pretrial conference may include:

1. The formulation and simplification of the issues and the elimination of frivolous issues
2. Amendments to the pleadings
3. The possibility of obtaining admissions of fact and of documents, which will avoid unnecessary proof
4. Stipulations as to the authenticity of documents
5. Advance rulings from the court on the admissibility of evidence
6. The avoidance of unnecessary proof and cumulative evidence and limitations on the use of expert testimony
7. The appropriateness and timing of summary adjudication under Federal Rule of Civil Procedure 56
8. The control and scheduling of discovery
9. The identification of witnesses
10. The identification of documents
11. The need and schedule for filing pretrial briefs
12. The date or dates for further conferences and for trial

13. The advisability of referring matters to a magistrate judge or master
14. Settlement and the use of special procedures to assist in resolving the dispute
15. The disposition of pending motions
16. Procedures for handling complex actions or issues, multiple parties, and difficult legal questions
17. Procedures for handling unusual proof problems
18. The form and substance of the pretrial order
19. An order for a separate trial with respect to any claim, counterclaim, cross-claim, third-party claim, or with respect to any particular issue in the case
20. An order directing the parties to present evidence early in the trial with respect to a manageable issue that could, on the evidence, be the basis for a judgment as a matter of law under Federal Rule of Civil Procedure 50(a) or a judgment on partial findings under Federal Rule of Civil Procedure 52(c)
21. An order establishing a reasonable limit on the time allowed for presenting evidence.

One of the objectives of these conferences is to come up with a schedule which manages the deadlines of time to join parties and amend pleadings and complete discovery. This schedule is called a pretrial order. (See **Form 8–12**) Pretrial orders can be agreed on and drawn up by the parties in some jurisdictions. The final pretrial conference takes place just prior to trial and manifests itself in a final pretrial order Some judges have standard pretrial orders which are used in their courts, filling in the appropriate dates for each case.

The pretrial order may limit the time:

1. To join other parties
2. To amend the pleadings
3. To complete discovery.

The pretrial order may also:

1. Modify the times for mandatory disclosure under Rule 26(a)
2. Modify the times for supplementation of disclosures under Rule 26(e)(1)
3. Modify the extent of discovery to be permitted
4. Include the date or dates for conferences before trial and a final pretrial conference
5. Include the date for trial
6. Include other matters appropriate to the case.

The schedule in the pretrial order may not be modified except upon a showing of good cause and by leave of the court.

New to the 1994 Federal Rules of Civil Procedure is Rule 26(f) which calls for a mandatory discovery planning meeting which is to take place no later than 14 days before either a scheduling conference is held or a scheduling order is due under Rule 16(b). The purpose of this meeting, according to Rule 26(f) is to discuss the possibilities of a "prompt settlement or resolution of the case, to make or arrange for the disclosures required by subdivision (a)(l), and to develop a proposed discovery plan."

A number of federal district courts have disapproved or modified the requirements of Rule 26(f).

At the planning meeting, attorneys are to discuss the proposed schedule for disclosure of discovery as provided for in Rule 26, the subjects which will be covered by disclosure rules, and whether there is a need for discovery to be conducted in phases or to be limited to particular issues, if any modifications to the limitation or imposition of discovery under the rules need to be implemented in the case (presumably by agreement between the parties), and the need for any other orders by the court to expedite or facilitate the process. All attorneys of record and all unrepresented parties who have appeared in the case at that point in time are responsible for appearing at the meeting and attempting to formulate the discovery plan in a good faith effort. According to Rule 26(f)(4), they then must prepare and submit to the court "a written report outlining the plan" within 10 days after the meeting. The Federal Rules of Civil Procedure contain Form 35, Report of Parties' Planning Meeting (**Form 8–11**), which may be used for fulfilling the report obligation created under Rule 26(f)(4). Paralegals should calendar all dates stated in the report immediately upon receipt of the document. Rule 16(b) provides that the court should not issue the scheduling order until it has received the report required by Rule 26(f).

§ 8.16   Sample Report of Parties' Planning Meeting

FORM 8-11
SAMPLE REPORT OF PARTIES' PLANNING MEETING
(FED. R. CIV. P. FORM 35)

IN THE UNITED STATES DISTRICT COURT
[judicial district] JUDICIAL DISTRICT OF [state]
[judicial division] DIVISION

[name]		)	
		)	
	Plaintiff	)	
		)	
vs.		)	Civil Action No. [case number]
		)	
[name]		)	
		)	
	Defendant	)	

§ 8.16 REPORT OF PLANNING MEETING

Report of Parties' Planning Meeting

1. Pursuant to Fed. R. Civ. P. 26(f), a meeting was held on [date] at [place] and was attended by:
    [name] for plaintiff[s]
    [name] for defendant[s] [party name]
    [name] for defendant[s] [party name]

2. Prediscovery Disclosures. The parties [have exchanged/will exchange by [date]] the information required by [Fed. R. Civ. P. 26(a)(1)/local rule [citation].

3. Discovery Plan. The parties jointly propose to the court the following discovery plan: [use separate paragraphs or subparagraphs as necessary if parties disagree.]

Discovery will be needed on the following subjects: [brief description of subjects on which discovery will be needed].

All discovery commenced in time to be completed by [date]. (Discovery on [issue for early discovery] to be completed by [date].)

Maximum of [number] interrogatories by each party to any other party. (Responses due [number] days after service.)

Maximum of [number] requests for admission by each party to any other party. (Responses due [number] days after service.)

Maximum of [number] depositions by plaintiff(s) and by defendant(s).

Each deposition (other than of [name]) limited to maximum of [number] hours unless extended by agreement of parties.

Reports from retained experts under Rule 26(a)(2) due:

  from plaintiff(s) by [date]
  from defendant(s) by [date]

Supplementations under Rule 26(e) due [time(s)/interval(s)].

4. Other Items. (use separate paragraphs or subparagraphs as necessary if parties disagree.)

The parties [request/do not request] a conference with the court before entry of the scheduling order.

The parties request a pretrial conference in [month and year].

Plaintiff(s) should be allowed until [date] to join additional parties and until [date] to amend the pleadings.

Defendant(s) should be allowed until [date] to join additional parties and until [date] to amend the pleadings.

All potentially dispositive motions should be filed by [date].

Settlement [is likely/is unlikely/cannot be evaluated prior to [datel/*may be enhanced by use of the following alternative dispute resolution procedure: [description of alternate procedure].]

Final lists of witnesses and exhibits under Rule 26(a)(3) should be due

> from plaintiff(s) by [date]
> from defendant(s) by [date]

Parties should have [number] days after service of final lists of witnesses and exhibits to list objections under Rule 26(a)(3).

The case should be ready for trial by [date] (and at this time is expected to take approximately [length of time]).

[other matters]

Date:[date]

_____

[name]

_____

[name]

§ 8.17   Pretrial Conference Checklist

Sometimes it is the paralegal's responsibility to help prepare conference. Use the following checklist to make sure that the pretrial conference runs smoothly:

____   1.   Are all pleadings in order?

____   2.   Has counsel upon whom request for certification is served withdrawn?

____   3.   Have all written and filed agreements to take depositions and produce party for physical examination been accomplished?

____   4.   Have all necessary ad litem and/or interpreter appointments been made?

____   5.   Have all matters preliminary to trial been accomplished and the case readied for trial?

____   6.   Have all parties and counsel of record been furnished with copies of requests for certification?

____   7.   Are there any venue or jurisdictional problems?

___ 8. Have all expert witnesses been designated?

§ 8.18 Sample Pretrial Order

FORM 8–12
SAMPLE PRETRIAL ORDER

No. _____

:   IN THE DISTRICT COURT OF
:   _____ COUNTY, _____
:   _____ JUDICIAL DISTRICT _____

JOINT PRETRIAL ORDER APPEARANCE OF COUNSEL

(List the parties, their respective counsel and the address and telephone numbers of counsel in separate paragraphs.)

STATEMENT OF THE CASE

(Give a brief statement of the case for the information of the Court.)

MOTIONS

(State if there are any pending motions.)

CONTENTIONS OF THE PARTIES

(State concisely in separate paragraphs what each party claims.)

ADMISSIONS OF FACT

(List all facts which have been stipulated and admitted and require no proof.)

CONTESTED ISSUES OF FACT

(List all factual issues in controversy necessary to the final disposition of this case.)

AGREED APPLICABLE PROPOSITIONS OF LAW

(Delineate those legal propositions not in dispute.)

CONTESTED ISSUES OF LAW

(State briefly the issue of law in dispute, with a memorandum of authorities supporting each issue.)

TRIAL READINESS AND SETTLEMENT

EXHIBITS

1. Each counsel will attach to the JOINT pretrial order a copy of the list of all exhibits to be offered and will make all such exhibits available for examination by opposing counsel. This rule does not apply to rebuttal exhibits, which cannot be anticipated.

2. Any counsel requiring authentication of an exhibit must so notify in writing the offering counsel within (5) days after the exhibit is made available to opposing counsel for examination. FAILURE TO DO SO is an ADMISSION of authenticity.

3. Any other objections to admissibility of exhibits must, where possible, be made at least three (3) business days before trial, and the Court notified in writing with copies to all counsel accompanied by supporting legal authorities and copies of the exhibits *in* dispute.

4. The offering party will MARK HIS OWN EXHIBITS.

5. All exhibits will be OFFERED and RECEIVED in evidence as the FIRST ITEM OF BUSINESS at the trial.

WITNESSES

1. List the names and addresses of witnesses who will or may by used with a brief statement of the subject matter and substance of their testimony.

2. Include in this section the following:

    "In the event there are any other witnesses to be called at the trial, their names, addresses and the subject matter of their testimony shall be reported to opposing counsel as soon as they are known. This restriction shall not apply to rebuttal or impeaching witnesses, the necessity of whose testimony cannot reasonable be anticipated before the time of trial."

SETTLEMENT

(Include a statement that all settlement efforts have been exhausted, that the case cannot be settled, and will have to be tried.)

TRIAL

(Include in this-paragraph the following:
 a.   Probable length of trial: AND
 b.   Availability of witnesses, including out-of-state witnesses.)

ATTACHMENTS

(Include the following REQUIRED attachments:

I   For a jury trial:Proposed Special Issues, including instructions or definitions.

ll   For a non-jury trial: Proposed findings of fact and conclusions of law, with
        supporting authorities in a memorandum of law.)

_____

Judge Presiding

_____   _____

Attorney for Plaintiff   Attorney for Defendant

§ 8.19   Motion for Continuance

Occasionally, for a variety of reasons, it may he necessary to ask the court for
continuance or postponement of a trial date. Normally, judges have their own special
unwritten rules about what reasons will be deemed good enough to rearrange the
trial schedule. Some judges are adamant about changing dates, and you would be
well advised to make note of such things in your judge's notebook for reference at
times like these.

   Your local court rules may vaguely spell out some of the acceptable and unac-
ceptable reasons for delaying a trial. Frivolous reasons will not be tolerated in any
jurisdiction, and failure to be ready for trial just because of bad planning and
preparation is not an excuse the court looks upon fondly. Acceptable reasons may
include the unavailability of a key witness or the illness of a party. Most matters are
decided by the discretion of the court, no matter what the local rules may say.

   You may be able to speak to opposing counsel and get him to agree on a
continuance without the necessity of asking the court to rule on such a motion.
Usually, however, the court will only allow one such agreed continuance. Either
way, the court will require a motion (**Form 8–11**) be it agreed or ex parte, so as to
rule and make the motion formal (**Form 8–14**).

FORM 8–13
SAMPLE AGREED MOTION FOR CONTINUANCE

[case number]

[name]	)	IN THE [type] COURT OF
	)	
vs.	)	[county] COUNTY, [state]
	)	
[name]	)	[judicial district] JUDICIAL DISTRICT

AGREED MOTION FOR CONTINUANCE

TO THE HONORABLE JUDGE OF SAID COURT:

TRIAL READINESS AND SETTLEMENT

COMES NOW [name], Plaintiff in the above cause, and pursuant to Rule [citation] of the [state/federal] Rules of Civil Procedure asking that this Court grant them a Continuance of their trial presently scheduled for [date], [20___] and for grounds would show the Court as follows:

I.

The Defendants herein have been properly cited to appear in this Court for trial on this cause on [date], 20[year], at [time] [A.M./P.M.].

II.

Plaintiff would show that their attorney [name] is further attorney of record for [name] in a pending matter currently set for trial in the [type] Court, in a case styled [plaintiff] v. [defendant]. That courtroom is in the County of [county], which is [number] miles from the city of [city] where this trial is scheduled.

III.

Counsel for Plaintiff and Defendant have agreed to reset the trial on this cause until [date] or such time as the Court deems appropriate. Defendant's willingness to allow this continuance is evidenced by its attorney's signature to the Agreed Order granting such a continuance which was submitted simultaneously with this Motion.

WHEREFORE, PREMISES CONSIDERED, Plaintiff [name] prays that the trial setting for [date], [20___], be continued until [date].

Respectfully submitted,
[name of firm]
By _____
   [name of attorney]
   [address]
   ATTORNEYS FOR PLAINTIFF

THE STATE OF [state]	)
COUNTY OF [county]	)

BEFORE ME, the undersigned authority, on this day personally appeared [name] who, being duly sworn by me, deposed and stated that he is attorney of record for the Plaintiff herein and that he has read the above and foregoing Motion for Continuance and that all facts stated herein are true and correct.

SUBSCRIBED AND SWORN TO BEFORE ME on this the [date] day of [month], [20___].

_____

Notary Public in and for
The State of [state] _____

_____

[notary's name typed or printed]
My Commission Expires: [date]

[Add certificate of service.]

FORM 8–14
SAMPLE AGREED ORDER GRANTING PLAINTIFF'S MOTION
FOR CONTINUANCE

[case number]

[name]	)	IN THE [type] COURT OF
	)	
vs.	)	[county] COUNTY, [state]
	)	
[name]	)	[judicial district] JUDICIAL DISTRICT

AGREED ORDER GRANTING
PLAINTIFF'S MOTION FOR CONTINUANCE

BE IT REMEMBERED that on this [date] day of [month] [20__] came on to be heard Plaintiff's Motion For Continuance, and the Court is of the opinion that it should be granted. It is therefore

ORDERED that this case previously set for [date], [20__] at [time] [A.M. / P.M.] shall now be placed on the docket for trial for [date], [20__], at [time] [AM./P.M.]

SIGNED this day of [date], [20__].

_____

Presiding Judge

APPROVED AS TO FORM
AND SIGNATURE REQUESTED:

[name of plaintiff's firm]

By: _____
[name of attorney]
[address]
ATTORNEYS FOR PLAINTIFF

[name of defendant's firm]

By: _____
[name of attorney]
[address]
ATTORNEY'S FOR DEFENDANT

§ 8.20   Motion in Limine

Part of the pretrial preparation includes consideration information which may be prejudicial to your case. In order to prevent the jury from hearing such information, a Motion in Limine (**Form 8-15**) is presented to the judge asking for protection against the introduction of the information. A motion in limine generally asks the court to make an evidentiary ruling prior to the trial. These motions are heard out of the presence of the jury, and if your motion is granted, opposing counsel is barred from introduction of the material in the presence of the jury. A motion in limine is best made before jury selection to ensure that no mention of the evidence in question is made in the jury's presence.

Motions in Limine are sometimes used similarly to declaratory judgments. In cases where a partial summary judgment has been obtained by one of the parties, Motions in Limine are often introduced to make sure that the points of the summary judgment are clarified and the boundaries drawn concerning what the jury should be told about the summary judgment.

§ 8.21   Motions in Limine Subjects

The following list should be helpful in preparing motions in limine:

1. Motions to exclude references to benefits plaintiff has received from insurance coverages, social security benefits, worker's compensation, and so forth;

2. Motions to prevent reference to the fact that one of the parties has been accused of, or has been found guilty of, a criminal offense which is unrelated to this case, as long as it is not a question of moral turpitude;

3. Motions to prevent reference to the receipt or nonreceipt of a traffic ticket by one of the parties in connection with a traffic accident which is the basis of the suit;

4. Motions to prevent reference to the plaintiff's involvement in prior or subsequent claims, lawsuits, or settlements, the only purpose of such references being that of detriment or prejudice;

5. Motions to prevent reference to the time or circumstances during which the plaintiff employed counsel;

6. Motions to prevent reference to the impending or subsequent remarriage of a surviving spouse in a wrongful death lawsuit;

516

7. Motion to prevent reference to the fact that damages recovered in a lawsuit are not subject to taxation by any governmental entity;

8. Motions to ensure the proper instruction of jurors regarding prior rulings, such as partial summary judgments in a case.

FORM 8–15
SAMPLE MOTION IN LIMINE

[case number]

[name]	) IN THE [type] COURT OF
	)
vs.	) [county] COUNTY, [state]
	)
[name]	) [judicial district] JUDICIAL DISTRICT

MOTION IN LIMINE

TO THE HONORABLE JUDGE OF SAID COURT:

COMES NOW [name] the [defendant/plaintiff] in the above cause, after the case has been assigned for trial but prior to the voir dire examination of the jury panel in connection with said trial, to file this first motion in limine, in support of which [defendant/plaintiff] respectfully shows to the Court the following:

I.

That [defendant/plaintiff] requests that counsel be instructed not to go into any of the matters numbered and set forth below in the presence of the jury, and that with repect to all of those matters set forth below that counsel be instructed to warn their clients and witnesses not to volunteer such matters or go into such matters in the presence of the jury (other than in response to a direct question):

1. [list matters that defendant/plaintiff want covered by this motion].

_____

2. _____

_____

3. _____

_____

Respectfully submitted,

_____

Attorney for [defendant/plaintiff]

§ 8.22 Trial Book

When an attorney goes to trial, he should have the nuts and bolts of his case at the trial table with him. Throughout the case, many documents and pieces of evidence are sifted through and culled out. Those which have the most importance and relevancy to his case are preserved in a trial book. A trial book is a large, three-ring binder which contains all the substantive pleadings in the case. It also contains a section entitled "Voir Dire," in which is kept questions for prospective jurors and any information you have managed to gather about those prospective jurors. An entire section should be devoted to witnesses and all pertinent information and testimony relating to them. Evidence has its own section and should include exhibit stickers ready to be filled out in court. The last portion of the trial book consists of the jury instructions you wish the judge to use. Both sides will submit instructions, and the judge may use one or the other, or a combination of both.

When the trial book is finished, it will contain the entire case in capsule form. It becomes the attorney's bible at trial and by necessity, should be one hundred percent accurate and complete.

§ 8.23 —Pleadings

The pleadings section of a trial book should contain all substantive pleadings in the case. It is not necessary to include any procedural motions or notices. Make sure that this section includes all amended petitions and answers. This is also the section in which to include all interrogatory answers. Documents should be clearly labeled with title and date of filing. If the title of the document is simply Answers to Interrogatories, be sure to designate in the title whether they are the plaintiff's answers or the defendant's answers. It is helpful to group documents of like kind together, such as all the interrogatory answers and the amended answers to the same interrogatories. Some attorneys also prefer to separate those documents filed by the plaintiff and those filed by the defendant. Others may prefer all pleadings placed in the chronological order in which they were filed. Check with your attorney for his preference.

§ 8.24 Voir Dire

Before trial begins, thought should be given to the type of person who would be beneficial to your case if seated on the jury. Attention should be given to values, attitudes, occupations, educational level, and whether there is anything in that person's makeup or background that would make him or her unable to render a fair and impartial verdict in the case. Each case will be different and will present its own distinctive set of circumstances, but some questions asked of a prospective jury panel during voir dire are fairly standard. One of the most revealing questions to ask a jury panel seated for a personal injury case relates to whether they or anyone in their family has been or is now a party in a personal injury lawsuit. If the answer to this question is affirmative, obviously you will want to find out if that person was a plaintiff or defendant. This type of close-to-home exposure to a similar lawsuit will usually bias your prospective juror and should be anticipated and dealt with accordingly.

The voir dire section of your trial book should contain the relative questions you have worked up as well as any information on prospective jurors you have been able to acquire in advance. In some jurisdictions, lists of the jury panels are available prior to trial. If they are available in your jurisdiction, by all means, do some research on the jurors. It is heartbreaking to go into a trial well-prepared and have opposing counsel leave you in the starting block because you did not prepare well for jury selection.

There are many effective ways of dividing a voir dire examination into topics and arranging them in order. The following sequence has been useful in many cases:

1. Introduction of parties and attorneys.
2. Inquiry as to juror's acquaintance with parties or attorneys.
3. Revealing the nature of the case.
4. Questions as to juror's knowledge or acquaintanceship with matters covered in narrative introduction.
5. Inquiry as to bias of jurors.
6. Inquiry as to disqualifying facts.
7. Conclusion.

In addition to arranging the overall format persuasively, the attorney should make sure that his individual questions dealing with a particular topic are arranged properly. Arranging the questions in a logical sequence permits a step-by-step development of a complicated point and increases the likelihood that the juror will comprehend the point the attorney is attempting to make.

If, however, a juror is being examined for the sole purpose of obtaining an admission from him that will substantiate a challenge for cause, the sequence of questioning should be like cross-examination. It is sometimes wise not to place questions in a purely logical sequence, thus preventing the witness from anticipating the course of future questions.

§ 8.25   Prospective Juror Questions Checklist

Subject to relatively few guidelines, the trial judge has wide discretion in controlling the scope of voir dire questions, and he will usually exercise this discretion in conformity with the established customs of his jurisdiction. In general, counsel can assume the trial judge will not permit subjects to be raised on voir dire that would require the granting of a mistrial if broached during trial, although sometimes it is possible to come closer to a forbidden subject, such as insurance, during voir dire than at any other time during trial.

In most situations, the judge's ruling on suggested questions will not be interfered with on appeal unless he clearly abuses his authority. When counsel is permitted to examine the jury, the trial judge, within his judgment and intelligence, may properly limit the extent of the examination within the bounds of fairness.

Because of the all-embracing nature of prejudice, a wide latitude should be allowed in the course of voir dire examination to probe the mental attitudes of jurors. Such free inquiry into the background and interests of jurors is especially necessary when a challenge for cause is not developed and counsel must question further to enable him to make a decision as to the advisibility of making a peremptory challenge.

Practice Guide

A checklist of questions that may be put to the prospective jurors on voir dire, where related to the parties or issues involved in a particular trial, is set out below:

____ 1. Nativity and ancestry of juror.

____ 2. Necessary property qualifications.

____ 3. Moral deficiencies.

____ 4. Education (schools and colleges attended) and knowledge of the English language.

____ 5. State of health and condition of the juror's ordinary faculties.

____ 6. Previous jury service.

____ 7. Possibility of membership on grand jury that returned the indictment to be tried by a petit jury.

____ 8. Possible membership on a previous jury that heard the same evidence as will be offered in the case at trial.

____ 9. Interest in another case pending for trial at the same term of court.

____ 10. Relationship to the parties or their attorneys.

____ 11. Direct or indirect financial interest in the outcome of the case.

____ 12. Relationship (as partner, employer, employee, landlord, tenant, debtor, creditor, or surety) to any of the parties.

____ 13. Membership in any organization to which one of the parties belongs.

____ 14. Marital status and children.

____ 15. Social, religious, fraternal, labor union, and political affiliations.

____ 16. Present and former places of residence.

____ 17. Present and former places of employment and, if married, the gainful employment, if any, of his or her spouse.

____ 18. In a criminal case, whether the prospective juror has been connected with any organization whose object is to suppress and punish crime, and

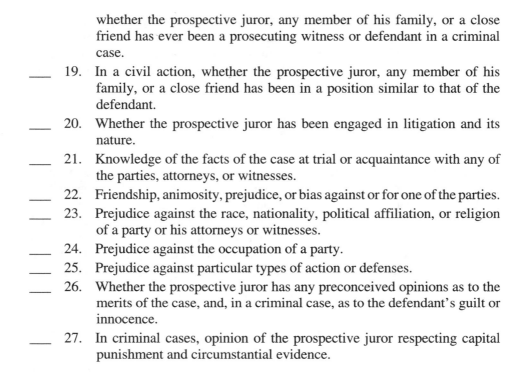

whether the prospective juror, any member of his family, or a close friend has ever been a prosecuting witness or defendant in a criminal case.

____ 19. In a civil action, whether the prospective juror, any member of his family, or a close friend has been in a position similar to that of the defendant.

____ 20. Whether the prospective juror has been engaged in litigation and its nature.

____ 21. Knowledge of the facts of the case at trial or acquaintance with any of the parties, attorneys, or witnesses.

____ 22. Friendship, animosity, prejudice, or bias against or for one of the parties.

____ 23. Prejudice against the race, nationality, political affiliation, or religion of a party or his attorneys or witnesses.

____ 24. Prejudice against the occupation of a party.

____ 25. Prejudice against particular types of action or defenses.

____ 26. Whether the prospective juror has any preconceived opinions as to the merits of the case, and, in a criminal case, as to the defendant's guilt or innocence.

____ 27. In criminal cases, opinion of the prospective juror respecting capital punishment and circumstantial evidence.

Voir dire questioning, in most jurisdictions, is not confined to subjects that constitute grounds for challenge for cause, and may extend beyond, in order to enable counsel to gain knowledge that will aid him in the exercise of peremptory challenges. Where counsel is allowed a major role in testing the jury on the voir dire, the cases generally hold that he should be carefully supervised by the court and not allowed to range far afield. Questions should be properly asked and not be too general, too involved, or too indefinite.

§ 8.26   Witness Files

During the course of the lawsuit, you will have accumulated testimony, documents, and background information relating to each witness. The witness file of a trial book should contain the following items for each witness:

1. Witness statements
2. Deposition transcripts
3. Deposition summaries
4. Documents addressed to, authored by, copied to, or mentioning the name of the witness
5. Excerpts from discovery responses directly relating to things within that witness' knowledge.

All documents should be clearly marked so that the attorney can put his hand on the information he needs while the witness is on the stand. Many times, the trial testimony of a witness differs from his sworn testimony earlier in the case, or may be disproved or strengthened by documents. In those instances, the information must be instantly available or it may lose its effectiveness.

§ 8.27   Evidence

As certain documents are pinpointed as beneficial for evidentiary purposes, index them and place them in the trial book. When you go into trial, the trial book will be as valuable to you as a bank vault. If you consistently place evidence in the trial book immediately, there is much less chance of it being misplaced or compromised. Keep an ample supply of exhibit stickers with the evidence, if they have not already been marked and indexed for filing with the judge. In many jurisdictions, this is required prior to trial, and may be exchanged between the plaintiff's and defendant's attorneys at the pretrial conference.

§ 8.28   Jury Instructions

Stock jury instructions are available in most form books for individual states. Once the issues to be addressed at trial have been determined, the stock jury instructions should be reviewed for relevance, and individual jury instructions should be written for those issues which are not standard. Both parties will be providing a set of jury instructions to the judge, and the judge will pick those which he feels are appropriate to read to the jury at the close of the trial. The jury instructions you have prepared should be placed in the trial book and taken to trial for presentation to the judge.

FORM 8–16
CHARGE OF THE COURT
(Wrongful Repossession and Deceptive Trade Practices Act)

NO. _____

[PLAINTIFF(S) NAMES] Plaintiffs,	)))	
	)	IN THE DISTRICT COURT OF
	)	
_____	)	_____ COUNTY,
	)	
v.	)	
	)	_____ JUDICIAL DISTRICT
[DEFENDANT(S) NAMES] Defendants.	))	

§ 8.28   JURY INSTRUCTIONS

CHARGE OF THE COURT
[WRONGFUL REPOSSESSION AND DECEPTIVE
TRADE PRACTICES ACT]

LADIES AND GENTLEMEN OF THE JURY:

This case is submitted to you by asking questions about the facts, which you must decide from the evidence you heard in this trial. You are the sole judges of the credibility of the witnesses and the weight to be given their testimony, but in matters of law, you must be governed by the instructions in this charge. In discharging your responsibility on this jury, you will observe all the instructions which have previously been given you. I shall now give you additional instructions which you should carefully and strictly follow during your deliberations.

1. Do not let bias, prejudice, or sympathy play any part in your deliberations.
2. In arriving at your answers, consider only the evidence introduced here under oath and such exhibits, and the rulings of the court; that is, what you have seen and heard in this courtroom, together with the law as given you by the court. In your deliberations, you will not consider or discuss anything that is not represented by the evidence in this case.
3. Since every answer that is required by the charge is important, no juror should state or consider that a required answer is not important.
4. You must not decide who you think should win, and then try to answer the questions accordingly. Simply answer the questions, and do not discuss nor concern yourselves with the effect of your answers.
5. You must not decide the answer to a question by lot or by drawing straws, or by any other method of chance. Do not return a quotient verdict. A quotient verdict means that the jurors agree to abide by the result to be reached by adding together each juror's figures and dividing by the number of jurors to get an average. Do not do any trading on your answers; that is, one juror should not agree to answer a certain question one way if others will agree to answer another question another way.
6. You may render your verdict upon the vote of five or more members of the jury. The same five or more of you must agree upon all of the answers made and to the entire verdict. You will not, therefore, enter into an agreement to be bound by a majority of any other vote of less than five jurors. If the verdict and all the answers are reached by unanimous agreement, the presiding juror shall sign the verdict for the entire jury. If any juror disagrees as to any answer made by the verdict, those jurors who agree to all findings shall each sign the verdict.

These instructions are given you because your conduct is subject to review the same as that of the witnesses, parties, attorneys, and the judge. If it should be found that you have disregarded any of these instructions, it will be jury misconduct and it may require another trial by another jury; then all of our time will have been wasted.

The presiding juror or any other who observes a violation of the court's instructions shall immediately warn the one who is violating the same and caution the juror not to do so again.

When words are used in this charge in a sense which varies from the meaning commonly understood, you are given a proper legal definition, which you are bound to accept in place of any other meaning.

Answer "Yes" or "No" to all questions unless otherwise instructed. A "Yes" answer must be based on a preponderance of the evidence. If you do not find that a preponderance of the evidence supports a "Yes" answer, then answer "No." The term "preponderance of the evidence" means the greater weight and degree of credible testimony or evidence introduced before you and admitted in this case.

Whenever a question requires other than a "Yes" or "No" answer, your answer must be based on a preponderance of the evidence.

Instructions/ Definitions

You are instructed that a fact may be established by direct evidence, by circumstantial evidence, or both. A fact is established by direct evidence when proved by witnesses who saw the act done or heard the words spoken or by documentary evidence. A fact is established by circumstantial evidence when it may be fairly and reasonably inferred from other facts provided.

Question No. 1

Did the Defendants engage in any false, misleading, or deceptive act or practice with respect to the replacement of the engine in the Plaintiff's car that was a producing cause of the damages to Plaintiff?

"Producing cause" means an efficient, exciting, or contributing cause that, in a natural sequence, produced the damages, if any. There may be more than one producing cause.

"False, misleading, or deceptive act or practice" means any of the following:

1. Representing that goods or services had or would have characteristics or benefits which they did not have;
2. Representing that goods or services are or will be of a particular standard, quality, or grade if they were of another;
3. Representing that an agreement confers or involves rights, remedies, or obligations that it did not have or involve or which are prohibited by law;
4. Knowingly making false or misleading statements of fact concerning the need for parts, replacement, or repair;
5. Failing to disclose information about goods or services that was known at the time of the transaction, with the intention to induce another into the transaction; or
6. In the course of collecting an alleged debt, threatening a person that nonpayment of an alleged debt will result in the seizure, repossession, or sale of any property of that person without proper court proceedings.

Answer "yes" or "no" as to each Defendant:

ANSWER: _____[NAME OF DEFENDANT]_____   YES   NO

_____[NAME OF DEFENDANT]_____   YES   NO

Question No. 2

Did the Defendants engage in any unconscionable action or course of action that was a producing cause of damages to the Plaintiff?

"Producing cause" means an efficient, exciting, or contributing cause that, in a natural sequence, produced the damages, if any. There may be more than one producing cause. An unconscionable action or course of action is an act or practice that, to a person's detriment, either

   a. Takes advantage of the lack of knowledge, ability, experience, or capacity of a person to a grossly unfair degree, or

   b. Results in a gross disparity between the value received and the consideration paid in a transaction involving transfer of consideration.

Answer "yes" or "no" as to each Defendant:

ANSWER: _____[NAME OF DEFENDANT]_____   YES   NO

ANSWER: _____[NAME OF DEFENDANT]_____   YES   NO

If you have answered Question Nos. 1 or 2 "yes," then answer Question No. 3.

Question No. 3

Was the Defendants' conduct, if any, committed knowingly?

"Knowingly" means actual awareness of the falsity, deception, or unfairness of the act or practice giving rise to the consumer's claim. Actual awareness may be inferred when objective manifestations indicate that a person acted with actual awareness.

Answer "yes" or "no" as to each Defendant:

ANSWER: _____[NAME OF DEFENDANT]_____   YES   NO

ANSWER: _____[NAME OF DEFENDANT]_____   YES   NO

Question No. 4

Did the Defendants make a conversion of the Plaintiff's car when it was repossessed on or about _____?

"Conversion" means the unlawful and wrongful exercise of dominion, ownership, or control by a person over the property of another person, to the exclusion of the exercise of the same rights by the rightful owner.

You are further instructed that in [state name], a mechanic or repair shop does not obtain a lawful lien over property until repairs have been made and the amount charged has not been paid, and then only if the mechanic retains possession of the car, or relinquishes his possession only after an insufficient-funds check has been given in payment of the repairs, or a check is given in payment on a closed account, or a stop-payment order is made on the check given.

Answer "yes" or "no" as to each Defendant:

ANSWER: _____ [NAME OF DEFENDANT] _____ YES   NO

ANSWER: _____ [NAME OF DEFENDANT] _____ YES   NO

If you answered Question No. 4 "yes" with regard to either Defendant, then answer Question No. 5 only with regard to the Defendant for whom you answered "yes" in No. 4.

Question No. 5

Do you find that the Defendants' conduct in taking or retaining possession of the Plaintiff's care was wanton and malicious?

Actual ill will or an intent to injure is not necessary. Wanton and malicious conduct may be implied from the knowing conversion of someone's property without justification.

Answer "yes" or "no" as to each Defendant:

ANSWER: _____ [NAME OF DEFENDANT] _____ YES   NO

ANSWER: _____ [NAME OF DEFENDANT] _____ YES   NO

Question No. 6

Did the Defendants commit fraud against the Plaintiff?

"Fraud" occurs when (a) a party makes a material misrepresentation, (b) the misrepresentation is made with knowledge of its falsity or made recklessly without any knowledge of the truth and as a positive assertion, (c) the misrepresentation is made with the intention that it should be acted on by the other party, and (d) the other party acts in reliance on the misrepresentation and thereby suffers injury.

"Misrepresentation" means a false statement of fact, or a statement of opinion based on a false statement of fact, or a statement of opinion that the maker knows to be false.

Furthermore, "misrepresentation" means an expression of opinion that is false, made by one claiming or implying to have special knowledge of the subject matter of the opinion. "Special knowledge" means knowledge or information superior to that possessed by the other party and to which the other party did not have equal access.

Furthermore, "fraud" occurs when (a) a party conceals or fails to disclose a material fact within the knowledge of that party, (b) the party knows that the other party is ignorant of the fact and does not have an equal opportunity to discover the truth, (c) the party intends to induce the other party to make some action by concealing or failing to disclose the fact, and (d) the other party suffers injury as a result of acting without knowledge of the undisclosed fact.

Answer "yes" or "no" as to each Defendant:

ANSWER: _____[NAME OF DEFENDANT]_____   YES   NO

ANSWER: _____[NAME OF DEFENDANT]_____   YES   NO

Question No. 7

Did the Defendants, on or about _____, make a trespass onto the Plaintiff's land when her car was repossessed?

A trespasser on land is a person who, not having title to the land, without consent of the true owner, makes entry thereon. Liability for trespassing is not dependent upon personal participation and a person who commands or requests a third person to enter land in possession of another is responsible for the third person's entry if it is a trespass.

Answer "yes" or "no" as to each Defendant:

ANSWER: _____[NAME OF DEFENDANT]_____   YES   NO

ANSWER: _____[NAME OF DEFENDANT]_____   YES   NO

If you have answered Question Nos. 6 or 7 "yes," then answer Question No. 8.

Question No. 8

Do you find that the Defendant's conduct referred to in Question Nos. 6 or 7 was committed with malice?

You are instructed that malice means: (1) conduct that is specifically intended by the Defendant to cause substantial injury to the claimant; or (2) an act that is carried out by the Defendant with a flagrant disregard for the rights of others with actual awareness on the part of the Defendant that the act will, in reasonable probability, result in harm or damage.

Answer "yes" or "no" as to each Defendant:

ANSWER: _____[NAME OF DEFENDANT]_____   YES   NO

ANSWER: _____[NAME OF DEFENDANT]_____   YES   NO

If you have answered Questions Nos. 1, 2, 4, 6, or 7 "yes," then answer Question No. 9.

TRIAL READINESS AND SETTLEMENT

Question No. 9

What sum of money, if any, if paid now in cash, would fairly and reasonably compensate Plaintiff for her damages, if any, that resulted from such conduct?

Consider the following elements of damages, if any, and none other.

Answer in dollars and cents, if any.

1. The difference, if any, between the price of the replacement engine agreed to between the parties and the amount actually paid by Plaintiff.

ANSWER: $_____

2. The reasonable and necessary cost for renting a car in _____ County, _____, for the period of time Plaintiff was deprived of the use of her car.

ANSWER: $_____

3. The reasonable value of the time lost by Plaintiff at work in attempting to correct the problems caused by the loss of the use of the car.

ANSWER: $_____

4. Mental anguish Plaintiff has suffered in the past as a result of the occurrence in question.

ANSWER: $_____

5. The reasonable value in _____ County, _____, of the ____ [make and model] _____ car on the date of the occurrence in question.

ANSWER: $_____

If you have answered Question No. 3 "yes," then answer Question No. 10.

Question No. 10

What sum of money, if any, do you find from a preponderance of the evidence should be awarded to Plaintiff as additional damages against Defendants?

"Additional damages" means an amount which you may, in your discretion, award as an example to others and as a penalty or by way of punishment or as compensation for the inconvenience and expenses of litigation, except attorney's fees and court costs, in addition to any amount which may have been found by you as actual damages.

Answer in dollars and cents, if any.

ANSWER: $_____.

If you have answered Question Nos. 3, 5 or 8 "yes," then answer Question No. 11.

Question No. 11

What sum of money, if any, is the Plaintiff entitled to receive from the Defendants as punitive damages?

Punitive damages means an amount that you may, at your discretion, award as an example to others and as a penalty or by way of punishment, in addition to any amount you may have found as actual damages.

It is not necessary to show that the Defendants were motivated by ill will or hatred of the Plaintiff.

In assessing punitive damages, if any, you may take into account not merely the act or acts of the Defendants themselves, but you may also take into account all of the circumstances, including any motives of the Defendants and the extent of damages, if any, suffered by the Plaintiff.

Answer in dollars and cents, if any.

Answer as to each Defendant:

_____ [Name of Defendant] _____ $_____

_____ [Name of Defendant] _____ $_____

Question No. 12

What sum of money do you find from a preponderance of the evidence to be reasonable attorney's fees for the services of Plaintiff's attorneys in her lawsuit against the Defendants _____ and _____ , as follows:

(A) For legal services rendered in the preparation and trial of this cause in this Court?

Answer in dollars and cents, if any.

ANSWER: $_____.

(B) For legal services if this case is appealed to the Court of Appeals?

Answer in dollars and cents, if any.

ANSWER: $_____.

(C) For legal services if application is made for writ of error to the Supreme Court of Texas?

Answer in dollars and cents, if any.

ANSWER: $_____.

(D) For legal services if the application for writ of error is granted by the Supreme Court of Texas?

Answer in dollars and cents, if any.

ANSWER: $_____.

Question No. 13

Did the Plaintiff, _____, exercise due diligence in effecting service of citation on the Defendant, _____?

You are instructed that the due diligence required to meet this test is that which an ordinary prudent person would use under the same or similar circumstances. An unexplained delay in effecting service constitutes a lack of due diligence. A reasonable explanation for delay constitutes due diligence.

Answer "yes" or "no".

ANSWER: _____

After you retire to the jury room, you will select your own presiding juror. The first thing the presiding juror will do is to have this complete charge read aloud and then you will deliberate upon your answers to the questions asked.

_____
Judge Presiding

CERTIFICATE

We, the jury, have answered the above and foregoing questions as herein indicated, and herewith return same into court as our verdict.

(To be signed by the presiding juror if unanimous.)

_____
Presiding Juror

§ 8.29   TRIAL CHECKLIST

(To be signed by those rendering the verdict if not unanimous.)

_____

_____

_____

(Number of spaces according to
number of jurors)

§ 8.29   Trial Checklist

As the discovery stage of the lawsuit draws to a close, this preliminary trial checklist should be consulted for a smooth transition into trial readiness.

____ 1. Request trial certification.
____ 2. Calendar all dates relative to trial as automatically ordered by the rules of civil procedure or as ordered by the court.
____ 3. File for summary judgment.
____ 4. Review pleadings to determine if they need amending.
____ 5. Notify parties and witnesses of confirmed trial date.
____ 6. Supplement discovery responses if necessary.
____ 7. Make sure all discovery requests to opposing party have been satisfactorily responded to.
____ 8. Check all evidence to make sure it has been properly proven-up.
____ 9. Review all statements and sworn testimony for inconsistencies.
____ 10. Make sure all medical records have been filed with the court
____ 11. Make sure all deposition transcripts have been filed with the court.
____ 12. Prepare subpoenas for witnesses.
____ 13. Prepare trial exhibits.
____ 14. Prepare voir dire questions for jury selection.
____ 15. Determine need for visual aids and trial exhibits.
____ 16. Prepare jury instructions.
____ 17. Organize exhibits.
____ 18. Prepare witnesses for trial.
____ 19. File list of exhibits with court.
____ 20. Complete preparation of trial book.
____ 21. Arrange for overhead projectors, easels, and so forth.
____ 22. Review witness files.

§ 8.30   Trial Kit

Whether you go to trial once a year or three times a month, it pays to be prepared. You will find it to your advantage to keep a large trial briefcase packed with necessary trial items so that everything you need for trial is in one place and ready to go at a moment's notice. With that chore already taken care of and out of the way, your time is free to follow up on the important last-minute details to which you need to attend.

The contents of the trial kit range from the very obvious legal tools you will need at trial, such as Rules of Civil Procedure and Rules of Evidence, to the myriad of office supplies you will take, such as pencils, pens, file folders, and labels to scissors, staplers, staples, and legal pads. Some of the contents of the trial kit, however, find their way onto the list only after experience has dictated their need following a conspicuous absence in the courtroom.

For example, while it may seem perfectly obvious to take a stapler and staples, it may not seem so obvious to include a staple remover. I can guarantee, however, that when the attorney sends you down into the bowels of the courthouse to make copies of the inch-thick document you both thought you would not need at trial, you will not find a staple remover sitting on top of the courthouse copy machine. Also, remember that you may need some petty cash or change of some sort for the copier.

The priceless value of a roll of duct tape is well known to people in many walks of life already. If you have not yet been introduced to its merits, let me remind you how embarrassing it would be to have your attorney or one of your witnesses trip over the extension cords you have trailed across the courtroom for your audiovisual aids. Duct tape can also temporarily fix just about anything which breaks at an inopportune time, and Murphy's Law dictates that that time will occur while you are in trial.

The toll of stress during time of trial should not be overlooked. The intensity of the situation often causes headaches for members of the trial team, and you should include ample supplies of both aspirin and nonaspirin pain relievers in your trial kit. Paper cuts are common, also, and you would be well advised to include a box of bandages.

When putting together your trial kit, you must remember that the courtroom will be your office for a few days, and anything you would have needed at your office you will need there also. Obviously, it is impossible to take everything you need with you, but with experience you will learn to make the transition as smoothly as you do a weekend trip for pleasure.

§ 8.31   Trial Kit Checklist

Keep a copy of the Trial Kit Checklist taped to the top of the inside of your trial briefcase and use it to check your kit's contents before leaving for every trial. Add to the list the things that you have found essential to your trial team which may not have appeared on this list.

§ 8.32 VISUAL AIDS AND EXHIBITS

____ 1. Rules of Civil Procedure for appropriate court,
____ 2. Rules of Evidence for appropriate court,
____ 3. Pencils, pens, ruler,
____ 4. Felt-tipped markers for charts and transparencies,
____ 5. Telescoping exhibit pointer,
____ 6. Exhibit labels,
____ 7. Manila file folders, expanding file folders,
____ 8. Stapler, staples, staple remover,
____ 9. Scissors,
____ 10. Pads of stick-on notes,
____ 11. File labels,
____ 12. Duct tape, extension cords,
____ 13. Petty cash (change for copy machines, telephones),
____ 14. Bandages,
____ 15. Aspirin or nonaspirin pain reliever,
____ 16. Legal pads,
____ 17. Paper clips,
____ 18. White correction fluid,
____ 19. Exhibit list forms.

§ 8.32 Visual Aids and Exhibits

No matter how good oral presentations are by either attorney in court, a jury will be duly impressed by a visual presentation. A complex idea or situation can be graphically displayed and simplified so that persons with no previous knowledge or experience in that subject are able to grasp the concept easily and quickly. Demonstrative evidence illustrates the depiction of crucial events or pivotal evidence to the jury. Sometimes, demonstrative evidence can be used for illustrative purposes even if it cannot be admitted as evidence at trial. Remember how difficult it was to understand fractions in the first grade until the teacher drew a picture of a divided pie on the blackboard?

The decision to utilize demonstrative exhibits at court is one which must be evaluated on several levels. Choosing an improper medium can be worse than using none at all. The subject matter itself may dictate which type of exhibit would be best. Remember that the goal of your exhibit is to magnify and clarify the issue to the jury in such a way that the most complex ideas are easily understood by persons with no previous background in that subject matter.

Cost should always be considered. Before large sums of money are spent on an elaborate exhibit, great thought should be given to what advantage may be gained by its use. Consideration should also be given to any potential problems which may arise with the admissibility of that particular exhibit, as it would not be prudent to spend a large sum of money when that factor may be in doubt. Economically, it also makes more sense to spend more of the money allotted for exhibits on those which have the potential for being able to be used over and over again during the trial. Before hiring new persons or firms to produce demonstrative exhibits, make sure you have seen examples of their work and have talked frankly about pricing structure. Prices can vary wildly from one vendor to another. I have gotten quotes from $80 to $350 on the same exhibit from different vendors.

Furthermore, the size of the exhibit and how easily it can be transported cannot be overlooked. Many small courtrooms, for example, may not be amenable to large and elaborate working models and oversized charts and graphs.

Visual aids and exhibits should have a clean, neat, and professional appearance. A jury is impressed with the completeness of an attorney's presentation, especially when he appears to have spent hours in the preparation of his client's case. It is possible to have professional quality trial exhibits at a surprisingly low cost these days. Using the services of the quick copy centers, you can produce fine-looking exhibits at a fraction of the cost that higher-priced advertising agencies or other litigation support companies might charge. Many of these copy centers now use computerized desktop publishing which can lower your costs even more. If you are uncertain how to display information visually to your best advantage, consult with a litigation support firm. Their experience in this format can be a valuable aid to you at trial. They specialize in converting written information to visual explanation.

The paralegal must have a ready list of contacts for producing demonstrative evidence and have a good rapport with those persons or firms. You must be able to express the objective of the exhibit and translate it to effectiveness. Make sure you see a draft of the exhibit or a mock-up before you sign off with your approval to be sure that the exhibit is not only professionally done but also reflects the objective you initially envisioned.

It is also vital that you understand the timing requirements of the vendor. It is generally advisable to wait as long as possible to produce trial exhibits because of the possibility of settlement of the case, but you must also allow the vendor enough time to produce a professional exhibit for you. Many of the processes they use require drying or setting-up time, in addition to the normal time constraints of working your project in among the others he has contracted to do. You will find that you will have a better rapport and be more satisfied with the product if you allow the vendor the time he needs to do his job properly.

One of the most dramatic moments of a trial is the revelation of physical injury. You may exhibit before the jury a part of plaintiff's body to show the extent or results of alleged injuries during your examination of an expert. This is an effective way to demonstrate the nature and extent of your client's injuries and any resulting disability. Obtain the court's permission prior to the exhibition. Scars and deformities must be presented in a very low-key style to avoid offending the jury.

For example, you may have a doctor manipulate the injured party's arms to show normal range of motion on the uninjured arm compared to restricted range of motion on the injured arm. In this way, limitation of motion, disability, and pain caused by the injury are graphically illustrated to the jury. You can also demonstrate disabilities effectively by having plaintiff, unaided, perform various routine physical movements (*e.g.*, walking, bending, reaching) before the jury.

In a tragic case, a young woman was dragged behind a trailer, and her ear was completely rubbed off. Despite numerous plastic surgeries, she remained seriously deformed, her facial muscles paralyzed and the latex replacement ear a poor substitute. Expert witnesses included a scholar from Oxford who was born without one ear and who has written eloquently about his experiences as an expert witness. The plastic surgeon testified tenderly about the plaintiff's devastating injury and, in a breathless silence, lifted the plaintiff's hair as she removed the latex ear. She turned in profile so the jurors could examine the wound, and in the five or six seconds that she stood, frozen in grief, tears began to stream down her face. Everyone in the courtroom was transfixed with empathy. Several jurors began to wipe away tears. They said afterwards that no amount of money could right the wrong. The delicate balance between the gruesome and the grandiloquent had been achieved.

§ 8.33 Overlays and Transparencies

It is often effective to present evidence in a visual manner which demonstrates degrees of change. A very effective way of doing this, especially for portraying disfigurement or the results of many operations, is to create a series of overlays over a primary normal picture. The resulting changes have a profound effect on a jury. You can contact local advertising agencies and litigation support agencies to perform this type of work.

Transparencies shown on an overhead projector are also useful trial tools. They can be marked on with grease pencils to illustrate a point. This is a very inexpensive way of producing trial exhibits, as the transparency paper can be fed into most duplication machines and will copy on to them from a standard typewritten sheet. If your duplicating machine does not have this capability, many quick print companies can do this for you very quickly and inexpensively.

§ 8.34 Photographs

The photograph is the most commonly used (and probably least expensive) type of demonstrative evidence used when examining the expert, and is often the most effective means of supplementing a witness's description of an item. For example, a wrecked automobile or a hazardous intersection is best explained by visual representation of the damage or hazard. Jurors are familiar with photographs, which provide an excellent, low-cost method of proving (or disproving) a fact in issue. Indeed, one good photograph is often more effective than several witnesses.

Consider the following example: In a rear-end collision case the plaintiff's treating chiropractor testified for four hours about the serious injury to the spine. Defense counsel cross-examined the chiropractor with one question: "Dr. Jones, did the plaintiff ever show you the photograph of the damage to her car?" The answer is usually, "No." Then in closing argument, with the photograph showing very minor damage in evidence, defense counsel destroys the chiropractor's testimony as self-serving, financially motivated, and based on inaccurate facts (he never saw the photo).

A proper foundation is necessary for admission of photographs in evidence. Show that the photographs are correct and accurate (though not necessarily exact) reproductions of the site or object purportedly depicted. Photographs are not inadmissible simply because they were taken after a change in condition of the place or object in question, or because unrelated objects are also included in the picture. However, explain to the jurors any variation from original conditions to avoid misleading them.

To authenticate a photograph, the testimony of a person present when the photograph was taken, stating that the photograph accurately depicts what it purports to show, is legally sufficient foundation for admission. Note, however, that it is not necessary to have at trial the photographer, or a person who was present when the photograph was taken, if a witness testifies that the photograph correctly represents the object that it portrays. (*See* Fed. R. Evid 901.) But where the proponent of the photograph fails to establish that it depicts a situation similar to that involved in the case at issue, the photograph is properly excluded as irrelevant.

If you anticipate a controversy regarding authenticity of a photograph, present it through testimony of the photographer, showing (1) circumstances under which the picture was taken, and (2) equipment and method used in taking the picture, developing the negative, and printing the photograph. For example, where lighting at the time of the accident or crime is an issue, show that photographs were taken under lighting conditions similar to those in the accident or crime. The trial court has wide discretion in determining whether photograph fairly depicts location and surrounding objects pertinent to case; conditions need not be identical to justify admission of photographs.

Photographs can be misleading. Since they are flat (two-dimensional) reproductions of scenes or objects, opposing counsel must take care to ensure that any photograph offered in evidence accurately depicts what the proponent says it depicts. Great variations in composition of photographs can be achieved by use of different lenses and camera angles. Familiarize yourself with basic photography principles and, if necessary, engage a qualified photographer to take or interpret photographs for the case.

In addition to the court's determination as to whether the photograph fairly depicts what it purports to show, the trial court always has discretion to exclude evidence if its probative value is substantially outweighed by probability that its admission will create substantial danger of undue prejudice, confusion, or misleading the jury (*See,* e.g., Fed. R. Evid. 403). When allegedly gruesome photographs are offered, the trial court must decide whether their probative value outweighs their probable prejudicial effect. Frequently, the court will allow a portion of the photos offered, but will not allow cumulative evidence.

The following is a sample authentication of a photograph for admissibility in evidence:

Counsel: May the record reflect that I am showing to opposing counsel a photograph which I am about to show to Mr. Smith?

The Court: The record will so reflect.

Opposing Counsel: I have examined the photograph.

Counsel: Your Honor, may this photograph be marked for identification?

The Court: May I see the photograph, Counsel? (Court reviews photo.) Madam Clerk, please mark this photograph as Plaintiff's Exhibit No. 6. You may proceed.

Q.   Mr. Smith, what is Plaintiff's No. 6 a photograph of?

A.   It is the intersection where the accident occurred.

Q.   Did you take that photograph?

A.   Yes.

Q.   When?

A.   On September 25, 1987.

Q.   At what time?

A.   7:00 p.m.

Q.   And what kind of camera did you use?

A.   A Minolta 35mm camera with a 50mm lens.

Q.   Any flash?

A.   No.

Q.   Where were you standing when you took the photograph?

A.   On the south side of Cabrillo Drive about 50 yards east of the intersection.

Q.   Mr. Smith, does this photograph accurately represent the condition of the intersection on September 25, 1987 at 7:00 p.m.?

A.   Yes.

Practice Note: Although a complete sample authentication has been included in this section, you will find that it is often unnecessary to present the portion concerning how the photograph was taken. More important is the portion where the witness states that the photograph accurately depicts the scene at the relevant time. Understand what foundation is required for admissibility, and do not get involved in unnecessarily complex foundational matters when not required.

Counsel: Your Honor, I offer Plaintiff's Exhibit No. 6 in evidence.

The Court: It will be received in evidence.

Counsel: Your Honor, may I take a moment to pass the photograph among the jury?

Practice Note: The Court may refuse the request to pass the photograph among the jury, perhaps because of time constraints, and may prefer instead that counsel simply hold up the photograph for the jury to see. Obviously, an enlargement would be preferable under such circumstances.

§ 8.35   Time Lines

Time lines are not only useful visual aids at trial, but are immensely helpful during the discovery and trial preparation process. Juries can easily understand time sequences and how events match up with them if they can see them laid our in a progressive, consecutive manner. Time lines can be done in-house, or they can be assigned to an advertising, or litigation support, agency. When the events of one party are placed above the line and the events of another are placed below the line, the effect is much like a rogue's gallery. All visual aids should be placed 15-20 feet away from the jury, and should be easy to read at that distance.

§ 8.36   Document Enlargements

You have heard the saying that a picture is worth a thousand words. So it is in a trial situation. Your attorney can tell the jury about a document, or he can read the document to them, but neither has the impact that a 3" x 6" enlargement of that document has in front of their eyes. Document blowups are surprisingly easy to have done and are relatively inexpensive. Most quick copy-type printing shops have the ability to produce the blowups and dry mount them on a cork-type board for easy handling. Blueprint shops, advertising agencies, litigation support firms, and printing or graphics firms also have these capabilities.

Once you have used these enlargements as trial exhibits, you will swear by them. Remember to have letter-sized or legal sized duplicates of these exhibits to hand to the judge for his convenience.

Photographs may also be enlarged and dry-mounted in this manner, and most firms will be able to assist you with either medium. You should be aware, however, that enlarging photographs is generally very expensive.

§ 8.37   Videotapes

More and more, the videocassette recorder (VCR) is finding its way into the courtroom. Because of today's society's sensitization to the visual film medium, this exhibit type is often the most effective which can be used. Day-in-the-life videos are routinely used, as are reenactments and reconstructions of incidents, accidents, and events. Some videotape may find its way into the courtroom with excellent evidentiary value in the form of television footage and even amateur videotaping.

With increased use in everyday life of video cassette recorders and videotape recording, videotapes can be produced quickly, efficiently, and without excessive cost. Videotapes are frequently used in conjunction with an expert's testimony. No distinction is drawn for evidentiary purposes between videotapes and motion pictures, and the terms are used interchangeably here.

Principles applicable to the introduction of photographs are equally applicable to proper introduction of silent videotapes and motion pictures; that is, both must be shown to be (1) relevant, (2) taken under conditions similar to the issue in controversy, and (3) a fair depiction of location and surrounding objects pertinent to the case. However, conditions need not be identical to justify admission. If necessary, establish the foundation for admission of a movie with testimony from the cam-eraperson.

Movies may be used in a variety of circumstances. In personal injury actions, "home" movies of the injured party taken prior to the accident can show the party's activities and condition before the injury. Movies are also effective to create a "day-in-the-life" film of the injured party, particularly where injuries are serious (*e.g.*, burn victim, paraplegic). Caution is advised, however. While such films dramatically show the extent of the party's injuries, pain, and suffering, juries may react adversely to a display which is unnecessarily graphic.

Practice Note: It is important to distinguish between videotapes that reenact or simulate an event and videotapes that are generic in nature and used to aid the testimony of an expert witness. The former are subject to strict evidentiary rules of admission, including hearsay objections. The latter are generally admissible if the videotape is utilized with the expert's testimony and is helpful to the judge and jury in understanding the issues of the case.

Defense counsel in personal injury or workers' compensation cases sometimes use surveillance films to impeach a claimant's testimony concerning his or her alleged injuries. For example, if the party claims a back injury, a surveillance film may show the person jogging, playing tennis, or lifting a heavy item during the alleged period of disability resulting from the injury.

Videotapes may generally be used to record testimony of witnesses at deposition and, in criminal cases, at preliminary hearing. Consult local rules. Where the witness is unavailable to testify at trial, these videotapes may properly be admitted into evidence in lieu of reading a transcript of testimony, provided all procedural safeguards are followed.

Stricter requirements may govern admission of audio recordings. For example, before admitting a recording in evidence, the proponent may be required to show (1) that the mechanical transcription device was capable of taking testimony; (2) that the operator of the device was competent to operate it; (3) that changes, additions, or deletions to the recording have not been made; (4) the manner of preservation of the record; (5) the identity of the speakers; (6) that the testimony of the speakers was freely and voluntarily made; and (7) the authenticity and correct-ness of the recording.

§ 8.38 Visual Aids and Exhibits Checklist

Remember to keep the following elements in mind during exhibit preparation and presentation:

____ 1. Exhibit is authentic representation of the subject matter it purports to portray.

____ 2. Exhibit will be authenticated by a qualified witness on the stand.

____ 3. Exhibit will clarify rather than confuse or mislead the jury.

____ 4. Exhibit is not cluttered, but simple and direct.

____ 5. Exhibit avoids excessive use of colors.

____ 6. Exhibit marked prior to being offered for admission.

____ 7. Exhibit utilizes horizontal, rather than vertical print.

____ 8. Each exhibit is focused on a single concept.

____ 9. Exhibit is the most effective exhibit type for the situation.

____ 10. Exhibit is used only when really needed so as not to dilute its effectiveness.

§ 8.39 Maps, Charts, and Diagrams

Diagrams can be very useful to an expert witness to illustrate relative locations of various objects or persons. Used in this manner, a diagram is not evidence of any fact or object. It is simply a figure drawn to suggest to jurors the relationship between persons or objects about which the witness is testifying. The diagram may be drawn on paper or blackboard.

The diagram takes on greater significance when coupled with a photograph. For example, if the diagram is a free-hand drawing of an intersection, not drawn to scale, the questioning could be as follows:

Q. When was the photograph taken?
A. I was standing here, at X, when I took it (pointing to the diagram).
Q. Why did you take it there?
A. That was the only place you could see both the stop sign and the hedge. From every other vantage point the hedge blocked the sign.

Next you would introduce the photographs to prove the point. This reinforces the power of the diagram and cements it in the mind of the jurors.

Although it is not absolutely necessary, wherever possible diagrams should be drawn to scale in order to foreclose objections based on distortion or unfairness; diagrams not drawn to scale are admissible, however, if there is a foundation that the diagram fairly and accurately depicts relevant information. The witness who testifies from a diagram must have personal knowledge of the subject matter depicted, so that the witness can verify correctness of the diagram in the respect for which it is used. To ensure an adequate record on appeal, and to avoid confusion and clarify testimony, the various points testified to by the witness should be marked on the diagram.

Use of illustrative charts and maps is also permitted, provided such exhibits are shown to be accurate and correctly representative of the area in question. For example, in a complex securities fraud case, it is helpful to "follow the money." A tagboard chart with clear plastic overlays is very impressive to the jury. Each step of the transaction is a different color, leading up to the fraud. Then with a second chart you can take the jury through the statutes so that they understand the violations and the reasons such conduct is proscribed.

Overhead projectors can be very handy in presenting diagrams, maps, and charts, as well as documentary evidence. Projectors create a large and easily readable image which can aid jurors' understanding of issues in the case. It is easy to make transparencies with a transparency kit and any photocopy machine. When a case involves many documents, such as a real-estate dispute, or a lender-liability case, it is essential that the jury be taken through the paper trail step by step. The overhead projector and a marking pen can often be teaching tools.

§ 8.40   Slides

Slides of color, or black-and-white, photographs or any other kind of charts, text, or graphs may be put together into a slide show which may be operated manually, remotely, or by computer. There are numerous graphics presentation software packages which available, such as PowerPoint, which enable you to produce automated graphics presentations. When producing these slide shows, remember to adhere to the general guidelines listed in the checklist for exhibits in § **8.34.**

§ 8.41   Computerized Animation

Computerized animation of accidents or incidents is being done by some litigation support firms. In these animations, the progression of events leading up to the subject matter of the litigation dispute is depicted in cartoon-like scenes which are projected onto a screen by a computer. This new technology is somewhat controversial, although it has been gaining acceptance in some courtrooms lately. The main objection to this new demonstrative medium is the the depiction of events may be somewhat less than accurate, or contrived, and the jury is given the wrong idea about how the events occurred. The key to acceptance of the computerized animation, as it is with any illustrative exhibit, is accuracy.

§ 8.42   Computer-Generated Evidence—In General

For purposes of litigation, "computer-generated demonstrative evidence" includes two separate kinds of evidence:

- Computer graphics refers to purely demonstrative evidence consisting of animated or static depictions prepared with the aid of a computer. Computer graphics are similar to drawings, photographs, films, and videotapes routinely used to illustrate objects, conditions, or events involved in litigation.

- Computer simulations refer to a type of evidence that employs computer modeling of simulated or experimental events in order to predict what will or has happened in a real case.

Computer simulations involve a form of experimental evidence, but they become particularly demonstrative when the output of the simulation is converted to a graphic animation that can be displayed on a computer or video monitor or projected onto a screen through the use of a liquid crystal display (LCD) panel or data projector. Without graphic illustrations of their output, computer simulations are relatively meaningless for litigation purposes. They are, therefore, clearly included in the category of computer-generated demonstrative evidence.

Until the early 1980s, computer-generated demonstrative evidence was rarely seen in the courts because its creation usually required access to a mainframe computer and an understanding of complicated software applications. The emergence of the microcomputer, however, and the development of graphic software packages set the stage for the remarkably rapid application of computer technology to courtroom demonstrative evidence. Accident reconstructionists now use microcomputers for purposes never envisioned a short time ago, such as calculating and showing the velocity and impact force of colliding automobiles, drawing accident-site diagrams, and obtaining scaled accident-site dimensions from photographs. (*See*, generally, Terry D. Day & Randall L. Hargens, *The Use of Computers in Traffic Accident Reconstruction* (Northwestern University Traffic Institute, 1989); this publication will hereafter be cited as "Day & Hargens, *Computers in Traffic Accident Reconstruction*.")

§ 8.43 —Accident Reconstruction by Computer

Computer simulations involve constructing a computer "model" of some real phenomenon or experiment and then using that model to predict what will happen in the real case [Gemignani, *Computer Law* § 4:4 (1985)]. In litigation, computer simulations are used primarily to reconstruct past events and demonstrate their occurrences graphically in the courtroom. Simulations can re-create automobile accidents, structural stresses, intrusion of toxic pollutants in underground aquifers, and many other real-world events. They are valuable as evidence in a trial because they produce visual reenactments of the events or conditions which brought about the loss complained of [Gemignani, *Computer Law* § 35:20A (1988 Supp)].

A computer simulation of an automobile accident can re-create the complex and rapid events that occur when automobiles slam into one another, and then display the re-creation visually in real time or slow motion. Data from the accident site, such as skid marks, vehicle crush, metal deformation, car positions, and biomechanical findings can be used to accurately calculate the speed of automobiles at impact, their angles of approach, their trajectories after a collision, and a host of other conclusions about the dynamics of the accident. Not only can the technique be used to re-create how the collision probably occurred, it also can be used to eliminate competing and conflicting hypotheses about what actually took place. When properly used, it is an invaluable accident investigation tool; when misused it can produce erroneous results and a misconception of what actually occurred during the accident [Day & Hargens, "Application and Misapplication of Computer Programs for Accident Reconstruction" (SAE Technical Paper No. 890738) in Motor Vehicle Accident Reconstruction: Review and Update at 129 (SAE Publ. No. SP-777, 1989); this paper will hereafter be referred to as "Day & Hargens, 'Application and Misapplication of Computer Programs for Accident Reconstruction' "].

Until recently, the speed and memory required to display computer graphics, particularly simulation animations, were generally restricted to large, costly main-frame computers with tremendous computing power. Desktop microcomputers today, however, incorporate sophisticated techniques to overcome the inherent limitations of microcomputer speed and memory in making computer graphics and animations [Pepe *et al.*, "Cost-Effective Real-Time Computer Simulation" at 15]. These improvements have been accompanied by the development of software applications designed for both graphic input and graphic output. Most of today's programs also reproduce high-resolution color drawings that can be printed or plotted on most standard computer hardware [Day & Hargens, *Computers in Traffic Accident Reconstruction* at 4].

Desktop computers are also used today to produce computer animations. Virtually any sequence of events can be graphically displayed once the motion has been defined, and three-dimensional objects can be animated accurately while being viewed from any point. Besides auto accident reconstructions, animation graphics can depict landslides, fault line propagation, human body dynamics, headlight visibility ranges, and line-of-sight obstructions [Pepe *et al.*, "Cost-Effective Real-Time Computer Simulation" at 19].

As opposed to computer simulations and animations, computer-aided graphic displays are relatively simple and inexpensive to produce. Some law firms have employed computer-trained graphic specialists to produce graphic illustrations in-house both for courtroom use and for management presentations within the firm.

§ 8.44 —Computer Animation Techniques

A computerized graphic simulation is a means of providing real-time representation of the particular characteristics of an incident. To animate the simulation, individual "frames," like pictures, are created every tenth or twentieth of a second and sequenced electronically to simulate real-time motion. Once the plotting of each picture is completed, the computer animation program is used. The animation program loads each picture from disk until the last picture in the sequence is reached. At that time, a file containing all the picture information compiled is saved to disk. This file is loaded to a special playback program, where it is played back at real time. Other playback speeds, ranging from accelerated to slow motion, are also available, as is the option of inserting preprogrammed stops at desired frames [Pepe *et al.*, "Cost-Effective Real-Time Computer Simulation" at 17].

Unlike computer-generated courtroom drawings, animation sequences can be complex and expensive. While the time sequence usually can be generated by a computer, the actual placement and drawing of the initial object is done manually. These animations often require a film choreographer to place a detailed drawing (*e.g.*, of a car or a plane) at different orientations and positions over time. An animation of a single simulation may cost $10,000, and the cost will escalate if the case involves more simulations playing out different scenarios.

§ 8.45 —Demonstrative Exhibits by Computer

The newest application for computers is the preparation of drawings, which grew out of the high-technology industries that use computers to design components and prepare final design drawings. These programs are ideal for some litigation purposes, such as preparing accident-site diagrams. An accident-site drawing program is actually a mapping program using the same coordinate system as other programs and containing a built-in library of representations of frequently seen objects such as highways, intersections, cars, road signs, and traffic controls [Day & Hargens, *Computers in Traffic Accident Reconstruction* at 17].

Drawing programs make it is easy to produce scale diagrams, an essential part of a reconstruction. CAD programs have essentially replaced rulers and pencils by enabling an operator to draw lines according to an established scale. Each line is positioned according to real-world coordinates, making it easy to locate lines and other objects precisely, using accident-site measurements. The investigator uses CAD to draw a scale diagram for purposes of analysis, and the same drawing can be enhanced or re-scaled on the computer for preparing reports or courtroom exhibits [Day & Hargens, *Computers in Traffic Accident Reconstruction* at 17].

Recent enhancements in the area of CAD systems include three-dimensional renderings. Sometimes called "animation" effects, these graphic representations can include shadowing, hidden-line removal, and perspective drawings over time. Originally used to simulate airplane crashes, these three-dimensional CAD simulations of motor vehicle accidents are being prepared on videotape for courtroom presentations.

"Paint" programs are designed to be used as an artist's tool by keeping track of points on the computer's screen rather than using real-world measurements, making it easy to draw and erase lines and circles and to produce multiple copies of certain areas on the screen. These same features place restrictions on their use in accident reconstruction, however, because it is usually not possible to place an object at a known coordinate location or produce scale diagrams using paint programs except by trial and error [Day & Hargens, *Computers in Traffic Accident Reconstruction* at 17].

Computer graphics are created in a variety of ways for courtroom presentation, and the following scenario is intended to illustrate merely one such method.

Plaintiff was injured in an accident while operating an industrial forklift truck, and suit has been brought against the manufacturer of the forklift alleging various defects in the vehicle's design. Plaintiff needs a simple line drawing of a forklift truck to illustrate for the jury the various features of forklift construction. From a government publication, the paralegal has selected a drawing of the type of forklift plaintiff was operating at the time of the accident.

The paralegal delivers the picture to the computer graphic artist with instructions to reproduce it as a courtroom exhibit. Typically, the artist will load the image into the computer by scanning. A scanned image is an image that has been converted from paper and ink to digital information that can be viewed and manipulated on a computer; it is like placing tissue over artwork for tracing with a pen.

After the image has been scanned into the computer, it can be manipulated in many ways until it is "just right" according to your specifications. The graphic artist can also reproduce the image in full color, using a computer palette of over sixteen million colors to paint from. Special effects can be employed to produce graduated screens and "fountains" in monochrome and color. A laser proof of the image can be used to compare it with the original for validation. The computerized image or tracing can then be printed by a digital photo imaging process that produces computer output on photographic paper at high resolutions.

If the attorney does not have a picture or drawing for the artist to work with, or the illustration provided is not suitable for scanning, the presentation can be developed in other ways. Often the attorney and the artist can go to standard texts covering the subject area, such as anatomy books for medical illustrations. When the desired picture is located, it can be traced by the artist or photocopied for later scanning into the computer. For example, the computer graphic artist can take an X-ray of a client's long-bone fracture provided by counsel, make a positive of the X-ray, photocopy the positive, scan the photocopy into the computer, and then color and manipulate the image until it serves its desired purpose.

Note: High-quality positives are essential for this use. When working with X-rays, the image to be scanned should be a photographic continuous-tone positive of the X-ray film and should be done by a quality vendor.

Caution: Computer graphics are not yet a panacea for courtroom exhibits. Despite the apparent ease and simplicity of the processes described above, some caveats are in order. First, cost is a factor. Simple drawings can still be done more quickly, cheaply, and often more accurately by hand. Second, optical character recognition (OCR) technology is still in a developmental stage, particularly with respect to graphics. Scanning rarely produces an exact duplicate of the image input to the computer. Very often, if not in most cases, the image must be redrafted by the operator when it is in the computer in order to make an accurate match of the original. This process can require substantial operator time. Hence, for simply reproducing an image in order to master it for a blowup or poster-size exhibit, a computer aid may be neither optimally accurate nor cost-effective.

Where you want to portray a defect in an object, or to manipulate the image in some way, computer assistance is essential and will generally be less expensive than manual drafting. For example, once the image has been scanned into the computer and then retraced by the operator to its original state, it can be turned, flipped, rotated, reversed, and zoomed quickly and accurately by the computer. This capability of computer-generated exhibits also allows for last-minute changes on the eve of trial. Once the exact image has been put into the computer, refinements, corrections, and other changes can be made at almost any time, even during trial if necessary.

Practice Note: When planning to use computer-generated courtroom exhibits, seek out an experienced demonstrative evidence specialist who is not exclusively dependent on computers. The vendor should have at least one fully qualified graphic artist on the staff. Not only are many courtroom exhibits produced better manually, many complicated exhibits require hybridization; that is, manual drafting will be required to complement the work generated by the computer to produce the desired effect. In other words, the computer has limitations, particularly for graphic presentations.

Observation: In-house graphic capabilities. Many law firms have developed in-house computer graphic capabilities. These systems work very well for in-house management presentation graphics, for nonlitigation graphics, and for artwork to enhance settlement brochures. For trial work, an outside vendor is still preferred. For one thing, the outside vendor comes to the project with a fresh, unbiased view that can often see flaws in graphic presentations that have been overlooked by in-house staff. They also tend to be more flexible and creative, and their graphic design input can be invaluable in preparing complex courtroom exhibits. When a foundation witness is required to identify and authenticate the exhibit in court, outside vendors tend to make better and more credible witnesses.

Outside vendors tend also to be more versatile in terms of the hardware and the software that is available to them. Most will have both PC and Macintosh capabilities. Apple Macintosh graphics technology is clearly superior at this time, but PC-generated graphics are improving. Outside vendors will also have greater flexibility to choose software applications to suit a particular job. For example, they will utilize both drawing programs and plotters, depending on the nature of the assignment. The latter are more accurate for presentation graphics, but they are less flexible overall than drawing programs, which are better for image presentation and manipulation.

§ 8.46   Easel with Flip Chart

Even with the technological revolution bursting into the courtroom, one of the oldest demonstrative exhibit aids is still one of the most preferred. The three-legged easel with a flip-chart of blank paper is used widely in courtrooms, especially during the testimony of expert witnesses. The flip-chart has replaced blackboards, in most cases, which no longer appear in every courtroom as they once did.

When purchasing an easel, be sure to buy one with a lip on which to rest the marking pens, as there will most likely be no other place to rest such objects in the courtroom. The easel should be easily collapsible, but steady when set in place. It should also have some sort of device at the top for holding the chart in place so that is will not fall off the easel when it is being written upon.

§ 8.47   X-Rays

In cases where x-rays are to be used in the courtroom, remember that a backlit board of some type is needed in order for the x-ray to be seen. You may also want to look into the possibility of developing the x-rays into slides or photographs for ease of showing in the courtroom, but you must also be aware that some judges will require the actual x-ray be produced at time of trial and may not allow a facsimile.

§ 8.48   Models, Demonstrations, and Physical Evidence

There are times when pictures or graphics are not enough, and you may want to contract with a litigation support firm to produce a working model of some mechanism which is important to your case. Models may also be non-working, three-dimensional mock-ups of just about anything, from groups of buildings to animate objects. Whenever possible, these models should be done to scale to avoid misleading the jury.

Expert witnesses may decide to do working demonstrations in the courtroom to demonstrate how something occurred which is important to the litigation. Because these demonstrations have the propensity to be dramatic in nature, the trial team must be very careful to follow the guidelines of the court in producing them. Some judges will not allow them at all, citing the theatrical quality of the demonstration, but most will decide on a case-by-case basis whether the demonstration will be allowed for illustrative purposes, but may not be given evidentiary value to be used by the jury in reaching a verdict.

Physical evidence is often brought into the courtroom when available. The impact of seeing the actual evidence is far greater in most cases than substitutions such as photographs or line drawings. Sometimes the actual physical condition of a plaintiff in a personal injury suit is in itself, physical evidence, although that too, can be controversial, if opposing counsel feels that it would be prejudicial for the jury to view it.

§ 8.49   Judge's Notebook

From the time a case is assigned to a specific court, the paralegal should begin to put together information relating to the judge seated on the bench in that court. The following types of information are helpful:

1. Whether the judge has a reputation for being plaintiff- or defendant- oriented;
2. Whether the judge has a reputation for being a scholar;
3. Whether he reads the briefs submitted to him or prefers to hear oral arguments;
4. Whether he has a preference for a particular formats or presentations of documents;
5. His political leanings;
6. The reputation of his attention span during trial;
7. A compendium of his rulings on similar cases or issues.

The more complete the attorney's knowledge is of the type of judge he must go before, the better prepared he will be to present his client's case effectively.

§ 8.50 Proving up Evidence

Before being able to offer testimony into evidence, it must be proven up, or proven to be original and credible evidence. All evidence must be in admissible form before it can be introduced as evidence. This can be accomplished in a number of ways, and it is something that the litigation paralegal should be concerned with throughout the case. The case should be managed in such a way that all documents, testimony, or physical evidence vital to the case should be proven up early in the litigation so as to avoid devastating problems at the time of trial when the admission of that evidence is crucial.

Testimony, of course, may be preserved for evidence at time of trial by gathering it in forms of sworn testimony in admissible form to be used at the time of trial. Documents, as well as physical evidence, must be authenticated. The generally accepted way of doing this is to introduce the document to a witness who is in a position to swear under oath to the document's authenticity.

As an example, the following are customary ways in which the legal profession seeks to prove up or authenticate documents:

1. Request the opposing party to provide a copy of the original document in his response to your Request for Production of Documents;
2. Attach a copy of the document to your Request for Admissions and ask the other party to admit its authenticity;
3. Introduce the document as an exhibit at a deposition and ask the witness to identify it;
4. If the document is a public document, get a certified copy of it from the appropriate office or agency;
5. Notice the deposition of the custodian of records and ask that person to bring the document with him to the deposition;

6. Subpoena a nonparty who may have possession of the document by using a Subpoena Duces Tecum;

7. If the document is a copy of an original, have the opposing party stipulate to its authenticity.

Under normal circumstances, the original of a document must be produced at trial. However, there are times when this is not possible. If the original is in the possession of the opposing party, you will have to make arrangements well in advance to have that person produce the original at trial. There is a procedural rule known as the best evidence rule which will allow a copy of the original to be used in trial under certain conditions. Rule 1003 of the Federal Rules of Evidence states: "A duplicate is admissible to the same extent as an original unless (1) a genuine question is raised as to the authenticity of the original or (2) in the circumstances it would be unfair to admit the duplicate in lieu of the original."

§ 8.51 Determining Admissibility

The main determining factor in whether or not a piece of physical evidence or a document is admissible at trial is whether that evidence can withstand the relevancy test. The issue of relevancy is twofold: (1) does the evidence have probative value?; and (2) is it material? Federal Rule of Evidence 401 states: "'Relevant evidence' means evidence having any tendency to make the existence of any fact that is of consequence to the determination of the action more probable or less probable than it would be without the evidence." Federal Rule of Evidence 402 states: "All relevant evidence is admissible, except as otherwise provided by the Constitution of the United States, by Act of Congress, by these rules, or by other rules prescribed by the Supreme Court pursuant to statutory authority. Evidence which is not relevant is not admissible."

Materiality goes to the issues at hand. The evidence may have peripheral relevance, or relevance to peripheral issues, but does it have direct relevance to the immediate issues at hand? The concept of probative value is less easily determined. Basically, the rule of thumb is to decide whether the evidence is of any assistance in determining whether a fact is more probable or less probable. In other words, if we have a certain fact before us, and we have evidence which we believe would help support or weaken that fact, then the evidence has probative value. It increases the probability of either the veracity or the falsehood of the fact.

If the evidence has passed the test of relevancy, including materiality and probative value, it then must be determined whether there is some other Rule of Evidence which may preclude the admissiblity of the evidence. One of your major concerns in this respect will be to determine if there is some reason why this evidence should not be considered competent. The evidence must be testified to by a credible witness who is competent to understand the sworn oath. In the absence of a credible witness, the document, or evidence, must be able to stand on its own. Therefore, the hearsay rule, and the rules regarding its exceptions are extremely important rules to be able to understand and apply.

An outstanding paralegal will become intimate with the Rules of Evidence, both federal and state, and be able to assist the trial team in assessing the evidence and documents for admissibility. Determinations of this nature should be made early enough in the case to make contingency plans in the event that certain evidence proves to be inadmissible at the time of trial.

§ 8.52 Motion for Directed Verdict

If, after all the evidence has been presented in a trial, one party feels that the other party has not presented evidence enough to satisfy the requirements mandated by the law under the " preponderance of the evidence" doctrine or that the evidence introduced is insufficient to support that party's allegations, a Motion for Directed Verdict may be made by the questioning party (**Form 8–17**). Additionally, on behalf of the court, the judge may decide to move for and order a directed verdict (**Form 8–18**) against a party who has not offered evidence to support his allegations and against whom no other possible verdict could be sustained.

Many times, Motions for Directed Verdicts are made spontaneously and verbally in a courtroom, but there are times when it is anticipated that the opposing side will not or cannot fulfill the obligation of sufficient evidence, and it is proper to prepare such a motion is writing in anticipation of such an event. If made on behalf of the defendant, the motion may be made as early as the close of presentation of evidence by the plaintiff, because the plaintiff has the burden of proof.

While certain portions of the motion may be prepared in advance and in anticipation of such a need, the motion must be extremely precise in stating the grounds upon which the motion is based. Therefore, it is necessary to reference specific passages of testimony from the trial in the motion itself, restating such testimony verbatim, and showing in detail how the offered testimony does not prove the allegations made.

FORM 8–17
SAMPLE MOTION FOR DIRECTED VERDICT

NO. [case number]

[name]		)	IN THE DISTRICT COURT OF
		)	
	Plaintiff	)	[county] COUNTY, [state]
		)	
vs.		)	[judicial district] JUDICIAL DISTRICT
		)	
[name]		)	
		)	
	Defendant	)	

§ 8.52   MOTION FOR DIRECTED VERDICT

MOTION FOR DIRECTED VERDICT

TO THE HONORABLE JUDGE OF SAID COURT:

COMES NOW [name], defendant in the above-entitled action, and pursuant to Rule [citation] of the [state/federal] Rules of Civil Procedure, files this his Motion for Directed Verdict, and for grounds would show unto the Court as follows:

I.

The plaintiff in this action has rested his case, and in doing so, has failed to produce any evidence which warrants the submission of this case to the jury.

II.

The evidence produced in this action by the plaintiff is wholly insufficient to warrant the submission of this case to the jury.

III.

The evidence in this action is of such a nature that a verdict other than for the defendant would be wholly contrary to the carriage of justice and intent of the law in requiring the plaintiff to prove his allegations with a preponderance of the evidence.

IV.

[State specific details which support your contention that the allegations of the plaintiff were not proven at trial. For clarity's sake, a separate paragraph should be devoted to each allegation and how specifically it was not proven by a preponderance of evidence.]

WHEREAS, PREMISES CONSIDERED, Defendant moves and requests that the Court instruct a verdict for the defendant, and against the plaintiff, and herewith tenders the following form of instruction:

Ladies and Gentlemen of the Jury:

You are hereby instructed to return a verdict in favor of the defendant and against the plaintiff.

Let the form of your verdict be:

"We, the jury, in obedience to the Court's instructions, find for the defendant and against the plaintiff."

[name of firm]

By: _____
       [name of attorney]
       Counsel for Defendant
       [address]
       [telephone number]

FORM 8–18
SAMPLE ORDER GRANTING MOTION FOR DIRECTED VERDICT

NO. [case number]

[name]	)	IN THE DISTRICT COURT OF
	)	
Plaintiff	)	[county] COUNTY, [state]
	)	
vs.	)	[judicial district] JUDICIAL DISTRICT
	)	
[name]	)	
	)	
Defendant	)	

ORDER GRANTING MOTION FOR DIRECTED VERDICT

On [date], [20__], the matter of the Defendant's Motion for Directed Verdict came on for hearing, and

It appearing to the Court after having considered all of the evidence presented in the case, that the evidence is legally insufficient to entitle plaintiff to recover against defendant,

It is therefore, ORDERED, ADJUDGED, and DECREED that the Defendant's motion for directed verdict be, and is hereby granted. The jury is instructed to render a verdict in favor of [name], defendant in this action, and against [name], plaintiff in this action; that plaintiff take nothing by his petition and that defendant be reimbursed by plaintiff for his costs of suit in the sum of [amount].

SIGNED and dated on this [date] day of [20__].

_____
Presiding Judge

ENTERED on this [date] day of [month], 20[__].

_____
Clerk of Court

§ 8.53 Motion for Temporary Restraining Order

FORM 8–19
MOTION FOR TEMPORARY RESTRAINING ORDER

Plaintiff, by counsel, pursuant to law, moves the court to enter its temporary restraining order forthwith and without notice, based upon the following reasons:

(1)   As appears from the accompanying affidavit of Plaintiff, immediate and irreparable loss will result to the Plaintiff from the delay required to effect notice or from the risk that notice will itself precipitate adverse action by Defendant before an order Carl be issued.

(2)   Plaintiff's counsel herewith certifies to the court in writing that no efforts have been made to give notice to Defendant, for the reason to do so is likely to result in Defendant wrongfully withdrawing the subject matter of this lawsuit and removing such assets beyond the jurisdiction of this court.

WHEREFORE, Plaintiff requests that the court enter its temporary restraining order as follows:

(a)   Restraining and enjoining Defendant, h— agents, employee, and attorneys, and those persons in active concert or participation with, them who receive actual notice of the order, from removing funds from account No. _____, pending a hearing on an order to show cause or until further order of the court and

(b)   Directing Defendant to appear before the court within 14 days and show cause, if there be any, why the temporary restraining order should not be converted to a preliminary injunction.

[Date]
[Attorney for Plaintiff]
[Business Address of Attorney]

§ 8.54   Motion for New Trial

Filing a Motion for a New Trial (**Form 8–20**) is one of the options available to a party when he disagrees with the judgment or verdict of the trial court. According to Rule 59 of the Federal Rules of Civil Procedure, a Motion for New Trial may be filed within 10 days of the entry of the judgment. The court may also initiate its own motion for any reason for which it would have granted a similar motion by one of the parties. Your state will have a parallel rule for this motion in its Rules of Civil Procedure.

The grounds for filing a Motion for New Trial are very similar to the grounds for filing an appeal. Generally, this motion is filed on grounds of procedural error such as errors in admissibility of evidence, jury instruction, excessive damages, or a verdict which is unfounded or directly contradictory or contrary to the law. (**Form 8–21** is a Sample Order Granting a New Trial.)

It is common for a Motion for Judgment Notwithstanding the Verdict to accompany a Motion for New Trial. Refer to § 8.56 for information on this motion.

TRIAL READINESS AND SETTLEMENT

FORM 8–20
SAMPLE MOTION FOR NEW TRIAL

NO. [case number]

[name]	)	IN THE DISTRICT COURT OF
	)	
Plaintiff	)	[country] COUNTY, [state]
	)	
vs.	)	[judicial district] JUDICIAL DISTRICT
	)	
[name]	)	
	)	
Defendant	)	

MOTION FOR NEW TRIAL

TO THE HONORABLE JUDGE OF SAID COURT

COMES, NOW, [name], [plaintiff/defendant] in the above-styled cause of action, and moves this Court to set aside the judgement heretofore rendered against it on [date], [20__] and grant it a new trial in this cause, for the following good and sufficient reason:

I.

This Motion is presented within the time limits prescribed by Rule No. [citation] of the [state/federal] Rules of Civil Procedure for a Motion for New Trial.

II.

The judgement of the court is contrary to the laws. [State basis in law.]

III.

(In the alternative) There was insufficient evidence to support the judgement as delivered. [State the facts supporting the above.]

IV.

(In the alternative) Movant's failure to file an answer before judgment was the result of an accident and/or mistake, rather than due to an intentional act or the result of conscious indifference. [State circumstance.]

V.

(In the alternative) Movant has a meritorious defense as to the full amount of the judgment sought herein. [State the defense and make reference to any supporting exhibits or affidavits.]

VI.

Movant is ready, able and willing to go to trial immediately and no delay, harm or prejudice will occur to the other parties as a result of Movant's motion.

Movant shall also reimburse the other parties for their reasonable expenses and attorney's fees incurred in this motion.

WHEREFORE PREMISES CONSIDERED, Movant [name] prays that after notice and hearing the judgement rendered in this cause be set aside and the Movant be granted a new trial.

Respectfully submitted,

[name of firm]

By: _____
    [attorney for movant]
    [address]
    [telephone number]

[Add certificate of service.]

FORM 8–21
SAMPLE ORDER GRANTING NEW TRIAL

NO. [case number]

[name]	)	IN THE DISTRICT COURT OF
	)	
Plaintiff	)	[county] COUNTY, [state]
	)	
vs.	)	[judicial district] JUDICIAL DISTRICT
	)	
[name]	)	
	)	
Defendant	)	

ORDER GRANTING NEW TRIAL

On [date], [20__], the court heard the motion of [name], [plaintiff/defendant], for a new trial in this cause.

The court, having fully considered the motion and having heard the argument of counsel on the motion, is of the opinion that the motion should be granted.

It is therefore ORDERED, DECREED, AND ADJUDGED that the judgment rendered in this cause on [date], 20[year] and the verdict of the jury on which the judgment was rendered, be and they hereby are set aside, and that the motion for a new trial in this case be granted. Motion is hereby granted.

Dated this [date] day of [month] [20___]

_____
Judge Presiding

Entered on this [date] day of [month], [20___].

_____
Clerk of Court

§ 8.55   Motion to Set Aside Default Judgment

FORM 8–22
MOTION TO SET ASIDE DEFAULT JUDGMENT

NO. _____

[PLAINTIFF(S) NAMES] Plaintiffs,	)))) IN THE DISTINCT COURT OF)) _____ COUNTY,)) _____ JUDICIAL DISTRICT))
v.	
[DEFENDANT(S) NAMES] Defendants.	))

MOTION TO SET ASIDE DEFAULT JUDGMENT

COMES NOW Defendant _____, by and through his attorney of record, _____ of _____ and moves that the Default Judgment signed on _____, 20___ be set aside, in the interest of justice and fairness, The entry of default judgment against Defendant in this action was due to inadvertence. In that the Plaintiffs Original Petition was inadvertently filed in this law firms files by a new member of the secretarial staff without being entered into the law firm's docket system. The entry of default judgment was discovered by the attorney of record on _____, 20___, and this motion was prepared and filed immediately.

WHEREFORE, PREMISES CONSIDERED, Defendant prays that the Default Judgment be set aside in the interest of justice and fairness.

Respectfully submitted,

NAME OP FIRM

_____

Name of Atty
Atty's Bar #
Address
City, State, Zip
Phone #

CERTIFICATE OF SERVICE

I hereby certify that a true and correct copy of the above and forgoing document has been forwarded to all counsel of record by facsimile and/or certified mail/R.R.R. on this ____ day of 20__.

ORDER

Having read the above motion and being otherwise advised in the law and the premises,

IT IS HEREBY ORDERED, ADJUDGED. AND DECREED that said motion is in all respects granted.

DATED this day of _____ 20____.

_____

JUDGE PRESIDING

§ 8.56   Motion for Judgment Non Obstante Veredicto (Judgment Notwithstanding the Verdict)

There may be instances where your trial team has moved for a directed verdict at trial because it did not believe that the opposing party sufficiently proved the elements necessary to prevail in the case. (See **§ 8.52** for further discussion on directed verdicts.) If the motion for directed verdict was denied and judgment was against your client, a Motion Notwithstanding the Verdict (**Form 8–23**) is in order.

This motion would be proper only in cases where a motion for directed verdict would have been proper. If the motion is granted (**Form 8–24**), the judge may enter findings in direct contradiction to any special issues or the entire jury verdict, providing that there is no evidence to support the jury verdict or particular special issues. Effective December 1, 1995, Federal R of Civil procedure 50(b) was amended to read:

> If, for any reason, the court does not grant a motion for judgment as a matter of law made at the close of all the evidence, the court is considered to have submitted the

action to the jury subject to the courts, later deciding the legal question raised by the motion. The movant may renew its request for judgment as a matter of law by filing a motion no later than 10 days after entry of judgment—and may alternatively request a new trial or join a motion for a new trial under Rule 59. In ruling on a renewed motion, the court may:

(1)   If a verdict was returned:
    (A)   allow the judgment to stand.
    (B)   order a new trial,
    (C)   direct entry of judgment as a matter of law; or
(2)   if no verdict was returned:
    (A)   order a new trial, or
    (B)   direct entry of judgment as a matter of law.

FORM 8–23
SAMPLE MOTION FOR JUDGMENT
NOTWITHSTANDING THE VERDICT

IN THE UNITED STATES DISTRICT COURT
[judicial district] DISTRICT OF [state]
[judicial division] DIVISION

[name]		)	
		)	
	Plaintiff	)	Civil Action No. [case number]
		)	
vs.		)	
		)	
[name]		)	
		)	
	Defendant	)	

MOTION FOR JUDGMENT NOTWITHSTANDING THE VERDICT

TO THE HONORABLE JUDGE OF SAID COURT:

Defendant, [name], respectfully moves this court to enter Judgment Notwithstanding the Verdict and to enter judgment for the defendant and that plaintiff take nothing in this case, and for its motion would respectfully show the court as follows:

I.

The court should enter a judgment for defendant notwithstanding the verdict for each and every of the reasons stated in defendant's Motion for Instructed Verdict, made before this court after plaintiff had rested his case, a true and correct copy of which is attached hereto as Exhibit A and incorporated by reference herein.

II.

Defendant would show the court that there is no evidence to support the jury's finding of [verdict] to issue No. [number], which reads in its entirety as follows:

[State issue verbatim as posed to jury.]

The evidence presented in this proceeding conclusively establishes the opposite of this jury finding and there is no evidence of probative value to support the jury's finding of [verdict] to this issue.

[Make specific statements here to allude to testimony which supports allegation that the jury finding is incorrect.]

III.

[Repeat previous paragraph for each and every issue for which maintains an incorrect jury finding.]

WHEREFORE, PREMISES CONSIDERED, defendant respectfully requests that the court disregard the above jury findings and enter a Judgment Notwithstanding the Verdict in favor of defendant and against plaintiff.

Dated [date], 20___ .

by _____
[name of attorney]
[address]
[telephone number]

FORM 8–24
SAMPLE ORDER GRANTING MOTION FOR JUDGMENT
NOTWITHSTANDING THE VERDICT

IN THE UNITED STATES DISTRICT COURT
[judicial district] DISTRICT OF [state]
[judicial division] DIVISION

[name]		)	
		)	
	Plaintiff	)	Civil Action No. [case number]
		)	
vs.		)	
		)	
[name]		)	
		)	
	Defendant	)	

559

ORDER GRANTING MOTION FOR JUDGMENT
NOTWITHSTANDING THE VERDICT

On[date],20[__],defendant, [name] in the above-entitled and numbered cause, brought a motion before this court to direct a verdict in its favor at the close of plaintiff's case in the trial, That motion was denied, and thereafter the jury returned the verdict in favor of the plaintiff.

On [date],20[__],defendant [name] brought a motion before this court that judgment be entered in its favor, notwithstanding the verdict. The court, having heard and considered the motion, is of the opinion that the motion should be granted.

It is therefore ORDERED, DECREED and ADJUDGED that judgment for defendant be entered on presentation of a form of judgment prepared by counsel for defendant.

SIGNED and DATED this [date] day of [month], 20[__].

_____

Judge Presiding

§ 8.57 Settlement

Generally, a paralegal will play less of a role in settlement and the negotiations leading up to it than in any other part of the lawsuit. Because much of this process takes place in telephone conversations and in meetings between attorneys, the paralegal is not often privy to the steps that a delicate settlement negotiation takes, The paralegal's importance in settlement procedures. is in maintaining current and concise records. Without up-to-date figures, it is conceivable that an attorney could make a mistake either in his settlement demand or in the acceptance or rejection of a settlement offer. Paralegals may also be asked to draft release documents using standard forms. (See **Forms 8–26** and **8–27.**) Under no circumstances, however, should those documents be used without an in-depth review by the attorney in charge of the case.

Paralegals may also play a role in drafting settlement offers (see **Form 8–25**).

FORM 8–25
SAMPLE SETTLEMENT OFFER

[name and address of
opposing attorney]

Re: [title of case]
         [court] Court
         Index No.   Calendar No.
         [your File No.]

§ 8.57 SETTLEMENT

Dear [opposing attorney]:

As your records indicate, we are the attorneys for [plaintiff's name].

This action is a claim for damages for personal injuries sustained by the plaintiff, [plaintiff's name] as a result of a [briefly describe occurrence]. Said occurrence took place on [date].

As a result of this occurrence, the plaintiff sustained personal injuries which resulted in extensive medical care and treatment including doctors treatments, hospital treatments, and physical therapy treatments, with residual permanent injuries.

The extent of the disability, injuries, special damages, and claims of our client have been submitted to you in the Bill of Particulars, which was served on or about [date].

The legal liability has been established by the events, the photographs exhibiting the condition of the step where the Occurrence took place the statement of the plaintiff, and the legal documents prepared for this action.

The injuries, treatment, disability, and prognosis have been established and confirmed by the records which have been delivered to you, and the permanency of the injury has been confirmed by medical reports served upon you. We have previously transmitted to you all requested medical authorizations, together with substantiation of the injuries and damages. We have duly complied with the applicable court rules relating exchange of information.

A review of all available documents confirms liability for the occurrence and injuries an your clients, [defendants' name].

As disclosed by you, the extent of the defendants' insurance coverage is in the sum of $____, with no excess or umbrella insurance policies.

Based upon the representations of insurance coverage, liability and injuries, and the assurance that there is no other liability coverage for this loss, we are prepared to accept the sum of $_____ in full settlement of the claims of [plaintiff's name].

Such offer to settle on behalf of the plaintiff is withdrawn if not accepted in writing within ten (10) days following your receipt of this letter. In the event such offer is rejected, this letter is intended to be used as a basis for a possible "bad faith action" which may be available to the plaintiff if a trial results in an award to the plaintiff in excess of the Insurance policy limitations.

We are herewith enclosing duplicate copies of this letter so that, if you deem it advisable, you may have a copy to forward to your clients, so that there is no claim of surprise or failure by the plaintiff to communicate his intentions.

Very truly yours.

_____

Enclosures

FORM 8–26
SAMPLE RELEASE IN FULL OF CLAIMS
(DEFENDANT CORPORATION)

RELEASE IN FULL OF CLAIMS

THE STATE [state]   )

)

COUNTY OF [county]   )

WHEREAS, the following persons [names] hereinafter referred to as [plaintiff], have asserted a claim against [name], hereinafter referred to as [defendant].

WHEREAS, the sum and substance of the complaint is [specify the substance of the complaint.]

WHEREAS there is considerable doubt, disagreement, dispute and controversy with reference to the validity of [plaintiff]'s claim against [defendant] and as to the legal or moral liability of [defendant] for any amount of damages or justification for legal relief and there is further doubt, disagreement, uncertainty and confusion as to the amount of said liability, if any.

THEREFORE I, as the duty authorized officer and agent of [name], in consideration of the sum of $[amount], receipt of which is hereby acknowledged and confessed, do hereby release, acquit and forever discharge, and by these presents do for [plaintiff], its heirs, executors, legal representatives, administrators, successors and assigns, release, acquit and forever discharge [defendant] and its successor corporations, their employees, representatives, successors, insurers and assigns, and all other persons, firms or corporations who might be liable from any and all claims, demands, charges, costs of court including but not limited to attorney's fees, and causes of action of whatsoever nature, or any other legal theory arising out of the circumstances described in _____ and more particularly in the papers on file in the following styled and numbered cause: [case number] from any and all liability damages of any kind known or unknown, whether in contract or in tort, property damages and any other damages which have accrued or may ever accrue to us, our heirs, executors, legal representatives, administrators, successors or assigns, for or on account of the facts and subject matter referred to in Cause No. [case number] and styled [plaintiff] v. [defendant].

The aforementioned consideration is accepted by the undersigned in full satisfaction of all damages or claims owed to us or that may be owed to us by [defendant] and its successor corporations. It is further understood that this is a compromise and settlement of all matters alleged by the undersigned including but not limited to those contained in [plaintiff' petition, styled [case caption] and pending in [specify court]. It is also agreed to by the parties hereto that upon acceptance by the undersigned of the consideration herein recited that the undersigned shall dismiss or cause to have dismissed the above-styled and numbered cause with prejudice.

It is further understood and agreed that there are no promises of any additional payments or of any further benefits to be received by the undersigned from [defendant] its employees, agents, successors, assigns and/or affiliates other than the consideration herein recited.

It is further understood and agreed that in making the settlement, the acceptance of the undersigned of the consideration herein stated is in full accord and satisfaction of disputed claims. The payment of the sums of money is not flow, nor at any time in the future, to be construed as an admission of liability or guilt by any respondent or defendant, all of which has been expressly denied and vigorously contested.

As further consideration for the payment of the above stated sum of money and as an essential part of this Release in Full, the undersigned parties hereby agree to keep confidential the facts, terms and conditions of this Release in Full including all terms and provisions thereof. The undersigned further agrees and acknowledges that this settlement is a confidential matter and that the performance of the parties being released herein is conditioned upon strict honoring of this confidentiality and not disclosing to any party any of the terms hereof.

As part of the consideration for the payment of the above mentioned sum of money by the parties hereby released, I expressly warrant and represent and do hereby state for the parties referred to above and thereby represent to each and all of the parties hereby released, that I am legally competent to execute this release and agreement and I am above the age of eighteen (18) years, that no promise or agreement which is not herein expressed has been made to me in executing this release, and that I am not relying upon any statement or representation of any agent of the parties being released hereby. I am relying on my own judgment and I have been represented by legal counsel in this matter. The aforesaid legal counsel has read and explained to me the entire contents of this release, as well as the legal consequences of this release, and I understand that this release shall operate as a full and complete and final release and settlement of any and all claims referred to above.

As part of the consideration for the payment of the above sum of money, the undersigned hereby agree to and do hereby indemnify and hold harmless each and all of the parties hereby released from any and all claims, demands, costs of court, attorney fees, actions and causes of actions which may hereafter be asserted by any person, firm or corporation claiming by, through or under us in connection with this release.

WHEREAS, it is acknowledged, agreed and understood that I have read this full release and that it is a complete, written statement of the terms and conditions of said release.

Signed this [date] day of [month], [20__].

[plaintiff]_____

_____

FORM 8–27
SAMPLE RELEASE IN FULL (ALTERNATIVE)

RELEASE IN FULL

THE STATE OF [state]   )
) KNOW ALL MEN BY THESE
COUNTY OF [county]   ) PRESENTS:

THAT I, [name] in consideration of the sum of [amount] DOLLARS ($_____) to me in hand paid, receipt of which is hereby acknowledged and confessed, have RELEASED, ACQUITTED and FOREVER DISCHARGED, and by these presents do for myself, my heirs, executors, administrators, successors and assigns, RELEASE, ACQUIT, and FOR-EVER DISCHARGE [name], and all other persons, firms and corporations to whom and for whose conduct the parties hereby released may be liable, from any and all claims, demands and causes of action of whatsoever nature, whether in contract or in tort, or arising under or by virtue of any statute or regulation, for personal injuries, property damage, and for all other losses and damages of every kind, including but not limited to loss of consortium, ensuing death, and exemplary and punitive damages, which have accrued or may ever accrue to me, or to my heirs, executors, legal representatives, successors or assigns, for or on account of an accident that occurred on or about [date], 20[year].

The aforementioned consideration is accepted by the undersigned in full satisfaction of all damages to the undersigned arising out of said accident. The payment of said sum by the parties released herein is not to be construed as an admission of liability, which has been denied.

I have heretofore brought suit in the [type] Court of [county] County, [state] in Cause No. [case number], to recover damages sustained by me as a result of the above-described accident. The consideration mentioned above is accepted by me in full compromise and settlement of all claims and causes of action for personal injuries and property damage being asserted in said suit, or which might have been asserted in said suit, and I agree that a judgment may be entered in that suit, denying me any recovery.

As part of the consideration for the payment of the above-mentioned sum by the parties hereby released, I have expressly warranted and represented and do hereby for myself, my heirs, legal representatives and assigns, expressly warrant and represent to each and all of the parties hereby released that: (1) I am legally competent to execute this agreement and release; (2) all medical, hospital and other expenses of any and every nature and character whatsoever incurred by me or on my behalf arising from the said described accident have been or will be hereafter paid in full; and upon request, I will furnish evidence to the parties hereby released of the payment in full by me of all expenses and bills; (3) I have not assigned, pledged or otherwise in any manner whatsoever, sold or transferred, either by instrument in writing or otherwise, any right, title, interest or claim that I have or may have by reason of the accident described above or any matters arising out of or related thereto, except to my counsel named in this instrument [list the pertinent documents].

§ 8.57 SETTLEMENT

As part of the consideration for the payment of the above sum of money, I, for myself, my heirs, executors, administrators and assigns, have agreed to and do hereby INDEMNIFY, DEFEND and HOLD HARMLESS each and all of the parties hereby released from any and all claims, demands, actions and causes of action of whatsoever nature or character which have been or which may hereafter be asserted by any person, firm or corporation whomsoever claiming by, through or under me, and from any and all legal actions, including third-party actions and cross-actions, asserted or brought against any of the parties hereby released by any firm, person, or corporation against whom I have asserted or brought, or may hereafter assert or bring, any action, arising out of or in any manner connected with the above-described accident.

As part of the consideration for the payment of the above-mentioned sum of money, the undersigned specifically agrees and consents that this instrument, as well as any judgment or order of dismissal used in connection herewith, will not be used in any existing or subsequent legal proceeding asserted against the undersigned resulting from the accident hereinabove described, as a pleas of res judicata, compulsory counterclaim, estoppel by judgment, or any similar doctrine of defense.

I, the undersigned, expressly warrant and represent to the parties hereby released, as part of the consideration for the payment of the above-mentioned sum of money, that before executing this instrument I have fully informed myself of its terms, contents, conditions and effect; that in making this settlement I have had the benefit of the advice of doctors of my own choosing; and no promise or representation of any kind has been made to me by the parties hereby released or by anyone acting for them, except as is expressly stated in this instrument. I have relied solely and completely upon my own judgment, and the advice of counsel in making this settlement; and I fully understand that this is a full, complete and final release, and that the sum of money that is to be paid to me as a result of the herein described accident.

I, [name], counsel of record for [name] do hereby acknowledge that the foregoing release was fully and completely explained to him prior to the execution thereof and acknowledge receipt of my fee out of the sum of money mentioned above.

SIGNED and EXECUTED this [date] day of [month], 20[__].

_____
[name of claimant]

_____
[counsel for claimant]

TRIAL READINESS AND SETTLEMENT

FORM 8–28
RELEASE

NO. _____

[PLAINTIFF(S) NAMES] Plaintiffs,	)))
	) IN THE DISTRICT COURT OF
	)) _____ COUNTY,
v.	)) _____ JUDICIAL DISTRICT
[DEFENDANT(S) NAMES] Defendants.	))

RELEASE

STATE OF _____	)
	) KNOW ALL MEN BY THESE
COUNTY OF _____	) PRESENTS:

That I, _____ (hereinafter referred to as "Plaintiff"), a resident of _____ County, _____, for and in consideration of the sum of ONE HUNDRED FORTY THOUSAND AND NO/100 DOLLARS ($140,0000.00) in hand paid on behalf of Defendant _____ (hereinafter referred to as "Defendant"), the receipt, sufficiency, and manner of payment of which is hereby acknowledged and confessed for myself, or anyone claiming through or under me, my heirs, executors, beneficiaries, and/or administrators, have and do hereby, fully and forever RELEASE, ACQUIT, and DISCHARGE said Defendant, her agents, employees, heirs, executors, beneficiaries, administrators, successors, and assigns, and any and all other persons, firms, and/or corporations in privity with her, from any and all liability now accrued, or hereafter to accrue, on account of any and all claims, demands, and/or causes of action which I, or anyone claiming through or under me may now have, or may hereafter have, against said Defendant, and all other persons, firms, and/or corporations whomsoever, in any way arising from, growing out of, or in any way connected with any alleged damages sustained by me in connection with the incident made the basis of this suit, which is more fully described in Plaintiff's pleadings on file in the cause of action described below.

This settlement is simply a compromise of a disputed claim and is not a confession or admission of liability or negligence on the part of the Defendant, and shall not be held or construed as a confession or admission in any suit or proceeding no matter by whom same may be brought.

The Plaintiff further agrees, as part of the consideration hereof, to enter into an agreed take-nothing Judgment as to the Defendant in that certain suit now pending on the docket of the _____ Judicial District Court of _____ County, _____, and

§ 8.57   SETTLEMENT

styled _____, the same being Cause No. _____ on the docket of said Court.

This Release includes a full, final, and complete settlement and satisfaction of any and all claims, demands, and/or causes of action asserted by the Plaintiff in any suit against said Defendant, as well as any and all claims, demands, and/or causes of action which might have been asserted by the Plaintiff, his heirs, executors, beneficiaries, and administrators, or anyone acting on behalf of the Plaintiff, in said suit.

As further consideration of the above sum, the Plaintiff hereby releases Defendant, her officers, employees, agents, and attorneys, from all claims, demands, and/or causes of action, known or unknown, based on or in any way related to any conduct, representation, or omission of Defendant, her officers, employees, agents, or attorneys, in the course of evaluating, negotiating, or otherwise handling the above-referenced claim. This Release includes any claim, demand, or cause of action based on allegations that Defendant, her officers, employees, agents, or attorneys, misrepresented or failed to disclose any fact, failed to deal fairly or in good faith, or failed to perform with reasonable care, skill, expedience, or faithfulness.

The Plaintiff further understands and agrees that the Defendant does not admit liability for any claim, demand, or cause of action released above and that any such liability is indefinite, uncertain, and incapable of being satisfactorily established.

This Release shall be construed and interpreted in accordance with the laws of the State of _____ and constitutes the entire agreement between and among the parties hereto with respect to the matters described herein. This Release supersedes any prior oral or written agreements, if any, between and among the parties relating to any aspect thereof. No other representations or terms of whatever nature shall constitute part of this agreement.

This Release may be modified or amended only by written instrument duly executed by the parties to this Release after the date hereof.

The invalidity of any provision of this Release shall not affect the enforceability of any other provision hereof.

I, _____, HEREBY REPRESENT AND WARRANT THAT I HAVE MADE NO ASSIGNMENT HEREIN OF MY CLAIM OR ANY PART THEREOF TO ANY OTHER PERSON, FIRM, AND/OR CORPORATION, OTHER THAN TO MY ATTORNEYS HEREIN, AND THAT THERE ARE NO CURRENT OR OUTSTANDING LIENS IN CONNECTION WITH OR ARISING OUT OF THE INCIDENT MADE THE SUBJECT OF THIS RELEASE. IN ALL EVENTS, IN CONSIDERATION OF THE PAYMENT OF THE AFOREMENTIONED SUM, I HEREBY AGREE TO INDEMNIFY AND HOLD HARMLESS THE PARTY RELEASED HEREIN FROM ANY AND ALL CLAIMS, DEMANDS, AND/OR CAUSES OF ACTION, OF ANY AND EVERY NATURE WHATSOEVER, MADE BY ANY PERSONS, FIRMS, AND/OR CORPORATIONS IN CONNECTION WITH THE MATTERS MADE THE SUBJECT OF THIS RELEASE.

SIGNED on this _____ day of _____, 20___.

_____

TRIAL READINESS AND SETTLEMENT

STATE OF _____   )
)
COUNTY OF _____   )

BEFORE ME, the undersigned authority, on this day personally appeared _____, known to me to be the person whose name is subscribed to the foregoing Release and who acknowledged to me that he executed the same for the purposes and consideration therein expressed.

GIVEN UNDER MY HAND AND SEAL OF OFFICE this the _____ day of _____, 20 ___.

                          _____
                          NOTARY PUBLIC,
                          State of _____

I, _____, hereby certify that I am the attorney of record for Plaintiff _____ in the above-described suit. I have read the foregoing Release to him, and have fully explained to him the legal effect thereof, and after such explanation, he was fully satisfied to release his claim. In consideration of the inclusion of my firm name as attorney for Plaintiff on the settlement draft, I join in the execution of this instrument.

                          _____

§ 8.58   Settlement by Infant

Most jurisdictions require court approval of settlements by infants (see **Form 8–29**).

FORM 8–9
INFANT'S COMPROMISE ORDER

                    At a Term, Part   ,
                    Of the [title of court] of
                    the State of [state] ,
                    County of [county]
                    on the _____ day of
                    _____, 20__.

PRESENT:
Hon. Justice

568

§ 8.58 SETTLEMENT BY INFANT

[name], an infant, by his father   )
and natural guardian, [name], and)
[name of guardian], Individually)
)
    Plaintiff(s),   )   Index No. _____
)
)   INFANT'S COMPROMISE
)
    -against-   )   ORDER
)
[name]   )
    Defendant(s).   )

Upon reading and filing the affidavit of [name], sworn to the _____ day of March, 20__, the parent and natural guardian of [plaintiff infant], an infant under the age of 14 years, the medical affirmation of [physician's name], M.D., dated _____ 20__, the affirmation of [plaintiff's attorney], Esq., dated _____, 20__; and it appearing to the satisfaction of the Court that it would be in the best interests of the infant, [name], to settle his action against the defendant in the sum of Twenty-Five Thousand Dollars ($25,000.00), and the infant, [name], along with his parent and natural guardian, [name], having appeared and having been examined before this Court, together with their attorneys, [name of firm] by [plaintiff's attorney], Esq., on the _____ day of _____, 20__.

NOW, on motion of [name of firm], attorneys for the plaintiffs, it is
ORDERED:

1. [name] as the parent and natural guardian of [name], an infant, be and he is hereby authorized and permitted to compromise and settle this action for and on behalf of the said infant against the defendant, [name], in the amount of Twenty-Five Thousand Dollars ($25,000.00), conditioned upon compliance with the remaining provisions of this Order;

2. Out of the aforesaid sum of Twenty-Five Thousand Dollars ($25,000.00), there shall be paid by the defendant, [name], to [firm name], the attorneys for the plaintiffs and infant the sum of $_____ in full settlement of said attorneys' claim for compensation for their services and the further sum of $_____ for disbursements, making in all the sum of $_____;

3. The balance of the settlement funds, to wit, the sum of $_____ shall be paid to [name], the parent and natural guardian of the said infant, to be held for the sole use and benefit of the said infant, jointly with an officer of the _____ Bank, located at _____ to be deposited at said Bank in an account yielding the highest rate of interest whether it be savings, money market, or a time deposit account. If all or part of said funds are deposited in a time deposit account, the date of maturity shall not extend beyond the date when the infant attains his majority and upon maturity of said deposit said funds shall be reinvested in some form of account yielding the highest rate of interest. The Bank shall, upon the infant's demand and without further order of the Court, pay over to the infant reaching majority, viz., 18 years of age, upon

presentment of proper proof of age, all the monies being held for the infant. A copy of this order shall be served on the aforesaid Bank;

4. This Order is conditioned upon compliance with the terms of the Order, the father and natural guardian of the said infant be and he is hereby authorized and empowered to execute and deliver a general release and all other instruments necessary to effectuate the settlement herein, and the filing of a bond is hereby dispensed with.

ENTER:

_____[judge's name]_____
Judge of [court]

§ 8.59   Settlement Negotiation File

Keep a separate file of copies of all correspondence and memos regarding settlement offers. This gives the attorney a quick reference of the settlement negotiation history of the case and shows in capsulized form the direction the opposing party is taking in the negotiations. It is a much more civilized way of retrieving the information, and wins hands down in a contest with scribbled notes on file folders, correspondence filed through several folders, and garbled telephone messages stapled on the inside of the correspondence file. Your job is to anticipate the needs of your attorney and make him more efficient. The mote details and loose ends that you attend to for him, the better able he will be to concentrate on the theory of the law, and how he can best serve his client's interests.

§ 8.60   Settlement Brochures

Because it is true that over ninety percent of civil litigation lawsuits settle before they ever get to trial a great deal of emphasis is placed on the importance of preparing the case for settlement negotiations. Before any party can enter into settlement negotiations, he must have a good working knowledge of the facts of the case, the applicable law, and, most importantly, the value of his case.

In order to facilitate that process, the paralegal is often charged with the responsibility of preparing a Settlement Brochure, or Portfolio, which contains all the pertinent past, present, and future damage calculations. The brochure is also a highly organized collection of documents and items of physical evidence such as photographs and newspaper articles designed to dramatize the loss and to legitimatize the damage calculations. A complete Settlement Brochure will contain the following sections:

Facts of the Case: This section contains a well-written, precise, and complete recapitulation of the causes of action and the details of the accident or incident which gave rise to the subject matter of the lawsuit. Also included in this section are witness statements and sworn affidavits, newspaper accounts relating to the incident, photographs of the accident and accident site (if appropriate), and other pieces of evidence which support the pleading allegations.

Personal History of the Plaintiff: Once again, writing style in this section is very important. This synopsis of the plaintiff's personal history will contain insights into his or her personality, lifestyle, goals, accomplishments and education. Special attention should be paid to describing the plaintiff's relationship to his family and friends and how the accident or incident has affected those relationships and lifestyle. It is appropriate to include a "before" photograph here.

Summary of Prior Medical History of Plaintiff: A complete summation of the plaintiff's prior medical history should be placed here, including a candid treatment of any other injuries or ailments which have plagued the plaintiff in the past. These issues should be dealt with thoroughly and with no exclusions. Leaking something out which may have been uncovered by the opposing side will lead to feelings of deception and is not conducive to effective settlement negotiations.

Injuries and Effects: This section contains an extremely detailed and graphic account of the injuries or damage incurred, and it should be accompanied by equally graphic "after" pictures to contrast with the "before" pictures in the introductory portion of the settlement brochure. The dramatic portrayal of the changes in lifestyle, psychological ramifications, and description of how the injuries have affected the plaintiff's plans and goals should be presented in the same fashion as evidence to a jury during trial. The information here is designed to elicit sympathy and to maximize the amount of the settlement potential. The opposing side will be given a glimpse of the powerful emotional impact that the case would have on a jury.

Medical Treatment Record: Incorporate here a general summary of the medical treatment received by the plaintiff in relation to the injuries incurred as a result of this accident and include copies of pertinent medical records such as x-rays, test results, operative reports, doctor's reports, hospital admission and discharge reports, and prognoses.

Medical Expenses: This is the section which should contain copies of all medical bills, expenses, and a ledger of same.

Wage Loss: Take advantage of this opportunity to enclose letters from the plaintiff's previous employers and documentation from the plaintiff's personnel file to show the quality of employee he was prior to the incident which is the subject of the present lawsuit. This is also the proper place to include wage loss calculations, including overtime pay missed, if that was a regular expectation of the plaintiff based on previous employment practices.

Other Damages: If there are other related expenses which cannot be categorized in the medical expense or prior wage loss area such as property (damage or lost income from lost business opportunity, categorize each separate area here, also listing a ledger of calculations to correspond. This is also the category into which lost earning potential will be placed, which will include such areas as passed over promotions and loss of ability to continue in the same line of work or to earn the same amount of money as before, due to a resulting disability, be it either mental or physical.

Evaluation of Claim: Sum up your entire case here, clearly demonstrating the devastating impact that this incident has had on the plaintiff's life, goals, and plans. Finalize the calculation of the total dollar impact that this ordeal has cost the plaintiff, and make poignant points designed to remind the defendant and his counsel what kind of effect this material would have on a jury.

§ 8.61 Transmittal Letter to Opposing Party Requesting Execution of Settlement Papers

When you are sending the settlement papers to the opposing party, it is necessary to include a transmittal letter as well. **Form 8–30** can be used for this purpose.

FORM 8–30
SAMPLE TRANSMITTAL LETTER TO OPPOSING PARTY
REQUESTING EXECUTION OF SETTLEMENT PAPERS

[date]

RE: Cause No. [case number], in the [judicial district] Judicial District Court in and for [county] County, [state], [plaintiff] v. [defendant]

Dear [name]:

I enclose an original, and [number] (copy/copies) of a [final judgment in this cause/settlement agreement], together with [number] multiple original releases and (a) settlement draft(s) in the agreed amount of $[amount].

Please make arrangements for the execution and return to me of the original and [number] [copy/copies] of [the final judgment/settlement] and [number] original release[s]. Please hold the draft(s) until [the judgment has been filed and has been signed by the Court/identify any other conditions]. The draft(s) will not be accepted for payment until that time.

Thank you for your courtesy and cooperation in this matter.

Very truly yours,

_____

[firm name]

§ 8.62   Dismissals

Dismissals take place in lawsuits for a variety of different reasons a dismissal with prejudice means that the case cannot be refiled. Therefore, obviously, a case dismissed without prejudice may be refiled. If your client is a defendant and has agreed to a settlement, make sure that the dismissal reads "with prejudice."

Cases may also be dismissed for want of prosecution. This happens when a judge reviews a file and feels that there has been a substantial lack of activity on either part. In this instance, the parties are given notice that the case is due to be dismissed and either party has the right to file a motion to retain the action. If neither party files, the case is dismissed.

Dismissals also can be handed down by the judge for sanctions, or punishment. For example if a party neglects to file answers to interrogatories, even after a direct order from the court, the judge may strike his pleadings or dismiss the case altogether.

There are probably hundreds of other reasons for dismissing a case. Each lawsuit is unique and should be treated as such. The most important thing to remember is to protect your client by making sure the phrases "with prejudice:" or "without prejudice" are properly used in each instance. (See **Form 8–31**.)

FORM 8–31
SAMPLE DISMISSAL

NO. [case number]

[name]		)	IN THE DISTRICT COURT OF
	Plaintiff,	)	
		)	[county] COUNTY, [state]
[name]		)	
	Defendant.	)	[judicial district] JUDICIAL DISTRICT

DISMISSAL

It is hereby stipulated and agreed between the parties [plaintiff] and [defendant], by and through their respective attorneys [plaintiff's attorney] and [defendant's attorney], that the above-titled action be, and the same hereby is dismissed with (without) prejudice, each party to pay its own costs.

Dated: [date]_____ Dated: [date]_____

[name]_____ [name]_____
Attorney for Plaintiff Attorney for Defendant

   It is so ordered this [date] day of [month], [20__].

_____
PRESIDING JUDGE

§ 8.63 Dismissal for Want of Prosecution

Courts sometimes use a housekeeping-type of measure such as the Dismissal for Want of Prosecution to eliminate those cases from the docket which have not been pursued or prosecuted by the plaintiff for long periods of time. The reasons for dismissal can be varied, but the plaintiff's lack of due diligence in its prosecution of litigation is generally the underlying cause of the dismissal. (**Form 8–32**) The plaintiff's refusal or failure to respond to motions before the court or the plaintiff's failure to appear at hearings can be reasons for dismissal by the court's own motion. Any other kind of behavior seen by the court as done for the purpose of delay only are common causes of dismissal for want of prosecution (**Form 8–33** is a Sample Order for Dismissal.)

   Dismissal on motion of the court is a drastic remedy which is usually not imposed unless no other remedies appear to be adequate. The cases are generally dismissed without prejudice to the plaintiff, and notice is given to each party, who in turn is given the opportunity to file a Motion to Retain the case on the docket and be heard at oral hearing. Failure of either side to request a hearing in such a matter or to respond to such a notice will generally result in an automatic dismissal by the court after the period of notice expires.

FORM 8–32
SAMPLE MOTION TO DISMISS FOR WANT OF PROSECUTION

NO. [case number]

[name]	)	IN THE DISTRICT COURT OF
	)	
Plaintiff	)	[county] COUNTY, [state]
	)	
vs.	)	[judicial district] JUDICIAL DISTRICT
	)	
[name]	)	
	)	
Defendant	)	

§ 8.63 DISMISSAL FOR WANT OF PROSECUTION

MOTION TO DISMISS FOR WANT OF PROSECUTION

TO THE HONORABLE JUDGE OF SAID COURT:

[name], Defendant in the above-entitled cause, by and through his attorney of record, [name of attorney], moves this court for an order dismissing this cause against the above-named defendant without prejudice and in support thereof would the court as follows:

I.

That the above-entitled action has been pending on the docket of said Court since [date], a period of [time period] (years, months, and so forth), during which time the plaintiff has failed to prosecute this action and to bring the matter to a speedy trial on the merits.

II.

That said failure to prosecute is not the result of any accident or excusable mistake, but rather is a conscious omission on the part of the plaintiff.

III.

That [define circumstances and facts which make the pursuit of the action to its logical conclusion impossible or unlikely] (such as, the amount of time elapsed preventing the gathering of evidence and potential witness, and so forth).

IV.

That as a result of the said want of prosecution on the part of the plaintiff, further prosecution of this action is improbable, if not impossible.

WHEREFORE, [defendant], by and through his attorney of record, [name] respectfully requests that this Court enter an order dismissing the plaintiff's action with prejudice, and further, defendant prays that plaintiff be ordered to pay all costs.

Respectfully submitted,

_____
(firm name)

By: _____
[typed name]
[address]
Attorney for Defendant

TRIAL READINESS AND SETTLEMENT

FORM 8–33
SAMPLE ORDER FOR DISMISSAL

NO. [case number]

[name]	)	IN THE DISTRICT COURT OF
	)	
Plaintiff	)	[county] COUNTY, [state]
	)	
vs.	)	[judicial district] JUDICIAL DISTRICT
	)	
[name]	)	
	)	
Defendant	)	

ORDER FOR DISMISSAL

On [date], [20__], came on to be heard Defendant's Motion to Dismiss the above-entitled cause for plaintiff's want of prosecution. The Court, having duly considered the motion, and finding that it has merit, hereby orders the motion granted.

IT IS THEREFORE ADJUDGED, ORDERED AND DECREED, that the above action is hereby dismissed without prejudice, that it be removed from the docket of the Court, and that all cost incurred herein be adjusted to plaintiff.

SIGNED this [date] day of [month], [20__].

_____
Judge Presiding

§ 8.64 Judgments

You've done all your homework, put in countless hours of hard work, walked in to trial totally prepared, and have won your lawsuit. Congratulations! There is just one more loose end to tie up now: the judgement. Getting that judgement may prove to be easier than collecting it. Get the judgement filed immediately and begin your collection process. It is common in many jurisdictions to file an abstract of judgement, which in effect will put a lien on that person's property so that it cannot be sold until your client receives his money and the lien is released. (See **Forms 8–34** and **8–35.**)

§ 8.64   JUDGMENTS

FORM 8–34
SAMPLE FINAL JUDGMENT FOR PLAINTIFF

NO. [case number]

[name]		)	IN THE [type] COURT OF
	Plaintiff,	)	
		)	[county] COUNTY, [state]
vs.		)	
		)	[judicial district] JUDICIAL DISTRICT
[name]		)	
	Defendant	)	

FINAL JUDGMENT

The above-entitled cause came on regularly for trial on [date], [20__], in the [judicial district] Judicial District of the above-entitled Court before the Honorable [name], judge presiding, and the issues having been duly tried and the jury having rendered its verdict.

IT IS ORDERED AND ADJUDGED AS FOLLOWS:

That the plaintiff recover from the defendant the sum of $[amount] dollars with interest theron at the rate of [rate of interest]% as provided by the law with his costs incurred.

DATED: [date], [20__]

_____
PRESIDING JUDGE

FORM 8–35
SAMPLE FINAL JUDGMENT FOR DEFENDANT

NO. [case number]

[name]		)	IN THE [type] COURT OF
	Plaintiff,	)	
		)	[county] COUNTY, [state]
vs.		)	
		)	[judicial district] JUDICIAL DISTRICT
[name]		)	
	Defendant.	)	

FINAL JUDGMENT

BE IT REMEMBERED ON THE [date] day of [month], [20__], came on for hearing the above-entitled and numbered case, wherein [name] [is/are] plaintiff(s) and [name] [is/are] defendant(s); (and [name] is invervenor,) all parties appeared by their respective

577

attorneys of record and announced that all matters in controversy had been compromised and settled and the consideration therefor paid in full; and the parties thereupon requested the Court to enter judgment that the plaintiff(s) take nothing by reason of this suit and that all court costs be taxed against the defendant(s).

This judgment is made and entered without prejudice to the rights of the defendant(s) herein to hereafter assert any counterclaim or third-party claim that [he/she/it/they] may have as a result of the incident made the basis of this suit and the entry of this judgment shall not constitute any res judicata or estoppel by judgment concerning any such counterclaim or third party claim that the defendant(s) herein may hereafter assert.

Accordingly, it is ORDERED, ADJUDGED and DECREED that the plaintiff(s) take nothing by reason of this suit against the defendant(s) and that all costs of court herein be taxed against the said defendant(s), (except deposition costs incurred by any party,) for which costs the Clerk may have execution if they be not paid in due course.

All relief sought herein by any of the parties herto which is not expressly granted is denied.

(The parties, in open court, hereby agree to waive the provisions of Rule [citation] of the [state/federal] Rules of Civil Procedure.

SIGNED this [date] day of [month], [20__].)

_____
Presiding Judge

APPROVED AND AGREED TO:

_____
Plaintiff

(_____)
(Plaintiff)

[name of firm]

(By) _____
    [attorney name]
    State Bar No. [number]
    Counsel for Plaintiff(s)

[name of firm]

(By) _____
    [attorney name]
    State Bar No. [number]
    Counsel for Defendant

FORM 8–36
FINAL JUDGMENT

NO. _____

[PLAINTIFF(S) NAMES]	)	
Plaintiffs,	)	
	)	IN THE DISTRICT COURT OF
	)	
	)	_____ COUNTY,
v.	)	
	)	_____ JUDICIAL DISTRICT
[DEFENDANT(S) NAMES]	)	
Defendants.	)	

FINAL JUDGMENT

On this the _____ day of _____, 20___, came on to be heard the above-entitled and numbered cause wherein _____ is the Plaintiff and _____ is the Defendant.

The Plaintiff and Defendant, by and through their respective attorneys of record, have announced to the Court that all matters in controversy between them have been compromised and settled, that the Plaintiff should take nothing by reason of his suit against Defendant, and that Defendant should have judgment.

IT IS THEREFORE ORDERED, ADJUDGED, AND DECREED that Defendant _____ shall have judgment and that the Plaintiff shall take nothing by reason of his suit against the Defendant, with taxable court costs to be paid by the party incurring same.

SIGNED this the _____ day of _____, 20___.

_____
JUDGE PRESIDING

APPROVED AS TO FORM:

NAME OF FIRM

By: _____
Attorney Name
Bar #
Address
City, State, Zip
Phone

ATTORNEYS FOR PLAINTIFF

NAME OF FIRM

By: _____
Attorney Name
Bar #
Address
City, State, Zip
Phone

ATTORNEYS FOR DEFENDANT

§ 8.65   Motion for Summary Judgment

In cases where there are no material issues of fact and the law states that the movant is entitled to judgment, he may move for summary judgment. If the motion is granted, the movant has, in effect, won the lawsuit without going to trial. This being the case, preparation for filing of this motion should be nothing short of preparing for trial.

Under the Federal Rule of Civil Procedure 56(a), a plaintiff may file a Motion for Summary Judgment twenty days after the action has commenced or after service of a motion for summary judgment by the adverse party. The following documents are a necessary part of the filing of this motion under the Federal Rules of Civil Procedure:

1. Motion for Summary Judgment (**Form 8–37**)
2. Notice of Motion (**Form 8–38**)
3. Affidavit in Support of Motion for Summary Judgment (**Form 8–39**);
4. Brief in Support of Motion for Summary Judgment (containing the argument for legal authority for the granting of the motion);
5. Request for Oral Argument;
6. Proposed Order

The affidavits in support of and opposition to a summary judgment motion must be made on personal knowledge. They must set forth such facts as would be admissible in evidence and they must show that the affiant is competent to testify to the matters stated in the affidavit.

FORM 8–37
SAMPLE MOTION FOR SUMMARY JUDGMENT

IN THE UNITED STATES DISTRICT COURT
[judicial district] DISTRICT OF [state]
[judicial division] DIVISION

§ 8.65 MOTION FOR SUMMARY JUDGMENT

[name]	)	
	)	
Plaintiff	)	
	)	Civil Action No. [case number]
vs.	)	
	)	
[name]	)	
	)	
Defendant	)	

MOTION FOR SUMMARY JUDGMENT

TO THE HONORABLE JUDGE OF SAID COURT:

COMES NOW, [name], Plaintiff in the above captioned cause and moves for Summary Judgment pursuant to Rule 56(a) of the Federal Rules of Civil Procedure, and in support thereof would show the Court as follows:

I.

Plaintiff is entitled to Summary Judgment as a matter of law because the pleadings, affidavits, and documents that comprise the Summary Judgment Record show that there are no issues of material fact in dispute.

II.

That Defendant [name] has answered in this case and all parties are properly before the Court, and this case is appropriate for Summary Judgment consideration.

III.

[Describe facts of the case]

WHEREFORE, PREMISES CONSIDERED, [plaintiff] prays that its Motion for Summary Judgment be granted and that it have judgment against [defendant] in the amount of $[amount] for reasonable attorney's fees through summary judgment and on appeal, costs of court and for such other and further relief as this Court deems just.

Respectfully submitted,

_____

Attorney for Plaintiff
[address]
[city, state, zip code]
[telephone number]

TRIAL READINESS AND SETTLEMENT

FORM 8–38
SAMPLE NOTICE OF MOTION FOR SUMMARY JUDGMENT

IN THE UNITED STATES DISTRICT COURT
[judicial district] DISTRICT OF [state]
[judicial division] DIVISION

[name]	)	
	)	
Plaintiff	)	
	)	Civil Action No. [case number]
vs.	)	
	)	
[name]	)	
	)	
Defendant	)	

NOTICE OF MOTION FOR SUMMARY JUDGMENT

TO: [name] _____

[address] _____

_____

You will take notice that on [day], the [date] day of [month], [20__], the attached Motion for Summary Judgment will be presented to the Court for a ruling without the necessity for an oral hearing, unless demand for one is made by you.

Respectfully submitted,

_____
Attorney for Plaintiff [address]
[city, state, zip code]
[telephone number]

[Add certificate of service.]

FORM 8–39
SAMPLE AFFIDAVIT IN SUPPORT OF MOTION FOR
SUMMARY JUDGMENT

IN THE UNITED STATES DISTRICT COURT
[judicial district] DISTRICT OF [state]
[judicial division] DIVISION

[name]	)	
	)	
Plaintiff	)	
	)	
vs.	)	Civil Action No. [case number]
	)	
[name]	)	
	)	
Defendant	)	

AFFIVAVIT IN SUPPORT OF MOTION FOR SUMMARY JUDGMENT

STATE OF [state]	)
	)
COUNTY OF [county]	)

BEFORE ME, THE UNDERSIGNED AUTHORITY personally appeared [name], a person whose signature is affixed before and after being duly sworn did depose and state on his oath as follows:

I.

My name is [name]. I am over the age of eighteen years and have never been convicted of a misdemeanor involving moral turpitude or a felony. I have personal knowledge of the facts stated herein and they are true and correct.

II.

This affidavit is submitted in support of the plaintiff's Motion for Summary Judgment herein for the purpose of showing that there is in this action no genuine issue as to any material fact, and that the plaintiff is entitled to judgment as a matter of law.

III.

[State all facts of evidence which support the motion and are part of the affiant's knowledge.]

_____
[title]

SUBSCRIBED AND SWORN BEFORE ME on this the [date] day of [month], [20__],
to certify which witness my hand and seal of office.

_____

NOTARY PUBLIC in and for
the State of [state]

My Commission Expires:
[date]

_____

[printed name of notary public]

§ 8.66 Motion for Nonsuit

A form of dismissal commonly used is the Motion for Nonsuit. Sometimes, at the
commencement of a case, an attorney is unsure if a defendant is actually liable in
the action, but will name him in the original petition to preserve the claim and
possibly, the statute of limitations. As the suit progresses, discovery may bring to
light the nonliability of that defendant, and the plaintiff may choose to excuse the
defendant from the lawsuit by way of this motion. A Motion for Nonsuit may also
he used when a settlement has been reached between some of the parties while others
remain in the suit. (See **Form 8–31.**)

FORM 8–40
SAMPLE MOTION FOR NONSUIT

NO. [case number]

[name]	)	IN THE [type] COURT OF
	)	OF [county] COUNTY, [state]
Plaintiff,	)	
	)	
vs.	)	
	)	
[name]	)	[judicial district] JUDICIAL DISTRICT
	)	
Defendant.	)	

MOTION FOR NONSUIT

COMES NOW, [name], Plaintiff(s) in the above styled and numbered cause, and
would show the court that all matters herein between [plaintiff] and [defendant] have
been compromised and settled, and that Plaintiff(s), [name] no longer desire(s) to
proseciute this suit against [defendant].

WHEREFORE, Plaintiff(s) [name], move(s) that this Cause be dismissed as to [state
reasons dismissal], with prejudice, to the right of Plaintiff(s) to ever refile said suit again.

Respectively submitted,

_____

By: _____
[name of attorney]
[state] Bar No. [number]
[name of attorney]
[state] Bar No. [number]
[name of law firm]
[address]
[telephone number]

ATTORNEYS FOR PLAINTIFFS

FORM 8-41
MOTION FOR NONSUIT

NO. _____

[PLAINTIFF(S) NAME]	)	
Plaintiffs,	)	
	)	
	)	IN THE DISTRICT COURT OF
	)	
	)	_____ COUNTY,
	)	
v.	)	
	)	_____ JUDICIAL DISTRICT
[DEFENDANT(S) NAMES]	)	
Defendants.	)	

MOTION FOR NONSUIT

Pursuant to Rule _____ of the _____ Rules of Civil Procedure, all Plaintiffs in the above-entitled and numbered cause hereby notify the Court that they no longer desire to prosecute their claims against Defendant _____. Plaintiffs retain their claims against all other named defendants. Taxable costs are to be borne by the parties incurring same.

Respectfully submitted,

NAME OF FIRM

_____

Name of Atty
Atty's Bar #
Address
City, State, Zip
Phone #

TRIAL READINESS AND SETTLEMENT

CERTIFICATE OF SERVICE

I hereby certify that on _____, 20___, a true and correct copy of the foregoing instrument was forwarded to all counsel of record by certified mail, return receipt requested, and that the above instrument was filed with the Clerk of the Court, together with this proof of service.

_____

NO. _____

[PLAINTIFF(S) NAMES] Plaintiffs,	)))
	) IN THE DISTRICT COURT OF
	)) _____ COUNTY,
	)
v.	)) _____ JUDICIAL DISTRICT
[DEFENDANT(S) NAMES] Defendants.	))

AGREED ORDER OF DISMISSAL WITHOUT PREJUDICE

Under consideration of Plaintiff's Motion for Nonsuit without Prejudice, it is hereby ORDERED, ADJUDGED, AND DECREED that all claims of all Plaintiffs against Defendant_____, in the above-captioned matter, are dismissed without prejudice to the refiling of same. Costs are to be taxed against the party incurring same.

SIGNED this the _____ day of _____, 20____.

_____

JUDGE PRESIDING

§ 8.67   Motion to Dismiss on Satisfaction of Judgment

One last form of dismissal is used after a judgment has been paid which provides a final clearing of the record after the satisfaction of the judgment. The following Motion to Dismiss on Satisfaction of Judgment (**Form 8–42**) is a general short form to he used for this purpose.

FORM 8–42
SAMPLE MOTION TO DISMISS ON SATISFACTION OF JUDGMENT

NO. [case number]

[name]	)	IN THE [type] COURT OF
	)	
Plaintiff	)	[county] COUNTY, [state]
	)	
vs.	)	[judicial district] JUDICIAL DISTRICT
	)	
[name]	)	
	)	
Defendant.	)	

MOTION TO DISMISS ON
SATISFACTION OF JUDGMENT

COMES NOW, [name], plaintiff in the above-entitled action, and respectfully moves this court for a dismissal of this cause, the defendant having satisfied the judgment to plaintiff in the amount of $[amount] on [date], [20__]. It is thereby agreed and stipulated by the parties that this action be dismissed.

Respectfully submitted,

_____

Attorney for Plaintiff

§ 8.68 Motion for Renewal of Judgment

There will be times after a judgment is granted that collection in one lump sum is not possible. When this happens, the statute of limitations on collection of the judgment should be researched and noted so that time does not run out before the judgment is no longer valid.

Several weeks before the running of the statute, the Motion for Renewal of Judgment (**Form 8–43**) should be filed. Attach copies of the original judgment and the affidavit of the Plaintiff as exhibits.

TRIAL READINESS AND SETTLEMENT

FORM 8–43
SAMPLE MOTION FOR RENEWAL OF JUDGMENT

NO. [case number]

[name]		) IN THE [type] COURT OF
		)
	Plaintiff	) [county] COUNTY, [state]
		)
vs.		) [judicial district] JUDICIAL DISTRICT
		)
[name]		)
	Defendant.	)

MOTION FOR RENEWAL OF JUDGMENT

COMES NOW, Plaintiff, [name] by and through [his/her] attorneys of record, [name of law firm], and moves this Honorable Court for an Order to Renew the Judgment in this action for all purposes. The Plaintiff respectfully shows:

1. That heretofore, on [date], [20__] plaintiff obtained judgment in this Court against Defendant, [name] for $[amount] to be paid with interest at the statutory rate front the said date of its rendition, and the costs of said action determined at $[amount]. Plaintiff is the owner of the Judgment.

2. That the Judgment remains due and partially unpaid, leaving a balance due of $[amount].

3. That the Plaintiff desires to have said Judgment renewed and extended before the expiration of the statutory period provided under [state] State Statute No. [citation].

4. That no cause exists why the Judgment should not be renewed.

This motion is made and based upon all of the papers, files and pleadings in the matter, and on any and all evidence or argument of counsel brought at the time of the hearing of this motion.

DATED this [date] day of the [month], [20__].

[name of law firm]

By: _____
       [attorney name]
       [firm address]
       Attorney for plaintiff

§ 8.69   Postjudgment Interrogatories

While securing a judgment for your client is an admirable feat, collecting the judgment is a more formidable challenge. The major thrust of post-judgment interrogatories is to locate assets of the judgment debtor to enable collection. The interrogatories which follow are to be used for individual judgment debtors and corporation judgment debtors, respectively. (See **Forms 8–44** and **8–45**). As with all other interrogatories, these questions are meant to serve as a guide so tailor them for the situation at hand. Be sure to check your local rules of civil procedure for filing, serving and number-limitation rules.

§ 8.70   Sample Postjudgment Interrogatories (Individual)

FORM 8–44
SAMPLE POSTJUDGMENT INTERROGATORIES (INDIVIDUAL)

1. Please state your full legal name and each other name you have used at any time, including nicknames, aliases, married, or maiden names.

2. Are you or your spouse named on an assumed-name certificate or partnership certificate for any business enterprise? If so, for each such certificate, please state:
    a. The full assumed or partnership name used;
    b. The full name of the person using it;
    c. The city, county, and state in which the assumed or partnership name was primarily used.

3. Have you or your spouse used an assumed name or partnership name without filing an assumed name or partnership certificate? If so, for each such name please state:
    a. The full assumed or partnership name used;
    b. The full name of the person using it;
    c. The city, county and state in which the assumed or partnership name was primarily used.

4. Please state your date and place of birth.

5. Please state your Social Security number.

6. Please state the number and state of issuance of any driver's license which you hold.

7. Please state your current residential address, post office box, city, state, and telephone number, including area code.

8. For each current business in which you own an interest, please state the street address, post office box number, city, county, state, and telephone number, including area code.

9. If you are now married, please state your spouse's full name and complete present address.

10. If you have previously been married to someone other than your present spouse, for each such prior marriage, please state:
    a. The full legal name of the former spouse;
    b. Whether the former spouse is still living;
    c. The date of the marriage to each such former spouse;
    d. The date of the termination of each such marriage and circumstances of each such marriage, (for example, divorce, death, and so forth);
    e. The complete residential address for each such former spouse.

11. If you are presently involved in a divorce or annulment action, please state the case number, case name, and name of the court in which the action is pending.

12. Have you and your spouse ever signed a prenuptial or postnuptial agreement which divides the community property? If so, please state:
    a. The date the agreement was signed;
    b. The substantive contents of the agreement;
    c. Whether the agreement has been filed with the county clerk of any county, and if so, the name of that county in which it is filed.

13. Regarding your father, please state:
    a. His full name;
    b. Whether he is living now;
    c. If he is alive, his complete present address;
    d. If he is alive, his present occupation and employer's name;
    e. If he is not living, the date of his death and his complete residential address at the time of his death.

14. Regarding your mother, please state:
    a. Her full name;
    b. Whether she is living now;
    c. If she is alive, her complete present address;
    d. If she is alive, her present occupation and employer's name;
    e. If she is not living, the date of her death and her complete residential address at the time of her death.

15. Regarding your spouse's parents, for each parent please state:
    a. The parent's full name;
    b. Whether he or she is still living;
    c. The complete present address of the parent, if living;
    d. The present occupation and employer's name or the parent, if living;
    e. The date of death and complete residential address at death if the parent is deceased..

16. If you have one or more children now living, for each such child, please state:
    a. The full legal name of the child;
    b. Whether or not the child is now married;

    c.   The date of birth of the child;

    d.   The complete residential address of the child.

17.   Please state the complete address of each place of residence where you have lived in the past five years and the dates that you lived there.

18.   If you own one or more residences, for each such residence, please state:

    a.   The complete address of the residence;

    b.   Whether the residence is mortgaged;

    c.   The full name, complete address, and telephone number of each mortgage holder;

    d.   The present balance of the mortgage;

    e.   The complete address, name, and amount of each escrow account maintained in connection with each mortgage;

    f.   The complete address of the property that you claim as a homestead.

19.   Do you rent one or more of the places you use as residences? If you do, for each residence you rent please state:

    a.   The complete address of the residence;

    b.   The full name and complete address of your landlord;

    c.   The amount of each rental payment, the day of the month when it is made;

    d.   The complete address where rental payments are made;

    e.   The amount of each deposit paid to the landlord.

20.   Do you have one or more boarders, tenants, or subtenants? If you do, for each one please state:

    a.   The person's full name:

    b.   The amount of rent paid by him or her;

    c.   The date on which the person began renting from you;

    d.   The rental agreement you have with him or her;

    e.   The amount of any deposit made by the person to you.

21.   What is your usual occupation?

22.   Are you presently self-employed (either full-time or part-time)? If so, please state:

    a.   The nature of your occupation in detail;

    b.   How long you have been self-employed in this business;

    c.   The full name under which you business is operated;

    d.   The complete address and telephone number of your place of business;

    e.   Your annual income for each of the last five years or for any portion thereof that you have been self-employed;

    f.   Your average monthly income for the last six months;

    g.   Whether any money is presently owed you and, if it is, from whom and in what amount is owed.

23.   Are you presently employed (either full-time or part-time) by someone other than yourself? If so, each such employer, please state:

    a.   The full name, complete address, and telephone number of the employer;

b.   Your wages or salary and how often you are paid (for example, daily, weekly, monthly);

c.   If you work for commissions, the average monthly total of your commissions;

d.   The day of the week on which you are paid every month, or the other regular day or dates on which you are paid;

e.   Whether any compensation is presently owed you and if it is, from what source and in what amount it is owed.

24.   Is your spouse presently employed? If so, for each such job your spouse has (including self-employment), please state:

a.   Whether any income is from self-employment;

b.   The full name, complete address, and telephone of each employer;

c.   The annual compensation that your spouse has received for each of the last five years or for any portion thereof during which your spouse has been employed by another or self-employed;

d.   Your spouse's average monthly income for the last six months

e.   Whether any compensation is presently owed you and your spouse and, if there is, from what source and in what amount it is owed.

25.   Are you the sole support of your family? If you are not, for each other person who contributes support, please state:

a.   The full name and complete address of the contributor;

b.   Your relationship to the contributor;

c.   The amount of each contribution and when it is normally made;

d.   The full name and address of each person or entity from whom the contributor acquires the assets to make the contribution.

26.   Do your receive income or benefits from any source other than your employment of family contributions listed above? If so, for each source, please state:

a.   The full name and complete address of the source;

b.   The amount of the income or benefits;

c.   Precisely when each payment is received throughout the year;

e.   The full name, complete address, and telephone number of each person, financial institution, or other entity with which you deposit the payments.

27.   For each of your expenses that recurs on a monthly or other regular basis and exceeds $100, please state:

a.   The frequency with which such payments are made;

b.   The amount of each payment and either (1) that this amount is the same for each payment, or (2) that this amount is an average for the past year;

c.   The full name and complete address of the recipient of the payments;

d.   The full name and complete address of each person or entity from whom you acquire the assets to make payments.

28.   For each of your spouse's expenses that recurs on a monthly or other regular basis and exceeds $100, please state:

a.   The frequency with which payments are made;

b.   The amount of each payment either (1) that this amount is the same for each payment or (2) that this amount is an average for the past year;

c.   The full name and complete address of the recipient of the payments;

d.   The full name and complete address of each person or entity from whom the assets to make payments are acquired;

e.   The full name of the person who pays the expense and, if not yourself, your relationship to that person.

29.   For each of your family's expenses that recurs on a monthly or other regular basis and exceeds $100, please state:

a.   The frequency with which payments are made;

b.   The amount of each payment and either (1) that this amount is the same for each payment or (2) that this amount is an average for the past year;

c.   The full name and complete address of the recipient of the payments;

d.   The full name and complete address of each person or entity from whom the assest to make payments are acquired;

e.   The full name of the person who pays the expense and, if not yourself, your relationship to that person.

30.   Have you or your spouse made any payment exceeding $500 to any person or entity during the last four months? If so, for each payment please state:

a.   The date and amount of the payment;

b.   The full name and complete address of the recipient;

c.   The total amount owed the recipient before the payment was made;

d.   The date on which the payment was due;

e.   The balance due the recipient after the payment was made;

f.   The name of the person (you, your spouse, or both) who made the payment.

31.   (1) Have you or your spouse received any real estate or personal property by inheritance? (2) Do you or your spouse expect to receive any inheritance? If the answer to either question is yes, for each property or inheritance please state, to the greatest extent possible:

a.   A complete description of the property;

b.   The present estimated market value of the property;

c.   The complete present location of the property;

d.   The full name of the estate or person from whom the property was or will be inherited;

e.   The full name and complete address of the executor or administrator of the estate;

f.   The name, number, and location of the court administering the estate;

g.   The name of the person (you, your spouse, or both) who inherited or will inherit the property;

h.   Whether there has been a final distribution of the estate and, if so, when it was made.

32.   Within the last year, have you or your spouse received as a gift any money or property worth more than $100? If so, for each gift please state:

    a.   The full name, complete address, and telephone number of the person or entity that made the gift;

    b.   The date it was received;

    c.   The name of the person (you, your spouse, or both) who received it;

    d.   A complete description of the gift;

    e.   The present estimated market value of the gift;

    f.   The gift's present location;

    g.   A detailed description of what was done with the gift if the recipient (you, your spouse, or both) who received it;

33.   Do you or your spouse have an ownership interest in, option to purchase, contract to sell, leasehold in, or other interest in any real estate? If so, for each such property, please state:

    a.   The legal and common descriptions and the location of the property;

    b.   The size of the property

    c.   A description of every improvement on the property

    d.   The name of the person (you, your spouse, or both) having the interest;

    e.   The full name and complete address of every other person or entity having any kind of interest in the property;

    f.   The present value of the equity of you or your spouse in the property;

    g.   Whether the property is encumbered. If it is, also please state:

        (1)   The nature of the encumbrance;

        (2)   The full name and complete address of the holder of the encumbrance;

        (3)   The amount of the encumbrance;

    h.   The cost of the property, excluding improvements;

    i.   When and how the property was bought or acquired;

    j.   Whether any part of the property is within the corporate limits of a town and, if so, the name of the town;

    k.   Whether any money or property has been placed in escrow. If so, also please state:

        (1)   The full name and complete address of the person or entity now having possession of the escrow amount or property;

        (2)   The amount of money or value of the property in escrow.

34.   Is there any checking account, money market, savings account, trust fund, pension plan, profit-sharing plan, mutual fund, or other account or fund money in which you, your spouse, or any family member now residing with you either owns an interest or has a right of withdrawal or deposit? If so, for each such account please state:

    a.   The full name and relationship to you of each person owning an interest in the account or having access to it;

    b.   The name (or title) and number of the account;

    c.   The full name and complete address of the person or entity holding the fund;

    d.   The present balance in the account.

35. Do you, your spouse, or any family member now residing with you have access to any depository (including but not limited to safes, vaults, and safe-deposit boxes)? If so, for each depository please state:
    a. The full name and complete address of each person or entity to whom the depository is rented or leased;
    b. The full name and complete address of the bank or other institution where the depository is located.
    c. The full name and complete address of each person having access to the depository;
    d. A complete description of the property contained in the depository on the date you are answering these questions;
    e. The date of each inventory of the depository;
    f. The complete contents of each inventory, quoting verbatim or (if you will do so without a court order) attaching copies of them to your answers.

36. Has anything been removed from any above-mentioned depository during the last twelve months? If it has, for each thing removed, please state:
    a. A complete description of the property removed;
    b. The date it was removed;
    c. Why it was removed;
    d. The full name and complete address of each person who removed it;
    e. The full name of the present custodian of the property and either (1) the complete address of the property's present location or (2) a detailed description of its disposition, whichever applies;
    f. Whether the property is worth more than $500, and if so, also please state the date of acquistion and the cost of acquisition of the property.

37. Do you, your spouse, or any family member now residing with you have access to any depository (including but not limited to safes, vaults, and safe-depository boxes)? If so, for each such depository please state:
    a. The full name and complete address of each person or entity to whom the depository is rented or leased;
    b. The full name and complete address of the bank or other institution where the depository is located;
    c. The full name and complete address of each person having access to the depository;
    d. A complete description of the property contained in the depository on the date you are answering these questions;
    e. The date of each inventory of the depository;
    f. The complete contents of each inventory, quoting verbatim or (if you will do so without a court order) attaching copies of them to your answers.

38. Has anything been removed from any above-mentioned depository during the last twelve months? If so, for each such thing removed, please state:
    a. A complete description of the property removed;
    b. The date it was removed;
    c. Why it was removed;

    d.   The full name and complete address of each person who removed it;

    e.   The full name of the present custodian of the property and either (1) the complete address of the property's present location or (2) a detailed description of its disposition, whichever applies;

    f.   Whether the property is worth more than $500, and if so, also please state the date of the acquisition and the cost of the acquisition of the property.

39.   Is there any real estate or personal property that any person or entity holds title to or possesses in the name or for the benefit of yourself, your spouse, or any member of your family now residing with you? If so, for each such property, please state:

    a.   The full name of the person in whose name the property is held and, if it is not in your name, your relationship with the person in whose name it is held;

    b.   The full name of the person for whose benefit the property is held and, if it is not for your benefit, your relationship with the person for whose benefit it is held;

    c.   A detailed description of the property;

    d.   The value of the property;

    e.   The full name, complete address, and telephone number of the person or entity holding the property;

    f.   The relationship between the person or entity holding the property and the person for whose benefit it is being held;

    g.   A detailed description of the arrangements under which the property is being held, including a description of the interest you, your spouse, or your family member has in the property.

40.   Have you or your spouse furnished a financial statement to any person or entity in the last five years? If so, for each such financial statement, please state:

    a.   The full name and complete address of each person or entity to whom it was furnished;

    b.   The date it was furnished;

    c.   The contents of the statement, quoting verbatim or (if you will do so without a court order) attaching a copy of it to your answers;

    d.   The name of the person (you, your spouse, or both) who furnished the statement.

41.   If you will do so without a court order, please attach to your answers a copy of each federal income tax return of the last five years for you, your spouse, or both of you. Please state:

    a.   The source and amount of each item of income listed;

    b.   The total income received for each year, whether or not reported;

    c.   The date each return was filed and the address of the Internal Revenue Service office where it was filed;

    d.   The amount and source of each amount of income received but not shown on any of the returns that you are attaching to your answers;

    e.   The full name and complete address of each person who worked on or helped prepare each return.

42.   Do you or your spouse have any life insurance? If so, for each such policy, please state:

   a.   The full name, complete address, and telephone number of the issuing
        company;
   b.   The policy number;
   c.   The date of issuance, amount, and type of the policy;
   d.   The cash value of it or that it has no cash value;
   e.   The full name and complete address of each beneficiary of the policy;
   f.   Whether the policy is encumbered in any way, and if it is, in what way and
        for what amount.

43. At any time in the last five years, have you or your spouse paid or had paid a
     premium on any life insurance policy payable to your estate or your spouse's
     estate? If so, for each such policy, please state:
   a.   The full name, complete address, and telephone number of the issuing
        company;
   b.   The number of the policy;
   c.   The face value of it on the death of the insured;
   d.   Each date on which a payment was made;
   e.   The amount of each payment.

44. Has any beneficiary designation of an insurance policy on yourself or your spouse
     been changed in the last five years? If so, for each change please state:
   a.   The date when the change took place;
   b.   The name of the new beneficiary;
   c.   The name of the old beneficiary;
   d.   Why the change was made.

45. If you will do so without a court order, please attach to your answers a copy of
     each insurance policy, contract, or document to which the preceding answers have
     pertained.

46. Do you or your spouse now own, claim any interest in, or have title to any vehicle
     (including but not limited to automobiles, trucks, boats, aircraft, motorcycles)? If
     so, for each vehicle please state:
   a.   A complete description of the vehicle, including (as applicable) its year, make,
        model, vehicle identification number, serial number, and other permanent
        identification numbers;
   b.   The general condition of the vehicle;
   c.   The complete address of its current location;
   d.   The full name and complete address of each person or entity having control
        over the vehicle;
   e.   The present estimated market value of the vehicle;
   f.   The name of the person (you, your spouse, or both) having title to or an
        interest in the vehicle and the nature of the interest.

47. Do you or your spouse now own, claim any interest in, or have title to any firearm?
     If so, for each such firearm please state:
   a.   A complete description of the firearm, including (as applicable) its year, make,
        model, serial number, and other permanent identification numbers;

     b.   The general condition of the firearm;

     c.   The complete address of its current location;

     d.   The full name and complete address of each person or entity having control over the firearm;

     e.   Its present estimated market value;

     f.   The name of the person (you, your spouse, or both) having title to or an interest in the firearm and the nature of the interest.

48.   Do you or your spouse now own, claim any interest in, or have title to any art object? If so, for each such object please state:

     a.   A complete description of the object;

     b.   The complete address of its current location;

     c.   The full name and complete address of each person or entity having control over the object;

     d.   The present estimated market value of the object;

     e.   The name of the person (you, your spouse or both) having title to or an interest in it and the nature of the interest.

49.   Do you or your spouse now own, claim any interest in, or have title to any collection (including but not limited to stamp collections and coin collections) that has not been described in a previous answer to these interrogatories? If so, for each such collection please state:

     a.   A complete description of the collection, including (as applicable) the year, make, model, serial number, and other permanent identification numbers of each thing in the collection;

     b.   The complete address of its current location;

     c.   The full name and complete address or each person or entity having control over the collection;

     d.   The present estimated market value of the collection (or of each thing in it if appropriate);

     e.   The name of the person (you, your spouse, or both) having title to or an interest in the collection and the nature of the interest.

50.   Do you or your spouse now own, claim any interest in, or have title to any manufactured home, mobile home, trailer house, recreational vehicle, camper trailer, trailer, or other item of a similar nature that has not been described in a previous answer to these interrogatories? If so, for each such item, please state:

     a.   A complete description of the item, including (as applicable) the year, make, model, vehicle identification number, serial number, and other permanent identification numbers;

     b.   The general condition of the item;

     c.   The complete address of its current location;

     d.   The full name and complete address of each person or entity having control over the item;

     e.   The present estimated market value of the item;

     f.   The full name and complete address of the person or entity having possession to the certificate of title or other document evidencing title to it;

g.   The amount of any lien against the item and the full name and complete address of the holder or owner of the lien;

h.   The name of the person (you, your spouse, or both) having title to or an interest in the item and the nature of the interest.

51.   Do you or your spouse now own, claim any interest in or have title to any animal of the value of $100 or more? If so, for each such animal please state:

a.   A complete description of the animal, including registration information as applicable;

b.   The complete address of its present location;

c.   The present estimated market value of the animal;

d.   The full name and complete address of the person or entity having possession of the animal;

e.   The date and the cost of acquisition of the animal;

f.   The amount of any lien against the animal and the full name and complete address of the holder or owner of the animal;

g.   The name of the person (you, your spouse, or both) having title to or an interest in the item and the nature of the interest.

52.   Do you or your spouse now own, claim any interest in, or have title to any farm machinery of any kind that has not been described in a previous answer to these interrogatories? If so, for each such item please state:

a.   A complete description of the item, including (as applicable) its year, make, model, motor number, serial number, and other permanent identification numbers;

b.   The complete address of its present location;

c.   The full name and complete address of its present location;

d.   Whether the item is subject to a lien and, if it is, the amount of such indebtedness and the full name and complete address of the holder or owner of the lien;

e.   The present estimated market value of the item;

f.   The date and cost of acquisition of the item;

g.   The name of the person (you, your spouse, or both) having title to or an interest in the item and the nature or the interest.

53.   Do you or your spouse now own, claim any interest in, or have title to any kind of aircraft that has not been described in a previous answer to these interrogatories? If so, for each such aircraft, please state:

a.   A complete description of the aircraft, including the FAA identification number, motor number, and other permanent identification numbers;

b.   The complete address of its present location;

c.   The full name and complete address of the person or entity having possession of the certificate of title, and if different, the present location of the certificate;

d.   Whether the aircraft is subject to a lien, and if it is, the amount of such indebtedness and the full name and address of the holder or owner of the lien;

e.   The present estimated market value of the aircraft;

f. The date and cost of its acquisition;

g. The full name and complete address of the person or entity having possession of the aircraft;

h. The name of the person (you, your spouse, or both) having title to or an interest in the aircraft and the nature of the interest.

54. Do you or your spouse now own, claim any interest in, or have title to any of the following kinds of property?

a. Stocks, bonds, futures contracts, or money in margin accounts or other securities;

b. Gold or silver bars or coins;

c. Mortgages or liens on real or personal property;

d. Promissory notes, drafts, bills of exchange, or other commercial paper;

e. Judgments;

f. Savings bonds or other government-issued bonds;

g. Any interest in oil, gas, or mineral leases;

h. Certificates of deposit, letters of credit, money orders, cashier's checks, traveler's checks, bank deposits or escrow funds;

i. Keough plans, individual retirement accounts, profit-sharing plans, deferred compensation plans, pension plans, prepaid funeral plans, retirement benefits, or other retirement plans;

j. Leases, life estates, remainder estates, remainder interests, or other interests in real property;

k. Patents, copyrights, trademarks, service marks, franchises, or other such licenses;

If you do and if the information sought in this question has not been provided in another answer, for each item of property please state:

a. A complete description of the item, including account number, registration number, other permanent identification numbers, and other specified identification;

b. The full name and complete address of the person in whose name the item is held;

c. The present value of the item;

d. The amount of the indebtedness outstanding against the item;

e. The name of the person (you, your spouse, or both) having title to or an interest in the item and the nature of the interest.

55. Do you or your spouse now own, claim any interest in, or have title to any personal property (including but not limited to household effects, furniture, tools, appliances, clothing, and jewelry) that is worth more than $500 and that has not been described in a previous answer? If so, for each such item please state:

a. A complete description of the item, including (as applicable) the year, make, model, serial number, and other permanent identification numbers;

b. The complete address of its present location;

c. The full name and complete address of the person or entity having possession or control of the item;

d. The present estimated market value of the item;

    e.   The name of the person (you, your spouse, or both) having title to or an interest in the item and the nature of the interest.

56.   Do you or your spouse now own, claim any interest in, or have title to any personal property now pledged as security for debt? If so, for each item please state:

    a.   A complete description of the item, including (as applicable) the year, make, model, serial number, and other permanent identification numbers;

    b.   The amount of the debt the property was pledged to secure and the current amount of the debt;

    c.   The full name and complete address of the person or entity to whom the property is pledged;

    d.   The date the debt is to be paid;

    e.   The date the debt was incurred;

    f.   The name of the person (you, your spouse, or both) having title to or an interest in the property and the nature of the interest.

57.   Have you, your spouse, or an agent of either of you moved any property that you or your spouse owns (or claims any interest in) from the county of residence on the date you received these questions, please state:

    a.   A complete description of the property including (as applicable) the year, make, model, serial number, and other permanent identification numbers;

    b.   The complete address of its present location;

    c.   The reason for removing the item from the county of the owner's residence;

    d.   The name of the person (you, your spouse, or both) having title to or an interest in the item and the nature of the interest.

58.   Do you or any member of your family now residing with you have an ownership interest in any business, partnership, joint venture, or other endeavor in which it is engaged;

    a.   The full name, complete address, and telephone number of the business or entity;

    b.   A detailed description of the type of business or other endeavor in which it is engaged;

    c.   The full name of the person (you or a family member) having the interest and, if applicable, you relationship to that person;

    d.   The date, manner, and cost of acquisition of it;

    e.   A detailed description of the interest;

    f.   A description of the legal nature of the entity;

    g.   The full name and complete address of each officer, director, or partner in the business;

    h.   The full name and complete address of each bank in which the business maintains any type of checking or deposit account or from which the business has borrowed money;

    i.   The present estimated market value of the interest and its percentage of the total value of the business;

    j.   The amount of any interest you or a family member has transferred within the last year and the full name and complete address of the person or entity receiving the interest.

59. Have you or any member of your family now residing with you been at any time an employee, officer, director, stockholder, or owner of any other kind of interest (including debentures, purchase options, beneficial interests) of a corporation? If so, for each such relationship or interest, please state:
   a. A description of the relationship or interest;
   b. The full name of the person (you or a family member) having the relationship or interest;
   c. The full name, complete address, and telephone number of the corporation;
   d. The nature, amount method, and date of payment of compensation received from the corporation by you or a family member at any time;
   e. The nature and extent of the duties or responsibilities of you or your family member in the relationship.

60. Are you or your spouse a beneficiary of any trust? If so, for each trust please state:
   a. The full name of the trust;
   b. The full name, complete address, and telephone number of the trustee;
   c. The full name, complete address, and telephone number of each beneficiary of the trust;
   d. A detailed description of the terms of the trust as they relate to you or your spouse as beneficiary;
   e. A detailed description of how the trust is funded;
   f. The total amount presently held in trust;
   g. The portion of the current balance held in trust for you or your spouse;
   h. The date on which rights in the trust will vest in you or your spouse;
   i. A description of the assets owned by the trust and their present estimated market value;
   j. The account number and location of each checking, savings, or other depository account of the trust;
   k. The date and period when trust disbursements are regularly made;
   l. The contents of every one of the trust's tax returns for the last five years, quoting verbatim or (if you will do so without a court order) attaching copies of the returns to your answers.

61. Do you or your spouse maintain any business or personal account with any bank, savings and loan association, credit union or postal savings department? If so, for each account please state:
   a. The full name and complete address of the institution holding the account;
   b. The full name and number under which the account is maintained;
   c. The balance of the account five calendar days before the day you received these interrogatories;
   d. The balance of the account on the day you answered these interrogatories.

62. Do you own an interest in a patent or copyright? If you do, for each such interest, please state:
   a. A full description of the thing patented or copyrighted;
   b. A description of the interest you own;
   c. The registration number of the patent or copyright

    d.   The amount of income you received from the patent or copyright during the last twelve months.

63.   Do you or your spouse hold any property as trustee of any type of trust? If so, for each trust please state:

    a.   A detailed description of all the property included in the trust;

    b.   The full name and complete address & each beneficiary of the trust;

    c.   Whether the trustee (you or your spouse) has a general power of appointment over any property in the trust;

    d.   The date the trust was created;

    e.   The full name of the trust.

64.   During the last five years, have you or your spouse created or contributed to any trust? If so, for each trust, please state:

    a.   When the trust was created;

    b.   A description of the property contributed;

    c.   The full name and complete address of each trustee;

    d.   The full name and complete address of each beneficiary.

65.   Does any person at entity owe you or your spouse money (including but not limited to promissory notes and accounts receivable)? If so, for each such debt please state:

    a.   The full name and complete address of the debtor;

    b.   The amount and due date of the debt and to whom owed.

66.   Has any account receivable of you or your spouse been assigned or disposed of (other than by collection in full) in the last twelve months? If so, for each such account please state:

    a.   The full name of the account;

    b.   The kind of disposition;

    c.   The date of the disposition;

    d.   The full name and complete address of the person or entity taking the account;

    e.   The amount of reserve due you or your spouse;

    f.   The extent to which future accounts receivable were covered;

    g.   The amount of payment received in exchange;

    h.   The name of the person (you, your spouse, or both) who owned the account.

67.   At any time in the last five years, have you or your spouse disposed of any personal property of a value of $100 or more by sale, gift, or other action? If so, for each disposition please state:

    a.   A full description of the property disposed of;

    b.   The date of the disposition;

    c.   The full name and complete address of each person or entity to whom disposition was made;

    d.   The payment or other consideration received in exchange;

    e.   The manner of disposition (gift, sale, and so forth);

    f.   The date you or your spouse had acquired the property;

    g.   The name of the person (you, your spouse, or both) who owned the property;

h.   The estimated market value of the property when you or your spouse acquired it;

i.   The contents of any gift tax return filed in connection with the disposition, quoting verbatim or (if you will do so without a court order) attaching a copy of the return to your answers.

68.   Have you or your spouse ever made any conveyance, transfer, gift, or other disposition of property with any reservation of rights, benefits, or options for the reacquisition of the property at some future date? If so, for each such disposition, please state:

a.   A full description of the property involved;

b.   When the disposition occurred;

c.   The full name and complete address of the transferee;

d.   The nature of the reservation, benefit, or option;

e.   The cost of the property when you or your spouse acquired it;

f.   The market value of the property at the time of disposition or the payment or other consideration received in exchange;

g.   The name of the person (you, your spouse, or both) making the transfer.

69.   At any time in the last five years, have you or your spouse disposed of any real estate by sale, gift, or other action? If so, for each such disposition, please state:

a.   A full description of the property disposed of;

b.   The date of the disposition;

c.   The full name and complete address of each person or entity involved in the transaction;

d.   The payment or other consideration received in exchange;

e.   The manner of disposition (gift, sale, and so forth);

f.   The contents of any gift tax return filed in connection with the disposition, quoting verbatim or (if you will do so without a court order) attaching a copy of the return to your answers;

g.   The name of the person (you, your spouse, or both) making the disposition.

70.   At any time in the last five years, have you or your spouse transferred any real estate or personal property to any other person or entity in exchange for a promise of future support? If so, for each such transfer, please state:

a.   A full description of the property transferred;

b.   When the transfer occurred;

c.   The full name and complete address of each person or entity to whom the transfer was made;

d.   A detailed description of the transaction;

e.   The name of the person (you, your spouse, or both) making the transfer.

71.   At any time in the past five years, have you or your spouse suffered any casualty loss from fire, wind, theft, or other cause? If so, for each such loss please state:

a.   A complete description of the property lost or damaged;

b.   The date of the loss;

c.   The cause, nature, and amount of the loss;

    d.   Whether the loss was covered by insurance and, if it was, the name of the insurance carrier, the policy limits, and whether any claim was filed;

    e.   If a claim was filed, the amount of the claim, the full name and address of the agent who processed it, and how much of the claim was paid;

    f.   In whose name (you, your spouse, or both) the lost or damaged property was held.

72.   At any time in the last five years, have you or your spouse made any agreement by which some entity or other person was granted an option to buy any assets of you or your spouse? If so, for each such agreement please state:

    a.   The date of the agreement;

    b.   The full name and complete address of each party to the agreement;

    c.   The payment or other consideration you or your spouse received in exchange for the agreement;

    d.   A complete description of the property covered by the agreement and the name of the person (you, your spouse, or both) in whose name it was held;

    e.   The terms of the agreement, quoting verbatim or (if you will do so without a court order) attaching a copy of it to your answers.

73.   Have you or your spouse ever been a plaintiff or defendant in a lawsuit? If so, for each suit please state:

    a.   The party designation (plaintiff, defendant, and so forth) of you or your spouse;

    b.   The names of the parties under which the suit was filed and indexed and the number of the suit;

    c.   The name, number, and location of the court;

    d.   The date the suit was filed;

    e.   The damages and other relief sought by each party;

    f.   The amount of any settlement offer in the case;

    g.   The present status of the suit;

    h.   The amount of any judgment entered against you or your spouse, the date it was entered, and the name of the person (you, your spouse. or both) against whom it was entered.

74.   Is there any judgment against you or your spouse that is unpaid? If there is, for each unpaid judgment please state:

    a.   The date of the judgment

    b.   The amount of it and how much remains unpaid;

    c.   The name of the plaintiff having the judgment against either or both of you;

    d.   The name of the present holder of the judgment if different from the plaintiff;

    e.   The name, number, and location of the court in which the judgment was obtained;

    f.   The case number of the judgment;

    g.   The name of each county and the volume and page numbers of each record book where it is recorded;

    h.   The name of the person (you, your spouse, or both) against whom it was entered.

75. Have you or your spouse ever: (1) filed a petition in a bankruptcy proceedIng; (2) entered into an assignment for the benefit of creditors; or (3) been a party to a composition agreement? If so, for each such occurrence please state:
    a. The nature of the proceeding or agreement;
    b. The date when the proceeding began or the agreement was made;
    c. The name, number, and location of any court that was involved;
    d. The disposition or present status of the proceeding or agreement;
    e. The name of the person (you, your spouse, or both) involved.

76. Has any person or entity ever filed an insolvency proceeding against you or your spouse (including a state receivership action or a federal bankruptcy proceeding)? If so, for each proceeding please state:
    a. The full name and complete address of the person or entity that filed it;
    b. The date it was filed;
    c. The name, number, and location of the court in which it was filed;
    d. The grounds alleged;
    e. The disposition of the proceeding or its present status;
    f. The name of the person (you, your spouse, or both) against whom it was filed.

77. Do you or your spouse now keep, or have you kept at any time in the last five years, any records (including but not limited to checkbooks, books, ledgers, memos, other written documents, tape recordings, and computer records) of receipts, disbursements, and other business or personal transactions, including those of any business you or your spouse now operates or has operated? If so, for each set of records pertaining to any part of the last five years please state:
    a. The name of the person (you, your spouse, or both) or business whose records are or were kept;
    b. The form in which they are or were kept;
    c. When they were first maintained;
    d. The accounting basis (cash or accrual) used;
    e. Whether a bookkeeper or accountant is now being used and, if so, his or her full name and complete address;
    f. The full name and complete address of each person or entity that prepared them;
    g. The full name and complete address of each person or entity now having custody of them;
    h. The complete address of each location of any such records;
    i. Whether the records accurately reflect the income reported in federal income tax returns of you, your spouse, and any business either of you now operates or has operated, for each year during which the records were kept;
    j. The contents of these records, quoting verbatim or (if you will do so without a court order) attaching a copy of them to your answers. If the records amount to more than 100 pages for all sets, you may comply by stating that you will permit inspection or make them available without a court order.

78. Has any record relating to income, disbursements, or business of you or your spouse been stolen or disposed of in the last five years? If so, for each such disposition, please state:

a.   The nature of the disposition (such as theft or intentional destruction);

b.   The date of disposition;

c.   The reason for disposition;

d.   The full name and complete address of the person making the disposition;

e.   If theft occurred, whether it was reported to the police.

79.   Are you or your spouse presently entitled to receive any money from a governmental office (such as a utility deposit or income tax refund)? If so, for each such payment, please state:

a.   The full name and complete address of the office owing the money;

b.   The reason they owe the money;

c.   The amount owed;

d.   When it will be paid;

e.   The name of the person (you, your spouse, or both) to whom it is owed.

80.   At any time in the last five years, has anyone taken an inventory of the property, either personal or business, of you or your spouse? If so, for each such inventory please state:

a.   The date of the inventory;

b.   The name and complete address of each person who made the inventory or supervised it;

c.   The name and complete address of each person or entity having a copy of the inventory;

d.   The contents of the inventory, quoting verbatim or (if you will do so without a court order) attaching a copy of it to your answers;

e.   The name of the person (you, your spouse, or both) whose property was inventoried.

81.   Has any written inventory relating to you or your spouse's business been stolen or disposed of in the last five years? If so, for each such disposition please state:

a.   The nature of the disposition (such as theft or intentional destruction);

b.   The date of the disposition;

c.   The reason for the disposition;

d.   The full name and complete address of the person making the disposition;

e.   If theft occurred, whether it was reported to the police;

f.   The name of the person (you, your spouse, or both) whose inventory was disposed of.

82.   Do you claim that any real estate or personal property of you or your spouse Is exempt from the claims of creditors? If so, for each piece of property claimed to be exempt, please state:

a.   The legal and common descriptions of the property;

b.   The present estimated value of the property;

c.   Your reason for claiming the property is exempt;

d.   The nature of the property (describing it as either "rural" or "urban" if it is real estate);

e. The complete address of its location;

f. The amount paid for the property when acquired by you or your spouse;

g. The name of the person (you, your spouse, or both) owning or having an interest in the property.

83. Do you or your spouse have an interest in a pension plan, retirement fund, annuity fund, or profit-sharing plan? If so, for each such interest please state:

a. The full name and complete address of the administrator of the plan or, if you cannot provide that information, the full name and address of the employer through which the plan is provided;

b. The present value of the interest of you or your spouse in the plan;

c. A detailed description of the terms under which you or your spouse may receive money or property pursuant to the plan;

d. The name of the person (you or your spouse) having the interest.

84. At any time in the last five years, have you or your spouse used the services of an accountant, bookkeeper, or certified public accountant or had such services employed in behalf of you or your spouse? If so, for each such person please state:

a. The full name and complete address of the person;

b. The dates during which the services were employed;

c. A description of the services the person performed;

d. The contents of resulting reports, quoting verbatim or (if you will do so without a court order) attaching a copy to your answers;

e. The name of the person (you, your spouse, or both) for whom the services were performed.

85. Do you or your spouse have any charge account or credit card? If so, for each please state:

a. The full name and complete address of the establishment carrying the account or issuing the card;

b. The account number or credit card number;

c. The name in which the account or card is listed;

d. The balance now owed on the account or card.

86. Is any state or federal tax lien filed or outstanding against you or your spouse? If so, for each lien please state:

a. The name of the person (you, your spouse, or both) against whom the lien applies;

b. The date the lien was filed or became effective;

c. The kind of tax from which the lien arose;

d. The date and amount of each payment made to reduce the lien.

§ 8.71   Sample Postjudgment Interrogatories (Corporate)

FORM 8–45
SAMPLE POSTJUDGMENT INTERROGATORIES (CORPORATE)

1. State the indicated information about yourself:
   a. Full legal name;
   b. Other names you have used;
   c. Date of birth;
   d. Social Security number;
   e. Driver's license number and state of issue;
   f. Business address;
   g. Business telephone;
   h. Residence telephone.

2. State the indicated information about the corporation:
   a. Exact corporate name;
   b. Each trade name or assumed name used by the corporation and the date and place of filing of any assumed name certificates
      1. Name;
      2. Date;
   c. Each trade name or assumed name used by the corporation and the date and place of filing of any assumed name certificates
      1. Name;
      2. Date;
      3. Place;
   d. Date of corporation;
   e. Date of last payment of franchise taxes.

3. With respect to each person who has been a director of the corporation during the past four years, state:
   a. Name;
   b. Present address;
   c. Date elected;
   d. Date resigned.

4. With respect to each person who has been an officer of the corporation during the past four years, state:
   a. Office held;
   b. Name;
   c. Present address;
   d. Date elected;
   e. Date resigned.

5. If the corporation has ever issued any stocks, bonds, or other securities, then state, with respect to each person owning, holding, or claiming any such, the

following (attach a schedule to your answers for each such stockholder or security holder):

    a.   Name of holder;

    b.   Address of holder;

    c.   Description of securities;

    d.   Number of shares;

    e.   Face value of securities;

    f.   Market value;

    g.   Consideration received by corporation for issuing securities;

    h.   Method of payment of consideration to corporation;

    i.   When issued;

    j.   Where certificate now located.

6. State the nature of each business engaged in by the corporation during the past four years.

7. If the corporation has furnished any financial statement during the past two years, then state (attaching additional schedules as needed):

    a.   Name and address of each person or institution to whom furnished;

    b.   Exact date that each financial statement was furnished;

    c.   Please attach to these answers a copy of each financial statement described above. Then list and describe each item shown on the statement with its present location and value.

8. Using the information on income tax returns of the corporation for the past two years, for each state:

    a.   Source and amount of each item of income listed.

9. If the corporation has an ownership interest or a leasehold interest in any real estate, then state, with respect to each parcel (attaching additional schedules as needed):

    a.   Street address;

    b.   Full legal description (use attachments if necessary);

    c.   Descriptions of each structure or improvement;

    d.   Name and address of other person who has an ownership interest in the property;

    e.   Ownership of property as stated in documents of title;

    f.   Recording reference and present location of each document of title;

    g.   Present value of corporation's equity interest in each property.

10. If any of the real property owned by the corporation is encumbered by any type of lien or real estate mortgage, then state (attaching additional schedules as needed):

    a.   Description of property encumbered;

    b.   Nature or type of encumbrance;

    c.   Date of encumbrance;

    d.   Name and address of holder of encumbrance;

    e.   Consideration received for encumbrance;

f.   Date and place of recordation of encumbrance including page number.

11.   If the corporation owns any motor vehicles, then state as to each motor vehicle:
   a.   Year;
   b.   Make;
   c.   Model;
   d.   License number;
   e.   Motor number;
   f.   Serial number;
   g.   State of registration;
   h.   Estimated value;
   i.   Usual location.

12.   If the corporation owns any other vehicles or trailers of any sort, then as to each vehicle or trailer state:
   a.   Year;
   b.   Make;
   c.   Model;
   d.   License number;
   e.   Motor number;
   f.   Serial number;
   g.   Estimate value;
   h.   Present location;
   i.   Usual location.

13.   If the corporation owns any boats or boating equipment, then as to each boat or item of boating equipment state:
   a.   Year;
   b.   Make;
   c.   Motor number;
   d.   Serial number;
   e.   Registration number;
   f.   Present location;
   g.   Usual docking location;
   h.   Estimated value;
   i.   Complete description of any boating equipment owned;
   j.   Present location of any boating equipment.

14.   If the corporation owns any aircraft, then state:
   a.   Year;
   b.   Make;
   c.   Model;
   d.   Registration number;
   e.   Motor number;
   f.   Serial number;
   g.   Exact present location of each aircraft;

h.   Complete description of any electronic or avionic equipment installed in each.

15. If the corporation owns any firearms, then state:
     a.   Make and model;
     b.   Serial number;
     c.   Exact present location.

16. If the corporation owns any collection of any kind (such as coin, stamp, and so forth), then as to each such item state:
     a.   Complete description;
     b.   Contents;
     c.   Estimated present market value;
     d.   Exact present location.

17. If the corporation owns any tools or equipment of any sort, then as to each state:
     a.   Complete description of tool or piece of equipment;
     b.   Registration number;
     c.   Estimated present market value;
     d.   Present location.

18. If the corporation owns any sporting goods or equipment, then as to each state;
     a.   Complete description of each;
     b.   Registration number or serial number;
     c.   Estimated present market value;
     d.   Present location.

19. If the corporation owns any paintings or other art objects of any kind, then as to each painting or object of art sale:
     a.   Complete description;
     b.   Artist, author, and so forth;
     c.   Estimated present market value;
     d.   Exact present location.

20. If any of the personal property described above as owned by the corporation is encumbered by any security agreement or any other type of lien, state:
     a.   Description of each property encumbered (use attachments if necessary);
     b.   Nature or type of encumbrance;
     c.   Date of encumbrance;
     d.   Name and address of holder of encumbrance;
     e.   Date and place of recordation of encumbrance including volume and page number if appropriate.

21. If any of the corporation property has been pledged to secure a debt, state:
     a.   Description of property pledged;
     b.   Amount of debt secured;
     c.   How debt was incurred;
     d.   Date on which debt was incurred;

    e.   Name and address of pledgee;

    f.   Date on which possession transferred to pledgee.

22.   If the corporation has any ownership interest in any business, state:

    a.   Full name of the business;

    b.   Full address of principal place of business or general office;

    c.   Address of each place where business is conducted;

    d.   Type of business conducted;

    e.   Form of business organization;

    f.   Date acquired such interest;

    g.   Exact present value of such interest;

    h.   Percentage of total interest represented;

    i.   Bank or other institution at which the business maintains any type of account, state:

       (1) Name and address of institution;

       (2) Type of account;

       (3) Name of account;

       (4) Number of account.

23.   If any articles of incorporation or partnership or certificates of doing business under a fictitious name were filed with a governmental agency by any business named above, state:

    a.   Nature of document filed;

    b.   Location of office where filed;

    c.   Date of filing.

24.   If the corporation owns any stocks, bonds, or other securities of any class issued by any government, governmental agency, company, firm, or corporation, state:

    a.   Name and address of each organization in which interest is owned;

    b.   Description of each;

    c.   Serial or certificate number of each security;

    d.   Date on which acquired;

    e.   Method of acquisition;

    f.   Name and address of person, firm, or corporation from which the security was acquired;

    g.   Name and address of any person, firm, or corporation with whom any joint ownership or community interest in shares;

    h.   Present location of each security;

    i.   Name and address of each person having custody of securities;

    j.   Name and address of any person, firm, or corporation to whom securities are pledged or mortgaged or subject to an option to repurchase.

25.   If the corporation maintains any business bank accounts, for each such account state:

    a.   Name of account;

    b.   Number of account;

    c.   Name of bank;

    d.   Address of bank;

    e.   Authorized signature;

    f.   Present balance.

26. If the corporation owns any interest of any kind in any patent or copyright, state:

    a.   Registry number;

    b.   Description of each patent or copyright;

    c.   Name and address of any persons sharing any copyright;

    d.   Percentage of interest owned;

    e.   Income received from patent or copyright annually.

27. If corporation has paid or had paid for its premiums on any life insurance policies during the past two years, then as to each policy state:

    a.   Name and address of each beneficiary;

    b.   Name and address of issuing company;

    c.   Policy number;

    d.   Face value of policy upon death of insured;

    e.   Present cash value;

    f.   Date policy issued;

    g.   Total premiums paid to present time;

    h.   Name and address of each premium payer;

    i.   Name and address of owner of policy;

    j.   Date of each payment;

    k.   Location of each contract of insurance;

    l.   Name and address of each person having contract of insurance.

28. If the name of the beneficiary of any insurance policy described above has been changed in the past twelve months, then as to each policy state:

    a.   Date of change;

    b.   Name and address of each new beneficiary;

    c.   Reason for change in each case;

    d.   Please attach to your answers to these interrogatories a copy of each document or contract of insurance referred to above.

29. If the corporation now has any claims for money against others by reason of notes, claims for damages, or the like, then state (use attachments if needed):

    a.   Complete description of claim;

    b.   Name and address of person indebted to corporation;

    c.   Amount claimed due.

30. If any suit or action has been brought to reduce any claim described above to judgment, then state:

    a.   Number and style of each case;

    b.   Court in which case in pending;

    c.   Date of filing;

    d.   Status of each case;

    e.   Amount of offers of settlement;

    f.   Name and address of person offering settlement;

    g.   Details of compromise, if any.

31.   If the property is not being held for the corporation in the name of some person other than its own, or if any person, firm, or corporation is holding anything for the corporation or for its benefit, then state:

    a.   Description of item;

    b.   Name and address of title holder;

    c.   Date of transfer;

    d.   Amount of consideration given.

32.   If the corporation has any accounts receivable, state:

    a.   Name and address of each person owing the corporation;

    b.   Amount due from each person.

33.   If any accounts receivable have been assigned or otherwise disposed of other than by collection in the past year, state:

    a.   Name of each account;

    b.   Date of assignment;

    c.   Name and address of each assignee;

    d.   Amount of reserve due;

    e.   Extent to which future accounts receivable are covered;

    f.   Amount of consideration received for each such assignment.

34.   If the corporation has sold or assigned any account receivable and has any reserve funds set up for its benefits out of such accounts receivable, state:

    a.   Name of each account;

    b.   Conditions for receiving reserves;

    c.   Name and address of the person or firm holding funds;

    d.   Amount of funds,

35.   If the corporation has conveyed or disposed of any property, either by sale, gift, or otherwise, in the past two years, state separately for each such item:

    a.   Description of each item disposed of;

    b.   Date of disposition;

    c.   Name and address of person receiving;

    d.   Manner of disposition;

    e.   Consideration received

36.   If the corporation has sold, transferred, or assigned in bulk all or a substantial part of its stock and trade or trade fixtures in the past six months, state:

    a.   Type of business sold;

    b.   Date of transaction;

    c.   Name and address of transferee;

    d.   Amount of consideration received;

    e.   Location of any recording of any notices of sale or transfer;

    f.   Name and address of any newspaper publishing notices of such sale or transfer;

    g.   Description of each item.

37.   If the corporation entered into any transaction with any stockholder, officer, or director involving a transfer, conveyance, assignment, or other disposition of any of its real or personal property in the past four years, then for each item of property involved in the transaction, state:

    a.   Description of each;

    b.   Date of transaction;

    c.   Consideration received;

    d.   Name and address of person involved.

38.   If the corporation has suffered any casualty loss from fire, wind, theft, or otherwise in the past two years, then for each loss state:

    a.   Description of each item of property lost or damaged;

    b.   Cause of each loss;

    c.   Date of each loss;

    d.   Amount of each loss;

    e.   Name of insurance carrier covering loss;

    f.   Policy number and limits;

    g.   Date of filing of claim;

    h.   Date of payment of claim;

    i.   Amount of claim paid.

39.   If the corporation has been a party to any contract or other agreement whereby it created an option to anyone to purchase any or all of its assets in the past two years, state:

    a.   Date of agreement;

    b.   Location where agreement was made;

    c.   Name and address of each person or firm who was a party to the agreement;

    d.   Amount of consideration received;

    e.   Name and address of person furnishing consideration;

    f.   Description of property covered by the agreement;

    g.   Description of terms of the agreement.

40.   If corporation owes any debts, then for each creditor state:

    a.   Name and address of creditor;

    b.   Amount owed;

    c.   Date debt incurred;

    d.   How debt incurred;

    e.   Security given.

41.   If the corporation has made any payment to any creditor within the past four months, state:

    a.   Name and address of each;

    b.   Amount of each payment;;

    c.   Date of each payment.

42. If the corporation has kept any books or written memorandum of its income in business affairs for the past three years, state:
    a. Form in which books are kept;
    b. Date books were first kept;
    c. Name and address of each person or firm who prepared books;
    d. Whether books accurately reflect income contained in tax returns for each year;
    e. Present location of all books for the last three years;
    f. Name and address of each person or firm who has custody of books;
    g. Please attach to these answers a copy of each such books and memoranda described above for the period of the past three years or state a time and place when and where such books and memoranda may be inspected.

43. If the corporation either destroyed or disposed of any books of account, memoranda, or other records relating to its business or income within the past three years, state:
    a. Date books or records destroyed;
    b. Reasons for destroying;
    c. Name and address of persons destroying.

44. If the corporation has employed or had employed in its behalf the services of an accountant in the past two years, then for each accountant state:
    a. Name and address of each;
    b. Exact period employed;
    c. Reasons for leaving;
    d. Services performed.

45. If the corporation has taken an inventory of its property at any time within the past two years, state:
    a. Date of inventory;
    b. Name and address of persons supervising or taking inventory;
    c. Name and address of persons having copy of inventory;
    d. Total dollar value of property as stated in inventory.
    e. Means of valuation;
    f. Reasons for taking inventory;
    g. Description of each item of property included in inventory;
    h. Please attach to these answers a copy of each inventory referred to above.

§ 8.72   Legal Research

Some types of litigation have a higher settlement rate than others, but every case has the possibility of going to trial. Keeping that thought in mind, it is smart business to begin to prepare for trial from the very beginning of the case. Much of the preparation can be done as you go along, and will prevent the mass chaos and confusion that generally manifests itself two weeks before trial. Expenditures on visual exhibits for trial, naturally, should be held off until you are relatively sure the case will not settle before trial. However, it is never too early to begin to earmark those documents you wish to have blown up or develop charts or other helpful evidence in readiness for trial.

Research should be done on the assigned judge to determine his rulings on issues similar to yours. This should be done early enough in the case so your attorney is able to effectively research and develop arguments in this vein.

Documents that you know will be used as evidence in trial should be kept in a separate file and their authenticity determined so that early attention can be paid to those documents which need to be proven up before introduction at trial.

Copies of all deposition summaries should be put into a three ring binder and labeled. A copy of each summary should also be placed in the appropriate witness file. These things are all easy to do as the lawsuit progresses, and will save large amounts of time in the weeks before trial.

§ 8.73   Cite Checking

Whether or not the paralegal is heavily involved with the legal research associated with the preparation of legal briefs, he or she will most certainty be involved with the cite checking in the finial preparation stages before filing. Cite checking is the legal terminology used for the highly technical and exacting proofreading done on a legal brief before the document is filed. Cite checking is a very long and involved, often tedious process, and must be undertaken with patience and caution. The cite checking aspect of the brief Is equally as important as the research and writing aspects.

Briefs may need to be cite checked at several stages of preparation. and each step should be done as thoroughly at each stage as if it were the final draft. One of the constant problems in the preparation of a brief is the fact that it will pass through a number of hands before finalization, and the chance of inadvertent deletions, changes, or mistakes increase with each handling. There are four main areas of proofreading which comprise the process of cite checking:

Grammar, spelling and punctuation.   If your document is being prepared on a word processor, as most are today, the spelling portion of the proofreading process is made easier and faster by employing the spell-check function of the software. Even so, there will almost certainly be words which are not recognized by the software's dictionary, and you should check these spellings with a good reference dictionary. Also, check the document for consistency in spelling variations. If there is more than one acceptable spelling of a word, make sure that one spelling is used consistently throughout. Also check for legal spellings which may be different from traditional spellings, such as "judgment" rather than "judgement."

Check punctuation using a reference such as Strunk and White's *The Elements of Style*. If a copy of this small reference book is not available in your law firm, consult a dictionary. Very often, the basic rules for punctuation are found in an appendix or preface of a comprehensive dictionary. *The Elements of Style* is also an excellent reference for grammatical form.

Form and style.   Pay special attention to the local rules of civil procedure which govern and dictate the prescribed style and format for the brief. Be sure the margins of the brief coincide with those designated by the rules and that titles, captions, and styles are procedurally correct. Some local rules also limit the length of briefs to be filed, so check the brief at every revision to make sure that it does not exceed the maximum length allowed. Page-numbering and footnote placement should also be checked at every revision to make sure they do not become displaced or deleted.

Legal citation accuracy.   *A Uniform System of Citation,* published by the Harvard Law Review Association, commonly called The Harvard Blue Book, is the ultimate authority on the format of citation sentences and quotations from legal sources. Proofread the brief for accuracy and consistency in application of the rules set forward in this reference source. The proper and acceptable ways of identifying a legal source expressed in *A Uniform System of Citation* are designed to provide universal recognition and uniformity. In general, a citation sentence, as it is called, contains the name of the case, the volume name, volume number, page number, the jurisdiction of the court deciding the case, and the year the decision was made. The proper format for writing the citation sentence varies with the source of the material. The citation sentence may also contain specific page references to quotations, and prior and subsequent history of the case.

There are also specific rules regarding the use of shortened or abbreviated citations used after the first incidence of the formal citation. Shortened citations forms other than those listed in *A Uniform System of Citation* are not to be used. One of the most common abuses in this category is the use of supra with a case name to indicate a reference to a previously cited case. Supra is not to be used with case names unless the case name is extraordinarily long. Be familiar with proper usage of such terms as supra and ibid. and be able to correct improper usage of such terms in the brief.

There are formatting rules other than those affecting citation sentences which you must address in cite checking the brief. Quotations, for example, are handled much differently than in other types of written documents. While in most other kinds of documents or writing other than legal writing, quotations are followed by footnotes which include the source of the material at the bottom of the page or at the end of the document, legal sources are cited directly after the quotation within the text. The citation should always follow the quotation directly, including the page number from which the quotation is taken, and a case should never be referred to without an appropriate citation.

Quotations over fifty words are indented from both margins, without quotation marks, and are single-spaced. The citation for the quotation appears at the left (nonindented) margin after returning to the double space format.

When indicated by the attorney, you should also check all citations, including both the prior and subsequent history by using citators.

If your law firm subscribes to Westlaw or LEXIS, you can also check citations by computer.

Substantive proofreading.   Read the entire brief for general clarity, conciseness, and accuracy. For example, it is not enough simply to check the accuracy of the citation sentence which follows a quotation. You must go to the cited volume of the source and check the substance of the quotation for absolute technical accuracy, paying special attention to use of special punctuation where additions, deletions, and modifications of the quoted material occur. Consult *A Uniform System of Citation* for rules on brackets, ellipses, and so forth.

Check the material cited or quoted in a brief to be sure it is the intended material and makes sense when included in that context. Not only should the source material be checked, but in general, the brief should be read to ensure that words have been used properly. When in doubt about the appropriate use or definition of a word, consult a dictionary or thesaurus.

§ 8.74   Checklist—Legal Research Guidelines

Use the following checklist to help establish the research guidelines for your case.

____   1.   Determine the significant facts of your research problem. Each fact should fit into one of the following categories:

       ____   a.   Group or class of people who are a party to the dispute and the legal significance of their relationship;

       ____   b.   Subject matter of the dispute;

       ____   c.   Legal theories giving rise to the assignment or defense of liability;

       ____   d.   Damages or relief sought.

____   2.   From significant facts, determine the starting point of your legal research by determining which categories have the most legal significance to your case.

____   3.   Determine lists of words which are pertinent to your significant facts. Many of these words will be alternate descriptive terms for your key facts.

____   4.   Define the legal issues, incorporating the facts of your case and how those facts apply to the law.

____   5.   Research background information on your topics in secondary authority, such as legal encyclopedias and treatises.

____   6.   Begin to look for primary authority to support your legal issues (statutes, ordinances, regulations, court rules, constitutional provisions, and stare decisis case law from your jurisdiction).

____ 7. Look for persuasive authority to support your legal issues. (Secondary authorities, which include materials from legal encyclopedias, treatises, statutes, ordinances, regulations and case law from other jurisdictions which are not binding on the court.)

____ 8. Follow through with all leads developed through both primary and secondary authority.

____ 9. Revise your legal issues, if necessary.

____ 10. Research subsequent history of every authority you intend to use by checking all of the citations.

____ 11. Draft your brief.

CHAPTER 9

COMPUTERIZED LITIGATION SUPPORT

§ 9.1   Introduction

The coming of the personal computer into the law office has revolutionized the job of the litigation paralegal. Even ten years ago, the cost of computerizing the documents in a lawsuit was prohibitive unless the litigation was enormous and the major parties shared the cost by using a shared document-retrieval database administrated by an independent mainframe contractor. Database software packages were a mystery to the average law firm.

The highly competitive personal computer market, the computer's acceptance into the mainstream of business, and the spiraling increase in computer literacy among the masses has fueled the revolution. Law firms no longer refrain from computerizing all but the most complex and sizable cases. It is commonplace for the average law firm to computerize most of its litigation cases now, regardless of size. Paralegal hiring criteria has expanded to include the desirability of computer literacy, and more specifically, database knowledge and experience.

There are drawbacks to computerized litigation support, however. Cost considerations are still a factor, but not in the same respect as they were years ago. A firm and the client must weigh the benefits of the computerization and its rapid retrievability qualities against the substantial up-front costs associated with the design, preparation, and loading of the database. Any cost savings derived by computerization are not generally recognized until close to the end of the case when instantaneous retrievability of information pays off in discovery response preparation or settlement and trial preparation. The paralegal instantly recognizes the value of being able to retrieve a list of all documents which will be used to prepare for the deposition of a witness rather than the old-fashioned manual method of reviewing all the hard copies of the documents in the file. This example alone could save thousands of dollars in billable time to the client and gives the paralegal many more hours to devote to other cases or other projects on the case in question. Being able to put your hands on a document instantaneously could also mean the difference in winning or losing a case in trial.

What, then, does a computerized litigation support system do? Put very simply, it manages information, including pleadings, motions, other court papers, discovery documents, and full-text depositions, giving one the ability to retrieve and sort information instantaneously by chronology, subject matter, or source and to generate reports from the manipulation of such data.

§ 9.2   Considerations

Overwhelming benefits aside, there are always things which could go wrong with your venture into computerization. In order to avoid those types of occurrences, it is necessary to anticipate the worst-case scenarios and plan accordingly. The most formidable foe to your success in computerized litigation support is a lack of consistency. The project must remain consistent and fluid or the integrity of the database is at extreme risk. The old adage "Garbage in, garbage out" should be foremost in your mind. The entire database must be designed with consistency in mind. That means that the average cost of inputting data into the database should not fluctuate wildly throughout the case, and it means that all the information input into the database should be consistent. For example, an automobile should always be called an automobile, if that is the preferred term, and not a car or vehicle in other occurrences throughout the database. Mr. John Paul Jones should always be entered into the database in the same way so that the person retrieving the information does not have to be a mind reader and guess that Mr. John Paul Jones is also entered in the database as Mr. Jones, J.P. Jones, John Jones, and John P. Jones. This can be accomplished by a sophisticated training session, standardization of terms for all persons working on the database, or simply by having one person do all the database data input.

Cost and time considerations are certainly other factors which need to be seriously weighed. The costs and manpower demands come early in the computerized case, and the small or medium-sized law firm may not have the manpower or expertise to handle these enormous demands. This does not mean that computerizing is not a viable option. Although you may find that the costs of using your in-house manpower may be prohibitive for this project because of your employees' salary base, there are many experienced vendors specializing in preparation of documents and databases for computerized litigation support. Because these vendors work on volume and use experienced personnel to perform these projects, their cost is generally lower for the delivery of a turnkey database than your firm would have been able to achieve. This is especially important to consider because using high-priced legal professionals to do this work can drive the price of your database to 15 to 20 times the cost quoted by these vendors. Another critical consideration is the time factor in which you firm will be able to complete the database and have it ready for search and retrieval. Time projections cannot always include the unanticipated emergencies which always seem to occur at the most inopportune times in law firms, and can have a devastating effect on the manpower needed to complete your project.

If you are considering using an outside vendor, quality control and confidentiality are as important as cost and turnaround time. If possible, visit the site of an ongoing project by the vendor and look for signs of breach of confidentiality. If those signs are present, they will also be present when your case is being worked on. Choose another vendor. What kind of checks and balances does the vendor have in place to assure the consistency and integrity of the data entered into the database? Have the vendor give you a detailed explanation of his system. It will do you no good to pay for a database which is full of inconsistencies and mistakes.

You will have to decide whether you want to use a full-text or abstract version of your database, or a combination of the two. (See § 9.5.) There are various references to the pros and cons of these systems throughout this chapter. The most commonly used system is a combination of full-text and abstract.

Finally a decision must be made regarding the hard copies of the documents which you put in your database. Will you want the hard copies of your documents close by to serve as working copies throughout the case, or do you want to use microfilm copies of the documents or a more advanced and expensive form of computerized optical imaging whereby the picture of the document actually appears on your computer screen? If the case is very large and space in your office is at a premium, you may want to consider the microfilming alternative, in which case, all documents must be microfilmed and assigned microfilm numbers which are entered into the database as identifiers. The database search then yields the information about the document, including the location on the microfilm cartridge where the image resides. To review the document, one only has to insert the microfilm cartridge in a microfilm reader/printer and go to the designated number. Hard copies can be printed out from this machine if desired.

§ 9.3   Software Selection

Resist the urge to buy your computer hardware before you decide on a software package. The software application is much more important than the choice of computers at this point, because you want to be happy with the things you can accomplish with the software and not be limited to the type of software you can use because it is not compatible with your computer. Refer to the checklist which follows to guide you in determining which software package is best for your needs. Stay away from generic database packages, as they require too much configuration and do not generally have the capacity to manipulate data with inverted indices that dedicated litigation support software packages do.

There are literally hundreds of litigation support software packages available on the market today. The best source for a listing of these types of packages with varied legal applications is a book called *LOCATE,* available for purchase from the American Bar Association. The most common type of litigation support search software in use in today's law firms is the combination full-text/abstract program, such as BRS SEARCH or MICRO LS/MICRO TEXT. Descriptions and ordering information for these and other software packages can be found in *LOCATE.*

The preferable software package to purchase will be a database manager, which is capable of manipulating all the data input into the software by way of an independent word-processing package. Choose software packages which are in the mainstream rather than obscure so that it will be easier to get training, support, and qualified personnel to assist you in your project. This is especially true of the word-processing package that you choose. If you choose a package such as Word-Perfect, for example, you will never have a problem finding knowledgeable, trained personnel to help you input your data. It is an easy-to-understand package with a plethora of trained workers available in the potential workforce. It is a package which is also compatible with most of the search software packages you may want to choose. Check to see if your DOS and word-processing editions are compatible with the requirements of the search software.

It is imperative that the word-processing package and the search software package be able to talk to each other so that data can easily be moved from one software package to the other. Check with the vendor of the search software for a list of appropriate word processing packages that are compatible with the search software.

§ 9.4   Software Selection Checklist

____ 1.   Ability to network the computer software packages if a decision to do so is made at a later date. If, however, you do not foresee any reason for the data in a computer to be able to be accessed by more than one person at a time, this will not be necessary.

____ 2.   It is not usually necessary for the litigation support software to be able to talk to the accounting, data, conflicts, or other software packages.

However, you may want this package to be compatible with desktop publishing, graphics, or spreadsheet packages to facilitate development of charts or graphs from the information.

____ 3.   You will want to be able to download information from this package to your word-processing package to create reports, or pleading board indices, and so forth.

____ 4.   Full-text capability is very desirable, but not absolutely necessary. Remember that depositions need full-text treatment.

____ 5.   Deposition treatment capability is very important. You will want to be able to load deposition disks in order to both search and summarize on line.

____ 6.   The software package should have the ability to create an unlimited number of fields in abstract format with unlimited field lengths.

____ 7.   The use of Boolean logic for search statements is preferable to any other kind.

____ 8.   You definitely want to be able to search by field name, key word, key phrase, or date.

____ 9.   You will want the ability to combine several different search statements into one, making several simple searches into one with the use of Boolean operators.

____ 10. You will want to be able to print the list of documents produced by the search as well as the full text of the abstracts of the individual documents.

____ 11. The ability to produce reports and chronological listings of documents is of paramount importance. Pay close attention to the vendor when he explains how the software package allows manipulation of the data.

____ 12. The speed of the search package is vitally important.

____ 13. The ability to use all functions of the software by telecommunications should be considered.

____ 14. The ability to use the package in remote locations should be considered strongly, especially if you know you will be going to trial in distant locales.

____ 15. The ease of editing of data is another vitally important function. If the editing is not easily done, then the data should be able to be very easily downloaded into a word-processing package to accomplish that same purpose.

§ 9.5   Full-Text and Abstract Retrieval

There are actually three distinct types of database retrieval systems for the average law firm to consider. Full-text databases contain the verbatim data of the hard copies and are input either by scanning or by manual data entry. Abstract databases are more common than full-text, and consist of brief outlines of information found on each hard copy, which is then input into the computer database into logical fields, or categories. The most common type of database retrieval system in use in today's law firms is a combination of both full-text and abstract, which gives one the ability to better control the size and cost of the database and to allow for choices of data which would be best suited for each type of treatment.

Full-text retrieval on first glance is very attractive until one starts to look at the possibilities for problems. Full-text systems are extremely expensive to input and maintain. The larger the database, the slower the retrieval time is, because the computer must search through more materials to generate an answer. Also, because of the amount of data entered into a full-text system, search attempts often turn up a very large hit list which can be very unwieldy and not much help in narrowing down or pinpointing occurrences of the sought-after data.

There are some scanners on the market which will read a hard copy of a document into the full-text database system, but not all scanners are capable of reading various typefaces or fonts, and few are capable of reading longhand entries. Full-text documents also require much preparation before they can be searched by the software package. Page stops and paragraph breaks, for example, must be manually input onto every page even if the document is scanned or input by disk. Also, all ambiguous references to dates, names, and times, such as last week, he, or she, and two months ago, must be annotated so that they will turn up usable information during a search.

Some documents, such as depositions and hearing transcripts, lend themselves extremely well to full-text treatment when annotated, and become a very desirous part of the database. Such documents are better suited to full-text treatment than to abstract treatment.

The abstract method is an excellent choice for your legal database, but care must be taken to control the quality and consistency in the decision making process when such data is categorized, or all effectiveness is lost and the integrity of the database is destroyed. All categories, definitions, and fields must be carefully analyzed and made to conform to consistent application, such as referring to an automobile, a car, and a vehicle the same way every time, so that it is possible to retrieve information without having to read the mind of the person who designed the database in order to know which term to search. With careful planning and forethought, most databases are well suited to abstract or bibliographic coding of objective materials and can easily be mastered by individuals with a short amount of preparatory training for the process. Therefore, the abstract method is a good one for containing costs.

The most important key to the success of the abstract method is the proper use of the field which calls for the description of the contents of the document. Care should be taken to make sure this field is made up of substantive identifying information rather than just a reiteration of the subjective information located elsewhere in the abstract. (See § **9.11** and § **9.13** for a more complete discussion of this matter.) Obviously, the combination of full-text and abstracting is most desirable for the law firm, and I strongly recommend this type of system for your litigation needs.

§ 9.6   Deposition Transcript Search

Deposition transcripts may be searched full-text by using either a proprietary software package available from your court reporter, or by inputting the deposition transcript data directly into your full-text/abstract search and retrieval software package that you use for all your other litigation needs.

Most of the off-the-shelf deposition-search packages are relatively the same. Software such as Discovery ZX and Cat-Links work on the principle of key word searches of indices of words created by the package. Some packages have the ability to generate reports and store data for future searches. Some have the ability to manipulate data and export it to the word processing package to be finished off in a pretty presentation.

The packages which are offered by your court reporter may require that the deposition transcript data disk be formatted into a special language so that it can be understood by the software. This necessarily results in another charge for you which is passed on to the client, and could possibly delay your work with that data. You may instead want to use your own system and ask your court reporter to convert the deposition transcript data disks into ASCII format, which is the universal language for IBM-compatible software packages. Most court reporters are able to make this conversion for you. Once you have secured the testimony on an ASCII disk, the testimony will have to be annotated to facilitate searches.

When searching for all references to a witness's name in a particular piece of testimony, we are likely to find that the witness has been referred to as him, her, my boss, she, and so on many times, which would not show up in our search results. Wherever such a pronoun occurs, annotations must be overlaid so that the proper name (for example, Jim Jones) is discernible in our search. Consider also the following example of annotations in parentheses to correct similar transcript problems:

Q.   When was the last time you saw him (Wilkins) before the incident?
A.   Oh, I'd say it was about ten days; no, it was more like a week. Yeah. It was a week. (870411)

§ 9.7   On-Line Deposition Summaries

Deposition summaries can be done on the computer with only a word-processing package and no other special software. This eliminates the need for duplicative dictating, typing and editing to produce an outstanding deposition summary.

To do on-line deposition summaries, simply obtain the deposition transcript in ASCII format from your court reporter and use the import or text-in function key on your word-processing package, following the directions in your word processing software user's manual. This will convert the ASCII language to that of your word-processing package. Now change the pitch to 12 so that you can get more lines of text on your screen at once, and call up the document and open a window to split the screen. If you are using WordPerfect, for example, this is accomplished by pressing the function key Control-F3. Designate the number of lines you wish your window to contain and use your switch key (Shift-F3) to enter the newly created document in which you will summarize the testimony resident in the deposition transcript text. The two documents are visible simultaneously. You may move down the deposition transcript by scrolling down with the down-arrow key.

§ 9.8 Database Design

Using the checklist which follows, discuss the particular needs of the case with your attorney and the client. As you move through the checklist and answer the specific questions, you will see the emergence of a viable database design, which will almost automatically define your parameters for you. The most important thing to remember is that the database must be designed with the thought in mind that the ultimate goal is ease of retrieval of the input data. Therefore, all your efforts should be channelled in the direction of coming up with retrieval fields which make sense for that particular case. (See § 9.12 for detailed explanations of each field recommended for the database design.) Note that not all fields are recommended for every database and that the fields should be specific to that type of case.

It is very difficult in most instances to add retrieval fields at a later time without emptying the entire database, redesigning the fields, and then reloading the database. Therefore, it is better to have too many fields, including some which you do not use, than it is to have too few. Any way that you can conceivably think of for retrieving documents is a potential field. For example, if your attorney asks you for all documents written by a witness, then AUTHOR might be a conceivable field.

After the fields have been decided on, the coding form should be developed. This is the form on which the information from the documents is manually written and given to the data-entry person for input. The coding form should be an exact replica of the input screen of your software package.

The Database Design Form (**Form 9–1**) is very helpful in designing your database.

FORM 9–1
SAMPLE DATABASE DESIGN FORM

Name of file: _____

Client/matter number: _____

Attorney on file: _____ Ext. _____

Paralegal on file: _____ Ext. _____

§ 9.8   DATABASE DESIGN

1.   Discuss standard retrieval fields and determine if any are to be eliminated. Eliminated fields: _____

_____

2.   How are documents to be organized? _____

_____

_____

3.   Deadline for turnkey database: _____

4.   Cost limits and considerations: _____

_____

_____

_____

5.   Who is designated to do substantive abstracting? _____

_____

_____

6.   Explain the use of macros to the trial team and how it eases data entry. Discuss the categories of Document Types which will be used in this case. Fill out Document Types sheet attached to this form.

7.   Is a list of issues to be created for this case? _____ If so, fill out issues sheet attached to this form.

8.   Fill out Names of Players sheet attached to this form.

9.   Will Document Significance Levels be assigned and coded? Yes ___ No ___ If so, explain four star coding system to trial team, or determine if another system is to be used. System to be used: _____

_____

_____

10.   Will Bates stamp numbers or computerized number labels be used? _____

_____

11.   Describe the definition the attorney prefers to be used on this case to describe documents subject to attorney/client or other privilege: _____

_____

COMPUTERIZED LITIGATION SUPPORT

12.   Where will the hard copies of the documents be stored after the coding process? _____

ADDITIONAL COMMENTS

DOCUMENT TYPES

1.   _____

2.   _____

3.   _____

4.   _____

5.   _____

6.   _____

7.   _____

8.   _____

9.   _____

10. _____

11. _____

12. _____

13. _____

14. _____

15. _____

16. _____

17. _____

18. _____

19. _____

20. _____

21. _____

22. _____

23. _____

24. _____

25. _____

§ 9.9   Taxonomies and Macros

Part of the necessary standardization process in the design of the database is to create *taxonomies,* or definitions of terms within a certain classification. For example, a Document-Types taxonomy might include the following terms as definitions of the term correspondence: letter, transmittal letters, memos, and so on. This list should be developed before the first document is coded or inputted into the computer to insure the uniformity of terms used in the database. Otherwise, someone sitting down to search for memorandum might search under memo, note, or letter before finding all the information resident in the program on that subject. (See Forms (**9–2** and **9–3.**)

The taxonomies are developed for the use of the coder and the end-user doing the search. The coder will be able to use the taxonomy as a guide to keep the information uniform, and the end user doing a search will be able to look at the taxonomy and get an idea of the logic with which the database was created, thereby speeding up the retrieval process significantly.

Taxonomies are vital to the success of a database. Think of how many different ways one person's name might be mentioned in documents. The searcher would have to personally be aware of each and every misspelling, abbreviation, initial, and nickname in order to find all relevant information on that person. However, if it were decided that John Paul Jones would be input into the database as J.P. Jones every time the name appeared in the documents, one would only have to search that particular variation to find all relevant documents. Try to develop taxonomies, especially for things such as document types, that remain fairly consistent from case to case.

A *macro* is nothing more than a series of stored keystrokes which can be used to designate a certain word or phrase, and which, when typed on the computer, will call up on the screen the lengthened version of the information without the necessity of keyboarding every single character of a repetitive entry. Not only does this substantially cut the hours for data input, but it eliminates many typographical errors or variations which might occur. Your word-processing package will describe in detail all the instruction you will need to create macros for this purpose.

FORM 9–2
SAMPLE DOCUMENT-TYPES TAXONOMY—OIL AND GAS CASE

Letter

Memo

Affidavit

COMPUTERIZED LITIGATION SUPPORT

FERC Document

Agenda

Drawing

Minutes

Handwritten Note

Telecopy

Table

Assignment

Agreement

Contract

Cancellation Notice

Division Order

Application

Weekly Marketing Report

Pleading

Deposition

Deliverability Test

FORM 9–3
SAMPLE ISSUES TAXONOMY—OIL AND GAS CASE

Deliverability

Deregulation

Daily Contract Quantity

Force Majeure

Least Cost Policy

Market Projections

Market-Out Contract Clauses

Pressure

Reserves

Supply Scheduling

Take or Pay Liability

Weighted Average Cost of Gas (WACOG)

§ 9.10 Document Preparation

Before the documents can be analyzed, or entered, into the database, they must be properly prepared and numbered. Every page of every document should be numbered in the lower right-hand corner of the document with either a Bates stamp or a label containing a computerized number. Before you begin to number, however, decide whether the documents should be kept in their original order or if they should be organized in some logical fashion first.

   If the documents have come to you in some sort of logical order, as in existing files, it is probably advisable to keep the documents in that original order. The origin, or the source, of the document is often just as important as the document itself.

§ 9.11 Coding

Coding is the first part of the information extraction process. Coders are personnel with good handwriting and grammar skills who go through the hard copies of the documents and extract the objective information such as document number, date, name of author, addressee, and so forth and enter this information on the coding sheet. (See **Form 9–4.**) Once the coding has been completed, the coding forms are used by the data entry person to input the information into the database.

FORM 9–4
SAMPLE DOCUMENT CODING FORM

FILE NAME: _____

1. Bates stamp number: _____

2. Microfilm number: _____

3. Microfilm cartridge number: _____

4. Document type: _____

COMPUTERIZED LITIGATION SUPPORT

5. Date: _____

6. To (individual): _____

_____

7. To (company): _____

_____

8. From (individual): _____

_____

9. From (company): _____

_____

10. cc (individual): _____

_____

11. cc (company): _____

_____

12. Names mentioned in body of document: _____

_____

_____

13. File Name: _____

14. Drawing (description): _____

_____

15. Privileged document? (X) _____

16. Significance level (*****, ****, ***, **, *) _____

17. Issues: _____

18. Draft? (X) _____

19. Attached to: _____

_____

20. Marginal notations: _____

_____

_____

_____

21. Attachments: _____

_____

_____

22. Text or document description: _____

_____

_____

_____

_____

_____

_____

_____

_____

§ 9.12   Coding Instructions

When all the decisions have been made regarding the design of the database and the coding form has been designed, a set of coding instructions should be developed for the use of all personnel helping with the coding process. (See **Form 9–5.**) These instructions, along with the taxonomies which have been created for the case, will assure the standardized input of data which you desire for your database. If the case is a large one in which there are a number of people working on the coding process, it is advisable to hold a group training session to go over the instructions and answer questions regarding the coding process.

FORM 9–5
SAMPLE CODING FORM INSTRUCTIONS

1.   BATES STAMP NUMBER

    a.   Write complete range of numbers using letters if present.

    b.   Letters always precede numbers, except sometimes A or B. (Example: TRY0001, TRY001A)

    c.   Always include at least four numeric digits. (Example: 0001)

    d.   Multiple pages of the same document are written in a series. (Example: TRY0001-TRY0043)

  2. <u>MICROFILM NUMBER</u>

    a.   Copy the number exactly as it appears, using above instructions for multiple pages.

  3. <u>MICROFILM CARTRIDGE NUMBER</u>

    a.   Copy the number exactly as it appears.

  4. <u>DATE</u>

    a.   List date of document as YYMMDD. (Example: 871231)

    b.   Contract dates generally appear in the first paragraph of text.

    c.   Financial statements are always calculated on a year-end basis. (Example: 1987 Financial Statement date is 871231)

  5. <u>DOCUMENT TYPE</u>

    a.   Select one from the Document-Type list you have been given for each separate document. Ask for help if you are not sure how a document should be classified.

  6. <u>TO (INDIVIDUAL)</u>

    a.   If instructed to do so, refer to the Names of Players list for the standardized spelling or abbreviation of the name of the individual, or individuals to whom the document is addressed.

    b.   Separate names of multiple addressees by commas.

  7. <u>TO (COMPANY)</u>

    a.   List the names of all companies to which the document is addressed. If the document was addressed to an individual, list the company with which he is affiliated. We may want to do a search to find all correspondence sent by anyone at Company A to Company B.

    b.   Separate names of multiple addressees by commas.

  8. <u>FROM (INDIVIDUAL)</u>

    a.   Use same instructions above as TO (INDIVIDUAL), except, of course, listing names of persons from which the document came, or by whom it was authored.

  9. <u>FROM (COMPANY)</u>

    a.   Use same instructions above as TO (COMPANY), except, of course, listing names of companies from which the document came, or by whom it was authored.

  10. <u>cc (INDIVIDUAL)</u>

    a.   Use same instructions above as TO (INDIVIDUAL).

    b.   Convert handwritten initials as well as typewritten initials to names.

  11. <u>cc (COMPANY)</u>

    a.   Use same instructions above as TO (COMPANY).

    b.   Convert handwritten abbreviations or initials as well as typewritten initials or abbreviations to names of companies.

12.   <u>NAMES MENTIONED IN BODY OF DOCUMENT</u>

a.   List individuals and companies mentioned in body of document omitting primary senders or receivers.

b.   Separate all names with commas.

13.   <u>FILE NAME</u>

a.   If the document is inside a file folder with a file name, list the name of that file here.

14.   <u>DRAWING (DESCRIPTION)</u>

a.   Give brief description of any drawing, using name of drawing if one appears.

b.   List all pertinent information, for example, title, author, date, and so forth.

15.   <u>PRIVILEGED DOCUMENT</u>

a.   (Do not fill in this blank unless you have been specifically designated to do so.) If the document is privileged, place an X in the blank space.

16.   <u>SIGNIFICANCE LEVEL</u>

a.   (Do not fill in this blank unless you have been specifically designated to do so.) Assign a significance level rating to the document using the following rating system:

*****	—HOT DOCUMENT
****	—VERY SIGNIFICANT
***	—MODERATELY SIGNIFICANT
**	—SLIGHTLY SIGNIFICANT
*	—NOT SIGNIFICANT AT ALL

17.   <u>ISSUES</u>

a.   (Do not fill in this blank unless you have been specifically designated to do so.) Using the list of issues that you have been provided, list all issues, separated by commas, to which this document relates. Do not add additional issues of your own.

18.   <u>DRAFT</u>

a.   Place an X in this blank if the document is referred to or marked as a draft.

19.   <u>ATTACHED TO</u>

a.   List all Bates stamp numbers of the document to which this was attached, if applicable.

20.   <u>MARGINAL NOTATIONS</u>

a.   Write verbatim any and all marginal notations which appear on the document, except cc's, which are listed in the cc blanks above.

21.   <u>ATTACHMENTS</u>

a.   List all Bates stamp numbers of the documents which are attached to this document, if applicable.

22.   <u>TEXT OR DOCUMENT DESCRIPTION</u>

a.   (Do not fill in this blank unless you have been specifically designated to do so.) This area is reserved for either full-text input of the document or an abstract of the main ideas contained within the document. Do not repeat the document type in this description.

§ 9.13 Abstracting

Abstracting a document is much like doing a deposition summary. This is the most vital part of the information extraction process. The person designated to do the abstracting should be a knowledgeable person with excellent analytical skills and writing ability. Experienced paralegals generally do excellent abstracts of documents.

The abstract of the document involves the summarization of the substantive points of the subject document. Because the coding form has already extracted objective information from the document such as names, dates, document types, and numbers, the description or abstract field should be devoted to a compact, concise summarization of the subject matter content of the document, emphasizing any particular significance the document may have. For example, if the document is a cover letter accompanying an executed copy of a document, the abstracted summary should read something like this: "Transmittal of executed copy of Widget contract. States that last revision leaves parties in full and final agreement. First shipment expected to be received within two months of date of execution of contract." A **BAD** example of an abstract might look like this: "Transmittal letter from Party X to Party Y dated [date]."

§ 9.14 Quality Control, Data Entry, and Loading

It is extremely important to check the database for quality control at various stages of the process. Any data which has been entered into the computer should be printed out in hard copy form for proofreading by someone other than the original coder. It is imperative that the quality control take place at this stage before the data is loaded into the search software package (database manager) because it is a massive undertaking to unload data, edit, and reload once the information has been made a part of the database.

Most search software has a resident utility program which verifies the fact that the input data has been formatted correctly and that no errors are present which will cause the search software to get hung up during loading. The verification utility will point out the problem and the data will have to be backed out, edited, and reverified before loading. Once reverified, the data should be loaded immediately; it can then be searched as a regular part of the database, even before the database is entirely loaded.

§ 9.15 Brief Banks

The same process which is used to computerize your litigation document production and evidentiary materials can be used for in-house libraries of legal research briefs. This allows all the legal research memoranda which have been developed in-house to be catalogued and abstracted so that the information may be easily retrieved and used over and over. (See **Form 9–6.**)

The briefs and memoranda are abstracted in the same fashion as discussed in the chapter under coding (**§ 9.11**) and abstracting (**§ 9.13**), with one exception. Because the brief or memo is a word-processing-generated document, it can be easily imported into the software package full-text under the description heading of the abstracted coding form. The in-house generation of the document also makes the process of removing hard returns and other word-processing codes unnecessary, as a general rule.

At minimum, the abstract fields for the brief bank input should include the following:

1. Document number (for identification purposes)
2. Date brief or memorandum was written
3. Author of brief or memorandum
4. Addressee of brief or memorandum
5. Client/matter number
6. Research topic involved
7. Statute topic and number, if any
8. West key number, if applicable
9. State or federal law research?
10. Description or full-text.

FORM 9–6
SAMPLE BRIEF BANK DATA ENTRY FORM

Doc # _____

DocDate _____

Author _____

Addressee _____

Client/Matter # _____

Topic _____

_____

_____

Statute Topic/# _____

_____

_____

West Key # _____

State _____ Federal _____

Description (or full text) _____

_____

_____

_____

_____

_____

_____

_____

§ 9.16 Search Strategy

Boolean logic is a form of logical reasoning which has its roots in a mathematical model. It is the same type of logic used in Algebraic equations. In computerized litigation support, we use Boolean logic to formulate a search request. To use the logic, the search requests are structured in a logical syntax of English language words that are expected to be found in the text. Words and symbols known as connectors are used to further define and limit the number of appropriate responses, or hits, with the search request. The connectors are the key operatives in broadening or narrowing the search.

The following list is a definitive explanation of the search connectors used most frequently in Boolean logic:

1. And—The most frequently used connector, it requires that all search items be found in the appropriate response. A hit is not made unless these conditions are satisfied. For example, a search request asking for documents containing the words litigation AND support would only retrieve documents containing both terms.

2. Or—A search request asking for documents containing the words litigation or support would retrieve all documents containing either term.

3. Not—This connector is often referred to as a negative connector. It requires that the first word of the search request be found, but not the second. (For example, laser NOT beam.)

4. >—This is the connector used in conjunction with numbers and dates to mean greater than. If a search request contained the terminology 1968, you would

expect the computer to bring up all documents having dates after, or greater than, 1968.

5. <—This is the connector used in conjunction with numbers and dates to mean less than. If a search request contained the terminology 1953, you would expect the computer to bring up all documents having dates before, or less than, 1953.

6. Near—This connector requires that both search request terms be found in the same sentence near each other. The near connector can be used with a slash and a numerical definer in most software packages to designate that the two terms should be found within a certain number of words of each other. (Example: postoperative near/6 syndrome.)

7. Adj—This connector requires that both the search terms be found adjacent to each other within the document before it is to be retrieved.

8. =—The equal sign means exactly what you would expect it to mean in Boolean logic. It is generally used with dates, but by its nature is rather redundant.

Other connectors can be used to define the field where the desired response may be located, such as [Auth] preceding a proper name, which delineates that the searcher wishes to see only those responses found within the AUTHOR field.

§ 9.17 Building a Search

Searching for terms and phrases within documents is a very simple and precise exercise. Start with a premise and decide on the key words to be found within the document. Narrow the possibilities with designation of fields in which the terms must be found or with Boolean connectors such as AND or OR.

Perhaps you were looking for a contract between Texaco and El Paso Natural Gas dated 4/25/81. Follow the logic of the following search pattern:

```
SIMPLE SEARCH:
        Search Request:
1:  contract
        Search Results:
1:  contract                                      186 documents
```

Narrow your search by using a "document-type" field.

```
        Search Request:
2: contract [docu]
        Search Results:
   contract                                       186 documents
2: contract [docu]                                 78 documents
```

Now narrow your search even more by using party names.

Search Request:
3:   (Texaco and El Paso Natural Gas) and 2

[In this search we combined the results of search 2, which was the "document type=contract" search, with the party names.]

Search Results:
contract [docu]   78 documents
3:   (Texaco and El Paso Natural Gas)
     and 2   2 documents

Now we want to narrow the search even more by date, using results from search #3.

Search Request:
4:   3 and 810425

[Notice that the date is entered in a specific format.]

Search results:
(contract [docu]) and (Texaco and El Paso Natural Gas)   2 documents
810425   25 documents
4:   (contract [docu]) and (Texaco and El Paso Natural
     Gas) and 810425   1 document

Notice how the last search could have been done in one step. This is called a Complex Search.

The following are additional search examples:

- The following is an example of a search using the *OR* operator:
  (letter or memo) and 820113
  [Looking for either a letter or a memo dated 1/13/82]
- The following is an example of a search using the *ADJ* operator:
  elevator adj shaft
  [Looking for the term "elevator shaft"]
- The following is an example of a search using the *NEAR* proximity operator:
  (deliverability near3 test)
  [Looking for the word "deliverability" within 3 words of the word test]
- The following is an example of a search using the *NOT* operator:
  (letter of correspondence) NOT 820210
  [Looking for all letters or correspondence other than the ones written on 2/10/82]

§ 9.17   BUILDING A SEARCH

- The following is an example of a search using the operator:
  letter > 820210
  [Looking for a letter written after 2/10/82]
- The following is an example of a search using the operators:
  (letter) > 820210 and < 820227
  [Looking for a letter written between 2/10/82 and 2/27/82].

CHAPTER 10

RESOURCES ON THE INTERNET

§ 10.1   Introduction

In addition to the Internet sites indicated throughout the book, there are hundreds of others that could make a paralegal's job easier and faster. It would be impossible to list them all here, and they change almost as soon as you list them. Instead, I have chosen to list a few of my favorites, which will lead you in an endless circle of more links to everything imaginable. You can literally search the world from your desk now.

§ 10.2   General Legal Research Sites

Here is what you will find at *http://www.findlaw.com:*

- Administrative law
- Admiralty
- Antitrust and trade regulation
- Banking law
- Bankruptcy law
- Civil rights
- Commercial law
- Communications law
- Constitutional law

- Contracts
- Corporation and enterprise law
- Criminal law
- Cyberspace law
- Dispute resolution and arbitration
- Education law
- Entertainment and sports law
- Environmental law
- Ethics and professional responsibility
- Family law
- Government benefits
- Government contracts
- Health law
- Immigration law
- Indian law
- Injury and tort law
- Intellectual property
- International law
- International trade
- Judges and the judiciary
- Labor and employment law
- Law and economics
- Legal theory
- Litigation
- Probate, trusts and estates
- Property law and real estate
- Securities law
- Tax law
- Year 2000

It also covers federal and state cases, federal and state codes:

Legislative branch
House, Senate, Library of Congress, THOMAS Legislative Service. . .

Executive branch
White House, President, Office of Management and Budget. . .

Judicial branch
Supreme Court, Courts of Appeal, District Courts. . .

§ 10.2   GENERAL LEGAL RESEARCH SITES

Executive agencies
Department of Defense, Department of Justice, Treasury Department. . .

Independent agencies
CIA, EEOC, EPA, FTC, NASA, USPS. . .

Federal boards and commissions

Quasi-governmental organizations
FinanceNet, Legal Services Corporation, National Academies. . .

Miscellaneous nongovernment
C-SPAN, The Hill, Public Interest Groups. . .

Federal resource indexes and guides

State resources from all 50 states that are available are:

- FindLaw Resources
  - FindLaw Library - Client Development
  - FindLaw Library - Law Practice
  - FindLaw Library - Legal Research
  - FindLaw Library - Marketing
  - FindLaw Lawyer Marketing
  - FindLaw Message Boards - Law Practice & Technology
  - FindLaw Experts - Law Practice Management Consultants
- Legal Practice Web Guide
  - FindLaw Bookstore
  - Law Practice Management Materials
  - Law Practice Software and Technology
  - Legal Publishers
  - Professional Development
- Related FindLaw Guide Pages
  - Continuing Legal Education
  - FindLaw Tech Deals - Internet Contracts
  - Infirmation.com
  - Legal Associations and Organizations
  - Legal Forms

There are more indexes, including legal consultants and experts, law schools, and legal organizations.

RESOURCES ON THE INTERNET

This one is my favorite: *www.lawschoolhelp.com*. It has incredibly complete tutorials on civil procedure, contracts, a legal research guide, and remedies. For example, you can search on the civil procedure site and it will give you a complete, easy-to-understand explanation of the procedure, with links to all appropriate rules of civil procedure (federal).

Another general all-inclusive site is *http://www.ilrg.com:*

I. ILRG Legal Forms Archive. A locally maintained archive of more than 80 legal forms. Keyword searchable.

II. America's Largest 250 Law Firms. Visit the websites of the largest 250 law firms in the United States. Compiled by the New York Publishing Company, this listing of law firms is known as the *National Law Journal 250*.

III. ILRG Web Index: Off-site web resources indexed:

1. Continuing Legal Education—Index to the CLE resources on the Web. See also the Index to CLE State Requirements (USA).

2. Lawyers & Law Firms—Features ILRG's index of lawyers and law firms, law firm rankings, essential lawyer locator databases including the West Legal Directory and the Martindale-Hubbell Lawyer Locator, legal employment databases, and a listing of other major Web indexes of law firm websites.

3. Legal Associations—Nonprofit associations and organizations on the Web, including professional associations at the local, state, national, and international levels. Also featured is an intelligent agent-based .ORG search.

4. Legal Experts—Index to sources on the Web to locate a legal expert and other consultants.

5. Legal Forms Sources—In case you do not find the legal form you need within the ILRG database, check here for a listing of all known sources for law-related forms on the Web.

6. U.S. Corporate and Business Forms, Filing Instructions—Check here to find a comprehensive index to legal forms that have been promulgated by U.S. state governments, as well as links to the applicable corporations acts and other information helpful to the registry of business entities. These forms have been designed to meet statutory requirements and to facilitate filing. Also, visit the Antitrust & Trade Regulation pages.

7. U.S. Federal & State Government Tax Forms—Check here to find a comprehensive index to taxation forms promulgated by the U.S. federal and state governments.

8. Practice Areas—A topical index of law-related resources on the Web, from administrative law to wills and estates.

9. Y2K Index—A meaningful compendium of Y2K resources, including sample form language.

10. Index to Recommended Free Services—A list of various completely free services of interest to lawyers.

Academic sites include:

I. Law School Course Outline Archive. A locally maintained archive offering freely downloadable outlines for civil procedure, constitutional law, contracts, criminal law, property, and torts. Other outlines include business associations, federal income tax, insurance, international litigation and arbitration, and professional responsibility. In total, 31 outlines.

II. StudyLaw.com: Legal Study Abroad HQ. The most extensive collection of online legal study abroad materials in existence anywhere, this feature of the ILRG is the brainchild of Steven Byle, President of the Texas International Law Society. Contains information, brochures, and contact information for all study abroad programs approved by the American Bar Association, as well as contact information for almost every law school in the world.

III. Law School Rankings
    1. The Rankings Web Index—An index to law school rankings that are accessible via the Internet.
    2. Thomas E. Brennan's Judging the Law Schools—Former Michigan Supreme Court Chief Justice releases his own rankings of American law schools in an effort to remove subjective criteria from "traditional" rankings.
    3. Cost-Benefit Analysis of American Law Schools. Compiled in July 1996 by Christopher Sgarlata, a graduate of the University of Texas School of Law, this report re-indexes "the top 50 law schools"—as designated by *U.S. News & World Report*—in terms of a cost-of-living adjusted median salary, ranked from lowest to highest.
    4. Median Salary, Employment Rate, Tuition—Rankings.

IV. ILRG Web Index: Off-site Web resources indexed.
    1. Law Journals—All law reviews and journals on the Web.
    2. Law Schools—All law schools with websites.
    3. Law Students—Categorized index of websites of interest to students of the law, hand-picked by a group of law students from the University of Texas.
    4. Pre-Law—Categorized index of websites of interest to those who wish to attend law school, hand-picked by a group of law students from the University of Texas.
    5. Index to Recommended Free Services—A list of completely free services of interest to students.

RESOURCES ON THE INTERNET

Legal research sites include:

I.   LawRunner: A Legal Research Tool. Offers more than 1,100 predefined intelligent agents found on more than 300 forms to facilitate usage of the most complex query parameters built into the AltaVista™ Software. Use LawRunner to limit searches of the AltaVista™ database of 30 million Web pages to a particular jurisdiction, or to websites with a particular domain suffix. See also LawRunner American State Index, LawRunner International Index, and the LawRunner home pages for Australia, Canada, and the United Kingdom.

II. U.S. Federal Caselaw Search. Search for free the online databases of the U.S. Supreme Court and all circuit courts and learn about every online source for U.S. federal case law.

III. ILRG Search. Use this search engine to create a custom page containing the URL's matching your keywords from the ILRG's database of select websites.

IV. ILRG Web Index: Off-site web resources indexed.

   1. U.S. Federal Government: Executive Branch—Every major division of the executive branch.
   2. Legal Indices—In case you do not find what you need here.
   3. Legal Usenet—Law-related newgroups.
   4. News Sources—Newspapers, newswires, and sources for legal news.

§ 10.3   Legal Organizations Pertaining to Paralegals

National Associations of Legal Assistants, *www.nalanet.org*

National Federation of Paralegal Associations, *www.paralegals.org*

American Association for Paralegal Education, *www.aafpe.org*

Legal Assistant Management Association, *www.lamanet.org*

American Association of Legal Nurse Consultant, *www.aalnc.org*

§ 10.4   Online Sources for Locating People

www.peoplelocator.com

www.altavista.switchboard.com

http://people.yahoo.com/

http://www.411locate.com/

www.whowhere.com

§ 10.5 Online Sources for Locating Expert Witnesses

http://www.mother.com/~randy/tools.html

http://expertpages.com/index.htm

http://www.expert4law.org/

http://lawlounge.com/services/expert/directory.htm

http://www.lawguru.com/users/law/consult/index.html

http://www.onlineexperts.net/

http://www.tabexperts.com/

http://www.medicalopinions.com/

THE FREEDOM OF INFORMATION ACT 5 U.S.C. § 552, AS AMENDED BY PUBLIC LAW NO. 104-231, 110 STAT. 2422

Below is the full text of the Freedom of Information Act in a form showing all amendments to the statute made by the "Electronic Freedom of Information Act Amendments of 1996." All newly enacted provisions are in boldface type.

§ 552. Public information; agency rules, opinions, orders, records, and proceedings

(a) Each agency shall make available to the public information as follows:

(1) Each agency shall separately state and currently publish in the Federal Register for the guidance of the public—

(A) descriptions of its central and field organization and the established places at which, the employees (and in the case of a uniformed service, the members) from whom, and the methods whereby, the public may obtain information, make submittals or requests, or obtain decisions;

(B) statements of the general course and method by which its functions are channeled and determined, including the nature and requirements of all formal and informal procedures available;

(C) rules of procedure, descriptions of forms available or the places at which forms may be obtained, and instructions as to the scope and contents of all papers, reports, or examinations;

(D) substantive rules of general applicability adopted as authorized by law, and statements of general policy or interpretations of general applicability formulated and adopted by the agency; and

(E) each amendment, revision, or repeal of the foregoing. Except to the extent that a person has actual and timely notice of the terms thereof, a person may not in any manner be required to resort to, or be adversely affected by, a matter required to be published in the Federal Register and not so published. For the purpose of this paragraph, matter reasonably available to the class of persons affected thereby is deemed published in the Federal Register when incorporated by reference therein with the approval of the Director of the Federal Register.

(2) Each agency, in accordance with published rules, shall make available for public inspection and copying—

(A) final opinions, including concurring and dissenting opinions, as well as orders, made in the adjudication of cases;

(B) those statements of policy and interpretations which have been adopted by the agency and are not published in the Federal Register; ~~and~~

(C) administrative staff manuals and instructions to staff that affect a member of the public;

(D) copies of all records, regardless of form or format, which have been released to any person under paragraph (3) and which, because of the nature of their subject matter, the agency determines have become or are likely to become the subject of subsequent requests for substantially the same records; and

(E) a general index of the records referred to under subparagraph (D); unless the materials are promptly published and copies offered for sale. **For records created on or after November 1, 1996, within one year after such date, each agency shall make such records available, including by computer telecommunications or, if computer telecommunications means have not been established by the agency, by other electronic means.** To the extent required to prevent a clearly unwarranted invasion of personal privacy, an agency may delete identifying details when it makes available or publishes an opinion, statement of policy, interpretation, ~~or staff manual or instruction,~~ **staff manual, instruction, or copies of records referred to in subparagraph (D)**. However, in each case the justification for the deletion shall be explained fully in writing**, and the extent of such deletion shall be indicated on the portion of the record which is made available or published, unless including that indication would harm an interest protected by the exemption in subsection (b) under which the deletion is made. If technically feasible, the extent of the deletion shall be indicated at the place in the record where the deletion was made.** Each agency shall also maintain and make available for public inspection and copying current indexes providing identifying information for the public as to any matter issued, adopted, or promulgated after July 4, 1967, and required by this paragraph to be made available or published. Each agency shall promptly publish, quarterly or more frequently, and distribute (by sale or otherwise) copies of each index or supplements thereto unless it determines by order published in the Federal Register that the publication would be unnecessary and impracticable, in which case the agency shall nonetheless provide copies of an index on request at a cost not to exceed the direct cost of duplication. **Each agency shall make the index referred to in subparagraph (E) available by computer telecommunications by December 31, 1999.** A final order, opinion, statement of policy, interpretation, or staff manual or instruction that affects a member of the public may be relied on, used, or cited as precedent by an agency against a party other than an agency only if—

(i) it has been indexed and either made available or published as provided by this paragraph; or

(ii) the party has actual and timely notice of the terms thereof.

(3) **(A)** Except with respect to the records made available under paragraphs (1) and (2) of this subsection, each agency, upon request for records which (A) **(i) reasonably** describes such records and (B) (ii) is made in accordance with published rules stating the time, place, fees (if any), and procedures to be followed, shall make the records promptly available to any person.

(B) In making any record available to a person under this paragraph, an agency shall provide the record in any form or format requested by the person if the record is readily reproducible by the agency in that form or format. Each agency shall make reasonable efforts to maintain its records in forms or formats that are reproducible for purposes of this section.

(C) In responding under this paragraph to a request for records, an agency shall make reasonable efforts to search for the records in electronic form or format, except when such efforts would significantly interfere with the operation of the agency's automated information system.

(D) For purposes of this paragraph, the term "search" means to review, manually or by automated means, agency records for the purpose of locating those records which are responsive to a request.

(4) (A) (i) In order to carry out the provisions of this section, each agency shall promulgate regulations, pursuant to notice and receipt of public comment, specifying the schedule of fees applicable to the processing of requests under this section and establishing procedures and guidelines for determining when such fees should be waived or reduced. Such schedule shall conform to the guidelines which shall be promulgated, pursuant to notice and receipt of public comment, by the Director of the Office of Management and Budget and which shall provide for a uniform schedule of fees for all agencies.

(ii) Such agency regulations shall provide that—

(I) fees shall be limited to reasonable standard charges for document search, duplication, and review, when records are requested for commercial use;

(II) fees shall be limited to reasonable standard charges for document duplication when records are not sought for commercial use and the request is made by an educational or noncommercial scientific institution, whose purpose is scholarly or scientific research; or a representative of the news media; and

(III) for any request not described in (I) or (II), fees shall be limited to reasonable standard charges for document search and duplication.

(iii) Documents shall be furnished without any charge or at a charge reduced below the fees established under clause (ii) if disclosure of the information is in the public interest because it is likely to contribute significantly to public understanding of the operations or activities of the government and is not primarily in the commercial interest of the requester.

(iv) Fee schedules shall provide for the recovery of only the direct costs of search, duplication, or review. Review costs shall include only the direct costs incurred during the initial examination of a document for the purposes of determining whether the documents must be disclosed under this section and for the purposes of withholding any portions exempt from disclosure under this section. Review costs may not include any costs incurred in resolving issues of law or policy that may be raised in the course of processing a request under this section. No fee may be charged by any agency under this section—

(I) if the costs of routine collection and processing of the fee are likely to equal or exceed the amount of the fee; or

(II) for any request described in clause (ii) (II) or (III) of this subparagraph for the first two hours of search time or for the first one hundred pages of duplication.

(v) No agency may require advance payment of any fee unless the requester has previously failed to pay fees in a timely fashion, or the agency has determined that the fee will exceed $250.

(vi) Nothing in this subparagraph shall supersede fees chargeable under a statute specifically providing for setting the level of fees for particular types of records.

(vii) In any action by a requester regarding the waiver of fees under this section, the court shall determine the matter de novo, provided that the court's review of the matter shall be limited to the record before the agency.

(B) On complaint, the district court of the United States in the district in which the complainant resides, or has his principal place of business, or in which the agency records are situated, or in the District of Columbia, has jurisdiction to enjoin the agency from withholding agency records and to order the production of any agency records improperly withheld from the complainant. In such a case the court shall determine the matter de novo, and may examine the contents of such agency records in camera to determine whether such records or any part thereof shall be withheld under any of the exemptions set forth in subsection (b) of this section, and the burden is on the agency to sustain its action. **In addition to any other matters to which a court accords substantial weight, a court shall accord substantial weight to an affidavit of an agency concerning the agency's determination as to technical feasibility under paragraph (2)(C) and subsection (b) and reproducibility under paragraph (3)(B).**

(C) Notwithstanding any other provision of law, the defendant shall serve an answer or otherwise plead to any complaint made under this subsection within thirty days after service upon the defendant of the pleading in which such complaint is made, unless the court otherwise directs for good cause shown.

[(D) Except as to cases the court considers of greater importance, proceedings before the district court, as authorized by this subsection, and appeals therefrom, take precedence on the docket over all cases and shall be assigned for hearing and trial or for argument at the earliest practicable date and expedited in every way. Repealed by Pub. L. 98-620, Title IV, 402(2), Nov. 8, 1984, 98 Stat. 3335,3357.]

(E) The court may assess against the United States reasonable attorney fees and other litigation costs reasonably incurred in any case under this section in which the complainant has substantially prevailed.

(F) Whenever the court orders the production of any agency records improperly withheld from the complainant and assesses against the United States reasonable attorney fees and other litigation costs, and the court additionally issues a written finding that the circumstances surrounding the withholding raise questions whether agency personnel acted arbitrarily or capriciously with respect to the withholding, the Special Counsel shall promptly initiate a proceeding to determine whether disciplinary action is warranted against the officer or employee who was primarily responsible for the withholding. The Special Counsel, after investigation and consideration of the evidence submitted, shall submit his findings and recommendations to the administrative authority of the agency concerned and shall send copies of the findings and recommendations to the officer or employee or his representative. The administrative authority shall take the corrective action that the Special Counsel recommends.

(G) In the event of noncompliance with the order of the court, the district court may punish for contempt the responsible employee, and in the case of a uniformed service, the responsible member.

(5) Each agency having more than one member shall maintain and make available for public inspection a record of the final votes of each member in every agency proceeding.

(6)(A) Each agency, upon any request for records made under paragraph (1), (2), or (3) of this subsection, shall—

(i) determine within **twenty days (excepting** Saturdays, Sundays, and legal public holidays) after the receipt of any such request whether to comply with such request and shall immediately notify the person making such request of such determination and the reasons therefor, and of the right of such person to appeal to the head of the agency any adverse determination; and

(ii) make a determination with respect to any appeal within twenty days (excepting Saturdays, Sundays, and legal public holidays) after the receipt of such appeal. If on appeal the denial of the request for records is in whole or in part upheld, the agency shall notify the person making such request of the provisions for judicial review of that determination under paragraph (4) of this subsection.

(B) (i) In unusual circumstances as specified in this subparagraph, the time limits prescribed in either clause (i) or clause (ii) of subparagraph (A) may be extended by written notice to the person making such request setting forth the unusual circumstances for such extension and the date on which a determination is expected to be dispatched. No such notice shall specify a date that would result in an extension for more than ten working days, except as provided in clause (ii) of this subparagraph.

(ii) With respect to a request for which a written notice under clause (i) extends the time limits prescribed under clause (i) of subparagraph (A), the agency shall notify the person making the request if the request cannot be processed within the time limit specified in that clause and shall provide the person an opportunity to limit the scope of the request so that it may be processed within that time limit or an opportunity to arrange with the agency an alternative time frame for processing the request or a modified request. Refusal by the person to reasonably modify the request or arrange such an alternative time frame shall be considered as a factor in determining whether exceptional circumstances exist for purposes of subparagraph (C).

(iii) As used in this subparagraph, "unusual circumstances" means, but only to the extent reasonably necessary to the proper processing of the particular requests—

(I) the need to search for and collect the requested records from field facilities or other establishments that are separate from the office processing the request;

(II) the need to search for, collect, and appropriately examine a voluminous amount of separate and distinct records which are demanded in a single request; or

(III) the need for consultation, which shall be conducted with all practicable speed, with another agency having a substantial interest in the determination of the request or among two or more components of the agency having substantial subject matter interest therein.

(iv) Each agency may promulgate regulations, pursuant to notice and receipt of public comment, providing for the aggregation of certain requests by the same requestor, or by a group of requestors acting in concert, if the agency reasonably believes that such requests actually constitute a single request, which would otherwise satisfy the unusual circumstances specified in this subparagraph, and the requests involve clearly related matters. Multiple requests involving unrelated matters shall not be aggregated.

(C) (i) Any person making a request to any agency for records under paragraph (1), (2), or (3) of this subsection shall be deemed to have exhausted his administrative remedies with respect to such request if the agency fails to comply with the applicable time limit provisions of this paragraph. If the Government can show exceptional circumstances exist and that the agency is exercising due diligence in responding to the request, the court may retain jurisdiction and allow the agency additional time to complete its review of the records. Upon any determination by an agency to comply with a request for records, the records shall be made promptly available to such person making such request. Any notification of denial of any request for records under this subsection shall set forth the names and titles or positions of each person responsible for the denial of such request.

(ii) For purposes of this subparagraph, the term "exceptional circumstances" does not include a delay that results from a predictable agency workload of requests under this section, unless the agency demonstrates reasonable progress in reducing its backlog of pending requests.

(iii) Refusal by a person to reasonably modify the scope of a request or arrange an alternative time frame for processing the request (or a modified request) under clause (ii) after being given an opportunity to do so by the agency to whom the person made the request shall be considered as a factor in determining whether exceptional circumstances exist for purposes of this subparagraph.

(D) (i) Each agency may promulgate regulations, pursuant to notice and receipt of public comment, providing for multitrack processing of requests for records based on the amount of work or time (or both) involved in processing requests.

(ii) Regulations under this subparagraph may provide a person making a request that does not qualify for the fastest multitrack processing an opportunity to limit the scope of the request in order to qualify for faster processing.

(iii) This subparagraph shall not be considered to affect the requirement under subparagraph (C) to exercise due diligence.

(E) (i) Each agency shall promulgate regulations, pursuant to notice and receipt of public comment, providing for expedited processing of requests for records—

(I) in cases in which the person requesting the records demonstrates a compelling need; and

(II) in other cases determined by the agency.

(ii) Notwithstanding clause (i), regulations under this subparagraph must ensure—

(I) that a determination of whether to provide expedited processing shall be made, and notice of the determination shall be provided to the person making the request, within 10 days after the date of the request; and

(II) expeditious consideration of administrative appeals of such determinations of whether to provide expedited processing.

(iii) An agency shall process as soon as practicable any request for records to which the agency has granted expedited processing under this subparagraph. Agency action to deny or affirm denial of a request for expedited processing pursuant to this subparagraph, and failure by an agency to respond in a timely manner to such a request shall be subject to judicial review under paragraph (4), except that the judicial review shall be based on the record before the agency at the time of the determination.

(iv) A district court of the United States shall not have jurisdiction to review an agency denial of expedited processing of a request for records after the agency has provided a complete response to the request.

(v) For purposes of this subparagraph, the term "compelling need" means—

(I) that a failure to obtain requested records on an expedited basis under this paragraph could reasonably be expected to pose an imminent threat to the life or physical safety of an individual; or

(II) with respect to a request made by a person primarily engaged in disseminating information, urgency to inform the public concerning actual or alleged Federal Government activity.

(vi) A demonstration of a compelling need by a person making a request for expedited processing shall be made by a statement certified by such person to be true and correct to the best of such person's knowledge and belief.

(F) In denying a request for records, in whole or in part, an agency shall make a reasonable effort to estimate the volume of any requested matter the provision of which is denied, and shall provide any such estimate to the person making the request, unless providing such estimate would harm an interest protected by the exemption in subsection (b) pursuant to which the denial is made.

(b) This section does not apply to matters that are—

(1)(A) specifically authorized under criteria established by an Executive order to be kept secret in the interest of national defense or foreign policy and (B) are in fact properly classified pursuant to such Executive order;

(2) related solely to the internal personnel rules and practices of an agency;

(3) specifically exempted from disclosure by statute (other than section 552b of this title), provided that such statute (A) requires that the matters be withheld from the public in such a manner as to leave no discretion on the issue, or (B) establishes particular criteria for withholding or refers to particular types of matters to be withheld;

(4) trade secrets and commercial or financial information obtained from a person and privileged or confidential;

(5) inter-agency or intra-agency memorandums or letters which would not be available by law to a party other than an agency in litigation with the agency;

(6) personnel and medical files and similar files the disclosure of which would constitute a clearly unwarranted invasion of personal privacy;

(7) records or information compiled for law enforcement purposes,but only to the extent that the production of such law enforcement records or information

(A) could reasonably be expected to interfere with enforcement proceedings,

(B) would deprive a person of a right to a fair trial or an impartial adjudication,

(C) could reasonably be expected to constitute an unwarranted invasion of personal privacy,

(D) could reasonably be expected to disclose the identity of a confidential source, including a State, local,or foreign agency or authority or any private institution which furnished information on a confidential basis, and, in the case of a record or information compiled by a criminal law enforcement authority in the course of a criminal investigation or by an agency conducting a lawful national security intelligence investigation,information furnished by a confidential source,

(E) would disclose techniques and procedures for law enforcement investigations or prosecutions, or would disclose guidelines for law enforcement investigations or prosecutions if such disclosure could reasonably be expected to risk circumvention of the law, or

(F) could reasonably be expected to endanger the life or physical safety of any individual;

(8) contained in or related to examination, operating, or condition reports prepared by, on behalf of, or for the use of an agency responsible for the regulation or supervision of financial institutions; or

(9) geological and geophysical information and data, including maps, concerning wells.

Any reasonably segregable portion of a record shall be provided to any person requesting such record after deletion of the portions which are exempt under this subsection. **The amount of information deleted shall be indicated on the released portion of the record,unless including that indication would harm an interest protected by the exemption in this subsection under which the deletion is made. If technically feasible, the amount of the information deleted shall be indicated at the place in the record where such deletion is made.**

(c)(1) Whenever a request is made which involves access to records described in subsection (b)(7)(A) and—

(A) the investigation or proceeding involves a possible violation of criminal law; and

(B) there is reason to believe that (i) the subject of the investigation or proceeding is not aware of its pendency, and (ii) disclosure of the existence of the records could reasonably be expected to interfere with enforcement proceedings, the agency may, during only such time as that circumstance continues, treat the records as not subject to the requirements of this section.

(2) Whenever informant records maintained by a criminal law enforcement agency under an informant's name or personal identifier are requested by a third party according to the informant's name or personal identifier, the agency may treat the records as not subject to the requirements of this section unless the informant's status as an informant has been officially confirmed.

(3) Whenever a request is made which involves access to records maintained by the Federal Bureau of Investigation pertaining to foreign intelligence or counterintelligence, or international terrorism, and the existence of the records is classified information as provided in subsection (b)(1), the Bureau may, as long as the existence of the records remains classified information, treat the records as not subject to the requirements of this section.

(d) This section does not authorize the withholding of information or limit the availability of records to the public, except as specifically stated in this section. This section is not authority to withhold information from Congress.

(e)(1) On or before February 1 of each year, each agency shall submit to the Attorney General of the United States a report which shall cover the preceding fiscal year and which shall include—

(A) the number of determinations made by the agency not to comply with requests for records made to such agency under subsection(a) and the reasons for each such determination;

(B)(i) the number of appeals made by persons under subsection(a)(6), the result of such appeals, and the reason for the action upon each appeal that results in a denial of information; and

(ii) a complete list of all statutes that the agency relies upon to authorize the agency to withhold information under subsection(b)(3), a description of whether a court has upheld the decision of the agency to withhold information under each such statute,and a concise description of the scope of any information withheld;

(C) the number of requests for records pending before the agency as of September 30 of the preceding year, and the median number of days that such requests had been pending before the agency as of that date;

(D) the number of requests for records received by the agency and the number of requests which the agency processed;

(E) the median number of days taken by the agency to process different types of requests;

(F) the total amount of fees collected by the agency for processing requests; and

(G) the number of full-time staff of the agency devoted to processing requests for records under this section, and the total amount expended by the agency for processing such requests.

(2) Each agency shall make each such report available to the public including by computer telecommunications, or if computer telecommunications means have not been established by the agency, by other electronic means.

(3) The Attorney General of the United States shall make each report which has been made available by electronic means available at a single electronic access point. The Attorney General of the United States shall notify the Chairman and ranking minority member of the Committee on Government Reform and Oversight of the House of Representatives and the Chairman and ranking minority member of the Committees on Governmental Affairs and the Judiciary of the Senate, no later than April 1 of the year in which each such report is issued, that such reports are available by electronic means.

(4) The Attorney General of the United States, in consultation with the Director of the Office of Management and Budget, shall develop reporting and performance guidelines in connection with reports required by this subsection by October 1, 1997, and may establish additional requirements for such reports as the Attorney General determines may be useful.

(5) The Attorney General of the United States shall submit an annual report on or before April 1 of each calendar year which shall include for the prior calendar year a listing of the number of cases arising under this section, the exemption involved in each case, the disposition of such case, and the cost, fees, and penalties assessed under subparagraphs (E), (F), and (G) of subsection(a)(4). Such report shall also include a description of the efforts undertaken by the Department of Justice to encourage agency compliance with this section.

(f) For purposes of this section, the term—

(1) "agency" as defined in section 551(1) of this title includes any executive department, military department, Government corporation, Government controlled corporation, or other establishment in the executive branch of the Government (including the Executive Office of the President), or any independent regulatory agency; and

(2) "record" and any other term used in this section in reference to information includes any information that would be an agency record subject to the requirements of this section when maintained by an agency in any format, including an electronic format.

(g) The head of each agency shall prepare and make publicly available upon request, reference material or a guide for requesting records or information from the agency, subject to the exemptions in subsection (b), including—

(1) an index of all major information systems of the agency;

(2) a description of major information and record locator systems maintained by the agency; and

(3) a handbook for obtaining various types and categories of public information from the agency pursuant to chapter 35 of title 44, and under this section.
* * * * *

Section 12. Effective Date [not to be codified].

(a) Except as provided in subsection (b), this Act shall take effect 180 days after the date of the enactment of this Act [March 31, 1997].

(b) Sections 7 and 8 shall take effect one year after the date of the enactment of this Act [October 2, 1997].

PRIVACY ACT

5 USC Sec. 552a (01/16/96)
[TITLE 5 - GOVERNMENT ORGANIZATION AND EMPLOYEES]
[PART I - THE AGENCIES GENERALLY]
[CHAPTER 5 - ADMINISTRATIVE PROCEDURE]
[SUBCHAPTER II - ADMINISTRATIVE PROCEDURE]

§ 552a. Records maintained on individuals
(a) Definitions

For purposes of this section—

(1) the term "agency" means agency as defined in section 552(f) of this title;

(2) the term "individual" means a citizen of the United States or an alien lawfully admitted for permanent residence;

(3) the term "maintain" includes maintain, collect, use or disseminate;

(4) the term "record" means any item, collection, or grouping of information about an individual that is maintained by an agency, including, but not limited to, his education, financial transactions, medical history, and criminal or employment history and that contains his name, or the identifying number, symbol, or other identifying particular assigned to the individual, such as a finger or voice print or a photograph;

(5) the term "system of records" means a group of any records under the control of any agency from which information is retrieved by the name of the individual or by some identifying number, symbol, or other identifying particular assigned to the individual;

(6) the term "statistical record" means a record in a system of records maintained for statistical research or reporting purposes only and not used in whole or in part in making any determination about an identifiable individual, except as provided by section 8 of Title 13;

(7) the term "routine use" means, with respect to the disclosure of a record, the use of such record for a purpose which is compatible with the purpose for which it was collected;

(8) the term "matching program"—

(A) means any computerized comparison of—

(i) two or more automated systems of records or a system of records with non-Federal records for the purpose of—

(I) establishing or verifying the eligibility of, or continuing compliance with statutory and regulatory requirements by, applicants for, recipients or beneficiaries of, participants in, or providers of services with respect to, cash or in-kind assistance or payments under Federal benefit programs, or

(II) recouping payments or delinquent debts under such Federal benefit programs, or

(ii) two or more automated Federal personnel or payroll systems of records or a system of Federal personnel or payroll records with non-Federal records,

(B) but does not include—

(i) matches performed to produce aggregate statistical data without any personal identifiers;

(ii) matches performed to support any research or statistical project, the specific data of which may not be used to make decisions concerning the rights, benefits, or privileges of specific individuals;

(iii) matches performed, by an agency (or component thereof) which performs as its principal function any activity pertaining to the enforcement of criminal laws, subsequent to the initiation of a specific criminal or civil law enforcement investigation of a named person or persons for the purpose of gathering evidence against such person or persons;

(iv) matches of tax information (I) pursuant to section 6103(d) of the Internal Revenue Code of 1986, (II) for purposes of tax administration as defined in section 6103(b)(4) of such Code, (III) for the purpose of intercepting a tax refund due an individual under authority granted by section 464 or 1137 of the Social Security Act; or (IV) for the purpose of intercepting a tax refund due an individual under any other tax refund intercept program authorized by statute which has been determined by the Director of the Office of Management and Budget to contain verification, notice, and hearing requirements that are substantially similar to the procedures in section 1137 of the Social Security Act;

(v) matches—

(I) using records predominantly relating to Federal personnel, that are performed for routine administrative purposes (subject to guidance provided by the Director of the Office of Management and Budget pursuant to subsection (v)); or

(II) conducted by an agency using only records from systems of records maintained by that agency; if the purpose of the match is not to take any adverse financial, personnel, disciplinary, or other adverse action against Federal personnel; or

(vi) matches performed for foreign counterintelligence purposes or to produce background checks for security clearances of Federal personnel or Federal contractor personnel; or

(vii) Repealed. Pub.L. 104-226, § 1(b)(3)(C), Oct. 2, 1996, 110 Stat. 3033.

(9) the term "recipient agency" means any agency, or contractor thereof, receiving records contained in a system of records from a source agency for use in a matching program;

(10) the term "non-Federal agency" means any State or local government, or agency thereof, which receives records contained in a system of records from a source agency for use in a matching program;

(11) the term "source agency" means any agency which discloses records contained in a system of records to be used in a matching program, or any State or local government, or agency thereof, which discloses records to be used in a matching program;

PRIVACY ACT

(12) the term "Federal benefit program" means any program administered or funded by the Federal Government, or by any agent or State on behalf of the Federal Government, providing cash or in-kind assistance in the form of payments, grants, loans, or loan guarantees to individuals; and

(13) the term "Federal personnel" means officers and employees of the Government of the United States, members of the uniformed services (including members of the Reserve Components), individuals entitled to receive immediate or deferred retirement benefits under any retirement program of the Government of the United States (including survivor benefits).

(b) Conditions of disclosure

No agency shall disclose any record which is contained in a system of records by any means of communication to any person, or to another agency, except pursuant to a written request by, or with the prior written consent of, the individual to whom the record pertains, unless disclosure of the record would be—

(1) to those officers and employees of the agency which maintains the record who have a need for the record in the performance of their duties;

(2) required under section 552 of this title;

(3) for a routine use as defined in subsection (a)(7) of this section and described under subsection (e)(4)(D) of this section;

(4) to the Bureau of the Census for purposes of planning or carrying out a census or survey or related activity pursuant to the provisions of Title 13;

(5) to a recipient who has provided the agency with advance adequate written assurance that the record will be used solely as a statistical research or reporting record, and the record is to be transferred in a form that is not individually identifiable;

(6) to the National Archives and Records Administration as a record which has sufficient historical or other value to warrant its continued preservation by the United States Government, or for evaluation by the Archivist of the United States or the designee of the Archivist to determine whether the record has such value;

(7) to another agency or to an instrumentality of any governmental jurisdiction within or under the control of the United States for a civil or criminal law enforcement activity if the activity is authorized by law, and if the head of the agency or instrumentality has made a written request to the agency which maintains the record specifying the particular portion desired and the law enforcement activity for which the record is sought;

(8) to a person pursuant to a showing of compelling circumstances affecting the health or safety of an individual if upon such disclosure notification is transmitted to the last known address of such individual;

(9) to either House of Congress, or, to the extent of matter within its jurisdiction, any committee or subcommittee thereof, any joint committee of Congress or subcommittee of any such joint committee;

(10) to the Comptroller General, or any of his authorized representatives, in the course of the performance of the duties of the General Accounting Office;

(11) pursuant to the order of a court of competent jurisdiction; or

669

APPENDIX A

(12) to a consumer reporting agency in accordance with section 3711(e) of Title 31.

(c) Accounting of certain disclosures

Each agency, with respect to each system of records under its control, shall—

(1) except for disclosures made under subsections (b)(1) or (b)(2) of this section, keep an accurate accounting of—

(A) the date, nature, and purpose of each disclosure of a record to any person or to another agency made under subsection (b) of this section; and

(B) the name and address of the person or agency to whom the disclosure is made;

(2) retain the accounting made under paragraph (1) of this subsection for at least five years or the life of the record, whichever is longer, after the disclosure for which the accounting is made;

(3) except for disclosures made under subsection (b)(7) of this section, make the accounting made under paragraph (1) of this subsection available to the individual named in the record at his request; and

(4) inform any person or other agency about any correction or notation of dispute made by the agency in accordance with subsection (d) of this section of any record that has been disclosed to the person or agency if an accounting of the disclosure was made.

(d) Access to records

Each agency that maintains a system of records shall—

(1) upon request by any individual to gain access to his record or to any information pertaining to him which is contained in the system, permit him and upon his request, a person of his own choosing to accompany him, to review the record and have a copy made of all or any portion thereof in a form comprehensible to him, except that the agency may require the individual to furnish a written statement authorizing discussion of that individual's record in the accompanying person's presence;

(2) permit the individual to request amendment of a record pertaining to him and—

(A) not later than 10 days (excluding Saturdays, Sundays, and legal public holidays) after the date of receipt of such request, acknowledge in writing such receipt; and

(B) promptly, either—

(i) make any correction of any portion thereof which the individual believes is not accurate, relevant, timely, or complete; or

(ii) inform the individual of its refusal to amend the record in accordance with his request, the reason for the refusal, the procedures established by the agency for the individual to request a review of that refusal by the head of the agency or an officer designated by the head of the agency, and the name and business address of that official;

(3) permit the individual who disagrees with the refusal of the agency to amend his record to request a review of such refusal, and not later than 30 days (excluding Saturdays, Sundays, and legal public holidays) from the date on which the individual requests such review, complete such review and make a final determination unless,

PRIVACY ACT

for good cause shown, the head of the agency extends such 30-day period; and if, after his review, the reviewing official also refuses to amend the record in accordance with the request, permit the individual to file with the agency a concise statement setting forth the reasons for his disagreement with the refusal of the agency, and notify the individual of the provisions for judicial review of the reviewing official's determination under subsection (g)(1)(A) of this section;

(4) in any disclosure, containing information about which the individual has filed a statement of disagreement, occurring after the filing of the statement under paragraph (3) of this subsection, clearly note any portion of the record which is disputed and provide copies of the statement and, if the agency deems it appropriate, copies of a concise statement of the reasons of the agency for not making the amendments requested, to persons or other agencies to whom the disputed record has been disclosed; and

(5) nothing in this section shall allow an individual access to any information compiled in reasonable anticipation of a civil action or proceeding.

(e) Agency requirements

Each agency that maintains a system of records shall—

(1) maintain in its records only such information about an individual as is relevant and necessary to accomplish a purpose of the agency required to be accomplished by statute or by Executive order of the President;

(2) collect information to the greatest extent practicable directly from the subject individual when the information may result in adverse determinations about an individual's rights, benefits, and privileges under Federal programs;

(3) inform each individual whom it asks to supply information, on the form which it uses to collect the information or on a separate form that can be retained by the individual—

(A) the authority (whether granted by statute, or by Executive order of the President) which authorizes the solicitation of the information and whether disclosure of such information is mandatory or voluntary;

(B) the principal purpose or purposes for which the information is intended to be used;

(C) the routine uses which may be made of the information, as published pursuant to paragraph (4)(D) of this subsection; and

(D) the effects on him, if any, of not providing all or any part of the requested information;

(4) subject to the provisions of paragraph (11) of this subsection, publish in the Federal Register upon establishment or revision a notice of the existence and character of the system of records, which notice shall include—

(A) the name and location of the system;

(B) the categories of individuals on whom records are maintained in the system;

(C) the categories of records maintained in the system;

(D) each routine use of the records contained in the system, including the categories of users and the purpose of such use;

671

(E) the policies and practices of the agency regarding storage, retrievability, access controls, retention, and disposal of the records;

(F) the title and business address of the agency official who is responsible for the system of records;

(G) the agency procedures whereby an individual can be notified at his request if the system of records contains a record pertaining to him;

(H) the agency procedures whereby an individual can be notified at his request how he can gain access to any record pertaining to him contained in the system of records, and how he can contest its content; and

(I) the categories of sources of records in the system;

(5) maintain all records which are used by the agency in making any determination about any individual with such accuracy, relevance, timeliness, and completeness as is reasonably necessary to assure fairness to the individual in the determination;

(6) prior to disseminating any record about an individual to any person other than an agency, unless the dissemination is made pursuant to subsection (b)(2) of this section, make reasonable efforts to assure that such records are accurate, complete, timely, and relevant for agency purposes;

(7) maintain no record describing how any individual exercises rights guaranteed by the First Amendment unless expressly authorized by statute or by the individual about whom the record is maintained or unless pertinent to and within the scope of an authorized law enforcement activity;

(8) make reasonable efforts to serve notice on an individual when any record on such individual is made available to any person under compulsory legal process when such process becomes a matter of public record;

(9) establish rules of conduct for persons involved in the design, development, operation, or maintenance of any system of records, or in maintaining any record, and instruct each such person with respect to such rules and the requirements of this section, including any other rules and procedures adopted pursuant to this section and the penalties for noncompliance;

(10) establish appropriate administrative, technical and physical safeguards to insure the security and confidentiality of records and to protect against any anticipated threats or hazards to their security or integrity which could result in substantial harm, embarrassment, inconvenience, or unfairness to any individual on whom information is maintained;

(11) at least 30 days prior to publication of information under paragraph (4)(D) of this subsection, publish in the Federal Register notice of any new use or intended use of the information in the system, and provide an opportunity for interested persons to submit written data, views, or arguments to the agency; and

(12) if such agency is a recipient agency or a source agency in a matching program with a non-Federal agency, with respect to any establishment or revision of a matching program, at least 30 days prior to conducting such program, publish in the Federal Register notice of such establishment or revision.

PRIVACY ACT

(f) Agency rules

In order to carry out the provisions of this section, each agency that maintains a system of records shall promulgate rules, in accordance with the requirements (including general notice) of section 553 of this title, which shall—

(1) establish procedures whereby an individual can be notified in response to his request if any system of records named by the individual contains a record pertaining to him;

(2) define reasonable times, places, and requirements for identifying an individual who requests his record or information pertaining to him before the agency shall make the record or information available to the individual;

(3) establish procedures for the disclosure to an individual upon his request of his record or information pertaining to him, including special procedure, if deemed necessary, for the disclosure to an individual of medical records, including psychological records, pertaining to him;

(4) establish procedures for reviewing a request from an individual concerning the amendment of any record or information pertaining to the individual, for making a determination on the request, for an appeal within the agency of an initial adverse agency determination, and for whatever additional means may be necessary for each individual to be able to exercise fully his rights under this section; and

(5) establish fees to be charged, if any, to any individual for making copies of his record, excluding the cost of any search for and review of the record.

The Office of the Federal Register shall biennially compile and publish the rules promulgated under this subsection and agency notices published under subsection (e)(4) of this section in a form available to the public at low cost.

(g)(1) Civil remedies

Whenever any agency

(A) makes a determination under subsection (d)(3) of this section not to amend an individual's record in accordance with his request, or fails to make such review in conformity with that subsection;

(B) refuses to comply with an individual request under subsection (d)(1) of this section;

(C) fails to maintain any record concerning any individual with such accuracy, relevance, timeliness, and completeness as is necessary to assure fairness in any determination relating to the qualifications, character, rights, or opportunities of, or benefits to the individual that may be made on the basis of such record, and consequently a determination is made which is adverse to the individual; or

(D) fails to comply with any other provision of this section, or any rule promulgated thereunder, in such a way as to have an adverse effect on an individual, the individual may bring a civil action against the agency, and the district courts of the United States shall have jurisdiction in the matters under the provisions of this subsection.

(2)(A) In any suit brought under the provisions of subsection (g)(1)(A) of this section, the court may order the agency to amend the individual's record in accordance with his request or in such other way as the court may direct. In such a case the court shall determine the matter de novo.

(B) The court may assess against the United States reasonable attorney fees and other litigation costs reasonably incurred in any case under this paragraph in which the complainant has substantially prevailed.

(3)(A) In any suit brought under the provisions of subsection (g)(1)(B) of this section, the court may enjoin the agency from withholding the records and order the production to the complainant of any agency records improperly withheld from him. In such a case the court shall determine the matter de novo, and may examine the contents of any agency records in camera to determine whether the records or any portion thereof may be withheld under any of the exemptions set forth in subsection (k) of this section, and the burden is on the agency to sustain its action.

(B) The court may assess against the United States reasonable attorney fees and other litigation costs reasonably incurred in any case under this paragraph in which the complainant has substantially prevailed.

(4) In any suit brought under the provisions of subsection (g)(1)(C) or (D) of this section in which the court determines that the agency acted in a manner which was intentional or willful, the United States shall be liable to the individual in an amount equal to the sum of—

(A) actual damages sustained by the individual as a result of the refusal or failure, but in no case shall a person entitled to recovery receive less than the sum of $1,000; and

(B) the costs of the action together with reasonable attorney fees as determined by the court.

(5) An action to enforce any liability created under this section may be brought in the district court of the United States in the district in which the complainant resides, or has his principal place of business, or in which the agency records are situated, or in the District of Columbia, without regard to the amount in controversy, within two years from the date on which the cause of action a rises, except that where an agency has materially and willfully misrepresented any information required under this section to be disclosed to an individual and the information so misrepresented is material to establishment of the liability of the agency to the individual under this section, the action may be brought at any time within two years after discovery by the individual of the misrepresentation. Nothing in this section shall be construed to authorize any civil action by reason of any injury sustained as the result of a disclosure of a record prior to September 27, 1975.

(h) Rights of legal guardians

For the purposes of this section, the parent of any minor, or the legal guardian of any individual who has been declared to be incompetent due to physical or mental incapacity or age by a court of competent jurisdiction, may act on behalf of the individual.

(i)(1) Criminal penalties

Any officer or employee of an agency, who by virtue of his employment or official position, has possession of, or access to, agency records which contain individually identifiable information the disclosure of which is prohibited by this section or by rules or regulations established thereunder, and who knowing that disclosure of the specific material is so prohibited, willfully discloses the material in any manner to any person or agency not entitled to receive it, shall be guilty of a misdemeanor and fined not more than $5,000.

(2) Any officer or employee of any agency who willfully maintains a system of records without meeting the notice requirements of subsection (e)(4) of this section shall be guilty of a misdemeanor and fined not more than $5,000.

(3) Any person who knowingly and willfully requests or obtains any record concerning an individual from an agency under false pretenses shall be guilty of a misdemeanor and fined not more than $5,000.

(j) General exemptions

The head of any agency may promulgate rules, in accordance with the requirements (including general notice) of sections 553(b)(1), (2), and (3), (c), and (e) of this title, to exempt any system of records within the agency from any part of this section except subsections (b), (c)(1) and (2), (e)(4)(A) through (F), (e)(6), (7), (9), (10), and (11), and (i) if the system of records is—

(1) maintained by the Central Intelligence Agency; or

(2) maintained by an agency or component thereof which performs as its principal function any activity pertaining to the enforcement of criminal laws, including police efforts to prevent, control, or reduce crime or to apprehend criminals, and the activities of prosecutors, courts, correctional, probation, pardon, or parole authorities, and which consists of (A) information compiled for the purpose of identifying individual criminal offenders and alleged offenders and consisting only of identifying data and notations of arrests, the nature and disposition of criminal charges, sentencing, confinement, release, and parole and probation status; (B) information compiled for the purpose of a criminal investigation, including reports of informants and investigators, and associated with an identifiable individual; or (C) reports identifiable to an individual compiled at any stage of the process of enforcement of the criminal laws from arrest or indictment through release from supervision.

At the time rules are adopted under this subsection, the agency shall include in the statement required under section 553(c) of this title, the reasons why the system of records is to be exempted from a provision of this section.

(k) Specific exemptions

The head of any agency may promulgate rules, in accordance with the requirements (including general notice) of sections 553(b)(1), (2), and (3), (c), and (e) of this title, to exempt any system of records within the agency from subsections (c)(3), (d), (e)(1), (e)(4)(G), (H), and (I) and (f) of this section if the system of records is—

(1) subject to the provisions of section 552(b)(1) of this title;

(2) investigatory material compiled for law enforcement purposes, other than material within the scope of subsection (j)(2) of this section: Provided, however, That if any individual is denied any right, privilege, or benefit that he would otherwise be entitled by Federal law, or for which he would otherwise be eligible, as a result of the maintenance of such material, such material shall be provided to such individual, except to the extent that the disclosure of such material would reveal the identity of a source who furnished information to the Government under an express promise that the identity of the source would be held in confidence, or, prior

to the effective date of this section, under an implied promise that the identity of the source would be held in confidence;

(3) maintained in connection with providing protective services to the President of the United States or other individuals pursuant to section 3056 of Title 18;

(4) required by statute to be maintained and used solely as statistical records;

(5) investigatory material compiled solely for the purpose of determining suitability, eligibility, or qualifications for Federal civilian employment, military service, Federal contracts, or access to classified information, but only to the extent that the disclosure of such material would reveal the identity of a source who furnished information to the Government under an express promise that the identity of the source would be held in confidence, or, prior to the effective date of this section, under an implied promise that the identity of the source would be held in confidence;

(6) testing or examination material used solely to determine individual qualifications for appointment or promotion in the Federal service the disclosure of which would compromise the objectivity or fairness of the testing or examination process; or

(7) evaluation material used to determine potential for promotion in the armed services, but only to the extent that the disclosure of such material would reveal the identity of a source who furnished information to the Government under an express promise that the identity of the source would be held in confidence, or, prior to the effective date of this section, under an implied promise that the identity of the source would be held in confidence.

At the time rules are adopted under this subsection, the agency shall include in the statement required under section 553(c) of this title, the reasons why the system of records is to be exempted from a provision of this section.

(1)(1) Archival records

Each agency record which is accepted by the Archivist of the United States for storage, processing, and servicing in accordance with section 3103 of Title 44 shall, for the purposes of this section, be considered to be maintained by the agency which deposited the record and shall be subject to the provisions of this section. The Archivist of the United States shall not disclose the record except to the agency which maintains the record, or under rules established by that agency which are not inconsistent with the provisions of this section.

(2) Each agency record pertaining to an identifiable individual which was transferred to the National Archives of the United States as a record which has sufficient historical or other value to warrant its continued preservation by the United States Government, prior to the effective date of this section, shall, for the purposes of this section, be considered to be maintained by the National Archives and shall not be subject to the provisions of this section, except that a statement generally describing such records (modeled after the requirements relating to records subject to subsections (e)(4)(A) through (G) of this section) shall be published in the Federal Register.

(3) Each agency record pertaining to an identifiable individual which is transferred to the National Archives of the United States as a record which has sufficient historical or other value to warrant its continued preservation by the United States

Government, on or after the effective date of this section, shall, for the purposes of this section, be considered to be maintained by the National Archives and shall be exempt from the requirements of this section except subsections (e)(4)(A) through (G) and (e)(9) of this section.

(m) Government contractors

(1) When an agency provides by a contract for the operation by or on behalf of the agency of a system of records to accomplish an agency function, the agency shall, consistent with its authority, cause the requirements of this section to be applied to such system. For purposes of subsection (i) of this section any such contractor and any employee of such contractor, if such contract is agreed to on or after the effective date of this section, shall be considered to be an employee of an agency.

(2) A consumer reporting agency to which a record is disclosed under section 3711(e) of Title 31 shall not be considered a contractor for the purposes of this section.

(n) Mailing lists

An individual's name and address may not be sold or rented by an agency unless such action is specifically authorized by law. This provision shall not be construed to require the withholding of names and addresses otherwise permitted to be made public.

(o) Matching agreements—

(1) No record which is contained in a system of records may be disclosed to a recipient agency or non-Federal agency for use in a computer matching program except pursuant to a written agreement between the source agency and the recipient agency or non-Federal agency specifying—

(A) the purpose and legal authority for conducting the program;

(B) the justification for the program and the anticipated results, including a specific estimate of any savings;

(C) a description of the records that will be matched, including each data element that will be used, the approximate number of records that will be matched, and the projected starting and completion dates of the matching program;

(D) procedures for providing individualized notice at the time of application, and notice periodically thereafter as directed by the Data Integrity Board of such agency (subject to guidance provided by the Director of the Office of Management and Budget pursuant to subsection (v)), to—

(i) applicants for and recipients of financial assistance or payments under Federal benefit programs, and

(ii) applicants for and holders of positions as Federal personnel, that any information provided by such applicants, recipients, holders, and individuals may be subject to verification through matching programs;

(E) procedures for verifying information produced in such matching program as required by subsection (p);

(F) procedures for the retention and timely destruction of identifiable records created by a recipient agency or non-Federal agency in such matching program;

(G) procedures for ensuring the administrative, technical, and physical security of the records matched and the results of such programs;

(H) prohibitions on duplication and redisclosure of records provided by the source agency within or outside the recipient agency or the non-Federal agency, except where required by law or essential to the conduct of the matching program;

(I) procedures governing the use by a recipient agency or non-Federal agency of records provided in a matching program by a source agency, including procedures governing return of the records to the source agency or destruction of records used in such program;

(J) information on assessments that have been made on the accuracy of the records that will be used in such matching program; and

(K) that the Comptroller General may have access to all records of a recipient agency or a non-Federal agency that the Comptroller General deems necessary in order to monitor or verify compliance with the agreement.

(2)(A) A copy of each agreement entered into pursuant to paragraph (1) shall—

(i) be transmitted to the Committee on Governmental Affairs of the Senate and the Committee on Government Operations of the House of Representatives; and

(ii) be available upon request to the public.

(B) No such agreement shall be effective until 30 days after the date on which such a copy is transmitted pursuant to subparagraph (A)(i).

(C) Such an agreement shall remain in effect only for such period, not to exceed 18 months, as the Data Integrity Board of the agency determines is appropriate in light of the purposes, and length of time necessary for the conduct, of the matching program.

(D) Within 3 months prior to the expiration of such an agreement pursuant to subparagraph (C), the Data Integrity Board of the agency may, without additional review, renew the matching agreement for a current, ongoing matching program for not more than one additional year if—

(i) such program will be conducted without any change; and

(ii) each party to the agreement certifies to the Board in writing that the program has been conducted in compliance with the agreement.

(p) Verification and opportunity to contest findings

(1) In order to protect any individual whose records are used in a matching program, no recipient agency, non-Federal agency, or source agency may suspend, terminate, reduce, or make a final denial of any financial assistance or payment under a Federal benefit program to such individual, or take other adverse action against such individual, as a result of information produced by such matching program, until—

(A)(i) the agency has independently verified the information; or

(ii) the Data Integrity Board of the agency, or in the case of a non-Federal agency the Data Integrity Board of the source agency, determines in accordance with guidance issued by the Director of the Office of Management and Budget that—

(I) the information is limited to identification and amount of benefits paid by the source agency under a Federal benefit program; and

(II) there is a high degree of confidence that the information provided to the recipient agency is accurate;

(B) the individual receives a notice from the agency containing a statement of its findings and informing the individual of the opportunity to contest such findings; and

(C)(i) the expiration of any time period established for the program by statute or regulation for the individual to respond to that notice; or

(ii) in the case of a program for which no such period is established, the end of the 30-day period beginning on the date on which notice under subparagraph (B) is mailed or otherwise provided to the individual.

(2) Independent verification referred to in paragraph (1) requires investigation and confirmation of specific information relating to an individual that is used as a basis for an adverse action against the individual, including where applicable investigation and confirmation of—

(A) the amount of any asset or income involved;

(B) whether such individual actually has or had access to such asset or income for such individual's own use; and

(C) the period or periods when the individual actually had such asset or income.

(3) Notwithstanding paragraph (1), an agency may take any appropriate action otherwise prohibited by such paragraph if the agency determines that the public health or public safety may be adversely affected or significantly threatened during any notice period required by such paragraph.

(q) Sanctions

(1) Notwithstanding any other provision of law, no source agency may disclose any record which is contained in a system of records to a recipient agency or non-Federal agency for a matching program if such source agency has reason to believe that the requirements of subsection (p), or any matching agreement entered into pursuant to subsection (o), or both, are not being met by such recipient agency.

(2) No source agency may renew a matching agreement unless—

(A) the recipient agency or non-Federal agency has certified that it has complied with the provisions of that agreement;

and

(B) the source agency has no reason to believe that the certification is inaccurate.

(r) Report on new systems and matching programs

Each agency that proposes to establish or make a significant change in a system of records or a matching program shall provide adequate advance notice of any such proposal (in duplicate) to the Committee on Government Operations of the House of Representatives, the Committee on Governmental Affairs of the Senate, and the Office of Management and Budget in order to permit an evaluation of the probable or potential effect of such proposal on the privacy or other rights of individuals.

(s) Biennial report

The President shall biennially submit to the Speaker of the House of Representatives and the President pro tempore of the Senate a report—

(1) describing the actions of the Director of the Office of Management and Budget pursuant to section 6 of the Privacy Act of 1974 during the preceding two years;

(2) describing the exercise of individual rights of access and amendment under this section during such years;

(3) identifying changes in or additions to systems of records;

(4) containing such other information concerning administration of this section as may be necessary or useful to the Congress in reviewing the effectiveness of this section in carrying out the purposes of the Privacy Act of 1974.

(t) Effect of other laws

(1) No agency shall rely on any exemption contained in section 552 of this title to withhold from an individual any record which is otherwise accessible to such individual under the provisions of this section.

(2) No agency shall rely on any exemption in this section to withhold from an individual any record which is otherwise accessible to such individual under the provisions of section 552 of this title.

(u) Data Integrity Boards

(1) Every agency conducting or participating in a matching program shall establish a Data Integrity Board to oversee and coordinate among the various components of such agency the agency's implementation of this section.

(2) Each Data Integrity Board shall consist of senior officials designated by the head of the agency, and shall include any senior official designated by the head of the agency as responsible for implementation of this section, and the inspector general of the agency, if any. The inspector general shall not serve as chairman of the Data Integrity Board.

(3) Each Data Integrity Board—

(A) shall review, approve, and maintain all written agreements for receipt or disclosure of agency records for matching programs to ensure compliance with subsection (o), and all relevant statutes, regulations, and guidelines;

(B) shall review all matching programs in which the agency has participated during the year, either as a source agency or recipient agency, determine compliance with applicable laws, regulations, guidelines, and agency agreements, and assess the costs and benefits of such programs;

(C) shall review all recurring matching programs in which the agency has participated during the year, either as a source agency or recipient agency, for continued justification for such disclosures;

(D) shall compile an annual report, which shall be submitted to the head of the agency and the Office of Management and Budget and made available to the public on request, describing the matching activities of the agency, including—

(i) matching programs in which the agency has participated as a source agency or recipient agency;

(ii) matching agreements proposed under subsection (o) that were disapproved by the Board;

(iii) any changes in membership or structure of the Board in the preceding year;

(iv) the reasons for any waiver of the requirement in paragraph (4) of this section for completion and submission of a cost-benefit analysis prior to the approval of a matching program;

(v) any violations of matching agreements that have been alleged or identified and any corrective action taken; and

(vi) any other information required by the Director of the Office of Management and Budget to be included in such report;

(E) shall serve as a clearinghouse for receiving and providing information on the accuracy, completeness, and reliability of records used in matching programs;

(F) shall provide interpretation and guidance to agency components and personnel on the requirements of this section for matching programs;

(G) shall review agency recordkeeping and disposal policies and practices for matching programs to assure compliance with this section; and

(H) may review and report on any agency matching activities that are not matching programs.

(4)(A) Except as provided in subparagraphs (B) and (C), a Data Integrity Board shall not approve any written agreement for a matching program unless the agency has completed and submitted to such Board a cost-benefit analysis of the proposed program and such analysis demonstrates that the program is likely to be cost effective.

(B) The Board may waive the requirements of subparagraph (A) of this paragraph if it determines in writing, in accordance with guidelines prescribed by the Director of the Office of Management and Budget, that a cost-benefit analysis is not required.

(C) A cost-benefit analysis shall not be required under subparagraph (A) prior to the initial approval of a written agreement for a matching program that is specifically required by statute. Any subsequent written agreement for such a program shall not be approved by the Data Integrity Board unless the agency has submitted a cost-benefit analysis of the program as conducted under the preceding approval of such agreement.

(5)(A) If a matching agreement is disapproved by a Data Integrity Board, any party to such agreement may appeal the disapproval to the Director of the Office of Management and Budget. Timely notice of the filing of such an appeal shall be provided by the Director of the Office of Management and Budget to the Committee on Governmental Affairs of the Senate and the Committee on Government Operations of the House of Representatives.

(B) The Director of the Office of Management and Budget may approve a matching agreement notwithstanding the disapproval of a Data Integrity Board if the Director determines that—

(i) the matching program will be consistent with all applicable legal, regulatory, and policy requirements;

(ii) there is adequate evidence that the matching agreement will be cost-effective; and

(iii) the matching program is in the public interest.

(C) The decision of the Director to approve a matching agreement shall not take effect until 30 days after it is reported to committees described in subparagraph (A).

(D) If the Data Integrity Board and the Director of the Office of Management and Budget disapprove a matching program proposed by the inspector general of an agency, the inspector general may report the disapproval to the head of the agency and to the Congress.

(6) The Director of the Office of Management and Budget shall, annually during the first 3 years after the date of enactment of this subsection and biennially thereafter, consolidate in a report to the Congress the information contained in the reports from the various Data Integrity Boards under paragraph (3)(D). Such report shall include detailed information about costs and benefits of matching programs that are conducted during the period covered by such consolidated report, and shall identify each waiver granted by a Data Integrity Board of the requirement for completion and submission of a cost-benefit analysis and the reasons for granting the waiver.

(7) In the reports required by paragraphs (3)(D) and (6), agency matching activities that are not matching programs may be reported on an aggregate basis, if and to the extent necessary to protect ongoing law enforcement or counterintelligence investigations.

(v) Office of Management and Budget responsibilities

The Director of the Office of Management and Budget shall—

(1) develop and, after notice and opportunity for public comment, prescribe guidelines and regulations for the use of agencies in implementing the provisions of this section; and

(2) provide continuing assistance to and oversight of the implementation of this section by agencies.

The following section was enacted as part of the Privacy Act, but was not codified; it may be found at § 552a (note).

Sec. 7 (a)(1) It shall be unlawful for any Federal, State or local government agency to deny to any individual any right, benefit, or privilege provided by law because of such individual's refusal to disclose his social security account number.

(2) the provisions of paragraph (1) of this subsection shall not apply with respect to—

(A) any disclosure which is required by Federal statute, or

(B) any disclosure of a social security number to any Federal, State, or local agency maintaining a system of records in existence and operating before January 1, 1975, if such disclosure was required under statute or regulation adopted prior to such date to verify the identity of an individual.

(b) Any Federal, State or local government agency which requests an individual to disclose his social security account number shall inform that individual whether that disclosure is mandatory or voluntary, by what statutory or other authority such number is solicited, and what uses will be made of it.

The following sections were enacted as part of Pub.L. 100-503, the Computer Matching and Privacy Protection Act of 1988; they may be found at § 552a (note).

Sec. 6 Functions of the Director of the Office of Management and Budget.

(b) Implementation Guidance for Amendments— The Director shall, pursuant to section 552a(v) of Title 5, United States Code, develop guidelines and regulations for the use of agencies in implementing the amendments made by this Act not later than 8 months after the date of enactment of this Act.

Sec. 9 Rules of Construction.

Nothing in the amendments made by this Act shall be construed to authorize—

(1) the establishment or maintenance by any agency of a national data bank that combines, merges, or links information on individuals maintained in systems of records by other Federal agencies;

(2) the direct linking of computerized systems of records maintained by Federal agencies;

(3) the computer matching of records not otherwise authorized by law; or

(4) the disclosure of records for computer matching, except to a Federal, State, or local agency.

Sec. 10 Effective Dates.

(a) In General— Except as provided in subsection (b), the amendments made by this Act shall take effect 9 months after the date of enactment of this Act.

(b) Exceptions— The amendment made by sections 3(b) [Notice of Matching Programs - Report to Congress and the Office of Management and Budget], 6 [Functions of the Director of the Office of Management and Budget], 7 [Compilation of Rules and Notices] and 8 [Annual Report] of this Act shall take effect upon enactment.

TEXAS OPEN RECORDS ACT (REV. 1995)

Government Code Chapter 552. Public Information SUBCHAPTER A. GENERAL PROVISIONS § 552.001. Policy; Construction (a) Under the fundamental philosophy of the American constitutional form of representative government that adheres to the principle that government is the servant and not the master of the people, it is the policy of this state that each person is entitled, unless otherwise expressly provided by law, at all times to complete information about the affairs of government and the official acts of public officials and employees. The people, in delegating authority, do not give their public servants the right to decide what is good for the people to know and what is not good for them to know. The people insist on remaining informed so that they may retain control over the instruments they have created. The provisions of this chapter shall be liberally construed to implement this policy. (b) This chapter shall be liberally construed in favor of granting a request for information. § 552.002. Definition of Public Information; Media Containing Public Information (a) In this chapter, "public information" means information that is collected, assembled, or maintained under a law or ordinance or in connection with the transaction of official business: (1) by a governmental body; or (2) for a governmental body and the governmental body owns the information or has a right of access to it. (b) The media on which public information is recorded include: (1) paper; (2) film; (3) a magnetic, optical, or solid state device that can store an electronic signal; (4) tape; (5) Mylar; (6) linen; (7) silk; and (8) vellum. (c) The general forms in which the media containing public information exist include a book, paper, letter, document, printout, photograph, film, tape, microfiche, microfilm, photostat, sound recording, map and drawing and a voice, data, or video representation held in computer memory. § 552.003. Definitions In this chapter: (1) "Governmental body": (A) means: (i) a board, commission, department, committee, institution, agency, or office that is within or is created by the executive or legislative branch of state government and that is directed by one or more elected or appointed members; (ii) a county commissioners court in the state; (iii) a municipal governing body in the state; (iv) a deliberative body that has rulemaking or quasi- judicial power and that is classified as a department, agency, or political subdivision of a county or municipality; (v) a school district board of trustees; (vi) a county board of school trustees; (vii) a county board of education; (viii) the governing board of a special district; (ix) the governing body of a nonprofit corporation organized under Chapter 76, Acts of the 43rd Legislature, 1st Called Session, 1933 (Article 1434a, Vernon's Texas Civil Statutes), that provides a water supply or wastewater service, or both, and is exempt from ad valorem taxation under Section 11.30, Tax Code; and (x) the part, section, or portion of an organization, corporation, commission, committee, institution, or agency that spends or that is supported in whole or in part by public funds. (B) does not include the judiciary.

(2) "Manipulation" means the process of modifying, reordering, or decoding of information with human intervention. (3) "Processing" means the execution of a sequence of coded instructions by a computer producing a result. (4) "Programming" means the process of producing a sequence of coded instructions that can be executed by a computer. (5) "Public funds" means funds of the state or of a governmental subdivision of the state. (6) "Requestor" means a person who submits a request to a governmental body for inspection of copies of public information. § 552.004. Preservation of Information A governmental body or, for information of an elective county office, the elected county officer, may determine a time for which information that is not currently in use will be preserved, subject to any applicable rule or law governing the destruction and other disposition of state and local government records or public information. § 552.005. Effect of Chapter on Scope of Civil Discovery (a) This chapter does not affect the scope of civil discovery under the Texas Rules of Civil Procedure. (b) Exceptions from disclosure under this chapter do not create new privileges from discovery. § 552.006. Effect of Chapter on Withholding Public Information This chapter does not authorize withholding of public information or limit the availability of public information to the public, except as expressly provided by this chapter. § 552.007. Voluntary Disclosure of Certain Records When Disclosure Not Required (a) This chapter does not prohibit a governmental body or its officer for public information from voluntarily making part or all of its information available to the public, unless the disclosure is expressly prohibited by law or the information is confidential under law. (b) Public information made available under Subsection (a) must be made available to any person. § 552.008. Information for Legislative Purposes (a) This chapter does not grant authority to withhold information from individual members, agencies, or committees of the legislature to use for legislative purposes. (b) A governmental body on request by an individual member, agency, or committee of the legislature shall provide public information, including confidential information, to the requesting member, agency, or committee for inspection or duplication in accordance with this chapter if the requesting member, agency or committee states that the public information is requested under this chapter for legislative purposes. A governmental body, by providing public information under this section that is confidential or otherwise excepted from required disclosure under law, does not waive or affect the confidentiality of the information for purposes of state or federal law or waive the right to assert exceptions to required disclosure of the information in the future. The governmental body may require the requesting individual member of the legislature, the requesting legislative agency or committee, or the members or employees of the requesting entity who will view or handle information that is received under this section and that is confidential under law to sign a confidentiality agreement that covers the information and requires that: (1) the information not be disclosed outside the requesting entity, or within the requesting entity for purposes other than the purpose for which it was received; (2) the information is labeled as confidential; (3) the information be kept securely; or (4) the number of copies made of the information or the notes taken from the information that implicate the confidential nature of the information be controlled, with all copies or notes that are not destroyed

or returned to the governmental body remaining confidential and subject to the confidentiality agreement. (c) This section does not affect: (1) the right of an individual member, agency, or committee of the legislature to obtai information from a governmental body under other law, including under the rules of either house of the legislature; (2) the procedures under which the information is obtained under other law; or (3) the use that may be made of the information obtained under other law. SUBCHAPTER B. RIGHT OF ACCESS TO PUBLIC INFORMATION § 552.021. Availability of Public Information Public information is available to the public at a minimum during the normal business hours of the governmental body. § 552.022. Categories of Public Information; Examples Without limiting the amount or kind of information that is public information under this chapter, the following categories of information are public information: (1) a completed report, audit, evaluation, or investigation made of, for, or by a governmental body; (2) the name, sex, ethnicity, salary, title, and dates of employment of each employee and officer of a governmental body; (3) information in an account, voucher, or contract relating to the receipt or expenditure of public or other funds by a governmental body, if the information is not otherwise made confidential by law; (4) the name of each official and the final record of voting on all proceedings in a governmental body; (5) all working papers, research material, and information used to estimate the need for or expenditure of public funds or taxes by a governmental body, on completion of the estimate; (6) the name, place of business, and the name of the municipality to which local sales and use taxes are credited, if any, for the named person, of a person reporting or paying sales and use taxes under Chapter 151, Tax Code; (7) a description of an agency's central and field organization, including: (A) the established places at which the public may obtain information, submit informa- tion or requests, or obtain decisions; (B) the employees from whom the public may obtain information, submit information or requests, or obtain decisions; (C) in the case of a uniformed service, the members from whom the public may obtain information, submit information or requests, or obtain decisions; and (D) the methods by which the public may obtain information, submit information or requests, or obtain decisions; (8) a statement of the general course and method by which an agency's functions are channeled and determined, including the nature and requirements of all formal and informal policies and procedures; (9) a rule of procedure, a description of forms available or the places at which forms may be obtained, and instructions relating to the scope and content of all papers, reports, or examinations; (10) a substantive rule of general applicability adopted or issued by an agency as authorized by law, and a statement of general policy or interpretation of general applicability formulated and adopted by an agency; (11) each amendment, revision, or repeal of information described by Subdivisions (7)-(10); (12) final opinions, including concurring and dissenting opinions, and orders issued in the adjudication of cases; (13) a policy statement or interpretation that has been adopted or issued by an agency; (14) administrative staff manuals and instructions to staff that affect a member of the public; (15) information regarded as open to the public under an agency's policies; (16) information that is in a bill for attorney's fees and that is not privileged under the attorney-client privilege or confidential under other law; (17) information that is also contained in a public court record; and (18) a settlement agreement to which a governmental body is a party unless the agreement is confidential under other law. § 552.023. Special Right of Access to Confidential Information (a) A person or a person's authorized representative has a special right of access, beyond the right of the general public, to information held by a governmental body that relates to the person and that is protected from public disclosure by laws intended to protect that person's privacy interests. (b) A governmental body may not deny access to information to the person, or the person's representative, to whom the information relates on the grounds that the information is considered confidential by privacy principles under this chapter but may assert as grounds for denial of access other provisions of this chapter or other law that are not intended to protect the person's privacy interests. (c) A release of information under Subsections (a) and (b) is not an offense under Section 552.352. (d) A person who receives information under this section may disclose the information to others only to the extent consistent with the authorized purposes for which consent to release the information was obtained. (e) Access to information under this section shall be provided in the manner prescribed by Sections 552.229 and 552.307. ¤ 552.024. Electing to Disclose Address and Telephone Number (a) Each employee or official of a governmental body and each former employee or official of a governmental body shall choose whether to allow public access to the information in the custody of the governmental body that relates to the person's home address, home telephone number, or social security number, or that reveals whether the person has family members. (b) Each employee and official and each former employee and official shall state that person's choice under Subsection (a) to the main personnel officer of the governmental body in a signed writing not later than the 14th day after the date on which: (1) the employee begins employment with the governmental body; (2) the official is elected or appointed; or (3) the former employee or official ends service with the governmental body. (c) If the employee or official or former employee or official chooses not to allow public access to the information, the information is protected under Subchapter C. (d) If an employee or official or a former employee or official fails to state the person's choice within the period established by this section, the information is subject to public access. (e) An employee or official or former employee or official of a governmental body who wishes to close or open public access to the information may request in writing that the main personnel officer of the governmental body close or open access. § 552.025. Tax Rulings and Opinions (a) A governmental body with taxing authority that issues a written determination letter, technical advice memorandum, or ruling that concerns a tax matter shall index the letter, memorandum, or ruling by subject matter. (b) On request, the governmental body shall make the index prepared under Subsection (a) and the document itself available to the public, subject to the provisions of this chapter. (c) Subchapter C does not authorize withholding from the public or limiting the availability to the public of a written determination letter, technical advice memorandum, or ruling that concerns a tax matter and that is issued by a governmental body with taxing authority. § 552.026. Education Records This chapter does not require the release of information contained in education records of an educational agency or institution, except in conformity with the Family Educational Rights and Privacy Act of 1974, Sec. 513, Pub.L. No. 93-380, 20 U.S.C. Sec. 1232g. § 552.027. Exception: Information Available Commercially; Resource Material (a) A governmental body is not required under this chapter to allow the inspection of or to provide a copy of information in a commercial book or publication purchased or acquired by the governmental body for research purposes if the book or publication is commercially available to the public. (b) Although information in a book or publication may be made available to the public as a resource material, such as a library book, a governmental body is not required to make a copy of the information in response to a request for public information. (c) A governmental body shall allow the inspection of information in a book or publication that is made part of, incorporated into, or referred to in a rule or policy of a governmental body. Text of section 552.027 as added by Act of May 18, 1995, HB 949, section 1, 74th Leg., R.S. (effective immediately): ¤ 552.027. Request for Information From Incarcerated Individual (a) A governmental body is not required to accept or comply with a request for information from an individual who is imprisoned or confined in a correctional facility. (b) Subsection (a) does not prohibit a governmental body from disclosing to an individual described by that subsection information held by the governmental body pertaining to that individual. (c) In this section, "correctional facility" has the meaning assigned by Section 1.07(a), Penal Code. SUBCHAPTER C. INFORMATION EXCEPTED FROM REQUIRED DISCLOSURE § 552.101. Exception: Confidential Information Information is excepted from the requirements of Section 552.021 if it is information considered to be confidential by law, either constitutional, statutory, or by judicial decision. § 552.102. Exception: Personnel Information (a) Information is excepted from the requirements of Section 552.021 if it is information in a personnel file, the disclosure of which would constitute a clearly unwarranted invasion of personal privacy, except that all information in the personnel file of an employee of a governmental body is to be made available to that employee or the employee's designated representative as public information is made available under this chapter. The exception to public disclosure created by this subsection is in addition to any exception created by Section 552.024. Public access to personnel information covered by Section 552.024 is denied to the extent provided by that section. (b) Information is excepted from the requirements of Section 552.021 if it is a transcript from an institution of higher education maintained in the personnel file of a professional public school employee, except that this section does not exempt from disclosure the degree obtained or the curriculum on a transcript in the personnel file of the employee. § 552.103. Exception: Litigation or Settlement Negotiations Involving the State or a Political Subdivision (a) Information is excepted from the requirements of Section 552.021 if it is information: (1) relating to litigation of a civil or criminal nature or settlement negotiations, to which the state or a political subdivision is or may be a party or to which an officer or employee of the state or a political subdivision, as a consequence of the person's office or employment, is or may be a party; and (2) that the attorney general or the attorney of the political subdivision has determined should be withheld from public inspection. (b) For purposes of this section, the state or a political subdivision is considered to be a party to litigation of a criminal nature until the applicable statute of limitations has expired or until the defendant has exhausted all appellate and postconviction remedies in state and federal court. § 552.104. Exception: Information Related to Competition or Bidding Information is excepted from the requirements of Section 552.021 if it is information that, if released, would give advantage to a competitor or bidder. § 552.105. Exception: Information Related to Location or Price of Property Information is excepted from the requirements of Section 552.021 if it is information relating to: (1) the location of real or personal property for a public purpose prior to public announcement of the project; or (2) appraisals or purchase price of real or personal property for a public purpose prior to the formal award of contracts for the property. § 552.106. Exception: Certain Legislative Documents A draft or working paper involved in the preparation of proposed legislation is excepted from the requirements of Section 552.021. § 552.107. Exception: Certain Legal Matters Information is excepted from the requirements of Section 552.021 if: (1) it is information that the attorney general or an attorney of a political subdivision is prohibited from disclosing because of a duty to the client under the Texas Rules of Civil Evidence, the Texas Rules of Criminal Evidence, or the Texas Disciplinary Rules of Professional Conduct; or (2) a court by order has prohibited disclosure of the information. § 552.108. Exception: Certain Law Enforcement and Prosecutorial Information (a) Information held by a law enforcement agency or prosecutor that deals with the detection, investigation, or prosecution of crime is excepted from the requirements of Section 552.021. (b) An internal record or notation of a law enforcement agency or prosecutor that is maintained for internal use in matters relating to law enforcement or prosecution is excepted from the requirements of Section 552.021 § 552.109. Exception: Certain Private Communications of an Elected Office Holder Private correspondence or communications of an elected office holder relating to matters the disclosure of which would constitute an invasion of privacy are excepted from the requirements of Section 552.021. § 552.110. Exception: Trade Secrets, Commercial Information, or Financial Information A trade secret or commercial or financial information obtained from a person and privileged or confidential by statute or judicial decision is excepted from the requirements of Section 552.021. § 552.111. Exception: Agency Memoranda An interagency or intraagency memorandum or letter that would not be available by law to a party in litigation with the agency is excepted from the requirements of Section 552.021. § 552.112. Exception: Certain Information Relating to Regulation of Financial Institutions or Securities (a) Information is excepted from the requirements of Section 552.021 if it is information contained in or relating to examination, operating, or condition reports prepared by or for an agency responsible for the regulation or supervision of financial institutions or securities, or both. (b) In this section, "securities" has the meaning assigned by The Securities Act (Article 581-1 et seq., Vernon's Texas Civil Statutes). § 552.113. Exception: Geological or Geophysical Information Information is excepted from the requirements of Section 552.021 if it is : (1) an electric log confidential under Subchapter M, Chapter 91, Natural Resources Code; (2) geological or geophysical information or data, including maps concerning wells, except information filed in connection with an application or proceeding before an agency; or (3) confidential under Subsections (c) through (f). (b) Information that is shown to or examined by an employee of the General Land Office, but not retained in the land office, is not considered to be filed with the land office. (c) In this section: (1) "Confidential material" includes all well logs, geological, geophysical, geochemical, and other similar data, including maps and other interpretations of the material filed in the General Land Office; (A) in connection with any administrative application or proceeding before the land commissioner, the school land board, any board for lease, or the commissioner's or board's staff; or (B) in compliance with the requirements of any law, rule, lease, or agreement. (2) "Basic electric logs" has the same meaning as it has in Chapter 91, Natural Resources Code. (3) "Administrative Applications" and "administrative proceedings" include applications for pooling or unitization, review of shut-in royalty payments, review of leases or other agreements to determine their validity, review of any plan of operations, review of the obligation to drill offset wells, or an application to pay compensatory royalty. (d) Confidential material, except basic electric logs, filed with the General Land Office on or after September 1, 1985, is public information and is available to the public under Section 552.021 on and after the later of: (1) five years from the filing date of the confidential material; or (2) one year from the expiration, termination, or forfeiture of the lease in connection with which the confidential material was filed. (e) Basic electric logs filed in the General Land Office on or after September 1, 1985, are either public information or confidential material to the same extent and for the same periods provided for the same logs by Chapter 91, Natural Resources Code. A person may request that a basic electric log that has been filed in the General Land Office be made confidential by filing with the land office a copy of the written request for confidentiality made to the Railroad Commission of Texas for the same log. (f) The following are public information: (1) basic electric logs filed in the General Land office before September 1, 1985; and (2) confidential material, except basic electric logs, filed in the General Land Office before September 1, 1985, provided, that Subsection (d) governs the disclosure of that confidential material filed in connection with a lease that is a valid and subsisting lease on September 1, 1995. (g) Confidential material may be disclosed at any time if the person filing the material, or the person's successor in interest in the lease in connection with which the confidential material was filed, consents in writing to its release. A party consenting to the disclosure of confidential material may restrict the manner of disclosure and the person or persons to whom the disclosure may be made. (h) Notwithstanding the confidential nature of the material described in this section, the material may be used by the General Land Office in the enforcement, by administrative proceeding or litigation, of the laws governing the sale and lease of public lands and minerals, the regulations of the land office, the school land board, or of any board for lease, or the terms of any lease, pooling or unitilization agreement, or any other agreement or grant. (i) An administrative hearings officer may order that confidential material introduced in an administrative proceeding remain confidential until the proceeding is finally concluded, or for the period provided in Subsection (d), whichever is later. (j) Confidential material examined by an administrative hearings officer during the course of an administrative proceeding for the purpose of determining its admissibility as evidence shall not be considered to have been filed in the General Land Office to the extent that the confidential material is not introduced into evidence at the proceeding. (k) This section does not prevent a person from asserting that any confidential material is exempt from disclosure as a trade secret or commercial information under Section 552.110 or under any other basis permitted by law. § 552.114. Exception: Student Records (a) Information is excepted from the requirements of Section 552.021 if it is information in a student record at an educational institution funded wholly or partly by state revenue. (b) A record under Subsection (a) shall be made available on the request of: (1) educational institution personnel; (2) the student involved or the student's parent, legal guardian, or spouse; or (3) a person conducting a child abuse investigation required by Section 34.05, Family Code. § 552.115. Exception: Birth and Death Records A birth or death record maintained by the bureau of vital statistics of the Texas Department of Health is excepted from the requirements of Section 552.021, except that: (1) a birth record is public information and available to the public on and after the 50th anniversary of the date on which the record is filed with the bureau of vital statistics or local registration official; and (2) a death record is public information and available to the public on and after the 25th anniversary of the date on which the record is filed with the bureau of vital statistics or local registration official. § 552.116. Exception: State Auditor Working Papers An audit working paper of the state auditor is excepted from the requirements of Section 552.021. § 552.117. Exception: Certain Addresses, Telephone Numbers, Social Security Numbers, and Personal Family Information Information is excepted from the requirements of Section 552.021 if it is information that relates to the home address, home telephone number, or social security number, or that reveals whether the following person has family members: (1) a current or former official or employee of a governmental body, except as otherwise provided by Section 552.024; or (2) a peace officer as defined by Article 2.12, Code of Criminal Procedure, or a security officer commissioned under Section 51.212, Education Code. § 552.118. Exception: Triplicate Prescription Form Information is excepted from the requirements of Section 552.021 if it is information on or derived from a triplicate prescription form filed with the Department of Public Safety under Section 481.075, Health and Safety Code. § 552.119. Exception: Photograph of Peace Officer or Certain Security Guards (a) A photograph that depicts a peace officer as defined by Article 2.12, Code of Criminal Procedure, or a security officer commissioned under Section 51.212, Education Code, the release of which would endanger the life or physical safety of the officer, is excepted from the requirements of Section 552.021 unless: (1) the officer is under indictment or charged with an offense by information; (2) the officer is a party in a fire or police civil service hearing or a case in arbitration; or (3) the photograph is introduced as evidence in a judicial proceeding. (b) A photograph exempt from disclosure under Subsection (a) may be made public only if the peace officer or security officer gives written consent to the disclosure. § 552.120. Exception: Certain Rare Books and Original Manuscripts A rare book or original manuscript that was not created or maintained in the conduct of official business of a governmental body and that is held by a private or public archival and manuscript repository for the purpose of historical research is excepted from the requirements of Section 552.021. § 552.121. Exception: Certain Documents Held for Historical Research An oral history interview, personal paper, unpublished letter, or organizational record of a nongovernmental entity that was not created or maintained in the conduct of official business of a governmental body and that is held by a private or public archival and manuscript repository for the purpose of historical research is excepted from the requirements of Section 552.021 to the extent that the archival and manuscript repository and the donor of the interview, paper, letter, or record agree to limit disclosure of the item. § 552.122. Exception: Test Items (a) A test item developed by an educational institution that is funded wholly or in part by state revenue is excepted from the requirements of Section 552.021. (b) A test item developed by a licensing agency or governmental body is excepted from the requirements of Section 552.021. § 552.123. Exception: Name of Applicant for Chief Executive Officer of Institution of Higher Education The name of an applicant for the position of chief executive officer of an institution of higher education is excepted from the requirements of Section 552.021, except that the governing body of the institution must give public notice of the name or names of the finalists being considered for the position at least 21 days before the date of the meeting at which final action or vote is to be taken on the employment of the person. § 552.124. Exception: Records of Library or Library System (a) A record of a library or library system, supported in whole or in part by public funds, that identifies or serves to identify a person who requested, obtained, or used a library material or service is excepted from the requirements of Section 552.021 unless the record is disclosed: (1) because the library or library system determines that disclosure is reasonably necessary for the operation of the library or library system and the record is not confidential under other state or federal law; (2) under Section 552.023; or (3) to a law enforcement agency or a prosecutor under a court order or subpoena obtained after a showing to a district court that: (A) disclosure of the record is necessary to protect the public safety; or (B) the record is evidence of an offense or constitutes evidence that a particular person committed an offense. (b) A record of a library or library system that is excepted from required disclosure under this section is confidential. Text of section 552.124 as added by Act of May 9, 1995, H.B. 2473, 14, 74th Leg., R.S. (effective immediately): ¤ 552.124. Exception: Certain Audits Any documents or information privileged under the Texas Environmental, Health, and Safety Audit Privilege Act are excepted from the requirements of Section 552.021. Text of section 552.124 as added by Act of May 27, 1995, S.B. 1, 31, 74th Leg., R.S. (effective immediately): ¤ 552.124. Exception: Name of Applicant for Superintendent of Public School District The name of an applicant for the position of superintendent of a public school district is excepted from the requirements of Section 552.021, except that the board of trustees must give public notice of the name or names of the finalists being considered for the position at least 21 days before the date of the meeting at which a final action or vote is to be taken on the employment of the person. SUBCHAPTER D. OFFICER FOR PUBLIC INFORMATION § 552.201. Identity of Officer for Public Information (a) The chief administrative officer of a governmental body is the officer for public information, except as provided by Subsection (b). (b) Each elected county officer is the officer for public information and the custodian, as defined by Section 201.003, Local Government Code, of the information created or received by that county officer's office. § 552.202. Department Heads Each department head is an agent of the officer for public information for the purposes of complying with this chapter. § 552.203. General Duties of Officer for Public Information Each officer for public information, subject to penalties provided in this chapter, shall: (1) make public information available for public inspection and copying; (2) carefully protect public information from deterioration, alteration, mutilation, loss, or unlawful removal; and (3) repair, renovate, or rebind public information as necessary to maintain it properly. § 552.204. Scope of Responsibility of Officer for Public Information An officer for public information is responsible for the release of public information as required by this chapter. The officer is not responsible for: (1) the use made of the information by the requestor; or (2) the release of information after it is removed from a record as a result of an update, a correction, or a change of status of the person to whom the information pertains. SUBCHAPTER E. PROCEDURES RELATED TO ACCESS § 552.221. Application for Public Information; Production of Public Information (a) An officer for public information of a governmental body shall promptly produce public information for inspection, duplication, or both on application by any person to the officer. (b) An officer for public information complies with Subsection (a) by: (1) providing the public information for inspection or duplication in the offices of the governmental body; or (2) sending copies of the public information by first class United States mail if the person requesting the information requests that copies be provided by mail and agrees to pay the postage. (c) If the requested information is unavailable at the time of the request to examine because it is in active use or in storage, the officer for public information shall certify this fact in writing to the requestor and set a date and hour within a reasonable time when the information will be available for inspection or duplication. (d) If an officer for public information cannot produce public information for inspection or duplication within 10 calendar days after the date the information is requested under Subsection (a), the officer shall certify that fact in writing to the requestor and set a date and hour within a reasonable time when the information will be available for inspection or duplication. § 552.222. Permissible Inquiry by Governmental Body to Requestor (a) The officer for public information and the officer's agent may not make an inquiry of a requestor except to establish proper identification or except as provided by Subsection (b). (b) If what information is requested is unclear to the governmental body, the governmental body may ask the requestor to clarify the request. If a large amount of information has been requested, the governmental body may discuss with the requestor how the scope of a request might be narrowed, but the governmental body may not inquire into the purpose for which information will be used. § 552.223. Uniform Treatment of Requests for Information The officer for public information or the officer's agent shall treat all requests for information uniformly without regard to the position or occupation of the requestor, the person on whose behalf the request is made, or the status of the individual as a member of the media. § 552.224.

Comfort and Facility The officer for public information or the officer's agent shall give to a requestor all reasonable comfort and facility for the full exercise of the right granted by this chapter. § 552.225. Time for Examination (a) A requestor must complete the examination of the information not later than the 10th day after the date the custodian of the information makes it available to the person. (b) The officer for public information shall extend the initial examination period by an additional 10 days if, within the initial period, the requestor files with the officer for public information a written request for additional time. The officer for public information shall extend an additional examination period by another 10 days if, within the additional period, the requestor files with the officer for public information a written request for more additional time. (c) The time during which a person may examine information may be interrupted by the officer for public information if the information is needed for use by the governmental body. The period of interruption is not considered to be a part of the time during which the person may examine the information. § 552.226. Removal of Original Record This chapter does not authorize a requestor to remove an original copy of a public record from the office of a governmental body. § 552.227. Research of State Library Holdings Not Required An officer for public information or the officer's agent is not required to perform general research within the reference and research archives and holdings of state libraries. § 552.228. Providing Suitable Copy of Public Information Within Reasonable Time (a) It shall be a policy of a governmental body to provide a suitable copy of public information within a reasonable time after the date on which the copy is requested. (b) If public information exists in an electronic or magnetic medium, the requestor may request a copy either on paper or in an electronic medium, such as on diskette or on magnetic tape. A governmental body shall provide a copy in the requested medium if: (1) the governmental body has the technological ability to produce a copy of the requested information in the requested medium; (2) the governmental body is not required to purchase any software or hardware to accommodate the request; and (3) provision of a copy of the information in the requested medium will not violate the terms of any copyright agreement between the governmental body and a third party. (c) If a governmental body is unable to comply with a request to produce a copy of information in a requested medium for any of the reasons described by this section, the governmental body shall provide a paper copy for the requested information or a copy in another medium that is acceptable to the requestor. A governmental body is not required to copy information onto a diskette or other material provided by the requestor but may use its own supplies. § 552.229. Consent to Release Information Under Special Right of Access (a) Consent for the release of information excepted from disclosure to the general public but available to a specific person under Sections 552.023 and 552.307 must be in writing and signed by the specific person or the person's authorized representative. (b) An individual under 18 years of age may consent to the release of information under this section only with the additional written authorization of the individual's parent or guardian. (c) An individual who has been adjudicated incompetent to manage the individual's personal affairs or for whom an attorney ad litem has been appointed may consent to the release of information under this section only by the written authorization of the designated legal guardian or attorney ad litem. § 552.230. Rules of Procedure for Inspection of Public Information A governmental body may promulgate reasonable rules of procedure under which public information may be inspected efficiently, safely, and without delay. § 552.231. Responding to Requests for Information That Require Programming or Manipulation of Data (a) A governmental body shall provide to a requestor the written statement described by Subsection (b) if the governmental body determines: (1) that responding to a request for public information will require programming or manipulation of data; and (2) that: (A) compliance with the request is not feasible or will result in substantial interference with its ongoing operations; or (B) the information could be made available in the requested form only at a cost that covers the programming and manipulation of data. (b) The written statement must include: (1) a statement that the information is not available in the requested form; (2) a description of the form in which the information is available; (3) a description of any contract or services that would be required to provide the information in the requested form; (4) a statement of the estimated cost of providing the information in the requested form as determined in accordance with the rules established by the General Services Commission under Section 552.262; and (5) a statement of the anticipated time required to provide the information in the requested form. (c) The governmental body shall provide the written statement to the requestor within 20 days after the date of the governmental body's receipt of the request. The governmental body has an additional 10 days to provide the statement if the governmental body gives written notice to the requestor, within 20 days after the date of receipt of the request, that the additional time is needed. (d) On providing the written statement to the requestor as required by this section, the governmental body does not have any further obligation to provide the information in the requested form or in the form in which it is available until the requestor states in writing to the governmental body that the requestor: (1) wants the governmental body to provide the information in the requested form according to the cost and time parameters set out in the statement or according to other terms to which the requestor and the governmental body agree; or (2) wants the information in the form in which it is available. (e) The officer for public information of a governmental body shall establish policies that assure the expeditious and accurate processing of requests for information that require programming or manipulation of data. A governmental body shall maintain a file containing all written statements issued under this section in a readily accessible location. SUBCHAPTER F. COST OF COPIES § 552.261. Determining Cost of Copies The cost of obtaining a copy of public information shall be an amount that reasonably includes all costs related to reproducing the public information, including costs of materials, labor, and overhead. If a request is for 50 or fewer pages of paper records, the charge for the public information may not include costs of materials, labor, or overhead, but shall be limited to the photocopying costs, unless the pages to be copies are located in: (1) more than one building; or (2) a remote storage facility. § 552.2611. Charges for Public Records by State Agency (a) The General Services Commission by rule shall specify the methods and procedures that a state agency may use in determining the amounts that the agency should charge to recover the full cost to the agency of providing copies of public records under this chapter. (b) Each state agency by rule shall specify the charges the agency will make for copies of public records. A state agency may establish a charge for a copy of a public record that is equal to the full cost to the agency of providing the copy. (c) A state agency shall pay to the comptroller for deposit in an unobligated account designated by the comptroller in the general revenue fund all money collected by the agency for providing copies of public records. (d) Of the total amount of money deposited in the general revenue fund under Subsection (c), the comptroller may transfer 25 percent of the money collected for providing copies of mailing lists and 15 percent of the money collected for providing copies of other public records to the general revenue fund. (e) The comptroller shall adopt rules to administer Subsections (c) and (d). (f) In this section, "state agency" has the meaning assigned by Section 1.02, State Purchasing and General Services Act (Article 601b, Vernon's Texas Civil Statutes). § 552.262. Rules of the General Services Commission (a) The General Services Commission shall adopt rules for use by each governmental body in determining charges under this subchapter. The rules adopted by the General Services Commission shall be used by each governmental body in determining charges for copies of public information, except to the extent that other law provides for charges for specific kinds of public information. The charges for public information may not be excessive and may not exceed the actual cost of producing the information. A governmental body, other than an agency of state government, may determine its own charges for producing public information but shall not charge more than a 25 percent variance from the rules established by the General Services Commission unless the governmental body requests an exemption under Subsection (c). (b) The rules of the General Services Commission shall prescribe the methods for computing the charges for copies of public information in paper, electronic, and other kinds of media. The rules shall establish costs for various components of charges for public information that shall be used by each governmental body in providing copies of public information. (c) A governmental body may request that it be exempt from part or all of the rules adopted by the General Services Commission for determining charges for public information. The request must be made in writing to the General Services Commission and must state the reason for the exemption. If the General Services Commission determines that good cause exists for exempting a governmental body from a part or all of the rules, the commission shall give written notice of the determination to the governmental body within 90 days of the request. On receipt of the determination, the governmental body may amend its charges for public information according to the determination of the General Services Commission. (d) The General Services Commission shall publish annually in the Texas Register a list of the governmental bodies that have authorization from the General Services Commission to adopt any modified rules for determining the cost of public information. (e) The rules of the General Services Commission do not apply to a state governmental body that is not a state agency for purposes of Subtitle D, Title 10. § 552.263. Bond for Payment of Costs or Cash Prepayment for Preparation of Public Information An officer for public information or the officer's agent may require a deposit or bond for payment of anticipated costs for the preparation of a copy of public information if the charge for the copy is estimated by the governmental body to exceed $100. § 552.264. Copy of Public Information Requested by Member of Legislature One copy of public information that is requested from a state agency by a member of the legislature in the performance of the member's duties shall be provided without charge. § 552.265. Certified Record Provided by District or County Clerk The charge for a copy made in a district or county clerk's office may not be more than the actual cost of copies, as provided by Sections 552.261 and 552.262, unless a certified record, the cost of which is set by law, is requested. § 552.266. Copy of Public Information Provided by Municipal Court Clerk The charge for a copy made by a municipal court clerk shall be the charge provided by municipal ordinance. § 552.267. Waiver or Reduction of Fee for Copy of Public Information (a) A governmental body shall furnish a copy of public information without charge or at a reduced charge if the governmental body determines that waiver or reduction of the fee is in the public interest because furnishing the information primarily benefits the general public. (b) If the cost to a governmental body of processing the collection of a charge for a copy of public information will exceed the amount of the charge, the governmental body may waive the charge. § 552.268. Efficient Use of Public Resources A governmental body shall make reasonably efficient use of supplies and other resources to avoid excessive reproduction costs. § 552.269. Overcharge or Overpayment for Public Information (a) A person who believes the person has been overcharged for a copy of public information may complain to the General Services Commission in writing of the alleged overcharge, setting forth the reasons why the person believes the charges are excessive. The General Services Commission shall review the complaint and make a determination in writing as to the appropriate charge for the requested information. The governmental body shall respond to the General Services Commission to any written questions asked of the governmental body by the commission regarding the charges made for the public information. The response must be made to the General Services Commission within 10 days after the date the questions are received by the governmental body. If the General Services Commission determines that a governmental body has overcharged for requested public information, the governmental body shall promptly adjust its charges in accordance with the determination of the General Services Commission. (b) A person who overpays for a copy of public information because a governmental body refuses or fails to follow the rules for charges adopted by the General Services Commission is entitled to recover three times the amount of the overcharge if the governmental body did not act in good faith in computing the costs. § 552.270. Cost of Government Publication (a) The cost provisions of this subchapter do not apply to a publication that is compiled and printed by or for a governmental body for public dissemination. If the cost of the publication is not determined by state law, a governmental body may determine the charge to be made for the publication. (b) This section does not prohibit a governmental body from providing a publication free of charge if state law does not require that a certain charge be made. Text of section 552.270 as added by Act of May 26, 1995, H.B. 2891, 17, 74th Leg., R.S. (effective September 1, 1995): ¤ 552.270. Report by State Agency on Cost of Copies (a) Not later than

December 1 of each even-numbered year, each state agency shall file a report with the Legislative Budget Board, Comptroller, and General Services Commission describing the agency's procedures for charging and collecting fees for copies of public records. (b) In this section, state agency has the meaning assigned by Section's 1.02(2)(A) and (C), State Purchasing and General Services Act (Article 601b, Vernon's Texas Civil States). § 552.271. Inspection of Paper Record If Copy Not Requested A charge may not be imposed for making available for inspection any public information that exists in a paper record, except that if a requested page contains confidential information that must be edited from the record before the information can be made available, the governmental body may charge for the cost of making a copy of the page from which information must be edited. No charge other than the cost of the copy may be imposed. § 552.272. Inspection of Electronic Record If Copy Not Requested (a) In response to a request to inspect information that exists in an electronic medium and that is not available directly on-line to the requestor, a charge may not be imposed for access to the information, unless complying with the request will require programming or manipulation of data. If programming or manipulation of data is required, the governmental body shall notify the requestor before assembling the information and provide the requestor with an estimate of charges that will be imposed to make the information available. A charge under this section must be assessed in accordance with this subchapter. (b) If public information exists in an electronic form on a computer owned or leased by a governmental body and if the public has direct access to that computer through a computer network or other means, the electronic form of the information may be electronically copied from that computer without charge if accessing the information does not require processing, programming, or manipulation on the government-owned or government-leased computer before the information is copied. (c) If public information exists in an electronic form on a computer owned or leased by a governmental body and if the public has direct access to that computer through a computer network or other means and the information requires processing, programming, or manipulation before it can be electronically copied, a governmental body may impose charges in accordance with this subchapter. (d) If information is created or kept in an electronic form, a governmental body is encouraged to explore options to separate out confidential information and to make public information available to the public through electronic access through a computer network or by other means. § 552.273. Interim Charges for Geographic Information Systems Data (a) A municipality that does not collect records preservation funds may provide access to geographic information systems (GIS) data at low cost or no cost to requestors. A means by which the municipality may provide access to the information at low or no cost may include public access terminals, dial-up services, or any similar type of access. (b) If a municipality provides access as provided by Subsection (a), the municipality may set charges for providing copies of the GIS database. The factors considered in setting the charges may include data collection costs, system operation costs, and an estimation of the value of the information on the commercial market. (c) The General Services Commission shall conduct a study to determine reasonable charges for geographic information systems data. The study shall be completed not later than September 30, 1996, with full participation of parties, including; (1) the Geographic Information Systems Planning Council; (2) representatives of county and municipal governments; and (3) other interested parties. (d) This section expires August 31, 1997. SUBCHAPTER G. ATTORNEY GENERAL DECISIONS § 552.301. Request for Attorney General Decision (a) A governmental body that receives a written request for information that it wishes to withhold from public disclosure and that it considers to be within one of the exceptions under Subchapter C must ask for a decision from the attorney general about whether the information is within that exception if there has not been a previous determination about whether the information falls within one of the exceptions. The governmental body must ask for the attorney general's decision and state the exceptions that apply within a reasonable time but not later than the 10th calendar day after the date of receiving the written request. (b) A governmental body that requests and attorney general decision under Subsection (a) must within a reasonable time but not later than the 15th calendar day after the date of receiving the written request: (1) submit to the attorney general written comments stating the reasons why the stated exceptions apply that would allow the information to be withheld; (2) submit to the attorney general a copy of the written request for information; (3) submit to the attorney general a copy of the specific information requested, or submit representative samples of the information if a voluminous amount of information was requested; and (4) label that copy of the specific information, or of the representative samples, to indicate which exceptions apply to which parts of the copy. § 552.302. Failure to Make Timely Request for Attorney General Decision; Presumption that Information is Public If a governmental body does not request an attorney general decision as provided by Section 552.301(a), the information requested in writing is presumed to be public information. § 552.303. Delivery of Requested Information to Attorney General; Disclosure of Requested Information; Attorney General Request for Submission of Additional Information (a) A governmental body that requests an attorney general decision under this subchapter shall supply to the attorney general, in accordance with Section 552.301, the specific information requested. The governmental body may not disclose the information to the public or the requestor until the attorney general makes a final determination that the information is public or, if suit is filed under this chapter, until a final determination that the information is public has been made by the court with jurisdiction over the suit, except as otherwise provided by Section 552.322. (b) The attorney general may determine whether a governmental body's submission of information is sufficient to render a decision. (c) If the governmental body failed to supply to the attorney general all of the specific information that is necessary to render a decision, the attorney general shall give written notice of that fact to the governmental body and the requestor. (d) A governmental body notified under Subsection (c) shall submit the necessary additional information to the attorney general not later than the seventh calendar day after the date the notice is received. (e) If a governmental body does not comply with Subsection (d), the information that is the subject of a person's request to the governmental body and regarding which the governmental body fails to comply with Subsection (d) is presumed to be public information. § 552.304. Submission of Public Comments A person may submit written comments stating reasons why the information at issue in a request for an attorney general decision should or should not be released. § 552.305. Information Involving Privacy or Property Interests of Third Party (a) In a case in which information is requested under this chapter and a person's privacy or property interests may be involved, including a case under Section 552.101, 552.104, 552.110, or 552.114, a governmental body may decline to release the information for the purpose of requesting an attorney general decision. (b) A person whose interests may be involved under Subsection (a), or any other person, may submit in writing to the attorney general the person's reasons why the information should be withheld or released. (c) The governmental body may, but is not required to, submit its reasons why the information should be withheld or released. Text of section 552.306 as amended by H.B. 1718 applies only to request for attorney general decision under section 552.301 made on or after January 1, 1996: § 552.306. Rendition of Attorney General Decision; Issuance of Written Opinion (a) The attorney general shall promptly render a decision requested under this subchapter, consistent with the standards of due process, determining whether the requested information is within one of the exceptions of Subchapter C. The attorney general shall render the decision not later than the 60th working day after the date the attorney general received the request for a decision. If the attorney general is unable to issue the decision within the 60-day period, the attorney general may extend the period for issuing the decision by an additional 20 working days by informing the governmental body and the requestor, during the original 60-day period, of the reason for the delay. (b) The attorney general shall issue a written opinion of the determination and shall provide a copy of the opinion to the requestor. § 552.307. Special Right of Access; Attorney General Decisions (a) If a governmental body determines that information subject to a special right of access under Section 552.023 is exempt from disclosure under an exception of Subsection C, other than an exception intended to protect the privacy interest of the requestor or the person whom the requestor is authorized to represent, the governmental body shall, before disclosing the information, submit a written request for a decision to the attorney general under the procedures of this subchapter. (b) If a decision is not requested under Subsection (a), the governmental body shall release the information to the person with a special right of access under Section 552.023 not later than the 10th day after the date of receiving the request for information. § 552.308. Timeliness of Action by Mail When this subchapter requires a request, notice, or other document to be submitted or otherwise given to a person within a specified period, the requirement is met in a timely fashion if the document is sent to the person by first class United States mail properly addressed with postage prepaid and: (1) it bears a post office cancellation mark indicating a time within the period; or (2) the person required to submit or otherwise give the document furnishes satisfactory proof that it was deposited in the mail within the period. SUBCHAPTER H. CIVIL ENFORCEMENT § 552.321. Suit for Writ of Mandamus A requestor or the attorney general may file suit for a writ of mandamus compelling a governmental body to make information available for public inspection if the governmental body refuses to request an attorney general's decision as provided by Subchapter G or refuses to supply public information or information that the attorney general has determined is public information. § 552.322. Discovery of Information Under Protective Order Pending Final Determination In a suit filed under this chapter, the court may order that the information at issue may be discovered only under a protective order until a final determination is made. § 552.323. Assessment of Costs of Litigation and Reasonable Attorney Fees (a) In an action brought under Section 552.321 or Section 552.353(b)(3), the court may assess costs of litigation and reasonable attorney fees incurred by a plaintiff or defendant who substantially prevails. (b) In exercising its discretion under this section, the court shall consider whether the conduct of the governmental body had a reasonable basis in law and whether the litigation was brought in good faith. Text of section 552.324 as added by H.B. 1718 applies only to suit filed on or after September 1, 1995: § 552.324. Suit by Governmental Body The only suit a governmental body or officer for public information may file seeking to withhold information from a requestor is a suit that is filed in accordance with Sections 552.325 and 552.353 and that challenges a decision by the attorney general issued under Subchapter G. Text of section 552.325 as added by H.B. 1718 applies only to suit filed on or after September 1, 1995: § 552.325. Parties to Suit Seeking to Withhold Information (a) A governmental body, officer for public information, or other person or entity that files a suit seeking to withhold information from a requestor may not file suit against the person requesting the information. The requestor is entitled to intervene in the suit. (b) The governmental body, officer for public information, or other person or entity that files the suit shall demonstrate to the court that the governmental body, officer for public information, or other person or entity made a timely good faith effort to inform the requestor, by certified mail or by another written method of notice that requires the return of a receipt, of: (1) the existence of the suit, including the subject matter and cause number of the suit and the court in which the suit is filed; (2) the requestor's right to intervene in the suit or to choose to not participate in the suit; (3) the fact that the suit is against the attorney general; and (4) the address and phone number of the office of the attorney general. (c) If the attorney general enters into a proposed settlement that all or part of the information that is the subject of the suit should be withheld, the attorney general shall notify the requestor of that decision and, if the requestor has not intervened in the suit, of the requestor's right to intervene to contest the withholding. The attorney general shall notify the requestor: (1) in the manner required by the Texas Rules of Civil Procedure, if the requestor has intervened in the suit; or (2) by certified mail or by another written method of notice that requires the return of a receipt, if the requestor has not intervened in the suit. (d) The court shall allow the requestor a reasonable period to intervene after the attorney general attempts to give notice under Subsection (c)(2). SUBCHAPTER I. CRIMINAL VIOLATIONS § 552.351. Destruction, Removal, or Alteration of Public Information (a) A person commits an offense if the person wilfully destroys, mutilates, removes without permission as provided by this chapter, or alters public information. (b) An offense under this section is a misdemeanor punishable by: (1) a fine of not less than $25 or more than $4,000; (2) confinement in the county jail for not less than three days or more than three months; or (3) both the fine and

confinement. § 552.352. Distribution of Confidential Information (a) A person commits an offense if the person distributes information considered confidential under the terms of this chapter. (b) An offense under this section is a misdemeanor punishable by: (1) a fine of not more than $1,000; (2) confinement in the county jail for not more than six months; or (3) both the fine and confinement. (c) A violation under this section constitutes official misconduct. § 552.353. Failure or Refusal of Officer for Public Information to Provide Access to or Copying of Public Information (a) An officer for public information, or the officer's agent, commits an offense if, with criminal negligence, the officer or the officer's agent fails or refuses to give access to, or to permit or provide copying of, public information to a requestor as provided by this chapter. (b) It is an affirmative defense to prosecution under Subsection (a) that the officer for public information reasonably believed that public access to the requested information was not required and that the officer: (1) acted in reasonable reliance on a court order or a written interpretation of this chapter contained in an opinion of a court of record or of the attorney general issued under Subchapter G; (2) requested a decision from the attorney general in accordance with Subchapter G, and the decision is pending; or (3) not later than the 10th calendar day after the date of receipt of a decision by the attorney general that the information is public, filed a petition for a declaratory judgment, a writ of mandamus, or both, against the attorney general in a Travis County district court seeking relief from compliance with the decision of the attorney general, and a petition is pending. (c) It is an affirmative defense to prosecution under Subsection (a) that a person or entity has, not later than the 10th calendar day after the date of receipt by a governmental body of a decision by the attorney general that the information is public, filed a cause of action seeking relief from compliance with the decision of the attorney general, and the cause is pending. (d) It is an affirmative defense to prosecution under Subsection (a) that the defendant is the agent of an officer for public information and that the agent reasonably relied on the written instruction of the officer for public information not to disclose the public information requested. (e) An offense under this section is a misdemeanor punishable by: (1) a fine of not more than $1,000; (2) confinement in the county jail for not more than six months; or (3) both the fine and confinement. (f) A violation under this section constitutes official misconduct. Source: Office of the Attorney General of Texas Website
http://www.oag.state.tx.us/WEBSITE/OPENGOVT/ora.txt

APPENDIX B

THE BILL OF RIGHTS THE FIRST 10 AMENDMENTS TO THE CONSTITUTION OF THE UNITED STATES

Amendment I

Congress shall make no law respecting an establishment of religion, or prohibiting the free exercise thereof; or abridging the freedom of speech, or of the press; or the right of the people peaceably to assemble, and to petition the government for a redress of grievances.

Amendment II

A well regulated militia, being necessary to the security of a free state, the right of the people to keep and bear arms, shall not be infringed.

Amendment III

No soldier shall, in time of peace be quartered in any house, without the consent of the owner, nor in time of war, but in a manner to be prescribed by law.

Amendment IV

The right of the people to be secure in their persons, houses, papers, and effects, against unreasonable searches and seizures, shall not be violated, and no warrants shall issue, but upon probable cause, supported by oath or affirmation, and particularly describing the place to be searched, and the persons or things to be seized.

Amendment V

No person shall be held to answer for a capital, or otherwise infamous crime, unless on a presentment or indictment of a grand jury, except in cases arising in the land or naval forces, or in the militia, when in actual service in time of war or public danger; nor shall any person be subject for the same offense to be twice put in jeopardy of life or limb; nor shall be compelled in any criminal case to be a witness against himself, nor be deprived of life, liberty, or property, without due process of law; nor shall private property be taken for public use, without just compensation.

Amendment VI

In all criminal prosecutions, the accused shall enjoy the right to a speedy and public trial, by an impartial jury of the state and district wherein the crime shall have been committed, which district shall have been previously ascertained by law, and to be informed of the nature and cause of the accusation; to be confronted with the witnesses against him; to have compulsory process for obtaining witnesses in his favor, and to have the assistance of counsel for his defense.

Amendment VII

In suits at common law, where the value in controversy shall exceed twenty dollars, the right of trial by jury shall be preserved, and no fact tried by a jury, shall be otherwise reexamined in any court of the United States, than according to the rules of the common law.

Amendment VIII

Excessive bail shall not be required, nor excessive fines imposed, nor cruel and unusual punishments inflicted.

Amendment IX

The enumeration in the Constitution, of certain rights, shall not be construed to deny or disparage others retained by the people.

Amendment X

The powers not delegated to the United States by the Constitution, nor prohibited by it to the states, are reserved to the states respectively, or to the people.

RULES OF THE CIVIL TRIAL DIVISION
HARRIS COUNTY
DISTRICT COURTS

Rule 1. OBJECTIVE OF RULES.

The objective of the rules of the Civil Trial Division of the District Courts of Harris County is to obtain a just, fair, equitable and impartial adjudication of the rights of litigants under established principles of substantive law and established rules of procedural law. To the end that this objective may be attained with as great expedition and dispatch and at the least expense, both to the litigants and to the state, as may be practicable, the rules shall be applied to ensure that, so far as reasonably possible, all matters are brought to trial or final disposition in conformity with the following standards:

(a) Civil jury cases within 18 months from appearance date;

(b) Civil non-jury cases within 12 months from appearance date.

Rule 2. REPORTS TO ADMINISTRATIVE JUDGE.

The district clerk shall supply to the Administrative Judge of the Civil Trial Division, on a monthly basis, information concerning the number of filings, dispositions, trials and other judicial activities in each court in the Civil Trial Division.

Rule 3. FLOW OF CASES.

3.1 FILING AND ASSIGNMENT. On being filed, a case in the Civil Trial Division shall be assigned randomly to the docket of one of the courts in that Division. Once assigned to a court, a case will remain on the docket of that court for all purposes unless transferred as provided in Rule 3.2.

3.2 TRANSFER.

3.2.1 *Prior Judgment.* Any claim for relief based upon a prior judgment shall be assigned to the court of original judgment.

3.2.2 *Prior filings.* Any matter filed after a non-suit, dismissal for want of prosecution, or other disposition of a previous filing involving substantially-related parties and claims shall be assigned by the Administrative Judge of the Civil Trial Division to the court where the prior matter was pending.

3.2.3 *Consolidation.*

(a) *Consolidation of Cases.* Subject to subpart c, a motion to consolidate cases must be heard in the court where the first filed case is pending. If the motion is granted, the consolidated case will be given the number of the first filed case and assigned to that court.

(b) Consolidation of Discovery. Subject to subpart c, a motion to consolidate discovery in separate cases must be heard in the court where the first filed case is pending. If the motion to consolidate discovery is granted, the case will not transfer, but the case management will be conducted by the consolidating court.

(c) *Consolidation to Special Dockets.* Special dockets for the management of multi-court cases may be created by order of the Administrative Judge of the Civil Trial Division according to policies approved by the judges of the Civil Trial Division.

3.2.4 *Severance.* If a severance is granted, the new case will be assigned to the court where the original case pends, bearing the same file date and the same number as the original case with a letter designation; provided, however, that when a severed case has previously been consolidated from another court, the case shall upon severance be assigned to the court from which it was consolidated.

3.2.5 *Agreement.* Any case may be transferred from one court to another court by written order of the Administrative Judge of the Civil Trial Division or by written order of the judge of the court from which the case is transferred; provided, however, that in the latter instance the transfer must be with the written consent of the court to which the case is transferred.

3.2.6 *Presiding for Another.* In all cases where a court presides for another court, the case shall remain pending in the original court. If available, the judge who signed an order shall preside over any motion for contempt of that order, except as otherwise provided in Sec. 21.002, Tex. Gov. Code.

3.2.7 *Administrative Transfers.* The Administrative Judge of the Civil Trial Division may transfer cases between courts or may assign cases from one court to another court for hearing due to illness, trial schedule, or other sufficient reasons.

3.2.8 *Improper Court.* If a case is on the docket of a court by any manner other than as prescribed by these rules, the Administrative Judge of the Civil Trial Division shall transfer the case to the proper court.

3.3 MOTIONS.

3.3.1 *Form.* Motions shall be in writing and shall be accompanied by a proposed order granting the relief sought. The proposed order shall be a separate instrument, unless the entire motion, order, signature lines and certificate of service are all on one page.

3.3.2 *Response.* Responses shall be in writing and shall be accompanied by a proposed order. Failure to file a response may be considered a representation of no opposition.

3.3.3 *Submission.* Motions may be heard by written submission. Motions shall state Monday at 8:00 a.m. as the date for written submission. This date shall be at least 10 days from filing, except on leave of court. Responses shall be filed at least two working days before the date of submission, except on leave of court.

3.3.4 *Oral Hearings*. Settings for oral hearings should be requested from the court clerk. The notice of oral hearing shall state the time and date.

3.3.5 *Unopposed Motions*. Unopposed motions shall be labeled "Unopposed" in the caption.

3.3.6 *Extension of Certificates of Conference*. The certificates of conference required by the Texas Rules of Civil Procedure are extended to all motions, pleas and special exceptions except summary judgments, default judgments, agreed judgments, motions for voluntary dismissal or non-suit, post-verdict motions and motions involving service of citation.

3.4 TRIALS.

3.4.1 Manner of Setting. Cases shall be set for trial by order of the court.

3.4.2 *Date of Setting*. Cases shall be set for trial for a date certain. If a case is not assigned to trial by the second Friday after the date it was set, whether because of a continuance or because it was not reached, the court shall reset the case to a date certain. Unless all parties agree otherwise, the new setting must comply with all requisites of T.R.C.P. 245.

3.4.3 *Assignment to Trial.* A case is assigned to trial when counsel are called to the court to commence the jury or non-jury trial on the merits. For purposes of engaged counsel, no court may have more than one case assigned to trial at any one time.

3.4.4 *Dead Weeks.* Except with the consent of all parties, no court will assign cases to trial on the merits, or set oral hearings on motions, during:

(a) The week of the spring state or regional judicial conference

(b) The week of the State Bar Convention;

(c) The week of the Conference of the Judicial Section (September); and

(d) Any December week or weeks where the Monday of that week begins with the dates, Dec. 22-31.

3.5 ANCILLARY DOCKET.

3.5.1 Ancillary Docket. The ancillary docket consists of temporary restraining orders.

3.5.2 *Ancillary Judge*. The Ancillary Judge is responsible for hearing all matters on the ancillary docket. Each judge will serve as Ancillary Judge for one-half of a calendar month according to a schedule adopted by the judges of the Civil Trial Division. The Ancillary Judge will be available at the courthouse on business days during regular business hours, and will provide the county switchboard with the means to locate the Ancillary Judge at all other times.

If not available to serve at any time during the term, the Ancillary Judge will designate, in writing, another judge to serve ad interim, and will notify the

Administrative Judge of the Civil Trial Division, the ancillary clerk, and the county switchboard of that designation.

In the absence or unavailability of the Ancillary Judge or designee under the rule, matters requiring judicial attention will be presented to the Administrative Judge of the Civil Trial Division for ruling or assignment to another judge for ruling.

3.5.3 *Authority to Grant Ancillary Relief.* No judge other than the Ancillary Judge may grant ancillary relief without a written order from the Ancillary Judge or Administrative Judge of the Civil Trial Division. In requests for ancillary relief, the Ancillary Judge shall hear the matters as "Judge Presiding" for the court in which the case is pending.

3.6 DISMISSAL DOCKETS. The following cases are eligible for dismissal for want of prosecution pursuant to T.R.C.P. 165a:

(a) Cases on file for more than 120 days in which no answer has been filed or is required by law;

(b) Cases which have been on file for more than eighteen months and are not set for trial;

(c) Cases in which a party or his attorney has failed to take any action specified by the court.

Rule 10. CONFLICTING ENGAGEMENTS.

10.1 **INTER-COUNTY.** The Rules of the Second Administrative Judicial Region control conflicts in settings of all kinds between a Harris County court and a court not in Harris County. The Rules of the Second Administrative Judicial Region are available in the District Clerk's office.

10.2 **INTRA-COUNTY.** Among the trial courts sitting in Harris County:

(a) Trial/Non-Trial. Trial settings take precedence over conflicting non-trial settings; and

(b) Trial/Trial. A trial setting that is assigned takes precedence over a conflicting trial setting not yet assigned.

10.3 **WAIVER.** The court with precedence may yield.

10.4 **LEAD COUNSEL.** This rule operates only where lead counsel, as defined by T.R.C.P. 8, is affected, unless the court expands coverage to other counsel.

Rule 11. VACATIONS OF COUNSEL.

11.1 **DESIGNATION OF VACATION.** Subject to the provision of subparts .2 and .3 of this Rule, an attorney may designate not more than four weeks of vacation during a calendar year as vacation, during which that attorney will not be assigned to trial or required to engage in any pretrial proceedings. This rule operates only where lead counsel, as defined by T.R.C.P. 8, is affected, unless the trial court expands coverage to other counsel.

11.2 **SUMMER VACATIONS.** Written designation for vacation weeks during June, July, or August must be filed with the district clerk by May 15. Summer vacation weeks so designated will protect the attorney from trials during those summer weeks, even if an order setting the case for trial was signed before the vacation designation was filed.

11.3 **NON-SUMMER VACATIONS.** Written designation for vacation in months other than June, July, or August must be filed with the district clerk by February 1. Non-summer vacation weeks may not run consecutively for more than two weeks at a time. Non-summer vacation weeks so designated will not protect an attorney from a trial by an order signed before the date the designation is filed.

Rule 12. ADMINISTRATIVE JUDGE OF THE CIVIL TRIAL DIVISION.

1. **ELECTION.** The Administrative Judge of the Civil Trial Division shall be elected for a term of one calendar year by the judges of the Civil Trial Division at the regular December meeting of the judges of the Civil Trial Division. No judge may serve more than two consecutive terms as Administrative Judge. If a vacancy occurs in the office of Administrative Judge, the judges of the Civil Trial Division must hold an election to fill the vacancy at their next monthly meeting.

2. **DESIGNEE.** The Administrative Judge of the Civil Trial Division may by written order designate any other judge of the Division to act for the judge when the Administrative Judge is absent or unable to act. The judge so designated shall have all the duties and authority granted by these Rules to the Administrative Judge of the Civil Trial Division during the period of the designation.

Rule 15. UNIFORMITY.

15.1 **TRIAL AND DISMISSAL DOCKETS.** The judges of the Civil Trial Division shall only use those docket management form letters and form orders which have been approved by the judges of the Civil Trial Division.

15.2 **APPOINTEE FEE REPORT.** Each person appointed by a judge in the Civil Trial Division to a position for which any type of fee may be paid shall file the designated uniform report before any judgment, dismissal, or nonsuit is signed. This report is required for every appointment made whether or not a fee is charged.

15.3 **RECORDING AND BROADCASTING OF COURT PROCEEDINGS.** Recording or broadcasting court proceedings in the Civil Trial Division is governed by uniform rules adopted by the judges of the Civil Trial Division.

Rule 16. MEETINGS.

The judges of the Civil Trial Division shall meet regularly on the first Tuesday of each month from 12:15 until 1:15 p.m. The Administrative Judge of the Civil Trial Division may call a special meeting by written notice distributed at least 72 hours in advance of the meeting. Any special meeting called will state an ending time for the meeting. The judges may vote to reschedule or cancel any monthly meeting. No more than two meetings in any calendar year may be canceled.

Rule 17. EFFECTIVE DATE.

Effective October 20, 1987; amended 1/22/90; 7/1/90; 8/31/91; 1/3/96; 7/2/97; 4/27/98; 5/26/99.

LOCAL RULES OF THE UNITED STATES DISTRICT COURT
Southern District of Texas, Houston Division

<u>**RENUMBERED LOCAL RULES**</u>
<u>**CIVIL RULES**</u>

LR3. COMMENCEMENT OF ACTION
Parties represented by counsel must file a civil action cover sheet (Form JS44c) with all original pleadings.

LR4. SUMMONS
Parties other than prisoners must provide completed summons forms for issuance by the clerk.

LR5. FILING REQUIREMENTS

LR5.1 **Place of Filing.** Papers are filed by delivery of the original to the clerk, not to the judge.

LR5.2 **Original and Copy.** An original and one copy of each document to be filed in a case must be provided to the clerk at the time of filing.

LR5.3 **Related Litigation Policy.** The parties must advise the Court of related current or recent litigation and of directly affected non-parties.

LR5.4 **Certificate of Service.** Papers must have at the end a certificate reflecting how and when service has been made or why service is not required. Federal Rule of Civil Procedure 5(b).

LR5.5 **Discovery Not Filed.** Depositions, interrogatories, answers to interrogatories, requests for admission, production, or inspection, responses to those requests, and other discovery material shall not be filed with the clerk.

LR5.6 **Service of Pleadings and Other Papers.** All motions must be served on all parties and contain a certificate of service. Motions for default judgment must be served on the defendant-respondent by certified mail (return receipt requested).

LR7. CIVIL PRETRIAL MOTION PRACTICE
LR7.1 **Form.** Opposed motions shall

A. Be in writing;

B. Include or be accompanied by authority;

 I. Be accompanied by a separate proposed order granting the relief requested and setting forth information sufficient to communicate the nature of the relief granted;

 II. Except for motions under Federal Rules of Civil Procedure 12(b), (c), (e), or (f) and 56, contain an averment that

 (1) The movant has conferred with the respondent and

 (2) Counsel cannot agree about the disposition of the motion.

LR7.2 Unopposed Motions. Motions without opposition and their proposed orders must bear in their caption "unopposed." They will be considered as soon as it is practicable.

LR7.3 Submission. Opposed motions will be submitted to the judge twenty days from filing without notice from the clerk and without appearance by counsel.

LR7.4 Responses. Failure to respond will be taken as a representation of no opposition. Responses to motions

 A. Must be filed by the submission day;

 B. Must be written;

 C. Must include or be accompanied by authority; and

 III. Must be accompanied by a separate form order denying the relief sought.

LR7.5 Oral Submission.

7.5.A. *By Request*. If a party views oral argument as helpful to the Court, the motion or response may include a request for it. If it is granted, the parties will be notified by the clerk.

7.5.B. *By Order*. When oral presentation is required by the Court, counsel will be notified by the clerk of a date for oral presentation irrespective of any submission day.

LR7.6 Consolidation. A motion to consolidate cases will

 A. Contain in the caption of the motion

  (1) The case numbers;

  (2) Full styles; and

  (3) Judge to whom each of the cases is assigned.

 B. Be filed only in the oldest case with a courtesy copy furnished to the other affected courts.

 C. Be heard by the judge to whom the oldest case is assigned.

 IV. The term "oldest case," as used in this Rule, means the case filed first in any court, state or federal, including cases removed or transferred to this Court.

LR7.7 **Supporting Material**. If a motion or response requires consideration of facts not appearing of record, proof by affidavit or other documentary evidence must be filed with the motion or response.

LR7.8 **Hearing.** The Court may in its discretion, on its own motion or upon application, entertain and decide any motion, shorten or extend time periods, and request or permit additional authority or supporting material.

LR10. FORM OF PLEADINGS

LR10.1 **Caption.** Papers must have a caption, including the name and party designation of the party filing it and a statement of its character, like "Defendant John Doe's Motion for Partial Summary Judgment." Federal Rule of Civil Procedure 10(a).

LR10.2 **Format.** Papers offered for filing may not be in covers. They must be on 8½" x 11" paper, stapled at the top only, punched at the top with two holes, double spaced, and paginated.

LR11. SIGNING OF PLEADINGS, MOTIONS AND OTHER PAPERS BY ATTORNEY IN CHARGE

LR11.1 **Designation.** On first appearance through counsel, each party shall designate an attorney-in charge. Signing the pleading effects designation.

LR11.2 **Responsibility.** The attorney-in-charge is responsible in that action for the party. That individual attorney shall attend all court proceedings or send a fully informed attorney with authority to bind the client.

LR11.3 **Signing of Pleadings.** Every document filed must be signed by, or by permission of, the attorney-in-charge.

11.3.A. *Required Information.* Under the signature shall appear:
   (1)   attorney's individual name,
   (2)   designation "attorney-in-charge,"
   (3)   State bar number,
   (4)   Southern District of Texas bar number,
   (5)   office address including zip code, and
   (6)   telephone and facsimile numbers with area codes.

11.3.B. *Allowed Information.* Names of firms and associate counsel may appear with the designation "of counsel."

LR11.4 **Sanctions.** A paper that does not conform to the local or federal rules or that is otherwise objectionable may be struck on the motion of a party or by the Court.

APPENDIX C

LR16.CIVIL PRETRIAL PROCEEDINGS

LR16.1 **Civil Initial Pretrial Conference; Scheduling Order.** Within 140 days after the filing of a complaint or notice of removal, the judge will conduct an initial pretrial conference under Federal Rule of Civil Procedure 16 and enter a scheduling order, except in these types of cases: (a) prisoner civil rights; (b) state and federal habeas corpus; (c) student and veteran loan; (d) social security appeals; (e) bankruptcy appeals; and (f) forfeiture of seized assets.

A judge may conduct an initial pretrial conference and enter a scheduling order in any of the types of cases excepted.

A scheduling order setting cut-off dates for new parties, motions, expert witnesses and discovery, setting a trial date, and establishing a time framework for disposition of motions will be entered at the conference. Should there be an earlier Rule 26(f) discovery conference, the scheduling order may be entered at that conference.

Additional pretrial/settlement/discovery conferences may be scheduled by the Court as the need is identified.

By individual notice, the Court will require attendance at conferences "by an attorney who has the authority to bind that party regarding all matters . . .", 28 U.S.C. § 473(b)(2).

LR16.2. **Pretrial Order.** The form of the pretrial order in Appendix B is acceptable to the judges who require one.

LR16.3. **Notice of Settlement.** Counsel shall notify the Court immediately of settlements that obviate court settings. Unnecessarily summoned veniremen or disrupted court schedules resulting from an unexcusable failure to notify may be the predicate for sanctions.

LR16.4. **Alternative Dispute Resolution.** Pursuant to 28 U.S.C.§ 652 (1998) and to facilitate the settlement or narrowing of issues in civil actions, the Court adopts the following Alternative Dispute Resolution Program:

16.4.A. *ADR Methods Available.* The Court approves the use of the following ADR methods in civil cases pending before district, magistrate, and bankruptcy judges: mediation, early neutral evaluation, mini-trial, summary jury trial, and, if the parties consent, non-binding arbitration pursuant to 28 U.S.C. § 654 (1998) (collectively, "ADR"). A judge may approve any other ADR method the parties suggest and the judge finds appropriate for a case.

16.4.B. *Timing of ADR Decision.*

(1) Before the initial conference in a case, counsel are required to discuss with their clients and with opposing counsel the appropriateness of ADR in the case.

(2) At the initial pretrial conference the parties shall advise the judge of the results of their discussions concerning ADR. At that time and at subsequent conferences, if necessary, the judge shall explore with the

parties the possibility of using ADR. The judge may require the use of mediation, early neutral evaluation, and, if the parties consent, non-binding arbitration pursuant to 28 U.S.C. § 654 (1998).

16.4.C. *ADR Referral.* A judge may refer any civil case to ADR on motion of any party, on the agreement of the parties, or on its own motion. If the parties agree upon an ADR method or provider, the judge will respect the parties' agreement unless the judge believes another ADR method or provider is better suited to the case and parties. The authority to refer a case to ADR does not preclude the judge from suggesting or requiring other settlement initiatives.

16.4.D. *Opposition to ADR Referral, ADR Method or ADR Provider.* A party opposing in a particular case either the ADR referral, ADR method, or the appointed ADR provider must file written objections within ten days of entry of the order for ADR, and must explain the reasons for any opposition. The objections and related submissions shall be filed with the judge presiding over the case.

16.4.E. *Standing Panel, ADR Administrator and List of Providers.*

5. **Standing Panel.** The Court shall maintain a Standing Panel on ADR Providers ("Panel") to oversee implementation, administration, and evaluation of the Court's ADR program. The Chief Judge of the District will appoint three members, one of whom shall be a district judge who shall serve as chairperson. Each Panel member shall be appointed for a three year term. The Panel shall review applications from prospective ADR providers and annually shall prepare an ADR List of those qualified under the criteria contained in this rule.

6. **ADR Administrator.** The Court shall designate a person in the Court clerk's office as ADR Administrator to assist the Panel with its responsibilities and to serve as the primary contact for public inquiries regarding the Court's ADR Program.

7. **ADR Provider List.**

a. Copies of the ADR Provider List shall be available to the public in the clerk's office.

b. To be eligible for initial listing as an ADR provider, the applicant must meet the following minimum qualifications: (i) membership in the bar of the United States District Court for the Southern District of Texas; (ii) licensed to practice law for at least ten years; and (iii) completion of at least forty hours training in dispute resolution techniques in an alternative dispute resolution course approved by the State Bar of Texas Minimum Continuing Legal Education department.

c. Each applicant for the ADR Provider List shall submit a completed application in December or January for consideration for the next ADR Provider List. The applicant must use the form available in the clerk's office. The application shall contain: (i) the ADR method(s) for which the applicant seeks to be listed; (ii) a concise summary of the applicant's training, experience, and qualifications for the ADR method(s) for which the applicant seeks to be listed; (iii) the subject matter area(s) in which the applicant has particular expertise (*e.g.*, the concentration of non-ADR practice, board certification); (iv) the applicant's fee schedule; and (v) a commitment to accept some cases for no fee or a reduced fee.

d. To maintain the listing, an ADR Provider annually, between January 1 and January 31, must certify in writing to the Panel that the provider has completed five hours of ADR training during the previous calendar year. Self-study of court decisions on ADR and authoritative writings on ADR techniques and/or ADR ethics may be used to satisfy this requirement, if the provider identifies the materials studied and the dates of study in the annual certificate.

e. Each ADR provider shall remain on the ADR Provider List for five years, provided the requirements of subparagraph E(3)(d) are met. After a five-year term, the ADR provider may apply for re-listing.

f. An applicant denied listing may request a review of that decision by sending a letter to the Chief Judge of the District. The Chief Judge shall have final decision-making authority on the matter.

g. In any particular case, a judge may approve any ADR provider on which the parties agree, even if the provider is not listed on the ADR Provider List or does not satisfy the criteria for eligibility for the list.

16.4.F. ***Attendance; Authority to Settle.*** Party representatives (in addition to litigation counsel) with authority to settle and all other persons necessary to negotiate a settlement, such as insurance carriers, must attend the ADR proceeding.

16.4.G. ***Fees.*** The provider and the parties generally will determine the fees for each ADR proceeding. However, the judge presiding over a case has the right to review the reasonableness of fees and to adjust them as appropriate. A judge also may at any time request a provider on the ADR Provider List or any other person to conduct an ADR proceeding *pro bono* or for a reduced fee.

16.4.H. ***Binding Nature.*** The results of all ADR proceedings approved by this rule are non-binding unless the parties agree otherwise in a written agreement or by announcement in open court.

16.4.I. ***Confidentiality, Privileges and Immunities***. All communications made during ADR proceedings (other than communications concerning scheduling, a final agreement, or ADR provider fees) are confidential, are protected from disclosure, and may not be disclosed to anyone, including the Court, by the provider or the parties. Communications made during ADR proceedings do not constitute a waiver of any existing privileges and immunities. The ADR provider may not testify about statements made by participants or negotiations that occurred during the ADR proceedings. This provision does not modify the requirements of 28 U.S.C. § 657 (1998) applicable to non-binding arbitrations.

16.4.J. *Standards of Professional Conduct and Disqualification of ADR Providers.*

(1) All providers are subject to disqualification pursuant to standards consistent with those set forth in 28 U.S.C. § 455 (1988). In addition, all ADR providers are required to comply with the State Bar of Texas Alternative Dispute Resolution Section's Ethical Guidelines for Mediators, the Code of Ethics for Arbitrators in Commercial Disputes promulgated by the American Arbitration Association, and the American Bar Association and such other rules and guidelines as the Panel specifies. Copies of these standards are available from the clerk's office.

(2) Issues concerning potential ADR provider conflicts shall be raised with the judge presiding in the case relating to the ADR proceeding.

16.4.K. *Conclusion of ADR Proceedings.* After each ADR proceeding the provider, the parties, and the Court will take the following actions:

(1) Within 10 days of completion of the proceeding, the parties jointly shall send to the ADR Administrator a memorandum stating the style and civil action number of the case; the names, addresses, and telephone numbers of counsel and party representatives in attendance; the type of case; the ADR method used; whether the case settled; and the fees paid to the ADR provider. A copy of this memorandum shall also be sent to the judge presiding over the case. This reporting provision does not apply to non-binding arbitrations conducted pursuant to 28 U.S.C. § 654.

(2) Within 10 days of completion of the proceeding, the ADR provider shall send a report to the ADR Administrator and the judge presiding over the case disclosing only the information listed in subparagraph K.(1).

(3) Thereafter, the ADR Administrator shall submit a questionnaire evaluating the ADR provider and proceeding to the parties and counsel; counsel and the parties must complete and return the questionnaires. The Court, attorneys, and the public may review the questionnaires in the clerk's office. Data in the questionnaires shall be compiled by the ADR Administrator each calendar year. The questionnaires shall be retained by the clerk's office for at least three years.

16.4.L. *Evaluations.* The Court annually shall evaluate and issue a public report on the use of ADR in the district, dispositions of ADR proceedings, and other matters the Panel requires.

16.4.M. *Sanctions.* Fed. R. Civ. P. 16(f) sanctions apply to violations of this rule.

APPENDIX C

LR26.**DISCOVERY**

LR26.1. **Use of Discovery.** When a discovery document is needed in a pretrial procedure, the required portions may be filed as an exhibit to a motion or response. Discovery material needed at trial or hearing may be introduced in open court under the Federal Rules of Evidence.

LR26.2. **Placement of Discovery.** Every answer, objection, or other response to any interrogatory, request for admission, or to produce shall be preceded by the question or request to which the response pertains.

LR30. **DEPOSITIONS**

LR30.1. **Video-Taped Depositions.** By this rule, leave of Court is granted, in civil cases, for video-taped depositions without contemporaneous stenographic recordation. The notice or subpoena must indicate that the deposition is to be by video-tape to allow anyone desiring stenographic recordation to arrange for it.

LR33. **INTERROGATORIES**_rLR33.1. **Limitation of Interrogatories.** No more than twenty-five interrogatories (counting sub-parts) may be served without leave of Court.

LR38. **JURY TRIALS**

LR38.1. **Jury Demand.** Pleadings in which a jury is demanded shall bear the word "jury" at the top, immediately below the case number.

LR44. **PROOF OF OFFICIAL RECORD**

LR44.1. **Authentication of Exhibits.** A party requiring authentication of an exhibit must notify the offering party in writing within five days after the exhibit is listed and made available. Failure to object in advance of the trial in writing concedes authenticity.

LR46. **OBJECTIONS TO EXHIBITS**

Objections to admissibility of exhibits must be made at least three business days before trial by notifying the Court in writing of the disputes, with copies of the disputed exhibit and authority.

LR47. **JUROR CONTACT**

Except with leave of Court, no attorney, party, nor agent of either of them may communicate with a former juror to obtain evidence of misconduct in the jury's deliberations.

LR54. **COSTS**

LR54.1. **Deposit for Costs.**

8. The clerk will not be required to perform any service requiring a payment unless

1.The payment is deposited with the clerk;

2. A law excuses the payment or the deposit in advance; or

3. Leave to proceed in forma pauperis has been granted. 28 U.S.C. § 1915.

9. The U.S. Marshal may require a deposit to cover fees and expenses. 28 U.S.C. § 1921(d).

LR54.2. Bill of Costs. The parties must maintain their own record of taxable costs. The clerk does not record taxable costs. An application for costs shall be made by filing a bill of costs within 14 days of the entry of a final judgment. When attorney's fees are taxable as costs, an application for them must be made with the application for other costs. Objections to allowance of the bill, the attorney's fees, or both must be filed within five days of the bill's filing. Rule 54(d). 28 U.S.C. § 1920.

LR65. BOND PROCEDURE

LR65.1. Sureties. No employee of the United States Courts or of the United States Marshal's Service will be accepted as surety on any bond or undertaking in any proceeding.

LR65.2. Non-Assignability of Receipts. A clerk's receipt or the claim for the refund of a deposit is not assignable.

LR72. UNITED STATES MAGISTRATE JUDGES

The magistrate judges are authorized to perform all of the duties allowable to magistrates under the Federal Magistrates Act, as amended, 28 U.S.C. §§ 631, 636, under General Order No. 80-5, General Order 91-26 and General Order 91-30. These rules apply to proceedings before the magistrate judges.

LR79. BOOKS AND RECORDS KEPT BY THE CLERK

LR79.1. Withdrawal of Instruments. No filed instrument shall be removed from the clerk's custody without an order.

LR79.2. Disposition of Exhibits.

10. Exhibits that are not easily stored in a file folder (like posters, parts, or models) must be withdrawn within two business days after the completion of the trial and reduced reproductions or photographs substituted.

11. If there is no appeal, exhibits will be removed by the offering party within thirty days after disposition of the case. When there is an appeal, exhibits returned by the court of appeals will be removed by the offering party within ten days after written notice from the clerk. Exhibits not removed will be disposed of by the clerk, and the expenses incurred will be taxed against the offering party.

LR81. REMOVAL

Notices for removal shall have attached only the following documents:

12. All executed process in the case;

1. Pleadings asserting causes of action, e.g., petitions, counterclaims, cross actions, third-party actions, interventions and all answers to such pleadings;

13. All orders signed by the state judge;

14. The docket sheet;

15. An index of matters being filed; and

16. A list of all counsel of record, including addresses, telephone numbers and parties represented.

LR83. MISCELLANEOUS LOCAL RULES

LR83.1. **Admission to Practice.**

A. *Eligibility.* A lawyer applying for admission to the bar of this court must be licensed to practice law by the licensing authority of one of the fifty states, the District of Columbia, or a Territory of the United States, and if licensed by a licensing authority other than the State of Texas, then an attorney must also be a member in good standing of a United States District Court.

B. *Division.* Lawyers who reside in the district must apply in the division where the lawyer resides. Applicants who do not reside in the district may apply for admission in any division.

C. *Application.* The lawyer shall file an application on a form prescribed by the Court.

D. *Committee on Admissions.* The district shall have one committee on admissions comprised of five attorney members chosen by the Chief Judge and who shall serve staggered three-year terms. The participation of three members, either in person or by electronic means, shall constitute a quorum.

E. *Action on the Application.* After a review of the application, the Court will admit or deny admission. A person not admitted may request a hearing to show why the application should be granted. The hearing will be conducted under the procedures for disciplinary matters.

F. *Uncompensated Assignments.* The pro bono representation of indigent clients is encouraged by this Court. It is hoped that as a matter of public service a member of the Bar of the Southern District of Texas will accept an uncompensated assignment to an indigent's civil matter as often as every twelve months.

G. *Workshop.* An approved applicant must attend a workshop held by the Court before being admitted, unless the applicant either is over seventy years old or resides out of the district and is a member of the bar of another United States District Court. Former Circuit, District, Bankruptcy and Magistrate Judges are exempt from attending the workshop.

(1)   On approval of an application, the clerk will notify the applicant, giving the locations and dates of the next workshops.

(2)   Applicants who reside in the Houston or Galveston Divisions must attend the workshop in Houston.

(3)   Applicants for admission in the Brownsville, Corpus Christi, Laredo, McAllen and Victoria Divisions may attend a workshop in any division.

H. *Expiration.* Members of the bar must reapply every five years from the date of admission by filing a new application and paying the fee. If a member fails to reapply before the expiration of the term, a later application will be treated as an original application, requiring reapproval and attendance at a workshop.

I. *Oath.* On admission, the lawyer will take this oath before any judicial officer of the United States:

I do solemnly swear [affirm] that I will discharge the duties of attorney and counselor of this court faithfully, that I will demean myself uprightly under the law and the highest ethics of our profession, and that I will support and defend the Constitution of the United States.

J. *Fee.* The applicant will pay the fee set by order. Should an applicant scheduled to take the oath unreasonably fail to notify the clerk that he will not appear as scheduled, the applicant forfeits the fee.

K. *Practice Without Admission.* A lawyer who is not admitted to practice before this Court may appear as attorney-in-charge for a party in a case in this Court with the permission of the judge before whom the case is pending. When a lawyer who is not a member of the bar of this Court first appears in a case, the lawyer shall move for leave to appear as attorney-in-charge for the client.

L. *Conduct of Attorneys.* The Rules of Discipline in Appendix A govern membership in the bar of the United States District Court for the Southern District of Texas.

LR83.2. **Withdrawal of Counsel.** Although no delay will be countenanced because of a change in counsel, withdrawal of counsel-in-charge may be effected by motion and order, under conditions imposed by the Court.

LR83.3. **Notices.** All communications about an action will be sent to the attorney-in-charge who is responsible for notifying associate counsel.

LR83.4. **Change of Address.** Notices will be sent only to the address on file. A lawyer or pro se litigant is responsible for keeping the clerk advised in writing of the current address. Counsel of record and pro se litigants must include in this advice the case numbers of all pending cases in which they are participants in this district.

LR83.5. **Parties' Agreement.** Agreements among the parties are enforceable by the Court only if they are announced in open court or reduced to writing and signed. Nevertheless, agreements of the parties are not binding on the Court.

LR83.6. **Preserving Confidentiality.**

83.6.A. *Civil Actions.* On the filing of a civil action that the party desires be sealed, the party shall present an application to the clerk attaching the complaint and accompanying materials in a sealed envelope marked "sealed exhibit." A miscellaneous case number will be assigned and the case file presented to the miscellaneous judge. Once that judge has ruled on the application, the case file and order will be returned immediately to the clerk for the drawing of a civil action number and random assignment to a judge.

83.6.B. *Jurors' Names.* The trial judge may hold the names of petit jurors confidential. Names of jurors held confidential shall not be disclosed other than to employees of the judiciary of the United States in their official duties.

LR83.7. **Electro-Mechanical Devices.** Except by leave of the presiding judge, no photo- or electro-mechanical means of recordation or transmission of court proceedings is permitted in the courthouse.

LR83.8. **Courtroom Behavior.** Traditional, formal courtroom etiquette is required of all who appear in court as specified in Appendix C.

SUPPLEMENTAL ADMIRALTY RULES

A. **DESIGNATION AS "ADMIRALTY CASE"** - Papers in cases arising within the admiralty or maritime jurisdiction shall bear the word "admiralty" at the top, immediately below the case number.

E. **ADMIRALTY SALES** - In the absence of conflicting requirements in the order of sale, these are the procedures for sales of property under marshal's seizure in admiralty actions:

E.1. **Notice**. The notice of sale shall be published in a daily newspaper of general circulation in the division of the seizure on at least four days, between three and thirty-one days before the sale date.

E.2. **Payment.**

17. Payment to the marshal shall be by cash, cashier's check, or certified check; acceptance of cashiers' checks is conditioned on their payment.

18. Accepted bids of less than $1,000 shall be paid to the marshal on their acceptance.

19. For accepted bids of $1,000 and more, the higher of ten percent of the bid or $1,000 shall be deposited immediately and be paid in full within three business days of the sale. If an objection is filed within the three days, the buyer may defer payment of the balance until the sale is confirmed.

E.3. **Default.** If the buyer does not pay the bid on time, (1) the deposit is forfeited to the action, applied to costs, then paid to the registry; and (2) the Court may accept the second bid or order a new sale.

E.4. **Objections.**

E.4.1. *Time*. Objections must be written and filed with the marshal within three business days of the sale date.

E.4.2. *Deposit.* Objections shall be accompanied by a cost deposit of seven days of estimated expenses of custody.

E.4.3. *Disposition.*

1. If sustained, the deposits by the bidder and objector will be refunded immediately.

2. If overruled, the balance of the objector's deposit that remains after deduction of the expenses of custody from the day of the objection until the day of the confirmation will be paid to the objector.

SUPPLEMENTAL HABEAS CORPUS RULES

1.**STAYS OF EXECUTION**.

A. **Application Requirements.** A party who seeks to stay the execution of a Texas death warrant shall include in the application:

20. A copy of each state court opinion and judgment in the matter;

21. A description of the relief sought from any United States Court, including action number and court name;

22. The reasons for denying relief given by the courts that have considered the matter, by written opinion or portions of the transcript; and

23. An explanation why issues urged in the application have not been raised or exhausted in state court.

B. **Appeal.** If a certificate of appealability is issued, the stay of execution will continue until the court of appeals acts.

C. **Successive Applications.** All applications for relief from state orders in a single matter will be assigned to the judge to whom the first application was assigned. All applications for relief from state orders after the first will be strictly and promptly considered.

INDEX

INDEX

INDEX

INDEX

INDEX

INDEX

INDEX

INDEX

INDEX

INDEX

INDEX

INDEX

INDEX